REFUGEES IN AMERICA
IN THE 1990s

Refugees in America in the 1990s

A Reference Handbook

EDITED BY
DAVID W. HAINES

Greenwood Press
Westport, Connecticut • London

Library of Congress Cataloging-in-Publication Data

Refugees in America in the 1990s : a reference handbook / edited by
David W. Haines.
      p.   cm.
   Includes bibliographical references and index.
   ISBN 0–313–29344–9 (alk. paper)
   1. Refugees—United States. I. Haines, David W.
  HV640.4.U54R425   1996
  362.87'0973—dc20   95–50902

British Library Cataloguing in Publication Data is available.

Library of Congress Catalog Card Number: 95–50902
ISBN: 0–313–29344–9

First published in 1996

Greenwood Press, 88 Post Road West, Westport, CT 06881
An imprint of Greenwood Publishing Group, Inc.

Printed in the United States of America

The paper used in this book complies with the
Permanent Paper Standard issued by the National
Information Standards Organization (Z39.48–1984).

10 9 8 7 6 5 4 3 2

Copyright Acknowledgment

The editor and the publisher gratefully acknowledge permission to use the following:

Excerpts from *The Ambivalent Welcome: Print Media, Public Opinion and Immigration*,
by Rita J. Simon and Susan A. Alexander. 1993. Westport, CT: Praeger. An imprint of
Greenwood Publishing Group, Inc. Copyright © 1993 by Rita J. Simon and Susan A.
Alexander.

To Howard and Grace Haines

Contents

Preface

This volume began with the intention simply to update a reference volume on refugees published by Greenwood Press in 1985. However, the sharp changes in the situation of refugees over the last decade, the expansion in the quantity and quality of research on refugees, and the need to recognize a broader range of refugee groups have resulted in an entirely new book—two thirds of this volume is completely original; the remaining third is substantially revised.

Now, as then, the experience of refugees is complex and compelling. While it must be understood through the specific experiences of particular refugees, its understanding benefits from a comparative consideration of multiple refugee groups. This volume attempts to balance those two needs. Thus, although the heart of the volume is Part II with its individual group chapters, the two introductory chapters of Part I and the more documentary chapters of Part III attempt to provide a broader, comparative focus.

My debts are many. The contributors themselves deserve credit for being willing to structure their broad experience into relatively condensed presentations. I must note particular pleasure at having some refugee groups included for the first time: Juliene Lipson and Pat Omidian on Afghans, Elzbieta Gozdziak on Eastern Europeans, Tekle Woldemikael on Ethiopians and Eritreans, and Mehdi Bozorgmehr on Iranians. The chapters on these groups greatly expanded the scope of the book and the understanding of refugees that it aims to encourage. I am also particularly pleased that Phil Holman was willing to take on the task of introducing the U.S. refugee program, a program that he understands better than anyone else I know.

Comments and suggestions from a variety of people have been helpful along the way: Joe Coleman raised some intriguing comparisons between Cubans and Vietnamese, Beatrice Hackett made a variety of helpful suggestions, Steve Gold provided wise counsel on potential chapter authors, Jeff Sulik helped me rethink my own views on "refugees as refugees" versus "refugees as immigrants," and fellow anthropologists like Carol Mortland and Janet Benson have produced some excellent work that greatly encouraged me about the status of refugee research. Appreciation for thoughts along the way also goes to Jeff McDonald, Nguyen Manh Hung, Karen Rosenblum, Cynthia Harris (whom I was delighted to find still with Greenwood Press), and valued former colleagues at the Office of Refugee Resettlement (ORR): Barbara Chesnick, Linda Gordon, and David Howell. Toyo Biddle and Loren Bussert at ORR were helpful with reports and data and Bridget Austiguy-Preschel, Shelia Barrows, and Susan Badger provided invaluable assistance in manuscript preparation. A few institutions also deserve thanks: Virginia Commonwealth University and Georgetown University have both managed to maintain credible library collections on refugee-related issues, and the American Anthropological Association's Committee on Refugee Issues has been a very congenial forum within which to rethink issues of refugee policy, research, and praxis.

Part I

Introduction

Chapter 1

Refugee Resettlement in the United States

Philip A. Holman

The United States has a long and deeply rooted tradition of accepting refugees from all parts of the world. The depth and endurance of this tradition will be tested during the final years of the twentieth century as the nation's immigration and refugee policies once again come under detailed and critical reexamination.

During the half century since the end of World War II in 1945, the United States has admitted more than 3 million refugees. The largest groups have come from Cuba, Vietnam, and the former Soviet Union, but refugee admissions have represented well over a hundred countries worldwide. To understand the reasons for the admission of these refugees, it is useful to examine the history of U.S. refugee policy and its relationship to the nation's overall immigration and foreign policies.

THE DEVELOPMENT OF U.S. REFUGEE POLICY

Immigrants and Refugees

America's early open-door immigration policies made no distinction between immigrants—persons fleeing economic hardship or otherwise seeking a better life—and refugees—persons fleeing persecution. Since all were admitted, if not always welcomed, no such distinction was necessary.

Federal legislation to regulate immigration into the United States began in 1875 with an act barring the entry of convicts and prostitutes. Seven years later, the Chinese Exclusion Act and the Immigration Act of 1882 placed further restrictions on immigration: The Chinese Exclusion Act was the first legislation to base eligibility for entry on national origin. The 1882 Immigration Act established a head tax of $.50 per immigrant, gave the secretary of the treasury authority over immigration, and continued the bar against undesirables, including mental defectives and paupers. This legislation marked the beginning of an active federal role in immigration. Laws prohibiting the importation of foreign laborers under contract were also enacted in the 1880s. Legislation during World War I added literacy requirements for immigrants and expanded the exclusion of Chinese to cover most immigration from Asian countries.

Numerical restrictions on immigration came in the 1920s. A temporary Quota Act in 1921 was followed by a permanent National Origins Quota Act in 1924. This act established quotas based on the ethnic ancestry of the U.S. population in 1920—that is, the larger the proportion of the U.S. population having a particular national origin, the larger would be that nation's proportion of the immigration quota (Bean, Vernez, and Keely 1989:12). The act also placed an overall limitation on immigration of 150,000 persons per year, beginning in 1929. This combination of restrictions translated into country quotas such as 17,853 persons a year from Ireland, 5,802 from Italy, 869 from Hungary, and 252 from Spain. Only Great Britain and Northern Ireland combined retained a moderate quota of 65,721. The numerical limitations did not apply to Western Hemisphere immigrants, who had composed only a small portion of U.S. immigration. But the door that had been wide open to European immigration was now nearly closed.

Immigration to the United States had averaged 879,500 persons per year during the decade 1901–1910; 573,600 during 1911–1920; and 410,700 during 1921–1930. During the entire decade 1931–1940, the United States received a total of only 528,000 immigrants, fewer than the annual rate two decades earlier. The country-by-country limits within the 150,000 quota, combined with the economic depression in the United States, had dealt immigration a double blow.

With prohibitions on the entry of Communists added in the 1950s, the national origins quota system remained in effect until its removal by the Immigration and Nationality Act Amendments of 1965. The 1965 amendments were the most far-reaching revision of U.S. immigration policy since the first quotas had been enacted in 1921. Gone were the exclusions of specific nationalities; gone also were numerical proportions based on the national origins of the existing U.S. population. Previous country-by-country quotas were replaced by an Eastern Hemisphere ceiling of 170,000 with a 20,000 per country limit and a Western Hemisphere ceiling of 120,000 without per country limits. Certain immediate relatives of U.S. citizens were not counted within the ceilings. Subsequently, the separate ceilings for the hemispheres were combined into a worldwide ceiling of 270,000, with immediate relatives continuing not to be counted against the ceiling. The Immigration Act of 1990 further revised the immigration system to provide for a worldwide annual level of approximately 700,000 in fiscal years 1992–1994, followed by a permanent annual level of at least 675,000 beginning in fiscal year 1995. Separate provisions are included for family-sponsored immigrants and employment-based immigrants. In addition, provision is made for so-called diversity immigrants to provide additional opportunities for countries that have been underrepresented in immigrant admissions.

Because quotas had not been part of U.S. immigration policy before the 1920s, there had been no need for consideration of separate legislation for refugees. As a result, potential refugees suffered the same fate as potential immigrants when the immigration door virtually closed. The timing was tragic as Adolf Hitler rose to power in Germany and Jews attempted to flee from the Nazis but were generally denied entry into the United States. The United States accepted an estimated 250,000 refugees from Nazi persecution before its entry into World War II (Congressional Research Service 1991:556). The need was infinitely greater.

At the end of World War II, there were 11 million displaced persons in Europe living outside their country of nationality or customary residence. During the next few years, 1 million were resettled overseas, of whom the United States accepted 400,000. President Harry Truman took the first step to address the needs of the displaced persons by issuing a directive under which 90 percent of the regular, limited immigration quotas for central and eastern Europe would be used for displaced persons; 42,000 were admitted to the United States under this directive (Holborn 1956:410). The number of admissions available under existing law was clearly insufficient. This was followed by enactment of the first refugee legislation in U.S. history, the Displaced Persons Act of 1948. By the end of 1951, it had enabled the admission of more than 400,000 displaced persons. Subsequently, the Refugee Relief Act of 1953 and amendments to it in 1954 authorized the admission of another 200,000 refugees from war-torn Europe and escapees from Communist-dominated countries (Congressional Research Service 1991:556–558). This reference to escapees formally identified the preoccupation with refugees from Communist regimes that was to characterize U.S. refugee policy during the more than 40 years of the post–World War II cold war era.

Several developments in U.S. refugee policy occurred during this period: First, refugee admissions were handled separately from general immigration (although refugee admissions continued to be counted against immigration quotas); second, admissions focused almost entirely on refugees from communism; third, voluntary refugee resettlement agencies, working both overseas and in the United States, played a major role in arranging for and effecting resettlements; and fourth, in the absence of any government program for domestic assistance for refugees after their arrival, help in adjusting to American society necessarily came from the private sector. Indeed, under these laws, refugees could not be admitted unless it was guaranteed that they would not become public charges.

When Soviet forces suppressed a general insurrection in Hungary in late 1956 and refugees fled into Austria, the same policy prevailed as President Dwight Eisenhower agreed to admit the first of what ultimately became 38,000 refugees. Although the federal government opened and operated a processing center at Camp Kilmer in New Jersey, the federal assistance continued to be limited to entry, processing, and transportation costs to final destinations. Again, it was the voluntary agencies that took responsibility for resettlement, once the refugees left Camp Kilmer. The federal government was explicit that even the $40 per capita that it was willing to give to voluntary agencies for transportation of refugees to their final destinations did not "constitute a precedent for giving payment to the voluntary agencies for similar costs for other refugee movements" (Taft, North, and Ford 1979:55). The provision of per capita payments was important. The statement that they did not constitute a precedent—like other federal pronouncements from time to time—proved incorrect.

The next legislation established the statutory definition of refugees and refugeelike persons that would define U.S. refugee policy for the next 23 years:

The Act of September 11, 1957, sometimes referred to as the "Refugee-Escapee Act," provided for the admission of certain aliens who were eligible under the terms of the Refugee Relief Act, as well as "refugee-escapees," defined as persons fleeing persecution in Communist countries or countries in the Middle East. This was the basis for the definition of "refugee" incorporated in the Immigration and Nationality Act from 1965 until 1980. (Congressional Research Service 1991:558)

In addition, the 1957 act established the concept that refugee admissions would be addressed entirely separately from immigrant admissions: Not only did refugees continue to be identified separately; now they were no longer counted against the regular immigration quotas.

The Cuban Program

In January 1959, Fidel Castro came to power in Cuba, and the United States entered a new era in refugee resettlement. For the first time in history, the United States became a country of first asylum for large numbers of refugees. Cubans began fleeing as soon as the Batista regime had fallen; in fact, some had already moved to the United States in anticipation of a Castro victory. At first, the numbers were small, beginning with the pro-Batista political elite in 1959. Then came predominantly the business elite in 1959–1960; mainly the upper-middle socioeconomic group in 1960–1961; and a mix of the upper-middle, middle, and lower socioeconomic groups beginning in mid-1961.

Many of the early refugees brought funds out of Cuba or had previously deposited funds in U.S. and other foreign banks in anticipation of political upheaval. But as the refugee flight continued and as members of all socioeconomic groups began to join the exodus, the Castro government imposed increasingly stringent restrictions on those requesting permission to depart: All real and personal property was confiscated, and a refugee was allowed to depart from Cuba with only one suit of clothing, a few changes of underwear, and a maximum of five pesos, then worth about U.S. $.50. Later, the five pesos were eliminated.

Most of the Cuban refugees had a single destination—Miami. At that time,

Miami was distinguished by two important characteristics: Housing was plentiful as a result of recent overbuilding; and jobs were scarce because the economic growth that the real estate development had anticipated had not occurred.

The movement of Cuban refugees was in sharp contrast to earlier refugee flows to the United States. In previous refugee situations, other countries had provided initial asylum, and refugees were screened in European camps and carefully processed for movement to the United States. Prior to the arrival of a refugee, thorough preparations were made by the sponsoring voluntary agency and the receiving community. A place of residence and a job awaited the refugee on arrival.

The Cubans simply came—by commercial airline when they could get permission to leave, illegally by small boat or raft when they could not. Many had previous ties to the United States. Some already had permanent-resident status in the United States; others came on tourist, business, or student visas. Thousands of Cuban parents who were themselves unable to leave Cuba sent their children to the United States to escape Communist indoctrination, in some cases to avoid being sent to Russia or one of the Soviet satellite countries for such indoctrination. They entrusted their children to the United States in the hope of eventual reunion with them in this country or, preferably, in a future democratic Cuba. An estimated 13,000 unaccompanied Cuban children reached the United States. Five thousand were cared for by friends and private agencies without any participation by the federal government; the remaining 8,000 were placed in federally funded foster care in many locations throughout the United States.

By the end of 1960, more than 100,000 Cuban refugees had reached the United States, mostly in the Miami area. It was clear that state, local, and voluntary resources were insufficient to address the needs of the refugees or of Miami. In response, President Eisenhower established a Cuban Refugee Emergency Center in Miami in December 1960 with an initial allocation of $1 million from the president's contingency fund under the Mutual Security Act. Then President John Kennedy, two weeks after his inauguration, directed his secretary of health, education, and welfare, Abraham Ribicoff, to undertake a nine-point Cuban Refugee Program consisting of assistance to voluntary relief agencies; obtaining employment opportunities; resettlement from Miami to other areas; financial assistance to meet basic maintenance requirements of needy Cuban refugees; provision of health services; providing federal assistance for local public school operating costs; providing training and educational opportunities (with the emphasis on English-language instruction and job training); care of unaccompanied children; and surplus food distribution (later replaced by the food stamp program).

Federal funding was provided for these activities—first from the president's contingency funds under the Mutual Security Act of 1954 and the Foreign Assistance Act of 1961 and then from appropriations under the Migration and Refugee Assistance Act of 1962, which was enacted June 28, 1962. This was the first legislation specifically authorizing a broad array of domestic assistance and services for refugees within the United States and federal funds to pay for them.

Given the urgent nature of the Cuban refugee situation, the federal government used existing authorities in the Immigration and Nationality Act (INA) to legalize the presence of the refugees in the United States. After the United States terminated diplomatic and consular relations with Cuba on January 3, 1961, it was no longer possible to issue permanent-resident (immigrant) visas. Some refugees were granted the status of "indefinite voluntary departure"; most were "paroled" into the United States under the attorney general's authority under section 212(d)(5) of the INA. Both of these statuses enabled the refugees to remain legally in the United States indefinitely. The parole authority was used throughout the two decades' duration of the Cuban Refugee Program. Although legislators had included this authority in the INA in order to provide a means to allow particular individuals of special interest and concern to the government to be legally present in the United States, there was nothing to prevent its being used for large groups of refugees.

Through the Cuban Refugee Program, the federal government provided substantial funding to offset costs that would otherwise have fallen on the state of Florida, Dade County, and the city of Miami. The major such activities were health services and public education. Federally funded health services were provided through a Dade Country–administered medical and dental clinic located in the federal Cuban Refugee Center in Miami and through local hospitals. Funding to the Dade County public schools covered half of the operating costs incurred for Cuban refugee pupils. By the 1962–1963 school year, approximately 20,000 Cuban schoolchildren were enrolled—a considerable impact in a brief period. In the absence of federal refugee funds, the costs associated with health services and the public education of children would have had to be borne locally.

Another set of federally funded activities had the primary purpose of assisting the refugees during their initial time of need and then enabling them to become self-supporting: First, federal financial assistance was provided to needy refugees. Without such assistance, refugees would have been without publicly funded assistance because citizenship and durational-residency requirements in Florida's public welfare programs would have precluded their eligibility for aid. (Such requirements then existed in public welfare programs in a number of states; later, they were struck down by the courts.) Federal refugee funds were also available to reimburse other states for any public assistance provided to refugees who had been resettled from Miami. Very few of these resettled refugees required this assistance.

Second, federal funds financed extensive training for refugee adults, including hundreds of thousands of hours of adult English-language instruction and vocational training through the Dade County public school system; training for Cuban doctors, dentists, and other professionals to enable them to practice their professions in this country; and a program of loans for needy Cuban college students similar to those for U.S. citizen students.

Third, given the inevitable impact of large numbers of arrivals in Miami and the high unemployment there, the major activity of the Cuban Refugee Program was resettlement from Miami to job opportunities in other areas. Resettlements were carried out by four national voluntary refugee resettlement agencies with long experience in refugee resettlement both in the United States and abroad: United States Catholic Conference; Church World Service (Protestant); International Rescue Committee (nonsectarian); and HIAS (Hebrew Immigrant Aid Society). Throughout the nation, local churches, synagogues, and civic organizations participated with these agencies in the resettlement program. As in the Hungarian program, the federal government provided per capita funding to the resettlement agencies to offset their resettlement costs; the amount was now $60.

In 1962, between 1,600 and 1,800 refugees a week were arriving in Miami on twice-daily Pan American flights and twice-weekly KLM Royal Dutch Airlines flights from Havana. Then, as quickly as it had begun and grown, the refugee flow decreased to a trickle: On October 22, 1962, President Kennedy announced the existence of missiles in Cuba and the imposition of a quarantine on the importation of offensive weapons into the island. The next day, Castro banned all civilian flights to and from Cuba. For the first time in nearly four years, Miami did not have a large, steady influx of new refugees. Thus ended the first phase of the Cuban Refugee Program. During this period, 154,000 Cubans had registered at the federal Cuban Refugee Center, and 48,000 of them had been resettled outside the Miami area to all states except Alaska. (Later, 1 Cuban refugee was resettled in Alaska.) An estimated additional 100,000 Cuban refugees had not registered because they never needed federal assistance.

During the next three years, only two small streams of refugees continued: those who escaped illegally from Cuba by small boat and made the perilous trip across the Florida Straits and those who reached the United States after first going to another country. During this period, fewer than 30,000 refugees arrived in the United States and registered at the Cuban Refugee Center.

Then, on September 28, 1965, Castro—concerned about being blamed for refusing to let refugees leave Cuba and for the loss of life of persons who drowned while attempting to escape from the island by raft—announced in a speech that he would open a port in Cuba to which all Cubans in the United States could come and pick up their relatives who were still in Cuba.

"Now it will be known," Castro said, "who is at fault if someone drowns trying to reach the American paradise, the Yanqui paradise. That! for the well-prepared imperialists. Let's see what they say or do" (U.S. Department of Health, Education and Welfare 1971:3). Five days later, President Lyndon Johnson responded as he signed the new Immigration and Nationality Act of 1965 at the Statue of Liberty: "I declare this afternoon to the people of Cuba," Johnson stated, "that those who seek refuge here in America will find it. The dedication of America to our traditions as an asylum for the oppressed is going to be upheld'' (U.S. Department of Health, Education and Welfare 1971:3).

As a result of the statements by Fidel Castro and Lyndon Johnson, hundreds of small boats of all sizes and descriptions set out from Florida to the Cuban port of Camarioca to pick up relatives. Many were unseaworthy, and loss of life ensued. The U.S. Coast Guard set up a line of ships to rescue persons from small crafts and bring them safely to the United States. As a consequence, hundreds of refugees were pouring into Key West at all hours of the day and night. The situation was chaotic as efforts were made to provide them with emergency aid and accommodations.

In an attempt to create a safe and orderly flow of refugees, the United States negotiated a Memorandum of Understanding with Cuba. Under this memorandum, which was announced on November 6, the United States agreed to provide air transportation for 3,000 to 4,000 refugees a month, with priority given to the relatives living in Cuba of Cubans in the United States. The airlift began December 1, 1965. Until August 1971, about 42 flights a month brought about 3,500 refugees a month to Miami. In August 1971, a series of interruptions began to occur at the request of the Cuban government, which advised the U.S. Department of State that there remained in Cuba only a relatively small number of persons whom the Cuban authorities considered eligible to depart on the airlift. Only 26 flights occurred during 1972, and in April 1973, the airlift ended. During the period of the airlift, more than 265,000 refugees had registered in Miami, and more than 200,000 of them had resettled to join relatives in other parts of the United States. The flow that began with small boats making a dangerous crossing of the Florida Straits was over. But in 7 years, this same scenario, with variations, would repeat itself. And 14 years after that, it would happen again.

The Indochinese and Soviet Programs

From the beginnings of the Cuban Refugee Program in 1960 until 1975, it remained the sole program of domestic assistance to refugees in the United States. Then, in the spring of 1975, the American-supported governments in the countries of former French Indochina collapsed. Refugees fled immediately. Nearly 130,000, mostly Vietnamese, entered the United States. They went first through staging areas in the Pacific, then to processing centers in the continental United States, and then into communities under the sponsorship of the voluntary agencies. Congress moved rapidly to pass the Indochina Migration and Refugee Assistance Act of 1975, which President Gerald Ford signed into law on May 23, 1975. This act provided, for refugees from Vietnam and Cambodia, the same authority for domestic assistance and services as had been used for Cuban refugees under the Migration and Refugee Assistance Act of 1962. (A year later, on June 21, 1976, the act was amended to include refugees from Laos.)

Four processing centers in the United States were quickly established in April

and May 1975 at Camp Pendleton, California; Fort Chaffee, Arkansas; Eglin
Air Force Base, Florida; and Fort Indiantown Gap, Pennsylvania. Nine national
voluntary refugee resettlement agencies arranged resettlement opportunities for
the refugees. In addition to the four agencies that had participated in the Cuban
program, there were the Lutheran Immigration and Refugee Services, the Tol-
stoy Foundation, the American Council for Nationalities Service, the American
Fund for Czechoslovak Refugees, and the Travelers Aid International Social
Service of America. In addition, several state and local resettlement agencies
participated. These included the states of Washington, Iowa, Oklahoma, Maine,
and New Mexico; Jackson County, Missouri; the city of Indianapolis; the Chinese Consolidated Benevolent Associations of Los Angeles and New York; and
the Church of Jesus Christ of Latter Day Saints in Salt Lake City.

On December 20, 1975, the final 24 refugees left the Fort Chaffee processing
center—the last of the four centers to remain open—and the center closed.
Nearly 130,000 refugees had been resettled in all states of the United States in
seven months. As in the case of the Cubans, the attorney general's parole authority had been used to admit the Southeast Asian refugees. Some observers
thought the flow of Southeast Asian refugees to the United States was over.
They were wrong.

The federal program established for domestic assistance and services for the
Vietnamese, Cambodian, and Lao refugees was known as the Indochinese Refugee Assistance Program, or IRAP (pronounced I-RAP). Like the Cuban Refugee Program, it provided federal refugee funds to states for financial assistance
to needy refugees; for health services (now known as medical assistance); for
social services, again with the emphasis on English-language instruction and
employment-related services; and for assistance to impacted school districts.
Assistance payment levels were based on each state's program of Aid to Families with Dependent Children (AFDC); the scope of medical services was based
on each state's Medicaid program. Needy aged, blind, and disabled refugees
were eligible for the regular program of supplemental security income (SSI).

Unlike the Cuban program, which had a principal focus in a single locality—
Miami—because the first refugees had arrived, settled, and established a vital
Cuban community there, IRAP had to have a nationwide focus because the
refugees were resettled after brief stays in the U.S. processing centers to all parts
of the United States. In many areas, they were the first Vietnamese, Cambodian,
and later, Laotian residents.

The basic work of orientation, employment, and acclimation rested with the
resettlement agencies, their affiliates, and local sponsors. These efforts were
supplemented by several federal activities: The government established a nationwide toll-free telephone hotline, staffed by refugees, to provide information
and referral services in the languages of the refugees. It published a newspaper,
New Life, distributed to refugees, in separate Vietnamese, Cambodian, and Laotian editions. It established a special unit to work with refugees in establishing

self-help organizations, known as mutual assistance associations (MAAs), in order to further orientation, self-support, and participation in American life.

In Southeast Asia, the flow of refugees continued, first ebbing and then flooding, seriously impacting countries of first asylum, especially Thailand and Malaysia. In the United States, temporary legislation was extended, parole spaces were increased, and more refugees were accepted. By September 30, 1977, another 17,600 Southeast Asian refugees had been resettled in the United States. Then in fiscal year (FY) 1978 (October 1, 1977–September 30, 1978), 20,400 were resettled. In FY 1979, the number rose to 80,700, and in FY 1980, it peaked at 166,700. The major flow involved refugees escaping by boat from Vietnam, who quickly became known as the "boat people." The journey across the South China Sea was longer and more dangerous than that of Cubans across the Florida Straits. To the perils of nature and of overcrowded, unseaworthy vessels were added rape, murder, and looting by pirates who roamed the seas. In January 1979, the Department of State began negotiations that would eventually lead to the in-country processing of refugees within Vietnam, lessening the impetus to set out on the dangerous boat trips.

Meanwhile, the Soviet Union was easing its restrictions on emigration, and the number of Soviet refugees to the United States was increasing. Most were Jewish refugees. In 1977, the American Jewish community had spent over $20 million to help resettle 6,800 Soviet refugees in the United States; in the fall of 1978, the number was running nearly twice that of the previous year. The increases were straining the financial abilities of the private sector. In response, Congress included $20 million in the FY 1979 Foreign Operations Appropriations Act "for the resettlement in the United States of Soviet and other refugees not currently covered by existing federal refugee programs." The statutory language also specified that the funds "be expended only by HEW"—that is, the Department of Health, Education, and Welfare, which was responsible for the existing programs for Cuban and Indochinese refugees (*Congressional Record* 1978). The legislative history made clear that these funds were to be provided to the voluntary agencies that were sponsoring the refugees, that the amount was to be $1,000 per refugee, and that the voluntary agencies were to provide equal matching funds.

Thus, by FY 1979, the federal government was providing funds for assistance and services to refugees in the United States regardless of their national origin: to Cubans through the Cuban Refugee Program; to Vietnamese, Cambodians, and Laotians through the Indochinese Refugee Assistance Program; and now to non-Cuban, non-Indochinese refugees through what became known as the Voluntary Agency Matching Grant Program. The patchwork quilt of federally funded domestic refugee programs was now complete, if somewhat jumbled. This set the stage for the Refugee Act of 1980, which was already being developed.

The Refugee Act of 1980 and Its Aftermath

"The Congress declares," states title I of the Refugee Act of 1980,

that it is the historic policy of the United States to respond to the urgent needs of persons subject to persecution in their homelands, including, where appropriate, humanitarian assistance for their care and maintenance in asylum areas, efforts to promote opportunities for resettlement or voluntary repatriation, aid for necessary transportation and processing, admission to this country of refugees of special humanitarian concern to the United States, and transitional assistance to refugees in the United States. The Congress further declares that it is the policy of the United States to encourage all nations to provide assistance and resettlement opportunities to refugees to the fullest extent possible.[1]

This was, in fact, an accurate statement of what U.S. refugee policy had been during the 35 years of the post–World War II era preceding the 1980 act. Some might have questioned—and often did question during that period—the operational definition of "special humanitarian concern" as having been applied almost exclusively to refugees from Communist countries to the exclusion of a comparable concern for refugees from oppressive governments of non-Communist countries. In this respect, U.S. refugee policy mirrored and supported U.S. foreign policy—a relationship that is likely to continue.

"The objectives of this Act," title I of the 1980 act went on to say, "are to provide a permanent and systematic procedure for the admission to this country of refugees of special humanitarian concern to the United States and to provide comprehensive and uniform provisions for the effective resettlement and absorption of those refugees who are admitted."

The act incorporated the United Nations definition of a refugee into U.S. law; established an annual consultation procedure between the executive branch and Congress regarding refugee admissions; established a program of postarrival assistance for all refugee groups in the United States, regardless of national origin; set goals for the resettlement effort; and made a variety of other management, program, and admissions changes and clarifications (cf. Anker 1984; Kennedy 1981).

The 1980 act removed the previous requirement that a refugee must have fled from a "Communist or Communist-dominated country." The new definition of a refugee was included at section 101(a)(42) of the INA:

(42) The term "refugee" means (A) any person who is outside any country of such person's nationality or, in the case of a person having no nationality, is outside any country in which such person last habitually resided, and who is unable or unwilling to return to, and is unable or unwilling to avail himself or herself of the protection of, that country because of persecution or a well-founded fear of persecution on account of race, religion, nationality, membership in a particular social group, or political opinion, or (B) in such circumstances as the President after appropriate consultation [with Congress on

refugee admissions] (as defined in section 207(e) of this Act) may specify, any person who is within the country of such person's nationality or, in the case of a person having no nationality, within the country in which such person is habitually residing, and who is persecuted or who has a well-founded fear of persecution on account of race, religion, nationality, membership in a particular social group, or political opinion. The term "refugee" does not include any person who ordered, incited, assisted, or otherwise participated in the persecution of any person on account of race, religion, nationality, membership in a particular social group, or political opinion."

Under the act's procedures for determining refugee admissions, before the start of each fiscal year the president advises the Senate and House Judiciary Committees regarding proposed refugee admissions during the coming year; cabinet-level representatives of the president consult with members of the committees; committee members react to the president's proposal; and the president makes a final determination. The authority for the final determination rests entirely with the president, who may modify his original proposal in response to congressional reaction or may ignore congressional views. In the event that emergency refugee situations arise, additional consultations may be held, and determinations made, at any time. The act visualizes an annual flow into the United States of not more than 50,000 refugees, but admissions have never fallen to that level.

In conjunction with establishing a comprehensive definition of refugees and regular procedures for their admission, the act also sought to lessen the use of the attorney general's parole authority, which had been the vehicle for the admission of large numbers of refugees in the past. Thus, the act added this paragraph to section 212(d)(5) of the INA: "(B) The Attorney General may not parole into the United States an alien who is a refugee unless the Attorney General determines that compelling reasons in the public interest with respect to that particular alien require that the alien be paroled into the United States rather than admitted as a refugee under section 207."

Organizationally, the act called for the president to appoint a U.S. Coordinator for Refugee Affairs who would be responsible to the president for the development of overall refugee admission and resettlement policy and for the coordination of U.S. domestic and international refugee programs. The utility and effectiveness of this position varied over the years, and it was discontinued in 1993.

The act also established an Office of Refugee Resettlement within the Department of Health and Human Services (successor to the earlier Department of Health, Education, and Welfare) to fund and administer the federal domestic refugee programs. These are described below in the section on resettlement roles.

The legislators' desired nonuse of the attorney general's parole authority, except for individual cases of "compelling reasons in the public interest," lasted for 35 days after the Refugee Act of 1980 became law on March 17 of that year. On April 20, 1980, Castro announced that all Cubans wishing to emigrate to the United States were free to board boats at the port of Mariel. Within hours, Cubans living in the United States were on their way to pick up relatives. Between April 21 and April 30, more than 7,600 arrived. By the end of May, the total exceeded 94,000. The situation in south Florida was more chaotic than it had been during the first Cuban influx in 1959–1962.[2]

By September 26, 1980, when Castro finally closed the Mariel Harbor, nearly 125,000 Cubans had used it as their point of departure for the Florida Keys. During this same five-month period, 40,000 Haitians had also arrived illegally in the United States, most in Florida. Congress had moved quickly to provide emergency funding to offset the impact of the Cubans and Haitians and to provide for their reception, care, processing, and resettlement. By October 1980, some $375 million had been used for these purposes (Cuban-Haitian Task Force 1980).

A few weeks after the Cuban boat lift began, the Carter administration decided that the Cubans and Haitians would not be treated as refugees. Instead, a special immigration status of "Cuban/Haitian entrant (status pending)" would be established, using the attorney general's parole authority. The administration initially resisted the idea of providing refugee program benefits to the Cuban/Haitian entrants, but this resistance was short-lived in the face of congressional action. By October 10, Congress had passed, and President Jimmy Carter had signed, the Refugee Education Assistance Act of 1980. Title V of that act is entitled "Other Provisions Relating to Cuban and Haitian Entrants," generally known as the Fascell/Stone Amendment, after Congressman Dante Fascell and Senator Richard Stone, both of Florida. It requires the president to "exercise authorities with respect to Cuban and Haitian entrants which are identical to the authorities which are exercised under chapter 2 of title IV of the Immigration and Nationality Act"—the authorities that apply to refugees. Under this provision, any Cuban or Haitian who is paroled into the United States or who is in the United States and has applied for political asylum is eligible for refugee benefits. This was the first expansion of the refugee program, as established by the Refugee Act of 1980, to cover persons who are not actually classified as refugees. Within six months of enactment, the rigorous definitions and procedures contained in the Refugee Act had given way to the realities of migration impact and assistance.

One further expansion of refugee program coverage has occurred: Beginning in 1988, immigration law was amended by the Foreign Operations Appropriations Act to provide for the admission as immigrants, and their coverage under the refugee program, of Amerasians from Vietnam who were fathered by U.S. citizens—principally U.S. servicemen—together with their immediate relatives.

After the peak flow of 207,000 refugees in FY 1980 (plus the 165,000 Cuban and Haitian entrants that year), the number of refugee admissions decreased to 159,000 in FY 1981 and 97,000 in FY 1982. During FYs 1983 to 1987, the flow remained unusually stable, ranging between 61,000 and 71,000 annually, with Southeast Asians continuing to be the largest group. In FY 1988, the total rose to 76,000 and during the next six years exceeded 100,000 a year. The predominant trend during this period has been an increase in the number of refugees from the former Soviet Union, primarily Soviet Jewish refugees, ranging between 38,000 and 61,000 annually.

In the 1990s, the flow of Cuban and Haitian entrants began to increase once again. The entrants were setting out in small boats and rafts and either reaching U.S. shores undetected or after being intercepted and picked up by the Coast Guard. More than 10,000 Haitian entrants and 2,500 Cuban entrants arrived in FY 1992; in FY 1993, the figures were 700 Haitians and 3,500 Cubans. In 1994, the flow of Cubans became a flood. During January through June, the Coast Guard rescued 3,700 Cuban rafters in the Florida Straits; in July, the figure exceeded 1,000. On August 13, Castro ordered Cuban authorities not to hinder the departure of rafters. Within days, the Coast Guard was intercepting over 500 Cuban rafters a day. In response, the attorney general announced on August 18 that the Cubans would be detained rather than admitted into the United States, and the following day, President Bill Clinton announced that they would be sent to the U.S. Naval Base at Guantánamo Bay, Cuba. The United States' 35-year policy of accepting Cuban boat people had been reversed. Apparently unconvinced, the number of Cuban rafters increased, with more than 18,000 leaving Cuba between August 20 and 31. The number detained at Guantánamo soon reached 28,000; another 4,000 were in a refugee camp in Panama, the capacity of Guantánamo having been exceeded.

By September 9, the United States and Cuba had reached an agreement under which at least 20,000 Cubans a year would be admitted from Cuba to the United States through orderly procedures under a variety of immigration authorities—as permanent residents, refugees, and parolees. This did not include those who were being detained. Several months later, the Justice Department announced that it would admit parents and children among the Guantánamo detainees for humanitarian reasons. For other Cuban detainees, the outlook remained uncertain until May 2, 1995, when the Clinton administration announced that all of the 21,000 Cuban refugees remaining at Guantánamo would be admitted to the United States but that, under an agreement with Cuba, future Cuban rafters would be returned to Cuba. "The new policy of repatriating Cuban rafters," the *Washington Post* noted, "completes a change, begun last summer, that ends 35 years of official U.S. treatment of Cuban refugees as heroic freedom fighters" (May 3, 1995, p. A1).[3]

THE RESETTLEMENT PROCESS

Roles in Resettlement

Refugee resettlement is one of the United States' broadest and most enduring public-private partnerships in behalf of humanitarian objectives: Voluntary agencies operate at international, national, and local levels; federal, state, and local governments are involved; and thousands of citizens serve as sponsors of refugees, usually working through their churches, synagogues, and civic organizations. As refugee communities begin to establish themselves, refugees themselves become involved in the resettlement of new arrivals, both personally with respect to newly arriving family members and professionally through refugee community and service organizations.

The Refugee Act of 1980 prescribed new requirements and procedures governing the admission of refugees into the United States and the duration of federally funded domestic assistance to refugees. But in terms of the actual program of resettlement assistance and services, it essentially took existing practice and enacted it into law.

Agencies generally referred to as national voluntary refugee resettlement agencies have played a principal role in all refugee resettlement in the United States since the end of World War II. In some cases, their work dates back much earlier. The International Rescue Committee, for example, was founded in 1933 to aid victims of Nazism and Fascism. HIAS's efforts on behalf of Jewish immigrants began in the nineteenth century.

In recounting the resettlement of displaced persons following World War II, Holborn (1956:145) captured the essence of the roles of governments and voluntary agencies:

The solution of far-reaching social problems always requires official action either on the national or international level. Yet private efforts, inspired by humanitarian impulses, are indispensable to public services which, by their very nature, are impersonal, and are supplemented by the service of voluntary agencies geared to the needs of the individuals concerned.

The traditional role of voluntary agencies in the U.S. resettlement program has been to arrange U.S. sponsorships for refugees while they are still overseas and, at their destination, to provide for their reception; for initial food, clothing, and shelter; for the referral of adults to English-language training and to jobs or employment services; and for a variety of other services important to early functioning in a new environment, such as enrolling children in school.

Under the Cuban Refugee Program, federal relationships with the voluntary resettlement agencies were handled by the Department of Health and Human Services (HHS). More recently, for Indochinese and other refugees, these relationships were handled by the Department of State. The 1980 Refugee Act provided that this responsibility would be placed in the newly created Office of Refugee Resettlement in HHS unless the president determined otherwise. Early in 1981, President Carter decided that the responsibility would remain with the State Department, leaving existing practice intact.

Although the 1980 act did not refer specifically to the voluntary agency matching grant program, which had begun the previous year, it allowed the program to continue. When the matching grant program began, it was especially attractive to the voluntary agencies that were resettling non-Cuban, non-Indochinese refugees because federal refugee funding for domestic assistance was limited at that time to the Cubans and Indochinese. After the 1980 act provided for federally funded assistance regardless of a refugee's country of origin, this special attractiveness of the matching grant program disappeared. Nevertheless, several voluntary agencies have continued to participate over the years with respect to at least a small portion of their resettlements, and the American Jewish community has continued to participate, through HIAS and the Council of Jewish Federations, with respect to nearly all Soviet Jewish refugees.

Three federal departments have major responsibilities for refugee resettlement in the United States: The Department of State manages the program of initial resettlement, which is carried out under agreements with the voluntary agencies. It provides per capita funding to the voluntary agencies for this purpose under what are usually called reception and placement (R&P) grants. The State Department is also responsible for international aspects of refugee policies and programs, including U.S. relations with the United Nations High Commissioner for Refugees. It has also provided for English-language training and cultural orientation while U.S.-bound refugees are still in camps overseas—notably for Southeast Asian refugees, most of whom spent time in processing centers before reaching the United States.

The Department of Justice, through its Immigration and Naturalization Service, has the principal responsibility for determining the eligibility of applicants for refugee status. In addition, for the past several years, the Justice Department's Community Relations Service has been responsible for resettlement arrangements for Cuban and Haitian entrants who have been admitted to the United States.

The Office of Refugee Resettlement (ORR), within HHS, has overall responsibility for domestic assistance and services for refugees in the United States. The 1980 Refugee Act places most of this authority with the director of ORR, although a few authorities, such as issuing regulations, are reserved to the secretary of HHS. Also within HHS, the Public Health Service has major responsibilities for refugees as part of its overall health responsibilities.

Other federal agencies also play important roles with respect to refugees while carrying out their regular functions. Perhaps most important is the Social Security Administration since refugees, like other residents, must have social security cards in order to be employed.

The Refugee Act makes clear that the role of the states is to be central to the resettlement effort. In order to receive federal refugee funds, a state must have a federally approved plan for providing assistance and services to refugees and must designate a state coordinator to ensure coordination of all resources toward effective resettlement. The emphasis on the central role of the states has meant a deemphasis on the direct relationships between the federal government and specific localities that characterized the early years of the Indochinese program. Then, federal project grants for English-language training and employment services were made directly to a wide range of public and private nonprofit agencies at the local level. In contrast, current law and legislative history have established that, except for certain types of special projects, 85 percent of funds appropriated for refugee social services, such as language training and employment services, must be allocated among the states based on each state's proportion of the population of refugees who have entered the United States during the preceding three fiscal years. The states may then use these funds either to provide services directly or to contract with public or private service providers. Most states contract with a variety of providers, including voluntary agencies, refugee organizations, and local governments, rather than providing services directly.

Beginning in 1983, the federal government reemphasized the role of local governments through a program of targeted assistance grants for counties with large numbers of refugees and Cuban/Haitian entrants. Although these grants were awarded to states, they were to be administered at the county or equivalent level. Specific statutory authority for the targeted assistance program was subsequently added by the Refugee Assistance Extension Act of 1986.

Refugee Assistance and Services

Several types of assistance and services for refugees in the United States are authorized by the Refugee Act. The more important types are discussed below.

Care of Unaccompanied Minors. Full care is authorized for refugee unaccompanied minors—that is, minors who are in the United States unaccompanied by a parent or other close adult relative. This may include foster care, medical assistance, and any type of service necessary to the well-being of the child. Such care may be funded until the child is reunited with a parent or legally responsible relative or until the child reaches the age of majority under state law, whichever comes first. ORR has always considered the care of unaccompanied minors to be its first priority: Within available funding for the refugee program, the care of unaccompanied minors will be funded first.

Cash and Medical Assistance. Since most refugees reach the United States with few, if any, resources, transitional cash and medical assistance has been considered an essential component of federal domestic refugee funding since the Cuban Refugee Program began. Under both the Cuban and Indochinese programs, fully federally funded assistance was made available to needy refugees, regardless of family composition, age, or disability. In addition to meeting basic humanitarian needs, such assistance was intended to avoid the burden that would otherwise have fallen on state and local public and private resources.

The Refugee Act of 1980 continued the authorization of federal funding for cash and medical assistance but placed a time limitation on it. The act authorizes the director of ORR to provide funding to states and other public and private nonprofit agencies for cash and medical assistance that is provided to refugees during their first 36 months in the United States. If a refugee is eligible for the regular programs of AFDC and Medicaid, federal refugee funds are authorized to cover what would otherwise be the state share of AFDC and Medicaid costs during this 36-month period. Similarly, if an aged, blind, or disabled refugee is eligible for the federal program of SSI, federal refugee funds are authorized to cover the cost of any state supplementary payments (SSPs) for refugee SSI recipients during the 36-month period.[4]

If a refugee meets the same standards of financial need as apply in a state's AFDC program but does not meet the specific family composition, age, or disability requirements to qualify for the regular programs of AFDC, Medicaid, or SSI, then the refugee qualifies for the special federal programs of refugee cash assistance (RCA) and refugee medical assistance (RMA). RCA and RMA are usually administered by the same state agency as administers the state's AFDC program. The payment levels for RCA are the same as those in the state's AFDC program. The scope of medical coverage under RMA is the same as in the state's Medicaid program, plus any additional publicly funded health services that are available to other indigent residents through public institutions and would have to be met from state or local funds in the absence of federal refugee funding. In addition, a state may use federal RMA funds to provide health screening and follow-up.

The eligibility of refugees for AFDC, Medicaid, and SSI exists independently of the availability of federal refugee funds; therefore, the 36-month limit in the statute does not affect the duration of a refugee's eligibility for these programs. However, since RCA and RMA are special federal programs that would not exist in the absence of federal refugee funds, their scope and duration are governed by federal refugee regulations.

The major trend in domestic refugee assistance during the decade and a half since the 1980 Refugee Act has been reductions in federal funding for cash and medical assistance. This is discussed later in more detail.

Social Services. English-language training and employment services are the principal services emphasized in the Refugee Act, but any of a wide range of services related to adaptation and functioning in the United States may be provided. The overriding purpose of these services is to help refugees to become self-supporting and contributing participants in U.S. society. In 1982, Congress, concerned about increased refugee dependence on cash assistance, added language to the 1980 act, explicitly stating the intent of Congress that "employable refugees should be placed on jobs as soon as possible after their arrival in the United States" and that "social service funds should be focused on employment-related services, English-as-a-second-language training (in non-work hours where possible), and case management services." Case management services were intended to help ensure the timely participation of refugees in appropriate service programs and early job placement. In 1986, Congress added language requiring social service funds to be allocated among the states based on each state's portion of the three-year refugee population. This language translated recent practice into a statutory requirement. However, while prescribing a formula for allocating funds, the language did not impose a statutory limit on the time during which refugees could receive ORR-funded services; they could receive such services at any point before they became U.S. citizens. In addition to the 85 percent of social service funds allocated among the states according to the required formula, ORR has used the remaining 15 percent, which is awarded on a competitive basis to public and private nonprofit agencies, for special projects intended to advance resettlement.

Targeted Assistance. Under the Refugee Assistance Extension Act of 1986, targeted assistance grants are authorized to be made to states "for assistance to counties and similar areas in the States where, because of factors such as unusually large refugee populations (including secondary migration), high refugee concentrations, and high use of public assistance by refugees, there exists and can be demonstrated a specific need for supplementation of available resources for services to refugees." The grants must be "primarily for the purpose of facilitating refugee employment and achievement of self-sufficiency." The state, in turn, must make available to the county or other local entity at least 95 percent of the amount the state receives. Unlike social service funds, targeted assistance funds are not governed by a statutory formula. Instead, ORR publishes a notice of proposed allocations in the *Federal Register,* designating the counties and amounts proposed to be awarded, receives public comments, and then publishes a final notice. Some 20 states have received funds on behalf of 40 counties and multicounty metropolitan areas. In addition, Congress has traditionally earmarked a portion of the annual targeted assistance appropriation to be awarded to Florida for use by the Dade County (Miami) public schools and Jackson Memorial Hospital (Miami) to offset the local impact of Cuban/Haitian entrants and refugees. In recent years, Congress has also specified that 10 percent of the targeted assistance appropriation be used "for grants to localities most heavily impacted by the influx of refugees such as Laotian Hmong, Cambodians, and Soviet Pentecostals"; these funds are awarded on a competitive basis.

Preventive Health. The Refugee Act requires the secretary of HHS to "develop and implement methods for monitoring and assessing the quality of medical screening and related health services provided to refugees awaiting resettlement in the United States." It also authorizes the director of ORR to provide funds to state and local health agencies "to meet their costs of providing medical screening and initial medical treatment to refugees." ORR transfers to the Public Health Service the funds appropriated for these purposes.

Voluntary Agency Matching Grant Program. Although the matching grant program has continued under the Refugee Act, its parameters have been redefined over time. Originally a vehicle to provide federal domestic assistance for non-Cuban, non-Indochinese refugees, who were not covered under refugee legislation before 1980, it is currently seen more as an alternative to the state-administered refugee program. The Department of State's R&P grants to the voluntary agencies cover food, clothing, and shelter during a refugee's first 30 days in the United States. Therefore, the matching grant program, for those voluntary agencies and refugees participating in it, picks up with a refugee's second month in the United States and covers financial assistance and a wide range of other services from the second month through at least the fourth month. Ideally, the program will enable a refugee to become employed and self-supporting during this period and thereby avoid the need for public cash assistance through the welfare system. The federal contribution is still $1,000, despite price increases, and an equal private match has continued to be required. The private match, in cash and in kind, generally exceeds the requirement. In the early 1980s, the Office of Management and Budget (OMB) wanted to eliminate the matching grant program for reasons that were never made clear; in response, Congress included a provision in the Refugee Assistance Extension Act of 1986 requiring that the federal per capita contribution not be reduced and the required private match not be increased.[5]

Wilson/Fish Projects. In 1984, dissatisfied with high refugee dependence on cash assistance in some states, Congress amended refugee legislation to provide for the implementation of alternative resettlement projects to promote self-sufficiency. This provision became known as the Wilson/Fish Amendment, for Senator Pete Wilson of California and Congressman Hamilton Fish of New York, its sponsors. In this legislation, *alternative* meant an alternative to the regular state-administered assistance programs. Such projects could be administered by either public or private nonprofit agencies. A number of Wilson/Fish projects have been funded by ORR, most of which have resulted in lower need for cash assistance and greater self-support. In approving the Wilson/Fish Amendment, Congress specified that it would be budget neutral; thus, there is no additional appropriation for these projects. Instead, the projects must be funded from ORR's regular appropriations for assistance and services.

Trends in the Domestic Resettlement Program

Since 1986, the principal trend in the refugee resettlement program within the United States has been reduced federal funding in relation to the number of refugees admitted. The major effect has been considerably more cost borne by the states than was anticipated when the Refugee Act of 1980 was developed and enacted.

A secondary trend has been reductions in the availability of the special RCA and RMA programs. The first reductions in RCA/RMA were made for programmatic reasons; the most recent were a result of funding limitations.

Funding limitations began in FY 1986 in the refugee program, as in many other federal programs, as a result of the Balanced Budget and Emergency Deficit Control Act of 1985, known as Gramm-Rudman-Hollings, usually shortened to Gramm-Rudman. The refugee program achieved required savings by shortening the period for which federal refugee funds would pay the state share of costs for AFDC, Medicaid, and SSI SSPs. Although the Refugee Act of 1980 authorizes such costs to be paid during a refugee's first 36 months in the United States, this authority—like all of the authorities in the act—is subject "to the extent of available appropriations" (INA, section 412 [a] [1] [A]). The first such reduction was to 31 months, effective March 1, 1986. Subsequent reductions have been to 24 months, February 1, 1988; to 4 months, January 1, 1990; and to 0 months, October 1, 1990. Since refugee eligibility for AFDC, Medicaid, and SSI exists independently of the availability of federal refugee funding, these changes did not affect the receipt of such assistance; they simply shifted to the states the problem of meeting the regular state share of costs. States complained that these reductions in federal refugee funding were an abrogation of what they referred to as a "federal compact with the states." Given overall federal budget limitations, their complaints had no effect.

Congress had included a 36-month limit in the Refugee Act not only to define a maximum period of federal support to offset state costs but also because it believed that any special refugee assistance should be transitional—available during a refugee's initial months but not indefinitely. Congress was sensitive, too, to the fact that the RCA and RMA programs assist refugees who would not otherwise be eligible for such aid unless, in a given locality, there is a comparable state- or locally funded general assistance (GA) program for needy nonrefugees who do not meet the special requirements of family composition, age, and disability—technically known as "categorical" requirements—for AFDC, Medicaid, and SSI. The number of jurisdictions with broad GA programs was limited in 1980; over the years, the number has become more limited as states and localities have faced tightened budgets.

Although there had not been a time limit on the receipt of RCA and RMA in the Cuban and Indochinese programs prior to the 1980 Refugee Act, use of cash assistance had not been excessive. For Cubans, receipt of cash assistance was high in Miami during the early 1960s when large numbers of refugees were arriving and few jobs were available; for Cubans resettled outside Miami, it was extremely low. For Indochinese refugees, utilization of public cash assistance increased sharply at the end of the 1970s and reached 45 percent of the Indochinese refugee population in late summer 1980 due to the large number of new refugees, many without the occupational and educational skills of earlier arrivals. In the development of the 1980 act, both the executive branch and Congress agreed that any new refugee legislation should contain a time limit.

Use of cash assistance continued to increase in 1981 after the 36-month limit went into effect. This was due in part to large numbers of new arrivals and lower skill levels among the newly arriving refugees, but there was also an unforeseen factor connected with the imposition of a time limit: ORR reported to Congress in 1983 that "some refugees and service providers had interpreted the 36-month period of special refugee assistance as a 36-month guaranteed entitlement to cash assistance. During this time, instead of seeking employment immediately, newly arriving refugees could spend as much time getting education and training as possible'' (ORR 1983:8). In response, on March 1, 1982, HHS issued regulations reducing the time-eligibility period for RCA and RMA to a refugee's first 18 months in the United States. This also served to lessen the duration of any disparity between assistance available to refugees and that available to other residents. For similar reasons, HHS further reduced the RCA/ RMA time-eligibility period to 12 months, effective October 1, 1988.

More recently, on October 1, 1991, HHS reduced the period to eight months. This third reduction, which came a year after ORR had discontinued all federal refugee funding for state costs of AFDC, Medicaid, and SSI SSPs, was due solely to budget limitations.

In 1992, the Bush administration proposed to terminate the RCA and RMA programs and to provide cash and medical assistance through the voluntary agencies and a private medical program—with virtually no federal funds. The ensuing controversy engaged the resettlement community for the next several months. While leaving a final decision up to HHS, Congress appropriated sufficient funds to permit the continuation of an eight-month RCA/RMA program. Early in 1993, a federal court forbade implementation of the proposed private program because of HHS's failure to observe federal rule-making guidelines required by the Administrative Procedure Act. The incoming Clinton administration dropped the Bush proposal and began to try to repair the damage that had been done to the cooperative spirit of the public/private partnership that has been the essential ingredient of successful refugee resettlement in the United States.

More than a decade and a half of experience under the Refugee Act of 1980— although punctuated by a number of refugee emergencies and a variety of programmatic controversies—has demonstrated the resilience of both the legislation and the public and private participants in the resettlement effort.

Since 1980, a number of issues that dominated debate about the refugee program have become far less important or relevant. For example:

- *At the federal level, should HHS or the Department of State administer the initial resettlement grants with the voluntary agencies?* Many years of experience since President Carter's decision to leave this responsibility in the State Department have shown that this is probably as good an arrangement as any. It requires a functional relationship between the two federal agencies, but so would any alternative arrangement since initial resettlement encompasses the transition from the international sphere to the domestic one.

- *To what extent should refugees be provided domestic assistance not available to other U.S. residents?* This was a much-debated issue in the development of the Refugee Act and in the 1980s. It has been rendered nearly moot by the reductions in federal funding that have reduced the period of special assistance from a refugee's first 36 months in the United States down to 8 months. There is simply not much of a span to debate between zero months and 8 months.

Over the years since 1980, there have been changes in emphasis from time to time with respect to services to help refugees become self-supporting. These changes, however, do not constitute a discernible trend. Through its discretionary grant programs, ORR has encouraged, developed, and funded a variety of useful and often innovative projects to address the specific problems and needs of particular refugee groups in various locations in the United States. These projects are identified in ORR's informative annual reports to Congress, and some have been the subject of independent evaluations.

Despite such efforts at improving the quality of assistance and services, the dominant trend in domestic resettlement since 1986 has been continuing reductions in federal funding. These reductions have affected both refugees and their receiving communities by an abbreviated period of special refugee cash and medical assistance and an increased portion of costs dependent on state and local resources.

REFUGEE ISSUES: THE WIDER CONTEXT

Refugee resettlement in the United States is likely to be profoundly influenced in the next few years by three much larger areas of concern and reexamination: (1) U.S. immigration policy as a whole; (2) revision of cash and medical assistance systems within the United States; and (3) the worldwide refugee situation.

U.S. Immigration Policy

The congressionally mandated U.S. Commission on Immigration Reform is scheduled to issue its final report by September 30, 1997, assessing immigration policy and making recommendations regarding its implementation and effects. In a 1994 interim report, the commission addressed a number of areas of concern, including border management to prevent illegal entries while facilitating legal ones; work site enforcement of prohibitions against the employment of illegal aliens; denial of most publicly funded benefits to illegal aliens while maintaining eligibility of legal immigrants; development of the ability to respond effectively and humanely to emergencies involving the migration of large numbers of persons who have the United States as their destination; and curtailment of unlawful immigration at its source through U.S. foreign policy and international economic policy efforts to reduce the causes of unauthorized migration to the United States (U.S. Commission on Immigration Reform 1994).

All of these are areas that are both difficult to address and subject to continuing public debate as to appropriate policies and actions. Underlying the issues is a fundamental premise embraced by many that—whatever one's views on the specifics may be—in order for the United States to be able to maintain a national policy and program of legal immigration, illegal migration must be controlled.

Cash and Medical Assistance Systems

Cash and medical assistance available to needy refugees in the United States has been built around the systems and benefits available to U.S. citizens. Most refugees who have received such assistance have received it under the regular programs of AFDC, Medicaid, and SSI rather than under any special programs of refugee assistance. As the regular programs are subjected to national debate and potentially to major revision, the effect on refugee resettlement will need to be examined and addressed.

Because refugees comprise only a very small percentage of the nation's assistance recipients, their needs will not weigh much in the determination of changes in the welfare system. But such changes could weigh heavily on refugees and on the future of refugee resettlement in the United States.

Worldwide Refugee Situation

In early 1995, the United Nations High Commissioner for Refugees reported that there were 49 million refugees and displaced persons throughout the world. Of these, 23 million were refugees who had fled across borders, and 26 million were displaced persons in their own countries. As the *New York Times* reported, "An astonishing 1 in every 115 people on earth is now on the run or in some kind of exile" (1995: sec. 4: 3).

The United States' refugee admissions ceiling for FY 1995 was 110,000 persons. About 30,000 were expected to be persons outside their own countries, and about 80,000 persons within their own countries. Translated into a percentage, the United States had committed itself to resettling about two tenths of 1 percent of the world's refugees and displaced persons. Clearly, whether the United States were to resettle a few thousand more refugees, or a few thousand fewer would have little impact on the world refugee situation, although it would be profoundly important to the individual persons involved.

As federal funds continue to become more limited in the future, competition will increase between international and domestic concerns generally and, with respect to refugees, between resettlement in the United States and protection and assistance overseas. Decisions about the appropriate expression of the nation's tradition of humanitarian concern for uprooted and threatened people will become more difficult rather than less.

NOTES

1. Nearly all of the provisions of the Refugee Act of 1980 and subsequent amendments were enacted as parts of section 412 of the Immigration and Nationality Act. For clarity and ease of reference, they are cited here according to the acts that contained them.

2. Castro also seized the opportunity of the Mariel boat lift to release, and allow the departure of, criminals from jails and inmates from mental institutions. Although very

few had serious criminal records or were severely mentally ill, these few posed difficult problems (ORR 1982:6–8).

3. About 16,000 of the Haitian detainees at Guantánamo returned to Haiti voluntarily after U.S. military intervention returned Haitian president Jean-Bertrand Aristide to power in October 1994. Nearly all of the remaining 4,000 were involuntarily repatriated to Haiti in January 1995.

4. For nonrefugees, the regular federal share of AFDC and Medicaid costs varies from state to state and averages about 54 percent nationally. The basic SSI program is entirely federally funded, but there is no federal funding for SSPs, which are optional with the states.

5. OMB, as part of the executive office of the president, is responsible for overall executive branch budget proposals and concerns. Since OMB is usually associated with constraining federal spending, its proposed elimination of the matching grant program, which was drawing more than half of its funding from private sources, was puzzling. The effect would have been to shift all of the costs to the federal government since the refugees covered by the matching grant program would have been eligible for fully federally funded refugee assistance and services. As noted, Congress rejected the idea.

REFERENCES

Anker, Deborah. 1984. The Development of U.S. Refugee Legislation. In *In Defense of the Alien,* Vol. 6. Edited by Lydio F. Tomasi. New York: Center for Migration Studies. Pp. 159–166.

Bean, Frank D., Georges Vernez, and Charles B. Keely. 1989. *Opening and Closing the Doors: Evaluating Immigration Reform and Control.* Washington, D.C.: Urban Institute Press.

Congressional Record. 1978. September 22, 1978. Pp. S15804–S15809.

Congressional Research Service. 1991. Brief History of United States Immigration Policy. In *Immigration and Nationality Act.* Committee on the Judiciary, House of Representatives. (9th Edition.) April 1992. Pp. 548–569.

Cuban-Haitian Task Force. 1980. *A Report of the Cuban-Haitian Task Force.* Washington, D.C.: Department of State. November 1, 1980.

Holborn, Louise W. 1956. *The International Refugee Organization.* London: Oxford University Press.

Kennedy, Edward M. 1981. The Refugee Act of 1980. *International Migration Review* 15(1):141–156.

Office of Refugee Resettlement (ORR). 1982. *Report to the Senate Appropriations Committee on the Cuban/Haitian Entrant Program.* Washington, D.C.: HHS, Office of Refugee Resettlement.

———. 1983. *Refugee Resettlement Program: Report to the Congress.* Washington, D.C.: U.S. Department of Health and Human Services.

Taft, Julia, David North, and David Ford. 1979. *Refugee Resettlement in the United States: Time for a New Focus.* Washington, D.C.: New Trans Century Foundation.

U.S. Commission on Immigration Reform. 1994. *U.S. Immigration Policy: Restoring Credibility.* Washington, D.C.: U.S. Government Printing Office.

U.S. Department of Health, Education, and Welfare. 1971. *Fact Sheet: Cuban Refugees.* Washington, D.C.: Social and Rehabilitation Service, Cuban Refugee Program. March.

Chapter 2

Patterns in Refugee Resettlement and Adaptation

DAVID W. HAINES

Although the federal government's role in refugee resettlement has grown and changed, and although the numbers and origins of refugees to the United States have shifted, the initial difficulties of adjusting to a new society remain a constant. These difficulties are, in many ways, similar to those faced by immigrants to the United States, both those arriving in recent years and those who came in the major waves of immigration that ended in the early 1900s. However, the very nature of refugee status, particularly the dangers of exodus and the permanency of separation from home country, results in unique aspects to the resettlement of refugees.

The precise ways in which refugees adjust to the United States vary considerably, as would be expected from the divergent social and cultural heritages that refugees bring with them to the United States. There is additional variation in resettlement because of the different faces that American society presents to particular refugee populations in particular locations at particular times. Yet there are also some commonalities in refugee resettlement and in the factors that affect refugees' early adjustment to America. This chapter presents an overview of such factors based on what has become a very broad range of research. Reflecting their numbers, such research is most extensive for Southeast Asian and Cuban refugees, relatively serviceable for Soviet refugees, and rather limited for other, smaller groups. The introductory discussion that follows addresses, first, the capabilities, expectations, values, and experiences that refugees bring with them (including the aftereffects of exodus and transit), second, the initial situation they find in the United States (including the major problems they are most likely to confront), and third, the new lives they build over the longer term.

WHAT THEY BRING

General Population Characteristics

Much of the course of refugee adjustment to the United States hinges not on cultural characteristics or personal experiences but rather on such basic population characteristics as age and sex. Elderly refugees from many countries, for example, lack familiarity with English and with American customs and may find adapting to new ways particularly difficult. Children, on the other hand, adjust more quickly and completely to new customs, often at the expense of their relations with parents and other elders. Women, by virtue of their roles as wives and mothers, may remain more confined within their homes and thus be set off from experiences that would help them acculturate to the new society. The relative proportion of the sexes and of particular age groups thus helps determine the kinds of problems most likely to affect given refugee groups.

America's refugees over the past 35 years have differed markedly in general demographic characteristics. They also differ both from the general U.S. population and from immigrants to the United States. Age differences are the greatest. As Taft, North, and Ford (1979:18) pointed out in their early seminal report on the U.S. refugee program, the U.S. population had a median age of almost 29 in 1975, and immigrants arriving that year had a median age of about 24. Cuban refugees who had arrived since the late 1960s were considerably older, with a median age of over 37; Southeast Asian refugees, who were then becoming the country's new major refugee group, were considerably younger, with a median age under 20. Soviet refugees, the third largest of the refugee groups, were in between, with a median age 2 years greater than that of the U.S. population as a whole. In terms of the proportion of the population under age 15, the differences were similarly striking. Both the U.S. population and arriving immigrants in 1975 had about one fourth of their members under the age of 15, but for both Cuban and Soviet refugees, less than a fifth of the population was under the age of 15. For Southeast Asian refugees arriving in 1975, well over a third (38.7 percent) were under the age of 15.

This general pattern has continued over the succeeding years. Generally speaking, Southeast Asian refugees are still a young population, much younger than the U.S. population, younger than immigrants in general, and younger than other Asian-origin populations in the United States. Soviet, Eastern European, and Cuban refugees, on the other hand, have tended to be older, and with fewer children. Such differences have direct implications on virtually all areas of resettlement, from finding housing to obtaining work, to mixing separate incomes of husbands and wives, to planning for the economic future of succeeding generations.

Occupational and Educational Background

The second set of factors that influences adjustment to the United States involves the skills and competencies that refugees bring with them. One of the most important of these is occupational background. For early Cuban, Soviet, and Southeast Asian arrivals, more than two thirds of those who had been in the labor force in their country of origin had been in white-collar occupations. For the U.S. population as a whole, by way of comparison, only half of those in the labor force are in white-collar occupations. Perhaps more important are the percentages who were in professional and technical occupations. For the U.S. labor force, the relevant figure is about 15 percent, but for all the refugee populations, the figure has been much higher. Of Cuban refugees, one in four had been in a professional or technical occupation; for Vietnamese refugees, almost a third, and for Soviet refugees more than a third, had been in equivalent occupations (Fagen and Brody 1964; HIAS 1980; OSI 1977).

Educational levels also tend to be high, especially considering the relative lack of educational opportunities in most countries from which refugees come. A systematic sample of the roster of the Cuban Refugee Center (Miami) in 1963 indicated that more than 14 percent of male refugees over the age of 16 had completed 4 years of college. An additional 22 percent had completed high school, with or without subsequent college education. Less than 5 percent had completed no more than the third grade (Fagen and Brody 1964:392). Data from a survey of 1,574 Southeast Asian refugee heads of household in Illinois (Kim 1980:33) present a somewhat similar picture. Fewer Southeast Asian refugees had completed college (8.3 percent) but more had completed high school (32.8 percent). Only 7 percent lacked any formal education. Data from a 1980 national survey of 1,032 Southeast Asian refugee households give similar aggregate figures but also illustrate important differences among the different Southeast Asian nationalities. For Vietnamese males, almost 14 percent had completed college, and over 40 percent had completed at least the first of the two high school degrees. For Cambodian and Laotian males, the figures were generally lower. Among Laotian males, for example, only half as many had completed college and about one fourth as many had completed high school (OSI 1981). The federal government's major effort to look at other refugee groups also found relatively high educational levels for Afghans, Ethiopians, Poles, and Romanians (Cichon, Gozdziak, and Grover 1986).

Research on later groups of refugees has shown some decline in these relatively high occupational and educational levels. Although these shifts have sometimes been overstated, they do exist and have a variety of causes. One is the presence in later refugee flows, particularly those from Southeast Asia, of special populations whose background is rural (e.g., highland Lao groups such as the Hmong, rural refugees escaping from Cambodia) or who have been systematically excluded from educational and occupational opportunities in their home countries (e.g., young Vietnamese whose families were suspect because of ties to Americans). Despite such changes, the generalization remains that refugees come to the United States with relatively high occupational skills and educational levels as compared with their compatriots in country of origin, if not always with the general American population or other immigrant groups. Nevertheless, there are variations within and between particular refugee groups, and those variations have sharp effects. Those without education or relevant occupational skills face enhanced difficulties as they adjust to life in the United States; those with such skills have an important tool that may ease the transition to a new life.

Life Experiences, Values, and Expectations

The third set of factors that influences refugee adjustment involves the life experiences of refugees in country of origin, their basic values, and their expectations about life in the United States. Here the range of refugee experience is extensive. Refugees from the Soviet Union and Eastern Europe, for example, have spent their lives under planned, socialist economies. The state has restricted many of their freedoms, including for Soviet Jews the practice of their religion. The state has also, however, met many of their basic needs (including employment) without requiring any great individual initiative. These refugees thus have little experience that bears directly on the self-initiated job search that is important in the American labor market. Recent Cuban refugees share this experience, but earlier Cuban refugees, by contrast, came from a society that prior to 1959 shared many features with that of the United States. In particular, early Cuban refugees had experience with the workings of an open, competitive, capitalist economy. Aspects of American society, such as entrepreneurship, that may elude a Soviet refugee thus came naturally to such early Cuban refugees. Cambodians, Laotians, and Vietnamese, in turn, came to the United States having spent most of their lives under a situation of continuing war, itself preceded by nearly a century of direct or indirect French colonial rule. Likewise, Afghan, Ethiopian, Eritrean, Haitian, and Iranian refugees have their own distinct histories that similarly color their expectations about the structure of the American political and economic system—and about the agencies that aim to help them in their resettlement.

The cultural values and spiritual beliefs of refugees also affect their initial adjustment to the United States. For most of the refugees, for example, individualism per se is less valued than it is by Americans. Rather, the individual is an integral part of ongoing social units. The importance of the ''honor'' of the Cuban family, for example, has been a spur to the quest for economic success in the United States. Husbands and wives cooperated in constructing a self-sufficient and productive life in the United States (see discussion below). Equally if not more so for other refugees, the individual appears as less important than the social group, whether that group is based on kinship or unique community or religious traditions. Where they resettle with sufficient density, for example, the minority of Vietnamese who are Catholic, the minority of Hmong who are Protestant, and the minority of Iranians who are Jewish have maintained an important social context for their lives in America. Success in the United States can often be defined more as a social attribute than as an individual one.

The values and expectations that refugees bring with them can both hinder and facilitate adjustment. On the positive side, for example, teachers consistently note the respect and hard work they find among Southeast Asian refugee children, reflecting the near reverence for education in much of Asia (Caplan, Choy, and Whitmore 1991). Traditional Buddhist precepts may also help Cambodian refugees come to terms with their holocaust (Welaratna 1993; Mortland 1994a). On the negative side, refugees who have lived under a pervasive state bureaucracy (as in the Soviet Union) may have little understanding of the independence and role of the private agencies in the United States that are attempting to assist them, and cultural notions of gratitude may lead some refugees to acquiesce to pressures to convert to a new religion or to move away without warning when they can no longer maintain a culturally appropriate relationship with a sponsor. The specific effects of such existing values and expectations, whether positive or negative, are difficult to predict but are often decisive to the relative success of the resettlement process.

Family and Kinship

The fourth set of factors involves the primary web of social relationships within which the adjustment of the individual refugee takes place. The most important of these involves the family, both within the household and as an extended set of kin. Much of the importance of the family stems directly from such demographic considerations as fertility. Southeast Asian refugees, for example, have more children than do mainstream American families; Soviet refugees have fewer. Automatically, then, Vietnamese refugee households are larger, include more dependents, and will experience problems in the areas of housing, education, and household incomes. At least as important, however, is the way in which the family functions as the nexus of social identity. The structuring of roles within the household also has important effects. For example, early Cuban refugee women entered the U.S. labor force in large numbers despite cultural conventions that had often restricted them to the home. This shift reflected considerable flexibility in their roles as wives and mothers. Specifically, employment was seen as a way to contribute to the family without sacrificing rights and obligations within the home (Ferreé 1979; Boone 1980, 1994; Perez 1986; Prieto 1986). Similar flexibility in the wife's role has been noted for the Vietnamese (Hoskins 1975; Haines 1986; Kibria 1990; Benson 1994). If refugees bring with them to the United States the belief that women's work outside the home is both acceptable and important, then the family has an additional wage earner and enhanced flexibility in achieving economic self-sufficiency.

Another important aspect of kinship involves the multiplicity of function and extent of inclusion that characterize many refugee families. The structure of Vietnamese and Hmong kinship provides an illustration. For both groups, kinship is organized along patrilineal lines. This does not necessarily mean that the family itself is patriarchal but, rather, that blood relations between males are used to extend the family back to distant ancestors and laterally to include distant cousins. For both the Hmong and the Vietnamese, these sets of relatives linked through males can be extensive. The resulting kin group functions as a unit for a variety of social, political, economic, and ritual activities. In Vietnamese villages a particularly large kin group could act as the framework for the economic and political life of an entire village (Hickey 1964). For the Hmong, the extension of the kin group and the multiplicity of its functions are even greater. Leadership, for example, may be the result of belonging to a particular family and is likely to be validated through a series of (polygynous) marriages to women of other clans or family alliance groups (Geddes 1976; LeBar, Hickey, and Musgrave 1964).

For the Hmong and Vietnamese, then, the family extends directly into the areas that in the United States would be characterized as the arena of the community. It is a comment on the diversity of Southeast Asian cultures that the Lao and Khmer do not particularly resemble the Hmong and Vietnamese. The Khmer show some preference for relatively small nuclear households and, if anything, a tendency to extend the family through female, rather than male, blood relations. Khmer kinship terminology and residence patterns actually show considerable similarity to those of the United States. One result is that, for the Khmer, "community" may be quite similar to the American situation and relatively separate from kin relations.

As in the area of values and expectations, the different refugee populations differ both from one another and, by and large, from American society in the area of family and kinship. In some cases, distinctive characteristics may ease adjustment: Strong conjugal bonds may facilitate effective dual-wage-earning strategies; strong emphases on extended families may facilitate effective multigenerational strategies for achieving economic success in American society. In other cases, distinctive characteristics may have less desirable results: Movements by refugees to re-create extended family units may undermine resettlement efforts as refugees move away from the programs designed for them; strong patriarchal patterns may result in spousal abuse under the pressures of resettlement.

Exodus and Transit

Refugees are refugees because they flee from situations of danger. Flight is often chosen rapidly, and even when the dangers are not excessive, clandestine action, social and financial losses, and a sharp separation from homeland are necessary. All refugees share this experience to some extent, and it conditions their adjustment to the United States. However, there are great variations among refugees as to the precise nature of exodus and the nature and duration of the transit to the United States. For Cubans and Haitians, for example, the United States has usually been the country of first asylum (although during the mid-1960s some Cubans came to the United States by way of other countries, particularly Spain, and during 1994, camps in Guantánamo and Panama were used by the United States for those picked up from coastal waters). For most other refugees, however, arrival in the United States is the result of a long and complex transit.

Soviet Jews have had perhaps the most orderly transit, but even that has involved serious hardships. Until 1989, all those desiring to emigrate from the Soviet Union had to apply for exit visas to Israel. The time period from application to acceptance varied considerably, as did the overall likelihood of success. During this period the potential émigré was largely cut off from Soviet society, denied work, and subjected to harassment. When exit was approved, the émigré went first to Vienna, and it is only then that any desire to go to the United States could be made known. All Soviet refugees coming to the United States were technically "break-offs" (*noshrim*) from emigration to Israel. When their desire to not go to Israel was made known, they were then transferred to Rome for processing to the Western countries, including the United States. The entire process, from visa application to arrival in the United States, could be lengthy, and the émigré was likely to be exposed to some material hardship and considerable ideological pressure (Jacobson 1978; Simon 1985). More recently, the process has been changed to allow direct request for refugee status at the U.S. embassy in Moscow.

While the exit and transit processes for Soviet Jews were cumbersome and with considerable risk, it is for Southeast Asian refugees that the experience has been most severe. The initial exodus (largely Vietnamese) from Southeast Asia in 1975 followed the fall of the American-supported governments and occurred under panic conditions (Kelly 1977; Liu, Lamanna, and Murata 1979). People were caught up in the exodus with little, if any, prior planning. Families were splintered and fortunes were lost. Those going to the United States were transported to camps in the Pacific and then to others in the continental United States before being resettled by the voluntary agencies into local communities. Material needs, however, were met with considerable success, and at least some provision was made for orientation and language training.

For later Indochinese refugees, the problems were worse. Many refugees who fled Laos and Cambodia in 1975 ended in camps of temporary asylum in Thailand, rather than being resettled rapidly to third countries such as the United States. Camp conditions were frequently poor, with little security, limited supplies, and limited opportunity for planning a future in a country of final asylum. Those Cambodians who managed to flee the Khmer Rouge faced a potentially deadly walk to the border and long stays in camps that became havens for competing Khmer military factions. As these refugees languished in the camps, the surge in the boat exodus from Vietnam in 1978, partly encouraged by the

Vietnamese government, began to spark international attention. Many refugees lost their lives as boats sank; others experienced thefts, beatings, rapes, and murders by Thai pirates. Boats approaching land were sometimes pushed back to sea. Those refugees who reached shore found themselves placed in overcrowded camps, with an uncertain future (Grant et al. 1979; Burton 1983; USCR 1984).

The boat exodus led to a positive international response and the resettlement of very large numbers of refugees in the United States and in other Western countries (particularly Australia, Canada, New Zealand, and western and northern Europe). Concerted international response also began to reduce the extent of pirate attacks on refugees, to reduce the size of the temporary asylum camps for all the nationality groups, and to expand the number of Vietnamese refugees leaving directly from Vietnam in a relatively orderly fashion. The international humanitarian crisis in Southeast Asia, coupled with increasing concern in the United States about the effectiveness of resettlement programs, also led to the development of special refugee processing centers in Southeast Asia where refugees went after acceptance for resettlement, and where they received a variety of training and orientation courses for life in the United States. With such an extended period between flight and resettlement, the camp experience itself came to be a distinct stage of a refugee's experience. Many children were born in refugee camps; many others spent important segments of their formative years in camps; for yet others, long stays in refugee camps led not to resettlement but to repatriation—sometimes forcible—to their original country (see Long 1993; Hall 1992; Knudsen 1992; Donnelly 1992).

WHAT THEY FIND

The Situation in the United States

Refugees come to the United States with varying background characteristics, bring different skills and abilities, and arrive through a wide range of migration experiences. They also come to the United States at different times and settle in different parts of the country. In essence, they come to different Americas and must adjust to different environments. Their very reception by the American public varies. Early Cuban refugees came as exiles from a Communist nation strongly opposed by the U.S. government. Their stay was initially viewed as temporary (contingent on the fall of Castro), and they enjoyed strong political support. Southeast Asian refugees also fled from new Communist governments, but they brought memories of an unpopular war. They arrived when Asian immigration had risen significantly (because of the 1965 revisions to the Immigration and Nationality Act) and were eventually to be bystanders in the turbulent surge of antiimmigrant sentiment in the mid-1990s. Southeast Asian refugees thus became a visible part of a larger Asian presence and of a far larger and increasingly distrusted "alien" presence, particularly in California. Soviet refugees faced a different set of problems. Having lived their lives in a secular society, they have had to come to terms with a Jewish community that supports them extensively but also tends to expect from them an expressed religiosity with which they have little experience. They, like other refugees, thus not only bring their own set of expectations with them but are also affected by the expectations about them held by American society as a whole and by the individual Americans who interact with them as sponsors, fellow workers, neighbors, and friends (see Gold 1992; Simon 1985; Markowitz 1993; Orleck 1987).

Refugees also find, as have immigrants throughout American history, an America that is at varying stages of economic growth, constriction, and restructuring. Cuban refugees generally fared better in terms of employment prospects in the early 1960s than did Southeast Asian refugees in the late 1970s. The situation was particularly bleak for Southeast Asian refugees in the early 1980s. Although the public might consider that refugees were taking jobs from Americans, the extent to which refugees were first laid off suggests that this was not generally the case. Case study material notes the extent to which refugees lacked the necessary seniority to make it through the recession, for example, in the situation of refugees who had managed to move into good jobs in the light aircraft industry in Wichita, Kansas, only to lose those jobs in the recession (Finnan and Cooperstein 1983). National surveys of Southeast Asian refugees by the Office of Refugee Resettlement (ORR) during the recession also showed relatively high unemployment rates for refugees during that period—24 percent in late 1982 and 18 percent in late 1983 (ORR 1983, 1984).

The structure of public policy at the time of resettlement also has important effects on refugee adjustment. Different refugee populations, and the same refugee population at different times, have been subject to varying domestic resettlement provisions and regulations—much less varying admissions criteria and overseas training and maintenance. Cubans, for example, were allowed to congregate heavily in the Miami area. With Southeast Asian refugees, on the other hand, considerable efforts were made to disperse the refugees throughout the United States. The specific kinds of assistance available to refugees also make a difference. Support to early Cuban refugees was direct and localized in Miami through the Cuban Refugee Center. Since 1980, however, refugees have been increasingly brought under the dictates of mainstream public assistance programs as special programs for refugee services and assistance continued to constrict in amount and duration of eligibility.

Finally, the adjustment of refugees is subject to the particular features of the communities in which they settle. This is true both in terms of the resources available (jobs, housing) and in terms of more general features of the local environment. Starr and Roberts (Starr and Roberts 1982; Roberts and Starr 1989) have demonstrated that such general community characteristics as ethnic heterogeneity and median educational levels significantly affect the nature of Vietnamese refugee adjustment. It is also clear that the resources of an established ethnic community make a difference. The lack of an ethnic base has been a problem for smaller refugee groups and has been the instigating reason for several federal efforts to construct adequately sized clusters of refugees in areas where resources were available for resettlement (Kogan and Vencill 1984; Granville Corporation 1982). Vietnamese had very few compatriots in the United States before the 1975 exodus but were in a better situation than other Southeast Asian groups (Lao, Khmer, Hmong, Iu Mien, Thai Dam, Khmu). Even refugee groups with long-established ethnic communities, such as the Poles and Iranians, have difficulties in establishing coherent, untroubled relationships with an existing ethnic community based on very different socioeconomic dynamics. Even when there are large numbers of a particular group, the resulting "community" may be extraordinarily complex. Bozorgmehr and Sabagh (1991), for example, note the great diversity and segmenting within the Los Angeles Iranian community, and Gold (1994a) shows, also for Los Angeles, how complicated and multiethnic even the networks of ethnic Chinese-Vietnamese entrepreneurs can be.

Problems in Resettlement

The variety of possible situations and responses in the United States, coupled with the range of skills and characteristics that refugees bring with them, ensures that the resettlement and adjustment of the refugees constitute a complex, multifaceted process. It can be smooth, but it is more likely to be characterized by a variety of problems. Health deserves special note since the hazards of exodus, and the lack of preparation for it, are likely to result in serious problems. Even the relatively routinized exit of early Soviet Jewish refugees was attended by a "backlog of medical problems" (Gilison 1979:24). The health status of Southeast Asian refugees was predictably worse. In the early years, anemia and skin, respiratory, and gastrointestinal problems were often noted, along with more serious conditions, such as malaria, hepatitis, and tuberculosis (Catanzaro and Moser 1982). Concerns about Southeast Asian refugee health led to improved medical screening overseas before entry into the United States and were one factor in the creation of formal refugee processing centers (GAO 1983). Many of these problems have no complete resolution and themselves fade into another set of problems that can be characterized more as diseases of resettlement than as diseases of exodus. Rasbridge (1994), for example, notes the prevalence of hypertension, alcohol-related problems, and gastritis among various refugee groups in Dallas. Yet other health problems exist that are not resettlement related but may also take their toll on adjustment: Vietnamese men, for example, are notably heavy smokers (Phan 1994).

Housing is another frequent problem area in resettlement, There may be problems of affordability, of availability in general, or of availability of appropriately sized housing. The worst problems are probably for large families seeking to rent. Multibedroom apartments tend to be relatively few, and official codes about shared bedrooms are often strict. Even if housing is available, its location may be less than ideal in terms of employment or physical safety. Many Southeast Asian refugee families, for example, have moved into high-crime areas because of their need for modest-cost, multibedroom rental housing. Although this causes the refugees themselves problems, it may rebound to the benefit of the neighborhood as a whole, as when refugees moving into San Francisco's Tenderloin area had the net effect of stabilizing a previously transient area, making it safer for all (Finnan and Cooperstein 1983). It may also rebound to the advantage of landlords who have considerable leverage over tenants and can thus easily move them out if more profitable options emerge (Hagan and Rodriguez 1992; Conquergood 1992).

Another potentially difficult problem area in resettlement involves the refugees' interaction with those who seek to aid them. Many refugees, because of their prior experiences, have little understanding of social services as they are organized in the United States. American social services often emphasize an interventionist, counseling approach that may be alien to refugees. Soviet and Eastern European refugees, for example, have spent their lives under a government that supplies a variety of basic material needs but is also relatively unresponsive to demands. Such refugees are likely to perceive that social service agencies in the United States owe them a considerable amount of material aid but will be slow and unresponsive in furnishing that aid (e.g., Greenberg 1976; Gold 1994b).

A different set of problems in dealing with social service agencies exists for Southeast Asian refugees. Many, particularly those of nonelite background, have limited exposure to American-style social services and the ideas on which they are based. Such lack of exposure is reflected in refugee perceptions of agency helpfulness. Such perceptions are likely to be influenced by class status, with higher-status refugees more attuned to the working of service agencies (e.g., Aames et al. 1977:73). As well, Southeast Asian refugees have recognized the importance both of ethnic contacts within such service agencies (Mortland and Ledgerwood 1988) and of assistance and services that can be gained through separate, ethnically based networks and organizations (Gold 1992).

Finally, and on a more general level, refugees must learn how to deal with American society in general and with the institutions and people holding the keys to the success of the adaptation, whether they be potential employers, medical personnel, neighbors, government officials, or friends. The basic rule of thumb generally holds true: The greater the cultural differences between the United States and a refugee's country of origin, the more difficult the adjustment. Orientation programs, both in the United States and overseas in refugee processing centers, have been one mechanism to address this. Such programs, along with English-language training, are frequently noted as core needs by refugees themselves and underline once again the special difficulties that refugees face in adjusting to a new country without the advance knowledge and preparation that characterize most other American newcomers.

Employment

Refugees must find the financial resources necessary to support themselves and their households. For most, this entails finding work that almost never matches their previous skills or experience. Although the wages of refugees as individuals may not necessarily be sufficient to enable the self-sufficiency of the household, employment of one or more household members is the first step toward that self-sufficiency. Despite considerable public concern about refugee employment, most information has provided a relatively optimistic picture of the frequency of employment, if not necessarily of the quality of that employment.

Case study and small-survey data for Soviet refugees throughout the 1970s, for example, indicated high rates of participation in the labor force and reasonable success in actually finding employment (e.g., Gilison 1979; Gitelman 1978; Feldman 1977). The major survey effort on Soviet refugees (Simon 1985) had similarly positive findings, as have later research on Eastern European refugees (Cichon, Gozdziak, and Grover 1986) and Soviet refugees (Gold 1994b). The employment-related success of early Cuban refugees was also very clear. The 1970 census data, for example, showed a labor force participation rate of 84 percent for Cuban-born males, which was the highest rate for any reported group and well above the figure of 77 percent for all men. Cuban-born women had a labor force participation rate of 51 percent, a full 10 percentage points higher than the U.S. average for women (Urban Associates, Inc. 1974:102). Data for Cubans arriving in the early 1970s also indicated rapid employment (Portes, Clark, and Bach 1977). Later data sources, particularly from the 1990 census, have confirmed this generally positive portrayal, although the specific argument about the high labor force participation rate of Cuban women has faded as the participation of all U.S. women surged to 57 percent (U.S. Bureau of the Census 1993b).

The employment situation of the initial influx of Southeast Asian refugees in 1975 was similarly positive. By 1977, the refugees, mostly Vietnamese, had achieved labor force participation and unemployment rates similar to those of the general U.S. population (OSI 1977; Stein 1979; Marsh 1980). By 1980, the data, reflecting the situation of both 1975 and later arrivals, was somewhat less favorable. Interviews conducted with Vietnamese, Cambodian, and Laotian refugee heads of household in 1980 (OSI 1981) indicated labor force participation rates for men of about 60 percent, with some variation by country of origin, and for women from a low of 26.7 percent (Laotian) to a high of 42.4 percent (Vietnamese). Unemployment rates were, at that time, also somewhat high compared with the general U.S. population. However, length of residence was a decisive factor. Later arrivals were likely to have low rates of labor force participation, thus obscuring the gains made by earlier arrivals. Specifically, the combined labor force participation rate (both men and women) for 1975 arrivals was 64 percent—about the national average—whereas for 1979 arrivals it was only 32 percent. Length of residence also had significant effects on unemployment rates. For 1975 arrivals, the rate was less than 4 percent, compared with 17 percent for 1979 arrivals (OSI 1981).

Later surveys have indicated both similarities and differences in the employment patterns of Southeast Asian refugees. The pattern of improvement with increased length of residence continues, but there has also been a sharp decline in overall employment levels among more recent arrivals. Annual survey data from the federal Office of Refugee Resettlement indicate both the extent to which more recent arrivals have difficulty in finding employment and the way in which particular entry cohorts continue to make progress from year to year. For example, the percentage of working-age adults who arrived in 1990 who held jobs in 1990 (combining the effects of labor force participation and employment rates), was 14 percent, but rose to 25 percent in 1991, and to 29 percent in 1992 (ORR 1993). Yet even the 1992 rate was less than half of the equivalent figure (61 percent) for the overall U.S. working-age population.

A number of factors affect the employment of refugees. Age is one. Refugees in the middle years of adulthood tend to be more frequently in the labor force, and those refugee groups composed mostly of adults in those age groups, such as Soviet and Eastern European refugees, tend to have the most favorable employment situation overall. Household responsibilities are also an important factor, with women typically in the labor force far less frequently than men. Health problems can also be a factor, as can disadvantageous locations and simple lack of knowledge about the American world of work. One factor that merits particular attention is English-language competence. For most refugee groups, English-language competence appears to be an essential element in successful employment. Comprehensive data on Soviet refugees are lacking, but case study material supports the importance of English for obtaining employment (e.g., Feldman 1977; Gilison 1979; Gitelman 1978). For Cubans, the importance of competence in English has been less clear. Early needs assessments stressed the importance of providing more English-language training, particularly for the adult population (Hernandez 1974), but later, more academic research on Cubans (e.g., Portes and Bach 1985) has questioned the importance of English-language competence. The Cuban situation, however, is clouded by the strong Cuban ethnic economy and the general prevalence of Spanish in Florida and the Southwest. The importance of English-language competence for employment is clearer for other refugee groups. Annual federal surveys, for example, consistently show the significance of English-language competence for the employment of Southeast Asian refugees. The 1992 survey, for example, showed employment rates rising sharply with higher levels of English-language competence (ORR 1993: 55): 5 percent for those with no English, 26 percent for those with some English, and 44 percent for those who spoke English well. As a whole, then, the research emphasizes the importance of English for refugees—just as the more general research indicates the same point for immigrants (e.g., Chiswick and Miller 1995).

For some refugees, obtaining employment is a relatively rapid process. They have the English-language facility and the relevant job skills that allow easy entry into the U.S. labor force. For other refugees, obtaining employment involves overcoming serious obstacles of lack of English or difficult personal circumstances, such as health problems. For yet other refugees, employment is an unreachable and possibly irrelevant goal. The elderly and those with severe and continuing health problems are unlikely to obtain employment. Many refugees thus need and utilize public assistance during their initial years in the United States and sometimes for much longer periods. Almost inevitably, some assistance is necessary to maintain refugee households through the period when employment is not obtainable or when its rewards in wages and salaries are insufficient to meet household needs.

This use of public assistance by refugees has been a frequent cause of concern both for the federal government as it has increasingly restricted the extent of public assistance to refugees and for state governments that provide portions of the assistance that refugees receive under such mainstream programs as Aid to Families with Dependent Children (AFDC) and Medicaid. The so-called dependency rate emerged as an important policy issue at the very beginning of the first Reagan presidential term. Such concerns have resurfaced in the 1990s as part of a more general antiimmigrant sentiment. The debate is a complicated one for a variety of reasons. First, it is extremely difficult to provide a total picture of the contributions that refugees and other immigrants make to the United States either directly through taxes or indirectly through economic growth. It is thus impossible to assess adequately the net costs involved in providing such assistance. Second, refugee and immigrant use of assistance is greatly restricted to a few states where the numbers of refugees and immigrants are high and the use of assistance is at a disproportionately high rate. California, for example, accounted for 38 percent of all refugees and immigrants in 1994 but accounted for over half (52 percent) of all the refugees and immigrants receiving AFDC or supplemental security income (SSI) (GAO 1995; cf. Bach et al. 1984). Third, the very reasons for accepting certain refugee groups inevitably lead to situations of particular difficulty in resettlement and employment— especially when highly disadvantaged groups with long histories of direct and indirect abuse, and sharply truncated family and community structures, are accepted for admission precisely because of their need for escape and sanctuary.

This is to say no more than that even the initial adjustment of refugees to the United States is a complex process that takes time and poses serious difficulties for the refugees and for the programs that attempt to serve them. The very forces that bring refugees to the United States militate against easy solutions for their adjustment to an American society for which they are often ill-prepared and that is often uneasy with their presence—or with the presence of other immigrants with whom they are combined in the public mind.

WHAT THEY BUILD

Once refugees have adjusted to their new environment—or have simply survived the inevitable problems and traumas of dislocation—they inevitably move forward in their new lives. They are no longer fully strangers but rather another element in the complex class and ethnic fabric of American life. They are no longer operating in an unknown environment but rather trying to assess traditional goals, to utilize this new environment to meet these goals, and often to modify those goals in light of changed circumstances. Although it is possible to argue about the nature or dimensions of assimilation, or about the extent to which refugees retain cultural and political allegiance to their country of origin, it is inarguable that most do become "American" to some extent. The gaining of citizenship is an important indicator.

The building of a new life is a complex and difficult process for any newcomer, but it is potentially much more so for refugees. Refugees, by definition, are triply disadvantaged in this process. First, they have frequently experienced, and continue to bear witness to and suffer from, some of the most tumultuous events of the twentieth century. The Cambodian holocaust is the most severe example, but almost all refugees have personally experienced events well beyond the conception of most native-born Americans. Second, their exodus involves a rupture of cultural and social relations far more severe than the experience of other immigrants. Loss of relatives and friends and of social context is virtually inevitable. Third, their resettlement lacks the advance preparation and preexisting community structures that are often available to immigrants. Arriving refugees, for example, have often found themselves to be the first representatives in an area of a particular ethnic or national group.

The disadvantages that refugees face condition the course of their longer-term adjustment to the United States, making their frequent successes more impressive and their difficulties more understandable. That longer-term adjustment has three major features, which are discussed in the remainder of this chapter: first, the economics of a new life; second, the maintenance and development of family and community ties; and third, the reconstruction of meaning from often-fragmented personal experiences.

The Economics of a New Life

The achievement of minimal economic self-sufficiency hinges on employment. For refugees, as for the general U.S. population, there is often more than one wage earner per family. If those jobs are at the minimum wage—or lower—problems remain. Even two minimum-wage jobs, for example, are less than sufficient for the relatively large households that characterize some refugee groups—particularly those from Southeast Asia. In the longer term, unemployment remains a significant problem for some refugees, but it is underemployment that is the more pervasive problem. Most refugees come to the United States with relatively high occupational and educational backgrounds—at least compared to others in their country of origin. During their first few years in the United States, virtually all have difficulties in obtaining employment commensurate with their skills and abilities. Barry Stein, in an early, succinct review of research on refugee resettlement, notes the extent of this downward occupational mobility and its implications for refugee adjustment. The achievement of a level of employment consistent with prior occupational status is, he suggests, "of crucial importance to the degree of assimilation and satisfaction a refugee achieves in his resettlement" (Stein 1979:25). However, such a transfer of occupational status is difficult since "[t]he highly skilled refugees, who represent a majority of most refugee waves . . . have many barriers to successful resumptions of their careers. The major obstacles to the transfer of foreign-acquired skills are non-recognition of degrees and skills, licensing restrictions by trades and professions, the extensive retraining needed to adjust to national differences, the greater language demands of professional, managerial, and sales work, and the non-transferability of certain skills" (39).

The obstacles to finding employment commensurate with existing skills are many, and the extent of the resulting downward occupational mobility can be significant. The initial influx of Southeast Asian refugees, for example, occurred in 1975. That influx included a high proportion of refugees with significant occupational skills who entered a relatively open labor market. About two years later, in the summer of 1977, however, a survey (OSI 1977) found that half of those surveyed claimed professional or managerial occupations in Vietnam, but less than one in ten had an equivalent occupation in the United States. Specifically, 30 percent had been professionals in Vietnam, but only 7 percent were in professional employment in the United States. For managers, the corresponding drop was from 15 percent to 2 percent. In more recent years, the proportion of those with professional or managerial occupations in Southeast Asia has decreased, but the inability of those with such professional and managerial experience to find equivalent jobs in the United States has continued. In 1992, a national survey found that 11.2 percent of Southeast Asian refugees had professional or managerial backgrounds, but only 0.9 percent of the refugees had professional or managerial occupations in the United States (ORR 1993:54). These surveys also indicate a more general shift away from "white-collar" to "blue-collar work."

Extensive research on Cubans has indicated similar patterns in downward occupational mobility (Fagen, Brody, and O'Leary 1968; University of Miami 1967; Prohias and Casal 1973; Portes and Bach 1985). A broad range of research on Soviet Jewish refugees confirms the pattern (e.g., Gilison 1979; Gitelman 1978; Simon 1985; Gold 1994b; Markowitz 1993), as does more limited quantitative research on Eastern European, Iranian, and Ethiopian refugees (e.g., Cichon, Gozdziak, and Grover 1986; Koehn 1991). The net implication is that refugees tend to experience considerable downward occupational mobility during their early years in the United States. Although there is some indication that this process is partially reversed over time, the achievement of employment commensurate with existing skills and abilities is neither a rapid nor inevitable process. This downward occupational mobility has direct implications both for the amounts of income available to households and for the personal satisfaction that refugees find.

In terms of income, refugees not only have difficulty in obtaining jobs; even when successful, they receive relatively low wages. This is particularly true during their initial years in the United States but may well continue to be a problem throughout their lives (see Borjas 1995 for a discussion of the generally lower income that immigrants receive throughout their lives). A survey conducted in 1977 of the initial Vietnamese arrivals, for example, indicated that almost 85 percent of those working were working 40 hours a week or more. Nevertheless, almost a fifth had a weekly income lower than would be expected from working at the then-minimum wage (OSI 1977; cf. U.S. Bureau of the Census 1980). Similar data emerge from the 1990 census. Vietnamese participated in the labor force at virtually the same rate as the general U.S. population (64.5 versus 65.3 percent) but had much lower per capita income ($9,033 versus $14,420) (U.S. Bureau of the Census 1993a).

Individual wage and salary income do not, however, directly determine the adequacy of household income. One household may do fairly well financially by combining the minimal wages of several working household members, whereas another household may do poorly if a single wage earner making a less modest salary must support numerous nonworking dependents. Early information on Cuban refugees from the 1970 census is illustrative. Cubans had high rates of labor force participation for both men and women. They also had a rate of intact marriages similar to the national rate (Urban Associates, Inc. 1974; Prohias and Casal 1973). The result was reasonable household income. However, the results are not always so positive. The 1990 census, for example, found Vietnamese with a labor force participation similar to that of the U.S. population as a whole, and with a percentage of households with at least two wage earners well above the national level, but still with a percentage below the poverty line almost twice that of the general population: 25.7 percent versus 13.1 percent (U.S. Bureau of the Census 1993a). The household income situation was far worse for those Cambodian and Laotian households with fewer wage earners, and even somewhat worse for those from the Soviet Union who—despite impressive per capita earnings when they did find work—had relatively low labor force participation and relatively few multiple-earner households. Only with a few groups, like those born in Poland and Iran, did the strength of individual incomes outweigh the lack of multiple wage earners within the household (U.S. Bureau of the Census 1993b).

In terms of occupational satisfaction, most refugees must accept that they are unlikely to achieve an occupational status in the United States that matches their experience in their country of origin. Refugees face barriers of health, age, English-language competence, licenses and credentials, and even appropriateness of former employment to the U.S. labor market. Early research on Cuban refugees provides some hope for a satisfactory compromise as "refugees take into account a series of other factors in their subjective comparisons of situations" (Portes 1969:513) and as a strong ethnic community "can favorably influence the adjustment of its members by providing a comparison reference which does not demean the refugees' sense of worth" (Rogg 1971:481). Some such compromise is inevitable over time, but it may well be a painful one. That pain is seen in informal research with refugees and in various surveys. The job dissatisfaction of Soviet and Eastern European refugees has been widely noted (e.g., Gold 1994b; this volume), and the particular problems faced by high-status Southeast Asian refugees have appeared in various surveys (e.g., Vignes and Hall 1979; Lin, Tazuma, and Masuda 1979; Starr et al. 1979).

Family and Community

Both the practical concern with income and the personal concern with occupational status, however, point to the social groups and networks within and through which refugees structure their adjustment to the United States. Refugee adjustment is, after all, as much a function of social groups as it is of individuals. The effects of household structure on self-sufficiency and general income levels have been indicated above, as has the influence of the ethnic community in facilitating occupational satisfaction. The existing literature on refugees consistently stresses the importance of the family to adjustment and the extent to which refugees are constantly attuned to the possibilities of reconstructing family ties.[1]

Not only are families important to refugees, but they are also capable of easing many of the problems of adjustment to the United States. For example, the high labor force participation rates of Cuban women have contributed substantially to the economic progress of the families with which they live. In an early analysis, Ferreé (1979:48) noted that "there is no necessary conflict between traditional standards of female behavior and women's paid employment. Since the Cuban woman is working for her family, her employment is not seen as an expression of her independence or the loosening of traditional controls and restraints. . . . Because female employment is needed to maintain standards of respectability for the family, daughters are counseled to prepare for a lifetime career, and parents are willing to invest in such preparation." Boone (1980, 1994) notes a similar contribution to the family by Cuban women in the Washington, D.C., area. Wives and mothers not only fulfill traditional roles within the family but also directly contribute to the family's economic adjustment. Similar patterns emerged very early among Southeast Asian refugees, particularly those from Vietnam, in which the traditional role of women is also flexible enough to include management of the home and participation in the labor market (e.g., Hickey 1964; Hoskins 1975; Haines 1990). Although conjugal economic cooperation is a central feature, other kin relations, both within and outside the household, can also be important. Adult siblings among the Vietnamese, for example, were noted not only to furnish one another emotional support but also to cooperate in economic activities (Haines, Rutherford, and Thomas 1981), while extended family alliances among the Hmong were found to take an active part in bridging the distance between refugees and U.S. service providers (Dunnigan 1982).

Refugee families, however, also face problems. Not only are families often fragmented because of the conditions that caused them to flee, but the shifts in family roles necessary to construct a new life may cause strain. The incorporation of wives and mothers into the labor force may facilitate the family's economic adjustment, but it may strain domestic relations. Again, the early research on Cuban refugees is instructive. The positive contribution of the family is clear (e.g., Perez 1986), but so are the strains. On the basis of research with 100 Cuban women in Miami, for example, Gonzales noted that "conflicts between the economic pressure to work and the social need to maintain the domestic role have strained the smooth running of the traditional Cuban family" (Gonzales 1980:2). One result can be the frequent use of tranquilizers (e.g., Page and Gonzales 1980). Janet Benson (1994) portrays the severe strains on Southeast Asian refugee families in Kansas, where the dictates of both parents working at meat-packing plants—often at night—in order to increase their household income leaves no time for family interaction. Refugees may initially view this work as " 'easy money' and an opportunity for capital accumulation," she notes (122–123), but the costs are significant: "Even if workers escape serious injury or disability, families inevitably pay a price in terms of domestic stress, inadequate health treatment, substandard housing and child care, and other problems resulting from their incorporation in a labor system that places overwhelming emphasis on productivity."

Families also face severe generational strains. Children are caught between the demands of their traditional culture (represented by their parents) and American culture (represented by schools, peers, and the media). This can easily lead to conflict. An early assessment of the needs of Southeast Asian refugee youth (IRAC 1980:1) suggested that childhood and adolescence are the "battlefields over which and in which the most severe cultural conflicts emerge. Children are the key to any group's survival as a distinct cultural unit. As 'New Americans,' immigrant children find themselves charged by their elders with maintaining what often appears to be an increasingly remote and irrelevant cultural heritage." The very success of refugee children in the school system may engender both pride and problems at home as children's very competence in the new culture puts them at odds with their parents. Alternately, adherence to traditional cultural values and patterns, as represented by the home, may cause problems for children and youth in adjusting to the U.S. educational system. As Lipson and Omidian (this volume) note, Afghan refugee youth feel especially torn between their need to maintain respect for their elders but also to succeed on American terms and thus face "far more situational dissonance than do their elders." At the other end of the spectrum, the elderly may be cut off from the new world of work and from their usual social interactions, leaving them seriously isolated. This aspect of generational tension seems best resolved when the elderly have access to their own activities in addition to steady family interaction. That pattern holds in areas of Cuban resettlement in Miami (Hernandez 1974), Soviet Jewish settlement in Brighton Beach, Brooklyn (Orleck 1987), or Vietnamese resettlement in New Orleans—where the cultivation of Vietnamese-style gardens is the province of the elderly and serves important functions in binding together the unique Vietnamese community of New Orleans (Airriess and Clawson 1991, 1994).

Thus, although refugee families have a significant capacity to facilitate adjustment, whether in contributing to household income levels or in furnishing a supportive home environment, they face difficulties. Many refugees have lost family members, resulting in single-parent households that are at risk both financially and emotionally. Others may be intact but burdened by the different levels of accommodation to the United States that husbands, wives, and children have achieved. The ethnic community, like the family, can function as a mediator between the refugees and the wider American society, thus facilitating the adjustment process. The ethnic community can also furnish a wide variety of quite practical support, particularly in guiding its members toward the services they need or the opportunities they seek. On the social side, the community provides a set of people with common traditions, goals, and problems. The community, of course, also provides a basis for more direct economic aid. Its networks can provide access to jobs and the rationale through which particular jobs become desirable. Finnan (1980), for example, has described how certain features of electronics work in California were quickly interpreted by the Vietnamese community as signifying clean and good work, thus enhancing the social acceptability of work that could be characterized as professional instead of as repetitive and undemanding. That community determination has been essential in a continuing pattern of Vietnamese refugee involvement in technical occupations and education (Penning 1992, Zhou and Bankston 1994).

The ethnic community can also create jobs. Wilson and Portes (1980), for example, describe ethnic businesses in Miami. There the combination of sustained Cuban immigration and entrepreneurial skills that originated in Cuba led to significant economic benefits for both the entrepreneurs and those they hired. They suggest that such ethnic businesses provide special access to markets and sources of labor. These conditions can give them an edge over similar peripheral firms in the open economy since the "economic expansion of an immigrant enclave, combined with the reciprocal obligations attached to a common ethnicity, creates new mobility opportunities for immigrant workers and permits utilization of their past investments in human capital. Not incidentally, such opportunities may help explain why many immigrants choose to stay in or return to the enclave, foregoing higher short-term gains in the open economy'' (315). Their examination is part of a long academic fascination with the enclave (see Model 1992 for an overview of different academic approaches to enclaves). Such enclaves can draw on their own skills and resources to develop businesses that in the long run benefit both employer and employed. This ability is clearly contingent on community size, but it is also affected by the structure of the "enclave." For example, most national groups of refugees are highly diverse. The Iranian community of Los Angeles, for example, is not only geographically dispersed but also comprises four distinct and very different groups: Muslims, Baha'is, Christians, and Jews (Bozorgmehr and Sabagh 1991; Light et al. 1993). Furthermore, enclave activities often turn out to be very complex and multiethnic. Chinese-Vietnamese entrepreneurship in Los Angeles, for example, involves a complex mix of ethnic Vietnamese as clients, Latinos as workers, and non-Vietnamese Chinese as sources of capital (Gold 1994a). Such complexity strains the popular concept of an internally homogenous ethnic enclave or community.

In terms of both the family and the ethnic community, the situation of refugees is in many ways similar to that of other newcomers. Both the family and community furnish a sense of belonging and the basis for a positive self-identity. Both also make direct contributions to the economics of a new life in America. While families pool often-minimal individual wages and salaries, communities, through enclave businesses, develop the basis for community-wide rises in income. Where the refugee experience tends to differ, however, is in the extent to which both the family and community must be re-formed in the face of the aftereffects of enduring the refugee-creating situation in the home country, the rupture of exodus, and an unplanned adjustment to a new country that often lacks precisely the kin and community-based resources that are needed.

Rebuilding Meaning

From the perspective of service providers and researchers, the stress points of resettlement have often been couched in terms of "personal adjustment" or even "mental health" issues. Refugee exodus is a traumatic experience. It often involves a decision made within a few hours that irrevocably changes a person's life. It may occur under panic conditions. Even when longer-range planning occurs, exodus is still usually clandestine, dangerous, and with family members left behind or lost en route. The result is that refugees can be left "midway to nowhere" (Kunz 1973). The psychological manifestations can be serious and multiple. Segal and Lourie (1975:4), for example, reported on the situation of the Indochinese refugees who reached Guam after the fall of Saigon in 1975. They noted "feelings of grief and depression, anxiety about the welfare of separated family members, panic over an uncertain future, feelings of remorse and guilt, confusion, and a growing sense of bitterness, disappointment, and anger. The emotional burdens carried by the refugees are often reflected not only in a general sense of malaise, fatigue, and psychosomatic complaints, but by evidences of lethargy, withdrawal and seclusion, huddling, expressions of melancholy, and crying in private.''

Other more quantitative research also indicates the emotional stress that the first Vietnamese refugees were undergoing. The use of such standardized instruments as the Cornell Medical Index (CMI) during 1975 indicated levels of overall distress for the Vietnamese refugees that were higher than those for American, British, Asian, or other migrant populations (Rahe et al. 1978; Lin, Tazuma, and Masuda 1979). Furthermore, this emotional distress did not disappear rapidly after resettlement. Follow-up work in 1976 indicated that CMI levels remained as high as they had been in the previous year and differed significantly only in increased levels of anger and somewhat reduced levels of inadequacy (Lin, Tazuma, and Masuda 1979; Masuda, Lin, and Tazuma 1980). A survey of agencies involved in refugee mental health in 1979 also indicated the continuation of mental health problems (Pennsylvania Department of Public Welfare 1979). Among the findings from the survey were that mental health problems of refugees who had arrived in 1975 were, in many cases, only beginning to surface at the time of the survey in spring 1979; depression (plausibly an aftereffect of exodus) was a major problem, but anxiety and marital conflict were also frequent problems; middle-aged refugees were at particular risk owing to the loss of traditional roles and statuses; smaller ethnic groups were at risk because of the lack of a strong ethnic community.

All these findings had in common the implication that refugee mental health problems were serious and were unlikely to disappear. An extensive literature now exists on such problems and on the ways in which refugees do and do not access services to resolve these problems (e.g., Chung and Lin 1994). One element of all this is a consideration of clinical posttraumatic stress syndrome (e.g., Clarke, Sack, and Goff 1993; Abe, Zane, and Chun 1994). It is also clear that many problems are the effect of the resettlement process itself, whether because of the way in which refugees have been treated as if they were immigrants rather than refugees (Kelly 1977; Tollefson 1989) or because of having simply reached a deadend in the resettlement process. Rasbridge (1994), for example, notes how the initial health problems of refugees gradually shift into ''chronic and complex diseases of resettlement''—notably, gastric problems and heavy alcohol use among some Cambodians.[2]

Although the effects of the refugee experience are clear, the understanding of and solutions to such problems are rendered difficult by the cultural divergences between different refugee populations and between refugees and American society. For most refugees, even the basic concepts of mental illness show little consistency with American psychological assumptions.[3] Different refugee groups may share similar general problems in recovering from the trauma of exodus and in adjusting to American society. However, the specifics of these problems, their general phrasing, and the resolution of them are likely to vary among different refugee groups. For individuals within these groups, personal adjustment will take different paths, as the effects of cultural background, job skills, availability of family and coethnics, age, and sex all influence the direction and the pace of adjustment.

What all these paths are likely to share is some negotiation between adherence to traditional beliefs and behavior, on the one hand, and the embracing of American ways, on the other. For refugees, this negotiation involves the triple assault on the meaning of their lives: the challenge to their lives that led to flight, the rupturing of their social relations as a result of flight, and the unplanned nature of their move to America. Refugees are thus presented with special problems in constructing the meaning of their lives. These problems appear in both political and spiritual domains.

In terms of political meaning, refugees are, by definition, people who have lost out in serious political and military conflicts. Whether it is the Vietnamese celebrating national shame day (the anniversary of the fall of Saigon) or Cubans agitating against Castro for 35 years, refugees face a political situation in the home country with which it is difficult—or impossible—to be reconciled. With the loosening of Communist government rule in the 1990s, Southeast Asian and Cuban refugees were particularly torn between the desire to renew ties with the home country—to alleviate the rupture in their social relations—and the desire *not* to lend support to the governments that ruled the home country. The strain was redoubled in the case of Vietnamese arriving in recent years after being released from reeducation camps. They arrived in the United States only to find former colleagues who not only had a 20-year head start on adjusting to the United States but who were also in the process of attempting at least a partial reconciliation with the home country.

For other refugees, the initial cause of flight may have partially or completely disappeared. Although Communist governments continued in Cuba and Vietnam, in other countries enough improvement in conditions occurred to raise questions about exile. The return of President Aristide to Haiti in 1993, for example, was considered by many the end to the rationale for the exodus from that country—although serious instability and reprisals from those associated with the former government continued. The end of the Communist government in Ethiopia and Eritrean independence dramatically changed the home country experience for those refugees. As Koehn (1991) describes, the result was a difficult, forced reappraisal of the political significance of exile. For Afghans, the Soviet occupation ended in 1989, but the situation in the home country remained unsettled and very dangerous—and the speed of modern communications kept refugees painfully aware of the dangers faced by relatives who remained in, or had returned to, Afghanistan (Lipson and Omidian 1995). For Eastern Europeans and Soviets, the collapse of the Soviet bloc struck at the issue of their exile—moving it generally from an anti-Communist basis to an issue of their status as an oppressed ethnic or religious minority (Gozdziak, this volume; Gold, this volume).[4] Although the specifics differ, the common element is the constant confrontation with an unstable and largely unacceptable political situation in the home country.

Refugees also face tremendous challenges to their spiritual lives. Even when the reasons for exodus are religious in nature, and the United States offers both freedom of religion and an existing religious community, the challenges can be serious. Christian and Jewish groups, for example, may have unique beliefs, traditions, and practices that do not precisely meld with existing mainstream churches. A disproportionate number of Vietnamese in America, for example, are Catholic. Those traditions, coupled with language limitations, may suggest the need for separate services that are impossible except in areas of large refugee concentration. Furthermore, Vietnamese Catholics face the concern of Vietnamese Buddhists who question whether Catholics can be truly "Vietnamese" (Rutledge 1985:61). The problem is even more severe for Cambodians or Hmong who convert to Christianity since this moves them away from traditional religious practices that are wound very tightly into their ethnic identity (e.g., Smith-Hefner 1994; Capps 1994). For Soviet Jews, it is less the difference in traditions than the lack of opportunity in the Soviet Union to actively practice their faith that has sometimes created a gap between them and the American Jewish community that has been so active on their behalf. As Gold (1994b:35) suggests, their Jewish identity is more secular and nationalistic than religious. The situation of these groups with religious ties in the United States may thus not be so different from that of other refugee (and immigrant) groups who must diligently pool resources to re-create the religious institutions that serve as the focus of community activities. Without a strong community base, this recreation of a functioning religious community is not possible. The smaller the community, and the smaller the particular religious group, the more serious the practical problems.

These religious challenges are similar to those faced by other immigrant groups. However, again, refugees face additional difficulties since so much of the basic structure of meaning to their lives has been cast into doubt by their experiences before and during exodus. The situation of Khmer refugees is the clearest. They must deal with the knowledge and memories of a holocaust that was created by Cambodians. As Usha Welaratna—a Theravada Buddhist herself—notes, the Khmer Rouge not only "violated every Buddhist precept... [and] showed contempt for the first and perhaps most important precept, that one should not kill" but "also forced their victims to violate Buddhist precepts in order to survive" (Welaratna 1993:252, 254). Carol Mortland, examining the same issue, notes how this calls into question the very meaning of life since to many Khmer "to be Cambodian is to be Buddhist" (Mortland 1994a:6). Although Mortland finds that Khmer have found ways to describe their experience, including explicit comparison with the Jewish holocaust, they are not truly at rest with those descriptions and "continue to ask a range of questions that continue to bother them, questions most of them would never have thought to ask until their lives were turned upside down" (Mortland 1994b:90).

Refugees are both witnesses to and victims of some of the worst events in recent history. Because of that, their adjustment to life in the United States is necessarily a complicated one. As they construct new lives in America, they must confront persistent, recurring questions about the viability of their political views and even the veracity of their spiritual beliefs. They must re-create their relations of kinship and community—frequently out of fragmented, ruptured pieces—and then attempt to maintain those ties even as their children all too rapidly accommodate to American culture. In the process, they must also overcome, or become reconciled to, what is often a severe loss of occupational status. That loss has both economic and personal implications. For these reasons, the experience of refugees in the United States in the 1990s remains a vital issue not only in its own terms but also as a source of insight into the evolution of American society and into the global political tumult of the second half of the twentieth century.

NOTES

1. This, incidentally, is one of the areas where there is frequently a difference between refugees and service providers. For example, an extensive survey of Southeast Asian refugees in Illinois found that 77 percent of those questioned believed that broken families (as a result of exodus) were a "very serious" problem (Kim 1980:110). It was, from the point of view of the refugees, their most serious problem, even more than (English-) language problems. Confirming data come from another survey in California in which "worry about family or friends still in homeland" was rated as the second most serious problem by the refugees interviewed (Human Resources Corporation 1979). Interestingly, the concern about missing family members is one area in which there is significant difference between the perceptions of refugees and of service providers. In both the noted surveys, service providers were also asked to assess the seriousness of various problems facing refugees and in both cases rated such family problems as significantly less serious than did the refugees.

2. An interesting early indication of the length of time needed for alleviation comes from a survey of Southeast Asian refugees in Illinois (Kim and Nicassio 1980). The researchers constructed an alienation index on the basis of answers to ten standardized statements about the refugee's life situation in the United States. The results were broken down by ethnic group and by year of arrival. The Hmong had the highest score (indicating most alienation), and the Vietnamese had the lowest. Further, when respondents were resorted according to year of entry, there was a statistically significant and inverse relationship between length of residence and alienation. However, the individual scores showed a rise through the first three years before declining in the fourth and fifth years. Although the drops for those in the fourth and fifth years of residence imply that mental health problems are ameliorated after three years in the country, this finding may well reflect the social characteristics of those who arrived in 1975 and 1976.

3. For example, Cubans, culturally closest of the refugees to American society, have distinctive ideas about what constitutes acceptable behavior and therefore a normal mental health status. Analysis of value orientations in two separate samples of Cubans and native-born Americans indicated significant differences along a number of dimensions.

The Cubans tended to prefer lineality (e.g., hierarchical relations within the family), a present-time orientation, and subjugation to nature. The Americans, on the other hand, showed a preference for individuality, mastery over nature, and a future-time orientation (Szapocznik, Scopetta, and King 1978; Szapocznik, Kurtines, and Hanna 1979).

4. For Central Americans, who had been a major focus of public concern about non-legal refugee groups in the 1980s, the availability of legalization under the Immigration Control and Reform Act of 1986 tended to move them from the status of undocumented refugees to that of undocumented workers (Melville 1985; Burns 1993; Coutin 1994; Hagan 1994; Harman 1995).

REFERENCES

Aames, Jacqueline S., Ronald L. Aames, John Jung, and Edward Karabenick. 1977. *Indochinese Refugee Self-Sufficiency in California: A Survey and Analysis of the Vietnamese, Cambodians and Lao and the Agencies That Serve Them.* Report submitted to the State Department of Health, State of California.

Abe, Jennifer, Nolan Zane, and Kevin Chun. 1994. Differential Responses to Trauma: Migration-Related Discriminants of Post-Traumatic Stress Disorder among Southeast Asian Refugees. *Journal of Community Psychology* 22(2):121–135.

Airriess, Christopher A., and David L. Clawson. 1991. Versailles: A Vietnamese Enclave in New Orleans, Louisiana. *Journal of Cultural Geography* 12(1):1–13.

———. 1994. Vietnamese Market Gardens in New Orleans. *Geographical Review* 84(1): 16–31.

Bach, Robert, Linda Gordon, David Haines, and David Howell. 1984. Geographic Variations in the Economic Adjustment of Southeast Asian Refugees in the U.S. *World Refugee Survey* 1984:7–8.

Benson, Janet E. 1994. The Effects of Packinghouse Work on Southeast Asian Refugee Families. In *Newcomers in the Workplace.* Edited by Louise Lamphere, Alex Stepick, and Guillermo Grenier. Philadelphia: Temple University Press. Pp. 99–126.

Boone, Margaret S. 1980. The Uses of Traditional Concepts in the Development of New Urban Roles: Cuban Women in the United States. In *A World of Women: Anthropological Studies of Women in the Societies of the World.* Edited by Erika Bourguignon. New York: Praeger. Pp. 235–269.

———. 1994. Thirty Year Retrospective on the Adjustment of Cuban Women. In *Reconstructing Lives, Recapturing Meaning.* Edited by Linda A. Camino and Ruth M. Krulfeld. Basil, Switzerland: Gordon and Breach. Pp. 179–201.

Borjas, George J. 1995. Assimilation and Changes in Cohort Quality Revisited: What Happened to Immigrant Earnings in the 1980s? *Journal of Labor Economics* 13(2):201–245.

Bozorgmehr, Mehdi, and Georges Sabagh. 1991. Iranian Exiles and Immigrants in Los Angeles. In *Iranian Refugees and Exiles since Khomeini.* Edited by Asghar Fahti. Costa Mesa, California: Mazda Publishers. Pp. 121–144.

Burns, Allan F. 1993. *Maya in Exile: Guatemalans in Florida.* Philadelphia: Temple University Press.

Burton, Eve. 1983. Surviving the Flight of Horror: The Story of Refugee Women. *Indochina Issues* No. 34.

Caplan, Nathan, Marcella H. Choy, and John K. Whitmore. 1991. *Children of the Boat People: A Study of Educational Success.* Ann Arbor: University of Michigan Press.

Capps, Lisa L. 1994. Change and Continuity in the Medical Culture of the Hmong in Kansas City. *Medical Anthropology Quarterly* 8(2):161–177.

Catanzaro, Antonino, and Robert J. Moser. 1982. Health Status of Refugees from Vietnam, Laos, and Cambodia. *Journal of the American Medical Association* 247(9): 1303–1308.

Cejas and Toledo, Inc. 1974. Needs Assessment: The Prevention of Spanish-Speaking Dropouts in the Target Areas of "Little Havana" and "Wynwood" (Grades 7–12). Miami, Florida.

Chiswick, Barry R., and Paul W. Miller. 1995. The Endogeneity between Language and Earnings: International Analyses. *Journal of Labor Economics* 13(2):246–288.

Chung, Rita Chi-Ying, and Keh-Ming Lin. 1994. Help-Seeking Behavior among Southeast Asian Refugees. *Journal of Community Psychology* 22(2):109–120.

Cichon, Donald J., Elzbieta M. Gozdziak, and Jane G. Grover. 1986. *The Economic and Social Adjustment of Non-Southeast Asian Refugees.* Dover, New Hampshire: Research Management Corporation.

Clarke, Greg, William H. Sack, and Brian Goff. 1993. Three Forms of Stress in Cambodian Adolescent Refugees. *Journal of Abnormal Child Psychology* 21(1):65–77.

Conquergood, Dwight. 1992. Life in Big Red: Struggles and Accommodation in a Chicago Polyethnic Tenement. In *Structuring Diversity.* Edited by Louise Lamphere. Chicago: University of Chicago Press. Pp. 95–144.

Coutin, Susan. 1994. Redefining Legal Identities: Salvadoran "Refugees" and "Immigrants" in Los Angeles, California. Paper presented at the annual meeting of the American Anthropological Association, Atlanta, Georgia.

Donnelly, Nancy D. 1992. The Impossible Situation of Vietnamese in Hong Kong's Detention Centers. In *Selected Papers on Refugee Issues.* Edited by Pamela A. DeVoe. Washington, D.C.: American Anthropological Association. Pp. 120–132.

Dunnigan, Timothy. 1982. Segmentary Kinship in an Urban Society: The Hmong of St. Paul-Minneapolis. *Anthropological Quarterly* 55(3):126–134.

Fagen, Richard R., and Richard A. Brody. 1964. Cubans in Exile: A Demographic Analysis. *Social Problems* 11(4):389–401.

Fagen, Richard R., Richard A. Brody, and Thomas J. O'Leary. 1968. *Cubans in Exile: Disaffection and the Revolution.* Stanford, California: Stanford University Press.

Feldman, William. 1977. Social Absorption of Soviet Immigrants: Integration or Isolation. *Journal of Jewish Communal Service* 54(1):62–68.

Ferreé, Myra Marx. 1979. Employment without Liberation: Cuban Women in the United States. *Social Science Quarterly* 60:35–50.

Finnan, Christine Robinson. 1980. A Community Affair: Occupational Assimilation of Vietnamese Refugees. *Journal of Refugee Resettlement* 1(1):8–14.

Finnan, Christine R., and Rhonda Ann Cooperstein. 1983. *Southeast Asian Refugee Resettlement at the Local Level: The Role of the Ethnic Community and the Nature of Refugee Impact.* Menlo Park, California: SRI International.

Geddes, William R. 1976. *Migrants of the Mountains.* Oxford: Clarendon Press.

Gilison, Jerome M. 1979. *Summary Report of the Survey of Soviet Jewish Émigrés in Baltimore.* Baltimore, Maryland: Baltimore Hebrew College.

Gitelman, Zvi. 1978. Soviet Immigrants and American Absorption Efforts: A Case Study in Detroit. *Journal of Jewish Communal Service* 55(1):72–82.

Gold, Steven J. 1992. *Refugee Communities: A Comparative Field Study.* Newbury Park, California: Sage Publications.

———. 1994a. Chinese-Vietnamese Entrepreneurs in California. In *The New Asian Immigration in Los Angeles and Global Restructuring.* Edited by Paul Ong, Edna Bonacich, and Lucie Cheng. Philadelphia: Temple University Press. Pp. 192–226.

———. 1994b. Soviet Jews in the United States. *American Jewish Yearbook* 1994:3–57.

Gonzales, Diana H. 1980. Sociocultural Adaptations among Cuban Emigre Women in Miami, Florida. Paper presented at the annual meetings of the Caribbean Studies Association.

Grant, Bruce, et al. 1979. *The Boat People: An "Age" Investigation.* New York: Penguin Books.

Granville Corporation. 1982. *A Preliminary Assessment of the Khmer Cluster Resettlement Project.* Washington, D.C.

Greenberg, Martin. 1976. Agency Concerns: The Special Problems Confronting Agencies in Providing Services to Immigrants from the USSR. In *The Soviet Jewish Emigre.* Edited by Jerome Gilison. Baltimore, Maryland: Baltimore Hebrew College.

Hagan, Jacqueline Maria. 1994. *Deciding to Be Legal: A Maya Community in Houston.* Philadelphia: Temple University Press.

Hagan, Jacqueline Maria, and Nestor P. Rodriguez. 1992. Recent Economic Restructuring and Evolving Intergroup Relations in Houston. In *Structuring Diversity.* Edited by Louise Lamphere. Chicago: University of Chicago Press. Pp. 145–171.

Haines, David W. 1986. Vietnamese Refugee Women in the U.S. Labor Force: Continuity or Change? In *International Migration: The Female Experience.* Edited by Rita James Simon and Caroline B. Brettell. Totowa, New Jersey: Rowman and Allenheld. Pp. 62–75.

———. 1990. South Vietnamese Households. *Vietnam Forum* 13:192–217.

Haines, David W., Dorothy A. Rutherford, and Patrick A. Thomas. 1981. Family and Community among Vietnamese Refugees. *International Migration Review* 15(1): 310–319.

Hall, Kari René. 1992. *Beyond the Killing Fields.* Hong Kong: Asia 2000.

Harman, Robert. 1995. Intergenerational Relations among Maya in Los Angeles. In *Selected Papers on Refugees Issues: IV.* Edited by Ann Rynearson and James Phillips. Arlington, Virginia: American Anthropological Association. Pp. 48–66.

Hebrew Immigrant Aid Society (HIAS). 1980. *Statistical Abstract.* New York.

Hernandez, Andres R., Editor. 1974. *The Cuban Minority in the U.S.* Washington, D.C.: Cuban National Planning Council.

Hickey, Gerald C. 1964. *Village in Vietnam.* New Haven, Connecticut: Yale University Press.

Hoskins, Marilyn W. 1975. Vietnamese Women: Their Roles and Their Options. In *Being Female.* Edited by Dana Raphael. The Hague: Mouton. Pp. 127–146.

Human Resources Corporation. 1979. *Evaluation of the Indochinese Refugee Assistance Program in Private Agencies in California.* San Francisco, California.

Indochina Refugee Action Center (IRAC). 1980. *An Assessment of the Needs of Indochinese Youth.* Washington, D.C.

Jacobson, Gaynor I. 1978. Soviet Jewry: Perspectives on the ''Dropout'' Issue. *Journal of Jewish Communal Service* 55(1):83–89.

Kelly, Gail Paradise. 1977. *From Vietnam to America: A Chronicle of the Vietnamese Immigration to the United States.* Boulder, Colorado: Westview Press.

Kibria, Nazli. 1990. Power, Patriarchy, and Gender Conflict in the Vietnamese Immigrant Community. *Gender and Society* 4(1):9–24.

Kim, Young Yun. 1980. *Population Characteristics and Service Needs of Indochinese Refugees.* Vol. 3 of the Research Project on Indochinese Refugees in the State of Illinois. Chicago: Travelers Aid Society of Metropolitan Chicago.

Kim, Young Yun, and Perry M. Nicassio. 1980. *Psychological, Social, and Cultural Adjustment of Indochinese Refugees.* Vol. 4 of the Research Project on Indochinese Refugees in the State of Illinois. Chicago: Travelers Aid Society of Metropolitan Chicago.

Knudsen, John Chr. 1992. ''To Destroy You Is No Loss'': Hong Kong 1991–92. In *Selected Papers on Refugee Issues.* Edited by Pamela A. DeVoe. Washington, D.C.: American Anthropological Association. Pp. 133–145.

Koehn, Peter H. 1991. *Refugees from Revolution: U.S. Policy and Third-World Migration.* Boulder, Colorado: Westview Press.

Kogan, Deborah, and Mary Vencill. 1984. *An Evaluation of the Favorable Alternate Sites Project.* Berkeley, California: Berkeley Planning Associates.

Kunz, E. F. 1973. The Refugee in Flight: Kinetic Models and Forms of Displacement. *International Migration Review* 7(2):125–146.

LeBar, Frank, Gerald Hickey, and John Musgrave, Editors. 1964. *Ethnic Groups of Mainland Southeast Asia.* New Haven, Connecticut: Human Relations Area Files Press.

Light, Ivan, Georges Sabagh, Mehdi Bozorgmehr, and Claudia Der-Martirosian. 1993. Internal Ethnicity in the Ethnic Economy. *Ethnic and Racial Studies* 16:581–597.

Lin, Keh-Ming, Laurie Tazuma, and Minoru Masuda. 1979. Adaptational Problems of Vietnamese Refugees: Health and Mental Health Status. *Archives of General Psychiatry* 36:955–961.

Lipson, Juliene G., and Patricia A. Omidian. 1995. Human Rights Abuse: Health and the Transnational Connection. In *Selected Papers on Refugee Issues: IV.* Edited by Ann Rynearson and James Phillips. Arlington, Virginia: American Anthropological Association. Pp. 5–20.

Liu, William T., Maryanne Lamanna, and Alice Murata. 1979. *Transition to Nowhere: Vietnamese Refugees in America.* Nashville, Tennessee: Charter House.

Long, Lynellyn D. 1993. *Ban Vinai: The Refugee Camp.* New York: Columbia University Press.

Markowitz, Fran. 1993. *A Community in Spite of Itself: Soviet Jewish Émigrés in New York.* Washington, D.C.: Smithsonian Institution Press.

Marsh, Robert E. 1980. Socioeconomic Status of Indochinese Refugees in the United States: Progress and Problems. *Social Security Bulletin* 43(10):11–20.

Masuda, Minoru, Keh-Ming Lin, and Laurie Tazuma. 1980. Adaptation Problems of Vietnamese Refugees: Life Changes and Perceptions of Life Events. *Archives of General Psychiatry* 37:447–450.

Melville, Margarita. 1985. Salvadoreans and Guatemalans. In *Refugees in the United States.* Edited by David W. Haines. Westport, Connecticut: Greenwood Press. Pp. 167–180.

Model, Suzanne. 1992. The Ethnic Economy: Cubans and Chinese Reconsidered. *Sociological Quarterly* 33(1):63–82.

Mortland, Carol A. 1994a. Cambodian Refugees and Identity in the United States. In *Restructuring Lives, Recapturing Meaning.* Edited by Linda A. Camino and Ruth M. Krulfeld. Basel, Switzerland: Gordon and Breach. Pp. 5–27.

———. 1994b. Khmer Buddhists in the United States: Ultimate Questions. In *Cambodian Culture since 1975.* Ithaca, New York: Cornell University Press. Pp. 72–90.

Mortland, Carol, and Judy Ledgerwood. 1988. Refugee Resource Acquisition, the Invisible Communication System. In *Cross-Cultural Adaptation: Current Approaches.* Edited by Young Yun Kim and William P. Gudykunst. Newbury Park, California: Sage Publications. Pp. 286–306.

Office of Refugee Resettlement (ORR). 1983. *Report to the Congress: Refugee Resettlement Program.* Washington, D.C.: U.S. Department of Health and Human Services.

———. 1984. *Report to the Congress: Refugee Resettlement Program.* Washington, D.C.: U.S. Department of Health and Human Services.

———. 1993. *Report to the Congress: Refugee Resettlement Program.* Washington, D.C.: U.S. Department of Health and Human Services.

———. 1994. *Report to the Congress: Refugee Resettlement Program.* Washington, D.C.: U.S. Department of Health and Human Services.

———. 1995. *Report to the Congress: Refugee Resettlement Program.* Washington, D.C.: U.S. Department of Health and Human Services.

Opportunity Systems, Inc. (OSI). 1977. *Fifth Wave Report: Vietnam Resettlement Operational Feedback.* Washington, D.C.

———. 1981. *Ninth Wave Report: Indochinese Resettlement Operational Feedback.* Washington, D.C.

Orleck, Annelise. 1987. The Soviet Jews: Life in Brighton Beach, Brooklyn. In *New Immigrants in New York.* Edited by Nancy Foner. New York: Columbia University Press. Pp. 273–304.

Page, J. Bryan, and Diana H. Gonzales. 1980. Drug Use among Miami Cubans: A Preliminary Report. *Street Pharmacologist* 3(11):1–4.

Penning, Kerry. 1992. Tradition and Pragmatism: An Exploration into the Career Aspirations of Vietnamese Refugee College Students. In *Selected Papers on Refugee Issues.* Edited by Pamela A. DeVoe. Washington, D.C.: American Anthropological Association. Pp. 89–99.

Pennsylvania Department of Public Welfare. 1979. *National Mental Health Needs Assessment of Indochinese Refugee Populations.* Philadelphia, Pennsylvania: Office of Mental Health, Bureau of Research and Training.

Perez, Lisandro. 1986. Immigrant Economic Adjustment and Family Organization: The Cuban Success Story Reexamined. *International Migration Review* 20(1):4–20.

Phan, Tam C. 1994. Public Health Agenda Year 2000: Objectives for Vietnamese Americans. *The Bridge* 11(3):2–3, 10.

Portes, Alejandro. 1969. Dilemmas of a Golden Exile: Integration of Cuban Refugee Families in Milwaukee. *American Sociological Review* 34:505–518.

Portes, Alejandro, and Robert L. Bach. 1985. *Latin Journey: Cuban and Mexican Immigrants in the United States.* Berkeley: University of California Press.

Portes, Alejandro, Juan M. Clark, and Robert L. Bach. 1977. The New Wave: A Statistical Profile of Recent Cuban Exiles to the United States. *Cuban Studies* 1:1–32.

Prieto, Yolanda. 1986. Cuban Women and Work in the United States: A New Jersey Case Study. In *International Migration: The Female Experience*. Edited by Rita James Simon and Caroline B. Brettell. Totowa, New Jersey: Rowman and Allenheld. Pp. 95–112.

Prohias, Rafael, and Lourdes Casal. 1973. *The Cuban Minority in the U.S.: Preliminary Report on Need Identification and Program Evaluation*. Boca Raton: Florida Atlantic University.

Rahe, Richard H., John G. Looney, Harold W. Ward, Tran Minh Tung, and William T. Liu. 1978. Psychiatric Consultation in a Vietnamese Refugee Camp. *American Journal of Psychiatry* 135(2):185–190.

Rasbridge, Lance A. 1994. Health and Illness among Refugees: Acute and Long-term Consequences of Resettlement. Paper presented at the annual meeting of the American Anthropological Association, Atlanta, Georgia.

Roberts, Alden E., and Paul D. Starr. 1989. Differential Reference Group Assimilation among Vietnamese Refugees. In *Refugees as Immigrants*. Edited by David W. Haines. Totowa, New Jersey: Rowman and Littlefield. Pp. 40–54.

Rogg, Eleanor. 1971. The Influence of a Strong Refugee Community on the Economic Adjustment of Its Members. *International Migration Review* 5(4):474–481.

Rutledge, Paul James. 1985. *The Role of Religion in Ethnic Self-Identity*. Lanham, Maryland: University Press of America.

Segal, Julius, and Norman Lourie. 1975. The Mental Health of the Vietnam Refugees: Memorandum to Rear Admiral S. G. Morrison. Washington, D.C.: U.S. Department of Health, Education, and Welfare, National Institute of Mental Health.

Simon, Rita J., Editor. 1985. *New Lives: The Adjustment of Soviet Jewish Immigrants in the United States and Israel*. Lexington, Massachusetts: Lexington Books.

Smith-Hefner, Nancy J. 1994. Ethnicity and the Force of Faith: Christian Conversion among Khmer Refugees. *Anthropological Quarterly* 67(1):24–37.

Starr, Paul D., and Alden E. Roberts. 1982. Community Structure and Vietnamese Refugee Adaptation: The Significance of Context. *International Migration Review* 16(3):595–615.

Starr, Paul D., Alden E. Roberts, Rebecca G. LeNoir, and Thai Ngoc Nguyen. 1979. Adaptation and Stress among Vietnamese Refugees: Preliminary Results from Two Regions. Paper presented at the Conference on Indochinese Refugees, George Mason University, Fairfax, Virginia.

Stein, Barry N. 1979. Occupational Adjustment of Refugees: The Vietnamese in the United States. *International Migration Review* 13(1):25–45.

Szapocznik, Jose, William Kurtines, and Norma Hanna. 1979. Comparison of Cuban and Anglo American Cultural Values in a Clinical Population. *Journal of Consulting and Clinical Psychology* 47(3):623–624.

Szapocznik, Jose, Mercedes A. Scopetta, and Olga E. King. 1978. Theory and Practice in Matching Treatment to the Special Characteristics and Problems of Cuban Immigrants. *Journal of Community Psychology* 6:112–122.

Taft, Julia Vadala, David S. North, and David A. Ford. 1979. *Refugee Resettlement in the U.S.: Time for a New Focus*. Washington, D.C.: New TransCentury Foundation.

Tollefson, James W. 1989. *Alien Winds: The Reeducation of America's Indochinese Refugees*. New York: Praeger.

University of Miami. 1967. *The Cuban Immigration 1959–1966 and Its Impact on Miami–Dade County, Florida.* Coral Gables, Florida.

Urban Associates, Inc. 1974. *A Study of Selected Socio-economic Characteristics of Ethnic Minorities Based on the 1970 Census: Volume 1: Americans of Spanish Origin.* Washington, D.C.: U.S. Department of Health, Education, and Welfare.

U.S. Bureau of the Census. 1980. *Statistical Abstract of the United States.* Washington, D.C.

———. 1993a. *Asians and Pacific Islanders in the United States.* (CB 3-5). Washington, D.C.

———. 1993b. *The Foreign Born Population of the United States.* (CB 3-1). Washington, D.C.

———. 1993c. *Persons of Hispanic Origin in the United States.* (CB 3-3). Washington, D.C.

U.S. Committee for Refugees (USCR). 1984. *Vietnamese Boat People: Pirates' Vulnerable Prey.* New York: American Council for Nationalities Service.

U.S. General Accounting Office (GAO). 1983. *Improved Overseas Medical Examinations and Treatment Can Reduce Serious Diseases in Indochinese Refugees Entering the United States.* Washington, D.C.

———. 1995. *Welfare Reform: Implications of Proposals on Legal Immigrants' Benefits.* Washington, D.C.

Vignes, A. Joe, and Richard C. W. Hall. 1979. Adjustment of a Group of Vietnamese People to the United States. *American Journal of Psychiatry* 136(4):442–444.

Welaratna, Usha. 1993. *Beyond the Killing Fields: Voices of Nine Cambodian Survivors in America.* Stanford: Stanford University Press.

Wilson, Kenneth L., and Alejandro Portes. 1980. Immigrant Enclaves: An Analysis of the Labor Market Experiences of Cubans in Miami. *American Journal of Sociology* 86(2):295–319.

Zhou, Min, and Carl L. Bankston III. 1994. Social Capital and the Adaptation of the Second Generation: The Case of Vietnamese Youth in New Orleans. *International Migration Review* 28(4):821–845.

Part II

The Refugees

Chapter 3

Afghans

JULIENE G. LIPSON AND
PATRICIA A. OMIDIAN

Through the centuries, the area that is now Afghanistan has been fought over
by Greeks, Kushans, Indians, Huns, Persians, Arabs, Turks, Mongols, British,
and Russians. Most recently, it has been torn by more than 15 years of political
strife and war. Afghan citizens began leaving their country in 1979 after a coup
that preceded the invasion of Afghanistan by the former USSR. Prior to the
withdrawal of Soviet troops in 1989, Afghan refugees comprised the largest
refugee population in the world, some 6.5 million people living in refugee camps
and cities in Pakistan and Iran, with smaller numbers in India, Europe, and North
America; it remains the largest despite repatriation of some 3 million people.
Although many Afghans want to return to their country, ongoing civil war between political parties has discouraged most Afghans living in Europe and the
United States from returning.

This chapter introduces the Afghan refugee population in the United States,
based mostly on our research with those in the San Francisco Bay Area. We
attempt to depict both the heterogeneity of Afghans in the United States and
their common cultural characteristics and dilemmas. Readers should keep in
mind that for every common theme, there are variations and exceptions. The
Afghan community is like a mosaic in which the tiles can be viewed up close
to reveal their different colors and shapes or from afar to reveal an overall
recognizable pattern.

Afghans began coming to the United States under refugee status in 1980, with
2,000 to 4,000 arriving yearly until fiscal year 1989 after the withdrawal of
former USSR troops from Afghanistan (U.S. Committee for Refugees 1994a).
This withdrawal spurred a politically influenced decision that Afghans were no
longer legitimate refugees; most were thereafter denied priority-one category for
visas (in danger of immediate loss of life).

No one knows exactly how many Afghans live in the United States. Estimates range from 45,000 to 75,000 (Rahmany 1993), with 55 to 67 percent in the San Francisco Bay Area. Other large communities are in Los Angeles, New York, the Washington, D.C., area, and Portland. Of these, 27,050 Afghans were admitted under refugee status between 1982 and 1994 (U.S. Committee for Refugees 1994a). The 1990 census underestimates the Afghan refugee population because many Afghans misunderstood its purpose and were afraid to cooperate. In fiscal year 1994, only 21 Afghans were admitted to the United States as refugees; many others came through family reunification channels.

The Afghan population in the San Francisco Bay Area continues to grow through secondary migration. This area is attractive because of the size of the existing Afghan population, the presence of extended family members, the weather, and, before the 1994 elections, a relatively generous welfare system. We attempted to more accurately enumerate the size of the San Francisco Bay Area Afghan community through querying a variety of county and private social service agencies, local mosques, and school districts. However, complete data could not be obtained from any one source, and we estimate that there are 15,000 to 20,000 Afghans in the area (Lipson and Omidian 1993).

The Afghan population in the United States is heterogeneous in social class origin, ethnic group and religion, political stance, degree of acculturation, and financial stability. The cosmopolitan, urban, formerly wealthy, and highly educated elite began arriving in the early 1980s. Family reunification in the mid- to late 1980s brought their middle-class relatives who are less educated, some illiterate even in their own languages. Although few refugees of rural origin could afford to leave Pakistan or Iran, there is a small but significant group who maintain their very traditional lifestyle. As Muslims, Afghans generally are quite religious but vary from strictly observing all practices to being more informal (for example, praying by oneself rather than ritually). They also range from very cosmopolitan to very traditional, with more well educated people from Kabul tending to be more cosmopolitan, depending on family background, strength of religious adherence, and political stance. Families from other cities and rural areas tend to be more traditional, with women uneducated, wearing traditional dress, and secluded from contact with unrelated men.

AFGHANISTAN

Afghanistan is a land-locked, mountainous country with an agriculture-based economy located in southwest Asia between Iran, Pakistan, Tajikistan, and Uzbekistan.[1] No systematic nationwide census has been conducted since 1978, and as of 1994, population estimates ranged from 11 to 17 million. With an area only 6 percent smaller than Texas, Afghanistan was, and still is, one of the world's poorest countries. Its vital statistics reflect this poverty; for example, life expectancy at birth was 46 years for males and 44 years for females (*World Almanac* 1993).

It has only been in the past 30 years that Afghanistan has become more urbanized and modernized, including development of educational and transportation systems. Major cities were finally connected by highways and railway systems in the mid-1970s, yet 85 percent of the population still relied on donkey and foot travel (Canfield 1986). Before the 1979 invasion and subsequent war, educational opportunities for village children allowed them to obtain government jobs and settle in urban centers, although merchants have been urban for generations. However, 88 percent of the population is illiterate (*World Almanac* 1993).

Afghanistan is a mosaic of social groups that differ by social class, urban and rural origin, ethnic group and language, tribe, region of the country, and religion. What is common to Afghans, however, is Islam and several strong cultural values, such as the importance of the family.

In prewar Afghanistan, there was a small but growing middle class that included many people trained in the West or former USSR. They differed in education and experience from their rural relatives and in wealth from the elite. Yet middle-class people were connected to both the rural and the elite population by extensive kinship systems. The relatively few university-educated middle-class people became part of a new network made up of classmates.

Afghanistan has many ethnic groups, the most populous of which are Pashtuns (38 percent), Tajiks (25 percent), and Hazaras (19 percent) (*World Almanac* 1994). The official languages are Pashtu (spoken in the south and east primarily by Pashtuns) and Dari (spoken in the west, central region, and the north by Tajiks and Hazaras); Uzbeks and Turkoman peoples speak Turkic dialects. These ethnic groups sometimes have more in common with their neighbors outside Afghanistan than with other Afghans.

Afghanistan's social organization reflects its origin as a tribal society based on nomadic pastoralism, although agriculture and village life have become more prominent. The prewar rural population was about 87 percent of the total Afghan population (Canfield 1986). Ethnic diversity and regional and village loyalties characterize the country as a whole, and intergroup conflicts are part of its social fabric. This pattern is reflected in Afghan communities in the United States and elsewhere.

Nearly all Afghans are Muslims, although a small number of Sikhs, Hindus, Christians, and Jews live there as well. The strong Islamic identity creates a mask of homogeneity that does not really reflect Afghan society. Two thirds of the population are Sunni Muslim, and the remaining 5 million are Shi'a of the Imami and Ismaili sects (Nyrop and Seekins 1986). Afghanistan's history reflects the importance of religion, with riots and killings between sects within regions and discrimination by the majority of the minority (Dupree 1980). However, since 1979, when Afghanistan's Communist leaders, aided by the Soviet army, tried to impose secular laws at the local level, these schisms were put aside, and Islamic symbols motivated the population against the government (Canfield 1986; Nyrop and Seekins 1986). Islam symbolizes how Afghans, in

Afghanistan and elsewhere, define themselves and explain the world around them.

EXODUS AND TRANSIT

Modernization of Afghanistan ceased in 1978. In the years following the 1978 coup and 1979 Soviet invasion, Afghanistan has been devastated by three wars: against the Soviet army and the Afghan government it was trying to support (1979–1989); against Communist government forces after the departure of the Russian army (1989–1992); and among warlords and factions vying for power in a bloody civil war (1992–1995). Over 40 percent of the population has been killed or forced to leave the country. Much of the remaining rural population was forced out of the countryside and into urban centers. The United Nations estimates that over 1 million have died. There are still approximately 1 million internal refugees and 3.5 million waiting in Pakistan, Iran, India, Europe, and the United States. Soviet and Afghan government forces systematically devastated the countryside, destroying whole villages in order to clear the rural areas of havens for the resistance forces.

When Soviet troops withdrew in 1989, an even bloodier battle ensued as government troops battled the resistance for control of Afghanistan. In 1992, the Communist president Muhammad Najibullah resigned when competing factions began taking the capital, Kabul. Since the fall of the Communist government, Kabul has been subject to more bombings than during ten years of war against the Soviet army. The battle continues to rage as control of the capital shifts from one faction commander to another, and it appears likely that it will wax and wane into the next century. After a new wave of shelling in Kabul and the north occurred in 1994, Pakistan closed its borders to prevent entrance of a new flood of Afghan refugees. Some 600,000 Afghans fleeing the fighting in and around Kabul and Kunduz became internally displaced in the first quarter of the year (U.S. Committee for Refugees 1994b). Along with the violence, food and energy shortages have made life in some parts of Afghanistan nearly intolerable.

During this whole period, Afghan citizens have observed or experienced atrocities and traumas. Some were imprisoned in Kabul by the Communist regime, and a number of the imprisoned were also tortured (Psychiatry Centre for Afghan Refugees 1988). Many of these Afghans still suffer from posttraumatic stress syndrome years later. The story of Modeer Saheb,[2] a well-educated, older man who had worked for an international agency in Kabul, is typical but by no means the worst:

Communist soldiers knocked on the door of Modeer Saheb's home in the middle of the night, trying to catch him hiding Mojahed (resistance fighters). When he heard the first knock, he awakened his wife and adult daughter, Fatima, so they could dress and be ready for a search. By the time he got to the door, the soldiers fired a bullet through it, taking off the end of his finger. After searching the house and finding only the family, a guard picked up a family diary from Modeer's desk which included who traveled where, who married whom, who was born, and who died. All family members had contributed to writing about the events and their feelings. The guard read about the "martyrdom" of Fatima's friend, Naheed, who was killed by soldiers firing into a crowd of school children protesting the communists, and her anger describing the communists using very "bad" language. Using this "evidence," the soldiers arrested and imprisoned Modeer and Fatima. In prison, when the guards attempted to separate Modeer and Fatima, he protested that his daughter should not be alone with soldiers, so one kicked him so hard in the groin that he fainted. After eight hours, the soldiers returned to release them because of the intervention of a colleague's son in the civil police. The guard demanded a written apology for the words in the diary, then hooded both father and daughter and drove them home. Since this incident Modeer has continuously had lower back trouble. (Omidian 1992, also see Omidian 1996)

The political climate for middle- and upper-class Afghans was one of uncertainty and even fear. Family members could disappear in the night, never to be heard from again; young men would be conscripted into the army from the streets as they went to school or the market, and office workers distrusted everyone—the person at the next desk might be a spy. Those who had worked with Americans before the coup were particularly vulnerable.

Afghans escaped Afghanistan any way they could, usually with little notice, and many had traumatic experiences getting out and finding safety. Many walked over the 10,000- to 15,000-foot mountain passes at night because of the constant threat of Communist helicopters. They experienced freezing weather, shelling and destruction, injuries, and death of family members along the way. A 70-year-old widow described this: "When the Communists came, we escaped. We walked through back roads of high mountains of Afghanistan. I was on a donkey, I fell, my head break. They just did home remedies, but with mercy of God, it cured itself" (Lipson 1993). Many never made it over the border to safety as planes strafed the refugee caravans, killing and wounding women and children; thieves and thugs ambushed families to rob them of gold or jewels or to kidnap the young women. Others were captured near the border and sent back or, more often, imprisoned. Afghan refugees experienced multiple losses; relatives were killed or left behind; they lost their status, language, and vocational competencies. Loss of home is mentioned repeatedly: "I am depressed for my country, my home, my relatives . . . my heart breaks."

Life was difficult in the country of first asylum, especially for women. In Pakistan, for example, women in the 344 refugee camps were confined to the family tent or mud hut, and even those in the cities could go out only completely veiled. Those who worked with foreign relief agencies were often harassed or had their lives threatened by conservative Afghans for working with men. Many suffered from the intense heat that was so different from the climate of Afghanistan. Hypertension, depression, and other health problems were common, but the women had little access to care because there were few female health providers, and they were usually not allowed to be seen by a male doctor.

Moving On: Leaving the Region for Other Places

Life in the first country of asylum was difficult and often transitory. Refugees living in Pakistan experienced numerous problems, although they lived in the more familiar atmosphere of a country with a Muslim majority, and Afghan and Pakistani Pushtuns have ethnicity in common. But Pakistan is also a country of limited resources, intense poverty, and different climate. The Afghan educated and elite found life in Pakistan hard and uncompromising. Many men could not find work, and women were restricted in ways that they had not previously experienced in Afghanistan. Many families were fearful because of rumors of daughters being kidnapped for houses of prostitution in other countries. Because of these rumors and intermittent violence toward Afghans by Pakistanis, many families restricted their wives and daughters to home, which also limited their opportunities for education.

In Iran, Afghans faced other problems. Unlike Pakistan, Iran was at war with Iraq and needed laborers to replace Iranian men who went to war. Although this allowed many Afghans to find work, religious differences made these advantages tenuous. The majority of Afghans are of the Sunni sect, a minority in Iran. Some changed their surnames in order to avoid harassment. In addition, Afghans began to be blamed for many of the growing social problems in Iran, including violence, theft, and other social ills.

Educated and elite families often decided, prior to leaving Afghanistan, to resettle in the United States or Europe. Others found life too difficult in Pakistan or Iran and chose to apply for asylum and refugee resettlement while in their first country of asylum. Choice of country rested on two primary factors: (1) previous work and/or friendship with people from a particular country, which opened the door for sponsorship; and (2) the desire to join family members already resettled abroad. Family connections are very important in Afghan culture, and families could be counted on to assist the newcomers. Of those interviewed by Omidian (1992, 1996), few expressed a desire to live in the United States. Most said that had it not been for the war that pushed them, they would never have come to the United States. Several said that they knew what the United States was like from having obtained their U.S. college degrees in the 1970s. They thought that America was no place to raise a family. Once the war began, however, they had to risk losing their culture in order to save their children and to give them the best chance in life. Yet for still others, America was the first choice, a land of opportunity, a gathering place for Afghans living outside the region, and the country with the greatest amount of religious freedom, an important consideration.

INITIAL RESETTLEMENT

Most Afghans entered the United States as refugees, but since 1989, most have come under family reunification criteria, with a visa contingent on having family members or an organization guarantee their support for a period of time. Once a visa is obtained, Afghans are processed through one of several private or nonprofit resettlement agencies.

Family members usually meet new arrivals at the airport and transport them home, where they stay until they locate separate housing, preferably in close proximity; in some cases, a parent or unmarried children will move in permanently. Welcoming parties and social gatherings for the new arrival(s) are often held for weeks by family and friends. Family connections and close physical proximity are very important to Afghans, as noted by one student who was asked to define the concept of "health": "Health and illness are difficult to define because everyone has his or her own cultural definition for it. For instance, for an Afghan immigrant, being healthy is having family members all here and together; it does not matter too much if physically they aren't doing too well." Thus, being reunited with family members is an event that goes beyond the social realm into the individual's notion of well-being.

After the welcoming and excitement of reuniting family members, however, Afghan refugees' initial adjustment is far from easy. For most people, there are four crucial problem areas: inadequate finances, limited job opportunities, educational discrepancies, and neighborhood problems.

Finances

Afghans experience immediate problems with money, jobs, and school. New arrivals are financially supported by family members until they can obtain work or other monetary support. If they enter as refugees, they receive several months of special support with the stipulation that they take English as a Second Language (ESL) classes and obtain vocational counseling. When this funding runs out, California Afghans are often encouraged by other Afghans to apply for welfare as soon as possible.

Money is a chronic problem for many Afghans. Even formerly wealthy new arrivals experience financial difficulties. For example, families with three houses and many servants in Afghanistan now live in small and crowded apartments (e.g., nine family members in two bedrooms). It was possible to live a sumptuous lifestyle in Afghanistan on what in the United States is very little money, but many of the wealthy sold their possessions or had to leave precipitously without having done so. With Immigration and Naturalization Service (INS) quota changes by the mid-1990s, there is a small but growing number of Afghans who spent their entire assets in Afghanistan or a transit country on false documents so that they could request asylum once they were on U.S. soil. This did not work for one woman, who was apprehended and imprisoned for two years and now attributes being "mentally ill" to this experience.

Job Opportunities

One of the most significant resettlement challenges faced by refugees is earning a livelihood. Home country skills and status are not usually transferable to the United States. Men, in particular, experience stress and depression related to loss of status brought on by unemployment and loss of their traditional breadwinner role. Those from middle-class backgrounds are more willing to accept entry-level jobs than are well-educated or upper-class refugees, who are too proud to accept menial jobs. An example involves the many physicians unable to pass the licensure exam because of finances, English problems, or outdated medical training (Lipson and Omidian 1992a). Vocational counselors may inadvertently insult their Afghan clients by not recognizing the importance of former social status.

A newly arrived man described the problems he faces as he and his young family adjust to life here. Neither he nor his wife had extended family or social networks in the area, and connections and social interactions are critical to an Afghan's emotional well-being. With no family members to guide him, he had to obtain advice from strangers, who "cannot be trusted":

It is very difficult to be comfortable outside of your own country. I worked for six years in Pakistan for the United Nations vocational training program. I had deceived myself; I thought I could be busy here and happy, but I have been here nine months now and nine months with no job. This is the first time I have ever eaten for free. Welfare is not good; it makes people lazy. Welfare is deceptive—it is not enough money to live on. If you work, you have to report it, but if you do not work you cannot live. Every time you get a job you lose. There are some people here that like to stay on welfare. Their life in Afghanistan was very hard and they were poor. Here, being on welfare makes them feel better as they do not struggle.

A former director in Afghanistan's Ministry of Agriculture said:

I thought I could get a good job because I was American-educated. I applied for every job I thought was appropriate. The welfare department sent me letters saying I am capable of working and I should take any job. Honestly, taking a job in a fast food restaurant is very humiliating for me, but being on welfare is even more humiliating. (Lipson and Omidian 1992b)

In the opinion of some Afghan community members, 90 percent of the San Francisco Bay Area Afghan families are supported by Aid to Families with Dependent Children (AFDC). Afghans themselves have strong and mixed feelings about the issue of public assistance. Most families think that they do not really have a choice, considering what jobs are available to them. An Afghan social worker noted that "Afghans are not lazy; they want to work hard, but they cannot live on what they get paid. With the job or without the job, there is not enough money either way."

Educational Discrepancies

School and learning English are also sources of potential difficulty for newcomers. The education of many children was interrupted for several years by war and/or no education available in transit locations. Depending on the school, they may be placed in ESL classes until they are able to speak enough English to function at a minimal level. When they enter regular classes, they may be placed with children two or three years younger. Children are sometimes teased by their classmates for being different. In general, however, younger children learn English quickly and adapt far better than do their elders.

Adult newcomers who entered as refugees were provided special financial support originally for up to three years, but that period has declined sharply over the last decade. Funding cutbacks have decreased the number of ESL classes; even those available are inappropriate for many Afghans, such as women illiterate in their own language, who cannot manage public transportation, or are responsible for young children.

Neighborhood Issues

Finally, Afghans vary in where they settle. Most prefer to move into neighborhoods where other Afghans live, and they sometimes encounter hostility from non-Afghan neighbors, particularly when they wear traditional dress. Public anti-immigrant sentiment of the past few years, especially during California's economic crisis of the early 1990s, has made life difficult for all immigrant groups, particularly those who stand out in appearance and speak accented or little English. For example, a traditional older man complained about the following incident:

When I walk to the grocery store, people honk or yell at me from their cars. I don't know what they are saying, but it is embarrassing. I am proud to wear my own clothes and my hat that I wore in the JIHAD. My father and grandfather never wore pants! I wish I was martyred in Afghanistan! (Lipson and Omidian 1992b)

When they first arrive, Afghans tend to settle in neighborhoods with cheaper rents. Such neighborhoods tend to be more dangerous as well, causing some older people, women, and children to sequester themselves indoors all day until a man or someone with a car can come to take them out. Isolation and loneliness are quite common among newcomers who know little English or who cannot drive. This loneliness is magnified by the difference in social customs that they knew in Afghanistan, where doors were always open and visitors are welcomed;

women and older people, in particular, spend time each day visiting and being visited.

But transportation is still a problem for those who have been in the United States longer, especially when it is complicated by not knowing English, as an older man described:

It's again the question of transport. I have a lot of friends and want to go and meet them, [but] I have not a private car. I have not the money to buy it. Then I have to ask my children to give me a lift, they are busy. My friends, they go to the grocery store and want to buy something but do not know the name and are not able to ask somebody. Then they have to ask their children to go with them; [the children] have their own appointment with their doctors and [must] go to their work. Also, when they go to the doctor, it is very difficult for them to express their needs. Therefore, they feel that they are more dependent here while in [our] country they have not this problem. They are home-locked, they cannot go to their relatives.

INTEGRATION

While the Afghan community perceives great variation in adaptational success of different families in the United States, outsiders view the majority of families as having difficulty since many remain on welfare or on disability.

For Afghan refugees, integration into U.S. society means being able to earn a living, functioning at a sufficient level at work or in school, meeting minimal everyday needs, and experiencing some level of satisfaction and stability. For the great majority of Afghans, integration does not mean assimilation. There are considerable differences in acculturation between Afghans who have been in the United States for 14 years and new arrivals but very little assimilation in general, except among children and teens. However, such ''assimilation'' is really more surface appearance and behavior, and most young people attempt to maintain their Afghan identity.

Integration occurs at different rates, depending on a number of factors, such as education, the person's expectations, occupation in Afghanistan, time and age of arrival in the United States, English proficiency, and familiarity with Western ways. Gender and generation are especially critical in influencing how much and how quickly Afghans integrate, so the following sections separately address the issues experienced by men, women, and youth.

Men's Issues

Employment issues are most problematic for Afghan men[3] because relatively few women in Afghanistan worked or financially supported the family. Had they remained in Afghanistan, older men would have retired and turned their family affairs over to a son. In the United States, although not perceived as ''retired'' by social service agencies, cultural norms and expected roles and status prevent most older Afghans from starting over. Those who arrived at a younger age have been somewhat more successful in gaining employment, but most remain on public assistance if they have families to support. The major employment for this generation is buying and selling goods at local flea markets, an activity that brings in cash while allowing families to keep Medi-Cal (California's Medicaid program for low-income families) and other benefits to which they have become accustomed.

Men who arrived in the United States early in the refugee process, between 1979 and 1984, face a similar problem. Resettled throughout the United States and Canada, they rapidly learned the language and found jobs with the help of American friends. After working a few years, they began to miss the Afghan community and, on the advice of family and Afghan friends, moved to the San Francisco Bay Area. Most now regret having moved because they had to start over, for the second or third time, at the bottom. Most have not regained even the small advances they had made.

Men over 35 fall into two groups: (1) the educated elite, who are older and skilled and want to practice their professions but cannot because of the slow economy and licensing requirements (e.g., doctors) or of being technologically outdated (e.g., engineers); and (2) the unskilled, who have no transferable job skills. Men in both groups are unable to find "meaningful" employment. Only entry-level jobs may be available, on which they cannot support families and which usually do not provide health insurance, an important consideration for a family with five to nine children. Many are thus inclined to remain at home on public assistance for fear of losing status and benefits like Medi-Cal.

Some Afghans came to California believing themselves entitled to compensation because of having lost everything in Afghanistan. One resettlement counselor observed, "They have the impression that welfare is a must for making it in this country. They are misinformed from the first day they arrive by people already here, and even before they arrive by family members who told them what to ask for" (Lipson and Omidian 1992b). However, this is rarely the case in other states with fewer Afghans and more restrictive welfare policies.

During informal discussions on community problems, men described the work/welfare dilemma in two ways. Those struggling by on public assistance alone, such as this highly educated and very frustrated man, tended to say such things as:

There are three kinds of Afghans in the U.S. First the very rich that escaped with their money. The second are people who were in power to save their life, the communists; here they live the good life as they get more money than most of the people. They can go to any school and are not stopped by GAIN [a retraining program available to refugees but restrictive]. Then there are the rest of us who were not high up in the government and who only came looking for better opportunities.

The other view is expressed by men who work full-time and struggle to meet family and social obligations; they focus more on time than money and express anger at ''wealthy'' Afghans who do not work and parents who do not get ''real work'' to get off welfare:

The wealthy are those who have lots of red rugs and live on AFDC, SSI, and the flea market. Yet, they go where they want and can see friends and relatives when they want. They can observe the holy days without worry of the job. They do not see a reason now to work hard when they can socialize and travel all they want. Those who work are jealous and angry about those who do not.

Most men, whether employed or unemployed, find life difficult at best and feel that they have lost more than they have gained by living in California. Their worldview, including their ability to practice Islam, is under siege; if they work, there is no time for family; if they are unemployed, they have failed to provide for their families. It is a wound that does not heal. Time only makes the problem more acute.

A small proportion of families has gained financial security through all adult and adolescent members working, even though none of the jobs pay well (e.g., gas station attendant, hotel maid, fast-food clerk). This kind of family cooperation is comparable to the excellent economic adjustment of Cuban immigrants in the United States; their relatively high family income level is due to proportionately more workers per family than the U.S. population (Perez 1986). Among Afghans, this method of increasing family income is not without its costs, as expressed by one woman who worried that

[y]oung people need after-school sports like volleyball or baseball. Unfortunately, our children go after school to work, hard work, physical work. This kind of job makes them very exhausted. They are not able to do their homework like American students, and at school they are sleepy. (Lipson and Omidian 1992b)

Women's and Family Issues

Traditional customs related to women[4] in Afghanistan include arranged marriages and polygyny, when affordable. In this strongly patriarchal culture, women are generally less educated, marry young, have many babies (preferably boys), do not work outside the home, and are restricted to socializing mainly with women relatives. This pattern varied for urban-educated women in the 1970s. Many worked outside the home and may have even indicated their interest in a specific potential husband. However, even professional women had less freedom than women in the United States—''only going to the office and home.''

Afghan women's lives in the United States have changed, and they puzzle about their proper roles. Women seem to acculturate more quickly than men do; they become caught between the Afghan community's expectations that they behave traditionally and their desire for American-style freedom and independence. One man claimed that typical Afghan women in California prefer to stay home and cook for the family, take care of the children, clean house, and socialize with Afghan female friends, especially by telephone. In contrast, a woman stated: ''Ladies adjusted well to this society; they drive, they work, they speak English. It is easy to cook here; they have more time for visiting and shopping, going to the park; they are more active than the men.'' However, many work hard to support their families.

Obtaining a job is often easier for women and teens, and they are less upset by taking jobs beneath their ability or background. However, family conflict may result from the husband not working and the wife taking a menial job (e.g., hotel maid); disturbing the traditional patriarchal role can cause marital problems. But even when the wife works full-time, she is still expected to cook, clean the house, and care for the children.

Many women experience intergeneration and intergender conflicts over women's freedom, the conflict between maintaining traditional values and becoming Americanized, role overload from adding new American roles to their preexisting or expected Afghan roles, lack of role models and suitable spouses for single women, and parenting difficulties. Women's experiences vary with their age, background, and individual personalities. Elderly women appear the most stressed and unhappy of any Afghans in the United States. Often widows, they live with sons' or daughters' families; however, they are socially isolated and lonely because the adults are working and the children are at school. As they rarely speak English, they are essentially homebound, afraid of going out because they will get lost. Unable to take public transportation to visit friends or other family members (Omidian and Lipson 1992), they miss the constant visiting that is characteristic of social life in Afghanistan. They feel trapped, like a 75-year-old woman who said, ''At this age, for me America is nothing. I want to be in my country, die in my country, but because my kids are here and they need me, I have to be here, not go.''

Single Afghan women refugees face different challenges than do their married counterparts. Most single women live with parents or siblings; they continue to be called girls, no matter what their age. Because marriage and children are central to Afghan women's identity, remaining single is viewed as unnatural. However, finding an appropriate husband is difficult. Afghan women who have been in the United States longer than a few months may be perceived as contaminated by American ideas and not properly naive or submissive by Afghan men, who frequently marry women still living in Afghanistan or Pakistan. When they want to complete a college education, they despair of being an ''old maid'' whom no one will marry (Omidian 1992, 1996). Although divorce among Afghans is increasing, stigma and family pressure keep most women in bad marriages from divorcing; divorcees may be shunned by their families and they may be unable to marry again. Those who move back in with their parents find that their status has changed. It is only when parents recognize that the daughter was in an abusive relationship that they give her moral support.

Other family role changes are related to children acting in the role of family spokesperson for parents who speak little or no English, acting as interpreters with schools and social or health care services. As children are expected to respect and obey their parents, especially their fathers and anyone older, children's power to interpret the outside world creates considerable family stress.

Youth's Issues

Young people are the most torn between Afghan and American culture. Respect for their elders is still a strong part of Afghan culture for many young people. But they view the concept of respect in the context of new choices that they would not have had to make in Afghanistan. At the same time, they feel obligated to maintain as much Afghan identity as they can, being respectful and meeting family expectations whenever possible. Many young women attending college see themselves as having to struggle on two fronts: first, with family members who are suspicious of their interactions with young men on campus and their desire for a degree; and second, with the American public that stereotypes Muslims as radical fanatics.

Because of their increased contact with other American subcultures and their quicker adaptation to school and work, young people face more situational dissonance than do their elders. They struggle daily with the fit between the "ideal" and the "real" and thus are constantly redefining and evaluating their social identity. Young people complain that America forces people to ignore the needs of their extended family:

We fool ourselves that our life will be better. For the old, they came here for the young people. Their life will not get better. This puts pressure on the young to do well, and this is very difficult. As young, we got everything, but now we cannot help them [parents], so we feel bad. We cannot return the help. In this country you have to support yourself first, and that is hard. Sometimes the old people ask us to help and we cannot, so we feel real sorry. (Omidian 1992:195)

Young people understand their parents' views and also understand their own dilemma—how to stay socially interconnected and Afghan while in America: "The biggest worries that the parents have right now is that their kids would change, and the biggest worry that kids have is they don't want to change, but they change" (Omidian 1992, 1996).

But while parents are troubled by the rapidity with which their children adjust to American life, they are proud of the children who do well. High academic achievement is seen by others as a sign of successful parenting. They also hope that the children will have more opportunities in the United States. Highly educated parents expect their children to follow in their footsteps, but parents with little or no education do not understand the educational system and cannot assist their children with their educational goals. Whether or not they are educated, parents struggle to understand an educational system that, in their minds, undercuts their authority over their children. "Back home" the schools support parents' and families' full control over the children. As one high school girl said:

The boys, they stay out late and stuff. That's OK, I mean the parents can't do anything about it. But when they come home, the father goes, "Well, if you were back home you wouldn't do this. Our relatives, what would they say?" So, as much as he enjoys outside he'll pay when he comes home and I'm sure they would get in a fight. My family went through that, my brother and my dad.

Afghan youth often discuss freedom of expression in America, but most young people and their parents feel that the advantages of personal freedom are wasted on issues that are harmful to people, like taking drugs. They think that no one needs this much freedom because people should rely on others and be part of a social network to live a happy life. Both young people and their parents think that Americans live without enough guidance and discipline.

On a broader level, some Afghan refugee youth have experienced war stress similar to that experienced by young Americans who live in urban war zones and witness drive-by shootings. An Afghan man in his early twenties, who lived in Kabul until two years ago, connects living in war with growing up quickly. He described seeing a boy, late for school, run across the street between a jeep and a tank. The jeep hit him and threw his body under a tank that rolled over him:

Then another tank and another. The tanks never stopped. There was no meaning to them in this death. In the end, there was no way to see the body as a person and yet someone had to tell the family. For months after this I could not sleep as I kept seeing this boy and this body. It is still fresh in my mind and I see it clearly still. I could never forget it. I also decided that what happened to Afghanistan was from God. We were drinking and leaving the way of God and this is how we are punished. This was what we deserved. After this life, I am older than the old men who tell me to respect them. What do they know? (Omidian 1994b)

In Kabul, this young man was motivated to make high grades to be admitted to the university; as long as he was a good student, he would not have to die as a soldier. In the wake of this pressure, he is looking forward to university classes in the United States for their own sake. Many Afghan youth who arrived in the late 1980s and the early 1990s faced an existence that most Americans see only at the movies.

A significant unifying factor is added to this mosaic of variation based on age, gender, ethnicity, education, and time in the United States. All Afghans living outside of the region maintain close ties with family members left behind. With the war likely to continue well into the latter half of the 1990s, trauma to, and displacement of, loved ones is still a reality to be faced. Many who survived

the war against the Communist government are fleeing their homes as the political factions vie for power and bomb previously untouched civilian targets.
Most families send money to help newly displaced relatives because few organizations are currently helping new refugees.

At the same time, people living in the United States are traveling to Pakistan
and Afghanistan to visit and choose spouses for unmarried children and siblings.
These marriages strengthen ties that might otherwise be lost. Also, by marrying
a son or daughter to someone living in Pakistan or Afghanistan, families ensure
the continuity of Afghan culture. Many feel that children raised in the United
States cannot learn to be proper Afghans, and such marriages reinforce cultural
identity.

CONCLUSIONS AND PROSPECTS

The first Afghans arrived in the United States less than a century ago; as late
as 1977, the few who came to study returned home (Angary 1991). The past
15 years have seen many changes in the new Afghan population in the United
States; its short history reveals both problems and successes. As civil unrest and
war continue, fewer Afghans think that they can return to their country, and
more are now becoming U.S. citizens. In addition to the danger in Afghanistan,
parents are concerned that their children, raised in the United States, are too
Americanized to function in Afghanistan; they also want to continue to take
advantage of the educational and economic opportunities of America's industrialized society.

The Afghan community is heterogeneous in background, problems, and successes. As of 1995, problems for some Afghan families are the same as those
experienced by other families in the early and mid-1980s—culture conflict, isolation, financial and occupational problems, mental health and other health problems primarily based on stress and posttraumatic stress disorder, poor access to
health care and lack of culturally appropriate services, and family stress based
on changing roles in the context of American culture. These are likely to worsen
in the mid-1990s antiimmigrant climate and amid federal plans to disassemble
the welfare system in California.

Other families, however, are relatively satisfied with their lives in the United
States and appreciate the country's opportunities and technological time savers.
Many of these families have been in the United States longer, know English,
and have relatively stable jobs. However, they are now facing the dilemma of
maintaining Afghan culture with their acculturated children and coping with
stressful role changes within the family. Many men, for example, are threatened
by the increasing assertiveness of women who function responsibly in the public
sphere and help to support the family financially.

In the nine years that we have known the Afghan population in northern
California, we have seen a number of changes. One of these changes is increased

economic stability; for example, some families have been able to purchase homes and their own businesses. Some children have changed from being respectful young Afghans to Afghan gang members who vie for power with other ethnic gangs; others excel in school, many going on to college and university. These students are looking toward professional education, which should remedy one of the major problems faced by Afghans in the area, a lack of Afghan health, mental health, and social service providers.

The community has not yet become cohesive, but there are signs of change in this arena as well, particularly among young people and women, who are not involved in the men's politics and who are eager to work together for the good of the community. There are thriving Afghan clubs at local high schools, colleges, and universities where people socialize and support Afghan culture and community events. For example, the San Jose State University and Chabot College Afghan Clubs helped to put on an Afghan Community Health Fair in 1993. The Afghan Women's Association International, based in Hayward, accomplished what no other Afghan organization had been heretofore able to do— mobilize people and resources throughout the whole Bay Area to collect and donate clothing, blankets, and food to ship 100,000 pounds to Jalalabad, Afghanistan, to help the 600,000 new refugees who fled from Kabul beginning in early 1994.

It is difficult to predict the future prospects of the Afghan refugee community. There are many positive signs of integration and success in American society along with maintenance of Afghan ethnic identity and increased community cooperation, particularly among the young people. But along with those who are doing well are pockets of Afghans who may take many years to heal, if they heal at all. The lives of some remain miserable because of posttraumatic stress disorder, isolation, and loneliness; others appear to be becoming a passive "welfare subculture," working the system for what they can get and raising the ire of their fellow Afghans. Overall, the varying courses of adjustment to American society reflect the heterogeneity of Afghans as a refugee subculture. Like a mosaic of tiles, we must view this subculture from various distances and angles to appreciate its complexity and overall patterns.

NOTES

This chapter is based on nine years of research with Afghans in the San Francisco Bay Area. Large sections based on publications and presentations are identified by superscripts rather than citation.

1. The sections on Afghanistan and youth issues are based on Omidian's (1992) Ph.D. dissertation.

2. Names used in this chapter are fictional.

3. Description and quotes on men and jobs are based on Omidian (1994a, 1994b).

4. The section on women relies heavily on Lipson and Miller (1994).

REFERENCES

Angary, Mir Tamim. 1991. *Afghanistan: Fighting for Freedom.* New York: Dillon Press.

Canfield, Robert. 1986. Ethnic, Regional, and Sectarian Alignments in Afghanistan. In *The State, Religion, and Ethnic Politics: Afghanistan, Iran and Pakistan.* Edited by A. Banuazizi and M. Weiner. Syracuse: Syracuse University Press. Pp. 75–103.

Dupree, Louis. 1980. *Afghanistan.* Princeton: Princeton University Press.

Lipson, Juliene. 1991. Afghan Refugee Health: Some Findings and Suggestions. *Qualitative Health Research* 1(3):349–369.

———. 1993. Afghan Refugees in California: Mental Health Issues. *Issues in Mental Health Nursing* 14(4):411–423.

Lipson, Juliene, and Suellen Miller. 1994. Changing Roles of Afghan Refugee Women in the U.S. *Health Care for Women International* 15(3):171–180.

Lipson, Juliene, and Patricia Omidian. 1992a. Afghan Refugees: Health Issues in the United States. *Western Journal of Medicine* 157(3):271–275.

———. 1992b. We Don't Know the Rules: Afghan Refugees' Health and Interactions with the U.S. Social Environment. Presented at the American Anthropological Asociation annual meeting, San Francisco, December.

———. 1993. Health among San Francisco Bay Area Afghans: A Community Assessment. *Afghanistan Studies Journal* 4:71–86.

Lipson, Juliene, Patricia Omidian, and Steven Paul. 1995. Afghan Health Education Project: A Community Survey. *Public Health Nursing* 12(3):143–150.

Nyrop, Richard, and Donald Seekins. 1986. *Afghanistan: A Country Study.* Washington, D.C.: U.S. Government Printing Office.

Omidian, Patricia. 1992. Aging and Intergenerational Conflict: Afghan Refugee Families in Transition. Unpublished Ph.D. dissertation, University of California, San Francisco.

———. 1994a. Afghan Refugee Males: Betwixt and Between. In *Endangered Minority Male: Volume I.* Edited by J. Nieto and P. Rainey. Bakersfield, California: Heritage of Aztlan. Pp. 107–116.

———. 1994b. "I'm Doing the Best I Can!": Conflicting Cultures/Conflicting Realities for Children of Middle Eastern Parents. In *Endangered Minority Male: Volume II.* Edited by J. Nieto and P. Rainey. Bakersfield, California: Heritage of Aztlan. Pp. 53–59.

———. 1996. *Transitions and Transformations: Aging and Family in an Afghan Refugee Community.* New York: Garland Publishers, Inc.

Omidian, Patricia, and Juliene Lipson. 1992. Elderly Afghan Refugees: Tradition and Transition in Northern California. In *Refugee Issues Papers.* Edited by Pamela DeVoe. Washington, D.C.: American Anthropological Association. Pp. 27–39.

Perez, Lisandra. 1986. Immigrant Economic Adjustment and Family Organization: The Cuban Success Story Reexamined. *International Migration Review* 20:4–20.

Psychiatry Centre for Afghan Refugees. 1988. *The Impaired Mind.* Peshawar, Pakistan.

Rahmany, Khalil. 1993. *A Long Journey: The Psychological Adjustment of the Afghan Refugees in the United States.* Unpublished Ph.D. dissertation, The Rosebridge Graduate School of Integrative Psychology, Concord, California, 1992.

U.S. Committee for Refugees. 1994a. Refugee Reports 15(3).

———. 1994b. *Refugee Reports.* 15(12).

World Almanac and Book of Facts 1994. 1993. Rahway, New Jersey: Funk and Wagnalls Corporation.

Chapter 4

Chinese from Southeast Asia

JOHN K. WHITMORE

The years 1978 to 1980 were major in the movement of Chinese out of Vietnam and Cambodia. These people found themselves at the mercy of both political and economic change within Southeast Asia and international rivalries outside. Given the pressures, they decided that they wanted out—not just out in general but out to the United States. They came not as a separate and distinct group but mixed with ethnic Vietnamese and Khmer from Vietnam and Cambodia at the same time that Lao, Hmong, and other groups were also entering the United States. Once here, there is the question of their relations with the Chinese-Americans already in residence.

Generally, less is known of the Chinese refugees from Southeast Asia than of any other major group from that region. Many studies exist of the Chinese people themselves, as well as a good number on the Chinese in Southeast Asia. Yet little attention has been paid to the Chinese communities in Saigon/Cholon and Phnom Penh, not to mention the smaller ones in Haiphong and Hanoi. Tsai (1968) examined his own community in southern Vietnam in great detail, and Willmott (1967, 1970) studied the Chinese in Cambodia, particularly Phnom Penh. I have used these major studies as well as a number of other sources to describe these Chinese communities, with special attention to their historical background. Recent work (e.g., Amer 1991; Tran 1993) helps to fill out this discussion.

This chapter brings together the information available on the Chinese communities of Indochina (especially Vietnam but also Cambodia; the Chinese community in Laos does not concern us here) and joins it with data from surveys of Chinese refugee groups in the United States. The result is a description of these refugees, their lives, and their prospects in the United States through the 1990s.

BACKGROUND

Although Chinese have had contact with, and lived on, the eastern mainland of Southeast Asia for more than two millennia, the important growth of Chinese communities in Vietnam, Cambodia, and elsewhere in Southeast Asia has only come about in the past 400 years. The rise of regional and international trade in the sixteenth and seventeenth centuries, including the increasing involvement of the Europeans, brought Chinese into the ports of Vietnam, Cambodia, Thailand, the Philippines, and Indonesia (Whitmore 1983; Willmott 1967). Difficulties of trade with the Japanese and the Europeans in China led Chinese traders to Southeast Asia for easier contacts, and the fall of the Ming dynasty in China to the Manchu power, in 1644, resulted in a flood of loyalists onto the coasts of the southern seas.

The early Chinese communities formed close to the contemporary centers of power and contributed much to the growth of the capitals, as at Phnom Penh. On occasion, the Chinese (or people of Chinese ancestry) became involved in the wielding of local political power. In Vietnam the Chinese had a choice of becoming Vietnamese (being known as *Minh-huong*) or remaining Chinese. If they chose the former, they adopted Vietnamese ways and came under Vietnamese law; if the latter, they stayed in the Chinese communities and were treated as foreigners. Interestingly, the diplomatic corps of nineteenth-century Vietnam was made up largely of *Minh-huong,* including the great Phan Thanh Gian, who dealt with the French in the 1860s (Woodside 1971; Nguyen Hoi Chan; 1971).

Another important development involving the settlement of Chinese in Vietnam took place during the seventeenth century in the south (generally known as Cochin China). Vietnamese had begun settling in this area only in the previous century, and the Saigon area became Vietnamese only in the 1690s. When 3,000 Chinese arrived off the coast of central Vietnam in flight from the Manchu conquerors in the 1670s, the local Vietnamese lord took it on himself to suggest that they keep going to inhabit open land around what is now Bien-hoa, north of Saigon. This land had been in the Cambodian domain, but the Chinese settlements there and elsewhere helped, ultimately, to bring it into the Vietnamese realm (Nguyen Hoi Chan 1971; Tsai 1968).

Trade and Chinese settlement did not flourish to nearly the same degree around the cities of the north, the capital Thang-long (now Hanoi) and the provincial centers, during the seventeenth and eighteenth centuries. It was mainly in the mountains, near the Chinese border and in the mining areas, or along the coast, that the Chinese population could be found. In the south the final quarter of the eighteenth century brought war and destruction to the Chinese communities. Out of the dynastic conflagration of the times emerged the settlement called Saigon by the Vietnamese and T'ai-ngon by the Chinese as the major trading center of the Mekong Delta area. By 1801 the Vietnamese were calling the Chinese community there "Cho-lon," or "Large Market" (Nguyen Hoi Chan 1971; Tsai 1968; de Poncins 1957).

With the establishment of the Nguyen dynasty in the first years of the nineteenth century, the new rulers drew a sharp line between the *Minh-huong* and the Chinese sojourners. The latter were officially recognized through their *bang.* Such organizations were natural to the overseas Chinese, being based on dialect and home province. Hence, the *bang* served as fairly autonomous and self-governing administrative units for the Vietnamese government, and their chiefs acted as the links between the Vietnamese bureaucracy and the Chinese population. The various chiefs accepted the responsibility for collecting taxes and controlling the flow of Chinese immigrants for the capital in Hue (Nguyen Hoi Chan 1971; Nguyen The Anh 1971; Tsai 1968).

Substantial though the Chinese population was in Vietnam by the middle of the nineteenth century, the major growth in the Chinese community came during the 90 years of the French colonial period. The European powers of the late nineteenth century, including the French, were drawing coolie labor out of China by the thousands. Encouraged by the French, the Chinese also took the opportunity to move south into better economic conditions, and from the 1860s, boatloads of Chinese immigrants arrived in Vietnam (hence, the Vietnamese term *nguoi tau,* "boat people," for them). The French had conquered the far south of Vietnam, called by them Cochin China, in the 1860s and removed it from the control of Hue. Saigon and the Mekong Delta would officially remain a separate colony under French law into the 1940s, whereas from the 1880s the north and center (called by the French Tonkin and Annam) were ostensibly under Vietnamese administration. The Chinese tended to gather in the French-controlled areas, the south and the urban centers, particularly the ports. Hence, Cholon, adjacent to Saigon, Haiphong, the French port of the north, and Hanoi, the French administrative center for Indochina, became the major places of Chinese settlement. Phnom Penh in Cambodia and, to a much lesser degree, Vientiane in Laos were also French administrative centers and locations of Chinese communities. Other Chinese lived in lesser population centers scattered across Vietnam and Cambodia. The main point to be made here is that the Chinese formed almost entirely an urban population, pursued economic advancement in urban occupations, and had access to all parts of the colony (Tsai 1968; Ky 1963; Marsot 1993).

The number of Chinese in the south of Vietnam grew rapidly. By 1889, almost 60,000 (according to official French count) lived scattered about the south alone. Seventeen years later the figure had doubled. Through the colonial period and into the 1950s the Chinese population of southern Vietnam greatly outstripped that of the north and center. In the early 1930s the French counted more than 200,000 Chinese immigrants in the south (with more than 70,000 *Minh-huong*), more than 50,000 in the north, but only 10,000 in the center. The Chinese community in Cambodia expanded rapidly in the 1920s as well, to more than 200,000. Twenty years later, at the end of the colonial period, the number of Chinese in southern Vietnam may have quadrupled to more than 800,000 and that in Cambodia almost doubled to more than 400,000, whereas the numbers in the north and center of Vietnam had only grown slightly. (Some 40,000 of Chinese descent are supposed to have come south in 1954–1955.) The Saigon/ Cholon metropolitan area seems to have had more than 575,000 Chinese and other urban areas in the south more than 90,000; another 130,000-plus appeared to be scattered among villages of the south. Thus, about 84 percent of the Chinese in southern Vietnam were urban, and 16 percent, rural. Some 35,000 were in Haiphong in the north, and another 15,000 were in Hanoi. The urban/ rural ratio in Cambodia was much closer, being 59 percent to 41 percent. These figures tend not to include those of Chinese descent whose families had lived in Vietnam before the French, that is, for Vietnam, the *Minh-huong* (Tsai 1968; Ky 1963; Willmott 1967; Tran 1993; Marsot 1993).

The Chinese tendency to organize themselves by dialect group and region of birth in the homeland was accepted and reinforced by the French administration. In this way the French refrained from direct interference into Chinese affairs, unless necessary, and placed responsibility for the activities of the Chinese community in the hands of the organizational leaders, whom they could replace. These organizations, the *bang,* took care of taxation, immigration, and police matters for the French within their own groups. In Vietnam the largest group of Chinese—perhaps half—were the Cantonese from Kwangtung province in China, with the Teochiu from the northeast coast of Kwangtung almost a third. In Cambodia (as in Thailand) the situation was reversed (Teochiu more than three quarters and Cantonese a tenth). Other major dialect groups of some size (2 to 10 percent) in Vietnam and Cambodia were Hakka, Hokkien (from Fukien province), and Hainanese (Tsai 1968; Willmott 1967; Skinner 1951; Marsot 1993). The dominant language for the entire Chinese community in Vietnam (unlike elsewhere in Southeast Asia) was Cantonese, and a large proportion of those in Cholon knew neither Vietnamese nor French (nor, later on, English) (Tsai 1968; de Poncins 1957). From the 1880s the French colonial system recognized these five dialect groups as the official congregations (*bang*), with Chinese not belonging to any of them included with the Hakka. These five remained the basic organization of the Chinese community through the colonial period. They had their own temples, schools, hospitals, and cemeteries. As Willmott (1967:84) noted for Cambodia, "[A] speech group was the constituency for business relationships, marriage partners, associations, and relations with the administration." Local branches of the *bang* officially served the Chinese population scattered among the towns of the countryside. Saigon, Cholon, Tra Vinh, and Long Xuyen in Vietnam and Phnom Penh and Kompong Cham in Cambodia had branches of all five *bang;* other towns of any size had two, three, or four *bang.* Smaller towns only had one, encompassing all the local Chinese of whatever group (Tsai 1968; Willmott 1970; Skinner 1951; Marsot 1993).

The importance of the Chinese community in twentieth-century Indochina lay in its economic function. The French facilitated the Chinese participation in the colonial economy, thus greatly advancing the French extractive powers. The Chinese had greater liberties than the Vietnamese, Khmer, and Lao. They could move among the five *pays* of French Indochina (Tonkin, Annam, Cochin China, Cambodia, and Laos), and they had access to the countryside and its peasants. They handled goods and accumulated large commercial fortunes. The Chinese profited greatly from the alcohol, salt, and opium monopolies imposed by the French on Vietnamese and Cambodian societies. Not only did the Chinese merchant community help underwrite the French administration by way of the monopolies, but it was also most important in supplying the colonial structure and instrumental in the major export from the colony, rice. With French encouragement, their contacts in the rural towns and villages, their ownership of the rice-hauling junks and the rice mills, and their monetary loans to the peasants, the Chinese merchants controlled the movement of rice within Vietnam and Cambodia and facilitated its export abroad from Saigon/Cholon (amounting to two thirds of French Indochina's total export value). Pepper was another agricultural product controlled by the Chinese. Through the international network of Chinese firms, such exports moved from the Chinese communities of Vietnam and Cambodia to Chinese firms in the major port cities of Southeast Asia and China. It was the Chinese who kept the flow of commercial goods going into and through the colony, profiting greatly thereby. With such advantages, the bulk of the Chinese community within Vietnam and Cambodia was involved in business of one sort or another (Ky 1963; Ngo 1971; Murray 1980; Tsai 1968; Willmott 1967; Marsot 1993; Brocheux 1995).

To quote Tsai Maw-kuey (1968:135), a Chinese from southern Vietnam, "All observers, whatever their nationality, are in accord that in South Vietnam the Chinese held and still hold all the levers of commerce, of industry, and of handicrafts and that they continue to play the most important role in the economic life of the country." Compared with other countries of Southeast Asia, the Chinese communities in Indochina were much more involved in business than in laboring occupations (a majority in commerce and another third in industry and artisanry). Saigon/Cholon was the hub of the Chinese economic network, and Phnom Penh was the center of its Cambodian hinterland during the colonial period.

As noted earlier, the major activity of the Chinese was the rice trade. Besides the control of the rice market, Chinese merchants strongly dominated the handling of foodstuffs in general, both wholesale and retail. Their enterprises supplied the major cities and extended deep into the villages of the countryside. The Chinese businessmen were also heavily involved in buying and selling numerous other items in Vietnam and Cambodia, and diversity was one of their economic strengths. Hundreds of Chinese firms controlled the production and trade of textiles and wood and metal goods. (See the Appendix to this chapter for detail on the economic activities of the different dialect groups.) Fundamental to such Chinese economic success were two elements: (1) commercial organization and networks (within the colony and without) and (2) the extension of credit (within their own community and to others).

The strength of the Chinese community lay, according to Tsai (1968:116), in its "perfect internal organization . . . whose power and efficacy are often underestimated or ignored." *Hui* (as opposed to the official *bang*) were groups formed to achieve any one of a number of specific goals. They were interlinked to create an informal network or series of networks that stretched throughout the colony and abroad. Any Chinese could belong to one such grouping or several, depending on personal interests. Three general types of *hui* existed: (1) by common family name or locality of origin; (2) by professional association; and (3) by shared interest (temples, schools, sports, etc.). Organized similarly, these groupings drew many people (and their families) into their workings and thus tied together the diverse Chinese community. Through such contacts were social ties and commercial links achieved, bringing trust to the relationships and providing access, in Lim's (1984) terms, "to labour, credit, information, market outlets, and security." Under the overarching structure of the five *bang,* such ties and links reached from the big cities into the countryside and to other big cities, at home and abroad. The urban connections and greater efficiency in operation led the Chinese to be preferred intermediaries (Tsai 1968; Willmott 1967; Ky 1963; Barton 1984).

The economic links that followed these social ties included better terms of credit and loans and went beyond the Chinese community to link members of the local population to the resulting economic structure. Based on the "confidence and spirit of cooperation" built up through the commercial and social networks, as Tsai (1968) described it, the Chinese system of credit, a "system both ingenious and original," further tied the Chinese networks together and stretched into the countryside. Among themselves, the Chinese merchants would often pool funds and take turns sharing the proceeds. In the process of handling commerce in the countryside (particularly in rice), these merchants would advance credit to their customers, mainly in the dry season, before the monsoon. As buyer from and seller to the peasant farmers, the Chinese village shopkeeper kept the flow of goods going in both directions, using loans of cash and other items to maintain this flow. The village shopkeeper in turn dealt with the town merchant, also receiving credit to facilitate local commerce. The provincial merchant himself operated on credit extended by the major merchants in the large cities (Saigon/Cholon, Phnom Penh). Ultimately, credit came from the Chinese banks in these cities (Tsai 1968; Ky 1963; Willmott 1967; Barton 1984; Menkhoff 1993).

A major interest for all Chinese groups was education. The five *bang* had public schools for their own members (that still required some tuition), and there were many expensive private schools. By the end of the colonial era, there were well over 200 schools with a total of more than 50,000 students, male and female, mainly at the primary level and spread across southern Vietnam. Cambodia had about half as many schools and students. Chinese families were prepared to make sacrifices for their children to attend these schools, but inevitably, attendance rose and fell with commerce. The schools were enmeshed in the local Chinese social structures. Mandarin, the official language of China, served as the language of instruction among almost all groups, some Cantonese being the exception, and problems existed in the quality of both teaching and texts. The desire for education was so great that it led to overcrowding in the classrooms. A variety of approaches (traditional, modern, nationalist, etc.) complicated the situation further. A French-Chinese high school supplied many of the intermediaries between the colonial regime and the Chinese commercial sector. The educational goal was mainly to provide a basic literacy and competence with numbers as well as to make contacts within the Chinese community, thus aiding the business sector. In general, Chinese education in Indochina lagged behind that found elsewhere in Southeast Asia (Tsai 1968; Willmott 1967, 1970; Skinner 1951).

The situation of the Chinese in Vietnam and Cambodia changed considerably with independence in the mid-1950s. The next 20 years saw major restrictions placed on the Chinese community in its economic and professional pursuits. Both the Saigon and Phnom Penh regimes put important limits on the economic activities open to nonnationals (mainly the Chinese). In Vietnam, such activities included many of those dominated by the Chinese (shopkeeping, the rice trade, fish, tea, soy, transportation, scrap iron, textiles, and general dealing, among other fields). This situation affected more than 40 percent of the Chinese enterprises in Saigon/Cholon and more than 60 percent of all firms in the forbidden activities. The purpose was to convert the Chinese into Vietnamese citizens. The result was that some Chinese became Vietnamese, others officially turned their businesses over to their Vietnamese wives or children, others (illegally) found a Vietnamese to front for them, and quite a few (almost a thousand) simply closed up shop. Even though about a half million Chinese apparently accepted Vietnamese citizenship during 1956 and 1957, the economic system slowed drastically as many middlemen ceased operations. Other restrictions included immigration, travel, the practice of Western medicine, books, and schools. Cambodia, on independence, did not restrict the Chinese quite so widely as did the Vietnamese but tried to keep them out of rice, salt, shipping, general trade, secondhand dealing, and loans. It also removed the restrictions of the *bang* system, the result being a loosened boundary between the Chinese and the Khmer communities and a greater opening for Cambodian citizenship. Tighter controls did exist for Chinese schools (Tsai 1968; Willmott 1967, 1970; Fall 1959; Tran 1993).

The disappearance of the official *bang* in both countries left the way open for the growth in variety and importance of the voluntary organizations (*hui*). At the same time, with the great decline in rice exports and the rise of American aid, both linked to the war, the economic role of the Chinese shifted somewhat from the commercial to the industrial and service sectors. Urbanization and commerce boomed. Many of the older economic pursuits thrived and grew with the flood of foreign wealth, mainly into southern Vietnamese society but also into Cambodia (Tsai 1968; Willmott 1970). Clifton Barton (1984:49) felt ''that a figure of seventy to eighty percent was a fairly accurate representation of the portion of the total volume of commercial and industrial activity that was controlled by overseas Chinese businessmen during the decade 1965–1975,'' and Tsai Maw-kuey (1968:76) could say in that year, "Incontestably, Cholon is, after Singapore, the greatest Chinese city outside China.''

The Chinese in northern Vietnam benefited from rapprochement between Hanoi and Peking and were allowed to remain Chinese citizens at the same time as they held the same rights as Vietnamese (Amer 1991). A well-to-do Chinese from Hanoi noted that the Chinese had the privileges, but not the disadvantages (as military duty), of their Vietnamese compatriots. The Chinese continued their urban and intermediary occupations within the context of the developing socialist system through the two decades of war. This included the privilege of visiting China and carrying on clandestine trade between the two countries. As Charles Benoit (1981:146) has noted, "[T]heir stellar success at running what amounted to an alternative economic system" meant the continuation of the Chinese community serving the Vietnamese economic system.

THE REFUGEE MOVEMENT

The mid-1970s saw little change in the situations of the Chinese communities in southern Vietnam, northern Vietnam, and Cambodia. The war in all three zones restricted the Chinese activities, as it did everybody's, but the role of the Chinese remained the same. They continued to operate in the urban sector, keep the economy going, and act as the intermediaries. With the end of the fighting, in 1975, the situation for the Chinese in northern Vietnam changed little, whereas that in the south underwent the strains of the transition from Saigon to Ho Chi Minh City (Amer 1991; Tran 1993). Some Chinese were in the first wave of refugees (an unpublished Michigan survey in 1980 showed that about 15 percent of Chinese respondents came before 1978). Nevertheless, the Vietnamese government policy toward the cities and the Chinese was initially moderate, particularly in comparison with that of the new Cambodian government. The fall of Phnom Penh to the Khmer Rouge in mid-April 1975 marked an immediate effort to clear from the cities not only the accumulated mass of refugees from the countryside but the urban population as a whole. The Chinese were thus removed from the towns and pushed into the countryside (with no protest from Peking). Many of the Chinese left, going either east into southern Vietnam, particularly Saigon/Cholon, or west into Thailand.

The major flood of Chinese refugees came in the midst of international power struggle and Vietnamese policy change. Increasing tensions with China led initially to security measures concerning those of Chinese descent on the northern border, in late 1977 and early 1978. Then the Vietnamese government both began to speak of forcing Vietnamese citizenship (and thus military duty) on the Chinese and decided that a change in economic policy was needed. That spring the government moved directly to control the urban economic sector, one that they had largely left alone in prior years. This move took place not only in the recently reunified south but also in the north, in Haiphong and Hanoi. Since, even in the north, it was the Chinese who were heavily involved in urban commerce, this effort to bring central control into the cities meant that the Chinese community was greatly affected. At the same time, relations between Vietnam and Cambodia worsened, and the friction along their common border became bloody. The Chinese regime was strongly behind that of Pol Pot against the Vietnamese. In addition, the autumn of 1978 saw the breakdown in the talks between the Vietnamese and the United States, with the Americans formally recognizing the People's Republic of China in December. In November the Socialist Republic of Vietnam joined the Council for Mutual Economic Assistance, the eastern European economic bloc, and moved much closer to the Soviet Union.

Thus, the Chinese in Vietnam were caught two ways. Official Vietnamese economic policy acted against their interests at the same time that China was beginning to lean heavily on the Vietnamese. Peking took the occasion both to make an example of the Vietnamese regarding the handling of overseas Chinese in Southeast Asia and to lean on the Vietnamese as being pro-Soviet. The Vietnamese in turn saw China on all sides of them, to the south and west (in Cambodia) as well as to the north and east. The Chinese in Vietnam, and eventually even those of longtime Chinese descent, were caught in both an economic squeeze and a security fear. They were being forced to leave the cities and any areas, particularly in the northern mountains and coasts, in which the Vietnamese thought they were a risk, a potential fifth column. They were to go to designated areas in the countryside or up into the highlands. The Chinese did not like the choices being offered them within Vietnam, and many took the opportunity to leave. The Vietnamese initially tried to calm their fears, but ethnic tensions continued to rise through 1978, and with the heavy fighting on the border in early 1979, the Vietnamese became active in getting the Chinese out (Grant et al. 1979; Benoit 1981; Amer 1991).

By the middle of 1978, the atmosphere of impending war and tales of good reception in China led more Chinese refugees to leave Vietnam. Rumor, panic, and propaganda sent over 150,000 across the border from northern Vietnam into China, where they were stuck away in the hills of Kwangsi province. Thereafter, most left by sea as China closed its border, those in the north going to Hong Kong and those in the south going to Malaysia, Indonesia, or the Philippines. These were the "boat people." Technically, this was illegal emigration, but testimony indicates that it evolved into a semilegal system as Vietnamese officials took payments to allow the flow of Chinese out of the country to continue. The organization of the departure was handled through the old commercial channels, and the boats lying offshore were arranged by the local and international networks of Chinese contacts. Thus, the blame for the poor conditions of the refugees must lie with both the government that allowed it to occur and the community that organized it, under however trying conditions (Grant et al. 1979; Benoit 1981; Amer 1991).

The flow of Chinese refugees continued from 1978 through 1979. Vietnam invaded Cambodia in late December 1978, hoping to end the dirty border war with Pol Pot. Deng Xiaoping then visited the United States and, on leaving, declared that China would "punish" Vietnam. The United States did not demur. The subsequent invasion led to three weeks of fighting that were bloodier than any three weeks in the first or second Indochina wars. Tensions rose steeply, and the Vietnamese began to make it clear to the Chinese that they should leave. Other Chinese refugees came out of Cambodia to the Thai border after the Vietnamese destruction of the Pol Pot regime and the subsequent fighting and famine. By 1980, over 200,000 Chinese had left Indochina and were seeking refuge in countries beyond Asia, particularly in the United States.

The sea voyages were horrendous for the overloaded craft, and many of the refugees were lost at sea or ravaged by pirates in the Gulf of Siam. Estimates of the losses range up to 50 percent of all those who left Vietnam. Problems still remained for the survivors on their arrival at foreign shores. The countries of first asylum, particularly Malaysia, but also Indonesia, the Philippines, and Hong Kong, were nervous about taking so many illegal Chinese into their populations. The first camps for the refugees were hastily improvised in deserted locations, the island Pulau Bidong off the east coast of the Malay Peninsula being the prime example. Here the refugees were kept alive through international efforts until they could be screened and admitted into a third country for permanent settlement. Later, transitional camps were set up at Bataan (in the Philippines), on Galang (an island in Indonesia), and in Hong Kong for those being admitted to the United States. There the refugees received orientation to American life, English training, and instruction in some vocational skills. The procedures whereby the Chinese refugees entered the United States were the same as those for the Vietnamese, Lao, Hmong, and others—once screened by the Immigration and Naturalization Service, they had to have personal sponsors, generally found by one of the voluntary agencies (VOLAGs) that had signed a contract with the State Department to take responsibility for the refugees. In this way the Chinese refugees were placed as single nuclear families (parents and children) in scattered localities across the country. One problem in examining the Chinese as a separate refugee group is that official records were usually kept on country of origin rather than ethnicity (Peters et al. 1983), and sorting them out from the Vietnamese and Khmer refugee populations, especially the former, is often difficult.

SOCIAL AND ECONOMIC STATUS IN THE
UNITED STATES

The Chinese refugees were, on the average, the earliest of the ethnic groups coming to the United States in the second wave of Indochina emigration (1978 on). The Lao and Hmong, although they were in the Southeast Asian camps longer than the Chinese, tended to arrive here only after the boat people. The

Vietnamese of the second wave mainly came later still. A study of Vietnamese, Chinese from Vietnam, and Lao refugees who arrived in the years from 1978 to 1982 conducted by the Institute for Social Research (ISR) of the University of Michigan for the Office of Refugee Resettlement, U.S. Department of Health and Human Services [HHS] (Caplan, Whitmore, and Bui 1984; Caplan, 1989) shows the Chinese to have been here an average of 28.5 months; the Lao, 25 months; and the Vietnamese, only 23 months.

The ISR study surveyed the three refugee groups in five sites around the country (Boston, Chicago, Houston, Seattle, and Orange County, California). The resulting data provide a profile of the Chinese refugees from Vietnam and enable preliminary comparisons between this group and the Vietnamese and Lao (see also Haines 1989). Of the total adult population of 4,160 in the survey, 836 were Chinese from Vietnam (20 percent, compared with 50 percent Vietnamese and 30 percent Lao). Fifty-five percent of these adults were male and 45 percent female. The Chinese refugee population tended to be older than the Lao and the Vietnamese, with an average age among adults of 33. Eighteen percent were 16 to 19 years of age, 36 percent in their twenties, 18 percent in their thirties, 13 percent in their forties, 8 percent in their fifties, and 7 percent 60 and over, a much flatter distribution than for the other two groups, which had a higher percentage of younger adults. The highest percentage of Chinese among the local survey populations lived in Seattle (39 percent), with Chinese making up 29 percent of the Chicago survey, 18 percent in Orange County, and only 9 percent and 8 percent, respectively, in Houston and Boston. Seventeen percent of the Chinese in the survey had moved, a percentage slightly higher than for the Vietnamese and the Lao.[1]

As would be expected from a historical view of the Chinese in Vietnam, the refugees were predominantly urban (87 percent), and their occupations there reflect this—31 percent of all the adults had held such urban jobs as proprietors, clerks, assistants, construction workers, auto mechanics, machine operators, and factory workers. Another 33 percent had been students. Their educational background was not high—more than half the adults had had no more than a primary education in Vietnam, another 40 percent had had some secondary education but no more, and only 4 percent had ever studied at a university.

Half the Chinese households (50 percent) were single nuclear families, and another 29 percent were extended families. The remaining fifth of the households contained at least one single, unrelated adult (whether living alone, with other singles, or with one or another type of family unit). Compared with the Vietnamese and the Lao in this survey, the Sino-Vietnamese tended to have both a higher percentage of single-person households and a higher percentage of extended family households. Yet these Chinese households were on the average the smallest (5.2 persons) and had the fewest children (1.6), the fewest children under age six (0.44), and the highest percentage of adults (75 percent). The average age of the youngest child was over six years old, the highest of the three groups, and thus this average child was in school. Overall, the Chinese refugees from Vietnam had households that were smaller, with more adults and older children, and possessed moderate levels of education and occupation in Southeast Asia compared with the Vietnamese and Lao refugees.

The question of English proficiency was a major one for the refugees. Because knowledge of English was strongly correlated with education, the Sino-Vietnamese were likely to be only moderately proficient in English, and this proved to be the case. Not quite half the Chinese households (478) had anyone who knew any English when they arrived in the United States, and in less than a tenth (8 percent) of the households did anyone know English even fairly well. In less than a fifth of the households (17 percent) did half the adults know some English. These figures are slightly higher than the Lao figures but are much lower than the Vietnamese. The relative pattern for current English among the three ethnic groups generally follows that for English on arrival, as all three groups showed consistent gains. Although fewer Chinese in the survey had taken English classes in the Asian camps (14 percent as compared with the overall mean of 23 percent), there was little difference among the three groups in taking English classes in the United States (40 percent were currently taking classes, and more than three quarters had had such classes at one time or another). The major reasons for Chinese respondents not taking current English classes were that the respondents were too old or too busy.

The Chinese from Vietnam, seeking contacts, were more involved in general employment services (40 percent) than were either the Vietnamese or the Lao (28 percent each), whereas vocational training, which requires more education and better English, had fewer Chinese (6 percent) than Vietnamese (9 percent) but more than Lao (4 percent). The unemployment rate for the Chinese from Vietnam (46 percent) was slightly worse than that for the Vietnamese (43 percent) and the Lao (40 percent) in the sample, despite the Chinese having been in the country longer. A partial explanation for this difference might be that the smallest numbers of Chinese in the sample came from the two areas with the best economic conditions, Houston and Boston. Moreover, such aggregate figures are misleading and need to be examined in terms of the length of time the refugees have been in the country. Thus, the Chinese unemployment rate dropped steadily, from more than 90 percent for those here a year or less to about 30 percent for those here between three and four years.

Another aspect of employment for the Chinese from Vietnam also reflects that for the Vietnamese and the Lao. When they were able to find work, the jobs were most often lower in status and poorer paying and had less of a future than the ones they held in Southeast Asia. If lucky, the refugee found a similar job; more often, it would be less than what he or she had had. For example, although operating a machine is a relatively common job for the refugees here, those (like many Chinese) who used to operate machines in Vietnam have had difficulty getting jobs here, undoubtedly because of poor English. The jobs obtained by the refugees tended to be in less stable sectors of the economy, where the work is part-time, seasonal, and irregular, with low wages. The Chinese held

jobs that were less likely than those held by either the Vietnamese or the Lao
to have employment benefits in general (55 percent) or health benefits (49 percent), paid vacations (45 percent), or retirement pensions (18 percent) in particular; they were, however, about equal in dental plans (27 percent). Even though
the Chinese had a higher unemployment rate than the Lao, they had been employed for a slightly longer average time (14 months to 13 months) and had a
slightly higher average hourly wage ($4.89 to $4.76). In general, the Chinese
from Vietnam tended to fall between the Vietnamese and the Lao in job status,
being lower than the former and higher than the latter (11 percent with high-
status jobs, 9 percent being professionals or managers).

The Sino-Vietnamese who were not in the labor force included current students (working and nonworking), housewives, the disabled, retirees, and those
who were simply not looking for work at the time. They again fell between the
Vietnamese and the Lao in the percentage of adults fitting these categories (56
percent), and the same is true for the percentage of students (17 percent).

An important aspect of the ISR study was its focus on the household rather
than on the individual. In the short time that the refugees had been here at the
time of the survey (fall 1982), few of them, as individuals, had been able to get
jobs good enough to lift them out of poverty. What is important, then, is the
combination of resources the household was able to bring together in order to
support all its individuals. Those on public assistance, for example, tended to
have a mix of available resources. The Chinese from Vietnam had 67 percent
of their households receiving some sort of public cash assistance, and almost
all of them also received food stamps. This was higher than for the Lao and
slightly lower than for the Vietnamese. As with unemployment, the percentages
of those on cash assistance declined steadily from the first year of residence to
the fourth. Another important instance of the mix of resources for the household
is the number of jobs held by individuals in the household. For the Chinese, as
for the refugees as a whole, there was a steady and significant progression
upward in the number of households having more than one job.

On this basis of mixed resources in the household, the key question is not
whether any one individual (or, for that matter, household) receives any kind of
public assistance; rather, it is whether the household has any earned income.
Fifty-nine percent of the Chinese households had some form of earned income,
slightly lower than for the Lao but higher than for the Vietnamese. The next
question is the source of the refugee household's total income (public assistance,
earned, or a combination of the two). The Chinese households were high on
combined incomes, slightly low on public assistance alone, and fairly low on
earned income alone. This is understandable, considering the tendency of the
Chinese to live in more complex extended families. The adults of these households were pooling their resources, both earned income and assistance, to further
their mutual aim. Over time the number of households on only cash assistance
dropped sharply from the first to the fourth year of residence, the number with
combined incomes peaked in the third year and then fell off, and the number

on earned income alone rose from the first through the fourth year. An important point to be made here is that the search for work continued through time, irrespective of eligibility for assistance or its cutoff.

One important reason for this, besides the desire for work itself, is that earnings are needed for households to rise significantly above the federal poverty level. In general, the households in the survey averaged 79 percent of the poverty level if they received only cash assistance, 146 percent if they combined income sources, and 218 percent if they had earned income alone. Approximately the same percentages held true if the households had no jobs, one job, or more than one job. The Chinese from Vietnam fit this pattern. Although half the Chinese households were living below the poverty level (essentially the same as the Vietnamese and the Lao), there was a steady rise in the percentage of the poverty level met from those in the country only a few months to those who had been here longer than three years.

Overall, Caplan and others (Caplan, Whitmore, and Bui 1984; Caplan, Whitmore, and Choy 1989) suggested that among the Vietnamese, Chinese from Vietnam, and Lao in the sample, ethnicity was a less important factor than a number of others—length of time in the United States, Southeast Asian education and occupation, arrival English proficiency, site, and household composition. Arrival English, which has a certain correlation with education in Southeast Asia, was a strong predictor of economic self-sufficiency. Household composition, in terms of the number of employable adults, was also of significance. The single nuclear family had the worst economic standing, particularly if it was large, except in cases in which some of the members had a decent level of English.

Dunning (1982) examined Sino-Vietnamese refugees in southern California and Texas within a year or two of their arrival. He found them falling short of the ethnic Vietnamese refugees (many of whom had been here since 1975) in economic performance. Actually, when compared with other 1979 arrivals, the Chinese were doing fairly well. One area Dunning examined that the ISR survey did not was sociocultural adjustment. Dunning's data showed the Chinese to have been more adaptive culturally to the surrounding environment than were the Vietnamese, considering the longer time spent here by the Vietnamese. Yet Peters and others (1983) showed in their study of Sino-Vietnamese from West Philadelphia that the Chinese from Vietnam had not integrated appreciably with any surrounding groups. The area in which they lived was quite mixed (blacks, whites, Asians, and native Americans), and a Chinatown existed in downtown Philadelphia. There were Korean establishments, and—to quote the study (1)— ''in the past two years there has been an explosive expansion of Southeast Asian refugee fruit and vegetable vendors as well as small food stores, many of which are owned by Sino-Vietnamese.'' Nevertheless, tensions pervaded the neighborhood and existed between the Vietnamese and Chinese; the different Chinese groups from Southeast Asia (mainly Vietnam and Cambodia) had not mixed appreciably (partly owing to language differences—Cantonese versus Teochiu), and, to quote from the report again (6), "in general, very little interaction or integration has occurred between the Sino-Vietnamese refugees and the local Chinatown community." First of all, few of the refugees could afford to live there, but, more basically, a line existed between the "Hong Kong-and-Taiwan-connected" community and the Southeast Asian Chinese.

Little information has come to hand concerning Chinese refugees from Cambodia. Their experiences were quite different from their compatriots in Vietnam (unless they passed through Vietnam on their way out). Many of them would have settled in the Khmer cluster projects, and indications are that they left those sites to settle elsewhere. Their educational and occupational backgrounds are undoubtedly quite similar to those from Vietnam, and we need to know more about their ability to establish themselves in this country. One major point to consider is that they would have arrived here about two years later, on the average, than the Chinese refugees from Vietnam, in mid-1981 compared to 1979. The work of Hackett (1989) on such refugees in and around the Washington, D.C., area during the mid-1980s showed a situation similar to that in Philadelphia. They, too, tended to stay out of the Chinatown in the city and to operate in the Indochinese community on the outskirts. In both these cases, the Chinese refugees were, for the time being, left to develop both their Chineseness and their Americanness largely on their own.

Educational Achievement

The interest of the Chinese community in education has always been strong. Its schools had provided both competence in reading and numbers as well as broader social contacts within the community for the students and their families. Yet the ISR study showed a majority of the Chinese adults with no more than primary schooling, 40 percent with some secondary schooling but no more, and less than a twentieth having any contact with higher education. This illustrated the needs of the community—its heavy commercial involvement and little opportunity for government or professional roles.

Arriving in the United States, the Chinese refugees joined the other ethnic groups from Southeast Asia in taking advantage of the American public school system. The broad desire for education that was hemmed in by so many social, economic, and political forces in Indochina found an outlet here. The second ISR study drew 200 households from the original 1,384 to examine the efforts of the refugee children in American schools (Caplan, Whitmore, and Choy 1989; Caplan, Choy, and Whitmore 1991, 1992). The finding was a consistent level of quality among the students (kindergarten to twelfth grade) both at the local level (as seen in grades) and on the national level (standardized tests). While the study looked predominantly at urban dwellers whose children attended inner-city schools, the focus on education of the refugee families allowed the schools to teach and the students to absorb the preferred information.

The Chinese students consistently placed between the Vietnamese and the

Lao in grade-point average (GPA). On a 4.0 scale, the overall GPA for the Chinese was 2.99. As might be expected, they did better in mathematics (3.23) than in fields requiring more English usage. In science, for example, it was 2.87, and lower for the social sciences and the humanities. Interestingly, there was a strong correlation of proclaimed religious belief with GPA; the children of Vietnamese and Chinese families claiming Confucian belief had 3.37, while Mahayana Buddhists had 3.13. Yet no correlation existed between either ethnicity or religion and performances on the standardized tests. All ethnic groups and religious beliefs did equally well. Overall, 60 percent of the refugee children placed in the top half of the national total. In mathematics, the figure was 85 percent, with 49 percent in the top quartile, almost double the national average, while the reading and language test had only 45 percent in the top half. Interestingly, 70 percent of the refugee students placed in the top half of the spelling test.

None of the standard variables provided a strong correlation with these results. Neither prior socioeconomic status nor educational background of the refugee families explained anything. The range of GPA and test results was generally narrow, and scholastic success ranged through all elements of the refugee community. What was equal among these elements was, first, desire for and focus on education and, second, accessibility to the public school system.

The study's approach, then, was to look to the refugee family and its values for an explanation of the children's success. One interesting detail, unlike almost every other known population, was that as the number of children per family increased from two up, the GPA tended to hold steady or even rise. Our explanation is that the family, like the household economically, joined forces here to encourage and support the students. A very strong consensus existed for education, cooperation, harmony, and responsibility. This was opposed to the values those families believed to be held by their nonrefugee neighbors: material goods and fun/excitement, which the refugees themselves put last. The Chinese refugees actively employed the value system brought with them from Southeast Asia within their new environment. Rather than simply assimilating and blending into the surrounding community, they maintained their own counsel and urged their children on in the classroom. Family involvement and hard work fit well into the American opportunity structure and provided the basis for the student's success.

The Importance of Contacts

The strength of the Chinese communities in Vietnam and Cambodia, as described earlier, lay in the strongly interlocked nature of their social and economic networks, sources of both information and funds. Barton (1984) has shown how strongly personal integrity meshed within these networks, such that individual and family success depended on maintaining contacts across the community and beyond. In this vein, one can see the significance of the many groups and associations, organized for a great number of social purposes, in setting the scene for such contacts to take place. Involved here were both informality and a strong sense of propriety in carrying out one's economic dealings.

What does this mean for the Chinese refugees from Southeast Asia in the United States? To succeed as they succeeded in Vietnam and Cambodia, they have to re-form the type of networks and the access to capital that were available to them there. This has already occurred to a limited degree in some places. The *New York Times* reported on the success of some Sino-Vietnamese refugees who had arrived in 1975 and linked up with contacts in New York City's Chinatown. To quote Seth Mydans (1984), "As a Chinese, Mr. Chao benefits from a worldwide network of more than 21 million overseas Chinese whose family and clan connections link them across national boundaries as a powerful economic force." According to this report, "many" of the New York Chinese refugees moved into Chinatown, where links reached out to California, Houston, Louisiana, and Washington, not to mention Singapore, Malaysia, Thailand, and Taiwan. The specific links mentioned here were Teochiu.

Such linkages had not yet appeared among the Chinese refugees in locations like Philadelphia and Washington, D.C. Both Peters and others (1983) and Hackett (1989) showed developments that may have been only in a nascent stage. Certainly, the "Food Cart Network" around the University of Pennsylvania would seem to have been a classic case of such economic organization. But the Philadelphia area had not shown any strong tendency to establish the multitude of associations that flourished so successfully in Southeast Asia. As a consequence, both information and capital would have been difficult to obtain. Nevertheless, the potential for developing contacts and building trust still existed.

Moving from the small numbers of Chinese refugees on the East Coast in the early and mid-1980s to the large community in California through the entire decade, one can see what the overseas Chinese pattern can accomplish. Gold (1994) has described the impact of the refugee Chinese on the local economy. Utilizing both their Southeast Asian background and experience and their broad contacts with other overseas Chinese here and abroad, a number of these refugees have established major enterprises, including, to quote Gold (198), "almost complete dominance" in areas such as "wholesale, import/export, real estate development, and manufacturing concerns." How have they achieved this dominance?

Essentially, they applied the strategy and tactics that had gained them such a strong position in Indochina to the situation at hand in the United States. Within the context of the American urban economy, these Chinese refugees made contact with and brought together ("integrated") a number of local elements, Asian and otherwise, to take advantage of opportunities offered. As in Southeast Asia, where they gained trust and access through their contacts, here again they have made their connections, both within and outside their own community. Operating within the context of local, national, and international patterns, the Chinese refugees have, through these multiple contacts, gained a place within the southern California economy and, in the process, have played a major role in re-forming it.

Gold describes how, through the use of overseas capital, cheap immigrant labor, and government benefits, these refugees "catalyze the economic trans-formation of southern California" (202). By being aware of available opportu-nities, of the variety of resources at hand, and of the contacts needed to take advantage of these, many Chinese refugees have set themselves up in thriving businesses. These businesses, ranging from tiny family operations to large com-mercial enterprises, tie together the variety of different elements from their own kin group, their own dialect group, overseas Chinese here and abroad, other ethnic groups, refugees and nonrefugees, and local, state, and federal govern-ments. These elements include capital, advice, trust, imported goods, cheap la-bor, markets, benefits, and local dynamics. While difficulties and high risk continue to hamper the economic development of Chinese refugees (such as a need for skilled workers and managers and the tendency to jump into uncertain situations), the gains have often been great.

One specific result has been a large, positive impact on urban areas. By pro-viding jobs, low-cost goods and services, and stable neighborhoods, the Chinese refugees have helped to renovate the inner cities and integrate the local econ-omy. On the one hand, stepping into low-paying jobs while simultaneously creating other low-paying jobs for other ethnic groups and, on the other, bringing this economy in contact with international supply and demand, these refugees have tied all these elements together through their own expansive contacts and connections.

Thus, the characteristics of the Chinese refugee community in this country—urban, small and medium business backgrounds, and moderate levels of educa-tion—mean that economic success and social integration (into Chinese-American society) depend on the opportunity and ability to reach out and make contact. Developing networks is a key to this success. Chinese refugees who remain isolated, however hardworking, stay at the mercy of their poor English, undeveloped educations, and lack of capital. For them, success will depend on their children and the American school system.

APPENDIX

The Chinese wholesale commerce in foodstuffs included fish products, pep-per, tea, livestock, market gardening, and raising fowl (ducks in Vietnam, chick-ens in Cambodia). Beyond the wholesale stage lay the retail groceries, butcher shops, street vendors, soup stalls, cafes, restaurants, and so on. Overall, the Chinese handled 85 percent of the commerce in foodstuffs and 90 percent of the preservation and sale of meat and fish. More than 1,400 firms in Saigon/Cholon alone handled textiles and their products; almost 900 firms dealt with metal products, including jewelry; and more than 200 firms were involved with wood products, including paper. The Chinese in South Vietnam handled all the textile production, almost half (48 percent) the commerce in textiles, almost all (98 percent) the commerce in metals, and 40 percent of forestry exploitation (Tsai 1968; see also Ky 1963; Tsung 1959). Willmott (1967) demonstrates a similar pattern for Cambodia.

Tsai Maw-kuey (1968), a member of the Hokkien *bang*, has broken down these economic activities in terms of the five dialect groups. Although the Cantonese and Teochiu were dominant numerically (this being the only place in Southeast Asia where the Cantonese were the largest group), the Hokkien were dominant in commercial circles. The other two groups (Hakka and Hainanese) had their own limited specialties. The Cantonese concentrated on urban general stores, restaurants, groceries, butcher shops, and other aspects of the food trade; the clothing and cloth business; construction and wood products; Chinese hotels and theaters; beauty salons; and mechanics. The Teochiu worked mainly in the tea business, wholesale and retail, but also in fish (from both the Mekong Delta and Cambodia) and their products, Chinese medicinal herbs, metalworking, and trucking. The Teochiu also had the most extensive international contacts and hence foreign trade and banking. The Hokkien, for their part, had a role far greater than their numbers. This group controlled the rice trade, with its shipping and milling, as well as the secondhand, hardware, and junkyard businesses. Living and intermarrying in the countryside, the Hokkien shopkeepers provided the key economic link between the mass of the Vietnamese population and the urban Chinese merchants. Through this link came rice and scrap iron, the products of agriculture and war, to the international market. The last two groups, Hakka and Hainanese, restricted themselves to limited and well-defined specialties: medicinal herbs, baked goods, leather products, textiles, plastics, ceramics, and rubber goods for the Hakka, who were much more involved in artisanry and industry than the other groups; European-style cooking—with its restaurant and cafe trade—Western films, and pepper growing for the Hainanese.

In Cambodia, Willmott (1970) shows the Teochiu, rather than the Cantonese and the Hokkien, to be dominant in number and through the countryside as the shopkeepers who handled local commerce and the rice trade. As in Vietnam, the Teochiu handled import-export but here were more widely involved in dry goods and groceries as well as pharmacies, vegetable farming, and street peddling. The Cantonese lived mainly in Phnom Penh, Battambang, and Kampong Cham and, with their great diversity of businesses, served as extensions of the commercial interests of Cholon. Occupations of specialization were construction, transportation, carpentry, mechanics, and wine. The Hokkien focused on banking, import-export, foodstuffs, and as in Vietnam, hardware. The Hakka and Hainanese were like their fellows in Vietnam. The former worked in bakeries, medicinal herbs, and leather, and the latter concentrated on restaurants and hotels. Here the Hainanese also included textile products, however.

Gold (1994) has pointed out that in southern California the Teochiu (Chao Zhou) were restauranteurs, Hainanese owned grocery stores, and the Hakka were herbalists. The majority of Cantonese were presumably involved in the major enterprises he described.

NOTE

1. I wish to thank Mr. Bui Long Quang for his aid in providing me with these figures.

REFERENCES

Amer, Ramses. 1991. *The Ethnic Chinese in Vietnam and Sino-Vietnamese Relations.* Kuala Lumpur: Forum.
Barton, Clifton A. 1984. Trust and Credit: Some Observations regarding Business Strategies of Overseas Chinese Traders in South Vietnam. In *The Chinese in Southeast Asia, Vol. 1, Ethnicity and Economic Activity.* Edited by L. Y. C. Lim and L. A. P. Gosling. Singapore: Maruzen Asia.
Benoit, Charles. 1981. Vietnam's "Boat People." In *The Third Indochina Conflict.* Edited by D. W. P. Elliot. Boulder, Colorado: Westview Press. Pp. 139–162.
Brocheux, Pierre. 1995. *The Mekong Delta: Ecology, Economy, and Revolution, 1860–1960.* Madison, Wisconsin: Center for Southeast Asian Studies, University of Wisconsin.
Caplan, Nathan, Marcella H. Choy, and John K. Whitmore. 1991. *Children of the Boat People: A Study of Educational Success.* Ann Arbor: University of Michigan Press.
———. 1992. Indochinese Refugee Families and Academic Achievement. *Scientific American* 266(2):36–42.
Caplan, Nathan, John K. Whitmore, and Quang L. Bui. 1984. *Economic Self-sufficiency among Southeast Asian Refugees.* Report to the Office of Refugee Resettlement. Ann Arbor, Michigan: Institute for Social Research.
Caplan, Nathan, John K. Whitmore, and Marcella H. Choy. 1989. *The Boat People and Achievement in America: A Study of Family Life, Hard Work, and Cultural Values.* Ann Arbor: University of Michigan Press.
de Poncins, Gontran. 1957. *From a Chinese City.* Garden City, New York: Doubleday.
Dunning, Bruce B. 1982. *A Systematic Survey of the Social, Psychological and Economic Adaptation of Vietnamese Refugees Representing Five Entry Cohorts, 1975–1979.* Washington, D.C.: Bureau of Social Science Research.
Fall, Bernard B. 1959. Commentary. In *Vietnam, the First Five Years.* Edited by R. W. Lindholm. East Lansing: Michigan State University Press. Pp. 111–117.
Gold, Steven J. 1994. Chinese-Vietnamese Entrepreneurs in California. In *The New Asian Immigration in Los Angeles and Global Restructuring.* Edited by Paul Ong, Edna Bonacich, and Lucie Cheng. Philadelphia: Temple University Press. Pp. 196–226.
Grant, Bruce, et al. 1979. *The Boat People: An "Age" Investigation.* New York: Penguin Books.
Hackett, Beatrice Nied. 1989. Overlapping Self- and Other-Defined Ethnic Identities: Adjustment and Chinese Cambodian Refugees in the Washington Metropolitan Area. Unpublished paper.
Haines, David W., Editor. 1989. *Refugees as Immigrants: Cambodians, Laotians, and Vietnamese in America.* Totowa, New Jersey: Rowman and Littlefield.

Ky Luong Nhi. 1963. The Chinese in Vietnam. Unplublished Ph.D. dissertation, University of Michigan, Ann Arbor.

Lim, L. Y. C. 1984. Chinese Activity in Southeast Asia: An Introductory Review. In *The Chinese in Southeast Asia.* Edited by L. Y. C. Lim and L. A. P. Gosling. Singapore: Maruzen Asia. Pp. 1–29.

Marsot, Alain G. 1993. *The Chinese Community in Vietnam under the French.* San Francisco: EMText.

Menkhoff, Thomas. 1993. *Trade Routes, Trust and Trading Networks: Chinese Small Enterprises in Singapore.* Fort Lauderdale, Florida: Breitenbach.

Murray, Martin J. 1980. *The Development of Capitalism in Colonial Indochina, 1870–1940.* Berkeley: University of California Press.

Mydans, Seth. 1984. Chinese Refugees from Vietnam Thrive in Chinatown. *New York Times,* February 11:29, 32.

Ngo Vinh Long. 1971. Use of the Chinese by the French in Cochinchina, 1886–1910. Harvard University *Papers on China* 24:125–145.

Nguyen Hoi Chan. 1971. Some Aspects of the Chinese Community in Vietnam, 1650–1850. Harvard University *Papers on China* 24:104–124.

Nguyen The Anh. 1971. *Kin-te va Xa-hoi Viet-nam duoi cac vua trieu Nguyen* (The economy and society of Vietnam under the Nguyen kings). (2nd Edition). Saigon: Lua-thieng.

Peters, H., B. Schieffelin, L. Sexton, and D. A. Feingold. 1983. *Who Are the Sino-Vietnamese? Culture, Ethnicity, and Social Categories.* Philadelphia, Pennsylvania: Institute for the Study of Human Issues.

Skinner, G. William. 1951. *Report on the Chinese in Southeast Asia.* Ithaca, New York: Cornell University, Southeast Asia Program.

Tran Khanh. 1993. *The Ethnic Chinese and Economic Development in Vietnam.* Singapore: Institute of Southeast Asian Studies.

Tsai Maw-kuey. 1968. *Les Chinois au Sud Vietnam.* Paris: Bibliotheque Nationale.

Tsung To Way. 1959. A Survey of Chinese Occupations. In *Vietnam, the First Five Years.* Edited by R. W. Lindholm. East Lansing: Michigan State University Press. Pp. 118–125.

Whitmore, John K. 1983. Vietnam and the Monetary Flow of Eastern Asia, Thirteenth to Eighteenth Centuries. In *Precious Metals in the Later Medieval and Early Modern Worlds.* Edited by J. F. Richards. Durham, North Carolina: Carolina Academic Press. Pp. 363–393.

Willmott, William E. 1967. *The Chinese in Cambodia.* Vancouver: University of British Columbia.

———. 1970. *The Political Structure of the Chinese Community in Cambodia.* New York: Humanities Press.

Woodside, Alexander B. 1971. *Vietnam and the Chinese Model.* Cambridge, Massachusetts: Harvard University Press.

Chapter 5

Cubans

JOSEPH COLEMAN

The refugee experience is distinct from that of other immigrants. Refugees do not initially expect to remain permanently in their countries of asylum, and are not—again at least initially—oriented toward fully integrating into them. Instead, they arrive in their new countries in what they hope will be a temporary absence from their own home countries.[1] This sense of temporary absence is particularly important in understanding Cuban refugees. The extreme geographical proximity of Cuba and the United States, and the long-intertwined political histories make for a closeness that has often been oppressive for Cubans but has also kept alive the direct involvement of Cuban refugees in events in the home country and the possibility of return. For exiles in America, the traditional Cuban view of the United States as a sort of dominating ''monster'' remains important. José Martí, Cuban's revolutionary writer and poet around the turn of the century, believed that it was difficult—perhaps impossible—to live with the ''monster in its lair.'' That view persists today.

This chapter addresses the homeland from which the Cuban refugees fled, how they left, their resettlement in the United States, and their general situation as exiles in America. It begins, however, with a consideration of the emotional importance of Cuba to the revolution and to those who fled from it.

THE LOVED LAND

In the middle of the last century, J. G. Cantero wrote in his book *Los ingenios de Cuba* (The sugar mills of Cuba) that his country's soil was ''the favorite of Providence'' and that people would know of that preferment if they saw and felt Cuba's ''copious and clear rivers, the state and variations of its benign and humid atmosphere, and above all the vivifying warmth of its tropical sun'' (quoted in Williams 1984:363–364).[2] Cantero continued, noting the "majestic sight of the sun as it appears over the hills from which it bathes with its gilded rays the emerald fields covered with the transparent dew of the morning gently stirs the soul, elevating it to the sublime Creator of such a splendid picture."[3] Similarly, in the late 1980s a middle-aged Cuban refugee woman living in Florida told how she had been sent away to school in the United States when she was six years old to learn English. Then, when she was ten, Castro came to power, and she went into exile. "I had two exiles," she said. "I was sent away twice from the best place in the world." The two vignettes give some sense of what many Cuban refugees think and feel about their country. Such attachment remains an important and continuing part of their refugee experience. It is not too much of an exaggeration to say that for most Cubans, home is always Cuba.

Cuba itself, however, is ruled by a more ideological vision summed up in the phrase *Fidel-patria-revolution.* The triad (with *patria* best translated here as "motherland" or "homeland") has been a rhetorical and symbolic basis for the Cuban revolution from the beginning. The phrase is still invoked regularly in Cuba, although there has been substantial loss of credibility in all three of the terms. Castro still affirms that he and the revolution can and must continue to protect *patria* and that the complete triad still has important meaning for the Cuban people and still provides them support. Others have suggested (e.g., Pérez-Stable 1993:11) that, in contrast, Cuba is no longer "in revolution" and that the transformation of Cuban society essentially began and ended in the 1960s.

Whether the revolution succeeded or failed, or whether it continues or ended decades ago, many Cubans have left, and many more continue to try to leave. Those who left first in 1959 and came to the United States were those who had been wealthy and influential in the pre-Castro society. They were followed by persons from the middle economic classes and eventually the lower economic strata—who were a significant component of the 1980 Mariel boat exodus. Over time, it is probably fair to say that the balance shifted from those who had been politically persecuted or threatened to include at least some who fled because of material deprivation.

HOME

The story of Cuban refugees in the United States is the story of events in Cuba as much as it is of a new life in America. Cuba became a Spanish colony in 1511, and its capital—Havana—has been an important and cosmopolitan city for almost 500 years. One early effect of the Spanish control, and of the several European diseases they introduced, was the virtual disappearance of native peoples from the island in that first century. Since that time, the population has been divided between those of Spanish descent and those descended from the hundreds of thousands of slaves imported from Africa to work in the sugar plantations and mills. Significant immigration from Spain in the early 1900s served to maintain large numbers of those with Spanish rather than African origins.

By the 1990s, Cuba's population was about 11 million people, with an annual growth rate of only around 1 percent. About 57 percent of the population is mulatto, 37 percent is white, and 11 percent is black.[4] Life expectancy is about 78 years for women and 74 for men. Literacy is high (95 percent for men and 93 percent for women), and infant mortality is low (about 11 per 1,000 live births—lower than in parts of the United States). The Cubans are generally a healthy and well-educated people. Medical care and public health have been strongly supported by the government. Educational opportunities for Cubans have also been extensive under Castro. As in many other socialist countries, technical and scientific subjects have been strongly emphasized, and the arts and humanities are heavily conditioned by socialist ideology. Similarly, the written language, fiction as well as nonfiction, has taken on much of the abstract, dull, and propagandistic characteristics of socialist discourse.

The country as a whole remains relatively underpopulated with its population spread over a territory about one third larger than South Carolina and slightly smaller than Pennsylvania. (In European terms, Cuba is substantially larger than Austria and about the size of Belgium, the Netherlands, and Switzerland combined.) The country is very narrow in parts but quite long east to west. Its 750-mile length is approximately the distance from Chicago to New York. At least as important as its own internal structure, however, is its geographic location: about equidistant from Florida and Mexico and commanding access to the Gulf of Mexico. Its location encouraged many in American government and politics to view it as a part of America's natural jurisdiction. Indeed, there was at times a belief that Cuba would eventually become a state.[5]

The Cuban experience with the United States has long-standing economic, social, and cultural aspects, and often involves sharp contrasts. In cultural terms, for example, Cubans are a passionate people, and the contents of their beliefs and passions are as varied as they are strongly held. They thus wonder at the strange, unemotional, undemonstrative ways of most Americans. Joan Didion, for example, notes Cuban attitudes toward Ted Koppel and his guests on *Nightline*. They were, she notes, "a constant source of novelty and derision" for well-educated, cultured Cubans. The term *Nightline* became a kind of shorthand description for powerful American leaders who lacked passion. Cubans watched with wonder as Americans "with very opposing points of view" talked "completely without passion" and "without any gestures at all" (Didion 1987:78–79). "Speaking from the heart," by contrast, is a commonly heard phrase in the Cuban enclave, and the expression represents a habit of mind among Cubans that they see as quite different from American manners.

In political terms, it is difficult even to separate the Cuban from the American. The Spanish-American War is perhaps the most telling junction of Cuban and U.S. history.[6] For the United States the war began in the summer of 1898. However, it was Cuba's second war of independence: It had begun for them in

1895 and ended very quickly after U.S. troops arrived. Americans remember Teddy Roosevelt and the Rough Riders at San Juan Hill, but most Cubans remember that their own forces already controlled the countryside when the Americans arrived. By 1898 the Cuban Army of Liberation had forced Spain to "concentrate in cities," and when the United States attacked, "there was nowhere to retreat" (Rudolph 1985:21).

After the war, Cuba's independence was shaped by American intentions, good and bad. Cubans were considered by the United States to need a strong hand if they were to become democratic, rational, and capitalist. This attitude was typified in the Platt Amendment of 1901. This amendment (to a U.S. military appropriations bill) contained several clauses that were forced into the new Cuban constitution. Under its terms, Cuba was required to accept as legitimate all acts of the military government of the United States that had been installed there; had to permit the United States to purchase or lease land it needed for "coaling and naval stations" (thus, the beginning of the Guantánamo Naval Base); and was required to allow the United States to intervene at any time to "preserve Cuban independence" or "to support a government capable of protecting life, property, and individual liberties" (Rudolph 1985:21). Although the Platt Amendment may have been intended by the United States as a relatively benevolent (if permanent) restriction on Cuba's independence, it was, from the Cuban perspective, an enormous humiliation. Elihu Root, secretary of war early in the century and a major force behind the Platt Amendment, briskly spelled out the nature of the relationship. Although he recognized that Cuba was "technically a foreign country," it "occupies an intermediate position, since we have required it to become part of our political and military system" (Paterson 1994:5).

Although the verbal stances of later American leaders were softened, Root's description of the relationship remained essentially correct until Fidel Castro. Castro's emphasis on achieving true independence from the United States helps explain the extent of his support among middle-class Cubans. Before Castro, under the dictatorship of Fulgencio Batista, there was widespread corruption as well as "profound inequalities" between the urban and rural sectors in Cuba (Pérez-Stable 1993:6). Castro often spoke of the revolution that would rectify such injustices, but, at least in the beginning, that revolution was not so much for communism as against the United States. For many reasons (see, for example, Paterson 1994), relations between the two countries worsened to the point that as President Dwight Eisenhower was preparing to leave office in December 1960, he broke diplomatic ties with the Castro government. By then Cuba had nationalized almost all American businesses, and also many belonging to Cuban entrepreneurs, who would soon become refugees. The attempted invasion by Cuban exiles at Playa Giron on the Bay of Pigs in the spring of 1961 made relations even worse. (The handling of the Bay of Pigs invasion also alienated many Cuban exiles who believed, often with a continuing sense of deep betrayal, that the American support had been inadequate.)

In December 1961 Castro proclaimed that Cuba was now a Communist state. In the following year, Cuba was expelled from the Organization of American States, which had also voted for a political and economic blockade of Cuba. The United States instituted a trade embargo, which has remained in effect at some level ever since. Castro in turn moved closer to the Soviet Union. In the fall of 1962, Russia began to place missiles and atomic warheads on the island, and the Cuban Missile Crisis followed. Communism and anti-Americanism remained pillars of the revolution from then on. Even in the late 1980s, as Eastern Europe was leaving the fold and the Soviet Union itself was beginning to collapse, Castro forcefully restated his own commitment to communism. At the same time, he moved against, and eventually executed, more than a dozen top military and government officials (including the revolutionary hero General Arnaldo Ochoa) who were accused of involvement in drug trafficking and ill-specified violations of national security.[7]

Three decades after the revolution, Castro remains central not only to Cuba but to the views and hopes of Cubans in America. For the exiles, the views are negative. Alina Fernandez Revuelta, Castro's refugee daughter (born out of wedlock), was asked if her father was a dictator. "That's not the right word," she said. "I looked it up once. A dictator is someone granted absolute but temporary powers in an emergency." She thought her father was a tyrant instead. "A tyrant," she explained, is an "absolute ruler unrestrained by law, who usurps people's rights" (Oppenheimer 1992:282). For others, the views are positive. There is a widespread perception across many countries of a sense of selflessness in Cuba, a generous spirit, and an enviable strength of character. A middle-class Dominican from Santo Domingo (personal communication), for example, said that he and many Latins still believe that U.S. foreign policy is driven almost entirely by material considerations, which are amoral and sometimes immoral. "I think," he continued, "Cuba has always been the one country almost everyone in Latin America admires. I mean, here we have this small, poor country, resisting and standing against the greatest power on earth!"

LEAVING HOME

After Castro took power and after it became clear that the influence of the upper economic classes would count for much less in the new regime than originally thought, the large-scale emigration of the wealthy and the near-wealthy began.[8] It was clear that the new regime, whatever political label it deserved at the time, was moving toward the egalitarian ideal of a new society for the *Hombre Nuevo* (New Man) it wished to develop. It was also clear that there would be a major distribution of wealth from rich to poor and from cities, notably Havana, to the countryside. For those who left at this time, it was relatively easy to bring much of their wealth with them. There were few restrictions or controls on those who wished to leave, or on their money.

The number of departures is not exactly known. Approximately 200,000 left for the United States in the early period that followed the exit of Batista and his immediate circle. Perhaps another 200,000 fled to other countries at the same time. The departure of the wealthiest Cubans was quickly followed by that of large numbers from the professional and managerial classes. This first wave of emigration slowed with the imposition of the trade embargo in 1962 and ended with the Cuban Missile Crisis later that year. By that time, Castro and his government had made a solid start in their attempt to reshape Cuba and its people through a system of pervasive education, rewriting of history, and constant exposure of individuals to group meetings and public events at which central themes were repeated.

The next major wave of emigration began in the fall of 1965 after the Cuban economy had deteriorated seriously. The political pressures on Cuba from the poor state of its economy (before Russian aid reached massive levels), and on the United States from rumors of chaotic, unimpeded exits from Cuba, were strong enough to bring the Cuban and U.S. governments to agreement on what became the so-called Freedom Flights, from the airport at Veradero in Cuba to Miami. Those who left were almost all close relatives of Cubans already living in the United States. The flights ended in 1973, after about 300,000 people on several thousand flights had been admitted to the United States (Portes and Stepick 1993:103–104). From then until the late 1970s, probably less than 40,000 Cubans were admitted to the United States. A large majority of these came from so-called third countries (i.e., did not come directly from Cuba) and were admitted as parolees rather than as refugees (see Gordon, this volume; Holman, this volume). Many were service workers, domestic servants, gardeners, hairdressers, taxi drivers, and others who had been employed by those in the wealthy economic classes who had exited Cuba earlier. In the late 1970s, in a brief warming between the administration of President Jimmy Carter and the Cuban government, Cuba released some 3,000 political prisoners and permitted them to travel to the United States. Including their accompanying family members, a total of between 10,000 and 15,000 people were admitted.

Then in early 1980 came the boat exodus from the port of Mariel, during which more than 120,000 Cubans came to the United States. Those trying to leave were assailed by those determined to stay. It was a time when "people turned against people, friends against friends." There were now many *actos de repudio*, staged mass acts of repudiation in front of the homes of people who were leaving Cuba. People began to "turn on each other like vicious animals, repeating the slogans" (Geldof 1991:302). As one Mariel refugee noted, Cuba had allowed nearly 100,000 Cuban exiles to return for visits in the late 1970s. Before that, she had been taught that they were all *gusanos* (worms) who had abandoned the *patria* (their country in the most spiritual sense). Now the Cuban government said the refugees were to be welcomed. The joke began to run through Cuba that the worms had turned into butterflies. It was no longer important, it seemed, that the visitors had left the country, or that they were capitalists. "They had many dollars to spend" (Geldof 1991:301); it seemed that it "really didn't have to do with ideology, it had to do with money." The myth and magic of the revolution were necessarily tarnished.

The general disillusionment and weak economy that brought on the Mariel exodus were followed by a more sharply deteriorating economy in the late 1980s and early 1990s as communism became weaker in the Soviet Union and Eastern Europe.[9] The economy was further weakened when President Bill Clinton tightened the existing embargo in 1993. Yet as communism elsewhere became less potent, Castro reaffirmed his commitment to the system and instituted what he called a "time of special sacrifice," a period of severe material restrictions for the Cuban people. One observer noted in 1990 that urban Cubans "who are dragging themselves through the day may be asked ('like Cambodians' they say indignantly) to go out and work in the fields" (Williams 1990:32).

In the summer of 1994, departures from Cuba increased greatly. By July, as many as 2,000 people a day were attempting the boat trip. In all of 1993, by way of comparison, only 3,000 to 4,000 had made the trip. In September 1994, President Clinton made the first of two profoundly significant changes in Cuban refugee policy: First, he ended the 30-year practice of giving refugee status to almost every Cuban who reached U.S. territorial waters or landed on U.S. soil. Cuba in turn agreed to "deter" those attempting to leave. Then in May 1995, Clinton took the second step. Apparently without consulting the Cuban refugee community, which had heretofore been a significant force in shaping U.S.-Cuban policy, he ordered the repatriation of Cubans seeking to enter the United States. At the same time, he determined that the United States would admit most of those who had been detained at the Guantánamo Naval Base since mid-1994. Any new attempts to reach the United States would be rebuffed, although the possibility of making refugee determinations in particular cases remained.

These changes in policy were criticized by many. The U.S. Committee for Refugees noted in its 1995 *World Refugee Survey* that "the recent policy shift by the Clinton Administration resulting in the near-automatic return of Cuban rafters to Cuba violates the right of Cubans to flee their country and seek asylum from persecution." The policy change "sets a dangerous example for other countries throughout the world who may make similar decisions to keep would-be refugees at bay" (news release, May 31, 1995). Human Rights Watch (news release, May 26, 1995) charged that Cuba was renewing its crackdowns on human rights activists, that it still had many hundreds of political prisoners, and that it had—following its deterrence agreement with the United States—recriminalized attempted exits from the country.

RESETTLEMENT

The resettlement of Cuban refugees has been a joint public and private sector responsibility. Many Cuban refugees have come to the United States to reunite with relatives, and thus unrelated volunteer sponsors have been rare. Still, each publicly funded refugee has at least a formal sponsorship from a voluntary agency responsible for ensuring that the initial "reception and placement" services funded by the U.S. Department of State have been provided. In many cases, an agency's only responsibility is monitoring to determine that the required services have been performed by the families receiving the refugees.

Beyond that general pattern, however, the resettlement of Cubans has involved a series of important precedents that have shaped the experience not only of Cuban refugees but also of U.S. resettlement efforts in general. When the United States began accepting and resettling Cuban refugees at the end of the 1950s, for example, it set a new precedent by paying for the majority of resettlement costs. Never before had the federal government been so involved in the financial costs of bringing refugees to America or of assisting them in learning to live in a new country. Indeed, the previous assumption had been that refugees "do it themselves" with the help of some private groups and volunteer sponsors. Despite the continuing importance of private and voluntary agency contributions, this new pattern of federal government support would become the standard for all refugees.

The Cuban refugee program set another important precedent: the provision of impact aid for localities providing services to refugees, particularly education. The large number of well-educated, successful Cuban parents expected and received high-quality educational resources for their children, including perhaps the first large-scale example of bilingual education for immigrant children. The effort was somewhat different from that later developed for other immigrant groups. Cuban parents did not believe their children needed bilingual support for learning or for living in their "own" culture; instead, they simply wanted education in Spanish because they thought their children were entitled to it. Unlike the situation for other groups, there was not much question whether Cuban children would learn English. A high percentage of the second generation became fluent, or very close to it, in both English and Spanish. For education and other impact aid, the federal government and the state of Florida have been engaged for many years in (usually polite) discussions about the extent of resettlement costs for Cubans and who should pay what portion of them. By the 1980s there was acceptance by Florida that the federal government would no longer pay 100 percent of all the costs of refugee "impact," though it would continue to pay some of those costs.

Another critical aspect of Cuban resettlement, both for Cubans and for government programs for all refugees, was the dense congregation of Cubans in Florida (see Table 5.1) and particularly in Miami (see Table 5.2). Not only was the result a transformed Miami and an unusually successful economic enclave but also a federal refugee program that thereafter was geared toward broader dispersal of refugees. Subsequent resettlement of Cubans away from Miami was supported by the federal government, and dispersal became a major, continuing policy issue in the later resettlement of Southeast Asian refugees. The issue of dense settlement reemerged in Miami with the 1980 Mariel boat exodus. Part of the sensitivity involved a segment of the arrivals who were either felons or

Table 5.1
Cubans by Selected States, 1990

State	Cuban Population	% of Total
Florida	674,052	64.57%
New Jersey	85,378	8.18%
New York	74,345	7.12%
California	71,977	6.89%
Illinois	18,204	1.74%
Texas	18,195	1.74%
Louisiana	8,569	0.82%
Massachusetts	8,106	0.78%
Georgia	7,818	0.75%
Pennsylvania	7,485	0.72%
Total: Top 10 States	974,129	93.31%
Total: United States	1,043,932	100.00%

Note: Ethnicity is self-assessed.
Source: U.S. Bureau of the Census 1992.

mentally ill–perhaps 5,000 to 10,000 of the 120,000 entrants. (Higher estimates include additional people jailed for political offenses.) The Mariel exodus was also an important precedent in its inclusion of refugees who had long lived under a Communist system. The arrivals were indeed ''new Cubans'' who had lived much—sometimes all—of their lives under the Castro regime. They arrived only to find the relatively weak condition of the U.S. economy in 1980. Both Americans and the old Cubans had very strong reactions to the Mariel exodus, although the former focused on the gross numbers of people who entered, while the latter concentrated more on the nature of the individuals and on the years of experience separating the Marielitos from earlier arrivals. A decade later, similar dilemmas would appear for Southeast Asian refugees.

Finally, and coming full circle, the Cuban resettlement is also unique because Cubans are the only recent refugee group to have been admitted to the United States in significant numbers under a privately funded admissions and resettlement system. The program began in 1988 and was administered by the Cuban American National Foundation and the federal government. (Several other groups had very small numbers admitted under the private program.) In the five years that the Cuban program functioned, almost 10,000 Cubans came to the United States from third countries[10] at almost no cost to federal, state, or local

Table 5.2
Cubans by Selected Urban Areas, 1990

Urbanized Area	Cuban Population	% of Total
Atlanta	5,227	0.5%
Boston	5,143	0.5%
Chicago	16,593	1.6%
Ft. Lauderdale	23,307	2.2%
Houston	7,496	0.7%
Las Vegas	5,531	0.5%
Los Angeles	52,437	5.0%
Miami	560,508	53.7%
New Orleans	5,891	0.6%
New York (metro)	150,021	14.4%
Orlando	9,006	0.9%
Philadelphia	5,257	0.5%
Tampa	30,846	3.0%
Washington, D.C.	8,564	0.8%
West Palm Beach	14,491	1.4%
Total: 15 Urban Areas	900,318	86.2%
Total: United States	1,043,932	

Notes: Ethnicity is self-assessed. Urban areas follow census definitions. Percentages do not add up exactly because of rounding.

Source: U.S. Bureau of the Census 1992.

governments. There was a separate allocation of admission numbers for the unfunded program. Refugees in this program had to meet the U.S. statutory definition of refugee, not be firmly resettled in another country, and be otherwise eligible for admission under immigration statutes and refugee program criteria. The program required that the private sector bear admission and resettlement costs for the first two years, or until the refugee attained permanent resident status, whichever came first. In addition, cases were prepared by privately paid staff for adjudication by immigration officers. As in the larger admissions program, the Immigration and Naturalization Service determined refugee status and eligibility for admission to the United States.

Unlike those who administered the regular refugee programs, Cuban Foundation staff were required to verify that the individual sponsors (who were mostly relatives of the refugees) had sufficient financial resources to prevent the refugees from qualifying for welfare assistance, Medicaid, or government refugee service programs. Federal, state, and local government officials were alerted to the specially altered immigration documents these refugees were given, which advised that the bearer was admitted under a special program and that if the refugee attempted to obtain government assistance or services, the foundation should be contacted. The program worked remarkably well, but it was not continued—in part because the government felt that the mainstream refugee program was capable of handling the reduced number of refugees it planned to admit. During the years the program operated, refugees were admitted to the United States from many countries in Latin America and the Caribbean, from Western Europe, and from Canada. A small number were also admitted from Russia.

INTEGRATION

Cubans have not been typical of either refugees or immigrants to the United States. They have not wanted to or had to make many of the accommodations to American society that other newcomers have faced. To a remarkable extent, they have been able, if they wished, to live independently and separately. This, along with the considerable knowledge of America that they often brought, helps explain the lack of culture shock and disruption they have experienced. The integration of Cubans has thus been less an integration into mainstream American society than an integration into a Cuban community that happens to be located in America.

The exact number of Cuban refugees who have come to the United States is difficult to reconstruct from government records. Gordon (this volume) estimates 735,000 refugees from Cuba and an additional 206,000 immigrants, for a total of 941,000 by the end of fiscal year (FY) 1994. The 1990 census provides a figure of 1,043,932 self-designated Cubans (see Tables 5.1 and 5.2, U.S. Bureau of the Census 1992). A separate estimate for foreign-born Cubans that year was 736,971 (U.S. Bureau of the Census 1993a). The population is concentrated in Florida (65 percent of the Cuban population), with sizable, though far smaller, numbers in New Jersey (8 percent of the total), New York (7 percent), and California (7 percent). The concentration by urban areas is equally impressive. Miami has about 54 percent of the total Cuban population, followed distantly by the New York metropolitan area (14 percent of the total) and Los Angeles (5 percent).

Census data from 1990 also provide some useful, general comparative information on the Cuban population in America. Comparison with the general U.S. population and the general Hispanic population (see Table 5.3) shows a relatively older population. Cubans had a median age of 38.9 years, well above that of the general U.S. population (33.0 years) and far above that of the general Hispanic population (25.6 years). The census data also suggest the frequently noted strength of the Cuban family. For example, 79 percent of Cuban family

Table 5.3
Selected Characteristics of Cubans, 1990

	Cuban	Hispanic	U.S.
Under age 16	16.1%	31.4%	22.9%
Median age	38.90	25.60	33.00
5 & older who don't speak English well	48.6%	39.4%	6.1%
Labor force participation (age 16 & up)			
All	65.0%	67.5%	65.3%
Female	55.6%	55.9%	56.8%
Per capita income	$13,786	$8,400	$14,420
% below poverty	14.6%	25.3%	13.1%
% of households with 2 or more workers	60.6%	57.6%	58.9%
% of family households with 2 parents	78.1%	69.9%	79.5%
% under 18 in 2-parent households	71.5%	66.0%	73.0%
% in linguistically isolated households	28.6%	23.8%	3.5%

Notes: Ethnicity is self-assessed. See source for exact definitions of variables.
Source: U.S. Bureau of the Census 1993b.

households included both parents (compared to 80 percent for the general U.S. population but 70 percent for the general Hispanic population), and 72 percent of the Cubans under age 18 lived in two-parent households (compared to 73 percent for the general U.S. population but only 66 percent for the general Hispanic population). The economic importance of the Cuban family is evidenced by the percentage of households with two or more workers: for Cubans the figure was 61 percent, compared to 59 percent for the U.S. population and 58 percent for the Hispanic population.

Somewhat surprisingly, the census data also indicate a population that does not rate its English-language ability as very high (see Garcia and Diaz 1992; Resnick 1988). When respondents were asked to assess their ability, 49 percent of Cubans said that they did not speak it "very well," versus 39 percent of Hispanics overall. By Bureau of the Census calculations, 29 percent of Cubans lived in linguistically isolated households, again a figure higher than that for Hispanics in general (24 percent). Despite their self-perceived lack of English ability, however, Cubans had a per capita income ($13,786) well above that for Hispanics ($8,400) and only slightly less than that of the general U.S. population ($14,420).

These census data also support the long-standing view of Cubans as a relatively old population with a strong family structure and an ethnic community strong enough to make the use of English less of a necessity than it has been for most immigrant and refugee groups. The data also support the more general notion, common in both the popular media and the academic literature, of Cubans as a success story, particularly that Cubans are more successful in a shorter period of time than other immigrants. Much of this difference reflects the great confidence Cubans have in themselves as a successful and cultured people. They expect to succeed, and often do. The image of Cuban success does not go unchallenged, however. The situation of many Cubans fails to match the image of success (e.g., Jorge and Moncarz 1987),[11] and the success itself has some negative consequences. Many non-Cubans, particularly in Miami, believe that Cubans have succeeded too rapidly and with too little gratitude to the United States. They did, after all, receive considerable public assistance in their early years in the United States.[12]

The impressive success of Cubans in the United States is not, however, necessarily an indication of their commitment to, or full integration into, American society. Many Cubans, particularly those born and raised in Cuba, are still in exile. The Spanish term used by the refugees is *el exilio*. The term has a long history and has been used by Cubans of many political positions for over 150 years. Cuba always remains close: emotionally, politically, and geographically. This closeness is reflected in the way Cubans construct their identity in the United States. Williams (1991:31) describes Cuban-Americans as "America's most restless immigrant group" who are "not quite sure on which side of the hyphen to hang their identities—and their future." This ambivalence reflects again the profound, enduring emotional link with Cuba. A poll conducted in the early 1990s asked members of various immigrant groups if the "old country" was better. The Cubans were "virtually alone" in saying that it was—and many of them "remain obsessed with events back in Cuba" (31).

A later survey of second-generation immigrant children in the Miami schools (Portes and Zhou 1994) indicated the continuing strength of a Cuban identity. Less than a fifth of all the Hispanic children identified themselves as non-hyphenated Americans. For Cuban students, "Cuban" alone was the most frequent choice, followed by "Cuban-American" and an occasional selection of

"Hispanic." (The proportion of Cubans choosing "Cuban" was highest among those children from high-status families who attended private schools.) By way of contrast, Nicaraguans chose the label "Hispanic" almost as often as they chose "Nicaraguan." On the basis of the survey, the researchers suggest the Cuban experience is best understood as one of "paced, selective assimilation" (30–31).[13]

The strong political influence of the relatively conservative refugee community is a final distinctive feature of the Cuban experience in the United States. Cubans' political activism and influence are unique among recently arrived refugees in this country and were instrumental for decades in maintaining the U.S. government's concern over Cuba. Castro's arrogance, spirit, and independence were offensive to both Washington and Cuban refugee conservatives, although for somewhat different reasons. To Washington, Castro was a tool of worldwide communism and one that was too close to the United States. To the Cuban refugees, however, he was the despised ruler of their country. Despite their internal differences, Cubans—at least in foreign policy—have been united, consistent, and effective. Particularly in Florida, the Cuban voting bloc has been tremendously important.

Central to that political effort has been the Cuban American National Foundation, the most powerful conservative Cuban organization in the United States. After some loosening in U.S.-Cuban relations in the late 1980s, the election of Ronald Reagan shortly after the Mariel boat lift provided a particularly opportune time for the foundation. It is still not entirely clear whether the Cubans found Washington or Washington found the Cubans. Anticommunism was one of the prime bases of the Reagan administration, and many of the administration's appointees were determined that no more "Mariels" would happen. Thus, just as the conservative Cubans were ready to exercise the power they had been building, the Reagan administration was ready for them. That influence continued under the Bush administration. One result was the program of private resettlement for Cubans from third countries. With the end of the cold war, and the shift to a Democratic administration, however, the "umbilical cord" (Booth 1994) was broken. As Cuba's outside support lessened, so did American concern about Cuba. Within the Cuban community in America there began to be more consideration of the possibility of normalizing relations with Cuba, but as one commentator (Booth 1994) noted, based on a survey of the refugees, over half favored both a U.S. invasion of Cuba and talks with Castro: "[A]side from the people in the organized groups, there is a feeling among Cubans to say yes to anything that might work. Yes to invasion. Yes to negotiations."

CONCLUSION

Nineteenth-century Cuban historian Luis Estévez y Romero said of Cuba's relations with the United States, "[P]oor Cuba always hopeful, always disappointed," and David Rieff (1993:115) adds, "and always ambivalent towards the United States." For Cubans in America, the ambivalence is doubled since they must construct an identity that hinges both on events in Cuba and on their own current lives in America.

Many believe that whatever happens to Castro, Cuba will participate more fully in the international "free market system." Without Soviet aid, this has become inevitable. Even those sympathetic to the revolution foresee change. Hildita, Che Guevara's daughter, for example, said of the revolution: "The dream is not dead. It's dormant, frozen in time. Capitalism has regenerated itself over the years. It has adopted new forms. But communism has failed to keep up with the times. There is no such thing as neocommunism. That's what I would like. Communism with a human face" (Oppenheimer 1992:277–278). Others sympathetic to Castro see not only a poor economy but a breakdown in socialism as the "second economy"—capitalistic and noncentralized—expands and becomes more entrenched. Ironically, these changes may result in economic improvements that strengthen the Castro regime.

In America, the general picture of Cuban refugees remains one of impressive individual economic advances; strong, traditional family structures; and the creation of a uniquely effective social, political, and economic enclave—an enclave that has transformed south Florida.[14] Whether that success in America implies Americanization remains an unresolved question. There is also the broader question of what role the Cuban community in America could and would play in a post-Communist Cuba. Geldof (1991:306) notes the comments of Mirta Ojita, a successful Marielita, who believes that when there is change in Cuba, "it will come from the inside. And I'm hoping that some of the people here in Miami will not have a lot of influence once we all go back to Cuba. . . . Most will not go back, except to visit, to open businesses, to buy a place in Veradero. But they will not live there, or help put the country back together." More forcefully, Maria Elena Cruz, the poet and dissident, has said, "First we were a Spanish colony. Then, we became an American colony. Then, we became a Soviet colony. The last thing we need now is to become a colony of Miami's Cuban exiles" (Oppenheimer 1992:329).

NOTES

1. In recent years the classical model of refugees as people with compelling reasons to flee persecution has been diluted. Many refugees have been classified by both the government and the public as simply another category of immigrant. The failure to distinguish them is due in part at least to decisions to admit persons who seem not to have fled from clear and severe persecution. To say this is not to say that it is easy to separate political persecution from the economic and other causes for emigration, but it is to say that the rigor with which the classic political definition has been applied in the United States and in other refugee-receiving countries does vary significantly from one time period to another and from group to group.

2. Cantero was the owner of an *ingenio*, a mechanized but labor-intensive sugar

refinery. The term has many other (related) meanings in Cuban Spanish, such as a talented or creative person, a wit, a kind of cleverness and sharpness, or a cutter (human or otherwise). The word's meanings sum up an important part of the Cuban national character.

3. Cantero omitted mention of the rich red-brown earth that in many parts of Cuba makes other colors even more brilliant by contrast.

4. Hutchinson's Encyclopedia, CompuServe Information Service. The racial categories follow the original. Other observers note instead that the Cuban population is divided between whites and mulattoes.

5. Why Cuba did not become a state is a complex and interesting question. Many (perhaps most) Cubans and at least some North Americans believe that it did, from time to time, become a state in all but name. José Martí, the early champion of Cuban independence and a gifted writer, who is "claimed" by both the Cuban Left and Right, said that Cubans had a kind of "geographic fatalism" (quoted by Geldof 1991:xvi).

6. Palmer (1956:622) might describe it as "Imperialism as Crusade." Imperialism rose from many different motives: Commercial, financial, and political ones were combined with humanitarian and religious ones.

7. As one scholar put it, "[T]he summer of 1989 notoriously highlighted the pitfalls of charismatic authority and the weaknesses of Cuban institutions, especially the Communist party" (Péréz-Stable 1993:164). Ochoa, a heavily-medaled hero of Cuba, and a close associate of Castro for many years, was arrested, tried, and then executed, along with the other officials, on charges of drug trafficking and not-clearly-laid-out violations of national security. Many who have looked at the affair believe there was reason to conclude Ochoa's actions had been approved or at least disregarded "at the highest levels of government" (Pérez-Stable 1993:164–165). Andres Oppenheimer (1992), in what is probably the most controversial part of his book, provides a great deal of attention to the Ochoa affair.

It seemed clear to refugees in Miami and to people inside Cuba that whatever the exact degree of complicity, the leadership had to have had substantial involvement for acts on the order of the offenses to have been committed. The affair was a serious blow to solidarity between the leadership and the people of Cuba and, if anything, a greater blow to the charismatic authority of Castro. Many refugees in the United States cheered, at the same time they were cheering the beginning of loss of support to Cuba from the Soviet Union and its Eastern European allies. Weakness and corruption at the top of government were out in the open and out on the street. Castro and Cuba were not the same thereafter.

8. "Without question," wrote Lynn Bender (1973:271), Cuba's most successful export from the very beginning of the Castro regime was not sugar or revolution but the "physical removal of its domestic enemies."

9. For a sympathetic account of the Cuban economy at the time, see Deere (1991).

10. The practice of emigration to third countries, other than the United States, usually—but not always—with the intention of reaching the United States ultimately, began soon after the revolution and has continued to the present. The U.S. government has welcomed this relatively small but significant movement of Cubans away from its shores and tried regularly through the years to prevent the later entry of these emigrants to the United States. At least some of those who traveled to third countries such as Spain or Venezuela did so thinking they had assurances from U.S. officials that they would in time be admitted to America.

For many years U.S. government policy prevailed, but in the late 1980s, the Cuban American National Foundation began a resettlement program for third country refugees that was accomplished without federal government funds for most of the approximately five years it existed. The program demonstrated, among other things, that many of those who had gone to third countries met both the refugee definition and the U.S. federal government requirement that they not be "firmly resettled" in those third countries. Many of the governments involved had not extended the benefits of permanent residency to the Cubans—such benefits being, in brief, the measure of "firm resettlement."

11. The Mariel exodus in 1980 raised a serious challenge to this image of success and also raised anew the question of Cubans exceeding the resources of Miami. Neither problem was as serious as originally feared. The differences turned out to be less economic than social. Rieff (1993:67–68) quotes a student at Miami-Dade Community College, speaking to the Cubans in his class who had grown up in the United States about what they—the long residents—thought of Cuba, "You're all like some guy who's in love with a girl who doesn't want nothing to do with him. You dream about her and write her name down over and over again, and pretty soon you've made her up, 'cause she's nothing like what you imagine. Well, I'm here to tell you, neither is Cuba!" For general discussions of the "Mariel" Cubans and their effects on Miami, see Bach, Bach, and Triplett (1981), Card (1990), Portes and Jensen (1989), and De la Campa (1994).

12. The Cuban use of significant amounts of public assistance in their early years in the United States reflected the federal government's decision to use public funds for resettlement. There was only a small federal bureaucracy administering the 100 percent reimbursement of costs to local government jurisdictions. Despite a general feeling that the federal government was giving Cuban refugees some sort of special status, reimbursement was not always obtained by state and local government. The author, for example, became, many years ago, the administrator of the Cuban program in a local jurisdiction outside Florida and found there were few rules for determining the eligibility of Cubans for the fully federally financed welfare and Medicaid programs. For Medicaid, the Cuban program had such low visibility and had been given such low priority by the agency that no request for the available 100 percent reimbursement of costs had been made for at least three years.

13. Another kind of example of this continuing Cuban identity occurred at the very end of the 1980s. When it began to become clear to Cubans in the United States that communism in the Soviet Union and Eastern Europe was severely weakened, and indeed disappearing in some countries, many refugees essentially stopped spending money. Some put their houses on the market. Seeing that Cuba was rapidly losing its support and believing this meant the early fall of Castro, they wanted to have the resources to return home quickly.

14. For discussions of the transformation of Miami, see Croucher (1994), Rieff (1987, 1993), Pérez-Stable and Uriarte (1993), Portes and Stepick (1993), and Lamphere, Stepick, and Grenier (1994).

REFERENCES

Bach, Robert L., Jennifer B. Bach, and Timothy Triplett. 1981. The Flotilla Entrants: Latest and Most Controversial. *Cuban Studies* 11:29–48.

Bender, Lynn Darrell. 1973. The Cuban Exiles: An Analytical Sketch. *Journal of Latin American Studies* 5:271–278.

Booth, William. 1994. Cuban Exiles Find Their "Umbilical Cord" to Washington Has Broken. *Washington Post,* June 18.

Card, David. 1990. The Impact of the Mariel Boatlift on the Miami Labor Market. *Industrial and Labor Relations Review* 43(2):245–257.

Croucher, Sheila. 1994. Mandela in Miami: The Globalization of Ethnicity in an American City. *Journal of Developing Societies* 10(2):186–202.

De la Campa, Roman. 1994. The Latin Diaspora in the United States: Sojourns from a Cuban Past. *Public Culture* 6(2):293–317.

Deere, Carmen Diana. 1991. Cuba's Struggle for Self-Sufficiency. *Monthly Review* 43(July–August):55–74.

Didion, Joan. 1987. *Miami.* New York: Simon and Schuster.

Franklin, Jane. 1993. The Cuba Obsession. *Progressive* (July):18–22.

Garcia, Ricardo L., and Carlos F. Diaz. 1992. The Status and Use of Spanish and English among Hispanic Youth in Dade County (Miami) Florida: A Sociolinguistic Study, 1989–1991. *Language and Education* 6(1):13–32.

Geldof, Lynn. 1991. *Cubans: Voices of Change.* New York: St. Martin's Press.

Haines, David W., Editor. 1985. *Refugees in the United States: A Reference Handbook.* Westport, Connecticut: Greenwood Press.

Jorge, Antonio, and Raul Moncarz. 1987. The Golden Cage Cubans in Miami. *International Migration* 25(3):267–282.

Koont, Sinan. 1994. Cuba: An Island against All Odds. *Monthly Review* 46:1–19.

Lamphere, Louise, Alex Stepick, and Guillermo Grenier, Editors. 1994. *Newcomers in the Workplace: Immigrants and the Restructuring of the U.S. Economy.* Philadelphia: Temple University Press.

Oppenheimer, Andres. 1992. *Castro's Final Hour: The Secret Story behind the Coming Downfall of Communist Cuba.* New York: Simon and Schuster.

Palmer, R. R. 1956. *A History of the Modern World.* New York: Alfred A. Knopf.

Paterson, Thomas G. 1994. *Contesting Castro: The United States and the Triumph of the Cuban Revolution.* New York: Oxford University Press.

Pérez-Stable, Marifeli. 1993. *The Cuban Revolution: Origins, Course, and Legacy.* New York: Oxford University Press.

Pérez-Stable, Marifeli, and Miren Uriarte. 1993. Cubans and the Changing Economy of Miami. In *Latinos in a Changing U.S. Economy.* Edited by Rebecca Morales and Frank Bonilla. Newbury Park, California: Sage Publications. Pp. 133–159.

Portes, Alejandro, and L. Jensen. 1989. The Enclave and the Entrants: Patterns of Ethnic Enterprise in Miami before and after Mariel. *American Sociological Review* 54:929–949.

Portes, Alejandro, and Alex Stepick. 1993. *City on the Edge: The Transformation of Miami.* Berkeley: University of California Press.

Portes, Alejandro, and Min Zhou. 1994. Should Immigrants Assimilate? *The Public Interest* 116 (summer 1994):18–33.

Resnick, Melvyn C. 1988. Beyond the Ethnic Community: Spanish Language Roles and Maintenance in Miami. *International Journal of the Sociology of Language* 69:89–104.

Rieff, David. 1987. *Going to Miami: Exiles, Tourists, and Refugees in the New America.* Boston: Little, Brown.

———. 1993. *The Exile: Cuba in the Heart of Miami.* New York: Simon and Schuster.

Rudolph, James D., Editor. 1985. *Cuba: A Country Study* (Foreign Affairs Studies, The American University). Washington, D.C.: U.S. Government Printing Office.

U.S. Bureau of the Census. 1992. *Census of Population. General Population Characteristics—United States.* (1990 CP-1-1). Washington, D.C.

————. 1993a. *The Foreign Born Population of the United States.* (CP-3-1). Washington, D.C.

————. 1993b. *Persons of Hispanic Origin in the United States.* (CP-3-3). Washington, D.C.

U.S. Committee for Refugees. 1995. *World Refugee Survey.* Washington, D.C.

White, Robert. 1989. Review of Dominguez, Jorge L. *To Make the World Safe for Revolution. Commonweal* (May 19, 1989):304–305.

Williams, Eric. 1984. *From Columbus to Castro: The History of the Caribbean, 1492–1969.* New York: Vintage Press.

————. 1990. The Self-Laceration of Cuba. *The Economist* 316:31–32.

————. 1991. Show Me the Way to Go Home. *The Economist* 321:31.

Chapter 6

Eastern Europeans

ELZBIETA M. GOZDZIAK

As long as there have been Germany and Russia, there have been refugees from
Eastern Europe seeking refuge or temporary safe haven in other countries. The
royalty and peasants, intelligentsia and rural shopkeepers: They had little in
common except their experiences of persecution, war, and famine. In New York,
Chicago, Detroit, Cleveland, Pittsburgh, and Los Angeles, they built their
churches, spoke their native languages, and published magazines filled with
nostalgic poetry and angry prose. They might speak wistfully of going back,
but totalitarian regimes refused them visas. They were forced to leave their
countries in waves, beginning in the nineteenth century, when Russia and the
Austro-Hungarian empire posed a threat for smaller nations. Each subsequent
upheaval, from the Russian revolution of 1917 through the Hungarian Uprising
of 1956 to the Prague Spring of 1968 and Polish martial law in 1981, sent more
people packing.

The east of the West or the west of the East? What is Eastern Europe? The
answer changes from country to country, affording interesting insights into the
motives involved in the perception of one's neighbors. Some scholars and indeed
many inhabitants of the region reject the term entirely, preferring *Central Europe;* others argue about the boundaries. Hungarians and Czechs tend to consider
the territory of the old Austro-Hungarian empire to be the historical core of the
region. For Poles, the "other Europe" covers the whole area between Germany
and the former Soviet Union.

Recognizing that Eastern Europe is far more of a political expression than a
geographical one and acknowledging its considerable ethnic diversity, I will
focus my attention in this chapter on three different countries—Poland, Hungary, and Romania—as refugees from these countries represent the largest
groups of Eastern Europeans resettled in the United States. This chapter provides

a synthesis of available research on resettlement experiences of different waves of immigrants and refugees from Eastern Europe in order to elucidate commonalities and differences in their resettlement experiences and to shed light on the processes of uprooting and adaptation.

POLES

The Country

Poland's borders have shifted countless times in the course of the country's turbulent history. At its peak, the union of Poland and the Grand Duchy of Lithuania expanded almost to Moscow at the end of the fifteenth century. Poland ceased to exist as an independent state after its neighbors—Prussia, Austria, and Russia—partitioned the country in 1795. Most recently, Poland's borders were significantly shifted westward after World War II. Poland lost such cities as Vilnius, Pinsk, Brest, and Lvov in the east but gained Wroclaw and Szczecin in the west. Modern Poland shares borders with Russia, Lithuania, Ukraine, the Czech Republic in the east, and Germany in the west. The Tatra Mountains form its border with Slovakia in the south, and the Baltic Sea constitutes a natural frontier in the north.

With a population of 38 million and an area of 120,725 square miles, Poland is the largest and most populous nation in the region. According to official Polish sources, ethnic Poles constitute 99 percent of the country's population. Of the approximately 500,000 reported as ethnic minorities, the Ukrainians and Byelorussians form the largest groups, with much smaller groups of Slovaks, Czechs, Lithuanians, Germans, Russians, Roma (Gypsies), and Jews.

History and Politics

The name of *Polska* (Poland) does not emerge until the tenth century—and then only as a domain of one small Slavonic tribe, the Polanie ("the people of the open fields") who settled on the banks of the Warta river in the vicinity of modern Poznan. The first Polish state was formed in 966 when Prince Mieszko I married Czech Princess Dabrowka from Prague and accepted Catholicism. The nation was frequently at war, against the Tartars in the east and the Teutonic Knights in the west. But in the fourteenth century, Poland thrived as an advanced European state, founding the Jagiellonian University in Krakow and establishing a strong monarchy that defeated the Teutons at Grunwald in 1410. The Jagiellonian period following the defeat of the Teutonic Order was Poland's golden age. The size of the combined Polish-Lithuanian empire grew to impressive proportions. In 1492 it stretched from the Baltic to the Black Sea and was twice the size of modern France. Literature and science were blooming; its achievements were crowned by the famous discovery by Mikolaj Kopernik (Copernicus) of the earth's movement around the sun.

However, in the following centuries, Poland fell behind the rest of Europe. Its famously independent nobles insisted on autonomy and the power of veto— excellent for liberty but bad for national strength. Poland's elected monarchs were no match for the surrounding absolute sovereigns, and between 1772 and 1795, Prussia, Austria, and Russia divided the country among them, erasing the Polish state from the political map of Europe for the next 150 years. The Poles, however, hung on to their national identity tenaciously while there was no Poland per se and in 1830, 1848, and 1863 rebelled against the foreign rule.

At the outset of World War I, both sides sought Polish support by promising Poland independence, which finally came about at the end of the war on November 11, 1918. The new nation's frontiers were determined partially by negotiations and partially on the battlefield. Despite a long history of constitutional government, Poland could not long sustain a democracy and by 1926 fell under the quasi-dictatorial rule of Marshal Jozef Pilsudski.

World War II began with the German attack on the Polish garrison outside Gdansk on September 1, 1939. Only a week earlier, the Nazis and Soviets had concluded the infamous secret pact that proposed a new partition of Poland. Accordingly, on November 1, Russia appropriated eastern Poland, and Germany occupied the rest. Although Polish units fought on the Allied side throughout the war, the territory of Poland was at the mercy of the occupiers. Over the next six years, 6 million Poles were killed, half of them Jews. In 1944 and 1945 the Red Army "liberated" Poland, using its presence to impose a socialist regime and to annex the eastern third of the country. Between the Holocaust and the annexation, Poland went from being a multiethnic state with large Jewish, Ukrainian, Lithuanian, Byelorussian, and German populations to one of the most ethnically homogeneous countries in the world.

In the decades after the war, Poles frequently agitated against communism, a form of government they bitterly resented. In 1956, 1968, 1970, 1976, 1980–1981, and 1988–1989, large-scale unrest broke out in Poland. The months of domestic strikes and protests in 1980–1981 spawned the creation of the Solidarity trade union under the leadership of Lech Walesa. In August 1980, the government signed an agreement with Solidarity allowing the independent trade union the right to strike and to print free publications. In December 1981, the government, with General Wojciech Jaruzelski at the helm, rescinded the agreement and banned Solidarity under the rule of martial law.

The government lifted martial law in 1983 but did not permit Solidarity to function officially until April 1989 when it agreed to Eastern Europe's first free parliamentary elections in 50 years. Solidarity overwhelmed the Communists in the June 1989 election, and by August, Solidarity journalist Tadeusz Mazowiecki took over as Poland's first non-Communist prime minister since World War II. The silver lining of freedom was soon to be tinged by dark economic thunder clouds. In 1990, the government embarked on a crash program to dismantle the Communist economy and introduce a free market–oriented capitalist system. While virtually all retail business was soon in private hands in Poland,

and a cornucopia of Western goods appeared in shops, prices rose dramatically, and as a result, the quality of life decreased substantially. Since economic change is slower than political restructuring, it was not possible to overcome rapidly the legacy of economic mismanagement and moribund bureaucracy so characteristic of the Communist economy. In December 1990, Poles elected former electrician Lech Walesa president. But three years later, in 1993, voters elected legislators who claimed that slowing the pace of reform, both economic and social, would soften the blows of transition.

The Exodus

Of all the Eastern European diasporas, the Polish is the biggest and one of the oldest. The first political exiles left after Poland was carved up by its neighbors in 1795. Most of them, however, went to Paris, not to America. In 1854, the first band of Poles who migrated "for bread" left Upper Silesia and struck out for east Texas, where they founded America's first Polish colony, Panna Maria, located 60 miles southwest of San Antonio. Farming colonies grew also in Missouri, Ohio, Indiana, Illinois, Arkansas, Oklahoma, and Minnesota. Rural Michigan drew seasonal agricultural workers from Detroit throughout the nineteenth century. By the end of the century, Polish immigrants began to take over abandoned and worn-out farmlands in the East. Poles worked as agricultural laborers in Connecticut, and Polish enclaves were established in the villages of Northampton, Greenfield, Hatfield, South Deerfield, and Sunderland, Massachusetts. In New Jersey and on Long Island, Poles took up truck farming, supplying the nearby urban market (Bukowczyk 1987).

The great period of Polish immigration to the United States began in the 1880s and lasted until the change in the American immigration law in 1924. The precise number of Poles who arrived in America during that interval is difficult to establish primarily because Poland was under foreign political domination during most of that time, and arriving immigrants were registered by country of residence, not by ethnicity. Thus, Polish immigrants were listed as Austrian, Austro-Hungarian, Russian, or German subjects.

The turn-of-the-century cohort consisted largely of labor migration predominantly from the peasant classes (Thomas and Znaniecki 1927; Radzialowski 1974; Golab 1977; Kleeman 1985). The group was characterized not only as being 90 percent peasant but also as being about one third illiterate, including people who looked to the church, and the parish priest in particular, for community leadership, guidance in their lives, and support in social, family and spiritual matters. The immigrants were mostly young men who imported their families, or went back to get them, after becoming established in a job and a community in the United States (Znaniecki Lopata 1976). Most settled in urban centers, near other Polish immigrants (Lieberson 1963). They tended to find work in industry. Hamtramck, Michigan, for example, attracted Poles from other settlements as the automobile industry expanded its needs for unskilled workers (Wood 1955).

The next wave of Poles arrived after World War II and the installation of Communist government in Poland. Between 1945 and 1969, approximately 162,000 Polish refugees came to the United States (U.S. Department of Justice 1969). These refugees were very different from their predecessors. The 1949 influx of 27,000 Poles (Znaniecki Lopata 1976), facilitated by the Displaced Persons Act, included primarily servicemen and others who refused to repatriate to Poland after the war, mainly for political reasons (Mostwin 1980). Poles who escaped Poland in the early 1950s were predominantly middle-class professionals. Many of them held university degrees or were highly skilled artisans (Goode and Schneider 1994). Because of their different backgrounds and experiences, these groups did not slip easily into the life of the Old Polonia as the Polish-Americans are called (Znaniecki Lopata 1976; Goode and Schneider 1994).

The 1968 wave included refugees expelled from Poland in that year after a series of student unrests and strikes as well as a number of people who came to the United States under the relaxed travel restrictions of the late 1960s and 1970s as Poland opened up to the West under the regime of Edward Gierek. Some of the latter émigrés intended to work in the United States to earn hard currency to be spent or invested in Poland. These "visitors" on temporary visas found employment within the working-class Polish ethnic communities of Chicago, Philadelphia, and New York. Some extended or overstayed their visas and remained illegally, while others were allowed to stay in the United States and work legally under the Extended Voluntary Departure (EVD) program.

The last wave were the post-Solidarity refugees (Goode and Schneider 1994). Polish refugees admitted under the Refugee Act of 1980 number more than 38,000, with the largest numbers having arrived in 1982 and 1983 (ORR 1993). This wave brought a fresh Polish presence to the United States. The newcomers included a number of young single men with skilled-craft backgrounds and young families in which the parents often came from the intelligentsia (Cichon, Gozdziak, and Grover 1986; Goode and Schneider 1994).

Arrival and Adaptation

The earliest arrivals from Poland might not have known a soul in this strange New World. Those who followed, on the other hand, might have received railroad tickets sent to them by their kin, been met by friends or relatives, or joined up with recruiters who would hasten them to their final destinations.

Polish immigrant farmers faced the challenge of life in a new land with the inevitable culture shock and adjustment to exotic and often difficult surroundings. The immigrants from Silesia who landed in Texas encountered foreign-looking Mexicans, and unfamiliar hot climate, and a wide diversity of new fauna and vegetation. They quickly learned, however, to rely upon wild game and corn, known to them as "Turkish wheat," and discovered new crops such as sweet potatoes. Few Polish newcomers grew cotton until after the Civil War, but Polish farm products did include corn, vegetables, cattle, oxen, pigs, and chickens. Incidentally, none of these Polish immigrants owned slaves (Bukowczyk 1987).

The Polish immigrants who arrived between the 1850s and 1880s took up farming because land in the West was still cheap. They considered themselves permanent settlers, and they wanted to put down roots in America. The Poles who came between the 1880s and World War I, on the other hand, confronted inflated land prices, high capital requirements, and low market prices for farm commodities (Bukowczyk 1987). They also viewed themselves as temporary sojourners and therefore eschewed farming and its inherent long-term commitment. Instead, they joined the ranks of unskilled laborers and went to work in the mines and factories of America's Second Industrial Revolution.

The first temporary sojourners were slow to adapt to America. They showed little upward mobility and lived in insular ethnic enclaves, trying to preserve their folk customs and peasant values oriented toward stability and family, security and steady work. Catholic to the core—their religion was a distinctive blend of magic and mysticism, rural superstition, and orthodox belief—they hoped for a better afterlife and venerated Matka Boska, the Blessed Virgin, Poland's patroness. Subsequent groups of Polish immigrants, although still mostly of rural background, represented a variety of types of peasants, differentiated by subclass, degree of urban influence, and region. They had "progressed from the first generation of largely uneducated former peasants living in poor, urban ethnic neighborhoods, to the financially well-off second generation that did not use higher education as a means of upward mobility and thus stayed in blue-collar jobs and life styles, to the increasingly educated third and fourth generations who can be expected to move up the socioeconomic ladder" (Znaniecki Lopata 1976: 116–117).

The post–World War II refugees present a distinctly different picture of adjustment and adaptation. The war did not exile only the elite of scholars, artists, and scientists. It uprooted thousands of Polish refugees—some fled Nazi oppression, others the Soviet "Iron Curtain" that fell over postwar Eastern Europe. Between the end of World War II and 1968, some 40,000 Polish ex-servicemen and underground insurgents came to the United States (Bukowczyk 1987). Unlike the Hungarian political refugees, most Polish displaced persons, whether they were veterans or not, did not come to America to continue political or ideological battles but to rebuild their own disrupted lives. They migrated as families and intended to stay here. Most of them were adults in their early middle age; about one third were infants, children, and adolescents, some of whom were orphans. They were resettled with sponsor families—not all Polish—throughout America but concentrated primarily in industrial states with large Polish-American communities: New York, New Jersey, Illinois, Connecticut, and Michigan.

Displaced children who came to the United States from Poland adjusted well, although traumatized orphans were often described by social workers as "undisciplined, unstable, primitive, even bestial, but longing for affection . . . precocious and hardened" (Korewa 1957: 58–59). In many cases, adults faced larger problems of transition and adjustment. Wrenching wartime experiences in labor and concentration camps, and later in refugee camps, had made them, according to one report, "sensitive, suspicious, and generally alert against real or imaginary threats to their dignity, security and welfare" (Heberle and Hall 1951: 3).

With scant information about the United States, gleaned mostly from literature, newspapers, movies, and American GIs, Polish refugees did not fit easily into American society. Because refugee policy favored persons with an agricultural background, many displaced Poles—most with urban backgrounds—lied in order to get into the country (Bukowczyk 1987). They soon found themselves placed in unsatisfying farm occupations for which they had no skills. Many left rural areas as soon as they could to search for higher wages (Heberle and Hall 1951). Middle-class refugees who made it into better-paying factory jobs, the only employment they were suited for, as they lacked English, felt declassé. Working-class people, artisans, and farmers fared better and integrated easily into blue-collar Polish America (Bukowczyk 1987; Znaniecki Lopata 1976).

Most Polish refugees of that era, however, fitted no better into Polonia than they did into mainstream America. Many shunned the older Polish-American working-class urban enclaves and gravitated toward suburbs. The intelligentsia rejected the lifestyle of working-class Polish-Americans, while older Polonia came to resent the displaced persons (or DPs as they were often called); felt jealous of their superior education, higher social status, and greater chances for upward mobility; and mockingly called them "princes," "barons," or "masters" because of their middle-class dress, educated speech, and predilection for Polish military titles. When the refugees attempted to speak for Polish America, older Polonians took offense because they expected to be followed, not to be led, by the newcomers (Bukowczyk 1987). The DPs, on the other hand, expected to assume the traditional class role that persons of their position had held in prewar Poland. They were dismayed by the "lack of respect for educated people" and shocked by the poor Polish spoken by the Polonians who retained peasant linguistic characteristics (Blejwas 1981).

More recent post-Solidarity refugees fit into Polish America no better than the displaced persons, perhaps even worse. However, their ambitions and good education fostered swift assimilation into the mainstream American society. They faced resentment from the Old Polonia, because their aspirations and lifestyles were different—European and more middle-class (Goode and Schneider 1994; Cichon, Gozdziak, and Grover 1986; Bukowczyk 1987). On their part, the newcomers criticized Americans and Polish-Americans for their "shallow view of freedom" (*Detroit Free Press* 1985). Exiled Solidarity activists were disheartened by the priorities of Polish-American ethnic leaders who found it more important to fight the proverbial Polish joke than to lend support to the new Polish cause (*New York Times* 1984).

While not very successful in getting along with the Old Polonia, the new-comers adjusted very well to mainstream America. They made a relatively rapid rise in occupational and socioeconomic status. They generally came to this country with a level of education comparable to or higher than that of an American secondary school. Usually, they had studied at least one foreign language and possessed a trade or professional skill. They either knew some English or learned it quickly, entered a trade related to their own, and advanced to a higher wage level and even supervisory positions within a few years. They were very ambitious and economically oriented and therefore highly motivated to work and move up the economic ladder. Among the Eastern Europeans surveyed by the Center for Applied Linguistics (CAL), Poles were the only ones who had more than one job at a time (Short 1988).

Almost all of the Polish refugees surveyed for the study of economic and social adjustment of Eastern Europeans, Afghans, and Ethiopians conducted in 1986 by the Research Management Corporation (RMC) for the federal Office of Refugee Resettlement (ORR) exhibited a substantial improvement over time in earnings and job status. They quickly moved into technical, administrative, sales, and skilled trade positions, often in the construction and manufacturing industries (Cichon, Gozdziak, and Grover 1986). All Polish refugees studied by RMC participated in the labor force and had equally high employment rates: 81 to 100 percent (Cichon, Gozdziak, and Grover 1986). Baker (1989) found that Poles settled in Boise, Idaho, were motivated, willing to work hard to get ahead, and committed to economic success. Even those who were not doing well economically were optimistic about their future economic position. Polish refugees in Philadelphia, especially those who secured employment in their fields, spent less time looking for their first job (anywhere from a couple of months to a year) than, for instance, Soviet Jews (anywhere from five months to five years) (Schneider 1988). Poles resettled in Dallas initially were working in service areas, such as housekeeping, dishwashing, and landscaping. In Chicago most initial positions held by Polish men were in building maintenance, construction, and factories, while women tended to have clerical jobs. Poles in New York City also obtained initial jobs in the service industry, but many also entered skilled and semiskilled trade positions in factories, sales, and administrative work (Cichon, Gozdziak, and Grover 1986). Goode and Schneider (1994) found that the newcomers from Poland who settled in Philadelphia worked as skilled craftspeople, in construction, in a variety of semiskilled service sector jobs, and sometimes in professional firms in the primary and secondary sectors. Poles studied by Baker in Boise, Idaho (1988, 1989) secured employment in a variety of low-income positions. The single largest employer was a producer of computer chips. Others worked as salesmen, janitors, auto mechanics, nurse's aides, and waiters. Some continued their crafts such as cabinet maker and barber. Five particularly successful males secured employment as computer programmers, but most professionals found their training to be nontransferable and exhibited less enthusiasm about their immigration experience than other types of workers. Seventy-five percent of the employed Polish refugees surveyed by RMC reported finding their jobs through informal referrals among acquaintances, 21 percent answered ads in newspapers or professional journals, and only one individual reported getting his job directly through a voluntary agency (Cichon, Gozdziak, and Grover 1986).

There was little variation in labor force participation by gender among the Polish refugees studied by RMC. The majority of both men and women worked. The exceptions were mothers of children under the age of six who had child care responsibilities (Cichon, Gozdziak, and Grover 1986). Baker's analysis (1988, 1989) demonstrates that the Polish refugee women in Boise were more likely to have lower economic status and lower-paying jobs. Fifty percent of the women in his study did not work outside the home. Most of the younger married females were seeking additional training. The most popular vocational goal of the refugee women was nursing.

Two years after the completion of the RMC study, I interviewed a number of the surveyed refugees by telephone (Gozdziak 1989) and found that the prospects for long-term self-sufficiency had increased even further. Many respondents had received promotions, found better jobs, completed recertification processes, or obtained additional skills (e.g., word processing, computer programming). The one subgroup that had more difficulty with rapid entry into the American labor force were the highly skilled professionals, doctors, and lawyers. In contrast, their less-educated countrymen, who had easily transferable skills (carpenters, masons, electronic technicians, etc.), were making the transition into the U.S. labor market far more rapidly (Gozdziak 1989).

In the mid-1980s, refugees from Poland had the lowest use of public assistance of all refugees resettled in the United States, at roughly 14 percent (ORR 1986). Use of public assistance among Poles was relatively low in the three sites visited by the RMC research team. In Dallas, no member of the sample had ever used welfare, partly because Texas provisions were inadequate for support. RMC reported that almost all Polish refugees were self-sufficient and attained that status within a fairly short period of time: between two weeks and 3 months. In Chicago and New York City, however, this positive picture of self-sufficiency was disrupted in some cases. After a year or two of being self-supporting, many Poles decided to go on public assistance. Data on refugee cash and medical assistance in Cook County indicate that Poles used assistance very little in the early months after arrival but used it considerably more in the 7 to 12 and 13 to 18 months after arrival. The explanation of the 7–12 months surge may be that the alternative resettlement project in Chicago prevented its clients, which included Polish refugees, from utilizing welfare during the first 6 months after arrival. However, the second surge, at 13 to 18 months, appeared to be a result of disillusionment with unsatisfactory jobs, layoffs, and adjustment difficulties after the initial novelty wore off (Cichon, Gozdziak, and Grover 1986).

There was controversy among service providers regarding the Polish refugees' attitudes toward adjustment. Some staff, usually representatives of the Old Polonia, claimed that the newcomers from Poland had unrealistic expectations of the lifestyles they should lead in the United States, that they wanted welfare and schooling provided for them until they could get the high-status jobs they held in Poland, and that they would accept nothing that came from thrift stores. Other service providers saw the same characteristics as sources of pride and motivation that prompted the Poles to pursue professional recertification and strive for economic and social self-sufficiency (Cichon, Gozdziak, and Grover 1986).

Overall, most recent newcomers from Poland experienced an initial period of disillusionment, followed by gradual adjustment to life in America. Initial adjustment problems included loneliness, sadness at separation from family, and depression. Coming from an extremely homogeneous society, many Poles experienced anxiety about the ethnic and racial diversity of American cities. Their initial insecurities were also exacerbated by the instability of employment in the United States and the lack of free health care, social welfare, and retirement benefits. Despite the initial adjustment problems, most Poles adapted well to their new lives in the United States, moving over time into middle-class neighborhoods and working and socializing in the broader American society.

HUNGARIANS

The Country

Hungary is a mostly flat country located in the Carpathian Basin, surrounded by mountainous neighboring countries. The two major rivers cutting through Hungary are the Danube and the Tisza. Bordered by the Czech and Slovak Republics, Austria, Romania, Serbia, Slovenia, Croatia, and Ukraine, Hungary is enveloped largely by Slavs. A small country of 35,000 square miles, the size of Indiana, Hungary is inhabited by about 11 million people. Hungary is relatively ethnically homogeneous. Some 93 percent of the population call themselves Magyars, descendants of nomadic plains people, and speak a Finno-Ugric language, most closely related to Finnish and Turkish. Gypsies make up the largest minority group. Other minorities include Germans, Slovaks, Croats, and Romanians. Along with Poland, Hungary is an eastern outpost of Roman Catholicism, a faith adopted by King Stephen in A.D. 1000. Today some 67 percent of the population remains Roman Catholic, with 20 percent Calvinist and 5 percent Lutheran (Heinrich 1986).

History and Politics

The Hungarians were the last of the major peoples of Eastern Europe to appear in the region. When the Magyar tribes, originally from the Asian side of the Ural Mountains, numbering around 250,000 people, took possession of the

Carpathian Basin at the end of the ninth century, they already had a sophisticated tribal organization and a distinct linguistic and cultural identity. Skilled horsemen who depended on pastures and spoils of war for survival, they quickly broke the resistance of the Slavic plowmen and, under the leadership of their chief, Arpad, easily subjugated the established Slavic tribes. This historical process is reflected in the vocabulary of modern Hungarians, whose agricultural terms are mostly of Slavic origin.

The successful conquest of the Danube Valley generated confidence, and the Magyars began to raid westward. By A.D. 924 they plundered as far as Champagne in what is now France. However, the Germans stopped their westward expansion in 955, and that forced the Magyars to settle permanently in Pannonia. In 1000 Arpad's great-great-grandson accepted Christianity and was crowned as King Stephen I. From the very beginning, the Hungarian state was inhabited by non-Magyars as the so-called crownlands of St. Stephen included Slovakia, Croatia, and Transylvania.

In 1241, Odgai, the son of Genghis Khan, and his "Golden Horde" (i.e., the Mongols) charged through and rampaged Hungary for two years. In the wake of the invasion, King Bela IV began serious fortification of Buda Hills, a project that continued until the middle of the nineteenth century. During the reign of Bela IV, Hungary became increasingly powerful and expanded into neighboring lands. When the last king of the Arpad dynasty died without an heir in 1301, a series of foreign-born kings held sway over Hungary as enemies slowly whittled down the empire. The threat of Ottoman invasion in the middle of the fifteenth century, however, galvanized the stagnant country. A Hungarian nobleman, Janos Hunyadi, led the Christian forces to a monumental victory over the Ottoman Turks in 1456 near modern-day Belgrade. His son, Matthias Corvinus, was crowned king in 1458. Under his rule, Hungary experienced a golden age of artistic and intellectual development. After his death, scheming nobles and an unsuccessful peasant revolt in 1514 considerably weakened Hungary. The Ottoman armies again swept north up the Danube and in 1526 defeated the Hungarians in the Battle of Mohacs. The Ottoman forces captured the fortified city of Buda in 1541, and an Ottoman pasha reined in Buda until Habsburg-led troops crushed the Turks in 1686, put down a rebellion led by Ferenc Rakoczi, and ruled Hungary from Vienna. The Habsburg emperor was the new master.

The early 1800s saw renewed attempts to regain independence from Habsburg Austria. These efforts culminated in the revolution of 1848, which proclaimed a separate Hungarian state, and was only put down after the Austrian government received help from Russian troops in 1849. A more stable settlement came with the Compromise of 1867, masterminded by Ferenc Deak, which recognized Hungary's independent status within the Habsburg Austro-Hungarian empire. Under the Compromise of 1867, Hungary, and especially its major city, Budapest, experienced rapid economic and cultural growth. The prosperity ended with the outbreak of World War I, the resulting defeat of the Habsburgs, and the division of the empire. Under the Treaty of Trianon, two thirds of Hungarian territory were distributed among Serbia, Croatia, Slovakia, Ukraine, and particularly Romania, which gained Transylvania. While the Treaty of Trianon accorded independence to some 10 million non-Magyars, it also severed 3 million ethnic Hungarians from their homeland, dooming many to oppression, discrimination, and violation of human rights under regimes committed to ethnic homogeneity, especially the ethnic cleansing policies of Ceauşescu's Romania. Hungary's misery was exacerbated by a bloody power struggle between Communist and rightist forces at the end of World War I, followed by the Great Depression that engulfed the whole continent. Power fell to the conservative forces led by Admiral Miklos Horthy, whose principal policy became the recovery of the territories lost at Trianon. This led to an alliance with Germany during World War II.

The country's occupation by Soviet forces after World War II resulted in the formation of a Communist government. In 1956, reformist currents appearing throughout Eastern Europe encouraged increased Hungarian opposition to the stifling presence of the Communist regime. On October 23, 1956, a mass meeting in front of the Budapest radio station was dispersed with gunfire. The result was a 13-day "Hungarian Uprising," which, in the early morning of November 4, was met by the armed forces of the Warsaw Pact and Soviet tanks. About 2,000 people died in the uprising, and approximately 200,000 Hungarians fled the country, seeking refuge in the West.

After order was brutally restored, Janos Kadar, the new Soviet-backed leader, slowly introduced economic reform. As a result, Hungary became one of the most prosperous and liberal of all Eastern European countries. The most significant of the reforms was the New Economic Mechanism (NEM) introduced in 1968. NEM decentralized many aspects of the economy and fostered limited forms of private enterprise. Political reform followed in the 1980s. In May 1989, six months before the fall of the Berlin Wall, Hungary began dismantling portions of the barbed-wire frontier with Austria, thus becoming the first country to create a gap in the Iron Curtain. A few days later, Janos Kadar was ousted after 33 years in power. In September, the government decided to let thousands of East Germans flee to the West through Hungary. The decision prompted an exodus of some 57,000 East Germans and eventually forced a desperate East German government to open the Berlin Wall.

The first free elections since World War II were held in April 1990 and resulted in a total defeat of the Communists. Unfortunately, like its neighbors, Hungary found life after communism difficult. By the mid-1990s, shops were full and new businesses booming, but unemployment was on the rise. Hungary's relationship with Slovakia was tainted by the aborted dam project at Nagyamaros, and relations with Romania were strained by unresolved minority issues.

The Exodus

Until very recently, Hungary was an emigration rather than an immigration country. Four distinct periods of Hungarian immigration to the United States can be identified. Within each of these periods, different waves can be distinguished. The first and the largest Hungarian immigration to America commenced in the mid-1800s and lasted until the end of World War I (Dovenyi and Vukovich 1994; Huseby-Darvas 1995). While the early wave was characterized as labor migration (Dovenyi and Vukovich 1994; Huseby-Darvas 1995), the importance of political, social, and cultural factors cannot be omitted, given the ethnic composition of the early cohort. Ethnic minorities were more likely to emigrate than ethnic Hungarians; there is evidence that entire ethnic rural communities sought refuge in the United States (Dovenyi and Vukovich 1994).

The second, interwar influx of Hungarian immigrants began a movement of political expatriates (Benkart 1980). It was numerically much smaller, as the flows of all Eastern Europeans were greatly reduced both by restrictive immigration policies and by the Great Depression. Despite these limitations, in the five-year period between 1922 and 1927, an estimated 70,000 ethnic Hungarians arrived in the United States: 40,000 from Hungary and 30,000 from neighboring territories (Dovenyi and Vukovich 1994).

The third, post–World War II period included four distinct waves of political refugees. The first wave consisted of some 16,000 displaced persons, including former concentration camp inmates and members of the retreating Hungarian army, who did not want to return to Hungary after the end of the war (Vardy 1985). The 45-ers, as they were also called, constitute the core of the postwar trans-Atlantic migration. The DPs were followed by a second wave of the so-called 47-ers, most of whom actually fled Hungary between 1947 and 1949. The elite among them were those political emigrants who participated in the various postwar coalition governments of Hungary but were eventually pushed out by the Communists. This wave included leaders and members of the Smallholder Party, the National Peasant Party, and the Social Democratic Party. The political elite among the 47-ers was followed by thousands of politically less exposed Hungarians who left their homeland between 1947 and the mid-1950s largely because of their growing disenchantment with the oppressive regime. Altogether, between the end of World War II and the Hungarian Revolution of 1956, 26,532 Hungarian refugees entered the United States (Vardy 1985).

In 1957, some 38,000 Hungarians, the vast majority of whom were young students, professionals, intellectuals, and scientists, were admitted to the United States under the Hungarian Parole Program. The period between the early 1960s and late 1980s saw another wave of Hungarian refugees in America, the so-called orphans of Kadar and Ceauşescu. The latter were ethnic Hungarians from Transylvania fleeing Romanian ethnic cleansing and villagization programs. These cohorts were not as numerous as their predecessors; according to the

Office of Refugee Resettlement, approximately 6,000 refugees from Hungary were resettled under the Refugee Act of 1980 (ORR 1993).

Arrival and Adaptation

All of the different waves of Hungarian immigration to the United States occurred in various political and social contexts and were characterized by diverse push-and-full factors, varied scope and destination, and distinct educational levels and social backgrounds impacting both people's desire and ability to adapt to the ways of the host society (Huseby-Darvas 1995).

Like other Eastern Europeans who arrived in the United States at the turn of the century, the Hungarian immigrants were, for the most part, unskilled agrarian laborers who came to America with the intention of saving money and returning to Hungary to improve their economic and social standing there. Broken families, with men outnumbering women, poor living conditions in overcrowded boarding houses, and hard work characterized the life of most Hungarian immigrants around the turn of the century.

At the outbreak of World War I, most Hungarians abandoned the idea of returning home; the "sojourners" became permanent immigrants. They settled mostly near the mines and steel furnaces of Ohio, Pennsylvania, New York, and New Jersey. However, large groups also settled in Illinois, Indiana, Michigan, and West Virginia (Szeplaki 1975; Huseby-Darvas 1995). Some cities and towns developed large Hungarian-American colonies that were much more noticeable than those in scattered mining camps. New York, Cleveland, Pittsburgh, and Chicago, in particular, counted many thousands of Hungarians among their vast immigrant populations. Smaller Hungarian settlements developed in Bridgeport, Connecticut, New Brunswick and Passaic, New Jersey, South Bend, Indiana, and Youngstown, Ohio (Benkart 1980).

While most of the early-immigrants came as unskilled workers, some gradually worked their way into skilled factory positions, after becoming familiar with industrial routines in the American mines and mills. The few women in the early Hungarian settlements went into partnership with their husbands as boardinghouse keepers. In 1910, for example, half of the Hungarian couples in the United States were taking in boarders (Benkart 1980). Opening small businesses in America required capital the sojourners did not have or did not want to invest. However, as their repatriation plans were abandoned, some opened meat markets and spice shops; others began to take interest in union organization to improve working conditions and to protect job security.

As permanent immigrants, Hungarians in the 1920s were willing to invest in building an American ethnic community. Separated from their homeland, they could no longer take their religious, linguistic, and cultural heritage for granted. Their concern for their homeland as expressed in fund-raising efforts to support Hungarian prisoners of war and maintenance of religious and cultural legacies (symbolized by their patronage of Hungarian churches) was combined with a greater interest in American politics. Although in 1920 fewer than a third of Hungarian immigrants were citizens of the United States, by the end of that decade, a majority of them were naturalized (Benkart 1980).

The interwar and post–World War II cohorts were quite unlike the older generation of immigrants both in their urban background and in the nature and intensity of their political convictions. The interwar immigrants included mostly middle-class business and professional people. Among them were four internationally acclaimed scientists—John von Neuman, Leo Szilard, Edward Teller, and Nobel laureate Eugene Wigner—as well as four future conductors of American symphony orchestras—Antal Dorati, Eugene Ormandy, Fritz Reiner, and George Szell. Composer Bela Bartok and novelist Ferenc Molnar both arrived in 1940 (Benkart 1980). Initially, some experienced downward mobility, but eventually most succeeded economically. In Cleveland during the 1920s, Hungarians began moving into better residential areas, a trend that the depression stalled only temporarily.

Although the DPs and the 47-ers were divided from each other only by a few years, they represented two different worlds that could hardly be expected to get along. Many of the DPs experienced downward social mobility. Classical training, unmarketable in America, diplomas from military academies, doctorates in Hungarian law, and an inability to speak English forced many of them to accept menial jobs in shops and factories. Former high-ranking judges, for instance, became unskilled workers in Detroit's automobile industry (Huseby-Darvas 1995). The artisans and shopkeepers fared much better and became skilled workers or shop owners.

The 47-ers, particularly the prominent personalities among them, were in a much better position. Not only were they not tainted as being pro-Nazi, they were held up as representatives of the Western-type democracy in Hungary and thus enjoyed the political and financial support of the American government. Upon arrival, many of them were given important positions in America's cold war institutions such as the Free Europe Committee and Radio Free Europe (Vardy 1985).

The 56-ers were possibly the most successful in their economic and social adaptation in the United States. They were a product of a powerful social transformation that had taken place before the revolution. The majority of the refugees were single men in their late teens, early twenties, or thirties. They were either students or at the outset of their professional careers. Their education was very practical and progressive; there were many engineers and medical doctors among them. Their practical training opened good prospects for them in American industrial establishments or in technical colleges and universities, and their lack of strong national sentiments fostered swift assimilation. They were the first to marry non-Hungarians in large numbers, and they consciously severed ties to Hungarian-American communities and organizations, perhaps with the exception of the church.

However, their achievements not only resulted from their demographic and

personal characteristics but were also nurtured by the reception of the host society. The publicity about the Hungarian Uprising encouraged American society
to think about those who were affected by the dramatic events as worthy of
assistance; the result was an outpouring of public support and generosity and a
very remarkable resettlement program. In November 1956, the National Academy of Sciences formally resolved to accord assistance to its Hungarian colleagues who might come to the United States, recognizing that as the minimum
assistance due to those who risked their lives on behalf of the fundamental
principles of freedom (Forbes 1988). As the newcomers arrived, the academy's
staff matched the individual aspirations and capabilities of the refugees with
positions in the academic or industrial world of the United States that would
enable them to contribute their particular talents to American society. The rationale for the special program was not to give advantage to the newly arrived
scientists or engineers but to eliminate some of the obstacles confronting the
refugees who arrived without resources, friends, or contacts, and who often had
no knowledge of English and lacked familiarity with the procedures for finding
a position in their professions in America. The objective of the academy's program was to enable the newcomers to become integrated into their local and
professional communities as quickly as possible. It is a pity that this approach
was not incorporated into the resettlement programs developed for other Eastern
European refugees under the Refugee Act of 1980.

ROMANIANS

The Country

Located on the Balkan Peninsula, Romania borders the newly independent
state of Moldova to the east, Ukraine to the north, Hungary and Serbia to the
west, and Bulgaria to the south. Much of Romania is mountainous or hilly, with
the Carpathian Mountains and Transylvanian Alps stretching across about a third
of the country from the north to the southwest. Victim of successive waves of
invaders, Romania has seen its borders change countless times over the course
of history. In modern times, as a result of the Treaty of Trianon signed after
World War I, Romania received the much-disputed Transylvania, home for some
3 million ethnic Hungarians. After World War II, Romania lost Bessarabia to
the Soviet Union. The country, about the size of Great Britain, has a population
of 23 million, of whom 90 percent are Romanians. The 10 percent who constitute Romania's ethnic minorities are Hungarian, German, Serbian, Turkish,
Ukrainian, Jewish, and Roma (Gypsies).

Romanians vociferously distance themselves from their Slavic, Magyar, and
Balkan neighbors, emphasizing instead the connection with imperial Rome.
They speak a language that sounds a bit like Italian, if not vernacular Latin, and
use the Latin alphabet—where one might expect Cyrillic script, since Orthodoxy

is a predominant religion. They claim to be Roman by descent and place much emphasis on this pedigree.

History and Politics

The Thracians, the ancestors of modern Romanians, inhabited ancient Romania as early as the sixth century B.C. The Romans came to conquer and colonize the newly consolidated Dacian empire in A.D. 106. Intense Romanization of the area over the next 200 years had a strong impact on its language and other aspects of Dacian culture. The Romans withdrew in A.D. 271 under the onslaught of invading barbarian tribes, but the Dacians retained Roman culture and the Latin language. From the third to the tenth century, successive waves of Goths, Slavs, Huns, Bulgars, and Magyars continued to invade the Dacians. Orthodox Christianity was brought in by the Bulgars in 846. By the early Middle Ages, the three states comprising present-day Romania—Transylvania, Wallachia, and Moldavia—formed separate feudal kingdoms. Continual Turkish occupation separated and dominated them for hundreds of years.

In 1600 the three Romanian states were briefly united, but it was not until 1862 that Alexandru Ion Cuza created a nation-state by joining Wallachia and Moldavia. In 1866, Alexandru abdicated and was replaced by Prussian Prince Charles Hohenzollern Siegmaringen. Prince Charles became King Carol I by a unanimous vote in 1881 and was crowned in the Bucharest Cathedral. After World War I, when the Austro-Hungarian empire was defeated, Transylvania was returned to Romania and joined Wallachia and Moldavia to form a new state. During World War II, the fascist Romanian Iron Guard ousted King Carol II, and Romania entered the war alongside the Axis.

On December 30, 1947, King Michael flew into exile, and Romania became a socialist state under the rule of Gheorghe Gheorghiu-Dej. Gheorghiu-Dej supported the Soviet suppression of the 1956 uprisings in Poland and Hungary, although soon afterwards he started edging toward an isolationist tack that took Romania out of Moscow's direct sphere of influence but was not less loyal to the precepts of Stalinism. In 1962, Romania stopped participating in Warsaw Pact military maneuvers. Gheorghiu-Dej died suddenly in March 1965 and was replaced by a seemingly gray little man who had worked his way up the Communist Party ladder by never rocking the boat. This was Nicolae Ceauşescu. Ceauşescu continued Romania's maverick foreign policy, condemning the Soviet invasion of Czechoslovakia in 1968. In 1984, Romania sent athletes to the Los Angeles Olympics, even though the rest of the Soviet bloc boycotted the games.

Despite the relative flexibility of its foreign policy, Communist Romania maintained one of Eastern Europe's most rigid and repressive societies. The realities of life for ordinary citizens have been compared to George Orwell's *Nineteen Eighty-four*. A vast police state grew to monitor its citizens, all forms of birth control were illegal, conversations with foreigners were suspect, and the

Ceauşescu personality cult was indescribable. Ceauşescu's economic policies, especially his obsessive attempt to rid the country of foreign debt, caused immeasurable hardship. He exported absolutely everything that could fetch hard currency, including food and oil, and correspondingly slashed imports. Once the "breadbasket of the Balkans," Romania emerged as the "basket case of the region." When Mikhail Gorbachev's reforms offered new economic hope for Eastern Europe in the mid-1980s, Ceauşescu remained the region's staunchest opponent of change, declaring perestroika to be in total contradiction to socialist principles.

Scattered public protests began to surface in 1987, and in the city of Brasov that year, they amounted to a riot. The anger of the Romanian people finally boiled over when security forces killed hundreds of pro-democracy demonstrators in the western city of Timisoara in December 1989. Protests spread across the country, and the army revolted against Ceauşescu. The bitter fighting that erupted in Bucharest and other Romanian cities was some of the worst seen in Europe since World War II. On Christmas Day, 1989, Ceauşescu and his wife, Elena, were executed.

In the first free postwar elections in May 1990, Romanians gave an overwhelming 89 percent support to the National Salvation Front and Ion Iliescu— a former Communist and Ceauşescu ally who helped lead the revolution. Despite the seemingly fair election, protests against the government continued through 1990, including a 53-day-long spring occupation of University Square in Bucharest. In June 1990, the Interior Ministry forces cleared away these protesters, killing several demonstrators and wounding hundreds. The following day, with the approval of the government, 7,000 miners swept through the streets to beat antigovernment protesters. In October 1990, the government accelerated its plans to introduce a free market economy by removing price subsidies and devaluing its currency. Protests and calls for the government to resign continued after these announcements.

Unlike elsewhere in Eastern Europe, political and economic reform proceeded very slowly in Romania. As indicated by the fall 1992 election, many of Ceauşescu's legacies, attitudes, and institutions remained intact. Romania continues to have the lowest standard of living in the region after Albania. An unemployment rate of 30 percent, inflation of over 300 percent, and frozen salaries cause much suffering and economic dislocation. It may take decades to recover from the consequences of Ceauşescu's regime that left the economy destroyed, the country polluted, and the people destitute from exploitation and numb from years of repression.

The Exodus

There were virtually no Romanians in America before 1870. Romanian immigration to the United States mounted between 1870 and 1900 when, according to one source, some 18,000 Romanian citizens entered the United States (Bob-

ango 1980). Another source estimated the number at 22,000 (Wertsman 1975).
In the next decade the number of Romanians increased to 62,153 and continued
at the rate of 27,000 per annum for the next four years, dropping to approximately 4,500 during World War I (Bobango 1980). However, until 1895 almost
all of them were Jews from Moldavia, Bessarabia, and Bukovina. Ethnic Romanians started arriving after 1895. They were mostly peasants from Transylvania, and a few Macedonian Romanians from the European parts of Turkey,
northern Greece, and Albania.

By 1920 an estimated 85,000 Romanians had come to the United States (Bobango 1980). These statistics, however, are tenuous at best. The majority of Romanians, approximately 85 percent, were from Transylvania, Bukovina, or the
Banat. These territories were not a part of the Romanian kingdom until 1918.
Therefore, many arrivals, although ethnically Romanian, were counted as Hungarians, Austrians, or Russians. As late as 1923, the "country of origin" designation used by the Immigration and Naturalization Service (INS) was based
on pre–World War I boundaries, which further confuses the figures.

The years 1920–1924 saw another influx of Romanians who hurried to reach
America before immigration restrictions closed the door. The Immigration Act
of 1924 set a Romanian quota of approximately 1,000 persons per year. Worldwide economic depression contributed to a further decline in immigration rates.
At the end of 1940, there were 115,940 Romanians living in the United States,
61,596 male and 54,344 female (Anagnastosache 1944). Approximately 10,000
Romanians entered the United States under the Displaced Persons Act of 1949.
A 30-year hiatus followed. The most recent wave of Romanian refugees came
to the United States in the early and mid-1980s, when about 40,200 Romanians
were resettled under the provisions of the Refugee Act of 1980 (ORR 1993).

Romanians were driven from their homeland by political, economic, and social conditions. Motivations for leaving home were many, including seeking
refuge from forced Magyarization and conversion to Catholicism in Transylvania, evading military service in the Austro-Hungarian army, escaping agricultural exploitation, and more recently, fleeing the Communist regime of
Nicolae Ceauşescu.

Arrival and Settlement

Unlike the pre-1895 Romanian immigrants who arrived in America with their
families, most of those who came afterward were single men between the ages
of 18 and 45. The vast majority were unskilled and only semiliterate laborers.
Not all Romanians came to the United States to stay. Some, particularly those
who arrived before 1920, intended to return home after saving enough money
to buy land and improve their economic and social standing in their native
villages. Approximately two thirds of the early arrivals returned home. Repatriation was especially high after World War I when many saw their native lands
incorporated into the Romanian kingdom (Bobango 1980).

Romanians settled in the industrial heartland of the mid-Atlantic and Great Lakes, establishing ethnic enclaves in New York, Philadelphia, Pittsburgh, Chicago, Detroit, and Cleveland. Few Romanians settled in the West or South before the 1960s, when many retired to California and some to Florida. On the other hand, Los Angeles and Orange County, California, proved to be a magnet for the largest group of Romanian refugees fleeing Ceauşescu's Romania.

There was a considerable secondary migration among the early Romanian immigrants. Single industrial workers would often remain in one city for a year or two, moving on to a different urban center in search of better-paying jobs. The second location sometimes became permanent, but a third or fourth move was not uncommon. This transitory lifestyle was abandoned once families arrived. The villages that produced the earliest and most numerous migrations were ethnically mixed. Romanians were thus used to living in diversified neighborhoods, and it was not unusual to find Romanians in America residing alongside Poles, Slovaks, and Russians.

The political refugees who arrived in the United States in the 1980s present a very different picture than their compatriots from the early part of the century. The older settlers call the newcomers *Noi-veniti* (newly arrived) and find that they have very little in common with them (Bobango 1980). The recent refugees tend to be better educated and far more politically aware than the earlier immigrants, who remain largely ignorant of current Romanian issues. The newcomers resettled primarily in New York City, Chicago, and Los Angeles. The majority were married adults in their twenties and thirties. The most common households were nuclear families with one to three children, although in Chicago the number of children was generally quite high, as the Windy City received quite a few Pentecostal families (Cichon, Gozdziak, and Grover 1986).

The educational levels of this cohort were fairly high. College graduates among those surveyed by RMC included some 45 percent in Los Angeles, 53 percent in New York City, and 11 percent in Chicago. Consistent with their educational backgrounds, the work experience of Romanians in Los Angeles and New York City was largely professional, including architecture, engineering, accounting, education, and medicine. While Chicago had its share of professionals, the majority were skilled tradesmen (Cichon, Gozdziak, and Grover 1986). Romanians' knowledge of English upon arrival followed the pattern of their educational backgrounds. Those in Chicago had little knowledge of English, with fewer than 5 percent claiming to know it reasonably well, while 30 and 24 percent of those in Los Angeles and New York City, respectively, reported knowing English well upon arrival (Cichon, Gozdziak, and Grover 1986).

Economic and Social Adaptation

Economic assimilation and ensuing upward social mobility were rapid among the early immigrant arrivals from Romania. By 1914 they accumulated enough capital to become small entrepreneurs, owners of restaurants, boardinghouses, saloons, pool halls, and immigrant banks. By the early 1920s traditional large families were disappearing. Fewer children, the acquisition of property, and willingness to finance their children's education may partially account for the early prosperity of this group.

There were three distinct groups among the early Romanian immigrants: (1) Those who lived in ethnic neighborhoods and whose lives centered around the factory, beneficial society, and the church; (2) those, mostly second generation, who moved away from the urban colonies into suburbs and detached themselves from Romanian culture; and (3) those who spent their workday in the old neighborhood and their leisure hours and Sundays at Romanian clubs and churches but chose to live elsewhere (Bobango 1980). The early Romanian immigrants quickly realized the need to assimilate into the larger American society. They sent their children to public schools to increase their exposure to mainstream America, reserving the role of parish schools to assist in the retention of Romanian language and culture. They also married outside the group, even crossing religious boundaries.

Two institutions, the boardinghouse and the mutual benefit society, have been credited with easing the transition between the Old and the New World. The boardinghouse provided camaraderie and helped perpetuate old ways: ethnic foods, musical traditions, and folkways. Because of the reluctance to use American banks, the boardinghouse boss served as custodian to the lodgers' savings, acted as agent for sending money home, and purchased their steamship tickets. The boardinghouse was a forerunner of the later widespread and colorful combination of saloon, pool hall, steamship agency, and money-lending and savings establishment known as the immigrant bank. The boardinghouse as an institution lasted well into the 1930s (Bobango 1980).

In 1902, Romanians in Cleveland organized a mutual benefit society called Carpatina (The Carpathian), and the following year the Vulturaul (Eagle) Romanian Society of Assistance and Culture was established in Homestead, Pennsylvania. The next decade saw the rapid proliferation of similar societies. They were organized along the lines of small insurance companies and were directly controlled by the policyholders' representatives (Wertsman 1975; Bobango 1980).

Economic adaptation of the most recent wave of Romanian refugees was as rapid as that of the earlier arrivals. Seventy-five to 95 percent of the newcomers participated in the labor force, and they had equally high (75 percent) employment rates. The survey of Romanian refugees conducted by CAL indicated that most of the refugees started working within 6 months of their arrival in the United States. The percentage rose from 69 percent in months 1 to 6 to 74 percent in months 7 to 18. Of those refugees who worked at the time of the survey, almost 70 percent found their first jobs within 3 months of arrival in this country (Short 1988). The majority of Romanians secured employment in building maintenance, factories, merchandise delivery or warehousing, and construction, with only slight variation in pattern across sites. In New York City some professionals obtained initial jobs in fields related to their own but at a lower skill level than they had practiced in Romania. For example, civil engineers worked as draftsmen and designers (Cichon, Gozdziak, and Grover 1986).

Most initial jobs paid between $3.35 and $8.00 per hour. However, Romanians with trade skills and reasonable ability in the English language earned markedly better wages. They sometimes landed jobs for $6.00 to $10.00 per hour soon after arrival in the United States (Cichon, Gozdziak, and Grover 1986; Short 1988). The RMC study indicates that Romanians who had initial wages of $5.00 per hour increased their earnings to approximately $6.50 per hour to $12.00 per hour within their first two years in the United States. Romanians made a relatively rapid rise in occupational and socioeconomic status. Those who advanced rapidly generally had smaller families; those who did not progress so swiftly had larger families and less education and were generally members of the Fundamentalist religious sects (Gozdziak 1989).

Concomitant with the high levels of labor force participation was a rather high but fairly short use of welfare among Romanians studied by RMC. Those in Los Angeles showed the highest usage level, with approximately 70 percent of the sample using it at some point in the three years studied. However, the majority used public assistance from 6 to 18 months. In Chicago, about 60 percent of Romanians reported using public assistance, but their use averaged under 7 months. Those who did stay on for longer periods of time were the elderly or those with larger families and only one employable adult. The New York City levels were much the same as in Chicago, but the reasons given for the longer-term use of public assistance focused more on needing support while refugees went to school to study English or pursued advanced degrees and professional recertification (Cichon, Gozdziak, and Grover 1986).

Approximately three fourths of the Romanians surveyed by RMC became self-sufficient within their first three years in the United States. This proportion was consistent across the sites studied. However, the length of time it took to become self-supporting varied across cities. In Chicago and New York City, it took the Romanians on average 2 to 6 months to become self-sufficient, while in Los Angeles it was 12 months, with a considerable number of families remaining on welfare for 18 to 24 months. As was the case with labor force participation, those with no trade skills, large families with young children, and poor English skills depended on public assistance the longest (Gozdziak 1989).

Social interactions of Romanian refugees, both among themselves and with the larger American society, defy easy characterization. It appeared that about half of the sample examined by RMC socialized very little, even within their own community. This lack of social ties was most often attributed to the fact that they were working so hard that they had little leisure time, and to rumors of spies sent by Bucharest to the United States to disrupt the refugee community and report on individuals. The latter perception was a unique barrier to the formation of any sense of trust among the newcomers. However, despite the fact that the larger Romanian community was divided, the bonds between family members and fellow church members were strong. The strength of those bonds contributed to the economic success of many Romanian families.

The newness of post–World War II Romanian immigration to the United States and the lack of commonalities between the Romanian-Americans and newcomers from Romania mean that there are few established Romanian institutions to which recent refugees can turn for community support. The activities of the Iuliu Maniu Foundation in New York, the orthodox Brotherhood, Romanian Welfare, Inc., and the Cultural Association for Romanians and Americans of Romanian Descent are very modest (Bobango 1980) and not always sensitive to the needs of the newcomers. Romanians surveyed by RMC reported difficulties finding help in upgrading their skills and identifying recertification and professional training programs. Staff in service agencies were unable to refer them or provide information about résumé banks, professional associations, or other mainstream services (Cichon, Gozdziak, and Grover 1986). Employment services were also of little help to large Romanian Pentecostal families, particularly those with small children and without easily transferable skills. Employment programs were set up to serve the breadwinner, rather than an entire household. Planning for household self-sufficiency, employment counselors did not apply multiple-wage-earner strategies and failed to realize that employment of a single family member was not sufficient to take large households out of poverty.

PROSPECTS

For the most part, the research provides good news—most Eastern European refugees and immigrants attain jobs within the first six months to a year in the United States, with many of them going to work even earlier. The prospects for long-term self-sufficiency are also good. With few exceptions, the majority of Eastern European households are moving out of poverty within the first two years. As their English-language proficiency increases with time in the country, many are able to obtain jobs in fields related to their professional background. The research indicates also that Eastern European refugees have been a tremendous resource for the local communities in which they resettled. Interviews with employers who had a long history of hiring Eastern Europeans yielded very positive comments about refugees as employees and their contribution to the local labor markets. Employers had to stretch to find enough adjectives of praise for their refugee employees—"hard working," "reliable," "honest," and "the best workers we have" were commonplace (Gozdziak 1989).

Although the majority are becoming economically self-reliant, the road to long-term self-sufficiency is considerably more difficult for Eastern Europeans with large families and young children and without easily transferable skills. Eastern Europeans who are advancing rapidly are "making it" not because of, but rather despite, a resettlement system that, on the whole, has not responded to the needs of this population. Service systems, as well as state and federal policies, tend to continue to focus—sometimes almost exclusively—on Southeast Asian refugees, even though the last decade saw an increased proportion of new arrivals from other parts of the world.

It would be impossible to write about Eastern European refugees in the 1990s without mentioning two very important phenomena: first, the possibility for some refugees to return to their homeland and, second, the fact that Eastern Europe has changed from a refugee-producing region into a region of refuge.

The possibility of return hinges on the policies of the home country. Different regimes developed different attitudes to their exiles. Hungarian and Polish Communists, always on the lookout for hard currency, realized the potential of their diasporas as early as the 1970s and tried to lure them back with publications, congresses, and encouragement to invest. But exiles were unwelcome in Romania, Czechoslovakia, and Russia, where hard-liners feared they might infect others with bourgeois ideas ("The Homecoming" 1993). Now the situation of displaced Eastern Europeans has changed, and many are returning home, at least for a visit, if not to stay. While they bring with them good things—capitalist skills, money to invest, knowledge of how democracy and civil society work—the reactions to the returnees vary. Some countries such as Hungary, Poland, Slovakia, and the Czech Republic have been welcoming; others, such as Romania, Albania, and Bulgaria, remain suspicious.

The other important change is that after being for centuries a refugee-producing region, Eastern Europe has recently become a safe haven for many people fleeing persecution. Of all the countries in Eastern Europe, Hungary, because of its proximity to the West and to the civil conflict between the Serbs and the Croats, and because of the large number of ethnic Hungarians living in neighboring states, has become a magnet not only for Hungarians from Transylvania but also for ethnic Romanians and, before the reunification of Germany, for East Germans. The influx began in 1987. By early 1991, over 50,000 refugees had arrived, of whom 85 percent were from Romania, and of those, 80 percent were ethnic Hungarians (Joly and Poulton 1992). Poland suffers greater economic problems than Hungary, and it has not attracted as many asylum seekers or refugees. It remains, however, a transit country for many Romanian Roma who want to get to the West (Gozdziak 1994).

REFERENCES

Anagnastosache, George. 1944. Romanians in America. *The New Pioneer* 2(3): 57–61.

Baker, Richard P. 1988. Eastern European Refugees: Implications for Social Work. *Journal of Sociology and Social Welfare* 16(3): 81–94.

———. 1989. Refugee Assimilation: A Study of Polish and Czech Refugees. *Humboldt Journal of Social Relations* 15(2): 157–183.

Benkart, Paula. 1980. Hungarians. In *Harvard Encyclopedia of American Ethnic Groups.* Edited by Stephan Thernstrom. Cambridge, Massachusetts: The Belknap Press of Harvard University Press. Pp. 462–471.

Blejwas, Stanislaus. 1981. Old and New Polonias: Tensions within an Ethnic Community. *Polish American Studies* 38(2): 55–83.

Bobango, Gerald. 1980. Romanians. In *Harvard Encyclopedia of American Ethnic Groups.* Edited by Stephan Thernstrom. Cambridge, Massachusetts: The Belknap Press of Harvard University Press. Pp. 879–885.

Bukowczyk, John J. 1987. *And My Children Did Not Know Me.* Bloomington: Indiana University Press.

Cichon, Donald J., Elzbieta M. Gozdziak, and Jane G. Grover. 1986. *The Economic and Social Adjustment of Non–Southeast Asian Refugees,* Vol. 1. Dover, NH: Research Management Corporation.

Detroit Free Press. 1985. August 19.

Dovenyi, Zoltan, and Gabriella Vukovich. 1994. Hungary and International Migration. In *European Migration in the Late Twentieth Century. Historical Patterns, Actual Trends, and Social Implications.* Laxenburg, Austria: International Institute for Applied Systems Analysis. Pp. 187–205.

Forbes, Susan S. 1988. Historical Overview of the Flows of Intellectual Refugees. In *Scientists in Exile. Issues and Perspectives on the Refugee Experience.* Edited by Kathie McClesky and Susan S. Forbes. Washington, D.C.: Refugee Policy Group and American Association for the Advancement of Science. Pp. 1–7.

Golab, Caroline. 1977. *Immigrant Destinations.* Philadelphia: Temple University Press.

Goode, Judith, and Jo Anne Schneider. 1994. *Reshaping Ethnic and Racial Relations in Philadelphia. Immigrants in a Divided City.* Philadelphia: Temple University Press.

Gozdziak, Elzbieta M. 1989. *New Americans: The Economic Adaptation of Eastern European, Afghan and Ethiopian Refugees.* Washington, D.C.: Refugee Policy Group.

———. 1994. Cyganed (Gypped) Out of Refuge: Romanian Roma in Poland. In *Selected Papers on Refugee Issues: III.* Edited by Geoffrey MacDonald and Amy Zaharlick. Washington, D.C.: American Anthropological Association. Pp. 46–59.

Heberle, Rudolph, and Dudley S. Hall. 1951. *New Americans: A Study of Displaced Persons in Louisiana and Mississippi.* Baton Rouge, Louisiana: Displaced Persons Commission.

Heinrich, Hans-Georg. 1986. *Hungary. Politics, Economics and Society.* London: Frances Pinter Publishers.

"The Homecoming." 1993. *The Economist,* December 26, 1992–January 8, 1993: 73–76.

Huseby-Darvas, Eva. 1995. Long Distance Nationalism among American-Hungarians in Southeast Michigan. Unpublished manuscript.

Joly, Danielle, and R. Poulton. 1992. *Refugees: Asylum in Europe?* London: Minority Rights Group.

Kleeman, Janice. 1985. Polish American Assimilation: The Interaction of Opportunity and Attitude. *Polish American Studies* 42(1): 11–26.

Korewa, Maria Barbara. 1957. Casework Treatment of Refugees: A Survey of Selected Professional Periodicals for the Period from January 1, 1939 to January 1, 1956. Master's thesis, Wayne State University.

Lieberson, Stanley. 1963. *Ethnic Patterns in American Cities.* New York: Free Press.

Mostwin, Danuta. 1980. *The Transplanted Family: A Study of Social Adjustment of the*

Polish Immigrant Family to the United States after the Second World War. New York: Arno Press.

New York Times. 1984. June 22.

Office of Refugee Resettlement (ORR). 1986. *Report to the Congress: Refugee Resettlement Program.* Washington, D.C.: U.S. Department of Health and Human Services.

―――. 1993. *Report to the Congress: Refugee Resettlement Program.* Washington, D.C.: U.S. Department of Health and Human Services.

Radzialowski, Thadeus. 1974. The View from a Polish Ghetto: Some Observations on the First Hundred Years in Detroit. *Ethnicity* 1: 125–150.

Schneider, Jo Anne. 1988. In the Big Village: Economic Adjustment and Identity Formation for Eastern European Refugees in Philadelphia, Pa. Unpublished Ph.D. dissertation, Temple University.

Short, Deborah. 1988. *Eastern European Refugee Survey.* Washington, D.C.: Center for Applied Linguistics.

Szeplaki, Joseph. 1975. *The Hungarians in America 1583–1974. A Chronology and Fact Book.* Dobbs Ferry, New York: Oceana Publications.

Thomas, William I., and Florian Znaniecki. 1927. *The Polish Peasant in Europe and America.* New York: Knopf.

U.S. Department of Justice. 1969. *Annual Report to the Commissioner of Immigration and Naturalization Service.* Washington, D.C.: Government Printing Office.

Vardy, Steven Bela. 1985. *The Hungarian Americans.* Boston, Massachusetts: Twayne Publishers.

Walters, E. Garrison. 1988. *The Other Europe. Eastern Europe to 1945.* Syracuse, New York: Syracuse University Press.

Wertsman, Vladimir. 1975. *The Romanians in America 1748–1974. A Chronology and Fact Book.* Dobbs Ferry, New York: Oceana Publications.

Wood, Arthur Evans. 1955. *Hamtramck: Then and Now.* New York: Bookman Associates.

Znaniecki Lopata, Helena. 1976. *Polish Americans. Status Competition in an Ethnic Community.* Englewood Cliffs, New Jersey: Prentice-Hall.

Chapter 7

Ethiopians and Eritreans

TEKLE M. WOLDEMIKAEL

Ethiopians and Eritreans are among the most recent groups of Third World refugees to come to the United States. Their number is small compared with other Third World refugees, such as the Vietnamese, Chinese, Cubans, and Haitians. The number of Ethiopians and Eritreans living in the United States was estimated to be between 50,000 and 75,000 in 1991 (USCR 1991a:11). Although the number of Ethiopians and Eritreans in 1995 could have reached to 100,000 people, the demographic impact of their presence is insignificant. They are, however, important symbolically. Since the end of the forced migration of Africans to the new world in the nineteenth century, Eritreans and Ethiopians represent the first African immigrants to come to the new world, especially the United States and Canada, in significant numbers. They are thus the first voluntary immigrants from Africa. Many other Africans want to immigrate to the United States voluntarily, but unlike Eritreans and Ethiopians, they have not had the opportunity to do so—although the number of other African refugees, mainly Somalis and Sudanese, began to increase considerably in 1992 (USCR 1994a: 12–13).

Until the passage of the Refugee Act of 1980, the U.S. government had no policy for allowing Africans to come to the United States as refugees. Ethiopians and Eritreans compose the first large group of Africans resettled in the United States. The first of these refugees to resettle in the United States were 169 refugees admitted in 1979 as seventh-preference immigrants (Koehn 1991:151; Scanlan 1980:105–106). After the enactment of the Refugee Act of 1980, the number increased dramatically. From 1975 to 1994, a total of 33,195 Ethiopians and Eritreans were resettled in the United States as refugees (USCR 1994a:10–11, 1983:5). In addition, between 1980 and 1994, 4,643 Ethiopians and Eritreans were granted asylum (USCR 1993a:12–13, 1994a:12–13; ORR 1993:A24). Of the 43,727 Africans allowed to enter the United States between 1982 and 1994 as refugees, the majority (around 68 percent) were Ethiopians and Eritreans. In the first ten years, from 1980 to 1991, Ethiopians and Eritreans constituted the overwhelming majority of African refugees in the United States. The data from 1982 to 1991 show that about 93 percent of the total number of African refugees were Ethiopians and Eritreans. However, from 1992 on, other Africans, especially Somalis and Sudanese, began to enter the United States as refugees in large numbers. The Somalis replaced Ethiopians and Eritreans as the largest group of African refugees to resettle in the United States in 1994. Out of the 5,856 Africans admitted in 1994, the Somalis constituted about 61 percent and the Sudanese around 21 percent, whereas the percentage of Ethiopians and Eritreans declined to about 5.6 percent (USCR 1994a:11–12).

The Ethiopian and Eritrean refugees came to the United States because of the terror, violence, torture, and persecution they experienced or feared they might experience in their country. This fear came from the hands of the provisional military government run by the Armed Forces Coordinating Committee, commonly known as the Dergue (meaning "committee" in Amharic), which ruled Ethiopia from 1974 to 1991. In February 1974, a popular uprising overthrew Emperor Haile Selassie's regime. The Dergue emerged to coordinate the activities of the various groups participating in the revolution and was expected to hand over power to civilians after stabilizing the nation. Instead, the Dergue took power into its own hands and unleashed a reign of terror for 17 years. During this period, it imposed on Ethiopia its own form of Marxist socialist program based on the Soviet model. The Dergue attempted to stamp out all opposition to its control and program. This included every person suspected of questioning the legitimacy of the provisional government or of having sympathies for Eritrean nationalist movements. Thus, the primary reason Ethiopians and Eritreans immigrated to the United States was political. Indeed, many of these refugees were relatively privileged and deeply attached to their home country. In a survey conducted in Washington, D.C., in 1984 (Koehn 1991:103–110), over half of the Ethiopian sample had high-level policymaking, professional, or managerial positions in their homelands, and 15 percent were primarily engaged in large-scale farming or other commercial activity. Approximately 80 percent of the Ethiopians, and 60 percent of the Eritreans, rated their personal or family income as "high" or "medium" at the time they left their country. Only 9 percent of the Ethiopians and Eritreans reported that their families' economic status or class position had influenced their decision to emigrate. Most came because of the dramatic political upheaval in their homelands and because of traumatic personal and family experiences, such as arrests and the death of relatives. Eritreans also cited fear that their nationality would be used to persecute them. Around 70 percent of the Eritreans stated that the failure to realize the objectives of a nationalist movement ranked as an important factor in their motivation to move to the United States.

The defeat of the Dergue army in May 1991 by a coalition of two opposition movements, the Ethiopian People's Revolutionary Democratic Front (EPRDF) and the Eritrean People's Liberation Front (EPLF), ended the Dergue's reign of terror. The EPRDF established a provisional government in Ethiopia and consented to the EPLF's demand that Eritreans be allowed to decide their fate through a popular referendum. In an internationally supervised referendum in April 1993, the overwhelming majority of Eritreans cast their ballots in support of an independent Eritrea. On May 24, 1993, Eritrea officially declared its independence from Ethiopia and soon afterward was admitted to the United Nations.

The emergence of an independent Eritrea and a nonmilitary government in Ethiopia have stemmed the tide of political refugees from Eritrea and Ethiopia. The slowing flow of political refugees was directly related to the end of the cold war. The Dergue was an unpopular regime propped up by the military and political support of the Soviet Union and the Soviet-influenced Eastern European countries and Cuba. With the implosion of the Communist block, external support to the Mengistu regime ended. Dergue power collapsed, and a new government emerged, led by the former liberation fronts of both Eritrea and Ethiopia. This has brought about major improvement in the political stability of the two countries. The exodus of refugees to neighboring Sudan and Somalia has slowed to a trickle. The United States stopped accepting applications for resettlement of Ethiopians and Eritreans who arrived in countries of first asylum after May 28, 1991, the date of the fall of the government of Mengistu Haile Mariam. As of November 21, 1991, the U.S. government officially stopped accepting new applications of Ethiopians and Eritreans to be resettled in the United States (USCR 1991a:10, 1991b:2). Thus, most of the refugees who were resettled in the United States between 1992 and 1995 were those who applied before November 21, 1991. By 1994, the annual number of Ethiopians and Eritreans resettled in the United States declined to 328 persons.

CONTEST FOR STATE POWER

The people of Ethiopia and Eritrea are a mixture of diverse cultures, religions, and races. The region was one of the earliest melting pots in the world. It was crisscrossed by people going from Asia to Africa, and vice versa, and saw widespread ethnic mixing, religious conversions, migrations, conquests, wars, and redefinitions of boundaries between states. The ethnic groups and nationalities that exist now are current labels, not natural groups that existed in isolation from one another in the past. Until the end of the nineteenth century, the core political unit in Ethiopia, then also known as Abyssinia, was a loose alliance of kingdoms (Moussa 1993:73). Because the majority of Eritreans and Ethiopians now in the United States spring from people who label themselves Abyssinians (Kiflu 1983), a brief description of the Abyssinians and their history is in order.

The Abyssinians are the core of the population in Ethiopia and a politically powerful group in Eritrea. They have considerable power in present-day Ethiopia and Eritrea. The Abyssinians are the product of a blending between indigenous Nilotic people, Cushitics and Semitic immigrants who came to the region presumably over three thousand years ago. The Abyssinians developed a unique culture that adapted Christianity to local conditions and created its own written language, called Geez, from which emerged many languages spoken in Ethiopia and Eritrea, including Tigrigna, Tigre, Amharic, Guragigna, and others. The Abyssinian political structure allowed for a fractured political order divided along provincial and regional lines but not among ethnic or cultural groups (Markakis 1987:12). A small segment of the Abyssinians, known as Jeberti, are Muslims.

Two regional and linguistic factions did compete for political supremacy: the southern Abyssinians, consisting of the Amharic-speaking peoples of southern and central parts of Abyssinia, versus the northern Abyssinians, consisting of Tigrigna speakers based in Tigray and southern Eritrea. The Abyssinians were united in their strong religious faith in Orthodox Christianity and in their fight against the competing Islamic powers in the region (Markakis 1987:12). They used the mythical history of the Solomonic Dynasty to announce that their kings could claim direct descent from the legendary King Solomon of the Bible. The throne was a basis for the unity of the state and was the most important institution in the country, next to religion. Throughout the history of Abyssinia, the throne was usually filled only after bitter internal strife and power struggles between various regional powers. The internal strife intensified between the seventeenth and the nineteenth centuries, a period known as Zemene Messafint (Age of the Princes), which led to fractured regional and provincial kingdoms. With the crowning of Teodros as emperor in 1855, the modern Ethiopian state, with its strong centralizing tendencies around southern Abyssinia, began. Following Teodros (1855–1868), three rulers fostered the centralizing process of the state. They claimed to be emperors of Ethiopia. They were Emperor Yohannes (1872–1889), Emperor Menelik (1889–1913), and Emperor Haile Selassie (1930–1974) (Tiruneh 1993:4). The last two emperors played important roles in shaping the recent history of Ethiopia and Eritrea.

Emperor Menelik of Shoa, a central province of Ethiopia, defeated several of his competitors. He marched north, south, east, and west of Shoa and colonized Oromoland and many eastern, southern, and western regions—thus establishing most of the state boundaries of present-day Ethiopia (Hassen 1990:198; Jalata 1993:50–74). Under Haile Selassie, the Ethiopian empire consolidated its control over the territories established by his predecessors. In an agreement to establish a federal state under his rule while maintaining Eritrea's administrative autonomy, he expanded the size of the country by acquiring the Ogaden in 1948 from the British, as well as Eritrea from the United Nations in 1952. A popular revolt in February 1974 against him ended the era of the Abyssinian throne and has come to be known as the Ethiopian Revolution.

Colonel Mengistu Haile Mariam led the Ethiopian Revolution and chaired the ruling committee, known as the Dergue. The Dergue eliminated not only the throne but the supremacy of the Orthodox Church. It declared Ethiopia a socialist Marxist state, eliminated private property and implemented land reforms, instigated large-scale resettlement into new areas of the country, organized urban populations into neighborhood associations known as *Kebeles,* enforced national service, and waged war against several nationalist and antiregime movements that challenged its power and policies. From 1977 to 1991, Colonel Mengistu Haile Mariam was the leader of the country. During his rule, Ethiopia was attacked by the Republic of Somalia and became entangled in several wars against Eritrean nationalists and the anti-Dergue Ethiopian movements. The political turmoil that ensued from the revolution wrenched the basic social fabric of the society. The major consequences of the upheaval were terror, death, and destruction waged on the whole nation. The people responded in one of three ways: (1) The majority chose passive resistance against the Dergue, (2) some joined the opposition forces, and (3) the rest fled to neighboring countries for safety and security.

The Ethiopian revolutionary state faced armed challenges in Eritrea, Tigray, and Ogaden (an area inhabited by Somalis and claimed by the Republic of Somalia) and from several resistance movements representing Oromos, Afars, and others. The conflicts caused large-scale destruction and displacement. The revolutionary government's attempt to centralize state power politicized the existing fissions along national and ethnic lines. This intensified the tensions to the point of armed conflict against the various national and regional movements representing Eritreans, Tigriyans, Afars, Somalis, Oromos, and others. This led to mass exodus of Eritreans and Ethiopians to neighboring countries including Sudan, Somalia, Djibouti, and Kenya. The next section of this chapter focuses on three such armed conflicts—the Eritrean Nationalist Front, the Ethiopian People's Revolutionary Democratic Front, and the Oromo Liberation Front—which have caused a massive influx of refugees into neighboring countries and are directly linked to the presence of Ethiopian and Eritrean refugees in the United States.

THE NATIONALIST WARS

The Eritrean Nationalist Front

Eritrea has an estimated population of 3.5 million, almost equally divided between Muslims and Christians, with nine different language groups. Eritrea was an Italian colony from 1884 to 1941. While Menelik was expanding his empire, the Italians consolidated their political control over the long strip of land shaped like a dagger along the Red Sea coast, north of Menelik's Ethiopia, and called it Eritrea (an ancient Greek name for the Red Sea). Italy attempted to expand its colony by attacking Menelik. In 1896, at the battle of Adua (a town in Tigray), Emperor Menelik and his army defended their territory by decisively defeating the Italian colonial army. The Italians and Menelik signed a peace agreement known as the Treaty of Ucciali in 1889, in which the Italians recognized Ethiopia's sovereignty, and the Ethiopians recognized the Italian occupation of Eritrea. Thus, modern-day Ethiopia and Eritrea were born at the same time.

After the Italians were defeated in World War II in 1941, the British colonial army established a military administration in Eritrea (1941–1952). Eritrea was federated with Ethiopia in 1952 by the United Nations, although there was considerable opposition from various segments of Eritrean society. From 1952 to 1962, the Ethiopian government slowly weakened the independent existence of Eritrea by suppressing the use of the Eritrean national languages, Tigrigna and Arabic, and replacing them with Amharic, the Ethiopian official language. The Eritrean flag was replaced by the Ethiopian flag. Local newspapers were censored. Political parties and trade unions were banned. Factories were closed and forced to relocate to Addis Ababa. The independent Eritrean police force was eliminated. The Eritrean parliament, under pressure from the Ethiopian government, voted to dissolve the federation in November 1962, and Eritrea was reduced to being the fourteenth province of Ethiopia. Although the act of federation was violated, the United Nations and most African nations tacitly accepted the dissolution, claiming this was an internal affair of an independent member of the United Nations and the Organization of African Unity (OAU).

The Eritrean armed struggle started in 1961 in western Eritrea, near the Sudanese border, with six men and five rifles in protest of the Ethiopian soldiers' encroachment upon their grazing and farming land. The protestors were primarily Muslims from the semipastoralist western Eritrea. In 1962, they linked up with members of the Eritrean Liberation Front (ELF), formed by Eritrean nationalists living in exile in Cairo and Saudi Arabia, and adopted the ELF for their guerrilla movement. The guerrilla movement grew in size and intensity from 1961 to 1966. In 1966, as more people joined the ELF, the leadership attempted to organize their fighting forces according to their regional and ethnic backgrounds. They created four regional and ethnic military units and added a fifth to accommodate to the increasing number of Christians from southern Eritrea joining the front. The five divisions led to a split of the movement along religious, regional, and ethnic lines. In 1970, a splinter group known as the EPLF emerged to challenge and compete with ELF's leadership. Between 1970 and 1973, a deep internal conflict between the two nationalist movements weakened the nationalist struggle. The ELF failed to eliminate the EPLF, which was gaining greater support from Eritrean workers; from urban-educated residents of Asmara, Addis Ababa; and from Eritreans exiled in Europe, the United States, and the Middle East (Woldemikael 1993:179–199).

During 1974–1975, the early stages of the Ethiopian revolution, the ELF and EPLF stopped their civil war, combined their forces, and controlled most of Eritrea except the capital city, Asmara, the ports of Massawa and Asab, and some smaller towns. In 1977, with strong Soviet and Cuban support, the Ethiopian government pushed the nationalist fronts back into their base areas in western and northern Eritrea. The two fronts resumed their internal conflict, and the bitter civil war intensified until the end of the 1970s, when it became the major killer of Eritreans. It ended with the EPLF defeating the ELF in 1981, pushing ELF forces from Eritrean land into Sudan (Woldemikael 1991:31–42). Some of the political refugees from Eritrea who entered the United States in 1980s were former ELF fighters.

The ELF never recovered from its defeat at the hands of the EPLF. It split into small groups, while the EPLF grew in size and strength. Between 1982 and 1984, the EPLF was severely weakened but not defeated when the Ethiopian government army waged "the Red Star" campaign. The government's goal was elimination of the nationalist movement by using all its firepower and military capability. The government army, receiving massive military support from the Soviet Union and Eastern Europe, included the combined forces of Ethiopian and Yemenese soldiers, with military advisers from Russia and Cuba. With the failure of the Red Star campaign, the defeat of the Ethiopian army became inevitable. On May 24, 1991, the EPLF defeated the Ethiopian army and captured Asmara, the capital city of Eritrea.

The Ethiopian People's Revolutionary Democratic Front

The EPRDF originated from another liberation front, the Tigray People's Liberation Front (TPLF), which was started by young students and ex-students, mostly from Tigray, in 1975. It aimed at eliminating the Dergue as well as gaining independence for Tigray. Although Tigray is the cradle of Abyssinian culture, it is one of the poorest provinces in Ethiopia. Haile Selassie kept it that way, so as to isolate and weaken the Tigrayans' sense of autonomy. The Tigrayans resented the Shoa-based Amhara rule. The majority of Tigrayans share the same culture, ethnic heritage, and religion of the highland Christians of southern Eritrea. The only difference has been the emergence of a new national consciousness among Eritreans who lived as a separate entity for over 60 years under Italian and British rule. During this period, generations of Eritreans grew up as colonized people with a sense of separate identity. The TPLF has had support and sympathy in Eritrea and a strong, though sometimes strained, relationship with the EPLF (Lefort 1981:106).

The TPLF grew in size and strength from 1975 to 1989, winning most of its battles against the Ethiopian army. In late 1989, it was estimated to have 20,000 fighters, with considerably more armed militia, and was the second-most powerful group in the region, next to the EPLF. In 1989, it captured Mekele, the capital of Tigray, and controlled the whole province. The same year, it formed the EPRDF, in coalition with other smaller Ethiopian groups. The TPLF and the EPRDF expanded their line of operations against the government army and took control of northern Ethiopia, including Wollo, Gojjam, Begemder, and finally the center of power, Shoa. On May 26, 1991, a few days after Mengistu

Haile Mariam fled the country, the EPRDF captured Addis Ababa, the capital
city of Ethiopia. Immediately, it established a transitional government based in
Addis Ababa. During the war, the Tigrayans suffered from famine as well as
indiscriminate killing and torture at the hands of the Dergue.

The Oromo Liberation Movement

The third major group is the Oromo, who wish to establish an independent
Oromo nation. The Oromos are believed to be more numerous than the Abyssinians. They are the largest ethnic group in the country, constituting almost 50
percent of the total population. They were first colonized by Abyssinian rulers.
Menelik expanded the centralized control over the Oromos, and Haile Selassie
consolidated it. Historically, they have been pastoralists specializing in cattle
raising. A widely dispersed population, Oromos are found in every province of
Ethiopia. They have adopted Amharic as their language as well as Amhara
culture and traditions in many parts of Ethiopia. They traditionally worshipped
an Oromo deity, but most of them converted to either Islam or Christianity
(Jalata 1993; Markakis 1987:20). The most important Oromo movement has
been the Oromo Liberation Front. It is based in Bale province in southern Ethiopia, a region bordering Kenya and Somalia. The Oromo nationalist movement
was widely dispersed and lacked a strong organizational capacity like that of
the EPRDF and the EPLF. Thousands of Oromos have fled to Somalia and
Kenya to escape the war between the Ethiopian government and the Oromo
nationalist movement in their region. The Dergue imprisoned and tortured Oromos suspected of supporting the nationalist aspiration of Oromo movements.
The demand of Oromo nationalists for self-determination still persists and now
poses a serious challenge to the legitimacy of the provisional government of
Ethiopia.

ESCAPE TO AND REFUGE IN SUDAN

Most refugees from Ethiopia and Eritrea escaped to Sudan, Somalia, Djibouti,
and Kenya. The estimated total number of refugees from Ethiopia and Eritrea
to neighboring countries was about 1,066,300 people in 1991, with about 66
percent fleeing to Sudan and 33 percent to Somalia (USCR 1991b:33–34). With
the termination of the nationalist wars in Eritrea and Ethiopia, a major cause of
human displacement in the Horn of Africa ended. It also led to repatriation of
some Eritrean and Ethiopian refugees to their homelands, and at the same time,
it triggered new refugees to neighboring countries. At the end of 1994, there
were still about 575,250 Eritrean and Ethiopian refugees (composed of about
67 percent Eritreans and some 33 percent Ethiopians) living in neighboring
countries, mostly Sudan and Somalia. From 1991 to 1994, around 100,000 Eritreans were repatriated from Sudan and about 19,000 from Yemen, Ethiopia,
and various Western countries. At the end of 1994, there were still about

380,000 Eritrean refugees in Sudan and 2,000 in Ethiopia, and 190,000 Ethiopian refugees in neighboring countries including 160,000 in Sudan, 20,000 in Djibouti, and 10,000 in Kenya (USCR 1995:56–57). The defeat of the Dergue sparked ethnic violence in southern Ethiopia, causing 80,000 Ethiopians to flee to Kenya during 1991–1992. A peace agreement between the fighting ethnic groups encouraged repatriation of most of the refugees with the aid of the United Nations High Commissioner for Refugees (UNHCR). By the end of 1994, some 10,000 refugees still remained in Kenya. An estimated 51,000 Ethiopian soldiers and their families who were based in Eritrea fled to Sudan after the EPLF took over all of Eritrea. Another 250,000 Ethiopian soldiers went south toward Addis Ababa after the EPLF captured Asmara. The UNHCR helped repatriate some of the ex-soldiers and their families from Sudan into Ethiopia (USCR 1992:42). In 1993 and 1994, some 26,000 Ethiopians repatriated from Sudan to Ethiopia (USCR 1995:58). About 100,000 Ethiopian Somalis, who had been refugees in Somalia following the Ethiopian-Somali war in the late 1970s and the subsequent civil unrest in the Ogaden region of Ethiopia in the 1980s, returned to Ethiopia, running from the civil war and famine in Somalia from 1991 on (USCR 1994b:53–54). During the nationalist wars, refugees from Eritrea, Tigray, and Wollo escaped to Sudan, while Somalis from Ogaden went to Somalia.

Throughout, Sudan has been the major destination of refugees and the major source of Ethiopian and Eritrean refugees resettled in the United States. Most of the Ethiopian and Eritrean refugees now resettled in the United States were in Khartoum, the capital city of Sudan, and the rest were scattered in different towns including Port Sudan, Kassala, Gedarif, and Wad Medani. In 1988, the UNHCR and the Office of the Sudanese Commissioners of Refugees (COR) estimated that over 250,000 refugees, mostly Ethiopians and Eritreans, lived in urban centers in Sudan (Kebbede 1992:111). They were mostly unemployed or living in poor conditions as domestics in Sudanese homes or as service workers for Sudanese families. They could not support themselves financially. They received help from remittances by family members abroad, from the offices of relief organizations, and from sharing resources among themselves. One study of 234 Ethiopian and Eritrean refugees in Khartoum conducted in 1988 found that slightly more than 50 percent of the sample was employed. Of those employed, only a third were full-time, and two thirds were relegated to low-paying service-type jobs or unskilled labor (Kebbede 1992:114). Another study of urban refugees, mostly in Khartoum, reported that in 1984, 20 percent of the urban refugees were unemployed, and an even higher percentage were underemployed in low-paying jobs. Two thirds of the sample reported that they received less daily income than was required to provide food, shelter, and basic necessities. Moreover, these urban refugees, who usually did not have identification cards allowing them to live in Khartoum, were subjected to exploitation by Sudanese landlords and employers. They were also subjected to arrest and involuntary relocation to other Sudanese towns and resettlement camps (Weaver 1985:152–155).

The economic plight of the refugees has to be understood in the context of the poverty of most Sudanese people and the limited economic development in the country. It is one of the poorest countries in the world. In early 1980, the International Labor Organization (ILO) estimated that in terms of satisfying basic needs of its people Sudan was close to the lowest in the world. In 1988, the World Bank estimated the per capita income of Sudan's 22.6 million population at $320 per year (Bernal 1991:24). What was unsettling about Sudan was that the government and the citizens used Ethiopian and Eritrean refugees as scapegoats for Sudanese economic and political crises. They were routinely refused credit, barred by law from owning fixed assets, and blamed for Khartoum's long-standing economic problems (Weaver 1985:154–155). They were accused of causing the shortage of housing, rising rents, pressure on public services, and insufficient supplies of consumer goods (Karadawi 1987:124).

In addition, the refugees were subjected to constant harassment and discrimination in public services. Refugees had difficulty obtaining, on their own, the identification cards required of every resident in Sudan; getting one required either the support of one of the major nationalist movements (which sometimes served as intermediaries with Sudanese officials, the government, and the voluntary agencies [Karadawi 1987: 121–122]), or bribing Sudanese public employees (Kebbede 1992:115). Government officials or anyone associated with the government could and often did threaten to send refugees to prison or have them deported to the borders of Eritrea or Ethiopia. To avoid being deported, refugees had to bribe public employees or those who posed as such, especially the police.

Refugees were advised to avoid the main streets of Khartoum or Port Sudan during times of "cleansing" (kesha, meaning "roundup" in Sudanese Arabic) of the cities from refugees, acts conducted several times a year. Those without identification cards were often loaded in military trucks and deported to a rural refugee community; ironically, most returned to the city within a few days' time on their own (Kebbede 1992:111–112). Even if a refugee possessed an identification card, Sudanese police and other government officials often ignored it and threatened to imprison him or her on any pretext. That way, they were able to extort money to augment their meager monthly income. Harassment of refugees, and targeting them for gaining money and other material or sexual favors, was an ongoing process obvious to the eyes of the Sudanese government and the international organizations.

The mistreatment and harassment often did not apply to Muslim Eritreans and Ethiopians, especially if they could create conversational intimacy in Arabic. The first thing the Sudanese would ask Eritrean and Ethiopian refugees was, "What is your name?" in order to find out their religion. Muslims were treated as acceptable foreigners rather than as undesirable intruders who were leading the society toward moral decadence and economic disaster. The worst harassment was directed toward Eritrean and Ethiopian women, who were seen as either prostitutes or potential prostitutes. Their Western-style dress or merely their walking unaccompanied by male friends or relatives exposed them to contempt from Sudanese men. Stones or other objects were thrown at them. Police officers often raped women refugees who were jailed for failing to produce an identification card. They were forced to disguise themselves to avoid recognition and the public eye. Still, many women were robbed and raped in their homes, and those who worked as domestics experienced rape and sexual assault at their workplace by their male employers or male members of the employer's family (Kebbede 1992:124–125).

The urban refugees stayed in the Sudan as a transitional place only until they could move to a third country. When an opportunity came for them to resettle in third countries in Europe or North America, most applied to the United States because they perceived the United States as the country that gives immigrants the greatest opportunities. Of the 1,656 Eritreans and Ethiopians resettled to a third country from 1981 to March 1983, for example, the largest number went to the United States (1,495), followed by Sweden (63), Germany (52), Canada (27), Switzerland (8), Somalia (5), the United Kingdom (4), Denmark (1), and Norway (1) (Kibreab 1987:12). In the 1984 Washington survey, the researchers found that around two thirds of the refugees interviewed had no expectations of migrating to the United States. This was especially true of Eritreans, 72 percent of whom had no expectation to migrate to the United States. A significant number of Eritrean refugees were ex-ELF fighters who became refugees when they lost their battle with the EPLF in 1981. They applied to come to the United States only because the opportunity to do so opened up while they were seeking refuge to a third country (Koehn 1991:161).

TRANSITION AND RESETTLEMENT

The passage of the Refugee Act of 1980 allowed Africans to enter the United States as refugees. The ceiling was set at 1,500 in fiscal year (FY) 1980, although only 955 persons were admitted that year. From 1981 to 1990, the ceiling fluctuated from a low of 2,000 in FY 1987 and FY 1989 to a high of 3,500 in FY 1986 and FY 1990. Yet the ceiling did not reflect actual admissions. For instance, although the ceiling for 1986 was 3,500, the actual number of refugees (1,315 persons) admitted in 1986 was lower than the actual number of refugees (1,994 persons) admitted in 1987 when the ceiling was set at 2,000 (USCR 1990:9). For 1991, the Bush administration made an increase to the African regional ceiling to 4,900, and this represented a 30 percent increase from 1990 actual admissions of 3,500 and a 70 percent increase over the original 1990 ceiling (USCR 1991a:4). In 1992 the ceiling went up to 6,000 persons, and in 1993 it was raised to 7,000. The ceiling remained at 7,000 for 1994 and 1995 (USCR 1994a:9). Despite these modest increases in the 1990s, the U.S. Congress has consistently set a low admission ceiling for refugees from Africa. There are several reasons: First, Africa had limited significance for the United States in the cold war. Second, in the early stages of the African refugee crisis of the

1980s, African governments, the OAU, the United Nations, and the UNHCR sought to repatriate or resettle Africans in African countries of asylum. They saw resettlement of Africans in third countries such as the United States as "unnecessary and counterproductive" (USCR 1981:4). Third, Africans do not have a constituency in the United States to advocate for the admission of Africans as refugees. Black Americans have ambivalent feelings toward admission of refugees because they fear that immigrants would compete with them for the scarce unskilled manufacturing and service jobs, and they see the plight of African refugees as an issue that does not directly concern them (USCR 1989:11). Fourth, racism exists in U.S. refugee and immigration policies with the U.S. Congress being slow in responding to the refugee crises of both Haitians and Africans. As Congressman Bruce A. Morrison stated, "The perpetuation of racism after slavery is a strain in American history, and we need to work hard to remove racist elements in U.S. immigration policies" (USCR 1989:11).

Compared with other Africans, Ethiopians and Eritreans have been relatively favored. For instance, in the first ten years, from 1980 to 1991, Ethiopians and Eritreans constituted the overwhelming majority of African refugees in the United States, and from 1982 to 1991 about 93 percent of the total number of African refugees were Ethiopians and Eritreans (USCR 1994a:11–12). By giving token refuge to Ethiopians and Eritreans who were fleeing a self-declared Communist country allied with the Soviet Union, the U.S. government effectively silenced its critics for not challenging Soviet power in the Horn of Africa. At the same time, this was a political gesture to the Sudan, next to Egypt, the closest ally of the United States in Africa in the 1980s, because Sudan blamed the refugees for being the primary threat to its political stability.

Yet unlike refugees from other Communist regimes, Ethiopians and Eritreans were the only groups not admitted in large numbers. Moreover, their transit to the United States took a long time. Most of the refugees spent one to five years waiting from the time they applied until they gained permission to enter the United States. Success in gaining entry depended on using appropriate admission strategy. The steps in the immigration process demanded a great deal of skill and luck. Convincing the screening agents—both the voluntary agency and the U.S. government person—that they were authentic and qualified refugees was a major hurdle for all would-be refugees. The most skillful individuals cultivated inside contacts and utilized their compatriots in community networks to find out and hone the stories that would secure the highest rate of acceptance. This meant that some denied participating in the antiregime political groups whose other members the U.S. government had refused admission on the ground that they were engaged in terrorist acts or the persecution of others. After an initial rejection, some would-be immigrants adopted a complete change of identity and tactics (Koehn 1991:167–201). Forged travel documents could be purchased on the black market for a fortune (Karadawi 1987:127; New York Times, May 26, 1987:6).

Once they arrived in the United States, most of the refugees were resettled and assisted by nongovernmental agencies. In the survey conducted in Washington, nongovernmental resettlement agencies were reported to have helped 85 percent of the Ethiopian and 95 percent of the Eritrean refugees. The largest numbers, 45 percent of both nationalities, were assisted by the U.S. Catholic Conference. Church World Service aided 18 percent of the Ethiopians and 10 percent of the Eritreans (Koehn 1991:201). The U.S. government and its authorized resettlement agencies followed the dispersal model in the resettlement of refugees from Ethiopia and Eritrea. The major concentrations of resettled Ethiopian and Eritrean refugees were in California, Washington, D.C., Maryland, Virginia, and Texas. Of the total 16,157 Ethiopian and Eritrean refugees resettled in the United States from 1983 to 1990, 22.3 percent were initially resettled in California, 12.5 percent in Texas, 6.6 percent in Maryland, 5.8 percent in New York, and 4.7 percent in Washington, D.C. (USCRa 1991:12).

After they were resettled, many Eritrean and Ethiopian refugees moved to major metropolitan centers where they could meet their compatriots. This secondary migration led to the concentration of the exiles in a few major urban centers—mostly Washington, D.C., Los Angeles, Dallas, and New York City. Washington, D.C., ranks as the number-one place of residence for Ethiopians and Eritreans in the United States. Since the 1960s, Washington, D.C., has been a hub for Ethiopian elites and their children, who were attending local schools. Around this core gathered other ex-students who came looking for jobs around Washington. The Ethiopian ambassador took an interest in the Ethiopian students in the United States and hosted the students during Ethiopian national and religious holidays. The reputation of Washington as the center of Ethiopian and Eritrean presence increased as it became the center of Ethiopian and Eritrean political activism. More and more students and ex-students joined their friends and families. Most students combined attendance at local colleges or universities with their work and political activism. The large service sector in the metropolitan Washington area provided ideal opportunities for jobs they could easily do in their spare time.

Ethiopian and Eritrean refugees had some unique demographic characteristics. The data on the refugees showed that those who arrived as political refugees were predominantly males. For instance, of the 2,929 Ethiopian and Eritrean refugees who arrived in 1992, 62 percent were males and 38 percent females (ORR 1993:10). Ethiopian and Eritrean societies are patriarchal and favor males over females in almost all spheres of public life, including education, employment, government, and business. Men predominate among those who were educated and employed in the modern sector. Thus, men in greater numbers than women met the complex criteria set by the U.S. gatekeepers in the refugee processing sites in the Sudan and in Europe.

In addition, contrary to the fact that the majority of the refugees in the Sudan were Eritrean Muslims, the resettled ones were Amharic-speaking Ethiopians and Tigrigna-speaking Eritreans, with some Tigrigna-speaking Ethiopians and some Oromos. Most of them were Christians, primarily Orthodox Christians.

Among Eritreans, large minorities were Catholics and Protestants. A few of the Eritrean refugees were Muslims. The explanation as to why this happened is complex. Those allowed in were Ethiopian and Eritrean immigrants whom the U.S. government defined as able to integrate into the society faster and better. This included those who were Christians, those not involved in nationalist movements, those who were better educated or young, and those who were deemed to contribute most to the host society or had work experience in the modern sector of the economy. The greatest influence in granting refugee status was the refugee's educational background. For instance, while fewer than 5 percent of the refugees from Ethiopia living in Sudan had attended a university, nearly 20 percent of the resettled household heads had attained this educational level (Koehn 1991:169). The Shoa-based Amharic-speaking Ethiopians were the most preferred for immigration to the United States because they had greater access to educational and occupational resources in Ethiopia, and they were less feared to be associated with "terrorist" organizations. They were mostly Christians as well. Therefore, they were perceived as the most likely to integrate successfully into U.S. society.

LIFE IN THE UNITED STATES

Economic Incorporation

Eritrean and Ethiopian refugees had been exposed to an idealized American way of life as presented in the media. They aspired to that ideal and expected to participate in it once they arrived. Their idealization of the American way of life made them ideologically committed to the attainment of the "middle-class lifestyle." Their desire was frustrated when they found themselves unable to function in everyday life in American society. Except for some professionals, who were employed as medical doctors, experts in international organizations, or researchers and professors in higher education, the majority found employment that would place them on the lower rungs of the economic ladder in the United States, mostly in unskilled service jobs. This created a sense of economic dislocation or downward mobility and challenged their sense of identity, status, and culture in the United States.

Generally, Ethiopian and Eritrean refugees faced difficulties in finding jobs that matched their educational and occupational experience and qualifications. They entered the U.S. economy as low-wage workers in the service sector. This pattern started when Ethiopians and Eritreans were going to school in the late 1960s and early 1970s and working as parking lot and gas station attendants, waitresses and waiters, busboys, taxi drivers, night guards, hotel and hospital maintenance personnel, nurse's aides, and providers of other services. Most hoped to return to their homeland and work in occupations based on their new qualifications. They treated their stay and their work in the United States as temporary until they finished their education or training. As the political crisis in their encounters worsened and as new refugees arrived as permanent residents, their dream of returning home faded. Many continued in their previous jobs. The earlier residents helped the newcomers find jobs in the service sector. So there occurred a cultural division of labor, in which most Ethiopians and Eritreans specialized in low-paying service jobs that required only minimum interaction with the host society. A few who have saved enough capital have broken from this trend and opened their own businesses, including liquor and convenience stores, restaurants, gas stations, taxi cabs, real estate agencies, and computer and printing services. Like other Third World immigrants, such as the Chinese and Indians, many Ethiopians and Eritreans have succeeded in creating a niche for Ethiopian and Eritrean restaurants in most major American cities. They specialize in Abyssinian cuisine, a cultural practice shared by both Tigrigna-speaking Eritreans and Amharic-speaking Ethiopians.

In a survey conducted in 1986 in three urban areas of high Ethiopian and Eritrean concentration, including Dallas, Washington, and Los Angeles, researchers found that Ethiopian and Eritrean refugees were participating in the labor force at high levels. They reported that 93 percent were either working or actively seeking work in Dallas, 100 percent in Washington, and 75 percent in Los Angeles. In contrast, the labor force participation level for the U.S. population age 16 and above was 65.4 percent during the times of the site visits. However, the actual employment rates were much lower. Of those participating in the labor market, 92 percent of the Dallas sample were employed full-time, but 67 percent of the Washington sample and only 47 percent of the Los Angeles sample were working in full-time jobs. These rates showed a higher unemployment rate than the U.S. general population in the respective countries. Thus, Ethiopians and Eritreans were facing economic hardship in Los Angeles and Washington, while they were very successful in Dallas (Cichon, Gozdziak, and Grover 1986:30). Los Angeles in the West and Washington in the Northeast represent the economic crisis and job loss experienced by the major cities and regions in the West and Northeast United States, and their economic difficulties had a direct effect on the lives of the refugees.

The first jobs for the Ethiopian and Eritrean refugees in the sampled sites were entry-level positions in the service sector, including hotel housekeeping, dishwasher, and landscaping. Among the refugees in Los Angeles, there were more diverse types of jobs such as security guards, gas station and parking lot attendants, busboys, mail sorters, sometimes cashiers, waiters and waitresses, and restaurant hosts and hostesses. In the case of Dallas and Washington, they would obtain the latter types of employment only after some work experience in the initial jobs listed earlier. Los Angeles provided more time for the refugees to stay on public assistance than Dallas and Washington so that they could improve their language and work skills in training programs and thus enter the job market at a different level than those who went to Dallas and Washington. In the three-year period studied, 1983 to 1985, the refugees showed only slight advancement in pay, skill, and responsibility (Cichon, Gozdziak, and Grover 1986:31).

In terms of economic self-sufficiency, the Dallas sample was considered 100 percent self-sufficient, while in Washington 50 percent of the sample was considered self-sufficient and in Los Angeles only 41 percent. However, the earned income of the self-sufficient families showed a grim economic picture. Most of the refugees in all three cities were living below the poverty level. Their incomes varied from 62 percent of the poverty level to 308 percent of the poverty level. Most lived in poorer sections of the cities, sometimes in dilapidated buildings, alongside other minorities (Cichon, Gozdziak, and Grover 1986:33–34).

This limited income suggests the likelihood of receipt of public assistance by the refugees. In fact, there was wide variation among the three sites studied. In Dallas, there was almost no welfare receipt among the sample, while in Washington half of the sample received it at some point, and in Los Angeles, 36 percent of the sample reported receiving cash assistance at the time of the site visit and another 23 percent had received it at some prior time. Therefore, Ethiopians and Eritreans seem to use welfare when and where it is available in adequate levels (Cichon, Gozdziak, and Grover 1986:32) and when needed.

Social and Cultural Incorporation

Ethiopians and Eritreans are immigrants from predominantly agrarian and pastoral societies whose semifeudal social structure remained intact until the Ethiopian revolution of 1974. In the case of Eritrea, the feudal social structure was modified by 50 years of Italian colonialism (1889–1941) and a brief occupation by the British (1941–1952). The cultural incorporation of both groups in America has been particularly painful for them because they now have to function in a highly industrialized, urbanized, and bureaucratic society. They often find the work discipline of the capitalist system, and the regimentation and regulation of time and space, bewildering and difficult. As an Eritrean writer has noted: "Coming from a less developed part of the world to a nation of mass production and mass consumption where everyone has to run to make ends meet, a newly arrived immigrant finds the fast pace of American life exhausting" (Kiflu 1983:99).

Once in the United States, the refugees suffer a shift in their social position, from being members of the dominant majority groups in their own societies to being among the nondominant immigrant minorities. Most are from the politically dominant ethnic groups in their countries, including the Amharic and Tigrigna speakers in Ethiopia and the Tigrigna speakers in Eritrea. This creates a reversal of status and a consequent conflict in their identity. The identity conflict manifests itself in gender and family relations, race relations, and generational frictions. This means that Ethiopian refugees feel pressure to find a new sense of identity that blends their home-country-based sense of self with the self they construct in the new society.

Gender Relations

Ethiopian and Eritrean refugees come from highly patriarchal societies. In Ethiopia and Eritrea a person's status is determined mainly by the class and ethnic position of his/her families in society. Still, gender cuts across class and ethnic lines. Men receive more respect than women regardless of their class and ethnic position. Men's identity is public, requiring continuous affirmation from their male peers. "Achieving the male gender ideals of personal autonomy, masculine honour and prestige—all available for public scrutiny and evaluation—protects both respect for the individual man as well as the family's and group's reputation" (McSpadden and Moussa 1993:211).

Coming to the United States, men and women experience the new society differently. Eritrean and Ethiopian women gain greater financial and personal independence and security than they had back home. Women experience greater freedom and rights in the home and at work in the United States. Men, on the other hand, find their dominant position contested both at home and at work. They often resist changing their attitudes and behavior. They avoid helping their wives in the kitchen when visitors come to their homes, even if they do help when they are alone. Most single men do their own housework, including working in kitchens to survive. But once they get married, the gender roles tend to be sharply defined. They are mainly concerned about their culturally defined male image as the patriarch of the family (McSpadden and Moussa 1993:217).

Thus, the ideal of equality between the genders in the United States generates tensions within the refugee families and between males and females. The number of cases of wife battery has risen along with some divorce. The dilemma for a battered woman is that her husband or male partner is often the only person she knows in their new country. The fighting husband and wife often have no mediating community or family relations to which they can turn. The absence of trusted community elders and extended families to mediate marital problems increases the family tensions and the isolation of women and their male partners. In addition, marriage in Ethiopia and Eritrea represents the bringing together of two extended families. Thus, it is hard for a woman to imagine that she has the right to break the relationship on her own (McSpadden and Moussa 1993:214). In the short run, most of the refugee women, like the men, work in low-paying service jobs. The relative gender equality in the United States, however, compared to the glaring inequality in their homelands, gives them some hope of improving themselves and attaining the American dream of a secure middle-class lifestyle—with or without their male partners in the long run.

Race Relations

In the eyes of the first generation of refugees, the question of racial identity is not a major concern in their new life in the United States. They focus their attention on "making it" in the system in spite of race-based social divisions.

Race becomes a serious concern as they set up families and have children. They are aware of the racial divide in American society and the assumptions different racial groups have about each other. However, they do not publicly and collectively acknowledge that racial issues affect their own lives. Instead, they relegate the racial issue to a private and often secondary level of concern. This pattern continues even when the significance of race increases as their children grow up in a society that has "naturalized" racial identities and denied the existence of ambiguity in the meaning of race and ethnic identity. The first-generation refugees continue to focus on acquiring basic survival skills such as language, vocational and professional skills, and even higher education. They emphasize national and regionally based ethnic identity as a way of mitigating any racially based ascribed identity. They do not try to understand the meaning of such contested identities as race or class in the United States. At the same time, they do not feel they are entitled to speak on issues that affect native-born American minorities because they are not part of the historical legacy of U.S. society. Eritreans and Ethiopians thus focus on the well-being of their families, relatives, and friends, in exile and in their homelands, and consider racial issues secondary in their lives.

Communal Concerns

Some writers have remarked that Ethiopians and Eritreans in the United States are extremely isolated from the host society (Cichon, Gozdziak, and Grover 1986:41), and this leads them to depression, mental health crises, and a high suicide rate (McSpadden 1988; McSpadden and Moussa 1993). The study conducted by Cichon and others in 1986 showed that refugees found support within the rather sizable Ethiopian and Eritrean presence in three sites of research— Los Angeles, Dallas, and Washington. The earlier immigrants served as resources with whom they could socialize, eat their own food, listen to their own music, use their own language, and share their experiences. In spite of this, most refugees experienced loneliness and isolation because the total number of Ethiopians and Eritreans in the United States was small and dispersed in different parts of the cities. They were also divided along ethnic, political, and, in the case of Eritreans, religious lines. Most suffered from the absence of family support and elders with the authority to direct and advise them. The alienation was most severe with single males in their twenties (Cichon, Gozdziak, and Grover 1986:41–42).

The earlier 1984 survey in Washington differed in its findings and suggested that Ethiopians and Eritreans did not suffer from higher rates of mental health problems compared with other refugees. In fact, most Ethiopian and Eritrean refugees were reportedly competing effectively in the mainstream economy and were involved in large-scale organizations. According to the study, "Many live among U.S. nationals and are comfortable interacting frequently with them on a social basis. In short, they have friends in the dominant society. . . . Most members of the . . . communities interact socially with fellow migrants and feel closer to their compatriots than the U.S. national'' (Koehn 1991:334).

The apparent contradictory findings between the 1984 survey in Washington and the 1986 survey of Dallas, Los Angeles, and Washington can be explained by taking several factors into account. First, the 1984 survey was conducted among the first wave of refugees who were better educated and had more work experience than did the second wave immigrants. Second, Washington is a city where blacks are the majority. The presence of blacks as a majority in Washington might serve as a protective shield for the refugees from the full impact of being a racial minority in the United States. Third, because of the relatively high concentration of Ethiopians and Eritreans in Washington, the refugees could live almost entirely within Ethiopian and Eritrean circles for their social and cultural life. Refugees who live in Washington have informed me many times that they feel comfortable living there and even forget that they are living in exile because it is inhabited predominantly by blacks and because they work and socialize with their compatriots every day.

In most cities of the United States the refugees cope with their reversal of status by participating in all-Eritrean and -Ethiopian political and cultural organizations. These include support groups, either for the nationalist movements, in the case of the Eritreans, or for the anti-Dergue movements, in the case of the Ethiopians. They also can choose to participate in almost all-male soccer teams that have been active for over ten years in the United States. Other organizations, such as friendship circles and peer groups, meet and play and socialize on weekends. Many participate in ''Ekub,'' a traditional Abyssinian rotating credit association, by means of which individuals accumulate capital while also socializing with their compatriots. Very often, husbands and wives participate together in networks of friendship, family circles, and political organizations. Recently, there has been a growing interest in providing religious services for the adults and teaching Tigrigna and Amharic to the second generation.

Repatriation

The end of the nationalist and civil wars in Eritrea and Ethiopia in May 1991 made repatriation of the refugees to their homelands a distinct alternative and a widely discussed issue among the refugees. Since they defined themselves as sojourners who were waiting to return to their homes after the end of the wars, the refugees had to decide whether to go back home or not. From 1991 to 1995, most refugees visited their families and relatives in their homelands but then returned to the United States. The most dramatic visit was when 360 Eritreans departed the United States on July 30, 1991, only three months after the end of the Eritrean nationalist war, on a charter fight bound to Asmara, Eritrea, to visit their families and loved ones after having not seen them in many years or even decades.

There are very few of the refugees who have not gone home at least once in the last four years. Among Eritreans, those who have yet to set foot in an independent Eritrea include some Muslim Eritreans who feel alienated from the perceived Christian dominance of the new government and economy, and some former ELF supporters who still hold a strong animosity and resentment to the EPLF—the liberation front that defeated them in 1981 and whose leaders run the present Eritrean state. Among Ethiopians, a large segment of the Amharic-speaking refugees have refused to accept the legitimacy of the EPRDF-dominated Ethiopian government. They have organized themselves into several political organizations with their own publications and a radio station aimed at discrediting the new Ethiopian government in the eyes of the American government and public. Their dream is to create followers within Ethiopia by linking with some dissident groups inside the country and eventually toppling the EPRDF-led Ethiopian government.

The reasons why the refugees decided not to repatriate have been explored in a small-scale comparative study of Eritrean men in northern California and Eritrean and Ethiopian women in Toronto conducted among those who had already visited and those who intended to visit the home country. The study showed that men's and women's decisions were strongly influenced by what would enhance their social power as men and women, respectively. For men, this meant restoring their social power "congruent with the patriarchal Eritrean socio-cultural understanding of masculinity, based in education, employment, family responsibilities, and social status. Women in contrast look[ed] for a creative tension between maintaining aspects of their cultural identity which . . . [were] fulfilling and at the same time asserting their rights as women in an egalitarian and democratic sense" (McSpadden and Moussa 1995:35).

The question of why most of the refugees decided not to repatriate after dreaming for so long about returning to their home of origin has to be explored in the context of the dilemma of being an exile or a person in diaspora. Many do not return home because the home they left does not exist after 30 years of war and destruction. The people they knew are old or dead or have also left. Those who stayed have been changed by the 30 years of rule of terror of the Dergue. The young children whom they left behind are adults with their own families now. Their neighborhoods and family homes have been changed, if not destroyed, during the war. New faces and new people live in the villages, towns, and places they consider home. Even the vocabulary and the expressions of language they spoke when they were young have changed. In addition, they find themselves alienated from the villages, towns, and cities they considered "home" because their experiences in exile in Sudan, in Italy, and in other places in which they lived before they were granted refuge in the United States have changed their sense of self and personhood. They find the society they left as too isolated, conformist, and critical of their statements, self-presentation, and behavior. The "home" they knew remains only in their imagination, where they can cherish and remember it while continuing to live in self-imposed exile.

FUTURE CONCERNS: THE SECOND GENERATION

The major long-term concern of Eritreans and Ethiopians in the United States has been how to continue their separate identity and pass on to their children their sense of connection to their homeland while also being full members of American society. Because of the strong assimilative mechanisms in the United States, the second-generation Eritreans and Ethiopians find it hard to follow their parents' cultural traditions. Their parents come from more communal and family-oriented societies. The parents' generation finds it hard to orient its children for coping with the demands of the competitive and individualistic U.S. society, which is also fractured along class, racial, and ethnic lines. They are often unable to control their children. When they try to use physical punishment or other authoritarian methods to discipline them, their actions draw public attention and they are then visited by police and government officials because of complaints of child abuse.

In the Eritrean and Ethiopian context, the older generation is respected because of their age and rank. Conversations follow a pattern in which the higher status is assigned to older men, followed by older women, followed by younger married men and married women, then the eldest sons, followed by the eldest daughters, and so on. In such gender- and age-based hierarchies, a child's or a young person's needs are hardly addressed. The children are forced to keep their mouths shut and pretend to conform to the wishes of their parents at home. But beyond the sight of their parents and outside their homes, they disregard their parents' wishes and hang around with youth in their neighborhoods and schools. Thus, the schools and neighborhoods where the children grow up play a significant role in shaping their identities and cultures. Families who live in poor minority neighborhoods, where gangs and drug-related criminal activities abound, find their children growing up exposed to such influences. As they grow older, they also become involved in gangs and drug-related activities. Children growing up in more affluent neighborhoods are more exposed to middle-class-oriented lifestyles and family life and thus are affected less by gangs and drugs.

There is no unique culture among the second-generation Ethiopians and Eritreans. The parental generation has been unable to pass its language, and to a large extent, its religious orientations, to the second generation. This failure to educate children about their faith and their language been a source of great anguish to them. Instead, the second generation has constructed and negotiated its own identity, blending its American and African cultural influences. The refugees' children are more individualistic and less nationalistic than their parents. Most of them confront American society as black persons with Ethiopian or Eritrean parents. What they become varies depending on their neighborhoods, their class backgrounds, and their own personal choice of friends and lifestyles. Some of them identify themselves as Eritreans/Ethiopians and Africans, and some as blacks. Many individuals assume different cultural identities depending on the social context. They use synthetic and racial identities as resources to manage socially challenging and often uncomfortable situations. When they apply to schools, they identity themselves as blacks. When they go to colleges, they participate in black-oriented associations, as well as African and international associations. They also take part in multicultural organizations. In the long run, the parental generation's strong pride in its national and ethnic heritage may help to give the second generation a strong basis for negotiating a meaningful collective identity for itself in the United States.

REFERENCES

Bernal, Victoria. 1991. *Cultivating Workers: Peasants and Capitalism in a Sudanese Village.* New York: Columbia University Press.

Bulcha, Mekuria. 1988. *Flight and Integration: Causes of Mass Exodus from Ethiopia and Problems of Integration in the Sudan.* Uppsala: Scandinavian Institute of African Studies.

Cichon, Donald J., Elzbieta M. Gozdziak, and Jane G. Grover, Editors. 1986. *The Economic and Social Adjustment of Non–Southeast Asian Refugees.* Dover, New Hampshire: Research Management Corporation.

Hassen, Mohammed. 1990. *The Oromo of Ethiopia: A History 1570–1860.* Cambridge: Cambridge University Press.

Jalata, Asafa. 1993. *Oromia & Ethiopia: State Formation and Ethnonational Conflict, 1868–1992.* Boulder, Colorado: Lynne Rienner Publishers.

Karadawi, Ahmed. 1987. The Problems of Urban Refugees in Sudan. In *Refugees: A Third World Dilemma.* Edited by John R. Rogge. Totowa, New Jersey: Rowman & Littlefield. Pp. 115–129.

Kebbede, Girma. 1992. *The State and Development in Ethiopia.* Atlantic Highlands, New Jersey: Humanities Press.

Kibreab, Giam. 1987. *Refugees and Development in Africa: The Case of Eritrea.* Trenton, New Jersey: The Red Sea Press.

Kiflu, Tesfai. 1983. Abyssinians in America: A Cultural Perspective. *The Mid-Atlantic Almanack: The Journal of the Mid-Atlantic Popular/American Culture Association* 2: 95–106.

Koehn, Peter H. 1991. *Refugees from Revolution: U.S. Policy and Third World Migration.* Boulder, Colorado: Westview Press.

Lefort, Rene. 1981. *Ethiopia: An Heretical Revolution.* Translated by A. M. Bennett. London: Zed Press.

Markakis, John. 1987. *National and Class Conflict in the Horn of Africa.* Cambridge: Cambridge University Press.

McSpadden, Lucia Ann. 1988. Ethiopian Refugee Resettlement in the Western United States: Social Context and Psychological Well-Being. Unpublished Ph.D. dissertation, University of Utah, Salt Lake City.

McSpadden, Lucia Ann, and Helene Moussa. 1993. I Have a Name: The Gender Dynamics in Asylum and in Resettlement of Ethiopian and Eritrean Refugees in North America. *Journal of Refugee Studies* 6(3): 203–225.

———. 1995. Power and Belonging: The Gendered Context for the Repatriation Decisions of Eritrean Refugees in North America. In *Selected Papers on Refugee*

Issues IV. Edited by Ann Rynearson and Jim Phillips. Arlington, Virginia: American Anthropological Association.

Moussa, Helene. 1993. *Storm & Sanctuary: The Journey of Ethiopian and Eritrean Women Refugees.* Dundas, Ontario: Artemis Enterprises.

ORR (Office of Refugee Resettlement). 1993. *Report to the Congress: Refugee Resettlement Program.* Washington, D.C.: U.S. Department of Health and Human Services.

Scanlan, John A. 1980. First Final Research Report Submitted to the Select Commission on Immigration and Refugee Policy. In *U.S. Immigration Policy and the National Interest.* Appendix C to the State Report. Washington, D.C.: The Commission. Pp. 105–106.

Tareke, Gebru. 1991. *Ethiopia: Power and Protest.* Cambridge: Cambridge University Press.

Tiruneh, Andargachew. 1993. *The Ethiopian Revolution 1974–1987.* Cambridge: Cambridge University Press.

U.S. Committee for Refugees (USCR). 1981. *Refugee Reports.* Washington, D.C.

———. 1982. *Refugee Reports.* Washington, D.C.

———. 1983. *Refugee Reports.* Washington, D.C.

———. 1984. *Refugee Reports.* Washington, D.C.

———. 1987. *World Refugee Survey.* Washington, D.C.

———. 1989. *World Refugee Survey.* Washington, D.C.

———. 1990. *Refugee Reports.* Washington, D.C.

———. 1991a. *Refugee Reports.* Washington, D.C.

———. 1991b. *World Refugee Survey.* Washington, D.C.

———. 1992. *World Refugee Survey.* Washington, D.C.

———. 1993a. *Refugee Reports.* Washington, D.C.

———. 1993b. *World Refugee Survey.* Washington, D.C.

———. 1994a *Refugee Reports.* Washington, D.C.

———. 1994b. *World Refugee Survey.* Washington, D.C.

———. 1995. *World Refugee Survey.* Washington, D.C.

Weaver, Jerry L. 1985. Sojourners along the Nile: Ethiopian Refugees in Khartoum. *Journal of Modern African Studies* 23(1): 147–156.

Woldemikael, Tekle M. 1991. Political Mobilization and Nationalist Movements: The Case of the Eritrean People's Liberation Front. *Africa Today* 38(2): 31–42.

———. 1993. The Cultural Construction of Eritrean Nationalist Movements. In *The Rising Tide of Cultural Pluralism.* Edited by Crawford Young. Madison: University of Wisconsin Press. Pp. 179–199.

Chapter 8

Haitians

FREDERICK J. CONWAY AND
SUSAN BUCHANAN STAFFORD

Haitians have a rich cultural and historical heritage, even though they come from one of the poorest countries in the Western Hemisphere. Haiti is the second oldest republic in the Americas, the product of an eighteenth-century revolution grounded in the "rights of man." Yet the struggle for the extension of human rights has been the most poignant theme of Haitian life in the 1990s.

Haiti is a mountainous country located on the island of Hispaniola, the second largest island in the Caribbean. Lying between Spanish-speaking Cuba and the Dominican Republic (with which it shares Hispaniola), Haiti retains its distinct linguistic and cultural identity. It is the largest country where French Creole and French are the major languages. Haiti is both the most densely populated and the most rural nation in the Caribbean region. Peasant agriculture is the basis of the economy, but the agricultural sector has been neglected for more than a century.

Although Haiti seems remote to many Americans, it has had a long and intimate relationship with the United States. The United States has been Haiti's most important trading partner since the nineteenth century and has played an important role in shaping Haiti's politics. The United States invaded Haiti twice in the twentieth century, most recently in 1994. In spite of the intimacy, Haitians remain exotic and in many ways invisible to many Americans.

The refugee status of Haitians in the United States is complex. Successive U.S. administrations have resisted giving refugee status to Haitians, even during times of fierce political repression in Haiti. Very few Haitians have been granted political asylum, and only a political and legal crisis in Florida in the early 1980s led to a quasi-refugee status of "Cuban/Haitian entrant." Nevertheless, many Haitian immigrants in the United States consider themselves to be in exile from their country. Others consider themselves to be nonpolitical immigrants.

This chapter will distinguish between the specific category of "Haitian entrant" and the more general categories of Haitian exile and immigrant.

An important theme in legal battles about Haitians' refugee status has been a comparison of their treatment with that of neighboring Cubans, who were almost always given refugee status until 1995. Thus, a chapter on Haitians as refugees must include some discussion of Cuban immigration, especially during the "Mariel crisis" of 1980. It is also necessary to consider U.S. policies that have resulted in the forced repatriation of thousands of Haitians desiring entry into the United States. These "refused refugees" are an important part of the Haitian story.

Proverbs are used frequently in Haitian conversations. The most famous Haitian proverb is *"Deye mon gen mon,"* which means "Behind mountains there are mountains." This is not only a physical image of Haiti's rugged landscape but a testament to the struggles of Haitians to establish a satisfying life and to their determination to overcome seemingly endless obstacles. These obstacles have been encountered both in Haiti and in the United States. The 1990s have been a period of significant political and cultural openings in Haiti and consequently of some of the fiercest political repression there in this century. The 1990s have also raised significant questions for Americans about their relationships with Haitians.

THE HOME COUNTRY

Early History

Haiti is the second oldest republic in the Americas, established on January 1, 1804, when an army of former slaves defeated Napoleon's forces. The Haitian Revolution ended more than three centuries of colonial rule by Spain and France. That rule began during Columbus's first voyage in 1492. By the 1550s, the indigenous Tainos had been almost exterminated, and the importation of African slaves by the Spanish was well under way. The French took possession of Saint-Domingue, as colonial Haiti was known, at the end of the seventeenth century. The French greatly increased the importation of slaves to work plantations of sugar cane, coffee, cotton, and indigo. By the middle of the eighteenth century, Saint-Domingue had become the most profitable colony in the world. It was far more valuable to the French than were the 13 North American colonies to Britain.

The wealth of Saint-Domingue was produced by slaves who worked in one of the most brutal plantation systems in the history of the Americas. In the decades before the start of the Haitian Revolution, the life expectancy of Africans, once they arrived in Saint-Domingue, was less than ten years. In the 1790 census, the 452,000 slaves constituted 87 percent of the population (Leyburn 1966:18).

Thirteen years of intermittent warfare during the revolution destroyed most of the infrastructure of the hated plantations. Early Haitian governments sought to reestablish the plantation system to restore export-oriented agriculture. The former slaves, however, had no interest in providing income to their rulers at the expense of their freedom. They left the plantations, taking up land granted by the government or simply removing themselves to the uninhabited mountains.

These new peasants developed an agriculture oriented toward subsistence and the local market, which required neither the capital nor the harsh labor exacted by exports such as sugar. Land was owned by individuals, worked by extended families, and passed on to their children. In the first 50 years after independence, Haitian land was transformed into a system of small holdings owned by individual peasants and large holdings owned by the state and leased out. Increases in population have resulted in smaller parcels being inherited by more individuals. Data from 1970 indicate that 85 percent of agricultural holdings were less than one hectare (Wilkie and Haber 1983:56). Haiti is a country in which the peasantry is desperately poor but tends to own land. Ties to the land are thus far more than sentimental, and Haitian peasants leave their land only under dire circumstances. In contrast to other Latin American countries, there is not a mass of landless peons working for an elite that owns most of the cultivated land. Conflicting class interests in Haiti have historically been more disguised.

Aside from temporary work groups, the extended family was the largest social group in rural areas. Attempts at establishing peasant organizations were suppressed. The relationship of the central state to a local area was channeled through the local *chef de section,* a military appointee. The direction of control and communication was entirely from the top down. With some embellishments, the same system operated through the end of the Duvalier regimes in the mid-1980s.

The ruling group consisted of two elements: an educated elite and the military leadership. From the beginning, the elite was largely mulatto, a group that had been partially free and often owners of slaves during the colonial period. The early military leadership consisted predominantly of former black slaves. Haitian law never recognized these color distinctions, but they remained important socially.

With the abandonment of the plantations, the elite group lost its chance to maintain dominance through control of land and agriculture. Some land remained in the hands of the elite, but their principal economic opportunities lay in the fields of commerce, the professions, and control of the political process. Politics soon became a struggle to gain control of government finances and patronage, removed from the agricultural base on which all depended. In spite of a number of uprisings, the peasant majority became irrelevant to Haitian politics—at least until the late 1980s—and no government in the past 150 years has made a significant investment in the rural sector.

Culture and Language

The ruling group, especially the educated elite, was oriented toward French cultural models. They sought to contrast themselves as sharply as possible with the peasantry, who were oriented toward their own cultural models forged from Haitian and African experiences. Thus, Haiti developed two cultures, a national peasant-based culture and an elite culture that was ambiguous in its identification, but that served to "delegitimize" the peasantry.

The use of language in Haiti is a good example of this, since language even more than color has been a class marker in Haiti. Creole is the language shared by all Haitians. Its vocabulary is largely derived from French, but its grammar is distinct, making the two languages mutually unintelligible. Historically, 5 to 10 percent of the population has also spoken French. Until the late 1980s, French was the only official language, the medium of law, oration, and literature, of all proper formality. Creole is viewed as the language of intimacy, humor, and through its proverbs, the wisdom of the lower classes.

With attitudes that pertain to all Haitian culture, both the monolingual Creole speaker and the bilingual Creole/French speaker are ambivalent toward the two languages. The elite are both sentimental toward Creole and disdainful of it. At the same time, there is a somewhat stilted quality to Haitian French; it is a language without slang. French symbolizes social dominance, but French utterances often lack substance, for example, in political oratory. The monolingual Creole speaker shares many of these attitudes. Creole is seen both as the truly Haitian form of expression and as a kind of baby talk without a grammar. Creole marks a person as "stupid." On the other hand, the Creole phrase *pale fwanse* ("to speak French") means "to be a hypocrite."

French does more than symbolize social dominance; it helps to reproduce it. Creole speakers who wish to become educated have until recently needed to do so in French. Literacy had to be acquired through a second language. The government official or the lawyer who insists on speaking French to a peasant even though both could use Creole continues the linguistic exploitation. Giving Creole legal equality with French was an important component of the political struggles of the 1980s.

Creole is not the only aspect of Haitian peasant culture that is denied legitimacy. The folk religion, vodoun, is perceived by the elite as powerful, even a necessary resort at times, but a threat to their status in Western civilization. Common-law marriage (*plasaj*), however long-standing, must be ratified in an expensive church ceremony to receive respectability. The physical features of the masses are despised and feared by many of their lighter-skinned compatriots. These characteristics of Haitian culture are the heritage of the colonial period, which ended formally almost two centuries ago.

From Independence to the Midtwentieth Century

After independence in 1804, neither France nor the United States gave Haiti diplomatic recognition, though trade links, especially with the United States, were very active. France waited 25 years before recognizing Haitian sovereignty—and then only at the crippling price of 60 million francs in "indemnities." The United States did not recognize Haiti until the U.S. Civil War. Even the Vatican considered Haiti "schismatic" until 1860.

Beginning with the need to pay the French indemnity, Haitian governments began to borrow heavily from French, American, and German sources. The late nineteenth and early twentieth centuries were marked by increased political and financial instability, as one group after another grabbed the presidency.

This period climaxed in 1915, when the U.S. Marines invaded Haiti, ostensibly because of the political crisis but principally to gain control of Haiti's finances at a time when German influence in Haiti was ascendant. The gold in the national treasury was removed to a bank in New York, and the Haitian currency, the gourde, was tied to the U.S. dollar by treaty. More than 3,000 Haitian guerrillas were killed by the U.S. Marines in the aftermath of the Occupation.

The U.S. Marines remained in control of Haiti until 1934. American financial control did not end until 1946. The U.S. Marines established temporary stability by forming the Haitian Army and through elections that gave the presidency to a series of elite politicians. During the Occupation the road system was improved, and attempts were made to reorient the classical French education system. None of these actions permanently changed Haiti's political or economic structure, however.

The lasting legacy of the Occupation was rather the intellectual and ideological ferment caused by the shock to Haitian sovereignty and pride. The Occupation confirmed that the United States, and not France, was to be the metropolitan center for Haiti in the twentieth century.

The Duvalier Era

The midtwentieth century saw the beginning of an unprecedented period of personal rule by the Duvalier family, which remained in power for almost three decades. The orientation of the François Duvalier government (1957–1971) was in part a reaction against the dominance of the mulatto elite. Duvalier's main program, however, came to be the establishment of absolute personal power. A period of terror in the early 1960s resulted in the departure of many professionals and businesspeople, as well as in the alienation of foreign governments and a sharp reduction in foreign aid and investments. The road system deteriorated, and many economic ventures halted. In 1964, François Duvalier had himself declared president for life. He maintained power through a reshuffled army and his own militia, commonly known as the Tonton Macoutes, as well as through the tacit support of the U.S. government. Duvalier did what no other Haitian president had done before him: he died a natural death in the National Palace and passed on the reins of power to his son.

The Duvalier period generated the first important wave of Haitian exiles to the United States. Most of these exiles were upper- and middle-class Haitians; they entered the United States legally, though generally as immigrants rather than refugees. They established vibrant, though class-divided, communities, especially in New York. Many intended to return to Haiti but had to wait as long as two decades before they felt safe to do so.

The 15 years (1971–1986) of the Jean-Claude Duvalier regime were a period of change for Haiti. Since most of the government's opponents were subdued, there was a reduction in political terror. The regime established a modus vivendi with the business elite. Foreign aid soared, resulting notably in the reconstruction of the road system and some infrastructure in the capital, Port-au-Prince. Investments created an important light-industry sector, with mostly American companies taking advantage of Haiti's low wages. These industries included the assembly of clothes, softballs and electronic equipment and even the sorting of grocery coupons. Remittances from Haitians abroad became an increasingly important element in the economy. Decades of government neglect unraveled the Haitian environment to the point that agriculture was in serious decline. Pressure for arable land forced people to cultivate steeper mountain slopes; stories were told of people "falling off their gardens." Deforestation has continued apace. With the tree cover gone, tropical rains that once nourished crops became a *lavalas,* a torrent that carried away the soil.

The influence of the United States on Haitian affairs, which was obscured under François Duvalier, again became apparent during his son's regime. The Carter administration pressured the Haitian government to relax controls on the radio and press in the late 1970s. Tight political control was resumed a few days after the Reagan victory in the American presidential election in 1980 and remained until the last weeks of the Duvalier regime. Jean-Claude Duvalier was supported by the Reagan administration until public unrest made his rule untenable early in 1986.

It was during the Jean-Claude Duvalier regime that the major flow of Haitians leaving for the United States occurred, beginning in the late 1970s and culminating in 1980. Most of the thousands who fled Haiti at this time left in boats without visas or other documentation. After a series of battles in American courts, most of these Haitians were given the status of "Cuban/Haitian entrant." This status did not certify them as refugees, but it did grant them an ambiguous legal position in the United States. During the last five years of the Duvalier period, however, Haitian "boat people" were intercepted by the U.S. Coast Guard. The great majority were forcibly repatriated to Haiti, with the cooperation of the Haitian government.

After the Duvaliers

In the hours after the Duvalier family was escorted from Haiti on a U.S. government airplane in February 1986, a new government announced itself to the nation. All of its members, except for a few who resigned in the following months, had been figures in the Duvalier regime. The politics of this and succeeding Haitian governments was widely called "Duvalierism without Duvalier."

The departure of Jean-Claude Duvalier opened a national dialogue on a level never previously experienced in Haiti. Peasant groups, labor unions, and political parties formed. The greatest achievement of this period was the adoption of a new constitution in 1987, the first drafted with widespread public participation. The constitution restricted the power of the executive, recognized Creole as the official language, and removed restrictions on practicing the vodoun religion.

The key political term of the late 1980s was *dechoukaj,* the "uprooting" of the Duvalierist past. An important focus of "uprooting" was the Tonton Macoutes, who sought refuge as attachés in the Haitian Army, remaining an important force for political repression. With the exception of the first months of the Aristide administration, the post-Duvalier period was marked by human rights abuses that surpassed even those of the François Duvalier regime. The repression was unusually broad in its scope. Because large numbers of urban and rural poor insisted on being part of the political process, they became the victims of political persecution in unprecedented numbers. During most of this period, the United States maintained its policy of intercepting and returning Haitians who attempted to enter the United States without visas.

The constitution provided for presidential elections in 1987 and the establishment of an independent electoral council. The election never took place. It was stopped by a massacre of people in Port-au-Prince as they waited to vote. After a series of coups, elections were again scheduled for December 1990. This time the elections were held successfully and were regarded by international observers as fair.

The Aristide Presidency

Father Jean-Bertrand Aristide won the presidential election of 1990 with 67 percent of the votes. He was swept into power by the *lavalas,* a torrential flood of popularity, especially among the poor. Aristide was a Catholic priest who served at the church of Saint Jean Bosco in a poor neighborhood of Port-au-Prince, where he began preaching for social justice in the last months of the Duvalier regime. A series of assassination attempts brought Aristide to national and international attention.

Aristide took an active role in the anti-Duvalier movement that was fostered by the Catholic Church. The Church hierarchy, however, was opposed to Aristide's activism, and he was expelled from his religious order. Later, the Vatican was the only state to recognize the military government that overthrew him.

The eight months of the Aristide administration were marked by decreases in human rights abuses (though anti-Aristide elements in the army remained active) and in numbers of Haitians attempting to leave the country. Aristide began to reform the civil service and the justice system. He spoke of economic as well as social justice, even though his economic policies were vague. Most important, the election of Aristide marked a symbolic shift: The man of the people had been elected. These changes were intolerable to many in the business sector, the military, and the old Duvalierists. In September 1991, the Haitian Army staged a coup against Aristide, who barely escaped to exile in Venezuela and the United States. Haiti was plunged into three years of political and economic turmoil.

In response to the coup, the Organization of American States (OAS) imposed an embargo on Haiti. The U.S. government refused to recognize the de facto military government but joined the embargo with considerable ambivalence. The coup leaders had close ties to the United States: They had previously received military training in the United States and funds from the Central Intelligence Agency (CIA) (Farmer 1994:219).

In June 1993, under pressure from the United Nations and the United States, the coup leader, General Raoul Cedras, and President Aristide signed the Governor's Island Accord, which provided for Aristide's return to Haiti in October 1993, supported by a multinational force to ''professionalize'' the Haitian Army. The military government had no real intention of permitting Aristide to return, however, and repression of his followers increased steadily. The stalemate ended in September 1994, when U.S. military forces occupied Haiti for the second time this century.

The U.S. invasion of Haiti, conducted peacefully because of last-minute negotiations, restored Aristide to the Haitian presidency but circumscribed his ability to implement his policies. The National Treasury was truly emptied after three years of corrupt military rule. Thousands of deaths had more than decimated the *lavalas*. American troops maintained order in the capital but did little to ''uproot'' the Duvalierist resistance. Political security in the countryside remained fragile at best. In March 1995, the unilateral American force was converted to a multinational United Nations force commanded by an American officer. The future of Haitian society, of the environment upon which it was based, and of the politics that directed it was as uncertain as ever.

EXODUS AND TRANSIT

Leaving Haiti

Given the conditions described above, it is not surprising that 1 million Haitians have emigrated since the 1950s (Allman 1981). An estimated 400,000 to

500,000 Haitians have settled in the United States, with major communities in the metropolitan areas of New York, Miami, Boston, Chicago, and Philadelphia.

Haitians have emigrated to the United States since prerevolutionary times and have come from all sectors of Haitian society. They started to arrive in great numbers when the elite and middle class fled the Duvalier regime in the late 1950s and resettled in the northeastern United States. They were joined by a steady stream from the urban working class seeking relief from declining political and economic conditions throughout the 1960s and 1970s. Joining those who legally immigrated and many who overstayed their tourist visas, a small but steady stream of Haitians entered the United States clandestinely by boat beginning in 1972. As conditions in Haiti declined precipitously, the number of Haitians risking their lives at sea increased dramatically in the late 1970s, culminating in an influx of 25,000 in 1980, at the same time as 125,000 Cubans flooded into south Florida. With its proximity to Haiti, south Florida, especially Miami, was the intended destination for thousands of "boat people" fleeing Haiti in the 1980s and 1990s.

For a number of years, the Bahamas had served as a focus of emigration for Haitian peasants. (Considerable migration to the Dominican Republic still takes place, especially during the cane-cutting season; the same was true of Cuba until 1959.) By the mid-1970s, however, the Bahamians showed less tolerance for Haitian workers as tourism waned and the economy declined. In 1978, when the Bahamian government threatened to deport illegal Haitians, many of them chose to continue their search for a better life in Miami rather than return to Haiti. The movement to Miami had begun.

As the Bahamas became less attractive and as smuggling operations from Haiti became more sophisticated (and commercialized), the outflow of people from Haiti to Florida increased. In addition, requirements for obtaining entry visas from the U.S. consulate in Haiti stiffened, making it more difficult than ever to travel to the United States legally. A series of favorable court rulings (see below) for Haitians seeking asylum in the United States, which included work authorization on release from detention, added impetus to the movement. Many Haitians who were determined to leave Haiti, but who could not afford documents or an airplane ticket, sold their meager assets to pay for the trip by sea or joined with others to build boats for the 700-mile voyage. Unknown numbers of Haitians have died in their attempt to reach the United States, as craft designed for coastal traffic foundered or dishonorable captains abandoned their human cargo to their fate.

Most Haitians were unable to make the voyage in a single crossing. They had to stop at Cuba or islands in the Bahamas to replenish supplies or make repairs. The Cubans generally provided the Haitians assistance and towed them back into the Gulf Stream to continue their voyage. The Bahamian reception was less than congenial and sometimes inhumane, as witnessed by the Cayo Lobos incident in early 1981, when the Bahamian government refused to rescue shipwrecked Haitians from a deserted, waterless island. The Haitian government also declined to intervene. Haitians who did make the voyage directly from Haiti to Florida often spent 10 to 14 days at sea and staggered ashore dehydrated, famished, and ill.

Although the majority of Haitians arrived in Florida by boat during this period, commercial airlines also brought undocumented Haitians directly from Port-au-Prince to Miami. The "Boeing people," as they were called, were more often from the more-educated working and middle classes than were the arrivals by sea. Well-organized commercial ventures that routed Haitians through the Dominican Republic, Jamaica, and Curacao often ended with sadly disappointed Haitians who discovered that their costly visas were not valid for the United States.

Prior to 1977, approximately 7,000 boat people were recorded by the U.S. Immigration and Naturalization Service (INS). In 1978–1979 alone, more than 8,300 entries were recorded. The influx jumped to 40,000 Haitian entries in 1980 and the first six months of 1981 (Cuban-Haitian Task Force 1981). The INS estimated that between 40 and 50 percent of the arrivals during this period may have escaped detection, so the figures may record only half of the actual arrivals.

Unlike Haitians arriving in south Florida in the 1970s, most of those who arrived during the 1980–1981 influx had embarked from Haiti (and not the Bahamas), pouring out from all areas of the country. The main areas of departure were from the northern and northwestern coasts of Haiti. The Department of the North was most frequently listed as the place of origin by arriving Haitians. The Department of the West, including Port-au-Prince, was the second largest sending area. (Many of the Haitians arriving from this region entered by airplane and were stopped at Miami International Airport.) The third major area of outflow was the Artibonite Valley, where large-scale thefts of peasant land have been alleged. The number of recorded arrivals listing southern regions as their origin was the smallest.

U.S. Policy towards Haitians Seeking to Leave Haiti

Haitians arriving in the United States have faced a public perception of themselves as illiterate, impoverished individuals who would drain public resources. Haitians were further stigmatized as health risks. In the 1970s they were identified with tuberculosis. In the early 1980s, they were declared to be a population at risk for the human immunodeficiency virus (HIV) by the federal Centers for Disease Control (CDC) and the New York City Health Department. In the 1990s, the HIV issue surfaced again in the Food and Drug Administration's ban on blood donations by Haitians.

The most consistent aspect of the U.S. federal government's response to the Haitian boat people is the view that they are not collectively entitled to be designated as refugees, as individuals who fear returning to their own countries because they fear persecution on the basis of race, color, national origin, religion, social group, or political opinion. In the view of the U.S. Department of State and the INS, Haitians are "economic" rather than "political" refugees; that is, their motivation to enter the United States stems from the desire for employment rather than from actual persecution or fear of persecution. Thus, since the 1970s, Haitians' claims for asylum as refugees have been almost uniformly rejected, despite evidence that human and civil rights have been regularly violated in Haiti and that persecution for political opinions occurs there. Opposition to this stance has taken two directions: first, that Haitians should be considered legal refugees and second, that their claims should be accorded due process in any case.

Haitians and their advocates have fought an unparalleled series of legal battles to ensure that claimants receive due process of law: fair treatment, including access to Creole interpreters and attorneys at INS hearings; and work authorizations on release from INS detention. In 1978, a flagrant violation of Haitians' rights occurred when the INS attempted to clear a backload of Haitian asylum cases by processing 150 per day and by revoking work authorizations. Advocates for the Haitians took the INS to court. In June 1980, a federal court, ruling in *Haitian Refugee Center v. Civiletti,* ordered new INS asylum hearings for approximately 5,000 Haitians and rebuked the federal government for intentional discrimination and racism.

Haitians and the Mariel Crisis

The Cuban Mariel exodus of April 1980 greatly complicated matters. Faced with the prospect of providing refugee status to 125,000 Cubans and pressured by the Haitian dilemma, the Carter administration equivocated, creating the ambiguous legal category of "Cuban/Haitian entrant (status pending)." The category included undocumented Haitians and Cubans who arrived in the United States before October 10, 1980. Cubans and Haitians entering the United States without documentation after that date were subject to exclusion and deportation by the INS, although they were eligible for the same social service benefits as entrants while they were in the United States.

Faced with the Mariel crisis, the Carter administration directed the Federal Emergency Management Agency to handle the immediate problems of shelter, food, and other necessities for the arriving Cubans and later for the Haitians. In June 1980, the Cuban-Haitian Task Force, a special interagency unit, attempted to institute a method for processing and resettling the entrants. Expecting to begin a new life in Miami, arriving Haitians who were encountered by the INS found themselves transported to the Krome South camp and later to the Krome North camp, parts of a former Nike missile base in the Everglades swamp. The camp was initially plagued with numerous problems: inadequate staff, especially Creole interpreters; lack of running water, sanitation, and supplies; lack of telephones and other means of communication for the Haitians; and lack of shelter other than tents and hangars. By the end of 1980, the government had begun to build permanent structures, including dormitories.

Anxiety, confusion, and pain marked the faces of Haitians who did not understand the chaotic resettlement process, were unsure of their fate, and tried their best to wait out the boredom of each day. Concertina wire atop the camp fence grimly reinforced the notion that the United States might not be the friendly haven the Haitians had sought.

In cooperation with voluntary agencies, such as the U.S. Catholic Conference, the Lutheran Immigration and Refugee Service, Church World Service, World Relief, and HIAS (Hebrew Immigrant Aid Society), the Cuban-Haitian Task Force developed a more systematic, responsible settlement approach requiring verified sponsors and reducing time spent in the camp. The Fascell-Stone Amendment to the Refugee Assistance Act of 1980 provided Haitians and Cubans with a limited range of federal benefits and made states eligible for 100 percent reimbursement for cash and medical assistance to them. Thus, funds became available to assist Haitians with their immediate needs and with longer-term social service needs.

Growing numbers of Haitian minors posed special problems during this period, as they often entered in the company of siblings, unrelated adults, or kin whose relationship could not be verified immediately, rather than with their parents. Many of these minors were declared to be "unaccompanied," in some cases according to a narrow American definition of kinship rather than the more extensive Haitian system. Thus, some minors were unnecessarily separated from bona fide relatives or adoptive parents. Unaccompanied minors were placed in a separate facility at Krome South until care and sponsorship were developed by the Office of Refugee Resettlement (ORR), which was responsible for them. The Haitian minors were gradually transferred to Greer Woodycrest, a facility in Millbrook, New York, where they received care and educational opportunities until appropriate placements were made. Krome South closed in July 1981, and all the minors were resettled out of Greer Woodycrest by January 1982.

The 1980s: Interdiction and the IRCA

The new Reagan administration, seeing the flow of Haitians unabated, addressed Haitian emigration in two ways: by halting the resettlement of undocumented Haitians and by preventing their arrival in the United States in the first place through a policy of "interdiction."

Beginning in May 1981, undocumented Haitians were detained rather than released. Krome North was turned into a permanent detention camp. Five federal prisons, the INS processing center in Brooklyn, and a former military base at Fort Allen, Puerto Rico, were also pressed into service. Except for those released on humanitarian parole, nearly 1,800 Haitians spent 15 months in bleak despair until they were released by federal court order. The court rebuked INS for failing

to follow proper administrative procedures. A federal appeals court further rebuked the federal agencies involved for racism and discrimination.

The interdiction policy began in September 1981, when the U.S. Coast Guard
began patrolling the Haitian coasts for the purpose of intercepting Haitian vessels on the high seas. Passengers were interviewed to determine whether they
had a legitimate claim to political asylum in the United States, and the great
majority were forcibly brought to Port-au-Prince. The Haitian government concurred in this policy, although its legality under international law has been questioned. The U.S. Supreme Court, however, ruled in 1993 that the U.S.
government was not barred from returning aliens found outside U.S. borders
(Mitchell 1994:76). The interdiction policy remained in effect for ten years. Only
28 of the 25,000 Haitians interviewed were granted political asylum (Mitchell
1994:73).

The interdiction policy greatly reduced the outflow from Haiti, with an occasional boat landing in full view of sunbathers basking on south Florida
beaches. Although the newly arrived Haitians were no longer singled out for
incarceration—Krome North now resembled a small United Nations with aliens
of many nationalities confined there—this fact did not make their detention
easier to bear as their claims for asylum were decided.

On a more positive front for some of the Haitian exiles, the Immigration
Reform and Control Act (IRCA) of 1986 helped to resolve the legal status of
Cuban-Haitian entrants and some illegal immigrants who arrived before 1982.
Through the IRCA, Haitians could regularize their status through the Cuban-
Haitian Entrant Adjustment and Special Agricultural Worker provisions. By do-
ing so, they became eligible for permanent residency, and their documentation
for employment became less confusing. In Florida, implementation of the IRCA
proceeded well, with 20,000 Haitians processing applications.

The 1990s: The Aftermath of the Coup against
President Aristide

At least 1,500 Haitians were killed during the first six weeks after the coup
against President Aristide in September 1991. The first response of the Bush
administration was to stop interviewing passengers on intercepted Haitian boats:
They were simply all repatriated. Soon the spectacle of Haitians being forced
to disembark at Port-au-Prince led to a shift in American immigration policy
toward Haitians. Undocumented Haitians were now sent to the U.S. military
base at Guantánamo, Cuba. The U.S. administration maintained that neither U.S.
nor international law regarding the treatment of refugees applied to the Haitians
at Guantánamo. In the seven months between September 1991 and March 1992,
some 34,000 Haitians were detained, more than during the entire previous decade (Farmer 1994:269).

A third of the Haitians interviewed at Guantánamo were given permission to
apply for political asylum in the United States, in sharp contrast to the figures

for Haitians who had been interviewed aboard U.S. Coast Guard vessels (Mitchell 1994:74). The growing numbers of Haitians at the Guantánamo base led the Bush administration to revert to its policy of interdiction and forcible return. The executive order for this change in policy authorized the INS to interview Haitian passengers to determine their refugee status, but interviews were not conducted.

In the meantime, the Haitians who had been taken to Guantánamo were tested for the presence of HIV, in contrast to other groups, notably Cubans who entered the United States by boat or airplane. Two hundred sixty-eight of the Haitians at Guantánamo were found to be HIV positive. They were isolated at Camp Bulkley on the Guantánamo base and were reported to be mistreated and forced to receive injections of medications and long-term contraceptives. In early 1993, a federal court found conditions at Camp Bulkley to constitute "cruel and unusual punishment" under the U.S. Constitution, and the HIV-positive Haitians were brought to the United States (Farmer 1994:277).

The Bush administration treatment of Haitians leaving their country became an issue during the 1992 U.S. presidential campaign. As the Democratic candidate, Bill Clinton denounced forced repatriation and delay in restoring Aristide to power. Shortly before his inauguration, however, Clinton reversed his campaign positions. Concerned with American political pressure against a new influx of Haitians, the Clinton administration continued the policy of forcible repatriation until just before the U.S. invasion of Haiti in October 1994. A few weeks after the invasion, the Clinton administration forcibly repatriated most of the remaining Haitians at Guantánamo in spite of continued insecurity and human rights abuses by members of the former military regime.

INITIAL RESETTLEMENT

Haitians seeking asylum in the United States are generally young men and women who, if they had remained in Haiti and been employed, would have formed part of the primary sector of the labor force and the country's hope for the future. Cuban-Haitian Task Force (1981) statistics indicate that approximately 30 percent of the 1980–1981 arrivals were female and 70 percent male. Less than 10 percent were minors under the age of 18. Fifty-five to 60 percent were between 18 and 29 years old, and 25 to 30 percent were between 30 and 44. Approximately 5 percent were over 45.

A Cuban-Haitian Task Force (1981) sample showed that although the majority of the Haitian boat people were illiterate, many possessed rudimentary reading and writing skills, usually in French. Occupational data show that most male arrivals had most frequently been engaged in unskilled work, primarily field cropping, with a minority possessing such skills as tailoring and mechanical repair work. Haitian women arrivals had work experiences as seamstresses, domestics, vendors, farmers, and factory workers. (The majority of the Haitian arrivals listed themselves as single, but these data are difficult to interpret, as common-law marriages may not have been included in the responses and because the question was also misinterpreted as having asked whether they arrived in the United States alone.)

A large percentage of the Haitian boat people, approximately 85 percent, settled in southern Florida, primarily in the Miami area. New York and New Jersey received most of the remaining 15 percent of the arriving Haitians. Secondary migration has occurred among these areas since 1981, as Haitians have become discouraged by employment and housing problems in Florida or find the northern winters too harsh.

The main problems of the Haitians are underemployment and substandard housing. Employment poses the most persistent problem for new arrivals, especially as they are unskilled, do not speak English or Spanish, and sometimes are illiterate. Employment is often seasonal or temporary and low paying with few benefits. Haitian men and women find work in service industries, factories, construction, or as domestics. They must compete with other immigrant groups, especially with Spanish speakers, whose language is an advantage in Miami. Although statistics are not available, lack of employment has forced many Haitians to become agricultural migrant laborers, traveling along the eastern seaboard to pick crops. Others have opted for a grueling life of cutting sugar cane in Belle Glade or Immokalee, Florida; they are the poorest of the Haitian immigrants. Haitians also compete for agricultural jobs in Homestead, south of Miami, and in Broward County, to the north. Opportunities for exploiting these Haitians abound.

In Miami itself, most of the Haitians have settled in the Edison-Little River section, now known as "Little Haiti." A poverty-stricken zone with substandard housing, the area is the center for Haitian business, social, cultural, and religious activities in Miami. Up to a dozen individuals, related or not, find themselves living together in houses built for single families. The housing is expensive, despite its delapidated state. Rats and other vermin create environmental and health problems. The Haitians have formed a highly mobile population, individuals moving from one residence to another as required by circumstances. Often, only a few members of a household are employed; their wages support the others who are less fortunate.

A survey (Stepick and Portes 1986:338) of post-1980 Haitian arrivals in south Florida provides evidence of the economic conditions faced by this group. The random sample of 499 recent arrivals living in Little Haiti, Fort Lauderdale, and Belle Glade showed an average educational level of less than elementary school for both men and women. About two thirds had been employed in Haiti, but 80 percent of the women and more than one third of the men were unemployed in Florida. This was a higher percentage of unemployment than that of Haitians arriving in the United States between 1970 and 1980. It was also higher than the level of unemployment for Mariel Cubans arriving in 1980.

In addition, many Haitians experienced downward mobility compared with occupations in the homeland. Their incomes in Miami barely hovered above the poverty line. Women arrivals were also at a greater disadvantage than men in finding employment and more likely to receive welfare assistance, mainly because of their children. Stepick and Portes (1986:346) found that key factors in finding jobs were knowledge of English and knowledge of the labor market. Even better-educated Haitians, however, faced high rates of unemployment and very low income.

Unlike Cuban arrivals who found work within the well-established and economically prosperous Cuban community in Miami, the existing local Haitian business community was neither large nor prosperous enough to offer a source of income for fellow countrymen (Stepick 1992). The Cuban community had been built for two decades by refugees with significant amounts of capital.

Social, educational, and health services were overwhelmed and unprepared to meet the needs of these particular arrivals. Agency personnel had little knowledge or understanding of Haitian cultural beliefs and social patterns; few Haitian Creole interpreters were available. Fear of detection by the INS also impeded access to health and mental health services (Spero 1985).

INTEGRATION

Social and Economic Change

Despite their problems, many of the Haitian boat people had the advantage of preexisting networks of kin and friends in the United States who eased the transition and adaptation process. A study of the boat people in the early 1980s showed that these Haitians had a remarkably positive outlook about their circumstances and prospects in the United States and were anxious to learn English and obtain an education (Stepick 1982). A follow-up survey in Little Haiti and Fort Lauderdale in 1986 showed some small improvement in Haitians' economic conditions. The improvement may stem from the ability of many of the Haitians to adjust their immigration status. However, the very low starting point ensured a continuing precarious economic profile (Portes and Grosfoguel 1994:67).

In the decade since the large influx of Haitians in 1980, a small Haitian business enclave has developed in Little Haiti with nearly 300 businesses. Most of these enterprises have been established by professional and middle-class Haitian-Americans who moved to Miami from the Northeast. The power to employ other Haitians is limited, as most Haitian businesses are small. Nevertheless, these businesses give Haitians a visible commercial presence in Miami and offer services and a sense of community to Little Haiti. An entire informal economy of child care, restaurants, and unlicensed taxi, repair, and construction services still offers Haitians an alternative route to making a living. More educated Haitians have gained a toehold in education, law enforcement, and the medical profession (Stepick 1992; Portes and Stepick 1993).

The educational system has been particularly responsive to addressing the needs of Haitian exiles. Haitians traditionally place a high value on education for its intrinsic worth and as an avenue of social mobility. Among the Haitian-born population in the United States, two in five have received some college education and only one in ten has less than eight grades of schooling (Miller 1994). Nearly 55 percent of the Haitian boat people interviewed in south Florida in the early 1980s had received some education in the United States, especially in English-language training (Stepick and Portes 1986:336). Although there can be no assertion about the Haitian boat people specifically, Miami-Dade Community College registered substantial growth in non-American black students, with the largest increase coming from the Haitian population (Vorp n.d.).

Ethnic Identity

For Haitians, the immigrant and exile experience has been strongly structured by issues of race and ethnicity. The issue of race hits Haitians squarely in the face on a daily basis, regardless of their social background. Phenotypically, and thus socially within American society, the majority of Haitians are perceived to be black. This categorization renders Haitian immigrants socially invisible within American society and subjects Haitians to the same kinds of discrimination faced by African-Americans. It also ignores a different system of complex social categorization within Haitian culture whereby skin color does not automatically translate into perceived social class status.

Haitians will proclaim their pride in being black and in being from the second free nation in the Western Hemisphere, a free nation of blacks. They do not deny their racial heritage. Thrust, however, into a dominant white culture where cultural characteristics can blunt ascription based on race, Haitians may use their cultural characteristics individually and collectively for access to resources and upward mobility. In the presentation of the self to white Americans, Haitians may draw upon the European side of their cultural heritage to engender more favorable reactions and treatment. By stressing French language and culture, as well as their willingness to work hard and their ambition, some Haitians try to combat the negative public perception of them as illiterate, impoverished people with nothing to offer the United States (Charles 1992; Fouron 1983; Woldemikael 1989).

The use of ethnicity and culture to minimize the negative connotations of race may distance Haitian immigrants from African-Americans, whose social position Haitians understand to be disadvantageous in American society. This stance causes tensions between Haitians and African-Americans. Although they often support each other on issues of racial discrimination, African-Americans and Haitians often share a negative opinion of each other based on perceived differences in culture. African-Americans are particularly wary of Haitians as competitors in the labor market and for community resources. The immigrant mentality of Haitians—their desire to make it in America and their resourcefulness—is viewed with considerable suspicion. At the same time, Haitians are largely unaware of the difficulties of the African-American experience. In Miami especially, where Cubans have achieved remarkable success, both Haitians and African-Americans are fearful of social and economic marginalization. They compete to avoid being on the lowest rung of the socioeconomic ladder (Stepick 1992).

The perceptions and attitudes of young Haitian exiles and especially of the American-born children of Haitian immigrants are reported to be strikingly different in this regard. Their identification with Haiti is relatively weak; it is an abstract homeland they do not remember or have never seen. Haitian high school students in Miami are reported to disguise their Haitian origins. The younger generation of Haitians in the United States identify as black, an identity they do not see as different from African-American. Haitian students model African-American cultural styles, in contrast to their elders' aspirations toward white American cultural styles. These differences in identity and style are an important part of the conflicts of assimilation that Haitian families have experienced (Woldemikael 1989).

At an organizational level, Haitians have leveraged various identities as ethnics, exiles, and blacks to gain access to resources made available to groups in American society on these bases. Haitian community-based agencies have been successful since 1980 as deliverers of social services such as translation, English-language classes and vocational training, employment counseling and placement, referral for local, state, and federal agencies, and legal advice. These centers have helped Haitian exiles to solve temporary and long-term problems associated with adaptation to American society. Even along the migrant worker routes, the Haitian presence had been addressed by agencies designed to meet their particular needs (Chierici 1991).

Definitions of self and community are also constantly informed and structured by Haitians' ongoing relations with their countrymen still at home. Haitians "of the diaspora" have an intense feeling of nationalism and investment in the future of their homeland. They are a significant force in the economy of Haiti through remittances to family members and through trade. Haitians abroad invest in Haiti as a hedge against their uncertain future in their countries of exile. Ties with Haiti are reinforced through visits, exchanges of audiocassettes, and news of Haiti reported in a variety of American-based Haitian newspapers. The Haitian-American press has both assisted with assimilation and maintained Haiti as an important focal point for its readership. Since 1986, many of these periodicals have taken on a new role since they are distributed in Haiti as well as in the United States.

The worlds of Haiti and the United States are not separate. Haitians live the reality of Haiti as well as of their daily lives in the United States. Both societies form the context of what it means to be Haitian. Jean-Bertrand Aristide made this link between Haitians inside and outside the country clear in his appeal for support and campaign funds from what he called the "Tenth Department," the community of Haitians living abroad. Regarding them as part of his constituency, Aristide spoke out strongly about issues affecting Haitians overseas, for example, being labelled as a population at risk for HIV (Richman 1992).

The few Haitian exiles admitted in the 1990s have not faced a warmer welcome than their compatriots who entered the United States in 1980. The image of thousands of ragged Haitians landing in barely seaworthy boats on the shores of Florida in 1980 is permanently etched in the minds of the American public. It is an image that repeatedly raised its head in the debate about U.S. policy toward Haitians in the 1990s, especially after the coup against Aristide. A beleaguered south Florida simply did not wish to receive another influx of people, either from Haiti or from Cuba. Public opinion, once again, did not favor the Haitians. A poll conducted in 1993 found that 65 percent of Americans thought that Haitians created problems for the United States; only 19 percent said that they benefited the country. Only Iranians fared as poorly as an immigrant group in the poll (Puente 1993).

Nevertheless, Haitians bring many strengths from the Haitian cultural heritage: a strong work ethic, fortitude, perseverance in the most arduous circumstances, deep religious faith, high self-respect, reliance on the extended family, and a tradition of sharing. These characteristics have enabled them to make a new life in the United States despite their problems and a welcome that has been less than open-armed.

CONCLUSIONS AND PROSPECTS

Haitians have faced enormous difficulties as exiles in the United States. Successive U.S. administrations have refused to recognize Haitians as legal refugees. Only strenuous legal battles have won for Haitians the right to have their cases for asylum heard by the INS. Having lost in court, three U.S. administrations have used other means for keeping Haitians out: turning them back at sea under a dubious arrangement with the Duvalier dictatorship or keeping them offshore to avoid U.S. constitutional responsibilities.

Two factors have generated U.S. policies toward Haitian exiles. The desire for political and economic control in a troubled neighbor has led to U.S. support for repressive regimes in Haiti. The fear of large numbers of Haitians needing public resources in the United States has made admitting Haitian immigrants politically expensive. These factors have resulted in denial that political abuses occur in Haiti and great ambivalence about the struggle for human rights there. American perceptions and attitudes about Haiti and its problems are unlikely to change. Haitians are not likely to be any more accepted as refugees in the future than they have been in the past.

Haitians in the United States, whether former boat people or long-term immigrants, continue to build their communities in spite of their lack of economic resources. Like other immigrant groups, they face questions of identity and cultural assimilation. Because of American notions of race and ethnicity, the issues faced by Haitians becoming Americans are particularly complex.

REFERENCES

Allman, James. 1981. Haitian Migration: Thirty Years Assessed. *Migration Today* 10(1): 7–12.

Buchanan, Susan Huelsebusch. 1979. Language and Identity: Haitians in New York City. *International Migration Review* 13(2):298–313.

Buchanan Stafford, Susan. 1987. The Haitians: The Cultural Meaning of Race and Identity. In *New Immigrants in New York City*. Edited by Nancy Foner. New York: Columbia University Press. Pp. 131–158.

Charles, Carolle. 1992. Transnationalism in the Construct of Haitian Migrants' Racial Categories of Identity in New York City. In *Towards a Transnational Perspective on Migration*. Edited by Nina Glick Schiller, Linda Basch, and Cristina Blanc-Szanton. *Annals of the New York Academy of Sciences* 645:101–123.

Chierici, Rose-Marie Cassagnol. 1991. *Demele "Making It": Migration and Adaptation among Haitian Boat People in the United States*. New York: AMS Press.

Cuban-Haitian Task Force. 1981. *Entrant Data Report* (May 31). Washington, D.C.

Farmer, Paul. 1994. *The Uses of Haiti*. Monroe, Maine: Common Courage Press.

Fouron, Georges. 1983. The Black Dilemma in the U.S.: The Haitian Experience. *Journal of Caribbean Studies* 3(3):242–265.

Leyburn, James G. 1966 (orig. 1941). *The Haitian People*. New Haven, Connecticut: Yale University Press.

Miller, John J. 1994. One Answer to the Haitian Dilemma: Let Them In. *The Wall Street Journal*, August 2.

Mitchell, Christopher. 1994. U.S. Policy toward Haitian Boat People, 1972–93. *Annals of the American Academy of Political and Social Sciences* 534:69–80.

Portes, Alejandro and Ramón Grosfoguel. 1994. Caribbean Diasporas: Migration and Ethnic Communities. *Annals of the American Academy of Political and Social Sciences* 533:48–69.

Portes, Alejandro, and Alex Stepick. 1993. *City on the Edge: The Transformation of Miami*. Berkeley: University of California Press.

Puente, Maria. 1993. USA Cool to Huddled Masses. *USA Today*, July 14. 1A.

Richman, Karen. 1992. A *Lavalas* at Home/A *Lavalas* for "Home": Inflections of Transnationalism in the Discourse of Haitian President Aristide. In *Towards a Transnational Perspective on Migration*. Edited by Nina Glick Schiller, Linda Basch, and Cristina Blanc-Szanton. *Annals of the New York Academy of Sciences* 645: 189–200.

Spero, Abby. 1985. *In America and in Need: Immigrant, Refugee and Entrant Women*. Washington, D.C.: American Association of Community and Junior Colleges.

Stepick, Alex III. 1982. *Haitians in Miami: An Assessment of Their Background and Potential* (Occasional Papers Series. Dialogue no. 12.) Miami: Florida International University Latin American and Caribbean Center.

———. 1992. The Refugees Nobody Wants: Haitians in Miami. In *Miami Now!: Immigration, Ethnicity, and Social Change*. Edited by Guillermo Grenier and Alex Stepick III. Gainesville: University Press of Florida.

Stepick, Alex, and Alejandro Portes. 1986. Flight into Despair: A Profile of Recent Haitian Refugees in South Florida. *International Migration Review* 20(2):329–350.

Vorp, Ronald. n.d. *Acculturation at Miami-Dade Community College, Fall Term 1981 through Fall Term 1991*. Miami, Florida: Miami-Dade Community College, Office of Institutional Research.

Wilkie, James W., and Stephen Haber, Editors. 1983. *Statistical Abstract of Latin America,* Vol. 22. Los Angeles: UCLA Latin American Center Publications.
Woldemikael, Tekle Mariam. 1989. *Becoming Black American: Haitians and American Institutions in Evanston, Illinois.* New York: AMS Press.

Chapter 9

Hmong

Timothy Dunnigan, Douglas P. Olney, Miles A. McNall, and Marline A. Spring

The Hmong were relatively unknown to the American public when they began arriving in the United States from Thailand refugee camps during the spring of 1976. This Laotian ethnic minority had been mentioned in news reports about "tribal" conflicts in Laos during the Vietnam War, but they were called the Meo, which is a derogatory Vietnamese term unacceptable to the Hmong. As the Meo, they were described as a primitive hill tribe who fought fiercely and effectively on the side of the democratically elected government of Laos against Communist insurgents called the Pathet Lao. The tragic results of Hmong involvement with the U.S. Central Intelligence Agency (CIA), a connection dating back to the early 1960s, did not fully come to light until after the Pathet Lao and North Vietnamese took over the country in 1975. Descriptions of the plight of these former allies in the news media fostered a sense of indebtedness toward the Hmong and stimulated concern for those languishing in Thailand refugee camps. Unfortunately, media exposure also created some misleading images of Hmong society.

Two decades have produced a generation of Hmong who have been through the entire kindergarten-through-college school system in the United States. The Hmong community in general has matured to the point where the 6,000 Hmong who continue to enter the country each year no longer have to deal with the same problems of physical survival as their predecessors. While finding good jobs remains difficult for many Hmong particularly for older persons, the young are now much better prepared to move into skilled and professional jobs. As a result, Hmong unemployment rates are falling. The early crisis of resettlement has abated, but new problems, as well as opportunities, have emerged.

Widely divergent views have developed in the Hmong community with respect to a number of issues that should be familiar to most Americans. Not surprisingly, there is much debate about how the Hmong should involve them-selves in politics as a way of influencing domestic and international policies. They are concerned about the quality and content of educational programs that will shape the values of their children. They are struggling with the meaning of gender and age-based differences in a society that seems to set no boundaries. And, of course, the Hmong are concerned about maintaining a unique cultural heritage while establishing, or continually creating, an American identity.

LAOS

The population of Laos is ethnically diverse. The politically dominant Lao, who speak a language closely related to Thai, are concentrated primarily in the alluvial plains of the Mekong River. Linguistically similar groups inhabit the mountain valleys of central and northern Laos. Living on the mountain slopes are populations of Mon-Khmer speakers. The Hmong and Mien, whose lan-guages have been classified as Sino-Tibetan, occupy the highest elevations. As LeBar and Suddard (1960:2) point out, "To the elite—virtually all Lao—the history of Laos is the story of the Lao." This is true despite estimates (Hickey 1955) that the nondominant minorities total half the population. The lowland bias is reflected in most historical and cultural surveys of Laos. Relatively little coverage is given the ethnic minorities, and their importance in recent history is only now being assessed.

Hmong are relative newcomers to Laos, having migrated from China and Vietnam beginning in the first part of the nineteenth century. The area of greatest settlement was the province of Xieng Khouang. Significant numbers also moved into adjacent provinces of Sam Neua, Luang Prabang, and Phong Saly. This concentrated the Hmong in northeastern Laos near the border with Vietnam, an area that became strategically important during the Vietnam War. Adequate documentation of early Hmong history is lacking (see Savina 1924; Dreyer 1976; Weins 1967; Larteguy 1979). Fortunately, additional information based on historical documents and oral traditions is being systematically recorded by a new generation of Hmong and non-Hmong scholars.

Observers writing in the 1950s and 1960s describe Hmong political organi-zation as being generally limited to the village (Hickey 1955; Halpern 1964; LeBar and Suddard 1960; LeBar, Hickey, and Musgrave 1964). Mention is made of Hmong "kings" in China and Vietnam who, for fairly brief periods, con-trolled large areas and dominated neighboring groups, situations that are called "unusual" by Hickey (1955:310; see also Tapp 1985). Although periods of Hmong hegemony were probably infrequent, they have managed on a number of occasions to unify into supralocal organizations against outside political threats, as at the time of the Vietnam War.

In the course of their long history, the Hmong have accommodated to a variety of political systems in China and Southeast Asia. When political soli-darity did not ensure their independence from some dominant nationality, they often enjoyed considerable autonomy because of the way they were integrated into state structures. For instance, LeBar and colleagues (1964:70) describe the following situation in sixteenth-century Kweichow, China: "Tribal chieftains, including Miao [Hmong] chieftains, were appointed to hereditary administrative positions, adopting Chinese surnames and entering into a kind of feudatory arrangement with the imperial government on behalf of tribesmen within their jurisdiction."

The Hmong in Laos sought similar arrangements with French colonial administrators and various Lao political leaders. Hmong strategy was to maximize their autonomy by supporting established authorities or emerging powers. The rewards consisted of increased control over their own affairs at the local level and a sharing in the benefits of national development. In areas where they were numerically and politically weak, they were subjected to discrimination and exploitation by other ethnic groups (Gunn 1990). The struggle for a measure of self-governance in Laos before 1975 has been interpreted by some critics of the U.S. involvement with the Laotian Hmong as a secessionist movement (see Adams and McCoy 1970). By 1975, however, Hmong integration into the political, military, economic, and educational institutions of Laos had progressed to a point where ethnic separatism would have been extremely unlikely, had the royalist government prevailed.

It must be acknowledged that the Hmong have long been perceived in Vietnam, Thailand, and Laos as politically suspect because of their cultural distinctiveness, independence, and ethnic loyalty. On a number of occasions the Hmong have rebelled against the exactions of hostile governments (Jenks 1985). An uprising lasting from 1918 to 1922 spread through parts of northeast Laos and northwest Tonkin (North Vietnam). Because one of the main leaders was Pa Chai, a native curer who prophesied the destruction of the Lao and French oppressors by supernatural means, French historians have denigrated the rebellion as "the crazy man's war" (Larteguy 1979:91–95; Smalley, Vang, and Yang 1990). It was after this rebellion was suppressed that other Hmong leaders were allowed greater political authority by the French in populous Hmong regions of Laos.

Another nativistic movement arose during the mid-1960s in Laos when intensified fighting between government troops and Communist insurgents began destroying many Hmong villages. The movement's prophet was Shong Lue Yang, who promoted Hmong unity and devised a special script for writing the Hmong language. Shong Lue was killed in 1971 by political rivals, but his followers continue to maintain active organizations in Laos, Thailand, and the United States. Some of its adherents, a small but undefined portion of the Laotian Hmong who are implacable enemies of the Pathet Lao and Vietnamese, have conducted resistance activities in Laos intermittently since 1975 (Smalley, Vang, and Yang 1990).

Notwithstanding these episodic revolts, the Hmong assiduously cultivated alliances with other groups and outside political leaders. The choosing of certain allies by Hmong leaders caused deep internal divisions. Two powerful lineages belonging to different clans began in the 1930s to compete for official French recognition in the Nong Het area of Xieng Khouang. The rivalry led to the formation of pro- and anti-French factions and eventually drew many Hmong into the Indochinese wars as combatants on both sides (Lee 1982). The Hmong who achieved political ascendancy during the late colonial period transferred their allegiance to the French-supported constitutional monarchy established in 1949. These same Hmong became allies of the United States as the latter replaced the French as the military backers of rightist elements in the Royal Laotian government. A much smaller Hmong faction joined with Lao Issara in agitating for an independent Laos, free from French influence. After independence, the disaffected Hmong became part of the Pathet Lao movement.

Lee (1982:203) describes the situation of the Hmong as the war was drawing to a close:

By 1973, the Hmong formed 32 percent of the 370,000 refugees on government support in Laos, and 70 percent of 155, 474 in Xieng Khouang—the biggest ethnic group affected by the war. About 12,000 are believed to have died fighting against the Pathet Lao from 1962 to 1975. This heavy toll was partly the result of the military draft introduced by the RLG [Royal Laotian government] in its offensive against the PL [Pathet Lao] and North Vietnamese forces.... An American refugee worker established that 20 percent of Hmong civilians died in the early 1960s as a result of sickness or enemy attacks during their flight to refugee camps.

The Hmong had become refugees in their own country long before it became necessary for many of them to seek sanctuary in Thailand.

The present status of the Hmong in Laos is difficult to ascertain. Hmong resistance movements continued throughout the 1980s, possibly with the covert help of China, Thailand, and the United States. The Chao Fa established a stronghold in the mountainous and forested region of Phu Bia, near the important strategic area known as the Plain of Jars. Although rumors of guerrilla actions still emanate from Laos, the government claims to have instituted programs and reconciliation and development for the Hmong and is now cooperating with the United Nations High Commissioner for Refugees (UNHCR) in the repatriation of Hmong refugees still left in Thailand camps.

For a time after 1976, refugees accused the Pathet Lao and their Vietnamese allies of carrying out lethal "gas" attacks against both resistance fighters and noncombatant Hmong in Laos. A Canadian research team conducted a small-scale epidemiological study of Laotian Hmong and Khmer from Kampuchea and concluded that chemical/biological warfare was being waged in Southeast Asia. The lethal agents, the researchers surmised, were mycotoxins (Humphreys and Dow 1982; Schiefer 1982). The U.S. State Department also took this position (Haig 1982; Schultz 1982). Strong denials were issued by the governments of Laos, Vietnam, and the Soviet Union. Evans (1983) dismissed the claims of

chemical/biological warfare as fabrications, but his arguments were more ideological and empirical. Whether Hmong were deliberately exposed to unusually
large amounts of mycotoxins by their political enemies has never been conclu-
sively determined.

The controversy concerning the possible use of various kinds of poisons by
newly established governments in Laos and Kampuchea in order to eliminate
pockets of resistance became much more narrowly focused when journalists
began reporting that Hmong "tribesmen" had experienced chemical attacks in
the form of "yellow rain" (Whiteside 1991a, 1991b). The metaphor was mis-
takenly attributed to the Hmong, and subsequent investigations centered on small
yellow droplets that had appeared on vegetation in areas where chemical attacks
were said to have occurred. When some scientific analyses indicated the presence of deadly fungus-produced poisons, the U.S. State Department believed
that they had conclusive evidence of chemical warfare (Seiders 1986). Other
scientists made a considerably more mundane and convincing case for the dep-
osition of feces excreted from swarming bees (Seeley et al. 1985; Marshall
1986a, 1986b).

Because early investigations were so limited, and the issue reduced to arguments about a single putative vector for a certain type of poison, outside observers still do not know what happened to convince many Hmong that they
had been targeted for "kemi" attacks. Extremely ethnocentric speculations
about Hmong "primitive" perceptions under conditions of extreme stress (e.g.,
Evans 1983; Whiteside 1991b) offer no answers. Accusations of chemical warfare during the early postwar period in Southeast Asia continue to be made
(Hamilton-Merritt 1993), but the issue may never be resolved.

THE EXODUS FROM LAOS TO THAILAND

When the Pathet Lao came to power in 1975, the United States abruptly
ceased aiding its Laotian allies. Most Hmong who had sided with the Royalists
believed that their position was untenable. General Vang Pao, who commanded
most of the Hmong troops and contingents from other ethnic groups, departed
by air from Laos for asylum in Thailand on May 14. He was accompanied by
his family and members of his support staff. Soon afterward, a great many
Hmong began fleeing overland to Thailand. By the end of the year, UNHCR
(1983) counted 44,659 "Lao hill people," most of them Hmong, living in the
refugee camps of Thailand. The flow of Hmong refugees out of Laos lessened
considerably during 1976 and 1977 but again increased to rather high levels in
1979–1980. There has since been a sharp decline in the rate at which Hmong
refugees have crossed from Laos into Thailand. According to the U.S. Committee for Refugees (1994b), only 1,155 Highland Lao entered Thailand in 1994.

Thailand camps were established at Nong Khai and Nam Phong to receive
the first waves of Hmong refugees. The Thai government began in 1979 to
concentrate ethnic and nationality groups at particular locations, the main

Hmong camp being Ban Vinai, which opened in December 1975. Smaller groups of Hmong were interned at Chiang Khong, Ban Nam Yao, Sop Thuang, and Chiang Kham. While waiting to be resettled in a third country, Hmong families spent some time at transit centers like Phanat Nikhom.

The Thai Ministry of the Interior assumed responsibility for setting up the refugee services and managing basic services, such as food, shelter, and sanitation. The UNHCR funds camp operations, and a number of voluntary agencies, or VOLAGs, provide additional services in Thailand, ranging from medical care to educational programs. Hmong residents of Ban Vinai were eligible to participate in more than 17 such services (CCSDPT 1982:3; Long 1993).

Several levels of organization, official and unofficial, evolved within the camps. A Thai served as commander of Ban Vinai and was assisted by a Hmong subcommander. The camp was divided into 7 residential areas, each having its own leader. A residential area was further divided into three subsections consisting of a number of ten-room dwellings encircled by smaller units. A leader was designated for every subsection and large dwelling. Persons were elected to these leadership positions by the residents and were expected to assign labor tasks, oversee the fair distribution of food, and ensure that information was disseminated properly (Smalley n.d.; CCSDPT 1982; Long 1993). In contrast to Ban Vinai, Sop Thuang was divided into 12 areas according to ethnic group distinctions, and the houses were arranged as they had been in the refugees' home villages.

The unofficial camp organization at Ban Vinai is nicely summarized by Smalley (n.d.:19).

The deeper cultural and emotional life of the Hmong refugees was not lived only within these loosely superimposed hierarchies. It was lived also within traditional families, lineages, subclans and other social relationships which people brought with them as they migrated. Some families had been shredded, with members lost in war and escape, others still back in Laos. But the intricate and extensive ways which Hmong have of relating people to people were brought with them. A lineage head might be in another section of the camp, but even so that was closer than a half day's walk or more distance than he might have been in Laos. The members of a village might be scattered all over Ban Vinai, but those who were there still looked to their village headman from Laos or some other leader they had known. . . . Decisions were made within the traditional frameworks, marriages were made within the traditional patterns, ceremonies were performed within traditional groupings. All this was constrained by the camp situations of course. Adaptations had to be made. But these fundamental parts of Hmong life went on in camp, and on that level the Thai, international, and even the Hmong camp hierarchy was relatively irrelevant.

For the first seven years, more Laotian Hmong entered Thailand than left for other countries. The Hmong refugee population in Thailand reached a peak of 55,000 in 1982 (DeVecchi 1982:23) and then slowly came down. The UNHCR has had a voluntary repatriation program in place since the early 1980s, but only about 5,000 Hmong have accepted the organization's help in returning to Laos (U.S. Committee for Refugees 1994a:4). The situation for the Hmong changed dramatically in the early 1990s when the Thai government decided to try speeding up both the resettlement and repatriation of refugees by closing camps and making the situation more uncomfortable for those who remained. Ban Vinai was closed late in 1992, as was Chiang Kham the following year. At the end of 1993, 23,220 Highland Lao were interned at two camps, Ban Na Pho and Phanat Nikhom, and this number was reduced to 10,044 by September 1994 (U.S. Committee for Refugees 1994b). With the closing of camps in Thailand, up to 12,000 Laotian Hmong left United Nations jurisdiction without authorization and settled around a monastery north of Bangkok.

It should be noted that the Thai government's recent push for repatriation has created considerable tension between competing political segments of the U.S. Hmong community. Some groups are cautiously supporting voluntary repatriation because they would like to see a rapprochement between the People's Democratic Republic of Laos and the United States that would lead to a substantial investment of American money in Laotian economic development. Opposing groups want Western countries to withhold their support in the hope that the present Communist regime in Laos will either collapse or at least undergo major democratic reform. They claim that Hmong who are repatriated from Thailand will face new persecutions and, therefore, should stay put for the time being.

RESETTLEMENT IN THE UNITED STATES

The magnitude of the refugee problem and the threat it posed to political stability throughout Southeast Asia was not immediately appreciated by the international community after the Vietnam War. Only 12,300 Laotians classified as belonging to "hill tribes" were resettled in third countries from 1976 through 1978. International concern for the refugees increased markedly with the fall of the Pol Pot regime in Kampuchea and the advent of the Vietnamese boat people crisis. As a result, more Hmong and refugees belonging to other ethnic groups were received by third countries. Resettlement figures for Laotian hill tribes for 1979 and 1980 were 13,000 and 29,000, respectively. After 1980, the Hmong showed less interest in permanent resettlement. Only 8,000 moved to third countries between January 1981 and May 1983 (UNHCR 1983).

By May 1983, the United States had accepted about 50,000 Hmong; France, 7,000; French Guiana, 1,200; Canada, 800; Australia, 300; Argentina, 200; and various other nations, including China and Japan, 300 or so (UNHCR 1983). Resettlement continued for the next decade, with another 66,000 going to the United States and only a few thousand going elsewhere.

The resettlement experience has been different for the Hmong in each country, ranging from participation in an extensive agricultural experiment in French Guiana (involving the creation of two self-sufficient Hmong villages in the jungle) to a bewildering variety of programs offered in the context of urban Amer-

Table 9.1
Hill Tribe Resettlement in the United States

Year	Number	% of Total
1975	301	0.3%
1976	3,058	2.7%
1977	1,655	1.4%
1978	3,873	3.4%
1979	11,301	9.8%
1980	27,242	23.7%
1981	3,704	3.2%
1982	2,511	2.2%
1983	738	0.6%
1984	2,753	2.4%
1985	1,944	1.7%
1986	3,668	3.2%
1987	8,307	7.2%
1988	4,168	3.6%
1989	8,476	7.4%
1990	5,207	4.5%
1991	6,369	5.5%
1992	6,833	5.9%
1993	6,741	5.9%
1994	6,253	5.4%
Total	115,102	100.0%

Source: U.S. Committee for Refugees 1994a.

ica. (See Table 9.1 for numerical data on Hmong resettlement in the United States.) The U.S. quota for accepting additional Laotian Hmong from Thailand continues to be 6,000 per year, a figure that has been met for the past seven years. The Hmong who remain in Thailand appear to be biding their time until some more acceptable option becomes available.

Approximately 90,000 Hmong were counted in the 1990 U.S. census. About 80,000 Hmong had been admitted to the United States by 1990, and considering their relatively high birthrate, the census estimate is undoubtedly much too low. Unfortunately, there have been no other official surveys that provide more reliable figures. In 1990, Hmong were found living in all but seven states, but just three states accounted for 90 percent of the Hmong population—California (46,892), Minnesota (16,833), and Wisconsin (16,373) (Schlader, Schwartz, and Detzner 1995). The largest concentrations of Hmong were located in the Central

Valley of California, the Minneapolis–St. Paul area of Minnesota, and the Wisconsin cities of Milwaukee, Appleton, and Wausau. This distribution is more a reflection of secondary migration than of initial resettlement. A majority of families have moved from locations where they were originally sponsored to areas where they could live close to relatives and have access to better employment, education, and social services.

HMONG KINSHIP

Barney (1967:275–276) describes the essential characteristics of Hmong (Meo) kinship categories and groups, which are formed primarily on the basis of descent through the male line.

The patrilineal clan system of the Meo dominates their social organization, serving as a primary focus for their culture as a whole by tying together social, political, economic and religious aspects of behavior. The basic unit of the Meo social structure is the "household" or patrilineal extended family, meaning not only those who live under one roof, but also including all those under the authority of one household head. Thus a single household could include a man's unmarried daughters, his sons and their wives and children, and possibly his sons' sons' children and might also include a few other feeble or otherwise dependent relatives. All members of the household carry the clan name of the household head in addition to their given name. The clan name refers to descent from a mythical ancestor, and common membership in a clan serves as a bond of kinship and friendship between people who would otherwise be strangers. Members of the same lineage, who can trace their common descent from a known ancestor, refer to lineage mates by a common term meaning "my olders and youngers" [*kwv tij*].

As an enclaved minority in Laos practicing swidden agriculture, the Hmong developed patterns of kin group formation that have helped them survive as refugees in Thailand and other countries of asylum. Members of the extended family were sometimes forced to separate in order to find sufficient agricultural land in the Laotian highlands. Nonetheless, they remained in contact with one another and made every effort to reunify in an area that would support the entire group. When families became fragmented during the flight from Laos to Thailand, and again in the course of permanent resettlement, the Hmong placed greater reliance on lineage and even clan ties as a basis for close cooperation. Solidarity among one's patrilineal relatives still provides the greatest security for the Hmong, even in urban America (Dunnigan 1982).

In the 1960s and early 1970s, some Hmong extended families and lineage groups were able to prepare for the future through occupational diversification. In addition to farmers, their membership included soldiers, traders, students, various kinds of technicians attached to the military and international development missions, and other people with special knowledge who served their respective kinship groups as circumstances changed. The expectation of mutual assistance among family and lineage members remains strong. Status and wealth differences do exist between nuclear families that make up the patrilineal group, but the general goal is to advance the socioeconomic position of all members.

Linkage through marriage entails additional reciprocity. Upon marrying, Hmong women customarily leave their "patrikin" and become fully integrated into the families of their husbands. This establishes an alliance of lineages belonging to different clans. Should there be marital discord, the wife's consanguineal relatives try to help arrange a reconciliation. A divorced woman returns to her natal group until she remarries. The children ordinarily remain with their father's group, but a variety of arrangements are becoming more common in the United States.

Married couples sometimes choose to live with the wife's patrikin. This is most likely to happen when the wife's relatives are better able to help the new couple. The couple's offspring will try to maintain understandings of mutual obligation with both the affiliated lineage and their own patrikin. The option of emphasizing relations of descent or marriage at different times, depending upon circumstances, further enhances the security of individuals and small family units.

ASPECTS OF HMONG RELIGION

Before being exposed to the missionizing efforts of Westerners in Laos, most Hmong believed in the existence of what they called *dab* or spirits. Various kinds of dangerous spirits inhabited the "wild" domain of the forests. Some had the power to possess people or capture souls and cause illness. Other "domestic" spirits of the home and garden protected families as long as family members acted properly. Deceased ancestors could also aid or punish their living relatives and had to be honored in prescribed ways. To these beliefs were added the philosophies and practices of Taoism, Confucianism, Buddhism, and beginning in the 1950s, Christianity. A relatively small number of Laotian Hmong were converted to Catholicism and Protestant fundamentalism, but about half the Hmong who resettled in the United States claimed adherence to a form of Christianity. Hmong Protestant congregations usually elect their own lay leaders and tend to separate themselves from non-Hmong for worship and socializing. Religiously trained Hmong have little difficulty gaining a following from among their own people.

The Hmong desire religious consensus within the kin group, or at least among its core members. The conversion of key leaders provides strong incentive for other members to follow the same course. Lineage organizations have sometimes directly addressed the problem of achieving religious unity by choosing as a group to accept a particular form of Christianity or to return to an earlier set of beliefs and practices. In part, the continued attraction of the pre-Christian religion can be attributed to the fact that sacred rituals help to define the boundaries of the kinship group. Shared funerary practices and ways of honoring the ancestors can be used to establish and reinforce lineage ties even when genealogical connections are unclear. Moreover, many Hmong continue to use native curers, a practice that strict Hmong Christians condemn. For the most part, religious differences have not prevented interlineage cooperation. Tensions that occasionally exist between non-Christian and Christian groups related by marriage are usually managed without overt conflict.

ECONOMIC ADAPTATIONS

The main occupation of the Hmong in Laos was swidden agriculture. Forest growth had to be cut and burned on the land that was cultivated. A variety of crops were planted for three or four years on average until soil exhaustion required the development of new plots. Old fields were sometimes replanted after a long period of fallow. Hmong strategies of field rotation, crop sequencing, soil selection, fertilization, and so on, were quite sophisticated and productive, although the long-term environmental effects of such slash-and-burn methods have been criticized and possibly exaggerated (see Geddes 1976). Hmong who had access to fertile areas with permanent sources of irrigation water practiced intensive agriculture. The Hmong also raised horses, pigs, cattle, carabaos, and chickens.

Besides planting varieties of rice, corn, and many types of vegetables, the Hmong cultivated opium poppies as an important cash crop. They were one of many ethnic groups producing raw opium for a market that had de facto legitimacy in Laos. A relatively small number of Hmong were itinerant traders who brought a variety of commodities to isolated settlements and collected opium from the producers for resale to higher-level distributors. Because the Hmong used opium as a broadly useful medicine (Westermeyer 1982), it has been difficult to convince some of the older, infirm Hmong living in the United States to cease using opium entirely.

As hostilities escalated after 1961 in northeastern Laos, more and more Hmong were prevented from supporting themselves by farming. Families that congregated in large refugee settlements in north central Laos at least tried to maintain gardens. Later, in Thailand, some of the Hmong were initially allowed to plant on land close to the refugee camps. Unfortunately, their harvests were eventually hijacked by armed local Thai, and afterward the Hmong only planted on scarce small plots within the camps.

Middle-aged and older Hmong would like to practice farming in the United States. Family groups have leased acreage in order to produce vegetables for home consumption and commercial sale through farmers' markets. Young Hmong men and women are also working family plots as a way of earning income. During the early 1980s there was considerable interest in publicly and privately funded farming projects that had the objective of training the Hmong to farm according to the production and marketing techniques generally practiced in the United States. As a result of participating in these experiments, many Hmong discovered that, like other American small farmers, they could not make a living solely from agriculture. The attraction of farming for the Hmong was apparent in the large migration to the central valley of California in 1982–1983 (Bays 1994). Although it is extremely difficult to become an established grower, some families were able to buy or lease land in the vicinity of Fresno and Merced where they raised labor-intensive commercial crops such as pea pods and tomatoes. For the vast majority of the migrants to the Central Valley, the dream of farming never materialized. A minority of Hmong families living in other states have been able to acquire rural land and raise some crops to supplement their income.

The economic history of the Laotian Hmong during the Vietnam War and postwar internment in Thailand has not been sufficiently researched. Yang (1976) describes some of the Hmong responses to economic opportunities that came with the political destabilization of Laos between 1961 and 1975. What has not been precisely documented is the extent to which Hmong increased their participation in sectors of the Laotian economy outside of agriculture. Data collected by researchers associated with the Life Course Center at the University of Minnesota show that a number of refugees living in Minneapolis–St. Paul, including women, had operated as small-scale entrepreneurs in Laos and Thailand (see also Bays 1994). These experiences may have provided a basis for undertaking business ventures in the United States such as butcher shops, grocery stores, restaurants, commercial sewing businesses, craft sale outlets, and automotive sales and repair shops. Middle-aged and older Hmong refugees often express a desire to own and operate small businesses, but only a small percentage ever achieve what could be called long-term success.

The fact that so few Hmong who resettled in the United States between 1975 and 1985 possessed the specific vocational skills and knowledge of English demanded by potential employers seemed to be reflected in the general psychological adjustment of the refugees (Westermeyer, Vang, and Lyfong 1983; Westermeyer, Vang, and Neider 1983a, 1983b, 1983c; Williams and Westermeyer 1983). Westermeyer, Vang, and Neider (1984) reported a high rate of depression among Hmong refugee subjects, with 40 percent achieving ''depressive'' scores on the Zung Depression Scale. They found some improvement over time, but the lack of employment opportunities seemed to contribute to the high rates of depression.

From the beginning of refugee resettlement in the United States, Hmong leaders have stressed the need for vocational training, and a great many Hmong have attended vocational/technical institutes. Young graduates are now finding employment in areas ranging from legal and medical services to domestic help. There are Hmong travel agencies that specialize in tours to Laos, Hmong real estate firms, and a growing variety of Hmong-owned retail businesses. Hmong with advanced education are providing some professional services to their own people, but, judging from 1988–1991 data (McNall, Dunnigan, and Mortimer 1994), most working Hmong still hold low-paying service, clerical, or light manufacturing jobs that require few skills and no more than a functional knowledge of English. One third of the employed Hmong engage in "bench work" as sewing machine operators or assemblers, and the most frequently reported service-type job is that of janitor.

Many Hmong continue to reside in public housing or substandard units located within the deteriorating inner city. The tendency for Hmong to cluster in certain areas appears to be determined not only by the availability of inexpensive housing but also by a strong desire on the part of the Hmong to reside near relatives. By being persistent and filling vacancies as they come available, Hmong have slowly taken over whole apartment buildings.

Disadvantaged minorities who had already established themselves in neighborhoods with relatively cheap housing stock initially resented the influx of Hmong refugees. The resentment was sometimes expressed in vandalism and physical violence. In some cases, local leaders representing the different groups were able to get together and work out strategies for reducing tensions. Attacks directed specifically at the Hmong have lessened, and much of the earlier concern has shifted toward the common problem of youth gang activity.

Owing a home is highly valued by the Hmong. If they have limited means, families will not hesitate to purchase a home close to relatives who rent in the inner city, but more affluent families have shown a pattern of outward movement similar to that followed by the general population. Hmong families tend to initially relocate to a first-tier suburb and, if their fortunes continue to improve, eventually seek housing in a relatively affluent outer-ring community. What is different about the Hmong compared with the general population is that the former show a tendency to migrate as a group. If a prominent family of an important Hmong leader settles in a new neighborhood or community, this encourages other family members and Hmong friends to investigate the possibility of moving into the same area.

EDUCATION

Despite current economic hardships and an historically limited experience with formal education, the Hmong community has had reason to be pleased with the educational accomplishments of its youth. Data gathered in St. Paul, Minnesota (McNall, Dunnigan, and Mortimer 1994) show the Hmong doing very well in high schools and pursuing postsecondary education at rates comparable to the general population. Hmong students in St. Paul spend more hours per week on homework and earn higher grade-point averages than their peers in all four years of high school. In addition, they less often get into trouble at school or drop out than non-Hmong. After high school, Hmong youth spend roughly the same amount of time in school as the non-Hmong (see Table 9.2). In addition, there are no differences between Hmong and non-Hmong in the type of schooling pursued, at least during the first year after high school. In other words, the two groups are enrolled in community, vocational, and four-year colleges at

Table 9.2
Percentage in School after High School: Hmong and Non-Hmong Compared

Year	Hmong	(N)	Non-Hmong	(N)	Chi-square	p
1	81%	64	77%	616	0.63	0.43
2	61%	53	60%	411	0.01	0.91
3	51%	43	58%	405	1.29	0.26

Note: None of the indicated differences are statistically significant.
Source: Youth Development Study (NIMH grant #42843).

nearly the same rates (see Table 9.3). For both, four-year colleges represent the schooling of choice.

While Hmong are generally doing well in school, graduating from high school, and finding work or matriculating at postsecondary institutions, there is a minority who are being drawn into the kinds of youth gang activities that have become a national concern. The extent to which Hmong youth actually join gangs and commit crimes has not been adequately researched, but public apprehension over "Asian gangs" has been fueled by alarmist stories in the mass media. Hmong parents living in high crime areas do fear that their children will be lost to the streets and the criminal justice system even though such tragedies are still uncommon. Moreover, Hmong secular and religious leaders strongly promote organized activities that give youth an opportunity to experience legitimate successes.

MARRIAGE AND FERTILITY

Hmong experience near-universal marriage and regard having children both as a natural process and as a necessary step in attaining a mature social status. Although marriage negotiations occur between the families of the engaged couple, our surveys indicate that a majority of Hmong who married in Laos chose their own partners with the approval of parents. Donnelly (1994) indicates that young Hmong persons often based their choice on the advice of others. Less than a quarter of Hmong in a 1992 Minnesota community survey (Spring n.d.) characterized their marriages as being arranged by parents. Another 10 percent reported having been married as the result of *zij pojniam,* which literally translates as "seizing a wife." While it can refer to the deviant and risky practice of taking a woman by force and trying later to mollify her family into accepting the marriage, it also applies to instances where males claim the right to propose to a woman by taking hold of her arm outside of her house and not relinquishing

Table 9.3
Postsecondary Schooling: Hmong and Non-Hmong Compared

Type	Hmong	(N)	Non-Hmong	(N)	Chi-square	p
Community College	9%	6	16%	99	2.51	0.11
Vocational College	16%	11	18%	106	0.05	0.82
Four-Year College	55%	37	47%	282	1.79	0.18

Note: None of the indicated differences are statistically significant.

Source: Youth Development Study (NIMH grant #42843).

it until senior members from both families arrive for purposes of marriage negotiation. The fascination among Westerners with Hmong customs of arranged
marriage and so-called marriage by capture has distorted the perceived prevalence of such practices.

Based on interviews with Hmong women in the United States, Donnelly
(1994) and Bays (1994) concluded that most women married in Laos between
the ages of 14 and 22. A 1992 Minnesota study (Spring n.d.) tallied a number
of marriages that fell outside this range. The lowest age was 10 years, and the
highest was 27 years. Hmong males indicated that they were somewhat older
when they first married, between 16 and 36 years of age. A couple's first child
usually arrived within the first 2 years and served to strengthen the marriage.
Hmong desire many children because they perpetuate the family and increase
its prospects for success (see "An Adaptation Model" below).

An issue of concern for social policymakers in the United States has been the
relatively early age at which Hmong, especially women, get married and have
children. Judging from several reports (Spring n.d.; Bays 1994), most Hmong
women marry in the United States between the ages of 11 and 23. One range
reported for Hmong males is 16 to 35 (Spring n.d.). Most Hmong women give
birth within the first year of marriage (Spring n.d.; Symonds 1984). Early marriages followed fairly quickly by childbirth are known to result in increased
fertility levels, and it is not surprising that researchers report high birthrates for
Hmong throughout the United States (Hahn and Muecke 1987; Hopkins and
Clarke 1983; Rumbaut and Weeks 1986; Weeks et al. 1989).

Of the approximately 30,000 Minnesota Hmong who were counted in the
1990 census, one third were born in the United States, and three fifths were
below the age of 18 (Yang and Murphy 1993). While Hmong compose at least

6 percent of the population of St. Paul, Minnesota, 25 percent of students entering first grade in 1992–1993 were Hmong. Nearly a third of a Hmong female cohort studied in St. Paul (Hutchison and McNall 1994) were married and gave birth by the end of their junior year of high school, and about half were married and had at least one child before the end of their senior year. It seems that not only do the Hmong marry and have children relatively early; they also appear to have more children.

Early marriage, early childbearing, and high fertility are all thought to have particularly damaging consequences for the educational and occupational achievement of young Hmong adults (Downing et al. 1984; Vangay 1989). Yet, as we have seen, Hmong females as well as males have attained educational success to a degree that is, in some respects, superior to that of the general population. Hmong marriage and fertility patterns do not produce lower grades, more high school dropouts, or lower levels of enrollment in postsecondary educational institutions. In general, early marriage and childbearing do not appear to serve as an impediment to young Hmong adults' pursuit of education. The reasons for this are not clear, but it seems reasonable to assume that, by virtue of the extended kin networks in the Hmong community, young Hmong women are able to take advantage of the child care services of older female relatives.

High fertility levels in the Hmong population are distinguished by short intervals between births. This pattern of childbearing is known to increase the risks of illness and death for both mother and child in other groups. Even though Hmong women appear to underutilize Western prenatal health care services, studies reveal that their birth outcomes are better than the national average (Spring et al. 1995; Helsel, Petitti, and Kunstadter 1992; Rumbaut and Weeks 1989; Erickson et al. 1987; Richman and Dixon 1985; Hopkins and Clarke 1983; National Center for Health Statistics 1989). Because they view pregnancy as a natural rather than a medical condition, are generally pleased with birth outcomes, and realize that mother and child survival rates have risen in the United States, Hmong have few incentives to fully utilize the reproductive services offered at medical clinics.

COMMUNITY POLITICS

Almost 15 years ago in St. Paul, Minnesota, the Hmong organized a national conference on resettlement issues. One of the best-attended sessions focused on the development of effective community leadership. Participants expressed the opinion that key leaders who had held the Hmong together in Laos and Thailand were being ignored by American authorities. If this continued, they reasoned, the Hmong would become fractionalized and incapable of exerting any political influence. The speakers recalled that they had advanced materially in Laos only after Hmong began serving as district officials, judges, military officers, legislative representatives, and even department ministers. In these positions, they were able to mobilize support for national goals while securing for the Hmong some of the economic and educational advantages enjoyed by the lowland Lao.

Early in the resettlement process, Hmong refugees began exerting pressure on the various service agencies to hire certain bilinguals. Some agency directors may have seen this as an attempt on the part of formerly powerful people or emerging leaders to selfishly promote themselves and their supporters, but many agencies understood the advantages of recruiting respected members of the client community to help solve difficult problems.

Not wanting to be entirely dependent on the established resettlement agencies, the Hmong formed mutual assistance associations in many parts of the country. Very quickly their efforts resulted in the formation of a national organization with regional branches for the purpose of providing a wide range of services directly to the refugees. These groups sought federal and local funds to support their new programs. The resulting competition for government dollars created some tensions between the Hmong and established agencies (Olney 1993).

So long as all the kin groups were struggling to survive in the United States, the appeal of a national mutual assistance association was strong. Divisions based on kinship, regional loyalty, dialect, and political alliance could be bridged by a coalition of leaders headed by General Vang Pao. As the situation improved for some groups, the perceived need for a single national organization became less general. Some Hmong wanted to concentrate exclusively on local and lineage-level concerns. Rather than being merely symptomatic of a kind of ethnic community breakup, these changes are indicative of a recurring cycle of alliance building in the face of a common threat, followed by segmentation when the need for general cooperation subsides (Dunnigan 1982; Olney 1993). As the needs of various groups and communities have changed, a variety of new forms of associations have developed to serve special segments of the population, such as women, youth, and elders. Still other associations have arisen in response to new political issues both within the United States and internationally.

AN ADAPTATION MODEL

As indicated above in the discussion of kinship and economics, Hmong in the United States have access to social resources often not available to members of the general population. The Hmong participate in rather extensive helping networks based primarily on kinship that afford individuals and nuclear families considerable security, economic as well as social and psychological. Reliance on kin group support is hardly unique to the Hmong. Kibria (1994) describes a similar system of reciprocity for Vietnamese refugees living in Philadelphia. Both her methods of study and conceptualization of Vietnamese adaptation suggest a way of understanding the coping strategies of the Hmong.

Using such standard ethnographic practices as in-depth interviewing, participant observation, and case study analysis, Kibria (1994:81) was able to determine that multifamily Vietnamese households tend to employ a "patchwork" strategy involving "gathering together a wide variety of resources from diverse social and economic arenas," which have the effect of mitigating "the instability and scarcity of resources." One factor reinforcing the gathering and sharing of essential goods within the Vietnamese household, according to Kibria, is an "ideology of family collectivism."

The Hmong household, which constitutes an important arena of resource sharing, often consists of three generations and may include several nuclear families of siblings. These siblings are usually, but not always, brothers. There are also larger kin groups upon which the Hmong often depend for certain kinds of assistance. The Hmong expression *tsev neeg* refers to all people under one roof, most specifically a resident family or household. Like the English word *family*, the meaning of *tsev neeg* can be extended to include all cooperating descendants of certain parents or grandparents. A number of nuclear and extended households may regard themselves as belonging to one *tsev neeg* and, as a result, feel strongly obliged to assist one another. Member households could be localized in a particular city or scattered across many countries. Although it is tempting to call such groups patrilineages, it must be recognized that the intimate involvement of affines, that is, relatives by marriage, in these reciprocal relationships tends to blur group boundaries, at least to some extent.

The pooling of resources within and between *tsev neeg*, particularly at the local level, has benefited the Hmong immensely. For instance, family associations consisting of linked patrikin and close affines (see Dunnigan 1982) have formed semicorporate organizations that offer loan and life insurance benefits to members. Of course, not all shared resources can be quantified in terms of cash values. Those who belong to large, highly diverse kin groups are also more likely to have direct access to persons with specialized knowledge and skills in areas of ritual performance, curing, marriage negotiation, adjudication of social conflicts, and so on. It is through the different contributions of many individuals that kin-based groups become more self-sufficient and prestigious.

Kibria's (1994) study of Philadelphia Vietnamese provides a good model for researching Hmong refugee adaptations. We would, however, suggest two modifications. Because the Hmong household is so thoroughly embedded in the larger kin network, at least in most instances, it would be a mistake to focus solely on the residence group as the unit of study. Behavior within the household often cannot be fully understood without an extensive examination of more encompassing kinship structures. We also have some doubt about the validity of the Western collectivism versus individualism dichotomy mentioned so often in cross-cultural research. Like the Vietnamese, the Hmong certainly do appear to have a distinctive ideology consisting of beliefs and values that facilitate cooperation among kin group members. However, the benefits of mutuality redound to each individual, and the strategy of supporting common interests in order to ensure one's own claim to group support can be viewed as a matter of practical self-interest. It is a strategy that cannot be reduced to the single premise that "the kin group is far more significant than the individual" (Kibria 1994:

90). Hmong youth, as they approach adulthood and face the prospects of marrying and establishing themselves in careers, usually discover significant personal advantages in staying closely allied with their extended families. What Kibria (1994) says about the Vietnamese of Philadelphia also applies to the Hmong. Only immediate relatives can be counted upon to help individuals survive the difficult problems that lie ahead.

REFERENCES

Adams, Nina S., and Alfred W. McCoy. 1970. *Laos: War and Revolution.* New York: Harper & Row.

Barney, Linwood. 1967. The Meo of Xieng Khouang Province, Laos. In *Southeast Asian Tribes, Minorities, and Nations.* Edited by Peter Kunstadter. Princeton: Princeton University Press. Pp. 271–294.

Bays, Sharon. 1994. Cultural Politics and Identity Formation in a San Joaquin Valley Hmong Community. Unpublished Ph.D. dissertation, University of California, Los Angeles.

Committee for the Coordination of Services to Displaced Persons in Thailand (CCSDPT). 1982. *CCSDPT Handbook: Refugee Services in Thailand.* Bangkok: Du Maurier Associates for the Committee for the Coordination of Services to Displaced Persons in Thailand.

DeVecchi, Robert. 1982. Politics and Policies of "First Asylum" in Thailand. In *World Refugee Survey, 1982.* Edited by Rosemary Tripp. New York: American Council for Nationalities Service. Pp. 20–24.

Donnelly, Nancy D. 1994. *Changing Lives of Refugee Hmong Women.* Seattle: University of Washington Press.

Downing, Bruce T., Douglas P. Olney, Sara R. Mason, and Glenn L. Hendricks. 1984. *The Hmong Resettlement Site Report: Minneapolis–St. Paul.* Submitted by the Northwest Regional Educational Laboratory, Portland, to the Office of Refugee Resettlement, Washington, D.C.

Dreyer, June. 1976. *China's Forty Millions: Minority Nationalities and National Integration in the People's Republic of China.* Cambridge: Harvard University Press.

Dunnigan, Timothy. 1982. Segmentary Kinship in an Urban Society: The Hmong of St. Paul–Minneapolis. *Anthropological Quarterly* 55(3):126–136.

Erickson, Deanne, Ingrid Swenson, Edward Ehlinger, Sheldon Swaney, Gertrude Carlson, and Karen Gleiter. 1987. Maternal and Infant Outcomes among Caucasians and Hmong Refugees in Minneapolis, Minnesota. *Human Biology* 59(5):799–808.

Evans, Grant. 1983. *The Yellow Rainmakers: Are the Soviets Using Chemical Weapons in Southeast Asia?* London: Verse Editions and NLB.

Geddes, William R. 1976. *Migrants of the Mountains.* Oxford: Clarendon Press.

Gunn, Geoffrey C. 1990. *Rebellion in Laos: Peasant Politics in a Colonial Backwater.* Boulder, Colorado: Westview Press.

Hahn, Robert A., and Marjorie A. Muecke. 1987. The Anthropology of Birth in Five U.S. Ethnic Populations: Implications for Obstetrical Practice. *Current Problems in Obstetrics, Gynecology and Fertility* 4:133–171.

Haig, Alexander M., Jr. 1982. *Chemical Warfare in Southeast Asia and Afghanistan.* Special Report 98. Washington, D.C.: U.S. Department of State.

Halpern, Joel. 1964. *Economy and Society of Laos: A Brief Survey.* Southeast Asia Studies Monograph Series, No. 5. New Haven: Yale University Southeast Asia Studies.

Hamilton-Merritt, Jane. 1993. *Tragic Mountains.* Bloomington: Indiana University Press.

Helsel, Deborah, Diana B. Petitti, and Peter Kunstadter. 1992. Pregnancy among the Hmong: Birthweight, Age, and Parity. *American Journal of Public Health* 82(10): 1361–1369.

Hickey, Gerald C. 1955. The Ethnic Minorities of Laos. In *Area Handbook on Laos.* Edited by Gerald C. Hickey. Chicago: University of Chicago Press.

Hopkins, David D., and Nancy G. Clarke. 1983. Indochinese Refugee Fertility Rates and Pregnancy Risk Factors, Oregon. *American Journal of Public Health* 73(11): 1307–1309.

Humphreys, G. R., and J. Dow. 1982. *Report of the Medical Team's Epidemiological Investigation of Alleged CW/BW Incidents in Laos and Cambodia.* Ottawa: Canada.

Hutchison, Ray, and Miles McNall. 1994. Early Marriage in a Hmong Cohort. *Journal of Marriage and the Family* 56:579–590.

Jenks, Robert D. 1985. The Miao Rebellion, 1854–1872: Insurgency and Social Disorder in Kweichow during the Taiping Era. Unpublished Ph.D. dissertation, Harvard University.

Kibria, Nazli. 1994. Household Structure and Family Ideologies: The Dynamics of Immigrant Economic Adaptation among Vietnamese Refugees. *Social Problems* 41(1):81–96.

Larteguy, Jean. 1979. *La fabuleuse aventure du peuple de l'opium.* Paris: Presses de la Cite.

LeBar, Frank M., Gerald Hickey, and John Musgrave, Editors. 1964. *Ethnic Groups of Mainland Southeast Asia.* New Haven: Human Relations Area Files Press.

LeBar, Frank M., and Adrienne Suddard. 1960. *Laos: Its People, Its Society, Its Culture.* New Haven: Human Relations Area Files Press.

Lee, Gary Yia. 1982. National Minority Policies and the Hmong. In *Contemporary Laos.* Edited by Martin Stuart-Fox. New York: St. Martin's Press. Pp. 199–219.

Long, Lynellyn D. 1993. *Ban Vinai: The Refugee Camp.* New York: Columbia University Press.

Marshall, Eliot. 1986a. Response to Seiders' Letter to the Editor. *Science* 234:528–529.

―――. 1986b. Yellow Rain Evidence Slowly Whittled Away. *Science* 233:18–19.

McNall, Miles, Timothy Dunnigan, and Jeylan T. Mortimer. 1994. The Educational Achievement of the St. Paul Hmong. *Anthropology and Education Quarterly* 25(1):44–65.

Meier, Peg. 1983. Hmong, Opium: A Culture Clash. *Minneapolis Star/Tribune,* October 1.

National Center for Health Statistics. 1989. *Advance Report of Final Mortality Statistics, 1987.* Monthly Vital Statistics Report 38, No. 5 supp. Hyattsville: Public Health Service.

Northwest Regional Educational Laboratory (NWREL). 1984. The Hmong Resettlement Study. Northwest Regional Educational Laboratory. (Unpublished)

Olney, Douglas P. 1983. Hmong Community Survey, Minneapolis–St. Paul. (Unpublished)

————. 1993. We Must Be Organized: Dual Organization in an American Hmong Community. Unpublished Ph.D. dissertation, University of Minnesota.

Richman, Debra, and Suzanne Dixon. 1985. Comparative Study of Cambodian, Hmong and Caucasian Infant and Maternal Perinatal Profiles. *Journal of Nurse Midwifery* 30(6):313–319.

Rumbaut, Rubén G., and John R. Weeks. 1986. Fertility and Adaptation: Indochinese Refugees in the United States. *International Migration Review* 20(2):428–466.

————. 1989. Infant Health among Indochinese Refugees: Patterns of Infant Mortality, Birthweight, and Prenatal Care in Comparative Perspective. *Research Sociology of Health Care* 8:137–196.

Savina, F. M. 1924. *Histoire des Miao.* Hong Kong: Imprimerie de la Societe des Missions-Etrangeres.

Schiefer, H. B. 1982. *Study of the Possible Use of Chemical Warfare Agents in Southeast Asia.* A Report to the Department of External Affairs. Ottawa, Canada.

Schlader, Jill, Michell Schwartz, and Daniel Detzner. 1995. *Southeast Asian Refugees: Statistics.* Southeast Asian Refugee Studies Project, Occasional Paper No. 12. Minneapolis: Center for Urban and Regional Affairs.

Schultz, George P. 1982. *Chemical Warfare in Southeast Asia and Afghanistan: An Update.* Special Report No. 104. Washington, D.C.: U.S. Department of State, Bureau of Public Affairs.

Seeley, Thomas D., Joan W. Nowicke, Matthew Meselson, Jeanne Guillemin, and Pongthep Akratanakul. 1985. Yellow Rain. *Scientific American* 253(3):128–137.

Seiders, Barbara A. B. 1986. Letter to the Editor. *Science* 234:528.

Smalley, William A. n.d. From Laos to the United States. (Unpublished)

Smalley, William A., Chia Koua Vang, and Gnia Yee Yang. 1990. *Mother of Writing.* Chicago: University of Chicago Press.

Spring, Marline A. n.d. Hmong Community Survey, Minneapolis–St. Paul. (Unpublished)

Spring, Marline A., Paul J. Ross, Nina L. Etkin, and Amos S. Deinard. 1995. Sociocultural Factors in the Use of Prenatal Care by Hmong Women, Minneapolis. *American Journal of Public Health* 85(7):1015–1017.

Symonds, Patricia V. 1984. A Flower Ready for the Bee: Hmong Perceptions of Adolescent Pregnancy. M.A. thesis, Brown University.

————. 1991. Cosmology and the Cycle of Life: Hmong Views of Birth, Death and Gender in a Mountain Village in Northern Thailand. Unpublished Ph.D. dissertation, Brown University.

Tapp, Nicholas. 1985. Categories of Change and Continuity among the White Hmong (Hmoob Dawb) of Northern Thailand. Unpublished Ph.D. dissertation, School of Oriental and African Studies, University of London.

United Nations High Commission for Refugees (UNHCR). 1983. *Monthly Statistics.* Bangkok, Thailand.

U.S. Committee for Refugees. 1994a. *Refugee Reports.* December 31. Washington, D.C.

————. 1994b. *World Refugee Survey.* Washington, D.C.

Vangay, Jonas Vang Na. 1989. *Hmong Parents' Cultural Attitudes and the Sex-Ratio Imbalance of Hmong Merced High School Graduates.* Merced: Mong Pheng Community Incorporated.

Weeks, John R., Rubén G. Rumbaut, C. Brindis, C. C. Korenbrot, and D. Minkler. 1989. High Fertility among Indochinese Refugees. *Public Health Reports* 104(2):143–150.

Weins, Harold J. 1967. *Han Chinese Expansion in South China.* Hamden, Connecticut:
    Shoe String Press.
Westermeyer, Joseph. 1982. *Poppies, Pipes and People: Opium and Its Use in Laos.*
    Berkeley: University of California Press.
Westermeyer, Joseph, Ton Fu Vang, and Gaohli Lyfong. 1983. Hmong Refugees in
    Minnesota: Characteristics and Self Perceptions. *Minnesota Medicine* 66:431–
    439.
Westermeyer, Joseph, Ton Fu Vang, and John Neider. 1983a. A Comparison of Refugees
    Using and Not Using a Psychiatric Service: An Analysis of DSM-III Criteria and
    Self Rating Scales in a Cross Cultural Context. *Journal of Operational Psychiatry*
    14(1):36–40.
———. 1983b. Migration and Mental Health among Hmong Refugees: Association of
    Pre- and Post-migration Factors with Self Rating Scales. *Journal of Nervous and
    Mental Disease* 171(2):92–96.
———. 1983c. Refugees Who Do and Do Not Seek Psychiatric Care: An Analysis of
    Premigratory and Postmigratory Characteristics. *Journal of Nervous and Mental
    Disease* 171(2):92–96.
———. 1984. Acculturation and Mental Health: A Study of Hmong Refugees at 1.5 and
    3.5 Years Post-migration. *Social Science and Medicine* 18(1):87–93.
Whiteside, Thomas. 1991a. Annals of the Cold War: The Yellow-Rain Complex—1. *The
    New Yorker,* February 11: 38–67.
———. 1991b. Annals of the Cold War: The Yellow-Rain Complex—2. *The New
    Yorker,* February 18: 44–68.
Williams, Caroline, and Joseph Westermeyer. 1983. Psychiatric Problems among Ado-
    lescent Southeast Asian Refugees: A Descriptive Study. *Journal of Nervous and
    Mental Disease* 171(2):79–83.
Yang, Dao. 1976. *The Hmong of Laos in the Vanguard of Development.* Translation of
    Les Hmong du Laos face au developpment. Vientiane, Laos: Siasavath Publishers.
    National Technical Information Service, order No. JPRS L/5562.
Yang, Pai, and Nora Murphy. 1993. *Hmong in the '90s: Stepping Towards the Future.*
    St. Paul: Hmong American Partnership.

Chapter 10

Iranians

MEHDI BOZORGMEHR

Right after the bombing in Oklahoma City on April 19, 1995, some Americans blamed Middle Easterners—and more specifically, the Iranian government—for masterminding this terrorist act. Although the terrorists were found to be Americans, the stereotype of the Iranian regime as a sponsor of terrorism endures. The widespread allegations are that Iran is trying to sabotage the delicate Arab-Israelis peace process and to acquire the raw materials and technology to build an atomic bomb. The terrorism stereotype does not stop at "state terrorism" and apply only to the Iranian regime since sometimes Iranians abroad are also perceived as Islamic fundamentalists. As such, the status of Iranians in the United States is precarious in a changing world order, where the alleged threat of Islamic fundamentalism has replaced communism. Ironically, Iranians in the United States have done nothing to perpetuate this stereotype. If anything, many Iranian exiles who arrived in the United States after the revolution are opposed to their government's policies—otherwise, they would have remained in Iran; and those who came to the United States before the revolution would have repatriated instead of staying on in the United States. But most Americans cannot make a distinction between the Iranian regime and Iranians, at least not in times of crisis when they become aware of Iranians among them. Iranians become scapegoats anytime conflict between Iran and the United States rages, which has been incessant in one form or another since the advent of the Islamic Republic of Iran in 1979. This is not unique to Iranians, however, and is often the fate of exiles fleeing revolutions in the Third World (e.g., Cubans and Nicaraguans), where new regimes take a vehemently anti-American position in light of past American support of their overthrown dictatorships. However, unlike the early waves of Cuban "golden exiles" before them, who were both

well-to-do and well received in the United States because they opposed socialism, Iranians did not enjoy a favorable reception.

There are two major stereotypes about Iranians in the United States; first, as
mentioned above, that they are Islamic fundamentalists; and second, that they
are affluent. Drawing on vivid images of Iran in the media, especially during
the "Iranian hostage crisis," Americans often think of Iranians in the United
States as devout Muslims and sometimes as religious zealots. The stereotype of
Iranians as very religious Muslims and extremists is inaccurate since most Iranian Muslims in the United States are secular; indeed, the religious Iranian
Muslims have no reason for leaving a strict Muslim society (Sabagh and Bozorgmehr 1994). Moreover, there are many non-Muslim Iranians in the United
States, including Christians, Jews, and members of other religious minorities, to
whom the Muslim label does not even apply (see Kelley, Friedlander, and Colby
1993).

Although religious diversity is not unique to Iranians, it is perhaps more
pronounced among them than many other refugee groups. The Iranian group
includes a sizable number of religious minorities because the revolution and its
outcome in Iran were Islamic and, as such, a threat to its non-Muslim minorities.
Despite Iran's relative religious homogeneity, where about 98 percent of its
prerevolution population was Muslim, all of Iran's religious minorities are present in the United States. Iranians are especially diverse in Los Angeles, partly
because of their concentration—about one out of every three Iranians in the
United States is in Los Angeles—and partly because they are drawn to this
metropolitan area by the presence of their non-Iranian coreligionists, especially
Christian Armenians and Jews.

The second major stereotype of Iranian exiles is that they are affluent, which,
unlike the first one, contains a kernel of truth but generally in terms of high
occupational status rather than imported wealth. This stereotype is very much
at odds with the image Americans have of refugees as the "wretched refuse of
teeming shores," inscribed on the Statue of Liberty. It is one thing to come to
the United States poor, start at the bottom, and move up through hard work and
perseverance, as so often have the immigrants and refugees of yesteryear; it is
quite another to arrive directly and obtain desirable jobs. The image of "rich
Iranians" dates back to the oil boom of the mid-1970s, when Iran and other
members of the Organization of Petroleum Exporting Countries (OPEC) cartel
benefited from skyrocketing oil prices. As one of the richest men in the world,
the shah of Iran also perpetuated a superrich image by his grandiose and lavish
displays of wealth. At that time, however, the vast majority of Iranians abroad
were college and university students. The shah's image was thus at odds with
the experience of most Iranian students who had to support themselves or were
financially helped by their families in Iran. Of course, the stereotype of rich
Iranians was reinforced by the exodus of the Iranian exiles in the late 1970s and
early 1980s. This stereotype has gone unchallenged to this day, because contrary
to the experience of other initially high-status refugees such as Cubans and

Vietnamese, the refugee flow from Iran has not yielded comparably lower social origins. This is not to say that recent refugees from Iran are not needy and deserving of the U.S. government's refugee assistance programs—but only that due to the problems of exit, cost of travel, and difficulties of obtaining a U.S. visa, poor Iranian refugees simply cannot make it to the United States, as have Cuban and Vietnamese "boat people." This feature sets the Iranian exiles apart from all other exiles in the United States since, as will be shown later, Iranians are one of the highest-status groups, not only compared with other refugees but even compared with economic migrants. That is why the term *exile*, which connotes a higher social class origin than *refugee*, is more appropriate for Iranians and is used frequently in this chapter.[1]

IRAN BEFORE THE REVOLUTION

Given the extreme socioeconomic selectivity and religious diversity of Iranians in the United States, it is important not to generalize from Iranian society to Iranian exiles. Nevertheless, a brief introduction to the social, economic, and political conditions of Iran may help the unfamiliar reader better understand the Iranians' backgrounds.

Direct U.S. influence in Iran dates back at least to the Central Intelligence Agency (CIA)–sponsored coup in 1953, which brought back the late shah to power and deposed Dr. Mohammed Mossadeq, the popular Iranian prime minister who advocated the nationalization of Iranian oil. Thereafter, Iran and the United States established close economic, social, and political ties, which in turn facilitated the movement of Iranians to the United States. The shah's new industrialization drive began in the 1960s and took off in the 1970s with the rising oil revenues. The upper classes of Iranian society disproportionately benefited from the booming economy. Unlike the less-populous oil-producing countries in the Persian Gulf (e.g., Kuwait), Iran had the labor force to operate its emerging industries. But the educational infrastructure was neither well developed nor sufficiently advanced to prepare Iranian students for the technical and managerial tasks. Overseas education was the only alternative as the need for skilled labor grew in Iran, outstripping the supply of universities to educate a burgeoning number of high school graduates. Whereas high incomes and savings made it possible for wealthy Iranians to travel and even invest abroad, even the less privileged sent their sons, but rarely daughters, abroad for higher education to avoid mandatory military conscription. Because of the patriarchal nature of Iranian society, females were less likely than males to be sent to study abroad unsupervised. Although Iranian students went to many countries in pursuit of postsecondary education, their favored destination was the United States. By the late 1970s, Iran had become the premier exporter of foreign students in the world and the largest country of origin of foreign students in the United States (Bozorgmehr and Sabagh 1987). The increasing presence of Americans in Iran, and the dominance of the English language globally, established English as the standard foreign language taught in Iranian high schools. By the time they graduated from high school, a basic familiarity with English directed Iranian high school graduates toward English-speaking countries when seeking higher education. The choices of destinations were narrowed down to advanced industrial countries because Iranian students were mostly interested in technical education such as engineering to prepare them for the rapidly industrializing Iranian economy. The United States was the preferred destination because its extensive college and university system could absorb Iranian students, whereas the extremely competitive English system did not offer similar opportunities. The United States also offered more job opportunities than England did, in case students needed to support themselves or supplement their income. This picture changed drastically after the Iranian revolution caught the world by surprise in 1978–1979.

The Iranian revolution came as a shock, not only to observers abroad but also to the people in Iran themselves. If anything, Iran was experiencing an economic boom in the early 1970s, although there was a sharp economic downturn just prior to the revolution. Thus, the causes of the Iranian exodus were initially more political than economic. Later, as the Islamic ideology and the Muslim clergy dominated the revolutionary process and its outcome, fear of religious persecution for the religious minorities (Jones 1984) and intolerable living conditions for the secular Muslims accounted for their mass flight. To the question, What was your main reason for leaving Iran? one Iranian in Los Angeles answered: "Being a Baha'i I was threatened. They threw acid at me. My son was kidnapped. My house was destroyed. I was imprisoned and lost my job." Another Iranian exile in Los Angeles gave the following answer to why he left Iran: "My life was in danger because I was well known and had close contact with the royal family." Early waves of exiles were drawn from the elites and most modernized segments of Iranian society often for political reasons such as the one mentioned above. The emergence of a theocratic state in Iran, the only one of its kind in the world at present, and its imposition of a strict code of behavior were particularly intolerable for the modernizing Iranian women. The following quote echoes the main reason for this group to leave their homeland: "lack of freedom in Iran, meaning limitations of women's work and activities." Iranian exiles also happened to be mostly educated, an education that was sometimes obtained in the United States and in Europe. Thus, there was no cultural, social, and economic gulf between them and Americans, resulting in little conflict on these grounds. In this sense, once more, Iranians do not fit the image of a typical refugee, that is, one who is poor, illiterate, and observes strikingly different customs, whose very presence creates cultural conflict with Americans.

The conflict between Americans and Iranians in the United States has operated at a political, rather than economic or cultural, level. There was hardly any conflict between Americans and Iranian students who lived in the United States before the Iranian revolution. The conflict started during the revolution around America's support of the late shah. The conflict between Iranians and Americans intensified in 1980–1981 when 52 Americans were taken hostage for 444 days in Iran. This sad event in Iranian-American relations coincided with the massive influx of Iranian exiles into the United States, who soon after arrival faced a presidential decree to deport Iranians who were out of legal status in violation of their visas. This was an unfair targeting and scapegoating of Iranians in the United States who had been persecuted by a regime that they had left behind. U.S.-Iran tensions have continued to the present, as shown by the withdrawal of Conoco's deal with Iran in 1995 due to presidential pressures. Unfortunately, every time these tensions break out as conflicts, Iranians in the United States become scapegoats and suffer the consequences.

EXODUS AND TRANSIT: FROM FOREIGN STUDENTS TO EXILES

Iranian migration to the United States came in two distinctive waves: before and after the Iranian revolution of 1978–1979. As pointed out above, Iranians who emigrated before the revolution were mostly students—although there were also a few economic migrants—while those who have left after the revolution are mainly exiles or political refugees. The consolidation of the Islamic Republic of Iran, on the one hand, and the growth of the Iranian community in the United States, on the other, have sustained the migration of Iranians to the United States. Data from the Immigration and Naturalization Service (INS) and the U.S. Census Bureau tell the same story: Iranian migration to the United States continues unabated, although not at the late 1970s high levels (see Tables 10.1 and 10.2).

From 1950 to 1992, 247,261 Iranians entered the United States as legal immigrants, that is, with a permanent residency visa. Illegal immigration from Iran to the United States is negligible, visa overstayers excepted. Although some of these had immigrant status upon arrival, most were admitted with student visas or as visitors for pleasure and subsequently changed their status to permanent residents. Given the difficulties of obtaining a U.S. visa, it is not surprising that most Iranians are not admitted to the United States directly as immigrants. The data in Table 10.1 further show that there was a sharp increase in the number of Iranian immigrants from 2,730 in the 1950s to 8,895 in the 1960s and 23,230 during 1970–1977. Starting with the Iranian revolution in 1978–1979, and in spite of the closure of the American embassy in Iran, there was a rapid acceleration in the number of immigrants admitted from Iran, reaching an annual average of over 10,000 in the early 1980s. Almost one quarter of all Iranian immigrants first entered the United States as refugees or were classified as asylees after their arrival, which qualifies the Iranian migration as part of an exile or refugee stream. Many of those who have arrived with immigrant visas are refugees from outside the United States. For the first 30 years, from 1950 to 1980, there were only 732 Iranian refugees and asylees, but this number jumped dramatically to 58,381 in the next 12 years, due to the Iranian revolution. The number of refugees/asylees would have been even higher if all Iranians who were exiles in a sociological sense were granted refugee or asylee legal status.

Table 10.1
Iranians Admitted to the United States, 1950–1992

Year	Immigrants	Refugees & Asylees
1950-59	2,730	
1960-69	8,895	
1970-76	18,969	
1977	4,261	732
1978	5,861	
1979	8,476	
1980	10,410	
1981	11,105	366
1982	10,314	701
1983	11,163	1,450
1984	13,807	3,544
1985	16,071	5,420
1986	16,505	6,022
1987	14,426	5,559
1988	15,246	6,895
1989	21,243	8,167
1990	24,977	8,649
1991	19,569	8,515
1992	13,233	3,093
Total	247,261	59,113

Source: Compiled from annual statistical yearbooks of the U.S. Immigration and Naturalization Service.

Of the almost 35,000 Iranian immigrants admitted before the revolution (i.e., 1950–1987), less than half (almost 14,000) were new arrivals (Bozorgmehr and Sabagh 1987; Table 10.1), whereas of a total of 108,694 Iranian immigrants admitted in 1987–1990, one third (30,565) were new arrivals. Thus, the trend among Iranians is toward obtaining permanent residency and settling down in the United States, a trend that has become more pronounced after the revolution. Data reported by the INS, but not shown here because they are no longer an important factor in Iranian migration, indicate that the number of nonimmigrants (mainly students but also visitors) from Iran has dropped precipitously from its peak in 1977–1979.

Iranians who came to the United States before the revolution were mostly students or economic migrants and were very distinctive from the exiles who

Table 10.2
Selected Characteristics of Foreign-Born Iranians, 1990

Characteristic		%
Sex	Male	57%
	Female	43%
Period of immigration	1985-1990	31%
	1980-1984	19%
	1975-1979	34%
	Before 1974	16%
Education*	College or higher	51%
	Some college	20%
	High school diploma	16%
	Some high school	7%
	Elementary school	6%
Occupation**	Higher white-collar	43%
	Lower white-collar	43%
	Blue-collar	14%

Notes:
*Education data are based on Iran-born persons aged 25 and over.
**Employment data are based on Iran-born persons aged 16 and over.
Higher white-collar = Managerial and professional occupations.
Lower white-collar = Technical, sales, clerical, and service occupations.
Blue-collar = Farming, craft, and transportation occupations, plus operators and laborers.
Source: U.S. Bureau of the Census 1993.

arrived after the revolution. Using period of arrival in U.S. census data, we have shown that the characteristics of the Iranian exiles differ from those of immigrants (Sabagh and Bozorgmehr 1987), which in turn affects their social and economic integration. However, the U.S. census data are imperfect for this purpose because the Iranian revolution occurred in 1978–1979, and the census data are reported for the 1975–1980 arrivals, thus resulting in a mixed group of exiles and immigrants. Our survey of Iranians in Los Angeles remedied this problem by asking the respondents about their motivation for leaving Iran. Those who stated that their motivation was either religious and/or political persecution were classified as exiles, and the rest were classified as immigrants. This intragroup comparison showed that less than half of the Iranian householders in Los Angeles (43 percent) were exiles, and over half (57 percent) were immigrants.

Moreover, this classification closely corresponded with the timing of the Iranian revolution. Yet, only one third of the sociologically defined exiles obtained legal refugee/asylee status. Surprisingly, one seventh of immigrants also obtained this status. Clearly, many Iranians could not prove a well-founded fear of persecution despite their original religious and/or political motivations for leaving Iran.[2]

It was relatively easy to acquire a U.S. visa before the seizure of the American embassy in Iran and its indefinite closure. It is now impossible to obtain a U.S. visa directly from Iran since there is no American embassy in that country. After the closure of the American embassy, Iranians have had to go to a third country to receive a visa to come to the United States. For Iranian exiles, the modal pattern has been to enter the United States on a tourist or visitor visa and subsequently to apply for political asylum. Some have applied for refugee status directly from Iran, but this process often has taken much longer. Other more fortunate ones who are immediate relatives of Iranian naturalized citizens have obtained an immigrant visa through the family reunification provisions of American immigration law.

Coming to the United States is becoming less economically feasible for Iranians since the Iranian currency is weak against the dollar, especially on the black market, thus requiring substantial money to finance the long trip. Moreover, the Iranian government levies a fee for leaving Iran and will not allow its citizens to take large amounts of money out. At the same time, given the anti-immigrant, and particularly antirefugee, backlash in Europe, most European countries have clamped down on their immigrant admissions. This is even more of a problem for Iranians because European countries are even more concerned than the United States about the threat of terrorism. Thus, the ultimate objective of Iranians who can afford it is to emigrate to the United States.

Religious minorities, in particular, fled Iran under treacherous conditions, often paying a middleman to get them across the border to neighboring Turkey and Pakistan, which did not require a visa for Iranians. From there, they usually migrated to European countries (Germany, Italy, Spain, Scandinavia) before obtaining a visa to come to the United States. Iranians, especially those who were not allowed to leave the country, recount horror stories about their flight. One such story was even portrayed in the otherwise sensational and stereotypical movie *Not Without My Daughter,* when an American woman tried to escape the wrath of her Iranian husband and leave Iran with her daughter.

Since official data do not report religion, our survey of Iranians in Los Angeles is important for examining the differences in patterns of migration of Muslims and religious minorities. The survey data on Iranians in Los Angeles tell a distinctive story about the exodus of non-Muslim minorities from Iran. While none of the Muslims left Iran for religious reasons, many Baha'is did so since they were singled out by the Islamic Republic for political persecution. Less than half of the Iranians in Los Angeles left Iran for political reasons, though this percentage was higher for Jews than it was for other groups. Combining political and religious reasons, a higher proportion of the more persecuted religious minorities (i.e., Baha'is and Jews) than of the less persecuted minority (Armenians) or the Muslim majority thus become exiles in a sociological sense. Among all Iranians who left Iran for reasons other than political ones, an insignificant segment did so for economic reasons. Similarly, education and family were much more important reasons for leaving Iran than were economic reasons, which shows that Iranians are not economic migrants (Bozorgmehr 1992: Ch. 4).

As far as the stereotypical issue of wealth is concerned, some of the earliest Iranian exiles to the United States managed to bring out considerable capital, although no one knows exactly how much. But many of them had to leave much of their assets behind, often in the form of not readily liquidable real estate. (Iranians invested in fixed assets such as real estate because of the erratic and uncertain economic climate in Iran under the shah.) As in many other refugee streams, the recent Iranian exiles to the United States, many of whom are members of religious minorities in Iran, are not as well-off as the early waves.

INITIAL RESETTLEMENT—WITHOUT A HELPING HAND

Unlike legally defined refugee groups such as Cubans and Vietnamese before them, Iranians for the most part received little help in their migration and resettlement from the U.S. government. Less than one in five of Iranian exiles in Los Angeles received any type of organizational help in moving from Iran to the United States, and those who did were mostly religious minorities from Iran, for example, Jews, who were assisted by international coreligionist organizations such as the Hebrew Immigrant Aid Society (HIAS).

One may argue that many of the Iranians who originally came to the United States as temporary migrants (e.g., students) have become "self-imposed exiles" by changing their mind about returning to Iran. But integration to American society can also bring about a change of mind among sojourners, in addition to the changing conditions in the homeland. Clearly, exiles left Iran more permanently than did the immigrants, which is reflected in their migration pattern. While half of Iranian immigrants migrated alone, only about one third of exiles did so. Moreover, religious minorities from Iran have migrated to the United States more in family units than have the Muslim majority due to the former's precarious status in Iran. Moving with the nuclear family, and even the extended one, has reduced the probability of return to the country of origin for the minorities. When asked about their plans upon arrival in the United States, about two thirds of Iranian exiles in Los Angeles indicated that they planned to stay in the United States permanently, and the rest said they would like to go back to Iran soon or someday. At the time of the survey in 1987–1988, an even greater percentage (83 percent) planned to stay in the United States. Even among Iranian immigrants, less than half (41 percent) of whom had originally planned to stay in the United States, the proportion had increased to 73 percent. Ironically, the main reasons behind change in plans for both exiles and immigrants were identical, namely, the Iranian revolution, political and religious persecution, and the Iran-Iraq war in the 1980s.

INS data on categories of Iranian admissions to the United States and our survey data on Iranians in Los Angeles are consistent in that they both show that, by and large, Iranians arrive in the United States under temporary student and visitor visas (Bozorgmehr 1992; Bozorgmehr and Sabagh 1988). This pattern has changed as Iranians have increasingly become naturalized citizens of the United States and can bring their immediate relatives over through family reunification. Iranian exiles suffered from a major change in the U.S. refugee laws in 1980. U.S. policy shifted from granting outright refugee and parolee status to migrant groups, as it had done with Cubans and Indochinese in the past, to a case-by-case evaluation of an individual migrant. Each applicant for refugee status now has to have proof of persecution beyond reasonable doubt if returned to his/her respective country of origin. Thus, it has become easier to arrive in the United States temporarily and subsequently apply for political asylum than to apply for refugee status from overseas. Iranians have faced serious difficulties in obtaining U.S. visas, especially after the Iranian hostage crisis of 1980–1981. An INS restrictive policy toward Iranians was in effect during those 444 days when Americans were held hostage in Iran. Simply, many more Iranians would migrate to the United States if they could obtain U.S. visas more easily. For instance, fleeing an antagonistic revolutionary regime, Iranian religious minorities in Los Angeles have relied on asylee/refugee visas more so than have Muslims, but the percentages admitted under this visa are low compared with the proportion of these subgroups who are sociological exiles. A lack of correspondence between political/religious reasons for leaving Iran and refugee/asylee visas points to the difficulty of obtaining refugee/asylee visas even among the persecuted Iranian religious minorities. Limited in options to get a U.S. immigrant visa, less than half of Iranians in Los Angeles have had to turn to visitor visas to come to the United States. However, a much higher percentage of religious minorities than Muslims were reclassified as asylees, indicating that religious minorities from Iran were in a better position to prove fear of persecution if returned to Iran than were Muslims.

ECONOMIC INTEGRATION

Immediately after the Iranian revolution in 1980, Iranians were one of the highest-status immigrant groups in the United States, as measured by their levels of education and occupation. At that time, however, Iranians consisted mainly of recent exiles fleeing the revolution and former college students. As such, it was not surprising that Iranians were highly educated professionals and affluent entrepreneurs. Over 15 years after the revolution, it is timely to know whether, and if so how, the arrival of recent refugees has affected the socioeconomic characteristics of Iranians in the United States.

Since the Los Angeles region has the largest concentration of Iranian immigrants in the United States, and the most comprehensive data are available through our survey of Iranians in Los Angeles, I will focus on this metropolitan area. Whenever applicable, however, the characteristics of Iranians in Los Angeles will be compared with their counterparts in the United States. The 1990 U.S. census enumerated about 285,000 Iranians in the United States, of whom 100,000, or 35 percent, were in the Los Angeles metropolitan area (five-county region), and about 80,000, or 28 percent, were in Los Angeles County. The vast majority of Iranians in Los Angeles were foreign born in both 1980 and 1990, mainly due to the influx of new exiles and refugees.

Most discussions of the economic integration of refugees have centered around the difficulty that these migrants face in transferring their skills and, as a result, experiencing more initial downward mobility than economic migrants. However, few studies have collected data on the occupational background of exiles/refugees in order to adequately address this issue, and when they have, the data are not often comparable since the economic structures of refugee sending and receiving countries are vastly different. To correct this problem, we used the U.S. census occupational classification for occupations in Iran and the United States. Although the broad U.S. census classification was also adopted in the Iranian census, it is admittedly less than perfect for the Iranian economy. Nevertheless, it serves a useful function in evaluating the occupational mobility of Iranian exiles and immigrants to the United States. Ultimately, a group's economic well-being should be evaluated in terms of the education and skills that it possesses, and in this sense, it is also important to examine the performance of Iranians in the United States.

According to the 1990 U.S. census, with half of its population 25 years and older holding a bachelor's degree or higher (see Table 10.2), foreign-born Iranians were the third-most highly educated major immigrant group (more than 100,000 persons) in the United States after Asian Indians and Taiwanese. As such, Iranians were the most highly educated group among exile or refugee groups. As Table 10.2 further indicates, less than half of Iranian immigrants and exiles in the United States hold higher white-collar (professional and managerial specialty) occupations. Only 14 percent of Iranians hold blue-collar jobs, but even this low rate is misleading since it contains occupations like hairdressers (a female-dominated Iranian occupation). Insofar as Iranians have opted for self-employment, they have sidestepped the usual problems of transfer of skills that wage and salaried refugees usually face. This is not to suggest that entrepreneurs do not experience downward mobility as their businesses are scaled down and/ or are often forced to venture into new and uncharted business territories. Nevertheless, there is some occupational continuity since the refugees could use their entrepreneurial acumen to become established in business and not be at the mercy of employers who might question their knowledge and skills.

Self-employment is also a well-established traditional route to upward mobility. The rate of self-employment is higher among Iranians in the United States (21 percent) than it is among many other groups. But unlike other immigrant groups who turn to self-employment because of disadvantages in the labor market (e.g., language handicaps), the presence of former commercial minorities such as Jews and Armenians and availability of capital partly account for the high self-employment rate of Iranians. The rate of Iranian self-employment is even higher in Los Angeles than it is in the United States as a whole due to the greater presence of Armenians and Jews. Iranians also have a much higher self-employment rate compared with the other groups—33 percent versus 24 percent, 19 percent, and 8 percent for non-Hispanic white, Asian, and Hispanic immigrant males, respectively, in 1990 in Los Angeles.

Like most other groups, the socioeconomic status of Iranian females is lower than males. Still, with 42 percent holding a bachelor's degree and higher, Iranian women in the United States are very highly educated. The most striking feature of the economic integration of Iranian females is their very low rate of labor force participation, which is mainly a carryover from Iran. Yet Iranian women have made great strides toward working outside the home in the United States, as evidenced by a substantial increase in their labor force participation over time. Although part of this is due to the fact that in 1980 many Iranian exiles from the 1978–1979 revolution had just arrived and were not yet in the labor force, as shown to be the case among males, the increase in the labor force participation of females is more substantial than that of the males. The female rate of labor force participation is noticeably higher in the United States than it was in Iran, where even in 1990 it was below 20 percent. But the overall Iranian rate is misleading in light of the extreme selectivity of Iranian immigrant women. Nevertheless, Iranian women are increasingly entering the labor market in the United States (Dallalfar 1994), which has significant effects for the changing sex roles and family life of this population.

Immigrants, such as Iranians, usually concentrate in specific occupations or industries to continue an economic heritage, to have greater opportunities of working with coethnics, to fill a void in the existing economic structure, and to avoid discrimination, among other reasons. To put it more succinctly, immigrants carve out occupational and industrial niches.[3] For Iranians, this pattern of occupational or industrial concentration has more or less persisted over time. Almost all of the top ten Iranian niches in Los Angeles are managerial, professional, and sales—highly desirable and lucrative niches. Remarkably, self-employment levels are very high for many of the niches. Self-employment rates exceed 30 percent, not only for high-status occupations (physicians) but also for blue-collar workers (hairdressers) (Bozorgmehr, Der-Martirosian, and Sabagh in press).

Ultimately, there are two ways to assess the occupational success of Iranians. First, the occupational distribution of Iranians is compared with that of other groups, particularly native-born whites.[4] Second, the earnings of Iranians are compared with those of the native-born white population. But since the two groups differ in characteristics that could influence earnings, we have to consider not only the actual earnings of Iranians but also the earnings they would receive if they had the same characteristics as native-born whites.[5]

In 1990, the occupational distribution of foreign-born Iranians in Los Angeles was most similar to that of native-born whites and least similar to that of native-born blacks.[6] This pattern has persisted since 1980, and holds true for industry with minor modifications. Thus, Iranians in Los Angeles are much more like native whites and Asians than like African-Americans and Hispanics in their occupational and industrial distribution. Since, on the average, native whites and Asians hold better jobs than Hispanics and blacks, occupational dissimilarity is a crude measure of economic well-being for Iranians.

In short, Iranian immigrants and exiles opt for managerial, professional, and entrepreneurial occupations. Whether they are successful, however, is more problematic to establish. Since Iranians have a high degree of professional and entrepreneurial experience, we would expect them to also have higher earnings generally.

Although foreign-born Iranians have relatively high earnings compared with other major foreign-born groups, they are not doing as well compared to native whites, at least not in Los Angeles. Some may argue that these are relatively new immigrants and as such they are expected not to do as well as native whites. If this is the case, then the earlier immigrant cohorts should do relatively better. In general, the longer the length of residence in the United States, the higher the earnings of immigrants. The best way to judge the economic performance of Iranians is to compare their earnings in dollars with the native-born whites, on the assumption that they have similar education, job experience, and so on.[7]

Actual earnings of Iranians are higher than the native whites'. But on the assumption that Iranians have the same characteristics as native whites, their adjusted earnings are lower than the native whites'. This suggests that even though Iranians have higher labor market skills, they are not treated like Anglos or whites despite their racial classification as such. This is also illustrated by the experience of the 1970–1979 Iranian cohort. Comparing the figures for 1980 and 1990, this group does not reap the same economic rewards as do native whites, but nonetheless its earnings have improved during a relatively short ten-year period. The 1970–1979 cohort included high-status exiles from the Iranian revolution, as well as former university students. The most recent immigrant cohort (1980–1990), however, is even more disadvantaged than the earlier cohort due to the influx of less educated and skilled refugees. For instance, among Iranians who immigrated before 1980, 72 percent of males and 42 percent of females aged 25 to 64 had 4 or more years of college education. The corresponding rates for the 1980–1990 cohort are 54 percent for males and 27 percent for females.

Exiles and refugees usually experience downward mobility during the initial phase of resettlement and only later, after improving their English and acquiring occupational skills, may recuperate economically. Iranian immigrants, and especially exiles, have experienced downward social mobility on their first job

and even current job compared to Iran. While 45 percent held managerial, executive, and professional specialty jobs in Iran, only 35 percent had similar first
occupations and current occupations in Los Angeles by 1987–1988 (Bozorgmehr
and Sabagh 1991: table 7). Although the passage of time may help the economic
progress of Iranian exiles in the United States, it is doubtful that those who are
reaching old age could ever surpass their former occupations.

SOCIAL INTEGRATION

Social integration or *assimilation* refers to the absorption of a minority group
into the dominant group. Sociologically speaking, a minority group, such as
Iranians, with high levels of education, occupation, and English-language proficiency, is expected to become rapidly integrated into American society. Since
Iranians by and large have not assimilated, why do they need and utilize ethnicity, despite their high status and ample resources? Answering this question
requires a systematic empirical and analytical explanation, which is beyond the
scope of this chapter. True, some Iranians are very assimilated, especially those
who arrived much earlier as students, subsequently married Americans, and settled down in places where there are few Iranians. But most, especially the post-
revolution exiles who have settled in areas of Iranian concentration such as Los
Angeles, New York, and Washington, D.C., have tenaciously resisted integration. One may argue that the difference between these two groups has less to
do with their migrant type than with the year of immigration—that is, the earlier
arrivals are more assimilated than the later ones. But it is not so much time of
arrival as the pattern of migration that accounts for the differences in social
integration. Iranian students were well on their way toward assimilation because
they had migrated on their own, until they were joined by parents and other
relatives or relocated within the United States to be near them. Often having
migrated with family members, or reunifying with them soon after, the exiles
have maintained close ties with relatives, thus reinforcing their ethnicity. This
is particularly the case among religious minorities from Iran, who have sometimes moved as entire families. If timing of arrival cannot fully explain remaining ethnicity, then what can? The economic explanation is that reliance on
coethnics confers economic advantages to the group such as information for
getting a job or starting a business. Some sociologists have argued that the
entrepreneurs or self-employed are more ethnic than their salaried counterparts
because the former's coworkers are often coethnics. Since Iranians are very
entrepreneurial (Light et al. 1993), it is tempting to accept this explanation. This
economic explanation of ethnicity, however, does not fully explain the Iranian
experience either. For one, there are many professionals among Iranians who
are expected to assimilate rapidly due to their English proficiency and high levels
of education, which puts them in direct contact with non-Iranians. Although
some Iranian professionals are also self-employed, and as such often work in
an ethnic milieu, we would expect professional status to promote integration

among those who are not self-employed. But even the latter are often very ethnic, though not nearly as much as the entrepreneurs. Therefore, other non-economic factors must account for the lack of integration of Iranians into the mainstream. Perhaps the most important and relevant one here is exile status, whose effect is both direct and indirect. Exile status, because of its involuntary nature, results in a stronger sense of loss for the homeland (Naficy 1993). Furthermore, exiles also include religious minorities from Iran, who are more solitary than most immigrants.

All indicators of ethnicity point to its maintenance among Iranians, at least in Los Angeles. Intermarriage is traditionally used as the best indicator of assimilation. In other words the higher the rate of intermarriage, the more assimilated the group. With 90 percent of Iranian females married to Iranian males (many in Iran), Iranian immigrants and exiles are very unlikely to have intermarried. Besides marriage in Iran, the sizable presence of endogamous minority groups, notably Jews and Armenians, accounts for the low rate of intermarriage.

The use and maintenance of ethnic language are particularly high among foreign-born Iranians, the majority of whom speak their mother tongues at home despite their facility with English. Although Iranians do not come from a country where English is commonly used, they show a remarkable degree of English proficiency. A good command of English reflects their high level of education, which in many cases was obtained in the United States. Among Los Angeles Iranians who speak a language other than English at home, about 80 percent claim that they speak English well or very well.

Iranians in Los Angeles are highly ethnic partly because they consist of religioethnic minorities, e.g., Armenians and Jews, with a long and well-defined history of minority experience. Among Iranian subgroups, the Muslims are the most assimilated, but even they are not fully assimilated because of their exile status and a strong sense of Iranian nationalism.

In Los Angeles, where all Iranian subgroups are present, the extreme diversity of Iranians results in a much more complex pattern of social integration than most other groups. This pattern is less complex in New York where Iranian Muslims and Jews are the two major subgroups. In both Los Angeles and New York, Iranians have non-Iranian coreligionists, a factor that figured partially in their initial settlement in these two metropolitan regions. Thus, if and when social integration occurs, the first tendency among Iranian subgroups is toward coreligionists of non-Iranian background. This is least likely among Muslims, however, who by the very dint of their secularism and their stronger identification with their nationality than religion are unlikely to mingle with devout non-Iranian Muslims. Thus, their integration, which also happens to be the most rapid of all other major Iranian subgroups, is very similar to the traditional assimilationist path, that is, into mainstream American society.

In the case of religious minorities from Iran, the issue of social integration becomes much more problematic than for Muslims. Of particular importance is the extent to which Armenians and Jews, the two largest religious minorities from Iran, have become integrated within the general community of Los Angeles Armenians or Jews. Data on friendship ties and participation in organizations indicate a lack of integration. The close friends of most first-generation Iranian Jews and Armenians are Iranian coreligionists. Furthermore, they are more likely than the Muslims to define their ethnicity in terms of both their nationality and religion, thus setting them apart from other Iranians. At the same time, however, these groups find themselves struggling with a set of coreligionists who define themselves more in religioethnic than in national-origin terms. Although minorities from Iran might find a congenial coreligionist community, cultural and class differences are pronounced enough to prevent social integration among the first generation.

These first-generation differences, however, are slowly disappearing among the second generation. Thus, less than half of Armenian and Jewish Iranian children, both second- and one-and-a-half generation (i.e., born in Iran and emigrated before the age of ten) have exclusively Iranian coreligionists close friends. These generational differences suggest that as Iranian Jewish and Armenian children grow up, they may move away from the Iranian community and become oriented toward the general Armenian and Jewish-American communities. However, this also depends on whom they marry. Not surprisingly, the first choice of almost all Iranian Jewish and Armenian parents is that their children marry Iranian coreligionists. Surprisingly, however, marrying a non-Iranian Jew or Armenian is the second choice, and marrying an Iranian only a third. The attitudes of young Iranian Jews in Los Angeles toward mate selection suggest that their selection of future husbands and wives very closely corresponds to their parents' wishes (Hanassab 1993).

Discrimination and prejudice are two other key factors that prevent or delay the social integration of Iranians, especially Muslims, into American society. Even in multiethnic Los Angeles, Muslims and other Iranians continue to experience discrimination, although the extent of this has decreased since the Iranian hostage crisis from about a quarter who indicated they experienced discrimination to a tenth. On the other hand, about half indicated that there is prejudice against Iranians. One Muslim Iranian in Los Angeles recounted his worst experience of discrimination during the hostage crisis:

With seven years of professional experience and education I received no responses from any companies to which I was sending my résumé. Then I changed my name from Mohammad to Mike in my résumé and immediately got four responses, including one from a company that had not responded to Mohammad.

Sadly, this experience could have been repeated during the Gulf War and the bombing of the World Trade Center in New York since *Mohammad* is also an Arabic name. The owner of an Iranian fast-food restaurant in Los Angeles told us that during the hostage crisis ''some of my customers have regretted having eaten at my restaurant after finding out I was Iranian.'' Another Iranian summing up the influence of the media on American public opinion toward Iranians said: "The daily behavior of Americans depends on what they said about Iranians on TV the night before."

CONCLUSIONS AND PROSPECTS

Iranian exiles and refugees are different from other contemporary exile and refugee groups in the United States. This is mainly due to the background of Iranians and the historical context of their migration, which in turn have affected their social and economic integration into American society and economy. Iran was a rapidly modernizing and Westernizing society when the revolution broke out in the late 1970s. The Iranian revolution and the establishment of the Islamic Republic of Iran had a dual effect: first, forcing the exodus of the elite and members of religious minorities from Iran; second, discouraging the return of Iranian college and university students who were pursuing a technical education in the United States. These two groups, although sociologically distinctive, were not unrelated. Indeed, many of the exiles were relatives of the students, and this factor accounts for the emergence of the United States as the largest concentration of Iranians in the Western world (Bozorgmehr in press). The combination of former students and elite exiles accounts for the highly educated, entrepreneurial, and professional Iranian community in the United States.

In spite of these characteristics and their corresponding contributions to the American economy and society, Iranians in the United States suffer from discrimination and prejudice because of negative stereotypes associated with the Iranian regime. Despite their high-status occupations and English-language proficiency, Iranian immigrants on the whole are surprisingly unassimilated. This level of ethnicity exceeds expectations for highly educated professionals but is congruent with the experiences of entrepreneurial minorities, who make up a large segment of Iranians. However, the main explanation for the maintenance of ethnicity is the presence of former religious minorities from Iran, who were forced into exile by the Islamic outcome of the Iranian revolution. But even Iranian Muslims are more ethnic than would be expected from their socioeconomic status because many are exiles, whether real or self-imposed, and as such have a strong sense of Iranian nationalism or attachment to the homeland. Given this surprisingly high level of retained ethnicity, it is unlikely that Iranians in the United States will become fully assimilated in the near future. If the children of Iranian Armenians and Jews assimilate, they will do so within the general Armenian and Jewish communities. The assimilationist trajectory of Iranian Muslim children is not clear, but they are likely to move toward middle-class American society.

ACKNOWLEDGMENTS

This chapter is based on research supported in part by grants from the National Science and Russell Sage Foundations. I would like to thank David

Haines, Claudia Der-Martirosian, and especially Georges Sabagh for their comments on drafts of this chapter.

NOTES

1. In this chapter, *exile* is a sociological term based on religious or political motivations for leaving the country of origin; *immigrant* refers to all others, including those whose motivations for emigration are social (e.g., to pursue education) and economic. *Refugee* is a formal legal status obtained from outside the country of refuge, and *asylee* is a formal legal status obtained from within the country of asylum.

2. Whenever data are available, the refugee/immigrant distinction is pointed out in this chapter. Unfortunately, this can be done for Iranians in Los Angeles only, for whom we have survey data. Thus, when Iranians in the United States are mentioned, or when other sources than our survey are used, it means Iranians irrespective of their exile or immigrant status.

3. An *ethnic niche* is an occupational or industrial specialization in which a group is overrepresented by at least 50 percent relative to its size in the labor force.

4. The term *native-born whites* is used to refer to native-born whites excluding the Hispanic population.

5. This analysis was carried out for the Los Angeles region to ensure that all groups face the same opportunity structure.

6. This comparison was done by deriving an index of dissimilarity.

7. These comparisons are made using regression analysis. Only the two most recent immigration cohorts (1980–1989 and 1970–1979) are included in the earnings regressions due to the small sample sizes of the two earliest cohorts (1960–1969 and before 1960). The 1980–1989 cohort consists mostly of refugees, whereas the 1970–1979 cohort includes former students and economic migrants. Because of the generally low level of labor force participation of Iranian females, the results are presented for males only to make the comparisons with other groups meaningful.

REFERENCES

Bozorgmehr, Mehdi. 1992. Internal Ethnicity: Armenian, Bahai, Jewish, and Muslim
    Iranians in Los Angeles. Unpublished Ph.D dissertation, University of California,
    Los Angeles.
————. In press. Diaspora in Postrevolutionary Period. *Encyclopedia Iranica*.
Bozorgmehr, Mehdi, Claudia Der-Martirosian, and Georges Sabagh. In press. Middle
    Easterners: A New Kind of Immigrant. In *Ethnic Los Angeles*. Edited by Roger
    Waldinger and Mehdi Bozorgmehr. New York: Russell Sage Foundation.
Bozorgmehr, Mehdi, and Georges Sabagh. 1988. High Status Immigrants: A Statistical
    Profile of Iranians in the United States. *Iranian Studies* 21(3–4):4–34.
————. 1991. Iranian Exiles and Immigrants in Los Angeles. In *Iranian Refugees and
    Exiles since Khomeini*. Edited by Asghar Fathi. Costa Mesa, California: Mazda
    Publishers. Pp. 121–144.
Dallalfar, Arlene. 1994. Iranian Women as Immigrant Entrepreneurs. *Gender and Society*
    8(4):541–561.
Hanassab, Shideh. 1993. Premarital Attitudes of Young Iranians regarding Mate Selec-

tion: Arranged Marriage vs. Inter-Marriage. Unpublished Ph.D. dissertation, University of California, Los Angeles.

Jones, Allen K. 1984. *Iranian Refugees: The Many Faces of Persecution.* Washington, D.C.: U.S. Committee for Refugees.

Kelley, Ron, Jonathan Friedlander, and Anita Colby, Editors. 1993. *Irangeles: Iranians in Los Angeles.* Los Angeles: University of California Press.

Light, Ivan, Georges Sabagh, Mehdi Bozorgmehr, and Claudia Der-Martirosian. 1993. Internal Ethnicity in the Ethnic Economy. *Ethnic and Racial Studies* 16(4):581–597.

Naficy, Hamid. 1993. *The Making of Exile Cultures: Iranian Television in Los Angeles.* Minneapolis: University of Minnesota Press.

Sabagh, Georges, and Mehdi Bozorgmehr. 1987. Are the Characteristics of Exiles Different from Immigrants? *Sociology and Social Research* 71(2):77–84.

———. 1994. Secular Immigrants: Religiosity and Ethnicity among Iranian Muslims in Los Angeles. In *Muslim Communities in North America.* Edited by Yvonne Yazbeck Haddad and Jane Idleman Smith. Albany: State University of New York Press. Pp. 445–473.

U.S. Bureau of the Census. 1993. *1990 Census of Population and Housing: Public Use Microdata Samples.* Washington, D.C.

Chapter 11

Khmer

CAROL A. MORTLAND

Khmer refers to the dominant group of inhabitants of Cambodia, a small country in Southeast Asia. Cambodia first came to American attention during the Vietnam War, spawning controversy and division within the United States that continues. In the late spring of 1970, President Richard Nixon announced that America and South Vietnamese troops had invaded Cambodia in pursuit of Vietnamese Communists who had for years been using the country as a staging area in their fight against South Vietnam. Four students were killed at Kent State University by the United States National Guard while protesting the invasion of Cambodia in what was only the most dramatic of thousands of protests that occurred throughout the United States.

Although the American government's stated aims in Cambodia were to help preserve peace and independence for Cambodians, much of America's attention resulted primarily from her own concerns, stated as maintaining American honor and withdrawing American soldiers as quickly as possible from Southeast Asia. And despite their claims, many opposing Americans were concerned less with the welfare of the Khmer people than they were with national concerns, for example, the safety of American soldiers and the effects of the war on the domestic economy.

This pattern in American-Cambodian relationships has continued to the mid-1990s, with the United States concerned primarily with easing the impact of resettled Cambodians on Americans rather than easing the impact of resettlement on Cambodians. Overlooked in Americans' concerns with their own realities are Khmer realities. This is especially relevant when looking at Cambodian migration to the United States.

Cambodians and their homeland, Cambodia, have experienced enormous change in the past quarter century. The country has been led by six governments since World War II: French colonizers, King Sihanouk monarchy, Lon Nol republic, Khmer Communists, Vietnamese-established socialism, and the coalition government. The Khmer themselves have been displaced. All have experienced change in their occupations, residence patterns, schooling, religious practice, and family and neighbor relationships. In the 1990s, Cambodians reside in numerous countries throughout the world, in circumstances unimaginable for most when they lived in Cambodia. Almost 150,000 Khmer live in the United States.

This chapter briefly reviews the history of Cambodians in the United States, focusing especially on the most important events of their lives: flight from their homeland, life in refugee camps and processing centers, and movement to America. The chapter also addresses the various strategies Cambodians have used to resettle in the United States: efforts to preserve their culture in the face of American pressure to change, the struggle to live near one another, and the reestablishment of patron-client ties and proper behavior. Cambodians go through predictable patterns of migration and resettlement, just as other migrants do. These patterns can be seen not only in the circumstances they face but in the ways they react to situations and the tactics they choose to deal with their new environment.

THE HOME COUNTRY

Cambodia before 1975

Although the archaeological record indicates that Cambodia was occupied by hunters and gatherers by 9,000 years ago (Mourer 1977; Higham 1989), Cambodians themselves anchor their roots in the majesty of Angkor. The Angkorean civilization, centered in northwest Cambodia, flourished from the beginning of the 800s A.D. to the mid-1400s. The center of Angkor was the court, occupied by the king. Angkorean rulers were absolute and semidivine. They used the labor of their subjects to grow rice that supported the kingdom and to construct the reservoirs and canals that aided intensive rice cultivation. Angkorean laborers also built the stone temple tombs and palaces, statues and relief sculptures, and roadways and bridges that demonstrated the power of Angkorean kings. Angkorean society consisted of sharply defined classes, including an elite composed of royalty and priests and a mass of commoners, many of whom were slaves. The elite were surrounded by luxury and servants—even a special vocabulary was used for them—while commoners served, labored, and obeyed.

From the mid-1200s, kingdoms both to the east and the west of Angkor began threatening Angkorean dominance, and by the mid-1400s, the city of Angkor was abandoned. Attacked repeatedly on both sides, areas of Cambodia for various periods of time came under the control of either Thai or Vietnamese rulers, sometimes both at the same time. In 1863, France pushed Cambodia's neighbors back and established a protectorate over Cambodia, thus preserving Cambodia as a modern entity (Chandler 1983). France governed Cambodia for 90 years. While protecting Cambodia from conquest by her neighbors, France allowed the Cambodian monarchy to continue, its officials now assisting the French in governing and collecting taxes. To assist in the civil service and on newly established rubber plantations and industries, the French brought in large numbers of Vietnamese; Cambodians consequently received little education as a result of colonization. They received few other benefits from the French, whose exploitation of Cambodia primarily benefited France.

Norodom Sihanouk, a young prince chosen to succeed his grandfather because of his apparent compliance with French interests, surprised France with his determination to secure independence for his country. Ninety years after France created the colony, he succeeded, and Cambodia became independent. In the period following, Sihanouk was just as determined to serve as predominant, sole ruler, and again he succeeded, dominating Cambodian life from 1955 to 1970 (Chandler 1991a). Like Cambodian leaders before him, Sihanouk found models for behavior for a modern world in an ancient, often mythical, past, believing himself an infallible leader ruling by divine right over childish subjects with no rights but those he granted them. He likened himself to the kings of Angkor, and his relationship to his people the same as that between Angkorean rulers and their people.

During the second half of the 1950s and the 1960s, Cambodia's neighbors again threatened Cambodia: Vietnam's war and both Vietnam's and Thailand's ties to the United States jeopardized Cambodia's neutrality, and Sihanouk's major accomplishment was the degree to which he was able to keep Cambodians free of the international tempest surrounding them.

The Sihanouk years are now seen as years of peace and prosperity by both Cambodians and observers. Despite the war to the east in Vietnam, most Cambodians continued to live as they had before: residing in rural villages where their parents had lived before them, supporting their families by rice cultivation, observing traditional Khmer Buddhism, and seeking protection and resources through a system of patronage (Ebihara 1968; Martel 1975). Public schools began to replace monastery schools, an occasional relative traveled to town to work, and Western technology and bureaucracy began a local appearance. Despite these changes, Cambodia remained by and large agricultural, traditional, Buddhist, and isolated.

But growing discontent from an increasingly educated population, effects from Vietnam's war, and a poorly managed economy began to affect Sihanouk's dominance and Cambodia's stability. A coup d'état in 1970 replaced Sihanouk with his prime minister, Lon Nol. After the coup, Cambodia's involvement in the Vietnam War increased enormously. American money, corruption, and incursions from soldiers from the various Vietnamese and allied armies who carried their war into Cambodia all contributed to the destruction of Cambodian society and agriculture and the growth of the Cambodian Communist rebellion. The United States, which had secretly begun bombing North Vietnamese border sanctuaries in Cambodia in March 1969 even before the coup, dropped as many bombs on Cambodia between 1969 and 1973 as were dropped in Japan during World War II (Shawcross 1979).

Cambodia rapidly fell to chaos in the early 1970s, and by 1975, even massive financial and military assistance from the United States could no longer bolster a corrupt and inept government and substitute for a collapsed economy. It has been estimated that between 600,000 and 800,000 Cambodians were killed during this period (Ea 1987; CIA 1980; Foreign Broadcast Information Service 1976). During the same period, the Cambodian Communists or Khmer Rouge grew from a meager few thousand in 1970 to a force large enough to occupy the country in 1975.

Democratic Kampuchea, 1975 to 1978

The Khmer Rouge marched into Phnom Penh, the capital of Cambodia, on April 17, 1975, and within hours began to evacuate the city. Khmer Rouge cadre turned the residents and war refugees of Cambodia's cities and towns into the countryside and set them to work farming. Cambodia became a labor camp. Over the next four years, the Khmer Rouge controlled the daily lives of everyone: telling people what work to do and how to do it, where to live and move, when to eat, whom to live with, even what to wear and say.

Describing events in Cambodia during the Khmer Rouge regime is an exercise in extremes; the enormity of change and the extent of horror endured by Cambodians are difficult to overstate, almost impossible to comprehend. The leaders of Democratic Kampuchea were a small group, most of whom had studied Marxism in Paris as students in the 1940s and 1950s. First among them was Pol Pot, whose name is used now by Cambodians to refer to the Khmer Rouge years. Pol Pot and his colleagues wished to create a new society in which the poor were free from exploitation by the rich, and all Cambodians were free from foreign powers. In Democratic Kampuchea, Cambodians would abandon their Western aspirations and return themselves to the days of Angkor, remembered as a time when Cambodians were independent, strong, and self-sufficient. But the ambitions of the Khmer Rouge leaders led them to disregard the realities of Cambodia's people and land. Weakened by years of war, Cambodian transportation, markets, and animals and resources for agriculture were disorganized or lacking, and townspeople were inexperienced at rural labor.

Ebihara (1985) notes the more dramatic transformations effected by the new rulers. First, the Khmer Rouge collectivized the economy by organizing families into work cooperatives and older children and youth into mobile work teams. These cooperatives and teams, often joined into larger groups, provided the labor for rice cultivation and building irrigation systems. Cambodians remember working from sunrise to sometimes long after sunset every day of the week, often walking long distances to work sites, usually eating little more than rice soup. Cambodians also remember vividly Khmer Rouge efforts to disrupt traditional family life. Work teams replaced the family as the basic economic unit. Children over eight or nine were placed in separate teams and occasionally sent away from their parents, smaller children were encouraged to spy on their parents, husbands and wives were often separated, and marriage was permitted only when and to whom the Khmer Rouge dictated. At weekly political meetings, Cambodians were reminded that their families were now replaced by Angka, the unseen but all-pervasive organization said to be running Democratic Kampuchea. A last change of enormous consequence to the Khmer was Democratic Kampuchea's efforts to erase religion. Cambodian Buddhism has long been a fundamental part of Khmer culture; Cambodians say, "To be Cambodian is to be Buddhist." But during the "Pol Pot" years, temples were destroyed, monks defrocked or killed, and rituals forbidden.

In the Cambodian revolutionaries' attempts to remake society into Democratic Kampuchea, one in five or seven or eight of all Cambodians died from execution, starvation, and illness (Vickery 1988; Chandler 1991a; Kiernan 1993). Estimates of how many Cambodians died as a result of Khmer Rouge activities from 1975 through 1978 have been a topic of disagreement, ranging from more than 2 million dead (Ea 1987) to far fewer than that (Vickery 1988). Vickery (1990) claims that between 700,000 and 1 million people above a normal peacetime death rate perished during the 1975–1978 period—about half from illness, hunger, overwork; the other half possibly executed—while the total population declined by 400,000. Banister and Johnson (1993) suggest a figure of 1.05 million dead. Kiernan's (1990, 1993) estimates are higher: concluding after extensive research that 1.5 million of Cambodia's 8 million people died during the Khmer Rouge regime.

Most writers agree with Chandler (1991a) that 1 million perished under the Khmer Rouge. One especially disastrous result of the above-normal death rate in Cambodia during the 1970s has been an imbalance in the sex ratio of Cambodians, both in Cambodia and in resettlement countries. It is estimated that a higher-than-usual number of widows head Cambodian households, both in Cambodia and in the United States (see, for example, Boua 1982; Ebihara 1985; United Nations Development Programme 1989; UNICEF 1990).

Government, education, religion, finance, markets, agriculture, transportation, communication, family, festivals—every aspect of special and everyday life was affected; virtually all was destroyed or changed. Most Cambodians had to move, most lost everything they owned, and virtually everyone had relatives and neighbors killed. Cambodians lost their past and their country; many feared they had lost their culture. By the end of the Khmer Rouge regime, they had only their memories and rumors of hope and food on the Western border.

After the Khmer Rouge

Although Vietnamese and Cambodian Communists had initially cooperated in founding their revolutionary movements, success brought hostility between the two groups, both of which in 1975 became seated governments (Chanda 1986; Evans and Rowley 1983). In late 1978, after a number of skirmishes between the Vietnamese and the Khmer Rouge along the Cambodian-Vietnamese border, Vietnam invaded Cambodia. By January 1979, Vietnamese troops occupied Phnom Penh, and the Khmer Rouge retreated to the west, toward Thailand.

Vietnam installed a new regime, called the People's Republic of Kampuchea. The Khmer population immediately went on the move, returning to home villages, looking for relatives, seeking food. The fighting and population movement hindered harvesting the rice crop in late 1978, and starvation was averted for many only with international assistance.

For the next decade, Cambodia, now called Kampuchea, slowly rebuilt herself under Vietnamese occupation. Cambodian Buddhism, family life, farming, and marketplaces were reestablished. This was done in the face of enormous obstacles, such as shortages of men to do male agricultural chores, poor health as a result of malnutrition and illness during the Khmer Rouge years, and an international aid blockade that denied Western developmental aid to the country. Another major obstacle was the growth of resistance armies in the West. First, there were the Khmer Rouge. Camped along the Cambodian-Thai border and supported by foreigners, including China and Thailand, the Khmer Rouge resumed the resistance fighting in which they had been engaged before 1975. They were joined by three other resistance armies, different in ideology and strategy but united in trying to replace the Vietnamese-backed government of Kampuchea with their own rule.

Disagreement over the nature of Vietnamese occupation existed both among Western observers and resettled Cambodians, ranging from accusations that Kampuchea was being Vietnamized at the expense of Cambodian culture to portrayals of Vietnamese as kindly protectors of a Cambodian-run country. What is evident is that Cambodians' initial relief at the relatively benign rule of the Vietnamese was replaced over time with increasing hostility toward their occupiers (Chandler 1991a). Although the Vietnamese appeared to many to have no intention of leaving Kampuchea, Vietnam withdrew its troops in the late 1980s.

In July 1991, the four Cambodian resistance groups agreed to a United Nations–brokered peace plan for Kampuchea, whose name had been changed to the State of Cambodia in 1989. The United Nations' peacekeeping mission to Cambodia lasted 18 months, cost nearly $2 billion, and involved 22,000 civilians and soldiers. The mission included organizing and managing a national election through which Cambodians elected a government and national assembly and drafted a constitution (U.S. Committee for Refugees 1994). National elections were held in May 1993, and in September the constitution was ratified. Sihanouk became head of state of a constitutional monarchy, now the "Kingdom of Cambodia," and Buddhism was restored as the state religion. Power was shared by the two leading parties, represented by First Prime Minister Prince Norodom

Ranariddh, Sihanouk's son, and Second Prime Minister Hun Sen, who was Cambodia's prime minister through the later 1980s. The Khmer Rouge signed the initial peace agreement but reneged and later attacked the peace process; although a reduced force, they continue to wage a brutal war in the northwest of the country.

In a sense, "Cambodia" includes approximately 250,000 Cambodians who have been resettled around the world (Chandler 1991a) in no less than 19 countries. Close to 150,000 Cambodians have been resettled in the United States. How they reached America is the next issue to be addressed.

EXODUS AND TRANSIT

Flight from Cambodia

For Cambodians in the United States, the flight from Cambodia to Thailand has become a major story in their repertoire, the focus of many of their memories (cf., for example, Ledgerwood 1990a; Marcucci 1986). Most Cambodian refugees are in the United States inadvertently, not because they wanted to live in America but because they wanted to escape Khmer Rouge rule. Their stories of flight reflect this reality, revealing a hiatus between a remembered Cambodia, both as it was in the horror days of the Khmer Rouge and in the relatively peaceful years before, and America.

The first wave of Cambodians to flee the Cambodian Communists did so in 1975 before the Khmer Rouge gained power, when approximately 35,000 Khmer fled west to Thailand and another 150,000 escaped east to Vietnam. Virtually all those in the first wave were resettled in Western countries, primarily France, the United States, Canada, and Australia. Cambodians initially escaping the Khmer Rouge included officials, professionals, and those of the moneyed or aristocratic classes who feared oppression or reprisals from the new Communist rulers and who had the means and connections to leave their homeland. Other early escapees were farmers and townspeople from western Cambodia who were able to slip across the border into Thailand (Ebihara 1985). Few Cambodians were able to escape their homeland during the Khmer Rouge years, although they report having fervently wished to do so; the severity of Khmer Rouge rule and their own weakened physical state made escape virtually impossible. Only with the fall of Democratic Kampuchea was flight again possible.

The second exodus of Cambodians from their country began with the invasion of Cambodia by Vietnamese in December 1978 and continued through the first months of 1979. As Khmer Rouge control broke down, 100,000 Khmer fled to Thailand, most fleeing the Khmer Rouge, others escaping the advancing Vietnamese soldiers, some eluding both. Khmer Rouge cadres also fled toward guerrilla bases in the northwest of Cambodia ahead of the invading Vietnamese troops, forcing many Cambodians to flee with them, using them as a shield, either before or behind them (Reynell 1989). These escapees came from a cross section of Cambodian life: urban professionals and businessmen, middle-class townspeople, and farmers, even Khmer Rouge cadres. Most began their flight to escape the horrors of the Khmer Rouge years, and many fled because they were hungry and had been hungry for four years.

A third major Cambodian exodus occurred from late spring of 1979 to the early months of 1980. During this period of worsening food shortages inside Cambodia, the number of fleeing Khmer increased drastically when rumors spread that food was available on the Thai-Cambodian border. In response to international dismay at the plight of Cambodians and the Thais' hostile reception, Thailand allowed international assistance, primarily in the form of food and basic medical supplies, to be given to Cambodians on the border in late 1979. Fighting between the Vietnamese army occupying Cambodia and Khmer insurgents in western Cambodia caused further flight toward Thailand. This wave of escapees also included a cross section of the Cambodian population: urbanites, townspeople, and peasants.

The United Nations and the International Committee of the Red Cross also established a "land bridge" on the Cambodian-Thai border to provide food, tools, and seed rice to Khmer inside Cambodia. The land bridge program brought as many as 1 million Cambodians to the border, many of whom traveled there to get rice and other assistance, carried it back to their families or to sell, returned to the border for additional assistance, and again hauled it home (Mason and Brown 1983). While intended to encourage Cambodians to stay within their country, the land bridge program did continue to draw Cambodians' attention, and their presence, to the border.

When Cambodians in these first three waves fled their country, they were not thinking of migration. They were thinking of temporary refuge, then of eventually returning home, of finding their children and parents, of finding food. They feared the Khmer Rouge, they feared the Vietnamese, they feared everything Cambodia had become. They fled "yet another army, yet another war" (cf. Ledgerwood 1990a:196; Smith 1989). They were thinking they would die if they stayed in Cambodia, and going was the only alternative they saw. This was especially true of those who fled to Thailand immediately after the fall of the Khmer Rouge.

Only later did Cambodians begin traveling to the border in order to gain admittance to a Thai refugee camp and, ultimately, resettlement in the United States. As the months passed, an increasing number of Cambodians began to see resettlement to a Western country as a possibility, even a goal. American embassy officials, for example, suspected that a number of middle-class Cambodians made the decision to leave Cambodia for Thailand refugee camps so they could be resettled in the United States. But they, and the majority of rice farmers who made up the refugee flow, never realized the extent of the process they had entered: its length, complexity, irreversibility, and short- and long-term consequences. Cambodians did not realize that they had commenced a new phase in their lives, that they were now setting out on their "refugee career" (Reynell 1989).

Those Cambodians who fled Cambodia during the 1980s comprise a fourth, much smaller wave of Cambodian escapees, most of whom were unsuccessful in their attempt to resettle in a third country. During the 1980s, some Cambodians returned to Cambodia voluntarily. Several hundred thousand additional Khmer remained in Thai refugee camps, and another several hundred thousand lived in a series of makeshift encampments along the Thai-Cambodian border. These camp Khmer were supported to varying degrees by assistance channeled through the United Nations.

Between March 1992 and May 1993, 362,200 Cambodians were trucked to Cambodia from Thailand as part of the United Nations' brokered peace plan for Cambodia. By that time, most of the camp residents had been there for years; Lynch (1989) found in 1989 that 89 percent of the adult population of Site II had been on the border by 1983 and thus in camps since that time. Over half of those repatriated had never seen Cambodia before, having been born in the refugee and border camps (cf. French 1994 for a vivid description of camp life). Another 5,300 Cambodians returned home on their own, and 576 were forcibly repatriated by Thailand (U.S. Committee for Refugees 1994).

Movement to America

The first wave of Cambodians to be resettled in the United States consisted of 6,000 people[1] resettled from 1975 to 1977 (Gordon 1984), most from the educated and urbanized Cambodian middle class and most connected to Americans or the American war effort in Southeast Asia. An additional 1,300 arrived in 1978 (*Refugee Reports* 1988).

A second wave came in 1979, when increased international concern over the refugee situation in Southeast Asia prompted the United States to enlarge relevant admission quotas and ease selection criteria. This allowed some 10,000 primarily rural Khmer who had fled Cambodia before the Khmer Rouge takeover but lacked sufficient ties to Americans or the American war effort to also enter the United States (Ebihara 1985). This second wave consisted of farmers, fishermen, and artisans who had more difficulty finding employment and housing and other necessities of life than did the first group of middle-class Cambodians due to differences in education, urban living, and English-language experience. While both groups struggled with life in a vastly different environment, neither had lived through the Khmer Rouge regime.

The third wave of Cambodians to come to America was by far the largest and longest. The number of Khmer arriving in 1980 was nearly triple that in 1979, and Cambodians continued coming in similar numbers each year through 1985. The number dropped in half in 1986, and to less than a sixth in 1987. The total number of Cambodians to arrive between 1980 and 1986 was 125,186 (*Refugee Reports* 1988, 1993). These Cambodians had endured nearly

four years of Democratic Kampuchea; most fled Cambodia at the earliest opportunity.

The fourth wave consists of Cambodians who arrived from 1987 to 1993,
when selection criteria for Cambodians entering the country stiffened considerably (Robinson and Wallenstein 1988). This wave totaled 8,627 and included
primarily family reunification cases: Cambodians coming to join relatives. Many
of these Khmer came as immigrants rather than refugees.

Resettlement to the United States for Cambodians in Thailand meant the end
of powerlessness, the beginning of a life with economic promise and hope.
Before resettlement or repatriation, however, most Cambodians spent years in
refugee camps. A comparison of resettled Cambodians' flight and refugee camp
stories reveals much about camp life. Like any transition experience, flight is
remembered as a specific, separating event: dangerous, harrowing, frightening.
But Cambodians remember themselves as active and capable in their flight from
Cambodia, as people who made decisions, were at least somewhat in control of
their destiny, and were daring, even heroic. Refugee camp stories, in contrast,
are condensed: Years are told in a sentence or two. Camp life is remembered
as a blur, a lengthy span of relative nonevents. Life in the camps—its beginning,
endurance, and ending—was controlled by others, and the passivity of the
Khmer made them anything but heroic in their own eyes. To remember that
time is to recall their powerlessness.

RESETTLEMENT AMERICAN STYLE

Although resettlement in the United States brought Cambodians escape from
the powerlessness of the refugee camps, they were in some sense moving into
yet another structured setting controlled by other people's perceptions and goals.
They found themselves part of a larger Southeast Asian population, including
Lao and a much greater number of Vietnamese. Many refugee programs and
Americans treated these refugees as a homogenous group, with similar experiences and expectations. The Khmer were categorized with people whose language they did not understand, often surrounded by those they had always
thought of as traditional enemies; in addition, social services often encompassed
refugee and immigrant clients from elsewhere in the world. This caused confusion and hardship for both Americans and refugees but led also to unique
personal and working contacts for some Cambodians, as their world was enlarged to include both Americans and other newcomers.

Americans were unaware of key social distinctions within Khmer society:
Villagers were lumped with Phnom Penh elite, farmers with bureaucrats, soldiers
with schoolteachers. They were now recognized as "Cambodians" and "refugees" by those around them, and distinctions among them that they considered
important were ignored, for example, factors such as: class, level of education,
and residence, that existed when they were in Cambodia; factors such as: type
of employment, English-speaking ability, utilization of social services, education, and residence in America.

When Americans recognized Cambodians as a distinct group, they noted the differences between Cambodians and other immigrant groups: less education, English, and familiarity with Westernization; more mental and physical problems. Virtually every popular and scholarly article on Cambodians emphasizes their problems, underscoring first the enormity of change Cambodians experience after resettlement. Observers note that most Cambodian refugees resettled in the United States went no further than the primary grades in Cambodia, there was virtually no exposure to English in the countryside, and most lived in rural settings without benefit of modern technology (e.g., Rumbaut and Ima 1988). In addition, Cambodians brought with them the scars of malnutrition, overwork, and anguish from the Khmer Rouge years. So Cambodians arrived, in Americans' views, wounded in body and mind and lacking language, work skills, or appropriate attitudes. Many American agencies and individuals concluded that Cambodians needed to be taught how to live in America.

Americans envision the United States as a refuge for immigrants and as a country built by immigrants who have contributed the best of themselves and their cultures. Hostility or ambivalence toward a group of migrants is usually expressed by reluctance to admit them or fund programs to serve them, even in verbal or physical attacks on people or their possessions. It was only after extensive lobbying of Congress by the Citizens' Commission on Indochinese Refugees in 1978, for example, that Cambodians were added to the list of Indochinese eligible for admission to the United States under presidential parole authority (Loescher and Scanlan 1986).

But for at least a century, the United States has treated immigrants as people whose difference is less an advantage than a handicap to their integration into American society. The American reception of Cambodians has mirrored that given to immigrants before; reflecting ideas first expressed toward immigrants in the Americanization movement of the late 1880s and early 1900s, most American immigrant education programs in the United States have been designed to teach immigrants to abandon their inferior traditions, seen to encompass notions of hierarchy and privilege, laziness, lack of self-reliance, and dependency. Instead, immigrants are taught American attitudes, values, and behaviors in the hope that they will become free, democratic, rational, hard working, and self-sufficient and thus better able to assimilate to American life (Tollefson 1989).

Americans' ambivalent welcome to Cambodians after their arrival in the United States can be seen among those closest to the immigrant situation: policymakers, resettlement workers, and volunteers. Some Americans have gone to extraordinary degrees to help Cambodians in their resettlement; American sponsors and volunteers have devoted literally millions of unpaid hours assisting Cambodians in a myriad of tasks (e.g., Criddle 1992). The American government, through resettlement and social service agencies, has spent hundreds of millions of dollars on the resettlement of Cambodians alone. The purpose of most of this money and effort has been to change Cambodians, teaching them not only English and employment skills but also American values and behavior.

Even before arrival in the United States, Americans began the attempt to transform Cambodian refugees into American citizens. From late 1980, Cambodians accepted for resettlement in the United States were sent to processing centers in Southeast Asia for up to six months of language, cultural orientation, and vocational training. But some observers questioned the value of such instruction in helping refugees adjust to America after they were resettled (Tollefson 1989; Mortland 1987), and most Cambodian refugees did not think they needed transformation at the hands of Americans.

The primary concern of the American refugee program has been that refugees become economically self-sufficient as quickly as possible after arrival (Refugee Act of 1980; ORR 1994). Americans state, and Cambodians agree, that English-language ability and job skills appropriate to the American workplace are the most important factors influencing Cambodians' employability. In addition, the level of education received in Cambodia, familiarity with Western culture, an urban background, literacy, and youth contribute to employability in America (ORR 1994). In the effort to create self-sufficient Cambodians as quickly as possible, educational programs for Cambodians continued after their arrival in the United States in the form of English-language, cultural orientation, and vocational training classes.

The quality and duration of programs and eligibility requirements for students varied greatly across the United States. In some locales, Cambodians were encouraged to study for as long as two years at government expense, then to continue their education at mainstream institutions if at all possible. Only after extensive training were they expected to seek full-time employment. In other locations, Cambodians were required to obtain employment as quickly as possible, studying English in their free hours. Sponsor expectations and connections, local job opportunities, and the national economic situation at the time of arrival also affected the rate and type of employment accessed by Cambodians. As the 1980s passed and increasing numbers of Cambodians arrived in the country, the refugee resettlement program shifted toward early employment above all else.

The federal government and resettlement programs continue this emphasis on early employment for refugee and immigrant arrivals, including the handful of Cambodians who have arrived annually in the 1990s (ORR 1994). Federally funded English-language, vocational training, and employment skills classes previously attended by Cambodians have been drastically reduced, and those that remain are usually local creations, often maintained by volunteers. Younger Cambodians now learn English in the public schools, where they are learning or have learned to speak without accent and often at the expense of Cambodian-language acquisition. Few older Cambodians any longer devote much time to learning English, although some continue to learn English on the job or from their children.

When Cambodian refugees were initally resettled in the United States, Americans were concerned with lessening the impact of Cambodians, and other refugees, on the United States (Refugee Act of 1980). In addition to attempts to change Cambodians in the processing centers and subsequently through language, vocational, and cultural orientation courses in the United States, efforts were made to place Khmer in areas where they would "blend" into surrounding communities. Khmer were thus "scattered" throughout the United States and initially placed with American sponsors because of the scarcity of Cambodians living in America. Through scatter placement and American sponsorship, policymakers tried to prevent Cambodians from settling into ethnic enclaves, hoping thus to reduce refugee visibility, increase their economic prospects, and decrease refugee costs to American taxpayers (Skinner and Hendricks 1979).

Cambodians, however, did not remain dispersed. They moved for a variety of reasons, most obviously to be with one another, and the immediate result of their movement was the rapid creation of Cambodian enclaves in several cities (Mortland and Ledgerwood 1987). An increasing number of resettled Cambodians became sponsors to their own relatives, adding to Cambodian clustering. In an effort to prevent secondary migration by new arrivals to areas of high Khmer concentration (for example, Long Beach, Seattle, and Philadelphia), the federal government clustered Khmer arrivals in 12 cities: Atlanta, Boston, Chicago, Cincinnati, Columbus, Dallas, Houston, Jacksonville, New York City, Phoenix, Richmond, and Rochester (Refugee Resource Center 1982). The program had mixed results (Bruno 1984, for example): Some Cambodians received little assistance, others moved to new locales despite pressure not to do so, and many felt coerced into particular options by program requirements and staff.

Efforts by the federal government to influence Cambodian residence in the United States continued into the late 1980s, although efforts in the early 1990s reflected an increased awareness by service providers and policymakers that Cambodians would move to join one another. The Office of Refugee Resettlement in the Department of Health and Human Services funded the research and publication of a report entitled *Profiles of Some Good Places for Cambodians to Live in the United States* (North and Nim Sok 1989). The report describes 22 communities where there were available jobs, generally self-sufficient Cambodian residents, a moderate-sized Khmer community, and minimum crime problems.[2] The report details job opportunities, size of Cambodian community, and town characteristics. The key for Americans is size of the Cambodian community: Five of the cluster cities[3] were dropped from this list, no longer considered desirable because "too many" Cambodians now lived there. Ironically, the presence of a Cambodian enclave with uniquely Khmer services, such as Buddhist temples, is one of the attractions of these "good places for Cambodians to live"; American program officials saw some value in ethnic community resources but not too concentrated or too many.

Americans also see Cambodian families as exhibiting numerous problems (Rumbaut 1995). Cambodian parents are learning what immigrant parents in the United States have learned before them: that immigrant children are concerned with the new land and ways, not the old (Steinberg 1989). While their parents struggle to retain their traditions, their children struggle to learn the new country. Since language learning ability is inversely related to age, children often need not even struggle in their efforts to learn English and American culture. Cambodian-American children (those who came to America as relatively young children or who were born in America), like the children of immigrants before them, are characterized by the experience of living in two worlds and, despite their wishes to fit in, not fully belonging to either.

American concerns about the Khmer, however, are sometimes shared by the Khmer themselves. Issues of family tensions and health problems provide examples. A gulf has grown up between Khmer who came to the United States as adults and will never be "Americans" by culture and their children who are trying desperately to be American. This loss of their children is an additional blow to Cambodians in the United States who now worry, among other things, that their children will not take care of them in their old age. Both Americans and Cambodians worry that Khmer children will follow less desirable models for American youth: dropping out of school, joining gangs, using drugs. American social service programs concentrate on helping Cambodian youth stay in school, providing counseling for families suffering from generational conflict, and facilitating after-school tutoring and recreational programs. Cambodian parents concentrate instead on trying to instill Cambodian values in their children: teaching them proper Cambodian behavior, encouraging their attendance at Cambodian Buddhist events, and cautioning them constantly about the dangers of American ways (for example, Ledgerwood 1990a; Kulig 1991).

Cambodians' health has been a major concern for both Cambodians and Americans since Khmer arrival in the United States (cf. Nguyen-Hong-Nhiem and Halpern 1989 and Welaratna 1993 for Khmer descriptions of life in America). The physical and mental consequences of the Khmer Rouge years are enormous, especially for first-generation immigrants, and include premature death, illness, and depression (Fryc 1991; Kulig 1991; Rasbridge 1991; Pickwell 1990; Mitchell 1987; Marcucci 1986). Many Cambodians came to America with serious medical conditions, for example, tuberculosis, extended malnutrition, and injury. Older women, especially, exhibit multiple problems: headaches, dizziness, confusion, even blindness. Cambodians are also seen as a population at risk emotionally (Bowlan and Bruno 1985; Kinzie 1987; Kinzie et al. 1984; Mollica 1988; Mollica, Wyshack, and Lavelle 1987; Eisenbruch 1991; Owan 1985; Williams and Westermeyer 1986). Similar physical and mental problems are experienced by the Khmer in Cambodia (Ebihara 1993).

Cambodian resettlement concerns have not always coincided with Americans' concerns for them; Khmer often comment, however, on the enormous efforts undertaken on their behalf by American organizations and individuals. But as government funding and programs for Cambodians have lessened, Cambodians have been left increasingly to their own devices.

RESETTLEMENT CAMBODIAN STYLE

When resettlement is viewed in terms of assimilation to American behavior and ideas, as most Americans view it, resettlement can be judged in terms of success and failure. But Cambodians view resettlement differently. For most Khmer, resettlement in America was initially a dream come true; for most, the dream changed as awareness of the permanency of their losses and the strangeness of America gradually settled over them. The ability to support themselves in America brings satisfaction, as it did before in Cambodia; yet their inability to regain what they have lost leaves them dissatisfied. All are occupied with the daily necessities of living with strangeness.

Although Cambodians find it extremely difficult to describe their experiences and losses, despite their interest and need to do so, their resettlement strategies in the United States are ways they express themselves in their new environment. By looking at their strategies for survival and renewal in America, we can "hear" through their actions what they find difficult to express: who they were, who they are.

Much of what Americans want to change about Cambodians is what Cambodians value most. Even when Cambodians themselves want the change, they often want it differently than do Americans. Language is a case in point. Cambodians know they must learn English and have made valiant efforts to do so. Their problem lies in the extreme differences between English and Cambodian, absence or scarcity of language training facilities, and competing obligations of work and school. But they also want to retain their language. Cambodians have major concerns that their children learn their own language. Some of their earliest efforts were to set up language classes for children. And a major disappointment has been that their children will not learn to write and speak Cambodian, although most understand it. Many parents have given up the effort, especially as it becomes obvious that children themselves are not interested.

The greatest concerns of the Khmer in the United States are finding means of successfully surviving in America, preserving their culture, and ensuring the future of their children. Cambodians say if they lose their culture, they will lose their identity as Cambodians (Ngor Haing 1987; May Someth 1986; Szymusiak 1986; Criddle and Mam 1987; Yathay Pin 1987). We see the same concern over loss in American writings about Cambodians (Coleman 1987; Crystal 1988; Florentine Films 1991; Marcucci 1986; Ebihara, Mortland, and Ledgerwood 1994; Mortland 1994a). Preserving their culture becomes the primary means Khmer use to secure their other aims. The strategies they use to achieve these goals follow methods that have worked for them in the past. These include, first, utilizing all available resources; second, reestablishing traditional relationships; third, reinstituting proper behavior; and fourth, reconstructing religion. Each of these is discussed in more detail below.

First, Cambodians have been active participants in utilizing all the resources of their environment, just as villagers in rural Cambodia had long drawn their income from a mix of farming and fishing and townspeople supplemented their primary incomes with part-time businesses or jobs, and they continue to do so. Realizing that employment is the swiftest and more respectable way in America to obtain resources, Khmer have sought employment at the highest levels of income and prestige (in traditional Khmer terms) available to them. Many study at night to enhance language and job skills. Since many Khmer are limited to entry-level positions by rudimentary English and American job skills, they increase income by pooling their resources, working more than one job, having multiple job holders in a household, and utilizing a family member's eligibility for social services. Often the adults in a family work outside the home, leaving child care, cooking, and household chores to a less employable member (for example, because of age or physical or mental difficulties). I have not found data to collaborate Welaratna's (1993; see also Rumbaut and Ima 1988) conclusion that many Cambodians seek human service employment in the United States, such as nursing. Rather, my data suggest that Cambodians with educational opportunities, thus able to escape entry-level positions, seek training in areas they feel are most likely to result in jobs, such as business, computer-related technologies, and electronics. The dream of many is to begin their own business, and some have done so: for example, donut shops, laundries, grocery stores, and restaurants. Over time, like immigrants before them, an increasing number of resettled Cambodians obtain employment and become economically self-sufficient (Gallagher 1988; ORR 1994).

Cambodian employment in the United States is an interesting phenomenon: Many of the educated and urbanized Cambodians resettled in the United States have experienced a decline in socioeconomic status; most never regain the status and wealth they enjoyed in Cambodia. For former peasants, however, American jobs have brought knowledge, possessions, and independence inconceivable for them in Cambodia. Women, too, have benefited from expanded opportunities in education and employment; in fact, women have sometimes been more successful than their menfolk in obtaining employment (Ui 1991). Cambodian women are more eager to seize these opportunities than men are to see them do so, for such employment can shift the traditional balance of power away from men. Because of the high percentage of widows, thus female-headed households, in the United States, employment is often a necessity rather than an option.

Cambodians utilize American services as provided and instructed by Americans (cf. Rasbridge and Marcucci 1992, for an interesting example). They have also taken advantage of other resources wherever available, often advising startled American neighbors on the best places to find little-known sales, overstocks, giveaways, and fishing sites. Some have utilized public services in unorthodox ways, usually by receiving benefits for which they are not eligible or working for cash (so that neither employer or employee has to pay taxes), always with an eye to maximizing resources and future opportunities. Some Khmer justify their actions by saying they are just doing what Americans do; others assert that what they are doing seems less criminal than what Americans are doing: drugs, crime, stealing, and stealing from other poor people; and some claim that Americans owe them for a variety of reasons: because of the tragedies they have endured, because of America's previous involvement in Cambodia.

Cambodians use the resources they obtain in America, such as money, jobs, and technology, to retain and reestablish Cambodian culture (e.g., Hopkins 1992). They use cars and telephones, for example, to communicate with family and friends within their own town and to keep in contact with the nearest temple, Cambodian stores, and relatives. They use cassettes and videotapes to correspond with relatives in Cambodia and other resettlement countries and to listen to the music, plays, and films of their homeland made in Hong Kong and California. They use whatever resources are at hand, including funding from Americans, to re-form dance troops and musical orchestras (Sam 1994; Ung 1988). College students have formed discussion groups to discuss, foremost among other topics, their own experiences and Cambodian politics.

An additional strategy Cambodians use to survive in America, invest in their children, and preserve their culture is to reestablish traditional social relationships among themselves and establish them with Americans, and they expend considerable effort on this from the time of their initial arrival in the United States. First, they seek to reassemble their families, often out of the fragments left by Khmer Rouge atrocities and resettlement procedures that separated nuclear from extended families. Cambodians often moved from their initial placement site in the United States to rejoin these extended family members, for example, aunts and uncles, married siblings, in-laws, and adopted kin, a relationship for which Cambodians use kinship terminology (Ebihara 1968).

Second, Cambodians attempt to contact, then often join, other relatives, fellow villagers, and friends, both from Cambodia and the refugee camps, as soon as possible after arriving in the United States. Living near one another in tenements or apartment complexes, or driving several hours on weekends to join countrymen, allows Cambodians to share information and resources. Smith (1989) gives an example of one migration: 400 Khmer who moved from Chicago to Madison because of its lower crime rate and more rural aspect. Their fishing and gardening activities in Madison, combined with specific economic strategies and cultural practices, has allowed the Khmer to reproduce many aspects of traditional Cambodian life. Over time, many Cambodian adults have in effect retired into their ethnic communities, restricting their contacts primarily to other Cambodians, having little to do with the larger surrounding community. Even if such residence patterns involve conflict with other Cambodians, conflict among one's own people is preferable for many Khmer than being alone among strangers. Cambodians continue to redistribute themselves in the United States (e.g., Smith-Hefner 1990) to join family or friends; to seek employment opportunities, lower living costs, or more generous assistance programs; and to join or escape particular Khmer enclaves.

Third, Cambodians reestablish patron-client ties in the United States (Mortland and Ledgerwood 1988; Ledgerwood 1990b). For Cambodians in America, a patron can be one of the best hedges against a repeat of past experiences. Thus, in traditional Khmer fashion, they have cultivated patrons both among more powerful and resourceful Cambodians and among Americans. These patrons provide resources, services, and information desired by Cambodians in exchange for loyalty and service. Cambodian patrons have gained additional access to resources by acquiring offical recognition as leaders of their community, forming organizations to receive additional benefits that are then funneled to both patron and followers (Mortland 1993); the federal government continues to fund these Cambodian self-help organizations (ORR 1994). These organizations have been engaged in a number of different activities, including providing social services, such as counseling, substance abuse treatment, job placement, and vocational training; and cultural preservation, such as teaching the Khmer language, forming dance troops or orchestras, and encouraging traditional crafts.

Sometimes, however, Cambodians have endeavored to escape their traditional ties to patrons in order to control areas of their own and their children's lives in the light of new options and constraints existing in America. For example, they seek social mobility through education and occupation, and escape from the control of local or religious leaders. As time goes on, an increasing number of Cambodians, especially the younger generation, are escaping or never experiencing the control of traditional patrons.

The tendency of the Cambodian people toward extravagant deference to superiors is backed by a religious tradition that relates position to meritorious behavior, with individuals deserving their place in life, and to a social structure that overwhelmingly favors those at the top with wealth and strength. Ordinary Cambodians have little choice but to defer. This tendency has contributed to what Chandler has called "Cambodia's tragedy" (Chandler 1991b). The best most Cambodians could do was to align themselves with a particular superior, seeking protection in exchange for their loyalty and labor. These ideas—of leaders' rights, followers' obligations, and patronage—continue to shape the attitudes and activity of many Cambodians in the United States and to vie for attention with their attempts to reestablish aspects of their lives over which they have traditionally prevailed: for example, family, food, and home life.

An important resettlement strategy Khmer use in the United States is to renew proper behavior and order among themselves. Cambodians have suffered a tremendous loss of order, even before the Khmer Rouge period, certainly during it, and following their escape to camps in Thailand. Their sense of lost order continues after resettlement in the United States, replaced by American concepts of what is proper and right. While Americans attempt to convert Khmer to an American sense of order, Cambodians have eagerly sought to re-create proper Cambodian order as quickly as possible in their new lives. They have done so by reestablishing proper etiquette toward one another, based on traditional Khmer hierarchical relationships. The sharp definition in class and behavior has continued throughout Cambodian history and remains evident among the Cambodians in America. Cambodians emphasize that inferiors must obey superiors:

thus, children must obey their parents; wives, their husbands; youth, their elders; and students, their teachers. Cambodians struggle especially to keep their women virtuous and their daughters pure, even to the extent of marrying them at even younger ages than in Cambodia (Ledgerwood 1990a). In this way, the Khmer regain a sense of security. What Chandler (1982) says of the nineteenth century is true for the twentieth: When Cambodians live in their proper places, they experience more balance, safety, and Cambodian identity than when they do not.

Lastly, Cambodians in America place tremendous importance on reestablishing their religion; they consider the practice of Khmer Buddhism vital to the preservation of their culture, even their identity. Almost immediately after arrival in the United States, the Khmer sought ways to practice their religious rituals, one of their first desires being to conduct rituals for their dead, which they had previously been unable to do, either for lack of means or permission. Cambodians soon set up temples in apartments, then houses, and after some years, some communities began constructing temple buildings. Khmer served as sponsors for monks to come to America from the Thai refugee camps, borrowed or purchased religious paraphernalia from other Buddhist countries, and held their rituals with whatever leadership was available.

Khmer religion consists of Buddhist practices along with beliefs in spirits. Cambodians in America devote considerable effort to propitiating a variety of spirits, from territorial spirits to ancestor spirits and including a sizable number of additional categories. Cambodians call on the spirits to prevent misfortune, especially illness, from striking them and to assist in bringing them fortune and happiness. These rituals may be conducted privately in one's own home or at a public gathering.

While many Cambodians have reduced their participation in Buddhist temple activities and spirit rites in the United States, primarily because of time and work constraints, most continue to hold to the traditional Buddhist and folk beliefs they were taught as children. Some conceal these beliefs by attendance at Christian churches or expressions of disbelief, but the majority of resettled Cambodians do not abandon their traditional ideas. Despite considerable obstacles—hostile American neighbors, lack of men wishing to go into the monkhood, fading memories of liturgy, prayers, and ritual detail—and competing American religions, schedules, and interests, most Cambodians continue to practice their religion at home and at over 50 temples across the country.

A resettlement problem unique to Cambodians in its severity results from the years they spent under the Khmer Rouge regime, during the years from 1975 to 1978 (Mortland 1994b). Cambodians find it difficult to explain what has happened to them and their country in the past several decades. Most Cambodians have struggled to find answers in their traditional religion; some have looked at alternate explanations, such as that provided by Christianity. For most, however, the enormity of the tragedies they experienced and the migration they have endured brings questions that continue to plague them: How could this have happened? Did they do something to cause what happened to them?

Additionally, successful survival in America and the preservation of Khmer culture are not inherently opposites. Cambodian notions of being "refugees" change with time. Some begin to find refugee status offensive, a way for Americans to pity Cambodians without listening to them, to decide what is best for Cambodians without consulting them. Some Khmer have become permanent residents, American citizens, or self-proclaimed "people without a country." Others have moved reluctantly or proudly on through immigrant status to citizenship.[4] Some Cambodians say they will always be refugees because the Khmer Rouge forced them from their land. Others continue their dependency as refugees, relying on social services and defining themselves (and being defined) primarily as victims. Children of Cambodians who were born in the United States may deal less with being Cambodian-Americans than with being a minority; for many who live in low-income urban areas, daily reality resembles that of other youth around them, with Cambodian concerns relevant primarily at home.

Similarly, Cambodian notions of "Americanness" and "Khmerness" vary. Cambodians go back and forth between what they perceive to be American and what they perceive to be Cambodian, using whichever fits their need of the moment. They thereby create Cambodian responses to American realities and reinvent their Cambodian past. They are aided in their recreation of identity by contrasting themselves and a "mythic" Cambodian past to Americans and America. As their leaders in Cambodia did before them (Chandler 1990, 1991b), Khmer Americans hark back to the splendors of Angkor in establishing and reestablishing their identity as Cambodians. Thus, they can speak of life as it was, as it should be, stating indirectly what is difficult to state directly, for example, that a life without Cambodianness is not life, that life in America is only bearable for Cambodians if they remain faithful to their cultural traditions.

CONCLUSIONS AND PROSPECTS

Americans cite a multitude of reasons to explain why Cambodians are unsuccessful in adjusting to America: their rural backgrounds, unfamiliarity with Western ways, lack of education or literacy in their own language, lack of English, lack of employable skills, and the physical and mental scars of the Khmer Rouge years. An alternate view is that Cambodians are successfully adjusting to life in the United States. As Welaratna (1993) notes, Cambodians are seeking to ensure the economic and emotional welfare of their families in ways that differ from Americans, placing family and social interaction above individual advancement. Many Cambodians conclude that they have been successful in their adjustment to America. Those who conclude otherwise judge Khmer success by American, rather than Cambodian, goals.

Because of their horrendous experiences under the Khmer Rouge and traumatic resettlement, Cambodians have been forced to examine themselves and their culture, to reflect on ultimate questions, on what is of highest priority to them (Mortland 1994b; Welaratna 1993). Their conclusions can be read in their strategies for living in America. These have included vigorously seizing opportunities for employment and education, utilizing traditional relationships such as family and patronage to obtain resources and services, redefining proper behavior for Cambodians who must live in such different circumstances, reestablishing places of worship, and reasserting the value of Cambodian culture and themselves as Cambodians. Finally and sometimes despairingly, Cambodians place their hopes on their children.

First-generation Cambodian immigrants continue to view reality in America through a traditional prism, through the meanings and relationships of their homeland. As American immigrants before them, they will always do so. Their children, however, have shifted perspective and now utilize an American prism to view their new homeland. Although Cambodia and Cambodian ways continue to affect the lives of these second-generation Cambodian-Americans, their sights are already and primarily trained on American culture.

ACKNOWLEDGMENTS

My gratitude to May M. Ebihara, Judy Ledgerwood, and David W. Haines for their comments on this chapter.

NOTES

1. Published numbers vary, depending on which government sources are used. In addition, both calendar and fiscal years have been used by the federal government in publishing statistics. Sources for resettlement figures used in this chapter are as follows: for 1975 through 1978, from Gordon (1984); from 1979 through 1981, from the Office of Refugee Resettlement, U.S. Department of Health and Human Services, as cited in *Refugee Reports* (1988); and for FY 1982 through FY 1993, from the Bureau for Refugee Programs, U.S. Department of State, compiled by the U.S. Committee for Refugees, cited in *Refugee Reports* (1993). Resettlement by year of Cambodians to the United States is thus:

1975	4,600
1976	1,100
1977	300
1978	1,300
1979	6,000
1980	16,000
1981	27,100
1982	20,234
1983	13,115

1984	19,851
1985	19,097
1986	9,789
1987	1,539
1988	2,805
1989	1,916
1990	2,166
1991	38
1992	141
1993	22
Total	**147,113**

2. The 22 cities are Mobile Bay, Alabama; Phoenix, Arizona; Denver, Colorado; Danbury/Hartford, Connecticut; Jacksonville and St. Petersburg in Florida; Atlanta, Georgia; Chicago and Joliet in Illinois; Des Moines, Iowa; Portland, Maine; Lincoln, Nebraska; Rochester, New York; Charlotte and Greensboro in North Carolina; Columbus, Ohio; Portland, Oregon; Providence, Rhode Island; Memphis and Nashville, Tennessee; Dallas, Texas; and Salt Lake City, Utah.

3. Boston, Cincinnati, Houston, New York City, and Richmond.

4. On average, Cambodians who become naturalized citizens do so in their tenth year after resettlement (ORR 1994).

REFERENCES

Banister, Judith, and E. Paige Johnson. 1993. After the Nightmare: The Population of Cambodia. In *Genocide and Democracy in Cambodia. The Khmer Rouge, the United Nations and the International Community.* Edited by Ben Kiernan. New Haven: Yale University Southeast Asian Studies. Pp. 65–139.

Boua, Chanthou. 1982. Women in Today's Cambodia. *New Left Review* 131: 45–61.

Bowlan, Jeanne, and Ellen Bruno, Editors. 1985. *Cambodian Mental Health. The Cambodian Women's Project Conference Proceedings.* New York: The American Friends Service Committee.

Bruno, Ellen. 1984. *Acculturation Difficulties of the Khmer in New York City.* New York: The Cambodian Women's Program, American Friends Service Committee.

Central Intelligence Agency (CIA). 1980. *Kampuchea: A Demographic Catastrophe.* Washington, D.C.: Central Intelligence Agency.

Chanda, Nayan. 1986. *Brother Enemy: The War after the War.* New York: Harcourt, Brace, Jovanovich.

Chandler, David P. 1982. Songs at the Edge of the Forest: Perceptions of Order in Three Cambodian Texts. In *Moral Order and the Question of Change: Essays on Southeast Asian Thought.* Edited by D. K. Wyatt and A. Woodside. New Haven: Yale University Southeast Asian Studies Monograph Series 24. Pp. 53–77.

———. 1983. *A History of Cambodia.* Boulder: Westview Press.

———. 1990. Reflections on Cambodian History. Cambodia 1990. *Cultural Survival Quarterly* 14(3):16–19.

———. 1991a. *The Land and People of Cambodia.* New York: HarperCollins.

————. 1991b. *The Tragedy of Cambodian History. Politics, War, and Revolution since 1945.* New Haven: Yale University Press.

Coleman, C. M. 1987. Cambodians in the United States. In *The Cambodian Agony.* Edited by David A. Ablin and Marlowe Hoods. Armonk: M. E. Sharpe. Pp. 354–374.

Criddle, Joan D. 1992. *Bamboo & Butterflies. From Refugee to Citizen.* Dixon, California: East/West Bridge Publishing House.

Criddle, Joan D., and Teeda Butt Mam. 1987. *To Destroy You Is No Loss: The Odyssey of a Cambodian Family.* New York: The Atlantic Monthly Press.

Crystal, Eric. 1988. Fragments of a Civilization. In *First International Scholars Conference on Cambodia. Selected Papers.* Edited by A. Judkins. Geneseo: Department of Anthropology and the Geneseo Foundation. Pp. 13–22.

Ea, Meng-Try. 1987. Recent Population Trends in Kampuchea. In *The Cambodian Agony.* Edited by David A. Ablin and Marlowe Hoods. Armonk: M. E. Sharpe. Pp. 3–15.

Ebihara, May M. 1968. *Svay. A Khmer Village in Cambodia.* Ph.D. dissertation, Columbia University. Ann Arbor: University Microfilms.

————. 1985. Khmer. In *Refugees in the United States. A Reference Handbook.* Edited by David W. Haines. Westport: Greenwood Press. Pp. 127–147.

————. 1993. A Cambodian Village under the Khmer Rouge, 1975–1979. In *Genocide and Democracy in Cambodia. The Khmer Rouge, the United Nations and the International Community.* Edited by Ben Kiernan. New Haven: Yale University Southeast Asian Studies. Pp. 51–63.

Ebihara, May M., Carol A. Mortland, and Judy Ledgerwood, Editors. 1994. *Cambodian Culture since 1975: Homeland and Exile.* Ithaca, New York: Cornell University Press.

Eisenbruch, Maurice. 1991. From Post-traumatic Stress Disorder to Cultural Bereavement: Diagnosis of Southeast Asian Refugees. *Social Science and Medicine* 33(6): 673–680.

Evans, Grant, and Kelvin Rowley. 1983. *Red Brotherhood at War.* London: Verso.

Florentine Films. 1991. *Rebuilding the Temple. Cambodians in America.* Haydenville: Florentine Films.

Foreign Broadcast Information Service. 1976. Asia and Pacific Daily Report. *Foreign Broadcast Information Service* 4:63.

French, Lindsay. 1994. Enduring Holocaust, Surviving History: Displaced Cambodians on the Thai-Cambodian Border, 1989–1991. Unpublished Ph.D. dissertation. Harvard University.

Frye, R. 1991. Cultural Themes in Health-Care Decision Making among Cambodian Refugee Women. *Journal of Community Health Nursing* 8(1):33–44.

Gallagher, Dennis. 1988. United States and the Indochinese Refugees. In *Indochinese Refugees: Asylum and Resettlement.* Edited by Supang Chantavanich and E. Bruce Reynolds. Bangkok: Institute of Asian Studies, Chulalongkorn University. Pp. 230–248.

Gordon, Linda. 1984. *Southeast Asian Refugee Migration to the United States.* Washington, D.C.: Office of Refugee Resettlement, U.S. Department of Health and Human Services, September.

Higham, Charles. 1989. *The Archaeology of Mainland Southeast Asia. From 10,000 B.C. to the Fall of Angkor.* Cambridge: Cambridge University Press.

Hopkins, MaryCarol. 1992. Becoming Bicultural: Preserving Culture through Adaptation. In *Selected Papers on Refugee Issues*. Edited by Pamela A. DeVoe. Washington, D.C.: American Anthropological Association. Pp. 71–80.

Kiernan, Ben. 1990. The Genocide in Cambodia, 1975–1979. *Bulletin of Concerned Asian Scholars* 20(2): 35–40.

———. 1993. Introduction. In *Genocide and Democracy in Cambodia. The Khmer Rouge, the United Nations and the International Community.* Edited by Ben Kiernan. New Haven: Yale University Southeast Asian Studies. Pp. 1–32.

Kinzie, J. D. 1987. The "Concentration Camp Syndrome" among Cambodian Refugees. In *The Cambodian Agony*. Edited by D. Ablin and M. Hood. New York: M. E. Sharpe. Pp. 33–352.

Kinzie, J. D., R. H. Fredrickson, Roth Ben, Jenelle Fleck, and William Karls. 1984. Posttraumatic Stress Disorder among Survivors of Cambodian Concentration Camps. *American Journal of Psychiatry* 141(5):645–650.

Kulig, Judith. 1991. Role, Status Changes and Family Planning Use among Cambodian Refugee Women. Doctor of Nursing Science, University of California at San Francisco.

Ledgerwood, Judy. 1990a. *Changing Khmer Conceptions of Gender: Women, Stories, and the Social Order.* Ph.D. dissertation, Cornell University. Ann Arbor: University Microfilms.

———. 1990b. Portrait of a Conflict: Exploring Changing Khmer-American Social and Political Relationships. *Journal of Refugee Studies* 3(2):135–154.

Loescher, Gil, and John A. Scanlan. 1986. *Calculated Kindness: Refugees and America's Half-Open Door, 1945 to the Present.* New York: The Free Press.

Lynch, James F. 1989. *Border Khmer: A Demographic Study of the Residents of Site II, Site B, and Site 8.* Bangkok: The Ford Foundation.

Marcucci, John. 1986. *Khmer Refugees in Dallas: Medical Decisions in the Context of Pluralism.* Ph.D. dissertation, Southern Methodist University. Ann Arbor: University Microfilms.

Martel, Gabrielle. 1975. *Lovea. Village des environs d'Angkor,* Vol. 98. Paris: Publications d'École Française d'Extrême-Orient.

Mason, Linda, and Roger Brown. 1983. *Rice, Rivalry and Politics: Managing Cambodian Relief.* Notre Dame: University of Notre Dame Press.

May Someth. 1986. *Cambodian Witness: The Autobiography of Someth May.* London: Faber and Faber.

Mitchell, F. 1987. *From Refugee to Rebuilder: Cambodian Women in America.* Ph.D. dissertation. Ann Arbor: University Microfilms International.

Mollica, Richard F. 1988. The Trauma Story: The Psychiatric Care of Refugee Survivors of Violence and Torture. In *Post-Traumatic Therapy and Victims of Violence.* Edited by Frank M. Ochberg. New York: Brunner/Mazel. Pp. 295–314.

Mollica, Richard F., Grace Wyshack, and James Lavelle. 1987. The Psychosocial Impact of War Trauma and Torture on Southeast Asian Refugees. *American Journal of Psychiatry* 144(22):1567–1572.

Mortland, Carol A. 1987. Transforming Refugees in Refugee Camps. *Urban Anthropology* 16(3–4):375–404.

———. 1993. Patron-Client Relations and the Evolution of Mutual Assistance Associations. In *Refugee Empowerment and Organizational Change. A Systems Per-*

spective. Edited by Peter W. Van Arsdale. Arlington: American Anthropological Association. Pp. 15–36.

—. 1994a. Cambodian Refugees and Identity in the United States. In *Reconstructing Lives, Recapturing Meaning. Refugee Identity, Gender, and Culture Change.* Edited by Linda A. Camino and Ruth M. Krulfeld. Basel, Switzerland: Gordon and Breach Publishers. Pp. 5–7.

—. 1994b. Khmer Buddhists in the United States: Ultimate Questions. In *Cambodian Culture since 1975. Homeland and Exile.* Edited by May M. Ebihara, C. A. Mortland, and J. Ledgerwood. Ithaca: Cornell University Press. Pp. 72–90.

Mortland, Carol A., and Judy Ledgerwood. 1987. Secondary Migration among Southeast Asian Refugees in the United States. *Urban Anthropology* 16(3–4):291–326.

—. 1988. Refugee Resource Acquisition, the Invisible Communication System. In *Cross-Cultural Adaptation: Current Approaches.* Edited by Young Yun Kim and William B. Gudykunst. Newbury Park, California: Sage Publications. Pp. 286–306.

Mourer, Roland. 1977. Laang Spean and the Prehistory of Cambodia. *Modern Quaternary Research in Southeast Asia* 3:29–56.

Ngor Haing. 1987. *A Cambodian Odyssey.* New York: Macmillan.

Nguyen-Hong-Nhiem, Lucy, and Joel Martin Halpern, Editors. 1989. *The Far East Comes Near: Autobiographical Accounts of Southeast Asian Students in America.* Amherst: University of Massachusetts Press.

North, David, and Nim Sok. 1989. *Profiles of Some Good Places for Cambodians to Live in the United States.* Washington, D.C.: Office of Refugee Resettlement, U.S. Department of Health and Human Services.

Office of Refugee Resettlement (ORR). 1994. *Refugee Resettlement Program. Report to the Congress. FY 1993.* Washington, D.C.: Office of Refugee Resettlement, U.S. Department of Health and Human Services.

Owan, Tom Choken, Editor. 1985. *Southeast Asian Mental Health: Treatment, Prevention, Services, Training, and Research.* Washington, D.C.: U.S. Department of Health and Human Services.

Pickwell, S. 1990. *Journey to the Promised Land: The Health Consequences of Refugee Status for Cambodians in San Diego.* Ph.D. dissertation. Ann Arbor: University Microfilms International.

Rasbridge, Lance A. 1991. Infant/Child Feeding among Resettled Cambodians in Dallas: Intracultural Variation in Reference to Iron Nutrition. Unpublished Ph.D. dissertation, Southern Methodist University.

Rasbridge, Lance A., and John L. Marcucci. 1992. Reactions to Coupon Coercion. Dallas Cambodian Women's Autonomy in the Acculturative Process. In *Selected Papers on Refugee Issues.* Edited by Pamela A. DeVoe. Washington, D.C.: American Anthropological Association. Pp. 81–88.

Refugee Act of 1980. 1980. *Public Law 96-212,* March 17, 1980, 96th Congress. Washington, D.C.

Refugee Reports. 1988. Statistical Issue. *Refugee Reports* 9(12):10.

—. 1993. Refugees Admitted to the United States by Nationality. *Refugee Reports,* December: 10–11.

Refugee Resource Center. 1982. *Cambodian Cluster Project. October, 1981–March, 1982. Final Report.* New York: Refugee Resource Center, Committee on Migration and Refugee Affairs, American Council of Voluntary Agencies in Foreign Service.

Reynell, Josephine. 1989. *Political Pawns. Refugees on the Thai-Kampuchean Border.* Oxford: Refugee Studies Programme.

Robinson, Court, and Arthur Wallenstein. 1988. *Unfulfilled Hopes: The Humanitarian Parole/Immigrant Visa Program for Border Cambodians.* Washington, D.C.: U.S. Committee for Refugees.

Rumbaut, Rubén G. 1995. Vietnamese, Laotian, and Cambodian Americans. In *Asian Americans. Contemporary Trends and Issues.* Edited by Pyong Gap Min. Thousand Oaks, California: Sage Publications. Pp. 232–270.

Rumbaut, Rubén G., and Kenji Ima. 1988. *The Adaptation of Southeast Asian Refugee Youth: A Comparative Study.* Washington, D.C.: U.S. Government Printing Office.

Sam, Sam-Ang. 1994. Khmer Traditional Music Today. In *Cambodian Culture since 1975. Homeland and Exile.* Edited by May M. Ebihara, C. A. Mortland, and J. Ledgerwood. Ithaca: Cornell University Press. Pp. 39–47.

Shawcross, William. 1979. *Sideshow. Kissinger, Nixon and the Destruction of Cambodia.* London: André Deutsch.

Skinner, Kenneth A., and Glenn L. Hendricks. 1979. The Shaping of Ethnic Self-Identity among Indochinese Refugees. *Journal of Ethnic Studies* 7(3):25–41.

Smith, Frank. 1989. *Interpretive Accounts of the Khmer Rouge Years: Personal Experience in Cambodian Peasant World View.* Madison: Center for Southeast Asian Studies, University of Wisconsin.

Smith-Hefner, Nancy J. 1990. Language and Identity in the Education of Boston-Area Khmer. *Anthropology and Education Quarterly* 21(3):250–268.

Steinberg, Stephen. 1989. *The Ethnic Myth. Race, Ethnicity, and Class in America.* Boston: Beacon Press.

Szymusiak, Molyda. 1986. *The Stones Cry Out.* Translated by L. Coverdale. New York: Hill and Wang.

Tollefson, James W. 1989. *Alien Winds: The Reeducation of America's Indochinese Refugees.* New York: Praeger.

Ui, Shiori. 1991. "Unlikely Heroes": The Evolution of Female Leadership in a Cambodian Ethnic Enclave. In *Ethnography Unbound. Power and Resistance in the Modern Metropolis.* Edited by M. Buraway. Berkeley: University of California Press. Pp. 161–177.

Ung, Chinary. 1988. The Regeneration of Khmer Music and the Performing Arts in the United States. In *First International Scholars Conference on Cambodia. Selected Papers.* Edited by Russell A. Judkins. Geneseo: State University of New York at Geneseo, Department of Anthropology and the Geneseo Foundation. Pp. 37–45.

United Nations Children's Fund (UNICEF). 1990. *Cambodia: The Situation of Children and Women.* Phnom Penh: UNICEF, Office of the Special Representative.

United Nations Development Programme. 1989. *Report of the Kampuchea Needs Assessment Study.* United Nations Development Programme. August 1989.

U.S. Committee for Refugees. 1994. *World Refugee Survey.* Washington, D.C.

Vickery, Michael. 1988. How Many Died in Pol Pot's Kampuchea? *Bulletin of Concerned Asian Scholars* 20(1):70–73.

———. 1990. Cambodian Political Economy, 1975–1990. *Cambodia 1990, Cultural Survival Quarterly* 14(3):23–27.

Welaratna, Usha. 1993. *Beyond the Killing Fields: Voices of Nine Cambodian Survivors in America.* Stanford: Stanford University Press.

Williams, Carolyn L., and Joseph Westermeyer, Editors. 1986. *Refugee Mental Health in Resettlement Countries.* Washington, D.C.: Hemisphere Publishing.

Yathay Pin. 1987. *Stay Alive My Son.* New York: The Free Press.

Chapter 12

Lao

PAMELA A. DeVOE

Over the last 20 years, particularly since the late 1970s, about 250,000 refugees from Laos have been resettled in the United States, about half of whom are ethnic Lao. Before coming to this industrial, technologically oriented, Judeo-Christian culture, they were a traditional, wet-rice agricultural group, following Buddhist traditions in their home country of Laos in Southeast Asia. While most Americans know the plight of Vietnamese or Cambodian refugees, few are aware of who the Lao are or even how they became homeless, displaced by the spillover of a war raging in neighboring Vietnam. This chapter will look at where these refugees came from; why they were forced to leave their home area; the initial dilemmas faced by the host country and by the refugees as they coped with a radically different sociocultural environment; and finally, how well they were able to adjust and to survive, sometimes by changing and sometimes through keeping and adapting essential traditional cultural characteristics.

THE HOME COUNTRY: LAOS

Topography and Its Impact

Today the landlocked country of Laos shares borders with Vietnam, Cambodia (Kampuchea), Thailand, Burma, and China. Its 91,425 square miles (Thee 1973:1) are defined in part by the Mekong River and the Mekong's fertile valley on the west side. In the north, however, the boundary wanders through extremely mountainous areas, separating Laos from China, Burma, and Thailand (Dommen 1985:1). It shares its longest border, over 1,300 miles, with Vietnam on the east.

The geographic relief of Laos is hilly and mountainous. Generally speaking, the land slopes from the north to the south and from the east to the west, with narrow river bottoms running between steeply sloped land. The mountain areas are often densely forested, particularly in the north. The south is characterized more by glade forest and savannas. The country's most significant alluvial plains are along the Mekong River. The Plain of Jars, an area of rolling hills, is in the north, and the Bolovens Plateau is in the south (Dommen 1985:2).

Transportation, and therefore intracountry communication, is and always has been problematic. Because of the nature of Laos' rivers, including the Mekong River, navigation is impossible except by small boats (Dommen 1985:2). Further, there are only a handful of major roads tying the country together. When the French left Laos, there were only about 1,500 miles of roads, few of which were completely passable in the rainy season. These roads were considerably expanded by the 1970s, although they still remained limited (Thee 1973:4). The country's major cities all lie along the banks of the Mekong River just across from Thailand, including Luang Prabang and Vientiane.

Ethnicity

Ethnically, while Laos is quite diverse, there are three major divisions (Thee 1973:5): the Thai-Lao group (also known as the Lao Loum, Valley Lao, or Lowland Lao), the Khas (also known as Lao Theung or Highland Lao), and the Sinitic and Tibeto-Burman group (called Lao Soung or Mountaintop Lao). Most refugees we refer to as Lao are members of the Lao Loum or Lowland Lao ethnic group. They came into the area in the sixth or seventh centuries from the southern provinces of China, driving the Lao Theung to the lower ranges of the mountains. Today, the Lowland Lao still occupy the valleys, particularly along the Mekong, where they were later influenced by the Khmer and Indian cultures. The Lao Theung, the descendants of the oldest inhabitants of the country, are concentrated in the central and southern part of Laos. The Lao Soung, a more recent addition to the area, came from South China in the early eighteenth century. Arriving late, they settled in the less populated mountains and hilltops of northern Laos. The best known of this group are the Hmong people, another important refugee group in America. (The Hmong refugees are not referred to by the term *Lao* and are discussed in a separate chapter in this volume.) *Lao* has come to refer only to the Lowland Lao people, and that is how the term will be used here. Occasionally, the term *Laotians* will be used in this chapter to refer to all of the citizens of the country of Laos, regardless of ethnicity.

The French Period

Historically, foreign colonies existed in the larger Laotian cities: Chinese, Vietnamese, Indian, Pakistani, Thai, as well as more recent additions of French and American groups (Thee 1973:5–6). Except for the French and Americans, who dealt with political and military issues, foreigners were traditionally most active as merchants and in the trades.

In the past, the whole of northeastern Thailand, the Mekong River Valleys, and south almost to the Gulf of Siam were ruled periodically by Lao rulers and then by Thai rulers. Before the French colonized the area, Laos was ruled by Thailand. Nevertheless, regardless of the changes in leadership, whether Thai or Lao, the common people lived out their everyday lives largely oblivious to the machinations of their ruling elites. In fact, the ethnic Lao lived and migrated throughout this area without major difficulty (Manich 1967:8–9).

Today there are more ethnic Lao people on the Thai side of the border than in Laos itself. The reason for this lies with French colonialism. In the late 1800s, the French took over both Vietnam and Cambodia. They intended to move into Laos and Thailand as well, but the British interfered, and the French ended up with the area east of the Mekong (which was part of Thailand at the time) (Manich 1967:9–10). Saying that they only wanted to give the area back to the Vietnamese, who also laid claim to the territory based on previous historical suzerainty, France took over Laos. Eventually, they gave a northeastern strip to Vietnam. However, this was not a historically Vietnamese area and had ethnic Thai living there. France then went on to give a southern section of Laos to Cambodia. Again, this section was not Cambodian, since the people there were ethnically Lao and still speak Lao. At the same time, the larger ethnic Lao population was divided by the Mekong River. The majority (six or seven times the number in Laos itself [Toye 1968:46]) ended up in former Laotian lands now subsumed politically by Thailand. The minority left behind in Laos lived on the relatively narrow plains along the eastern side of the Mekong River.

Making matters worse, the French included in Laos territory that had never been under Lao domination. Further, the territory held other ethnic groups with a long history of hostility toward the lowland peoples. These ethnic groups were also split into two different nation-states through French intervention: the Kha tribes in the southern highlands of Laos and their relatives in the central highlands of Vietnam (Toye 1968:46).

During France's 50-year colonial period in Laos, until the end of World War II, the country stagnated economically and culturally (Thee 1973:10; Toye 1968: 44–45). For example, under French influence, the use of a national Laotian language suffered. Laos became part of French Indochina, and French was the lingua franca of the area (Dommen 1985:1–2). Furthermore, the written script used for Lao was that used for Thai (Manich 1967:7–8). The script was developed in 1283 by King Rama Kamhaeng of Sukhotai and adopted by the Lao and the Thai since both were under his leadership at that time. Because of the French colonial policy of not encouraging the local language, Lao books ceased to be published, and only Thai books were available. Even the Buddhist priests had to study and use Thai since all of their religious books were in Thai.

Being much more oriented toward Vietnam and its people, France used Laos to alleviate population pressures in Vietnam by encouraging Vietnamese to migrate into Laos (Toye 1968:44). As a result, most of the Laotian political or public administrative offices were given to Vietnamese rather than Lao. A large portion of urban populations consisted of ethnic Vietnamese rather than local ethnic groups.

Further, while illiteracy was standard for most Lao, the available secondary schools were filled with children of immigrants. For example, in the 1930s, only 52 Lao completed secondary school (there was only one secondary school in the country, and it was in Vientiane) compared with 96 Vietnamese children. Most local Lao education remained the responsibility of the Buddhist temples, with monks as teachers. Out of approximately 160,000 school-age children, less than 13,000 attended schools. Thus, there was little development of a middle class. At the same time, the elite class, with their social standing secure under the French, apparently complied with colonial power without complaint (Toye 1968:60).

As a result, by 1945 when the French left, there were at least 50,000 Vietnamese in Laos, and two thirds of primary and assistant teachers in Laos were Vietnamese (Toye 1968:45). The former tradition of literacy and literature in the Lao language had disappeared. As a symbol of the stagnation France imposed on Laos, one need only look at the roads France built during its colonial period. If roads were built at all, it was only

to facilitate the movement of troops from Vietnam in case of civil emergency; Luang Prabang, Sam Neua, Savannakhet were connected by simple metalled roads with the road and rail system of Vietnam, but were not linked to each other. Thus Sam Neua could be reached from Hanoi by dry-weather road in a day, but it was still several days by mountain trail from Luang Prabang and Vientiane which administered it. (Toye 1968:59–60)

Although the French were ousted from Laos briefly between 1945 and 1946 by the Japanese, after the Japanese were defeated in World War II, the French reasserted their power. Between 1946 and 1954, however, France gradually gave Laos more and more rights of self-government (Thee 1973:11). Finally, in 1954 French rule ended. Still the Laotian peoples were not allowed to work out their own governmental system. For, with the French gone, the United States, afraid that Laos would be taken over by Communist leaders, stepped into the power vacuum and became a dominant intervening power.

By January 1, 1955, the United States Operation Mission opened in Vientiane, and the Royal government became a "tame client of Washington" (Thee 1973: 12). The following years were marked by civil war and unremitting aggression by North Vietnamese armies. Every American president, from Dwight Eisenhower through Richard Nixon, approved the use of U.S. forces in Laos (Thee 1973:379–380). By 1971, the *New York Times* estimated that almost 2 million tons of bombs had been dropped by the United States on Laos (which is comparable to *total* tonnage dropped during World War II). Others within Laos estimated that there were actually 3 million tons of bombs dropped on Laos. At the same time, a Staff Report of Edward Kennedy's Subcommittee to Investigate Problems Connected with Refugees and Escapees noted that the *official* count of Laotian refugees was almost 300,000 people. By 1971, figures indicated that one third of the country's people were homeless. The rate of refugee movement correlated directly with the intensity of U.S. bombings.

During this time, the Lowland Lao, who traditionally lived in the Mekong and other river valleys, were significantly affected by the political situation raging around them (Thee 1973:4–5). First, their population was unevenly distributed throughout the valley areas because of the war and the heavy U.S. bombing. Whole areas were depopulated. Second, refugees were forced from the countryside, as it came under the control of the Pathet Lao, to the cities which were under the control of the Royal government.

The Pathet Lao

The Lao People's Democratic Republic was established in 1975. The Communist takeover of Laos was a by-product of Communist takeovers in Vietnam and Kampuchea (Brown 1982:17–23). In the previous year, 1974, the United States and Thailand withdrew their military forces (in accordance with the Paris cease-fire agreement of February 21, 1973), but up to 40,000 Vietnamese soldiers remained in Laos along the Ho Chi Minh trail. Therefore, within a short time, the Pathet Lao, backed by the North Vietnamese, finally established the Lao People's Democratic Republic, ending their 30-year struggle for power.

A consequence of the Pathet Lao takeover was the 1975 "flight of the commercial and political elite" (Brown 1982:22) across the Mekong River and into Thailand. While a few thousand fled by the time of the Pathet Lao takeover, within the next five years (that is, by the end of 1980) an estimated 300,000 Laotian people, of mixed ethnicity, poured into Thailand as refugees (Van-es-Beeck 1982:324). Among these refugees, thousands had already fled their original homeland areas within Laos as the Pathet Lao took over their villages, only to have to flee again, this time into another country.

Concerned by the large number of people crossing their borders, Thailand took the stand that Laotian peoples fleeing to Thailand from their homeland after May 1975 were illegal immigrants with no protection under the law. Nevertheless, because of the large native Lowland Lao population in Thailand, tens of thousands of Lowland Lao and Sino-Lao refugees were able to "blend" into the largely ethnic Lao-Thai peoples in northeastern Thailand. By illegally purchasing identity documentation, their position within Thailand was assured. Others stayed illegally with no documentation and were easily exploited, often taking work at very low wages (Brown 1982:328). Most Laotians, however, tried to reach refugee camps established within Thailand's borders. Once in the camps, they were under the protection of the United Nations High Commissioner for Refugees—according to the Geneva Convention on Refugees of 1967 and its Protocol (Brown 1982:328). For those Lao refugees who made it to the refugee camps, the wait for resettlement to another country was often several years (Chan 1990:2–3; Crisp 1987; Haines 1985:22–23). Many children grew up only knowing camp experiences and camp life. By the time their families were resettled, these children had little, if any, memory of their home villages and traditional life. Their parents had memories of village life, but these, too, were overlaid with other memories of war, escape, and life interned as refugees in Thai camps.

INITIAL RESETTLEMENT[1]

Employment, Housing, and Neighborhoods

Initially, much of the research carried out with Southeast Asian refugees in the United States, including the Lowland Lao, centered on economic aspects of their adjustment (for example, Bach et al. 1983, 1984; DeVoe and Rynearson 1983; Haines 1987, 1989:14). Much of this early research was driven by governmental concern about how much refugee programs were going to cost and, therefore, how long it took each refugee or refugee family to become economically independent. A major consequence of this governmental concern was to push refugees to become self-sufficient as soon as possible. As a result, people were placed in whatever jobs were available, mostly low-paying, unskilled employment (DeVoe 1982, 1993a, 1993b; Hamilton 1986).

While some of the Lowland Lao who fled Laos were from the local elite, or from high military positions, the majority of Lao refugees coming to the United States were involved in nonmechanized labor, such as wet-rice farmers, or were simple soldiers. They had little or no contact with the technology common in an industrialized society. As the research I conducted over a period of several years in St. Louis, Missouri, indicated, much confusion emanated from this disjointed union of cultures. For example, one employer told of a middle-aged woman brought to him as a potential employee within a few days of her arrival in St. Louis. The employer needed more information to complete her application form. When handed a telephone so that she could call her sponsor to get the necessary information, she just looked uncomprehendingly at the phone, never having used one before. Such unfamiliarity, however, did not deter the refugees from accepting whatever jobs were available to them, nor did it keep them from succeeding in mastering their employment tasks to the satisfaction of their employers.

Further, many Lao refugees came with little or no education, could not read and write in their own language, and had held jobs that were nontransferable to the highly industrialized, urban environment in which they found themselves (Haines 1989:8). Since they were refugees, not immigrants, and therefore, had not had time to prepare for the end destination, a large number of people arrived without speaking English (except for what they were able to learn while in refugee camps). Nevertheless, one study indicated they had the highest rate of employment of all Southeast Asian ethnic groups (Hamilton 1986).

Both I (DeVoe 1982) and Blanchard and Harding (1984) found employers often had positive stereotypes concerning Lao workers. However, I also found (DeVoe 1982, 1993b:52) that employers indiscriminately lumped their Lao employees together with other Southeast Asian refugees, particularly with the Vietnamese who had already started coming into the area in large numbers. For example, most employers interviewed professed to have no trouble communicating with their refugee workers, regardless of their lack of English-language skills. Demonstrating the task to be done was often enough. Sometimes sponsoring agencies would be able to initially provide interpreters for the interview and the first few days on a new job. However, on occasion, employers would find an interpreter among the people already working in the factory or business. Unfortunately, because the employers did not recognize the differences among Southeast Asian refugees, it was not uncommon for employers to put Vietnamese workers with newly hired Lao workers to act as "interpreters." Despite such well-intentioned but misguided arrangements, many Lao managed to become productive workers. Employers often commented on their Southeast Asian workers' high degree of dependability, reliability, and general work ethic. On the other hand, perhaps due to the language difficulty, the employers also had very low expectations for their refugee employees, which affected their chances for job advancement and higher wages.

Besides being unskilled and lacking English, another problem related to employment was that when the Lao refugees came to the United States—especially because they were often lumped together with Vietnamese refugees—women's roles were misunderstood (DeVoe 1993a; Stier 1991). In Laos, women worked as entrepreneurs, as marketers, worked in their own fields, and generally were a significant factor in the family's financial success. Working outside of the home was considered normal and even desirable (Van Esterik 1980). This Lao attitude was counter to what many Americans expected. Among the St. Louis Lao, when Lao families first came to the United States, the adult males were often immediately found some kind of unskilled employment, but the married women, especially if they had children, were left unemployed. Women felt this lack of work not only as an economic handicap (less money in the family) but also as a psychological loss. They missed the interaction that they normally would have shared with fellow workers. Such interaction was all the more a loss since they lived in relatively isolated conditions in urban, multiethnic settings, a sharp contrast to when they were at home in their own villages, surrounded by family and long-term friends. As a result, even with language and literacy problems, the Lao women tried to find outside employment as soon as possible. Such commitment to work helped these struggling families handle some of the economic difficulties they faced but also raised another problem: child care.

Since the normal living pattern in the home country was for young Lao couples to move into or near the wife's family's compound, child care was never an important issue. There was usually another extended family member, grandparent, aunt, or cousin, to watch over the children (see also Zaharlick, Jobrack, and Calip-Dubois [1993:184–187] on family dynamics). In the new American environment, many Lao lived in nuclear families with no other blood relatives in the area. One consequence of this living pattern was that there were no inexpensive, reliable, caring adults to watch the children of working parents. As a result, other older, nonrelative Lao might be hired to care for the children. Sometimes, the children were left to their own devices, often watching television for hours, just as many American children do.

The two most obvious ramifications of these child care patterns are: First, a paid babysitter, even if not given much money, significantly diminishes the family's meager economic resources; and second, the children are overexposed to non-Lao values, behaviors, and ideas through mass media (and at the same time, are underexposed to Lao values, behaviors, and ideas because of their isolation from other Lao adults). As a result, whatever the child care solution, if a relative was not available to care for the children, this became another stressor for the family struggling to cope and survive.

Coincident with the low wages newly arrived refugees were able to make was the limited amount of money the family could allot to housing. This was very clear in St. Louis. People were initially resettled in apartments that had major problems, such as plumbing (so that they often only had cold water even in winter, and where the pipes in the walls burst from time to time) and poor maintenance (where the windows rattled in their frames, allowing the winter winds to chill the rooms' temperatures even more). Besides these physical problems, the housing was often in the more dangerous areas of the city (Rynearson and DeVoe 1984). When families moved from their initial apartments in an effort to find more secure living arrangements, they usually ended up in another poor, relatively unsafe, location. Random crime and violence were everyday concerns. People were robbed in their homes, and a few were attacked on the streets. If one family was attacked, the psychological sense of fear and vulnerability was shared by all within the Lao community as word of the event spread. The country they had come to as a safe haven from danger and the unknown was proving to be problematic, unreliable, and even dangerous. Nevertheless, they did not live their lives as paranoid hermits, hidden away from their surrounding neighbors. The neighboring Lao children played in front of their homes among themselves. Lao adults could often be seen chatting on the streets. Teenagers clustered in small groups outside their apartments. Although Lao of all ages sometimes formed friendships with non-Lao coworkers, fellow students, or fellow Christian church members, these neighborhood street scenes remained largely Lao.

Education and the Generations

Because the primary aim of the various levels of government (and therefore also of the sponsoring agencies) for adult refugees was rapid economical self-sufficiency, any schooling was limited. Most received English-language training until they started to work. However, education programs aimed at helping illiterate Lao refugee adults to read and write in English were few and far between. Adults who wanted to update (or "Americanize" by getting a license or certificate in the United States) their professional credentials, or earn a graduate equivalency degree (GED), or get a post–high school education achieved this on their own, on an ad hoc basis (personal communication with service providers).

Children were immediately enrolled in age-appropriate classes. Although there may not have been a large number of any one ethnic group coming into a particular school system, most refugees were resettled in metropolitan areas. Overall, these urban schools had to teach increased numbers of new multiethnic students with little or no English-language skills (personal communications with educators in the Midwest and the Southwest). While in the late 1970s, schools in certain areas (California and Arizona, for example) had bilingual programs for their Spanish-speaking students, this rapid increase in students speaking diverse languages created the need for another type of educational solution. Public schools responded by developing English as a Second Language programs and classes for their ethnically diverse children. The programs were set up to help students learn English as quickly as possible. Besides programs oriented toward students' needs (i.e., to help them adjust and succeed within the school environment), programs and workshops were also developed to aid teachers now faced with multicultural classrooms. These latter training programs encouraged cultural sensitivity on the part of the teachers and often gave concrete clues of what to expect from students of a particular ethnic background. The results of such training were mixed (e.g., DeVoe 1991, 1994). While teachers often learned to differentiate a Lao from a Cambodian from a Vietnamese from a Chinese student, they tended to overidentify students from these various groups with a certain list of cultural characteristics. This led to a more sophisticated form of ethnic stereotyping and affected the way teachers interpreted an individual student's work; for example, Vietnamese students are superior; Lao boys readily get into trouble; Cambodian parents are not interested in their daughters achieving a high school education. Teachers' efforts at helping some students were hampered because of these preconceived categories: The categories often determined the level and type of assistance given.

An example of one area where the attitudes and expectations of school personnel conflict with those Lao parents is the question of what age constitutes adulthood (personal communication with St. Louis service providers and school administrators and staff). In the home country's rural area, a young girl may be married by the age of 16 years, and boys in their late teens (high school age by American standards) may start to court girls of 13 or 14 years of age (middle-school age in the United States). These older Lao refugee boys may exhibit interest in the girls by hanging around the junior high schools they attend. Such behavior concerns school staff members because the boys are considered too old for the middle-school students, and their interest is interpreted as inappropriate by school personnel. Some Lao parents, who want their girls to take advantage of the education offered in the United States, also are unhappy with this and may take action. In one case, a family sent their child away to live with a relative in another city. To some parents, however, this behavior is not necessarily a problem, and so they do not interfere. Zaharlick, Jobrack and Calip-Dubois (1993) have also found that it is now more acceptable to consider marriage after a young person has graduated from high school. On the other hand, there were cases in St. Louis where parents themselves became a problem when they interpreted schooling past the early or middle teenage years to be excessive compared to the level of education their child would have received at home in Laos and excessive compared to the family's need for another employed worker. Family finances may ultimately determine whether a young person, considered a capable adult by home country standards, will remain in school and graduate with a high school degree.

Nevertheless, the end result of the Lao students' involvement in the American educational system is that they are better able to deal with their surrounding environment than their parents are. The students, even at a young age, often become and remain the family interpreter with non-Lao. This simple act of being the interpreter upsets the balance of power between the parent and the child. This is an issue that will not diminish within the Lao, or any refugee, community. Non-English-speaking adults may never achieve a comfortable level of proficiency with English, thereby giving their children a lifelong advantage over them in access to information, interpretation of such information, and interaction with the larger non-Lao community. Information access plays into the changing dynamics of power relationships and dependency, that is, of role reversal for these two generations.

INTEGRATION

Religion: Spiritual Adjustment Issues[2]

The differences in values, expected behaviors, languages, types of economic subsistence (e.g., nonmechanized agriculture versus industrialization), and even religion (Buddhism versus Christianity) cause considerable stress for arriving refugees. Under these circumstances, people frequently seek support from familiar sources. One of these is religion.

Many Lao refugees attend Christian churches in their American communities. The reason for attendance varies: The church may have sponsored them; they may have been Christian in the camps or in Laos; or they may be responding to active recruitment on the part of a given church. Nevertheless, Lao often do not consider their traditional religious beliefs and Christian religious beliefs to be mutually exclusive. Therefore, a Lao Christian may still feel the need to make *bun* (merit) or may go to a spirit medium to help resolve a problem. Such openness offers them flexibility in their struggle to survive in a stressful environment. On the other hand, such a multireligious approach can also create psychological difficulties.

Having access to a Lao *wat* gives the community a sense of ethnic mainte-nance and psychological support (Krulfeld 1994). For those Lao communities without a *wat* (Buddhist temple) and resident monks, stress results from *not* being able to carry out prescribed religious duties.

As Theravada Buddhists, Lowland Lao believe in reincarnation: the merit an individual accumulates in a past life determines what this life will be like. For example, a person born with *bun* or merit (somewhat equivalent to the Christian concept of "grace") will be long-lived, successful, and wealthy. Those born lacking *bun* will suffer poverty, sickness, and misfortune (Haarhoff 1973; Hanks 1965). And, of course, what one does and how one behaves in this life will have direct bearing on one's next life (Kaufman 1960; Keyes 1983; Tambiah 1970). Tambiah (1970) suggests that members of the Lao ethnic group in their homeland perceive merit making as having two main aspects: First, it ensures "a rebirth blessed with happiness, prosperity and wealth" (53); and second, it "produces a happy and virtuous state of mind" (53–54). So Tambiah found that villagers viewed merit making as more future oriented (e.g., rebirth) and abstract (e.g., a happy state of mind) than emphasizing immediate practical con-cerns.

Both in Southeast Asia and in the United States, Lao believe that the best way to make *bun* is through giving food daily, or giving other gifts and money periodically, to the Buddhist monks and the *wat.* Many Lao communities in the United States, such as the one in St. Louis, do not have a Lao *wat,* and therefore, there are no monks living in these communities either. Thus, for these Lao, there is no way for them to adequately make *bun* on a normal, daily basis, as they would in their homeland. One man (personal communication), who attended a Christian church, reflected the feelings of many when he said that if his com-munity had a *wat,* he could go there. As a member, he would give to the monks and the *wat* generally and thus accumulate merit. He added that he could not make merit in a Christian church and that he needed to make merit.

Merit making for the Lao in Southeast Asia performed an important social function. In their native villages, making *bun* was often a communal affair (Keyes 1983). As a communal activity, merit making clearly delimited the crit-ical social group. Village residents shared the responsibility of feeding and car-ing for the monks in the local *wat.* Another major source of merit making, and concurrently, village solidarity, in Southeast Asia was the special calendrical rites held at the *wat.* These occasions necessitated major collective action on the part of the villagers. Thus, while the benefits of merit making were accrued individually, the *process* served to promote the solidarity of the community.

In St. Louis, at least some Lao expressed a strong need to make *bun* in order to reap its immediate rewards; for example, they would have better health, good employment, and more money—all very concrete, immediate results. The im-plications of this present-oriented approach are even more serious when one considers that while it is rather difficult for many Lao in the United States to make *bun,* at the same time, they are constantly earning *baap.* (*Baap* can be translated as "demerit.") People make *baap* through bad thoughts and bad behavior. Examples are buying meat to eat and, therefore, having some part in causing another living being's death, and speaking unkindly to or about another person. Thus, while it is easy in America to build demerit (*baap*), at the same time, it is quite difficult to accrue merit (*bun*). A circular problem can result from this constant earning of *baap.* For example, for a community to have one or two residing monks and a *wat* in their community, they must have the financial resources to maintain them. Establishing a *wat* and maintaining monks is a financial drain on the community. Since the local St. Louis Lao perceive themselves as being poor (a sure sign of lacking merit), they cannot raise enough money. Without a temple and monks, they cannot acquire *bun* to counter the accumulating *baap.*

In their home country of Laos, being Buddhist was often equivalent with being Lao (Rutledge 1990:366), and in spite of participation in Christian activities in the United States, Buddhism continues to be an important ethnic identity marker. Krulfeld (1994) worked in a community in Virginia that was able to sponsor several monks and a *wat* in 1980, after only a few years in the United States (see also Ranard 1990). She notes how important this temple was in helping the community cope with their grief and stress, both psychological and spiritual. It gave the Lao, whose homes were geographically dispersed, a concrete sign of communality and solidarity. In many ways the temple and its monks reified their sense of Lao ethnic identity and of the traditional Lao values and behaviors versus those of the surrounding area.

Besides using Buddhism in accumulating *bun,* there is another resource in the Lao informal folk tradition (that is, not specifically Buddhist) for coping with a difficult environment, as well as with the unknown, the unexpected, or the tragic (which can be taken as a result of one's having *baap*). That is, one can have recourse to spirits, or *phii*[3] (Chotisukharat 1971; Tambiah 1970), as well as use of the *baci.* Belief in spirit intercession is a ubiquitous element in traditional Thai and Lao society (Chotisukharat 1971; Gandour and Gandour 1976; Haarhoff 1973; Kaufman 1960; Klausner 1964; LeBar and Suddard 1960; Tambiah 1970; Turton 1972). The spirits, *phii,* range from benevolent, prestigious figures to malevolent, violent beings (Tambiah 1970). The benevolent spirits function through mediums as curing agents and diviners in their homeland. The mediums can be considered a link in a broad-based support system. The *phii* continue to perform their helping functions within the Lao community. The belief in spirit possession may lie dormant until the need for a medium's services arises due to persistent illness or continued misfortune. At that point, particularly if the intervening services of a *wat* and its monks are not available, a medium may be sought to discover if a spirit is the cause of their problems. The following is an example of the use of a medium in St. Louis.

The Lao community in St. Louis had a medium living in the city from 1982 to 1983. Before coming to the area, the spirit medium lived for almost two years with her family as a cultural isolate in a rural American town. During this time, her spirits did not come to her; she attended a Christian church. Since she had a distantly related matrilineal relative in St. Louis, she and her family finally decided to move. During her residency in the St. Louis area, she was very active as a spirit medium. At least once a week, usually more often, the *nang tiam* (as the medium possessed by a spirit was called) was asked to perform healing rites and for divination, for example, for a winning lottery number or an answer to a serious family question.

Many people professed *not* to believe in her, saying that belief in spirit possession was not compatible with being a good Buddhist. When in need, however, these same people turned to the *nang tiam* for help. For example, one member of the Lao Buddhist Association repeatedly brushed aside the existence and activities of the *nang tiam* as not being Buddhist. However, when a woman neighbor became excessively tired and unable to work, and after the services of an American medical doctor proved fruitless, he agreed with the assessment by another Lao that his neighbor's troubles were due to *baap* (which the woman had acquired by not attending the local Laotian New Year celebrations). Since there were no monks available for her to make *bun* to counter her *baap,* this member of the Lao Buddhist Association further agreed with the opinion of other Lao that it might be necessary to bring in the spirit medium to cure the woman.

Thus, at least in this community that had no *wat* but did have a spirit medium present, the medium became a viable alternative in times of stress. While the Lao themselves speak of these two religious traditions as being antagonistic to each other in some respects, the two traditions come out of the same Lao cultural framework, and both reinforce basic concepts (e.g., *bun* and *baap*) and worldviews that are alien to the new urban, mid-American environment. By so doing, these ongoing religious traditions provide a sense of security and solidarity in the face of cultural change.

A third significant religious tradition that can help in times of stress as well as delineate what being Lao is, is the *baci* ceremony, sometimes called the *sukhuan* (which means calling back a person's soul) (Turton 1972). The *baci* is found among many Southeast Asian peoples, but it is especially important to the Lao who have developed a distinctive ceremony combining animist traditions and beliefs with Buddhist traditions (Peachey and Peachey 1983). The *baci* marks all important Lao occasions such as births and marriages, as well as assuring good health and well-being—and even acknowledging a farewell. Originating in animist beliefs that each person has 32 spirits (*kwan*), the *baci* is performed to keep the spirits from leaving or, in the case of illness, to call them back to the sick person. A *baci* often includes recitation of Buddhist Pali scriptures and ends with the symbolic act of tying strings around the wrists of the honored guests.

The *baci* is important to the Lao refugee community in several ways. It can be held with or without Buddhist monks. A religious specialist is not necessary. Thus, the existence of a *wat* in the area is irrelevant to the community's being able to resort to this religious tradition. Furthermore, the *baci,* while not actually a Buddhist tradition, is not considered to be in competition with Buddhism and even incorporates Buddhist scriptures. If Buddhist monks are available, they will perform this rite (Krulfeld 1994). As a part of the informal religious tradition, the *baci* is critical in alleviating stresses from other sources (jobs, health, family). It also serves as a public marker of Lao solidarity.

Gender Relations: Maintenance and Change

Women's positions vis-à-vis men's positions in Laos were economically strong; women were marketers and farmers, earning money for the family. Matrilocality remained the preferred residency pattern after marriage (i.e., the newly married husband and wife lived with or near her parents), and descent was traced through the female line. However, a significant overlay on this strong position of women was a Buddhist tradition that relegated women to a position subservient to men. For example, while men could be monks in search of enlightenment, women could only be nuns who acted as caretakers for the monks. The women had no significant religious role (Kirsch 1982; Krulfeld 1994; Van Esterik 1982). This, plus 50 years of French colonial government and hundreds of years of contact with Chinese, Vietnamese, and Indian cultural elements (all male-dominated cultural traditions), created a complex relationship between the genders. As the Thai (close cousins to the Lowland Lao) say, women are like the back legs of an elephant; men are the front legs (Potter 1977). That is, women are important, even critical, but they are behind the men and follow the men.

In the United States, Lao men complain that women have changed, that they no longer behave toward men as they used to in their home country (Rutledge 1990; Zaharlick, Jobrack, and Calip-Dubois 1993). This is possible and consistent with the impression in the community that there are more divorces in the United States (Rutledge 1990; Zaharlick, Jobrack, and Calip-Dubois 1993) than in Laos. However, given the difficulty of surviving on one income from the low-income jobs people have, it is possible that problems within the family only appear to be greater than they were in the past. Men have had to adapt and adjust in numerous ways, from work to their children's schooling, to available entertainment, to not being able to worship in the traditional, familiar way. As a consequence of these changes, they may have a heightened need for an eye of calm in the storm of change in which they find themselves. Unfortunately, it is not possible for the family to remain unchanged and ever peaceful since the women—pivotal to this scenario—have their own problems and losses to which they must respond and adapt.

There is considerable irony in the new sets of roles of Lao women in the United States. Often Americans think of their culture as being more open, free, supportive, and equal than other cultures, particularly where women are concerned. However, just the opposite is often the experience of Lao women. American society perpetuates greater gender inequalities on them than they left behind in their home country (DeVoe 1993a; Van Esterik 1980, 1982) First, the loss of the extended family, is an emotional burden for the Lao. The everyday consequences of the loss of the extended family are particularly hard for the women (Boserup 1970; Camus-Jacques 1989; DeVoe 1993a:31; Indra 1987; Loescher 1989:24; Montgomery 1991; Spero 1985). By coming to another country, they have effectively severed most or all ties with those who could offer psychological support, guidance, nurturance (Bell 1991; Knudsen 1991), and practical assistance with their family and household responsibilities. This isolation may cause the demoralized and depressed mindset Rumbaut (1989:155–156) found among Southeast Asian women compared to their male counterparts.[4]

Thus, within the home, women do not have their grandmothers, mothers, or even sisters to assist with the everyday domestic tasks of cleaning, cooking, and child care. At the same time, both men and women expect that the women will work and contribute to the family finances. It is not possible for the family to function in the same manner as in the home country. In this time of need, men often can be found helping within the home. In the St. Louis Lao community (Rynearson and DeVoe 1984), when the women worked or went to school, they maintained primary responsibility for home activities, but the men were capable and prepared to assist with domestic activities. On the negative side, because both adults work, the children often lack caregivers with them through the day and become too "Americanized" and apparently lacking in obedience and respect. Men, to whom the traditional extended family (usually matrilineally related) was not as important, do not suffer the same sense of loss at its absence. Men do, nevertheless, see their last bastion of familiarity and comfort, the nuclear family with themselves as head, altered without their desire or permission.

Ethnic Identity

In spite of the stress Lao contend with as refugees and as foreigners trying to adjust to a new sociocultural environment, the majority do not cling to their Lao ethnic identity. They see themselves as Lao-Americans or situationally, as Lao or American (see *Silk Sarongs and City Streets* 1986; Krulfeld 1992). Such ethnic flexibility or nesting of ethnic identity is not uncommon in Southeast Asia (Denton 1976; Rajah 1990). Interestingly, Krulfeld (1994) found that length of residence in the United States was not a factor in ethnic self-identification. One person who had lived in the United States for 15 years reportedly felt completely Lao and was not comfortable with Americans; others who had been in America for a much shorter time felt part of both cultures, Lao and American. Krulfeld also found that while the children were immersed in American culture through school, they identified as Lao-Americans, an identity that was acceptable to most of their parents. Parents did worry, however, that their children would lose their identity as Lao because, according to the parents, the children were quickly losing Lao values and forgetting Lao traditions. The children, however, said they were Lao by descent, so they could not possibly lose their Lao ethnicity. The minority of adults identifying mostly or exclusively as Lao connected negative morals and values with American culture and positive morals and values with their own Lao culture (e.g., obedience and respect for parents and the elderly). Their way of handling the stress of the new environment was to turn more completely toward an idealized traditional Lao culture and identity.

The majority of Lao, however, while maintaining Lao cultural traditions through activities such as dance and religious ceremonies, seem comfortable with the details of everyday American life—with its clothing styles, food, work patterns, housing, and urban life. This attitude allows them to identify as bicultural, as being a part of both cultures, Lao and American, and to forge a new ethnic identity—Lao-American.

CONCLUSIONS AND PROSPECTS

The Lao came to the United States as refugees, often unprepared educationally, socially, economically, and psychologically. They came bearing the scars of their prerefugee and refugee experiences but carrying the hope for a secure, stable, and prosperous life for themselves and their families in America. Since there were few Lao already living in the United States, most refugees settled in urban areas with no Lao community support systems, such as a *wat* or even a simple specialty grocery store selling Lao foods and condiments.

The thrust of aid from the larger American community was directed toward helping Lao adults achieve economic self-sufficiency. Diverse programs were set up to help in this process: English-language training classes, some health care, and job placement services. Schools were expected to be the adjustment vehicle for those 18 years of age and younger. Unless there were problems that interfered with employment or schooling, the Lao were left to their own devices in creating a new sense of self as individuals and as a community. This the Lao did by establishing *wats* if possible, by maintaining other informal traditional beliefs and behaviors, and by banding together to offer each other support in the face of everyday challenges.

After 20 years of resettlement in America, the majority of people appear to identify as Lao and Lao-American. Although parents worry about children maintaining their Lao identity, the children seem to take such an identity for granted, as a birthright. The children see themselves as Lao-American or as American of Lao descent. As with ethnic groups before them, each generation is more firmly rooted in the American way of life, yet there remains the possibility of reconfirming a unique Lao ethnic identity and maintaining distinctive Lao values and traditions.

NOTES

1. Unless noted otherwise, the case material for this chapter is based on ethnographic data gathered in the St. Louis refugee -community and from local employers, service providers, and school personnel. The author gathered this information from a variety of sources from 1981 to the present.

2. The St. Louis community differs from some other areas with respect to Lao refugees in that there is no Lao *wat* in the metropolitan area.

3. *Phii* as used here refers to spirits outside of oneself. Although the *phii* may possess a medium's body (as during a divination ceremony), they are not one's own spirits. The spirits belonging to each individual person are referred to as *kwan*.

4. Another factor influencing their depression may be the particular and traumatic experiences that women suffer during flight and during internment in refugee camps (see Agger 1995; Cha and Small 1994; Ramirez 1995).

REFERENCES

Agger, Inger. 1995. Abused Refugee Women: Trauma and Testimony. *Refuge: Canada's Periodical on Refugees* 14(7):19–22.

Bach, Robert L., Linda W. Gordon, David W. Haines, and David R. Howell. 1983. The Economic Adjustment of Southeast Asian Refugees in the U.S. In *World Refugee Survey 1983*. Edited by Rosemary E. Tripp. Washington, D.C.: U.S. Committee for Refugees (USCR) of the American Council for Nationalities Service (ACNS). Pp. 51–59.

———. 1984. Geographic Variations in the Economic Adjustment of Southeast Asian Refugees in the U.S. In *World Refugee Survey 1984*. Edited by Rosemary E. Tripp. Washington, D.C.: U.S. Committee for Refugees (USCR) of the American Council for Nationalities Service (ACNS). Pp. 7–9.

Bell, Robert A. 1991. Gender, Friendship Network Density, and Loneliness. *Journal of Social Behavior and Personality* 6(1):45–56.

Blanchard, Kendall, and John C. Harding. 1984. Economic Change and Adaptation among the Lowland Lao in Murfreesboro, Tennessee: The Viability of Network Exchange (1). Paper presented at the American Anthropological Association Annual Meeting, Denver, November.

Boserup, Ester. 1970. *Women's Role in Economic Development*. London: George Allen and Unwin.

Brown, MacAlister. 1982. The Communist Seizure of Power in Laos. In *Contemporary Laos*. Edited by Martin Stuart-Fox. New York: St. Martin's Press. Pp. 17–38.

Camus-Jacques, Genevieve. 1989. Refugee Women: The Forgotten Majority. In *Refugees and International Relations*. Edited by Gil Loescher and Laila Monahan. Oxford: Oxford University Press. Pp. 141–157.

Cha, Dia, and Cathy A. Small. 1994. Policy Lessons from Lao and Hmong Women in Thai Refugee Camps. *World Development* 22(7):1045–1059.

Chan Kwok Bun. 1990. Introduction. In *Indochinese Refugees 15 Years Later*. Edited by Chan Kwok Bun. [special issue of *Southeast Asian Journal of Social Science* 18 (1)]. Singapore: Department of Sociology, National University of Singapore.

Chotisukharat, Sanguan. 1971. Supernatural Beliefs and Practices in Chiengmai. *Journal of Siam Society* 59, pt. 1(January):211–231.

Crisp, Jeff. 1987. Refugees in Thailand. *Refugees* 45:18–34.

Denton, R. K. 1976. Ethnics and Ethics in Southeast Asia. In *Changing Identities in Modern Southeast Asia.* Edited by David J. Banks. The Hague: Mouton Publishers. Pp. 71–81.

DeVoe, Pamela A. 1982. Employers' Perceptions of Southeast Asian Refugee Employees in Metropolitan St. Louis: A report. St. Louis: Missouri Institute of Psychiatry, School of Medicine, University of Missouri at Columbia.

———. 1991. Refugee Children in School: Understanding Cultural Diversity in the Classroom. *Anthro Notes* (National Museum of Natural History Bulletin for Teachers) 13(2):1–4, 10–11.

———. 1993a. The Silent Majority: Women as Refugees. In *The Women and International Development Annual,* Vol. 3. Edited by Rita S. Gallin, Anne Ferguson, and Janice Harper. Boulder, Colorado: Westview Press. Pp. 19–51.

———. 1993b. Southeast Asian Refugee Employees and Their Employers in the American Mid-West: Proponents, Picadors, or Pawns? In *Refugee Empowerment and Organizational Change: A Systems Perspective.* Edited by Peter Van Arsdale. Arlington, Virginia: American Anthropological Association. Pp. 50–62.

———. 1994. Refugees in an Educational Setting: A Cross-Cultural Model of Success. In *Reconstructing Lives, Recapturing Meaning: Refugee Identity, Gender, and Culture Change.* Edited by Linda A. Camino and Ruth M. Krulfeld. Basel, Switzerland: Gordon and Breach Publishers. Pp. 235–249.

DeVoe, Pamela A. and Ann Manry Rynearson. 1983. *Social Relations in a Refugee Neighborhood: Indochinese in St. Louis, MO.* Report for the Office of Refugee Resettlement. Washington, D.C.: Division of Health and Human Services.

Dommen, Arthur J. 1985. *Laos: Keystone of Indochina.* Boulder, Colorado: Westview Press.

Epstein, T. Scarlett, and Rosemary A. Watts. 1981. *The Endless Day: Some Case Material on Asian Rural Women.* New York: Pergamon Press.

Gandour, M. J., and J. T. Gandour. 1976. A Glance at Shamanism in Southern Thailand. *Journal of Siam Society* 64, pt. 1 (January):97–103.

Haarhoff, J. P. 1973. People of Laos. In *Peoples of the Earth: South East Asia.* Edited by Andrew Turton. Danbury, Connecticut: Danbury Press.

Hackett, Beatrice Nied. 1988. Relative and Relational Power for Ethnic Chinese Cambodian Refugees: Economics with a Twist. Paper presented at the American Anthropological Association (AAA) Annual Meeting, Phoenix, Arizona, November.

Haines, David W. 1985. Initial Adjustment. In *Refugees in the United States: A Reference Handbook.* Edited by David W. Haines. Westport, Connecticut: Greenwood Press. Pp. 17–35.

———. 1987. Patterns in Southeast Asian Refugee Employment: A Reappraisal of the Existing Research. *Ethnic Groups* 7 (March): 39–63.

———. 1989. Introduction. In *Refugees as Immigrants: Cambodians, Laotians, and Vietnamese in America.* Edited by David W. Haines. Totowa, New Jersey: Rowman and Littlefield. Pp. 1–23.

Hamilton, Virginia, Managing Editor. 1986. Little-Known Ethnic Lao Refugees Resettle in Larger Numbers. In *Refugee Reports.* Nashville, Tennessee: A Project of the American Council for Nationalities Service. Pp. 1–6.

Hanks, Jane Richardson. 1965. A Rural Thai Village's View of Human Character. In *Felicitation Volumes of Southeast Asian Studies.* Bangkok: The Siam Society.

Indra, Doreen. 1987. Gender: A Key Dimension of the Refugee Experience. *Refugees* 6: 3–4.

Kaufman, Howard Keva. 1960. Concepts of *bun* and *bab*. In *Bangkhuad: A Community Study in Thailand*. New York: J. J. Augustin Incorporated Publisher. Pp. 196–209.

Keyes, Charles F. 1983. Economic Action and Buddhist Morality in a Thai Village. *Journal of Asian Studies* 42(4):851–868.

Kirsch, Thomas. 1982. Buddhism, Sex-Roles and the Thai Economy. In *Women of Southeast Asia*. Edited by Penny Van Esterik. Occasional Paper No. 9. Dekalb, Illinois: Northern Illinois University. Pp. 16–41.

Klausner, William J. 1964. Popular Buddhism in Northeast Thailand. In *Cross-Cultural Understanding*. Edited by F. S. C. Northrop and Helen H. Livingston. New York: Harper and Row. Pp. 87–92.

Knudsen, John Chr. 1991. Therapeutic Strategies and Strategies for Refugee Coping. *Journal of Refugee Studies* 4(1):21–33.

Krulfeld, Ruth M. 1992. Cognitive Mapping and Ethnic Identity: The Changing Concepts of Community and Nationalism in the Laotian Diaspora. In *Selected Papers on Refugee Issues 1992*. Edited by Pamela A. DeVoe. Arlington, Virginia: American Anthropological Association. Pp. 4–26.

———. 1994. Buddhism, Maintenance, and Change: Reinterpreting Gender in a Lao Refugee Community. In *Reconstructing Lives, Recapturing Meaning: Refugee Identity, Gender, and Culture Change*. Edited by Linda A. Camino and Ruth M. Krulfeld. Basel, Switzerland: Gordon and Breach Publishers. Pp. 97–127.

LeBar, Frank M., and Adrienne Suddard, Editors. 1960. *Laos: Its People, Its Society, Its Culture*. New Haven: HRAF Press. Pp. 44–46.

Loescher, Gil. 1989. Introduction. In *Refugees in International Relations*. Edited by Gil Loescher and Laila Monahan. New York: Oxford University Press. Pp. 1–33.

Manich, M. L. 1967. *History of Laos: Including the History of Lannathai, Chiengmai*. Bangkok: Chalermnit.

Montgomery, R. 1991. Predicting Vietnamese Refugee Adjustment to Western Canada. *International Migration* 29(1):89–113.

Peachey, Linda, and Titus Peachey. 1983. Religion in Socialist Laos. *Southeast Asia Chronicle* 91(October):16–19.

Potter, Sulamith Heins. 1977. *Family Life in a Northern Thai Village*. Berkeley: University of California Press.

Rajah, Ananda. 1990. Orientalism, Commensurability, and the Construction of Identity: A Comment on the Notion of Lao Identity. *Sojourn: Social Issues in Southeast Asia* 5(2):308–333.

Ramirez, Judith. 1995. The Canadian Guidelines on Women Refugee Claimants Fearing Gender-Related Persecution. *Refuge: Canada's Periodical on Refugees* 14(7):3–7.

Ranard, Donald W. 1990. A Buddhist Temple in Rural Virginia. *Refugees* 79(October): 32–33.

Rumbaut, Rubén G. 1989. Portraits, Patterns, and Predictors of the Refugee Adaptation Process: Results and Reflections from the IHARP Panel Study. In *Refugees as Immigrants: Cambodians, Laotians, and Vietnamese in America*. Edited by David W. Haines. Totowa, New Jersey: Rowman & Littlefield. Pp. 138–198.

Rutledge, Paul. 1990. Boon Vongsurith. *Journal of Refugee Studies* 3(4):365–369.

Rynearson, Ann Manry, and Pamela A. DeVoe. 1984. Refugee Women in a Vertical
    Village: Lowland Laotians in St. Louis. *Social Thought* 10(3):33–48.
Silk Sarongs and City Streets. 1986. Video produced by the International Institute of
    Metropolitan St. Louis, St. Louis, Missouri (28 minutes).
Southeast Asian Refugee Studies Newsletter. A publication of the Southeast Asian Ref-
    ugee Studies Project, Center for Urban and Regional Affairs, University of Min-
    nesota. Minneapolis, Minnesota.
Spero, Abby. 1985. *In America and in Need: Immigrant, Refugee, and Entrant Women.*
    Washington, D.C.: American Association of Community and Junior Colleges.
Stier, Haya. 1991. Immigrant Women Go to Work: Analysis of Immigrant Wives' Labor
    Supply for Six Asian Groups. *Social Science Quarterly* 72(1):67–82.
Tambiah, S. J. 1970. *Buddhism and the Spirit Cults in North-east Thailand.* Cambridge:
    Cambridge University Press.
Thee, Marek. 1973. *Notes of a Witness: Laos and the Second Indochinese War.* New
    York: Random House.
Toye, Hugh. 1968. *Laos: Buffer State or Battleground.* London: Oxford University Press.
Turton, Andrew. 1972. Matrilineal Descent Groups and Spirit Cults of the Thai-Yuan in
    Northern Thailand. *Journal of Siam Society* 217–256.
U.S. Committee for Refugees (USCR). 1990. 1989 World Refugee Statistics. In *World
    Refugee Survey 1989 in Review.* Edited by Virginia Hamilton. Washington, D.C.:
    U.S. Committee for Refugees of the American Council for Nationalities Service.
Van-es-Beeck, Bernard J. 1982. Refugees from Laos, 1975–1979. In *Contemporary Laos.*
    Edited by Martin Stuart-Fox. New York: St. Martin's Press. Pp. 324–334.
Van Esterik, Penny. 1980. Cultural Factors Affecting the Adjustment of Southeast Asian
    Refugees. In *Southeast Asian Exodus: From Tradition to Resettlement, Under-
    standing Refugees from Laos, Kampuchea and Vietnam in Canada.* Edited by
    Elliot L. Tepper. Ottawa: The Canadian Asian Studies Association. Pp. 151–171.
———. 1982. Introduction. In *Women of Southeast Asia.* Edited by Penny Van Esterik.
    Occasional Paper No. 9. Dekalb, Illinois: Northern Illinois University. Pp. 1–15.
Zaharlick, Amy, Steward Jobrack, and Theresa Calip-Dubois. 1993. Economic and So-
    ciocultural Influences on the Fertility Transition of Lao Refugees. In *Selected
    Papers on Refugee Issues:II 1993.* Edited by MaryCarol Hopkins and Nancy D.
    Donnelly. Arlington, Virginia: American Anthropological Association. Pp. 177–
    194.

Chapter 13

Soviet Jews

STEVEN J. GOLD

After three decades of emigration, there are now sizable communities of Jews from the former USSR in several nations and three continents, including Western Europe (some 40,000 live in Germany), North America, and Israel (Tress 1994). While the greatest number of émigrés reside in Israel, since the mid-1960s, almost 325,000 Jews from the former Soviet Union have settled in the United States (HIAS 1995). From 1988 to the present, persons from the former Soviet Union have been the largest refugee nationality to enter the United States (Littman 1992). Further, Soviet Jews[1] constitute the most numerous group of Jewish immigrants to enter the nation since the 1920s. Members of this population are notable for their high levels of skill and education, the intact status of their families, the extensive resettlement services they receive from both Jewish and government agencies, and—among Jewish migrants—their minimal premigration exposure to formalized Jewish training.[2] As educated Europeans who receive ample advocacy and support from a well established community of native-born coethnics, Soviet Jewish émigrés enjoy excellent prospects for a relatively smooth and rapid merger into the American middle class. In this, Soviet Jews are dramatically distinct from other major refugee groups of the period since 1980.

The presence of one third of a million émigrés is the result of enormous efforts expended by the American Jewish community over the last 25 years and, accordingly, represents the successful culmination of a campaign to save Soviet Jewry. However, despite their status as religious refugees and the generous support they have received from American coethnics, Jews from the former Soviet Union have been less religious and more Russian in their style of adaptation to the United States than was expected by the host community. Drawing upon their high levels of skill, Soviet Jews' economic adjustment to the United States has been a story of success. In contrast, their patterns of communal adaptation have generally reflected their own independent values and prerogatives rather than the model of rapid amalgamation planned for them by the American Jewish community.

EXODUS

As educated Caucasians exiting a relatively peaceful part of the world, Jews from the former Soviet Union may seem to have little reason to flee from their homeland. However, their historical and contemporary experience as Soviet Jews gives them ample reason to exit while the opportunity is available.

As an oppressed group under the czars, Jews played an important role in the Russian Revolution. However, from Joseph Stalin's time through the 1980s, the Soviet government maintained policies to limit Jews' influence in the nation's government and bureaucracy. Such steps were taken as part of an effort to discourage religion and extend control over all bases of power in the USSR. For example, between 1937 and 1974, the number of Jewish deputies in the Supreme Soviet was reduced from 47 to 6 (Simon 1985a: 8). Further, Soviet purges—from the show trials of the 1920s to the "Doctor's Plot" of the post–World War II era—included disproportionate numbers of Jewish victims (Chesler 1974; Simon 1985b).

Prior to the 1960s, the Soviet system offered Jews access to higher education because technical experts were required for the nation's military and industrial development. Soon, however, this path was restricted. "As Khrushchev pointedly indicated, 'we' no longer need the Jews because we have 'our own' experts" (Jacobs and Frankel-Paul 1981: 5). In 1960, Jews accounted for 3.2 percent of the students enrolled in higher education in the USSR. By 1971, the figure was less than 2 percent (Simon 1985b: 183). An electronics engineer described his confrontation with anti-Jewish quotas imposed by the Soviet bureaucracy:

I wanted to continue my education and get a promotion in my field. But as a Jew, I could not go above a certain level. It's not so much anti-Semitism among the people I worked with—I had good relations. But my bosses were limited with what they could do. It was Brezhnev time—it was State anti-Semitism. It wasn't much from the people. This is what is so outrageous—is that it's a State anti-Semitism, they just impose it. (Gold 1992: 33–34)

Anti-Zionism, a major plank in Soviet foreign policy from the 1960s onward, had dire consequences for Russian Jews. Articles condemning Israel appeared with increasing frequency in the official Soviet media after the 1967 Arab-Israeli war and thus gave government sanction to anti-Semitic attacks. "Getting the hint," ambitious officials would carry out personal projects of harassing, demoting, or refusing to hire Jews as a means of currying favor with superiors

(Gold 1992). Finally, while nearly all Soviet Jews confronted institutional discrimination, direct prejudice was also common, especially for those living in the Ukraine. An émigré from Odessa described the rampant anti-Semitism Jews encountered in Kiev during the 1970s:

When I came to Kiev, I took a bus usually from railway station or from airport. And I would ask myself, "How long will it take before I hear something about Jews?" Usually, it took 15 or 20 minutes and I would hear something already. These anti-Semitic feelings and thoughts, it's first place for them. Their anti-Semitic feelings and anti-Semitic conversations and everything, for them it's problem number one. (Gold 1992: 34)

As of the mid-1990s, the climate in the former USSR—characterized by impending economic crisis, social disorder, a revival of intolerant churches, and the rise of ultranationalism—appears to be a textbook example of a setting ripe for anti-Semitic outbreaks (Gitelman 1992). As Communist Party control of ideology has been replaced by freedom of expression, Jews have enjoyed greater access to communication and religious participation. At the same time, however, anti-Semites have also become increasingly open, active, and virulent. For example, in 1992, the Russian Nationalist Party published a manifesto featuring its 75 slogans. Of these, 52 were explicitly anti-Semitic or anti-Zionist (Gitelman 1992). In the 1990s, Vladimir Zhirinovsky, the leader of Russia's Liberal Democratic Party, became an important political force. His many anti-Semitic remarks have given Jews and other ethnic minorities cause for concern (Ingram: 1994: 8A). In 1994, he told the UN Correspondents' Association that "the majority of new business structures" in the former USSR "are headed mostly by Jews" and "most of the money is criminal." Accordingly, as of the mid-1990s, many Jews in the former Soviet Union still hoped to leave for the United States, Israel, or other Western nations (Brym 1993).

The post–World War II exit of Jews from the USSR has been shaped by a complex configuration of political relations between the United States, the USSR, and Israel. Prior to the 1970s, there was little Jewish emigration; during the entire decade of the 1960s, only 2,465 persons entered the United States from the USSR (Chiswick 1993: 262). However, during the late 1970s, and then a decade later in the late 1980s and early 1990s, thousands of Jews were able to leave. Peak years of entry into the United States were 1979, when 28,794 arrived, and 1992, when 45,888 Jews from the former Soviet Union entered (ORR 1990; HIAS 1995) (see Table 13.1).

Leaving the Soviet Union is only half of the story of migration. Once they exit, Soviet Jews must decide on a place to settle. The two major choices are the United States and Israel. There has long been a debate over who should be able to choose Soviet Jews' country of refuge. Prior to its downfall, the Soviet government permitted Jews to exit for either of two reasons. The first was family unification—allowing Soviet citizens to join relatives in other nations. This affected relatively few. The second reason for exit was the law of return. Since

Table 13.1
Soviet Jewish Refugee Arrivals by Calendar Year

Year	Number	As % of Prior Year
1965	12	
1966	36	300%
1967	72	200%
1968	92	128%
1969	156	170%
1970	135	87%
1971	214	159%
1972	453	212%
1973	1,449	320%
1974	3,490	241%
1975	5,250	150%
1976	5,512	105%
1977	6,842	124%
1978	12,265	179%
1979	28,794	235%
1980	15,461	54%
1981	6,980	45%
1982	1,327	19%
1983	887	67%
1984	489	55%
1985	570	117%
1986	641	112%
1987	3,811	595%
1988	10,576	278%
1989	36,738	347%
1990	31,283	85%
1991	34,715	111%
1992	45,888	132%
1993	35,581	78%
1994	32,622	92%
Total	322,341	

Source: Hebrew Immigrant Aid Society (HIAS) program information.

Jews' passports were stamped with "Jew" instead of the Soviet republic where they were born, they were allowed to go to Israel. Initially, the majority of Soviet Jews granted exit visas settled in Israel. However, from 1976 to 1989, at least half opted instead to dwell in the United States. Before the glasnost era, the official destination of all Jewish émigrés was Israel. Upon exiting the USSR, a large fraction "dropped out" as they applied for, and were almost always given refugee status by, the United States. By the late 1980s, less than 10 percent each year chose Israel (Gold 1994; Woo 1989).

Jews from the former Soviet Union cite several reasons for prefering the United States over Israel. These include greater economic opportunity, as well as a higher level of national security and no compulsory military service. (For a group who paid a great human price in World War II, the latter considerations are of major significance.) In addition, émigrés often assert that they feel more comfortable in the secular and pluralistic United States than in Israel, which they describe as "an Orthodox country."[3] Finally, Russian Jews are accustomed to identifying with a big nation and so prefer exchanging one superpower for another, as opposed to moving to a tiny country, which for many has a total population surpassed by that of their former city of residence.

From the early 1970s to the late 1980s, Soviet Jews coming to the United States would spend about a month in Italy while their resettlement applications were processed. After October 1, 1989, the United States no longer accepted Soviets who sought to enter the United States with Israeli visas (Woo 1989; Tress 1991). Instead, Jews who wished to enter the United States applied directly to the U.S. embassy in Moscow. The number of Soviet refugees permitted to enter the United States (Jewish and otherwise) is limited to 50,000 a year. As of 1995, priority is given to selected groups of former Soviets that the United States Congress has identified as likely targets of persecution. These include Jews, Evangelical Christians, Ukrainian Catholics, and followers of the Ukrainian Autocephalous Orthodox Church. Eligible persons with close, legal-resident relatives (parent, spouse, children, siblings, grandparents, and grandchildren) in the United States are granted priority for entry. Members of these denominations who have immediate U.S. citizen relatives (parent, spouse, or unmarried minor child) must apply as immigrants rather than refugees.

DEMOGRAPHIC INFORMATION

From 1965 through the end of 1994, HIAS resettled 322,341 Soviet Jews (HIAS 1995). (See Table 13.1.) The greatest number come from Russia and Ukrainia, which also have the largest Jewish populations among the former Soviet Republics. However, while Russia has the largest number of Jews, Ukrainia is the major source of émigrés. Of the 194,047 Soviet Jews who entered the United States between 1980 and May 1993, 42 percent (81,421) were Ukrainians, 24 percent (46,391) were from Russia, 13 percent (24,437) were Byelorussians, 6 percent (12,591) were Uzbeckis, 6 percent (11,113) were Mol-

Table 13.2
Origins of Soviet Jewish Refugees by Year of Arrival

Republic	1980-1989		1990-1993		1980-1993	
Ukraine	32,850	43.0%	48,571	41.3%	81,421	42.0%
Russia	20,237	26.5%	26,154	22.2%	46,391	23.9%
Byelorussia	10,419	13.7%	14,018	11.9%	24,437	12.6%
Moldavia	3,376	4.4%	7,737	6.6%	11,113	5.7%
Latvia	2,313	3.0%	2,173	1.8%	4,486	2.3%
Uzbekistan	3,111	4.1%	9,480	8.1%	12,591	6.5%
Azerbaijan	1,608	2.1%	3,107	2.6%	4,715	2.4%
Other	2,405	3.2%	3,632	3.1%	6,037	3.1%
Unknown	10	0.0%	2,846	2.4%	2,856	1.5%
Total	76,329	100.0%	117,718	100.0%	194,047	100.0%

Note: 1993 figures are through May.
Source: HIAS 1991, 1993.

davians, 2 percent (4,715) were from Azerbaijan, and 2 percent (4,486) were Latvians. The remainder (4 percent) came from other Soviet Republics or had unknown origins (HIAS 1993)[4] (see Table 13.2).

In terms of their patterns of settlement, state-level data from the 1990 census reveal that 30 percent of USSR-born American residents live in New York, 23 percent in California, 6 percent each in New Jersey and Illinois, and 5 percent each in Florida, Pennsylvania, and Massachusetts. Hence, 80 percent of those born in the Soviet Union reside in seven states. It should be noted that because federal statistics tabulate only the nationality and not the religion of refugees, there is no way of knowing what proportion of these are Jews. For example, Los Angeles is the major point of settlement for Soviet Armenians. Analysis of the 1990 census reveals that only 33 percent of post–1965 former Soviet residents in Los Angeles County *are not* of Armenian ethnicity. In contrast, only about 500 of the more than 60,000 former Soviets in New York City are of Armenian ethnicity[5] (see Table 13.3).

Key Characteristics: Age and Family Patterns

Three sociodemographic features of the Soviet émigré population are crucial for understanding their adaptation to the United States: their age; their intact, multigenerational families; and the class and culture-based patterns of interaction and support maintained within these social units.

Table 13.3
Location of Persons Born in the USSR, 1990

State	% of Total
New York	30%
California	23%
Illinois	6%
New Jersey	6%
Massachusetts	5%
Florida	5%
Pennsylvania	5%
Total	80%

Source: U.S. Bureau of the Census 1993.

Soviet Jews are the oldest refugee group entering the United States. Kosmin's 1989 study of Soviet Jews who had been in the United States at least 8 years found their median age to be 49. Of those entering the United States during 1991, 34 percent were over 50 and 15 percent were over age 65. About 18 percent of 1991 entrants were of school age. In fiscal year 1986, entering Soviet refugees' average age was 37, with women's median age being 41.4 years. However, since 1990, the median age has declined. For purposes of comparison, the average age of all immigrants entering the United States in 1991 was about 29 years (Kosmin 1990; ORR 1987; HIAS 1993).

The significant number of elderly among the Soviet Jewish population yields distinct patterns of adjustment. Refugee families experience problems because the elderly have difficulties learning English, finding employment, and making their way in the United States. At the same time, elderly émigrés help with child care and provide a strong sense of community as they congregate on streets, in parks, and in community centers in neighborhoods where they settle (Orleck 1987). Finally, since elderly émigrés are beyond working age, it is they who most commonly rely on government assistance for a considerable period after their arrival. In contrast, younger émigrés make rapid progress in their efforts to be self-supporting (see below).

Soviet Jewish families are often intact, have few children, and frequently include three generations. Because Soviet Jewish families are often extended and small in size, they are able to devote ample resources to child rearing—a pattern retained from the former USSR, where deep involvement across generations was typical and required for child rearing, since women as well as men worked outside of the home (Simon and Brooks 1983: 57; Markowitz 1994:

154–157). Prior to 1989, Soviet emigration policy worked to ensure the emigration of intact, multigenerational families by encouraging or even mandating the exit of elderly émigrés along with their more youthful offspring (Drachman and Halberstadt 1992). Since that time, family preferences and U.S. immigration policy have furthered this pattern of family unification (Gold 1994).

Additional evidence of the intact nature of émigré families involves high rates of matrimony. According to the 1990 census, 80 percent of post-1965 employed Russian male immigrants between the ages of 24 and 65 were married. This marriage rate exceeds that of all post-1965 male immigrants in the same age range by 17 percent (Chiswick 1995: 29). Thus, family composition, cultural orientation, and immigration regulations have all reinforced the Soviet Jewish family's ability to function as a source of support and stability for émigrés in America.

Soviet émigré families reveal many patterns that facilitate their smooth adjustment to American society. However, they also manifest certain characteristics that hinder adaptation. For example, in the Soviet Union, parents were highly involved in their childrens' lives, while the peer group—a central force in American adolescents' socialization—had relatively little influence (Shlapentokh 1984). This was especially the case among Jewish families, because parents felt their efforts were necessary to shield children from anti-Semitism and ensure chances for success. Carried over to the United States, parents' desire to protect children sometimes fosters excessive dependence and prevents émigré youth from establishing social relationships, developing a sense of autonomy, and dealing with American life on their own terms (Markowitz 1994; Hulewat 1981; Kozulin and Venger 1993).

Further, while generational conflicts exist among all immigrant families, such problems are aggravated among highly skilled Soviet Jews. The unprecedented ability of certain émigrés to adjust to America quickly widens the gaps in levels of adaptation that may exist within a single immigrant family (Gold 1989). For example, Sasha, a 35-year-old émigré, was making $30,000 a year as a computer programmer two years after his 1982 arrival in the United States. His position contrasted dramatically with that of his parents who knew almost no English, did not drive, and were unemployed. Consequently, Sasha had to provide their economic support, translation, and transportation in addition to managing his own career and family life. To offer the parents some independence, the family resided in a Russian-speaking neighborhood far from his job, thus requiring Sasha to make an 80-mile commute. He summarized his relationship with his dependent parents: "With my parents, it's not that they are just from a different country, they are from a different world. There are so many things they just don't understand. I have to take care of them. But I have my own life too" (Gold 1992: 70).

Becoming Americans: Language and Citizenship

Soviet émigrés (with the exception of the elderly) tend to make excellent progress with language acquisition. While about 50 percent spoke no English on arrival, within a few years, upwards of two thirds or more rate themselves as "good, very good, or excellent" at the English language. Between 50 and 70 percent have taken English classes (Simon 1985a; Kosmin 1990; Federation 1985). According to the 1990 census, 78.5 percent of employed, post-1965 Russian male immigrants to the United States speak English "well," "very well," or exclusively (Chiswick 1995: 29).

Soviets show a higher propensity to naturalize and do so more rapidly than the other major refugee groups (Cubans and Southeast Asians) who have entered the United States since 1975. From 1980 through 1991, almost 60,000 persons born in the USSR became citizens. This represents about 57 percent of those who arrived in the United States between 1975 and 1985 as refugees (ORR 1993: 61). The former Soviets' rapid naturalization provides members of this group with opportunities for political participation, eligibility for jobs and scholarships, and a higher priority ranking when assisting relatives to gain entry into the United States.[6]

EMPLOYMENT AND ECONOMIC FACTORS

When analyzing the economic progress of refugee groups, three main issues must be considered. First, one must evaluate the population's ability to find jobs. The second issue involves the level of income produced. Ideally, earnings should permit a refugee to survive without reliance on government benefits. Finally, if a refugee group is to achieve integration into the host society, prospects for economic mobility should exist. It is generally accepted that the first job a refugee finds in the United States may not be an ideal position. Nevertheless, employment itself does yield rewards in the form of income, work experience, and cultural orientation. As time passes, however, refugee workers should have the potential for promotion in order to increase their earnings, receive appropriate remuneration for their skills, and attain some level of occupational satisfaction. While many of these issues are determined by the economic environment within which a refugee seeks work, resettlement services and language, job training, and job placement programs can contribute to a group's positive economic integration.

As a result of their education, skills, and the benefits they receive, Jews from the former Soviet Union tend to do relatively well in the States after a short period of adjustment. Simon and Brooks (1983), in a nationwide sample, found their average educational level to be 13.5 years, a figure that exceeds the average for the U.S. population by a year and is among the very highest of all immigrant groups entering the country (Gold 1992: 43). Data from the 1990 census are consistent with Simon and Brooks' estimate. For employed male post-1965 Rus-

sian immigrants between 24 and 65 years of age, nationwide, the educational
level was 14.8 years (Chiswick 1995: 29). Average education was above 13
years for Soviet-born persons in both New York City and Los Angeles. Fifty-
eight percent of former Soviets in-New York City and 72 percent in Los Angeles
County had 1 or more years of college.

Soviet Jewish émigrés receive economic rewards for their high levels of education. The 1990 census revealed that employed Soviet men residing in New
York City who arrived in the United States between 1975 and 1981 were making
approximately $32,000 annually in 1990, while their counterparts in Los An-
geles were making over $43,000. For purposes of comparison, the average earn-
ings for all employed foreign-born men was about $26,000 in New York and
$24,000 in Los Angeles in 1990; while employed, native-born white men in
New York and Los Angeles earned approximately $46,000.

Employed Soviet women who entered the United States between 1975 and
1981 made about $22,500 in New York and approximately $26,000 in Los
Angeles. Their earnings were consistently between 58 percent and 72 percent
of those of employed Soviet men who arrived at the same time. For purposes
of comparison, the average earnings for employed, foreign-born women were
$19,000 in New York and $16,400 in Los Angeles in 1990; while employed,
native-born white women earned about $31,000 in New York and $26,000 in
Los Angeles in 1990. As might be expected, recently arrived Soviet men and
women made much less in 1990 than those émigrés with longer tenure in the
United States.

While the average income of former Soviets suggests a generally successful
merger into the American middle class, the economic adjustment of this population covers a wide range, from poverty to significant wealth. For example,
about 30 percent of those who had been in the United States for a year or less
in June 1991 were receiving cash assistance. Kosmin found that among émigrés
in the United States eight years or more in 1989, 42 percent of those households
in New York and 36 percent of those in Los Angeles were making less than
$20,000 per household. In contrast, 8 percent of former Soviets in New York
and 16 percent of those in Los Angeles had a household income of $60,000 or
more in 1989 (ORR 1992: A-18, 19; Kosmin 1990: 24–25).

Labor Force Participation

Labor force participation rates for Soviet Jews in the United States are generally quite high, with nearly 70 percent of working-age émigrés employed full-
or part-time. Between 10 percent and 28 percent are seeking work, depending
on the year of the survey and the part of the country sampled. With the large
numbers arriving since 1990 and the depressed economic conditions they encounter in many receiving communities, a sizable fraction of recent arrivals are
underemployed (Krautman 1990; Gold 1994: 20).

The 1990 census determined that the labor force participation rate for Soviet immigrant men in New York City was 76 percent, and 57 percent for women. Excluding recent arrivals, the labor force participation rate was 89 percent for men and 68 percent for women. Roughly similar trends were evident in Los Angeles, where the labor force participation rate for Soviet immigrant men was 79 percent and 63 percent for women. Excluding recent arrivals, the labor force participation rate in Los Angeles County was 88 percent for men and 71 percent for women. With the exception of those in the United States three years or less in 1990, unemployment rates were quite low, less than 7 percent for men or women in New York and Los Angeles. Between 32 and 59 percent of working-age women were not in the labor force.

One economic asset of the Soviet Jews over natives or other immigrant groups is the unusually high number of women with professional and technical skills. Sixty-seven percent of Soviet Jewish women in the United States were engineers, technicians, or other kinds of professionals prior to migration. In contrast, only 16.5 percent of American women work in these occupations (Simon 1985a: 17; Simon, Shelly, and Scheiderman 1986; Eckles et al. 1982: 29; U.S. Bureau of the Census 1984: 216). According to the 1990 census, 29 percent of post-1965 Soviet émigré women in New York City and 26 percent of émigré women in Los Angeles County work as professionals in the United States. The very high level of women's education and professional experience is one of the most noteworthy aspects of the Soviet Jewish population. In fact, the total number of women workers with former employment as ''Professionals'' or ''Engineers'' exceeds that of men (HIAS 1993; Gold 1994: 52).

Use of Cash Assistance

According to the Office of Refugee Resettlement (ORR), in 1986, about 26 percent of Soviet refugees were supported by cash assistance. This figure includes some Armenians and others as well as Jews (ORR 1987: 34–35). Data from the 1990 census show that 14 percent of Soviet-born men and 13 percent of Soviet-born women in New York City, and 7 percent of Soviet-born men and 11 percent of women in Los Angeles County, were on supplemental security income (SSI), Aid to Families with Dependent Children (AFDC), or General Relief in 1990. However, excluding recent arrivals, use of cash assistance declined to 5 percent for men and 10 percent for women in New York, and 5 percent for men and 9 percent for women in Los Angeles. Hence, once settled, refugees are able to reduce their use of government assistance.

According to data produced by the HIAS Matching Grant Department, the self-sufficiency rate for Soviet Jews in the United States after four months was 24.6 percent for those arriving in 1990, 23.8 percent for those entering in 1991, and 18.3 percent for those arriving in 1992. In general, it appears that émigrés arriving in smaller cities had a better chance of being self-supporting after four months than those who settled in larger cities. For example, in Baltimore there was an 80-percent-plus rate of self-sufficiency among Soviet Jews within four months of arrival in the years 1989 to 1992. In contrast, in Los Angeles émigrés had a four-mouth self-sufficiency rate between 22 and 11 percent for the same years, and in New York the largest point of settlement for the four-month self-sufficiency rate was about 5 percent after 1989. In addition to community size, other factors, such as the state-determined availability of public assistance, might also influence self-sufficiency rates. The fact that New York and California have much more generous benefit programs than does Maryland may partly explain the higher rates of self-sufficiency evident in Baltimore versus Los Angeles and New York (Gold 1994: 48–49).

The combination of large numbers of émigrés entering the United States and the recession of the early 1990s made initial job finding difficult for former Soviets. However, Soviets are noted for their rapid rates of exit from RCA (refugee cash assistance), which actually improved between 1990 and 1991, despite the generally sluggish economic conditions of the period. To quote from the 1993 Office of Refugee Resettlement *Report to the Congress:* "The RCA utilization rate for the Soviets is the lowest of any large group (28 percent) and represents a dramatic decrease from the previous year (50 percent), when a surge of arrivals in the winter and early spring of 1991 contributed to heavy RCA utilization" (ORR 1993:24). The high skill levels of émigrés, their motivation to find work, and the assistance provided them by agencies and community members can be credited with this impressive performance.

Areas of Employment

According to these statistics, Soviet Jews in the United States appear to be finding jobs and are earning a good living, considering their short stay in the United States. One problem they confront, however, is an inability to meet their previous level of occupational prestige. For example, a study of New York's Soviet Jewish community found that while 66 percent had professional, technical, and managerial occupations in the USSR, only half of these, 33 percent, found similar jobs in the United States (Federation 1985).

Soviet Jews experience problems in finding appropriate American jobs because of their lack of job-related licenses and certification, their limited English-language skills, and the incompatibility between certain Soviet and American occupations. For example, there are few American job opportunities for classical accordion players, coaches of sports seldom played in the United States, or engineers who formerly designed tundra-friendly (and by U.S. standards, hopelessly outdated) structures for the Siberian oil industry. Agency data reveal that a large fraction of formerly professional Soviet Jews are able to adapt to the U.S. economy by finding jobs in the skilled trades, bookkeeping and accounting, computer programming, and technical fields (Federation 1985).

The literature on Soviet Jewish émigrés includes several accounts of self-employment. Former Soviets gravitate toward several enterprises including engineering companies, restaurants and grocery stores, retail trade, and construction and real estate. In the 1980s, taxi companies in New York and Los Angeles included many Soviets, but émigrés often leave this risky enterprise after only a few years (Russell 1985).

Data from the 1990 census suggest that a sizable fraction of Soviets are involved in small business. In New York, 15 percent were self-employed (21 percent of men and 8 percent of women) with higher rates in Los Angeles, where 25 percent (33 percent of men and 17 percent of women) were self-employed. When compared with census data among various migrant groups, the Los Angeles figure puts Soviet Jews among those groups with the very highest rates of self-employment. This is an impressive finding, considering that as refugees from a Communist nation Soviet Jews lack two of the most essential resources for entrepreneurship—business experience and investment capital. On the other hand, high rates of entrepreneurship are common to Jewish immigrants to the United States. Their involvement in self-employment resonates with a literature that identifies entrepreneurship as a viable adjustment strategy for migrant groups (Gold 1992; Kestin 1985; Lubin 1985; Orleck 1987; Portes and Rumbaut 1990).

While many Soviets are becoming self-employed, others are entering white-collar and professional occupations. This pattern is consistent with that revealed by other highly skilled, educated, and English-speaking migrant groups such as Indians and Filipinos. Finally, it should be noted that various professions, such as doctor, dentist, and engineer (ones that involve a significant proportion of Soviet Jews) are often practiced independently and hence constitute both professional work *and* self-employment (Gold 1988; Mangiafico 1988: Portes and Rumbaut 1990).

INTERACTIONS WITH RESETTLEMENT ACTIVITIES AND SCHOOLS

Soviet Jews in the United States enjoy perhaps the most well-funded and professionally staffed resettlement system ever devoted to immigrants and refugees (Eckles et al. 1982; Gold 1994). Nearly all Soviet Jews have been resettled by the Hebrew Immigration Aid Society. The HIAS model of resettlement combines centralized policymaking, administration, and data collection with local-level service provision, thus giving each community the flexibility required to help clients according to local conditions and needs. For example, HIAS mandates certain program standards, such as reunion with relatives and "earliest appropriate job placement" in order to "avoid fostering reliance on public and private institutions." However, actual service provision is carried out by a team of local professionals in coordination with family members and community volunteers. "Consequently, the nature of programs developed within each community are often unique to that community's specific environment" (ORR 1993: C-10,11).

Compared with the refugee resettlement systems devoted to other ethnic and nationality groups, Soviet Jews' agencies are highly centralized and integrated, long established, well funded, and few in number. They enjoy a level of government and private funding per refugee that is considerably greater than that allocated for other groups. For example, during the early 1980s, the federal government gave each VOLAG (voluntary agency) $525 per Southeast Asian refugee. In contrast, Soviet Jews' resettlement agencies, which had access to nongovernment funds provided by Jewish charities, received $1,000 per refugee. Additional funding was made available by combining communal and governmental funds via a federal matching grant program (Eckles et al. 1982; HIAS 1991, 1993). In fiscal year 1992, the Council of Jewish Federations received almost $34 million in matching grants to resettle almost 34,000 refugees of whom 90 percent were Soviets (HIAS 1991).

Depending on the community of settlement, services to Soviet Jews are available from several coordinated agencies. Intake services, vocational and language training, and health care are often accessible from public agencies and community colleges or adult schools. The Jewish Family and Children's Service provides counseling, financial aid, and case management. The Jewish Vocational Service offers job placement and occasionally job training. Jewish Community Centers and Young Men's and Women's Hebrew Associations (YMHAs/ YWHAs) deliver social and recreational activities; the Bureau of Jewish Education contributes a variety of religious and cultural activities. Because of the constitutional separation of church and state, resettlement activities with religious content may not be supported with governmental funds.

Several synagogues, Jewish camps, and Jewish day schools have developed programs on their own or in consort with Jewish federations to welcome émigré families. In accordance with matching grant requirements, anchor families— established relatives of recently arrived émigrés—are expected to deliver certain benefits as well, valued at approximately $400 per refugee in Los Angeles during 1993. Resettlement agencies provide services for both immediate needs such as housing and health care as well as longer-term concerns of religious education, social integration, recreation, and cultural enrichment.

Finally, while the services available to Soviet émigrés may vary according to the Jewish agencies resettling them, benefits available through state and local sources also impact clients. For example, due to state regulations, a refugee family of four living in California in 1989 would be eligible for $734 monthly in AFDC benefits. The same family living in Texas would receive a maximum of $221. Further, while two-parent, indigent families are eligible for AFDC in California, they are not in Texas (Rumbaut 1989: 103).

Feelings about Agencies

Soviet Jews generally have positive evaluations of the services they receive in resettlement. Gitelman (1985: 62) found that 80.4 percent of émigrés to the United States rated their resettlement agencies as working ''very well; well;

or not badly'' (versus 44.3 percent for Soviet Jews in Israel). A New York–based study found that 71 percent of émigrés had a positive impression of NYANA (New York Association for New Americans) (their major resettlement agency), while only 29 percent had a negative impression (Federation 1985: 39). Nevertheless, émigrés also confront difficulties in adjusting to the United States. According to several studies, the major problems encountered by Soviet Jews in the United States are what Simon, Shelly, and Schneiderman (1986) call ''bread and butter issues.'' They include (in rank order) learning English, finding a job, earning enough money, and missing family and friends.

Unlike most immigrants who have little experience in obtaining government services, former Soviets come from a society where substantially more of life's necessities are distributed by government agencies than is the case in the United States. Accordingly, a unique problem that former Soviets confront is relearning ways of interacting with agencies in a dramatically different social context. A fairly large amount of literature has addressed Soviets' confrontations with this change in areas of service provision involving cash assistance, physical and mental health, job placement, and community socialization (Gold 1987, 1992; Markowitz 1993; Drachman and Halberstadt 1992; Ivry 1992).

Culture-based conflicts in several areas of service delivery are challenging to resettlement staff and clients alike. Moreover, since difficult interactions involving job placement, religious socialization, and mental health service provision account for a large proportion of the relations between Soviet Jews and American Jewish agencies, the two communities often develop their images of each other in a hostile setting that overwhelms the goodwill with which both parties initially regard one another.

Children's Academic Adjustment

School-aged émigrés are generally well educated and tend to excel in U.S. schools. For example, in a 1991 comparison of the 12 largest immigrant groups in the New York City public schools (grades 3–12) who had been in the country three years or less, students from the former USSR ranked first in reading scores, second in math, and fifth in English. Their reading and math scores were much higher than all students in the New York schools, including the native born. In addition, their mean increase in score over the previous year was the highest of all groups in both reading and English, and among the highest in math (New York City Public Schools 1991).

However, because of their lack of English skills and knowledge about the American educational system, émigré students experience frustration in attempting to achieve their goals. Schools in the former USSR are generally more rigorous and accelerated than their American counterparts, with students attending a 10-year (since the 1990s, 11-year) rather than 12-year system. Soviet students begin studying advanced subjects such as calculus and biology before Americans and consequently are years ahead of Americans of the same age.

Because of the lack of structural congruency between the two educational systems, Russian students are frequently required to repeat earlier work. Many émigré students find this to be destructive to the high levels of achievement motivation they initially bring to the United States (Gold and Tuan 1993).

SOCIAL ORGANIZATION

Soviet Jews have much interaction with each other but form few organized community activities (Orleck 1987; Markowitz 1991; Gorbis 1992). Their communities are often geographically concentrated, allowing the many aged émigrés to interact easily. Many ethnic businesses direct their goods and services to émigrés. Various publications, especially *Novoye Russkoye Slovo* (New York) and *Panorama* (Los Angeles), are available as well as Russian language television and radio.

While their communities are marked by divisions based in ideology, region of origin, educational level, occupation, and other factors, Jews from the former Soviet Union, especially the great majority from the European Republics, have many social similarities. They tend to be educated, urbanized, and Russian speaking and share many common values. Émigrés rely on frequent interaction for both a social life and obtaining important information and resources. In contrast, it appears that Soviet Jews do not form a great number of close relations with American Jews or gentiles. One reason for this is the rather broad cultural and linguistic gap between émigrés and American Jews.

For example, while American Jews tend to be Democrats, most Soviet Jews are politically to the right and, when naturalized, join the Republican Party (Gold 1992; Noonan 1988; Markowitz 1993; Lipset 1990). A journalist described Jews from the former Soviet Union as "a community that is staunchly conservative Republican and is quite puzzled by the left leaning liberalism of American Jews" (Frumkin 1993: 17).

Resistance to Organization

Émigrés generally avoid formal organizations. This is both because they lack experience in creating voluntary associations and because in the USSR such entities were imposed by government bureaucrats rather than voluntarily created by members. Consequently, émigrés assumed that persons who took leadership roles in communal activities did so only in order to obtain some personal benefit. According to a report on Soviet Jewish émigré organizations, émigrés "developed a very strong negative attitude toward such organizations and activities" and "the figure of the social activist acquired a permanent negative classification in the minds of many new immigrants" (Ilyin and Kagan 1991: 5).

As a result, the creation of formal organizations among this group has been difficult. Studies on both coasts describe émigrés' difficulties in creating viable associations (Gold 1992; Markowitz 1993). Nevertheless, several types of formal organizations have been identified. First are broad-based groups that seek to unite all Russian Jews or "new Americans"; second are veterans associations; and third are professional associations. Another type involves leisure and cultural activities such as sports teams and musical groups. Finally, Chabad has organized synagogues for Russian speakers in several localities (Freedman 1993). According to Ilyin and Kagan's (1991) report on Soviet émigré associations, in different ways, these organizations seek to help newcomers adapt to the United States, to retain Russian-language culture, and to develop a Jewish identity. These organizations vary widely in terms of their emphasis on a Russian or Jewish cultural orientation, their financial well-being, stability, and relations with American Jewish groups.

While émigrés have not developed an extensive network of formalized ethnic organizations, this does not always mean that they seek to avoid each other. Rather, reports continually emphasize Soviet Jews' deep social involvements and their immersion in an extensive array of informal networks that provides for both practical needs as well as a culturally rich social life (Markowitz 1993). For example, nightclubs that offer a lavish variety of Russian-style food and drink and feature entertainers versed in Russian, Jewish, and American popular music have become the centers of Soviet Jewish communities throughout the United States. These settings provide an environment where flashily dressed émigrés spend long evenings in celebration of religious and secular events in a style that combines their Russian, Jewish, and American identities. Former Soviets have also established networks within which they pursue a very wide variety of activities and interests ranging from literature, art, and poetry to politics, sports, various professions, and entrepreneurship (Gold 1992; Markowitz 1993; Simon 1985a).

Finally, when considering Soviet Jews' community patterns, it should be noted that the high levels of skill they possess together with the many benefits they receive from the Jewish community and the U.S. government may reduce their need to create mutual aid associations of the type common among other migrant communities, including earlier cohorts of Russian Jews. Consequently, by their very existence, resettlement services offer a disincentive to group formation.

JEWISH IDENTITY AND BEHAVIOR

Jewish identity is a complex issue for Soviet émigrés. While they have little formal Jewish education (only 4 percent had one year prior to migration), at the same time many appear to have deep feelings of connectedness and strong ethnic or national identification as Jews (Kosmin 1990; Markowitz 1988). The Soviet émigré population is marked by generational variation in religious experience. Three generations of Soviet émigrés in the United States—the elderly, the middle-aged, and the young—have each had a different experience with Judaism (Orbach 1980; Freedman 1993). The elderly are often familiar with traditional

Eastern European Judaism that they learned from their parents or before the
Stalinist restrictions of the 1930s. Middle-aged Soviet Jews grew up in an atheistic environment that encouraged the assimilation of Jews. Consequently, their
minimal experience of Judaism is secular. Finally, émigré children frequently
have had some exposure to contemporary Judaism, since numerous religious
activities and scholarships to Jewish camps, schools, and the like, are made
available as part of their resettlement program. So the meaning and experience
of Jewish identity for each generation on Russian Jews are so different that they
offer only limited potential for family unification. It is paradoxical that Soviet
Jews—religious refugees—are troubled by problems of religious unification
(Hyfler 1991).

A major question in the realm of émigrés' Jewish identity involves the ways
through which sentiments are manifested in behavior. A study conducted by the
Federation of Jewish Philanthropies in New York noted that these feelings are
often strongest when associated with distant, abstract, and symbolic elements of
Jewishness and are much weaker when émigrés confront actual, face-to-face
participation in organized Jewish life. Perhaps because of their origins in the
anti-Semitic USSR, émigrés maintain a private and personal approach to Judaism that does not lend itself to participation in organized Jewish activities
(Federation 1985: 24).

A number of surveys have explored Soviet Jews' involvement in Jewish rituals and behaviors and found them to be roughly similar to those of American
Jews'. Émigrés who have been in the United States longer and are financially
better off tend to be more involved in Jewish life (Kosmin 1990; Krautman
1990). In general, Jewish identification among émigrés is secular or nationalistic
rather than religious. Kosmin found that over 60 percent of émigrés surveyed
felt that the meaning of being Jewish in America was "cultural" or "nationality," while less than 30 percent felt it was "religious" (Federation 1985: 21;
Kosmin 1990: 35).

Despite their lower levels of Jewish education, émigrés from the former Soviet
Union are in various ways more "ethnic" (in terms of their involvement with
coethnic persons, networks, and outlooks) than many American Jews. This point
is illuminated by the work of sociologist Herbert Gans, who describes assimilated, third-plus generation American white ethnics (notably Jews) as maintaining "symbolic ethnicity" through self-selected, identity-related expressive
behaviors. This is contrasted with the more extensive reliance on ethnic communities and networks for the fulfillment of basic needs as maintained by first-
generation groups such as the Soviets (Gans 1979).

Soviet émigrés' strong ethnic ties are suggested by the responses to several
questions in the 1990–1991 New York Jewish Population Study. For example,
Jews from the former Soviet Union have higher rates of Yiddish competence,
membership in Jewish Community Centers and Young Men's and Women's
Hebrew Associations, and reading Jewish publications than all New York Jews.
They are much more likely to have close friends or immediate family living in

Table 13.4
Ethnic Ties: All Jews versus Post-1965 Soviet Arrivals

Question	Response	All	Soviet
Do you speak Yiddish?	Yes	38%	42%
Have you or any member of your household been a dues-paying member of a YMHA or Jewish Community Center within the past 12 months?	Yes	15%	17%
Do you regularly read any Jewish publications?	Yes	41%	49%
Do you or your spouse have any close friends or immediate family living in Israel?	Yes	46%	83%
Of the people you consider your closest friends, would you say that:	Few or none are Jews	6%	0.20%
	Most, almost all, or all are Jewish	66%	96%
When it comes to a crisis, Jews can only depend on other Jews:	Disagree	47%	25%
	Agree	50%	68%

Source: Horowitz 1993.

Israel than all New York Jews, exceed all New York Jews by 30 percent in terms of asserting that most or all of their closest friends are Jewish, and much more strongly believe that when it comes to a crisis, Jews can only depend on other Jews. Finally, Jews from the former USSR have more negative views of Jewish-Gentile intermarriage, even when the non-Jewish spouse converts to Judaism, than do all New York Jews. These measures suggest that despite Russian émigrés' lower rates of Jewish education and religiosity than American Jews, they are more involved with other Jews in certain ways than are members of the larger community (see Table 13.4).

Jewish Socialization

The Jewish community's resettlement system encourages Soviet émigrés to plan their adjustment to the United States in accordance with the values of

American Jewish life. Some émigrés have responded favorably to such pro-gramming. They have joined synagogues, sent their children to Jewish day schools and camps, participated in Jewish community activities, and raised funds for Jewish philanthropies. National and New York–based surveys have deter-mined that around 40 percent of Soviet Jews belong to synagogues—roughly the same proportion as members of the larger community (Kosmin 1990; Ho-rowitz 1993). In addition, anecdotal evidence suggests that religious amalga-mation is taking place. For example, the Chabad Russian Center of Los Angeles hosted 4,000 émigrés for its Yom Kippur services in 1993, while the Beth Shalom People's Temple in Brooklyn, New York, has attracted some 500 Soviet Jewish members (Estulin 1993; Ruby 1993).

In general, however, émigrés are only selectively concerned with American Jewish activities. Some émigrés remain unaffiliated because their most imme-diate priorities in the United States are finding jobs and getting their families established. Others avoid involvement with American Jewish institutions be-cause they resent the condescending way in which they are sometimes ap-proached by staff who, in one article, were urged "to create a Jewish need in him [the Soviet émigré] just as we would with a child, while at the same time understanding that he is no child" (Goldberg 1981: 161). Conflicts involving religious and cultural socialization for Soviet émigrés were most notable during the early years of resettlement (prior to the mid-1980s) when media exposure to the image of the pious refusenik made most American Jews assume that Soviet Jews would be both religious and anti-Soviet.

Just as émigrés sometimes resist efforts at religious training, most also retain a strong "Russian" identity. While Soviet Jews generally dislike communism, many retain a feeling of attachment to the culture, language, cuisine, literature, landscape, and way of life of their homeland and are unwilling to abandon these traditions in favor of Americanisms. When Americans approach former Soviets with strident criticisms of Russia and clear expectations that they should forsake their background, émigrés become alienated. Consequently, just as many Soviet Jews resisted the German-American Jews' assimilation programs early this cen-tury, so do today's former Soviets often dislike Americanization activities (Howe 1976; Mindel, Habenstein, and Wright 1988).

By the late 1980s, official acknowledgment was finally given to the fact that most Soviet Jews were not religiously active. Initial hopes for rapid religious assimilation were replaced by a more realistic acknowledgment of Soviet émi-grés' secular and ethnic rather than religious identification (Carp 1990). An American rabbi who works with Soviet Jews reflected on this realization: "One of the disappointments that many rabbis felt was that most of the Soviet Jews did not find a need to express their Jewishness. We should have understood this, because they come from a secular, atheistic country, but it was difficult to ac-cept" (Barber 1987: 41).

CONCLUSIONS

The patterns of economic and social adaptation and the political outlooks of Soviet Jewish émigrés appear to be fairly clear. Skilled, educated, and availed of excellent services, émigrés have achieved an enviable economic record. While they learn English quickly, most prefer to interact among themselves in an informal context that emphasizes their own language and culture. Identifying as Jews, most are not highly religious but maintain certain forms of ethnic attachment to their community that exceeds that of American Jews.

Accordingly, what remains to be seen is the degree to which these émigrés will become involved with Jewish life in the future, either on their own terms or in consort with the American Jewish community. While the general consensus regarding former Soviet Jews' communal and religious lives suggests that they are neither highly organized nor religiously involved, that image is beginning to be challenged as a number of reports reveal that groups of émigrés in various communities throughout the United States are creating organizations and becoming absorbed in Jewish life.

As today's émigrés often point out, Jews from the former Soviet Union are drastically different from the cohort of their coethnic countrymen who entered the United States from Russia almost a century ago. The early group were relatively unskilled and immersed in the collective folkways of Eastern European Judaism (Yiddishkeit). In contrast, today's contingent are religiously untrained, politically conservative, individualistic in outlook, and by and large, sophisticated urban professionals. Nevertheless both migrant communities cared deeply about the traditions of their European way of life and, while grateful to America for the opportunities and freedom it offered, strongly guarded their independence from established Jews, who they saw as overzealously planning their Americanization.

NOTES

1. While the Soviet Union no longer exists, the term *Soviet Jews* will be used interchangeably with *Jews from the former Soviet Union*. The less clumsy *Russian Jews* (a term often used by émigrés themselves) will not be used because most émigrés actually came from the Ukraine.

2. For this article, data on Soviet émigrés from the 1990 census (5 percent public use microdata sample) were drawn from the two largest locations of their settlement, New York City and Los Angeles County. These two locations accounted for over 50 percent of post-1965 migrants from the USSR tabulated in the 1980 census. A comparison of descriptive statistics of these two populations shows a very high degree of similarity. Since Armenians are a significant non-Jewish refugee group that has entered the United States from the former USSR since 1965, persons who claimed that they had Armenian ancestry or spoke Armenian at home were excluded from our analysis, as well as from

figures cited from Chiswick (1995). Additional data are from computer runs from *The 1991 New York Jewish Population Study* (Horowitz 1993).

3. According to the 1990–1991 Jewish Population Study of New York, the fraction of former Soviet Jews who have seriously considered living in Israel exceeds the rate of all Jewish New Yorkers by only 11 percent (30 percent of post-1965 Jewish immigrants from the former Soviet Union have considered living in Israel, while 19 percent of the entire Jewish community has done so).

4. Figures for 1990 entrants are unavailable and hence are not included in this tabulation.

5. According to the 1990 census, 41,995 persons born in the USSR have migrated to Los Angeles County from 1965 to 1990. Of these, 28,267 (67 percent) were Armenians (i.e., they reported Armenian ancestry or spoke Armenian at home). In contrast, of the 60,044 post-1965 émigrés from the former USSR in New York City, only 543 (1 percent) were Armenian.

6. According to the 1990–1991 Jewish Population Study of New York, 33 percent of post-1965 Jews born in the former Soviet Union are registered to vote.

REFERENCES

Barber, Jennifer. 1987. The Soviet Jews of Washington Heights. *New York Affairs* 10 (1):34–43.

Brym, Robert J. 1993. The Emigration Potential of Jews in the Former Soviet Union. *East European Jewish Affairs* 23(2):9–24.

Carp, Joel M. 1990. Absorbing Jews Jewishly: Professional Responsibility for Jewishly Absorbing New Immigrants in Their New Communities. *Journal of Jewish Communal Service* 66(4):366–374.

Chesler, Evan. 1974. *The Russian Jewry Reader.* New York: Behrman House Inc.

Chiswick, Barry. 1993. Soviet Jews in the United States: An Analysis of Their Linguistic and Economic Adjustment. *International Migration Review* 27:260–285.

———. 1995 Soviet Jews in the United States: Language and Labor Market Adjustments Revisited. Department of Economics, University of Illinois at Chicago, Mimeographed.

Dorf, Nina, and Fay Katlin. 1983. The Soviet Jewish Immigrant Client: Beyond Resettlement. *Journal of Jewish Communal Service* 60(2):146–154.

Drachman, Diane, and Anna Halberstadt. 1992. A Stage of Migration Framework as Applied to Recent Soviet Emigres. In *Social Work with Immigrants and Refugees.* Edited by Angela Shen Ryan. New York: Haworth Press. Pp. 63–78.

Eckles, Timothy J., Lawrence S. Lewin, David S. North, and Danguole J. Spakevicius. 1982. *A Portrait in Diversity: Voluntary Agencies and the Office of Refugee Resettlement Matching Grant Program.* Washington, D.C.: Lewin and Associates.

Estulin, Naftoli. 1993. Chabad Russian Immigrant Program and Synagogue. Leaflet, September.

Farber, Bernard, Charles H. Mindel, and Bernard Lazerwitz. 1988. The Jewish American Family. In *Ethnic Families in America.* Edited by Charles H. Mindel, Robert Habenstein, and Roosevelt Wright, Jr. New York: Elsevier. Pp. 400–437.

Federation of Jewish Philanthropies of New York. 1985. Jewish Identification and Affiliation of Soviet Jewish Immigrants in New York City—A Needs Assessment and Planning Study. Unpublished papers.

Frankel-Paul, Ellen, and Dan N. Jacobs. 1981. The New Soviet Migration in Cincinnati. In *Studies in the Third Wave: Recent Migrations of Soviet Jews to the U.S.* Edited by Dan Jacobs and Ellen Frankel-Paul. Boulder: Westview Press. Pp. 77–114.

Freedman, Jenny A. 1993. Soviet Jews, Orthodox Judaism, and the Lubavitcher Hasidim. *East European Jewish Affairs* 1(23):57–77.

Fruchtbaum, Irene, and Rodney Skager. 1989. Influence of Parental Values on Dating Behavior of Young Russian Women: A Cross-Cultural Perspective. UCLA Department of Education. Mimeographed.

Frumkin, Si. 1993. Who Are the Russians? *Jewish Journal* (Los Angeles), November 19–25:17.

Gans, Herbert. 1979. Symbolic Ethnicity: The Future of Ethnic Groups and Cultures in America. *Ethnic and Racial Studies* 2(1):1–20.

Gitelman, Zvi. 1978. Soviet Immigrants and American Absorption Efforts: A Case Study in Detroit. *Journal of Jewish Communal Service* 55(1):77–82.

———. 1985. The Quality of Life in Israel and the United States. In *New Lives: The Adjustment of Soviet Jewish Immigrants in the United States and Israel.* Edited by Rita J. Simon. Lexington, Massachusetts: Lexington Books. Pp. 47–68.

———. 1992. Soviet Jewry: A Global View. Paper presented at Wilstein Institute Board Retreat, University of Judaism, Los Angeles, December 12.

Glazer, Nathan, and Daniel Patrick Moynihan. 1963. *Beyond the Melting Pot.* Cambridge: The MIT Press.

Gold, Steven J. 1987. Dealing with Frustration: A Study of Interactions between Resettlement Staff and Refugees. In *People in Upheaval.* Edited by Scott Morgan and Elizabeth Colson. New York: Center for Migration Studies. Pp. 108–128.

———. 1988. Refugees and Small Business: The Case of Soviet Jews and Vietnamese. *Ethnic and Racial Studies* 11(4):411–438.

———. 1989. Differential Adjustment among New Immigrant Family Members. *Journal of Contemporary Ethnography* 17(4):408–434.

———. 1992. *Refugee Communities: A Comparative Field Study.* Newbury Park, California: Sage Publications.

———. 1994. Soviet Jews in the United States. *American Jewish Yearbook* 1994:3–57.

Gold, Steven, and Mia Tuan. 1993. Jews from the Former U.S.S.R. in the United States. San Francisco: Many Cultures Publishing.

Goldberg, Simcha R. 1981. Jewish Acculturation and the Soviet Immigrant. *Journal of Jewish Communal Service* 57(3):154–163.

Gorbis, Boris Z. 1992. Give Us Your Poor Homeless Organizations: A Review of California's Soviet-Jewish Organizations. In *New Voices: The Integration of Soviet Émigrés and Their Organizations into the Jewish Communal World.* Edited by Madeleine Tress and Deborah Bernick. New York: Council of Jewish Federations. Pp. 17–23.

Gorelick, Sherry. 1981. *City College and the Jewish Poor.* New York: Schocken Books.

Halter, Marilyn. 1995. Ethnicity and the Entrepreneur: Self-Employment among Former Soviet Jewish Refugees. In *New Migrants in the Marketplace.* Amherst, Massachusetts: University of Massachusetts Press. Pp. 43–58.

Hebrew Immigrant Aid Society (HIAS). 1991. *Annual Statistics 1979–1991.* New York: HIAS.

———. 1993. *Annual Statistics 1965–1993.* New York: HIAS.

———. 1995. *Annual Statistics 1965–1994.* New York: HIAS.

Horowitz, Bethamie. 1993. *The 1991 New York Jewish Population Study.* New York: United Jewish Appeal—Federation of Jewish Philanthropies of New York.

Howe, Irving. 1976. *World of Our Fathers.* New York: Bantam Books.

Hulewat, Phillis. 1981. Dynamics of the Soviet Jewish Family: Its Impact on Clinical Practice for the Jewish Family Agency. *Journal of Jewish Communal Service* 58(1):53–60.

Hyfler, Robert. 1991. When Is a Refugee No Longer a Refugee and Other Post-Resettlement Observations. *Journal of Jewish Communal Service* 67:285–288.

Ilyin, Pavel, and Mikaella Kagan. 1991. Finding a Niche in American Jewish Institutional Life—Soviet Jewish Émigré Organizations. Paper presented at the Wilstein Institute for Jewish Policy Studies Conference: Soviet Jewish Acculturation—Beyond Resettlement, Palo Alto, California.

Ingram, Judith. 1994. Zhirinovsky Blames Jews. *Lansing State Journal,* November 10: 8A.

Ivry, Joann. 1992. Paraprofessionals in Refugee Resettlement. In *Social Work with Immigrants and Refugees.* Edited by Angela Shen Ryan. New York: Haworth Press. Pp. 99–117.

Jacobs, Dan N., and Ellen Frankel-Paul, Editors. 1981. *Studies of the Third Wave: Recent Migrations of Soviet Jews to the United States.* Boulder, Colorado: Westview Press.

Jacobson, Gaynor I. 1978. Soviet Jewry: Perspectives on the "Dropout" Issue. *Journal of Jewish Communal Service* 55(1):83–89.

Kestin, Hesh. 1985. Making Cheese from Snow. *Forbes,* July 29: 90–95.

Kosmin, Barry. 1990. *The Class of 1979: The "Acculturation" of Jewish Immigrants from the Soviet Union.* New York: Council of Jewish Federations.

Kozulin, Alex, and Alex Venger. 1993. Psychological and Learning Problems of Immigrant Children from the Former Soviet Union. *Journal of Jewish Communal Service* 69:64–72.

Krautman, Jerry Allan. 1990. A Study of the Acculturation and Jewish Identity of Soviet Jews Emigrating to Los Angeles between 1972 and 1989. Master's thesis, University of Judaism.

Lipset, Seymour Martin. 1990. A Unique People in an Exceptional Country. In *American Pluralism and the Jewish Community.* Edited by Seymour Martin Lipset. New Brunswick, New Jersey: Transaction. Pp. 3–29.

Littman, Mark. 1992. *Monthly Data Report for September 1992.* Washington, D.C.: Office of Refugee Resettlement.

Lubin, Nancy. 1985. Small Business Owners. In *New Lives: The Adjustment of Soviet Jewish Immigrants in the United States and Israel.* Edited by Rita J. Simon. Lexington, Massachusetts: Lexington Books. Pp. 151–164.

Mangiafico, Luciano. 1988. *Contemporary American Immigrants: Patterns of Filipino, Korean, and Chinese Settlement in the United States.* New York: Praeger.

Markowitz, Fran. 1988. Jewish in the USSR, Russian in the USA. In *Persistence and Flexibility: Anthropological Perspectives on the American Jewish Experience.* Edited by Walter P. Zenner. Albany, New York: SUNY Press. Pp. 79–95.

———. 1991. The Not Lost Generation: Family Dynamics and Ethnic Identity among Soviet Adolescent Immigrants in the 1970s. Paper presented at the Wilstein Institute for Jewish Policy Studies Conference, Soviet Jewish Acculturation—Beyond Resettlement, Palo Alto, California.

———. 1993. *A Community in Spite of Itself: Soviet Jewish Émigrés in New York.* Washington, D.C.: Smithsonian Institution Press.

———. 1994. Family Dynamics and the Teenage Immigrant: Creating the Self through the Parents' Image. *Adolescence* 29(113):151–161.

Mindel, Charles H., Robert W. Habenstein, and Roosevelt Wright, Jr. 1988. Family Lifestyles of America's Ethnic Minorities: An Introduction. In *Ethnic Families in America: Patterns and Variations, 3rd Edition.* New York: Elsevier. Pp. 1–14.

New York City Public Schools. 1991. Test Scores of Recent Immigrants and Other Students, Grades 3–12. Mimeographed.

Noonan, Leo. 1988. Russians Go Republican. *The Jewish Journal,* November 18–24:31.

Orbach, Alexander. 1980. The Jewish of Soviet-Jewish Culture: Historical Considerations. *Journal of Jewish Communal Service* 57(3):145–153.

Office of Refugee Resettlement (ORR). 1987. *Report to the Congress: Refugee Resettlement Program.* Washington, D.C.

———. 1990. *Report to the Congress: Refugee Resettlement Program.* Washington, D.C.

———. 1991. *Report to the Congress: Refugee Resettlement Program.* Washington, D.C.

———. 1992. *Report to the Congress: Refugee Resettlement Program.* Washington, D.C.

———. 1993. *Report to the Congress: Refugee Resettlement Program.* Washington, D.C.

Orleck, Annalise. 1987. The Soviet Jews: Life in Brighton Beach, Brooklyn. In *New Immigrants in New York.* Edited by Nancy Foner. New York: Columbia University Press. Pp. 273–304.

Panish, Paul. 1981. *Exit Visa.* New York: McCann and Geoghegan.

Portes, Alejandro, and Rubén Rumbaut. 1990. *Immigrant America: A Portrait.* Berkeley: University of California Press.

Rischin, Moses. 1962. *The Promised City.* Cambridge: Harvard University Press.

Ruby, Walter. 1993. Russian Jews in America. *Jewish World,* April 2–8:16–19.

Rumbaut, Rubén. 1989. The Structure of Refuge: Southeast Asian Refugees in the United States, 1975–1985. *International Review of Comparative Public Policy* 1:97–129.

Russell, Raymond. 1985. *Sharing Ownership in the Workplace.* Albany, New York: SUNY Press.

Schiff, Alvin I. 1980. Language, Culture and the Jewish Acculturation of Soviet Jewish Emigrés. *Journal of Jewish Communal Service* 57(1):44–49.

Schwartz, Larry R. 1980. Soviet Jewish Resettlement: Operationalizing Jewish Consciousness Raising. *Journal of Jewish Communal Service* 57(1):50–55.

Shlapentokh, Vladimir. 1984. *Love, Marriage, and Friendship in the Soviet Union: Ideals and Practices.* New York: Praeger.

Simon, Rita J. 1983. Refugee Families' Adjustment and Aspirations: A Comparison of Soviet Jewish and Vietnamese Immigrants. *Ethnic and Racial Studies* 6(4):492–504.

———, Editor. 1985a. *New Lives: The Adjustment of Soviet Jewish Immigrants in the United States and Israel.* Lexington, Massachusetts: Lexington Books.

———. 1985b. Soviet Jews. In *Refugees in the United States.* Edited by David W. Haines. Westport, Connecticut: Greenwood Press. Pp. 181–193.

Simon, Rita J., and Melanie Brooks. 1983. Soviet Jewish Immigrants' Adjustment in Four United States Cities. *Journal of Jewish Communal Service* 60(1):56–64.

Simon, Rita J., Louise Shelly, and Paul Schneiderman. 1986. Social and Economic Adjustment of Soviet Jewish Women in the United States. In *International Migra-*

tion: The Female Experience. Edited by Rita Simon and Caroline Brettell. Totowa, New Jersey: Rowman and Allenheld. Pp. 76–94.

Tress, Madeleine. 1991. United States Policy toward Soviet Emigration. *Migration* 3/4 (11/12):93–106.

————. 1994. Research Note: The Soviet-Jewish Refugee Populations in Germany and the United States Compared. New York: HIAS.

Tress, Madeleine, and Deborah Bernick. 1992. New Voices: The Integration of Soviet Emigrés and Their Organizations into the Jewish Communal World. New York: Council of Jewish Federations.

U.S. Bureau of the Census. 1983. *1980 Census of Population, Detailed Population Characteristics,* Part 6, California Section 1. Washington, D.C.

————. 1984. *Statistical Abstract of the United States.* Washington, D.C.

————. 1993. *1990 Census of Population, Detailed Population Characteristics.* Washington, D.C.

Wirth, Louis. 1928. *The Ghetto Chicago.* Chicago: University of Chicago Press.

Woo, Elaine. 1989. Anticipated Reunion Turns into a Nightmare for Soviet Emigre. *Los Angeles Times,* November 24:B1, B12.

Chapter 14

Vietnamese

NGUYEN MANH HUNG AND
DAVID W. HAINES

Refugees from Vietnam constitute the second largest group of people ever formally accepted as refugees by the United States. Like the Cubans—the largest group—they play a major part in the history of the cold war. Their status as refugees from communism, and from Communist countries that the United States has directly confronted, is key to their history. For both Cuba and Vietnam, cold war–based conflicts have been particularly personal, either through extensive economic sanctions and abortive military action with the Cubans or through direct military involvement, withdrawal, and subsequent economic sanctions with the Vietnamese. The resettlement of refugees from both countries has thus been both a major humanitarian effort and an important political mechanism for showing continuing support to anti-Communist elements in both societies.

By the mid-1990s, formal support for accepting refugees from both countries was winding down. The number of refugees from Vietnam was still significant, but most were arriving through the Orderly Departure Program and involved two populations of particular importance to the United States: Amerasian children and reeducation camp survivors. In particular, 1994 was an important milestone for refugees from both Vietnam and Cuba. For Vietnam, the lifting of the trade embargo raised further possibilities for interaction with the home country; for Cuba, the United States discontinued its long-standing practice of automatically granting refugee status to those fleeing from Cuba and instead determined to classify them as a special kind of immigrant to be handled through formal processing in Cuba.

The movement of refugees from Vietnam has been extensive, complicated, and often dramatic. Refugees have come from a variety of social, religious, and ethnic backgrounds. Many were well educated and familiar with American and Western society; others were minimally educated and rural in origin. Some were government officials, military officers, businessmen, doctors, and teachers; others were farmers, fishers, and common soldiers. Many were swept up in a mass exodus as the Republic of Vietnam crumbled in April 1975; others left in later years through harrowing boat escapes; yet others came out in the relative safety of an orderly departure program, but after years of confinement in so-called reeducation camps. Some were able to bring family members with them or gradually reconstruct their families over time; others had to face a difficult adjustment to an alien society alone. For all, however, the loss of homeland and the ordeals of adapting to a rapidly changing new society remain acute despite some remarkable successes in surviving and adapting to a new life in America. They all have, as James Freeman (1989) aptly entitled his collection of Vietnamese refugees' stories, "hearts of sorrow."

This chapter focuses on these Vietnamese refugees, their origins, the factors that underlay their exodus, their journey to the United States, and their experience adapting to American society. The chapter begins with a brief status report on a group that has rapidly become one of America's largest Asian-origin populations and then turns to the history of this major group of American newcomers.

VIETNAMESE-AMERICANS IN THE 1990S

With the great influx of refugees in the second half of the 1970s, it was quickly clear that the Vietnamese would become a major segment of America's Asian-origin population. By the time of the 1980 census, they were already the sixth largest Asian-origin group (U.S. Bureau of the Census 1983), and the estimates were that they would be the fourth largest by 1985 (Gardner, Robey, and Smith 1985:5). Like most other Asian-origin populations (except Asian Indians), they were concentrated on the West Coast, although they were less concentrated there than other groups, and had a sizable representation in southern states where other Asian-origin groups were noticeably absent. The Vietnamese refugees were different in many ways from the established Asian-origin groups, with a much lower average age, much larger households, and lower educational levels. Compared with other Asian-origin groups, they were also much more frequently below the poverty line in terms of household income, though much of this reflected the recency of their arrival.

The early snapshot of Vietnamese refugee adaptation provided by the 1980 census showed an important new Asian-origin population that shared some of the characteristics that had made other Asian-origin groups relatively successful in recent American history but also a population that might face additional difficulties. By the time of the 1990 census, the expectations about increased size had been realized, with Vietnamese then over 600,000,[1] with particular concentration in California (see Table 14.1). Comparative information continued to suggest that despite similarities with other Asian-origin groups, particularly others who were arriving as immigrants, relatively large household size and

Table 14.1
Vietnamese by Selected States, 1990

State	Vietnamese Population	% of Total
California	280,223	45.60%
Texas	69,634	11.33%
Virginia	20,693	3.37%
Washington	18,696	3.04%
Louisiana	17,598	2.86%
Florida	16,346	2.66%
Pennsylvania	15,887	2.59%
Massachusetts	15,449	2.51%
New York	15,555	2.53%
Illinois	10,309	1.68%
Total: Top 10 States	480,390	78.17%
Total: United States	614,547	100.00%

Note: Ethnicity is self-assessed.
Source: U.S. Bureau of the Census 1992.

some limitations in education and English-language competence posed continuing problems. However, the data also indicated the relative advantage that Vietnamese had over other Southeast Asian refugee groups. This confirmed what virtually all research since 1975 had indicated about the relatively high educational levels of Vietnamese and their relative economic success in the United States compared with refugees from Cambodia and Laos (e.g., Gordon 1989b; Dunning and Greenbaum 1982; Caplan, Whitmore, and Bui 1985; Aames et al. 1977; Kim and Nicassio 1980; Rumbaut 1989).

By the time 20 years had passed since the fall of Saigon, the virtual end of Vietnamese refugee resettlement in the United States had thus left a sizable new Asian-origin population that shared much of the demographic profile of other Asian immigrants, particularly in settlement patterns and a rapid rise in business ownership (O'Hare 1992:37), appeared relatively well advantaged compared with other Southeast Asian refugee groups, and was progressing rapidly in adjusting to American society—although that process was clearly far from complete. The Vietnamese refugee population was also one that had emerged in the public media and in a broad range of research as one with some distinctive features. Three merit particular notice.

First, Vietnamese refugees had taken the task of adapting to American society very seriously, both individually and as a community. "Success" and the hard work needed to achieve it were staples of the Vietnamese refugee experience in America and were widely noted in the academic and popular press. That focus on success yielded some startling individual success stories within the first decade of resettlement: a concert violist, the first West Point female cadet, an astronaut, and some impressive entrepreneurs. Perhaps more important, much of that effort toward success was directed at education. Vietnamese valedictorians were common and pointedly lauded for their success. Vietnamese students flooded colleges and universities, with a strong emphasis on science and engineering where the prospects for a return on effort were likely to be highest.

Second, the emphases on success and education were wound into the core institution of Vietnamese life: the family. Nathan Caplan, John Whitmore, and their colleagues have emphasized the interlinked importance of family and education among Southeast Asian refugees (Caplan, Whitmore, and Bui 1985; Whitmore, Trautmann, and Caplan 1989; Caplan, Choy, and Whitmore 1991). Based on some of the best available survey data, they have identified the value of education as a pervasive cultural value that affects Southeast Asian refugees of all classes. Although they argue that this linkage exists for all Southeast Asian refugees, there is little argument that, if anything, it is most pervasive among the Vietnamese who, unlike those from Cambodia and Laos, have for millennia absorbed the classic East Asian emphasis on the value—even moral imperative—of education.

Third, as with America's other largest formal refugee group, the Cubans, the Vietnamese refugees have been highly political. Despite their commitment to achieving success in America and on American terms, they were quick to raise objections when they perceived inaccurate portrayals of Vietnam and of the Vietnam War (Nguyen Manh Hung 1984a, 1984b). In the 1980s, the release of *Vietnam: A Television History* was particularly painful to them since it raised concern among Vietnamese parents about negative stereotypes of the Vietnam War that were being used in educational situations. With losses in the war so much more severe than those of majority Americans, it was not possible for the Vietnamese to accept the dismissive way in which the Republic of Vietnam was often treated by the American media. A decade later in the 1990s, the increasing frequency of return visits to Vietnam and the increased opportunity for economic interaction represented by the end of the trade embargo raised anew the dilemmas of being in exile by virtue of political stands taken in the increasingly distant past.

By the mid-1990s, after 20 years of refugee exodus and resettlement, the Vietnamese were thus the second largest political refugee group ever formally accepted for resettlement in America, a major component of America's Asian-origin population, a group with both impressive successes and continuing problems in adjustment, and a people who emphasized the importance of success, were strongly family oriented, and had continuing political uneasiness (and sometimes fractiousness) about their status as exiles and their relationship with a changing—but still Communist—homeland. A fuller understanding of their experience hinges on a review of the political history of Vietnam, the patterns of their escape and transit to the United States, and the details of their encounter with a new society.

THE VIETNAMESE REFUGEES: WHO ARE THEY?

The Vietnamese refugees are the result—the fallout—of the Vietnam War. They came halfway around the world from a very old civilization to a very young country. Vietnamese think of themselves as descendants of the mythical King Hung, who founded the country more than 4,000 years ago. Recorded history traces the establishment of the kingdom of Nam Viet, a small country in the south of China, to the year 208 B.C. The over 2,000 years of Vietnam's subsequent history have been ones of continuous resistance to foreign domination and expansion to the south. In 111 B.C., China annexed Vietnam and ruled it for more than a thousand years. Although China succeeded in leaving a lasting cultural influence on Vietnamese society, the Vietnamese still retained their own distinct cultural and political identities. Chinese rule was interrupted by revolts, and in A.D 939, Vietnam finally succeeded in regaining its independence. In the thirteenth century, after defeating the invading armies of Kublai Khan, the Vietnamese began to move southward. They annexed the kingdom of Champa in 1471 and gained control over the Mekong Delta by the mideighteenth century. From a small country based in the Red River Delta, the location of Hanoi, Vietnam had expanded to a length of 1,300 miles from north to south, although only 100 miles wide at its narrowest in central Vietnam, near the former border between the northern and southern parts of the country.

As the European powers began their colonial expansion in Asia, Vietnam came under the sway of the French. The French established their first outposts in 1858 in Tourane (now Da Nang) and 1859 in Saigon. The inroads continued, and 25 years later in 1884, France was able to force the Vietnamese emperor to acknowledge French control of the entire country.[2] That control was imposed very differently in the north, central, and south of the country, amplifying regional differences that remain significant to this day. Although the court succumbed to French pressure, resistance against French rule, led by scholar-patriots and members of the imperial family, continued. Throughout the late nineteenth century, resistance was traditionalist with an emphasis on the pre-French political and cultural structure and the need to return to it. In the early twentieth century, spurred by Japanese military victory in the Russo-Japanese war of 1904–1905, more change-oriented opposition to the French developed under the leadership of Phan Boi Chau and Phan Chu Trinh.

The first formal, modern nationalist party, the Viet Nam Quoc Dan Dang (VNQDD), emerged in the 1920s. The aborted uprising at Yen Bay in 1930, a critical milestone in Vietnamese political history, led to the execution of its leaders and thus to its demise as the dominant anti-French force. It was into this vacuum that the Indochinese Communist Party (ICP) moved. As the French hold on Vietnam weakened in the early stages of World War II, the ICP in 1941 formed a broader resistance organization: the Viet Nam Doc Lap Dong Minh Hoi (Vietnam Independence League), known as the Viet Minh. In March 1945, Japanese forces overthrew the French colonial government in Vietnam and encouraged Emperor Bao Dai to declare Vietnam independent from France, which he did. Six months later, Japan surrendered to the Allies, and Viet Minh partisans seized their opportunity, took control of Hanoi, and set up a provisional government with Ho Chi Minh as president. Emperor Bao Dai abdicated in favor of the new government and was in turn immediately appointed its supreme adviser. In the South, government authority was exercised through the Provisional Executive Committee of the South, a coalition of various competing nationalist groups. Viet Minh control over this committee, unlike the situation in the North, remained precarious.

On September 12, 1945, British forces arrived in Saigon to disarm the Japanese. They permitted the French to stage a coup against the Committee of the South and to reestablish French control of the South before the British departed in January 1946. At roughly the same time, Chinese troops moved into the North to disarm the Japanese. With them came the leaders of two other organizations (the VNQDD and the Viet Nam Cach Menh Dong Minh Hoi—Vietnam Revolutionary League) that had organized the fight against French colonialism from their bases in China. Joining forces with their comrades at home, they demanded a share of government leadership. The ICP was officially dissolved, and a new coalition government was formed to cope with the return of the French. In March 1946, the new government (headed by Ho Chi Minh) signed an agreement with France, giving France unhampered access to North Vietnam in return for French recognition of Vietnam as ''a free state . . . belonging to the Indochinese Federation and to the French Union.'' The nationalists immediately accused the Communists of being too compromising on Vietnam's independence. The Communists used the breathing spell given by this agreement to move against their opposition. Caught between the Communists and the French, prominent nationalist leaders, one by one, left the government and went into self-imposed exile. In December 1946, the French provoked an incident in Hanoi to move against the Viet Minh. The colonial war began.

After the Chinese Communists took control of mainland China, the Viet Minh openly acknowledged its Communist ties. The ICP was reconstituted as the Vietnam Workers' Party, and the Democratic Republic of Vietnam established diplomatic relations with China and Russia. At the same time, the French, unable to defeat the Viet Minh on the battlefield, attempted a political solution. They agreed to the return of ex-Emperor Bao Dai who, as ''head of state,'' would have authority over the internal affairs of a unified Vietnam, while France still retained control over foreign relations and defense. France now could claim that it was at the front line of the cold war, helping a nationalist government in its struggle against communism. The United States moved to accord diplomatic recognition to the Bao Dai government and increased its financial support to the French military effort in Vietnam. The colonial war in Vietnam took on new dimensions: communism versus nationalism and totalitarianism versus democracy.

The war lasted eight years. In 1954, after the French were defeated at Dien Bien Phu, an international agreement ending the Vietnam War was signed in Geneva. Vietnam was divided at the seventeenth parallel; the North came under the control of the Communists, and the South belonged to the nationalists. The Final Declaration, which the United States and the Bao Dai government refused to sign, provided for national elections to be held in 1956 to reunify the country. In June, a new set of agreements was signed between France and Vietnam, providing the basis for genuine independence. Ngo Dinh Diem was appointed prime minister with full power but returned from exile to find South Vietnam in a state of near chaos. He began to take control of the armed forces, arranged for the withdrawal of French troops, and made significant strides toward reintegrating the country. In 1956, a new constitution was proclaimed, and Diem was subsequently elected president of the Republic of Vietnam. Among other accomplishments, his government was able to resettle nearly a million refugees who fled south from the Communist regime in the North. Many of these same people were among those who left Vietnam 20 years later when Saigon fell to that same Communist regime.

The elections originally planned for 1956 to reunify the country, as specified by the Geneva Final Declaration, did not take place. The result was renewed war. In 1959, the first Republic of Vietnam government post was attacked by guerrillas. In 1960, the National Front for the Liberation of South Vietnam (NFLSVN) was formed to lead the war against the government. The Front was tightly controlled by the Vietnam Worker's Party through its Central Office for South Viet Nam (COSVN). The United States was committed to help Diem mount a counterinsurgency campaign against the rebels. In 1962, the U.S. Military Assistance Command was established, and antiguerrilla special forces were sent to Vietnam. As the war progressed, Diem became increasingly authoritarian and was finally overthrown in 1963 by the military in a coup d'état, to which the United States acquiesced. The 1963 coup was followed by a period of political instability and military setbacks in South Vietnam. To stop this deterioration, the United States decided to send troops to South Vietnam and began to bomb North Vietnam. China and Russia, in turn, poured massive aid into North Vietnam, and the Socialist Republic of Vietnam increased its infiltration into South Vietnam. The war escalated. On Tet (the lunar New Year) in 1968, the Front launched a general offensive in several major cities. It was a costly campaign to the Front in terms of human lives, but it turned out to be a major political victory for them. The United States, knowing it could not win a quick military victory, decided to disengage. Troop withdrawal, "Vietnamization," and diplomatic negotiation began. In 1973, a cease-fire agreement was concluded in Paris. It provided for the total withdrawal of U.S. combat forces but not for the withdrawal of North Vietnamese forces. U.S. aid to South Vietnam was subsequently reduced, and Vietnamization could thus not proceed as originally planned. By 1975, the correlation of forces was utterly in favor of the Communists. Under the probing attack of Communist forces, President Thieu decided to redeploy South Vietnamese forces to defensible areas away from Central Vietnam. The withdrawal, originally from Pleiku and then from Hue, turned into a rout.

As Communist forces advanced toward Saigon, an American-organized evacuation was hastily implemented. The operation was able to evacuate approximately 130,000 Vietnamese but did not succeed in bringing out many Vietnamese who would be endangered by a Communist victory.[3] Hundreds of thousands of Vietnamese who grew up with the idea that they were fighting for a good cause alongside a committed ally were left to face an uncertain future. Within months after the Communist victory, that future became a more certain one: banishment from employment, loss of property, denial of access to education for children, and imprisonment in "reeducation" camps. Many of those left behind to this fate would eventually escape, but the path would be a long, painful, and often deadly one.

WHY DID THEY LEAVE?

Vietnamese refugees left their homeland for a variety of reasons. In 1975, most left because of the fear of communism and their fate under the new regime: possible imprisonment or even execution, and expected loss of social status and political freedom. Those leaving in later years had a different mix of reasons. Ethnic Chinese, for example, left because of racial and economic discrimination; some were even forced or "asked" to leave by a government worried that they would become a fifth column for Chinese action against Vietnam. These ethnic Chinese included those who had lived in North Vietnam for generations and those who clearly belonged to the working class. Religious leaders and their followers (both Catholics and Buddhists) left to avoid religious discrimination and persecution. Some left in panic, particularly in 1975; others left because life had become hard and unbearable to them and held no future for their children. It became common for Vietnamese parents to sacrifice everything in order to enable their children to escape the country, which helps explain why children and young people were such a major segment of those escaping by boat in the late 1970s.

Although economic hardship became one of the reasons for escape, it was rarely the root or sole cause for risking the dangers of departure.[4] Many people, especially those who were released from reeducation camps and those who were associated with the former government or with the American war efforts, suffered severe discrimination, and that discrimination had economic consequences. They did not get sufficient rations for necessities from government stores; they could not get jobs; their children were deprived of the opportunity to enter colleges and universities; and they were forced to go to the new economic zones, where their life became so hopeless that many came back to the cities to lead an illegal, barely subsistent life. The economic hardships they endured were thus very much the result of discrimination on political and social grounds. Such discrimination, and its often severe economic consequences, continued to fuel the refugee exodus that was at its peak in the late 1970s and continued sporadically through the 1980s. Conflict and warfare in Indochina (for example, the Sino-Vietnamese conflict and border war of 1979, the Cambodian invasion of 1979), political repression, worsening general economic and social conditions, and tales of a good life abroad have also been factors in that exodus.

THE FLOW OF REFUGEES FROM VIETNAM

By 1995, the total number of Indochinese refugees had amounted to nearly 2 million—about half of whom eventually came to the United States. Approximately 200,000 left during 1975 itself, and there were scattered escapes in the two years after that. The most extensive exodus, however, took place between March 1978, when the Vietnamese government began to enforce its socialist economic policy, particularly against ethnic Chinese who resided in Cholon (Saigon's sister city), and July 1979, when, under international pressure at the United Nations Geneva Conference on Indochinese Refugees, the Vietnamese government pledged to take "firm and effective measures" to stop the flow of refugees for a "reasonable period."[5] In order to understand this massive exodus, it is necessary to distinguish four general types of exodus from Vietnam, all of which had their own unique features. There have been first-wave refugees, second-wave refugees, escapees, and orderly departures.

The first-wave refugees left Vietnam during the spring of 1975 as Communist forces advanced toward Saigon and the United States began to airlift its nonessential employees out of Vietnam. This evacuation was organized by the U.S. government. Leaving before April 29 were Vietnamese dependents of U.S. servicemen and government workers,[6] people who worked for foreign companies and were not within draft age, people with connections to the Americans who organized the airlift, those sponsored by Vietnamese-Americans already living in the United States, and those who could talk or bribe their way into the U.S. processing center at Tan Son Nhat airport just outside of Saigon. Leaving in panic on April 29 itself, the day when U.S. military and civilian personnel were requested to leave within 24 hours, were those who could arrange to be at one of several designated locations in the city, could get into the American embassy itself, or could reach waiting barges on the Saigon River.

The first-wave refugees who left before April 29 (and a few who left on that date) boarded planes at Tan Son Nhat airport and were flown to Clark Air Base in the Philippines. Those who left on April 29 were flown by helicopters or taken by barges to waiting naval ships that carried them to Subic Bay in the Philippines. From the Philippines, refugees were flown to Guam and then to one of four refugee camps in the United States (Camp Pendleton in California, Fort Chaffee in Arkansas, Eglin Air Base in Florida, and Fort Indiantown Gap in Pennsylvania), where they waited for security clearance and sponsors to get them out of camps. Although this evacuation was in many respects admirably executed, it failed in its initial, prime objective of evacuating all Vietnamese whose lives would be endangered by the Communist takeover.

The second-wave refugees left Vietnam during the 1978-1979 period, at the height of the Sino-Vietnamese conflict. Resenting ethnic Chinese control of private business in South Vietnam, and fearing the possibility of a Chinese fifth column in Vietnam, the Vietnamese government clamped down on Chinese in business and forced them to leave the country. This evacuation was organized—although unofficially—by the Vietnamese authorities and was therefore labeled by refugees as ''unofficial departure.'' People who wanted to go had to register and pay in gold for a place on a boat. This was done through an intermediary called the organizer. When all the arrangements were made, they were told to assemble at a designated location, where they were brought to the waiting boat. Security agents would then escort their boat out of Vietnam's territorial waters. Second-wave refugees were predominantly ethnic Chinese, about 250,000 of whom went to China. But there were many ethnic Vietnamese who were able to buy false papers and register themselves as Chinese for the purpose of ''unofficial departure.''

The escapees, on the other hand, plotted their own departures. They were a continuing factor from 1975 on. Although a few took the land road through Kampuchea into Thailand, the majority took to the sea. They pooled resources to buy boats and gasoline for their trip; recruited a navigator (usually a former navy man); forged their papers; bribed local security agents; and left clandestinely, usually in the darkness of night, for the sea in small, unsafe boats. Their departure was the riskiest, and if caught by the authorities, they would be imprisoned. Once on the high seas, they fell prey to the sea and to the pirates who roamed the Gulf of Thailand.

The combination of these two flows during the late 1970s—second-wave ''unofficial departures'' and clandestine escapees—resulted in the ''boat people'' crisis that engaged world attention and action. Except for those Chinese and Vietnamese who found a place on the few ''big boats'' and arrived promptly and safely at ports of destination, most second-wave refugees shared the same risks as the escapees once they were on the high seas. Even if they survived the angry waves, mechanical failure, the lack of food and water, multiple robberies, assaults, and rapes, they still had to suffer humiliation, mistreatment, and internment in countries of first asylum. It is estimated that half the boat people were drowned at sea or killed during their journey in search of freedom and compassion (see Grant et al. 1979; USCR 1984). Both second-wave refugees and escapees landed in countries neighboring Vietnam where they lived in makeshift camps and began a long wait to be screened for acceptance by countries willing to resettle them permanently.

The final type of exit involves the Orderly Departure Program. That program was the result of the 1979 Memorandum of Understanding between Vietnam and the United Nations High Commissioner for Refugees (UNHCR), which was endorsed by all the major resettlement countries (including the United States). The Orderly Departure Program was initially mostly for those with family ties to people already living abroad, but the United States also accepted former employees of its mission in Vietnam and other Vietnamese who were closely associated with the U.S. effort in Vietnam before 1975. Their departure was the safest way out of the country but was not always easy to arrange. Entry permits from the country of destination and exit visas from the Vietnamese government had to be obtained. The waiting period was usually long, from two to five or more years, depending on one's connections, circumstances, luck, bribery, policies of each government, and the current status of U.S./Vietnamese relations. Although the program experienced ups and downs, it quickly became a major channel for Vietnamese exit.[7]

In subsequent years, the Orderly Departure Program has also been the vehicle for U.S. efforts to help two particular groups of Vietnamese. First, in December 1987, the United States recognized a special responsibility for Amerasian children. The situation of these children was particularly harsh after the American withdrawal. They, and their families, were subject to both official and popular abuse. Frequently they were reduced to a tenuous life on the streets. Since that time, a significant number of Amerasian children have been brought to the United States.[8] Second, in 1989 the United States made a broad offer to resettle those who had been placed in reeducation camps. This group of Vietnamese refugees had faced years of debilitating life in the camps and severe discrimination when they were released. Facing a new life in America would be particularly difficult for them because of their age and a long backlog of health and emotional problems resulting from up to 20 years of severe deprivation, as well as a culture gap that had developed between them and family members who had preceded them to the United States.

VIETNAMESE REFUGEES IN THE UNITED STATES

By 1995, the United States had received well over a million refugees from Indochina. Vietnamese refugees accounted for about two thirds of that total by nationality. In addition, some 200,000 Vietnamese arrived as immigrants, most through the Orderly Departure Program (ODP) (see Table 14.2). These refugees are a mixed group in terms of their background and in terms of their stage of resettlement. A large number of Vietnamese refugees are professionals, graduated from major universities and military academies in Europe and North America, and are familiar with the Western way of life. Others come from rural areas, have a much more traditional outlook, and lack much experience with urban, Westernized society. The initial, first-wave refugees tended to be more urban and professional in background, better educated, and more fluent in English;

Table 14.2
Vietnamese Arrivals by Fiscal Year

Year	Refugees	Immigrants	Total
1975	125,000	3,039	128,039
1976	3,200	4,230	7,430
1977	1,900	4,629	6,529
1978	11,100	1,890	12,990
1979	44,500	6,365	50,865
1980	95,200	4,104	99,304
1981	86,100	1,714	87,814
1982	42,600	2,452	45,052
1983	22,819	2,790	25,609
1984	24,856	4,878	29,734
1985	25,222	4,661	29,883
1986	21,700	5,514	27,214
1987	19,656	3,170	22,826
1988	17,571	3,922	21,493
1989	21,924	15,251	37,175
1990	27,796	27,677	55,473
1991	28,385	32,165	60,550
1992	26,856	40,213	67,069
1993	31,405	22,342	53,747
1994	34,110	10,400	44,510
Total	711,900	201,406	913,306

Notes: Immigrants include Amerasians and many of those arriving through the ODP. Chinese from Vietnam are included.

Sources: Gordon (1987) for refugees and immigrants through 1982; ORR (1995) for refugees thereafter; annual statistical yearbooks of the U.S. Immigration and Naturalization Service for arriving immigrants thereafter.

those coming later tended to be more frequently ethnic Chinese, more often from rural backgrounds, with lower English proficiency, and with fewer skills directly transferrable to an industrialized economy. Perhaps as important as their higher skill levels, earlier arrivals have had a longer time to adjust to the United States, faced better economic conditions on arrival in the United States, and survived a relatively smooth escape from Vietnam that limited at least their physical ordeal. Those coming later as boat refugees arrived as the United States was entering a serious recession in the early 1980s, bore the aftereffects of a dangerous escape and frequent long periods in camps, and faced a society whose compassion toward refugees was contracting. Those arriving recently, particularly such groups as Amerasians and reeducation camp survivors, face not only one of America's periodic surges of antiimmigrant sentiment but also a 20-year history of severe discrimination in their home country that has left both emotional and physical scars.

Vietnamese refugees have resettled in every state and many territories of the United States. Despite the initial government attempt to disperse them throughout the country, secondary migration has led to heavy concentration of refugees in a few states. By 1980, over two thirds of Indochinese refugees were living in only nine states (California, Illinois, Louisiana, Minnesota, Oregon, Pennsylvania, Texas, Virginia, and Washington). California had a third of the refugees, followed by Texas (10 percent) and Washington (4 percent). By 1990, the California figure had risen to nearly half (45 percent). California has been the major magnet for secondary migration of Vietnamese refugees, but it has not been the only one. Secondary migration has been prompted by a variety of causes that may create geographical clusters: climate, employment opportunities, reunification with relatives, accessibility to social services, and the pull of established ethnic communities. For example, Vietnamese refugees in Louisiana are predominantly Catholic, and the nation's capital area (including Washington, D.C., northern Virginia, and suburban Maryland) has a larger number of professionals working for international organizations and for federal and local governments. California and Texas have a large number of entertainers, writers, journalists, English as a Second Language teachers, and blue-collar workers. Ethnic Chinese have tended to concentrate in California and New York where they work in restaurants, grocery stores, retail sales, and commercial real estate. Southern California, with its warm climate, large population of Vietnamese refugees, thriving Vietnamese business community along Bolsa Avenue, major Vietnamese-language newspapers, and the possibility of leading a social life similar to that at home, has been called by Vietnamese "the refugees' capital."

The concentration of Vietnamese refugees in particular areas is significant (see Table 14.3) and has consequences. Large numbers of new arrivals, for example, may strain local resources. Geographic concentration also provides the basis for the development of functioning ethnic enclaves that have both positive and negative aspects. On the positive side, such enclaves provide uprooted refugees with a sense of identity and belonging. The enclave is a particularly effective mechanism for facilitating the exchange of information and mutual help, thereby aiding the resettlement process, reducing anxiety and mental distress, and providing vital employment and business-related information. The enclave has important economic functions in nurturing ethnic businesses by providing both an ethnic and "tourist" clientele. The disadvantaged who cannot function effectively in mainstream American society may also find a protective, navigable environment within the enclave. On the negative side, the formation and persistence of ethnic enclaves may lead to the development of a social ghetto, which provides a source of instability, ethnic conflict, and a shelter for criminals. This has largely been avoided in the Vietnamese experience in Amer-

Table 14.3
Vietnamese by Selected Urban Areas, 1990

Urban Area	Vietnamese Population	% of Total
Atlanta	5,541	0.90%
Boston	9,476	1.54%
Chicago	7,648	1.24%
Dallas/Ft. Worth	19,380	3.15%
Denver	5,867	0.95%
Houston	32,492	5.29%
Los Angeles	136,586	22.23%
Minneapolis/St. Paul	7,676	1.25%
New Orleans	11,274	1.83%
New York	14,967	2.44%
Philadelphia	10,061	1.64%
Portland/Vancouver	8,082	1.32%
Riverside/San Bernardino	7,586	1.23%
Sacramento	9,464	1.54%
San Diego	21,004	3.42%
San Francisco/Oakland	28,760	4.68%
San Jose	54,115	8.81%
Seattle	12,516	2.04%
Stockton	6,756	1.10%
Washington, D.C.	22,976	3.74%
Total: 20 Urban Areas	432,227	70.33%
Total: United States	614,547	

Notes: Ethnicity is self-assessed. Urban areas follow census definitions. Percentages do not add up exactly because of rounding.

Source: U.S. Bureau of the Census 1992.

ica, but antiimmigrant sentiments in America have often forced immigrant groups in on themselves, exacerbating such negative aspects of ethnic enclaves.

Economically, Vietnamese refugees have generally made a rapid adjustment to American society. Although persistent dependence on income support is still found among the youngest and the oldest refugees, and among those with little education and little English-language competence, labor force participation and employment rates of Vietnamese refugees do improve over time. The experience of early arrivals was particularly impressive. By 1982, those arriving from 1975 to 1977 were in the labor force at a higher rate than the general U.S. population:

72.1 percent for those who entered the United States in 1975 and 74.3 percent for those who entered the United States in 1976–1977, compared to 64.1 percent for the general U.S. population (ORR 1983). An extensive 1980 survey (Dunning and Greenbaum 1982; Dunning 1989) showed the predictable positive correlations between labor force participation, on the one hand, and the level of education, use of English, and length of residence of the refugees, on the other.

The experience of later arrivals has not been as uniformly positive but compares favorably with other recent arrivals to the United States. Employment continues to increase over time in the United States, and reliance on public support declines. Families continue to pool the returns from low-wage jobs, thus transforming them into workable household incomes. When possible, refugees move into jobs that pay better, even though these jobs are usually also relatively low status. Jobs in the electrical and electronic industries and in the machine trades are a particularly common option, but even such dangerous jobs as meat-packing (Stull, Broadway, and Erickson 1992) have attracted Vietnamese refugees because of their increased wages. Many other refugees have turned to setting up their own businesses. Bureau of the Census surveys of minority-owned businesses in the 1980s, for example, show a threefold increase in the number of Vietnamese businesses per 1,000 Vietnamese refugees from 1982 to 1987 (O'Hare 1992:37). Most of these have been family businesses that cater principally to ethnic clients (restaurants, laundries, grocery stores, hair salons, and tailor shops). Some Vietnamese have become involved in car dealerships, insurance, sales, and real estate; others have opened medical and dental offices; a few are engaged in wholesale, import-export, and manufacturing.

Behind an appearance of economic success, problems remain. Some Vietnamese refugees have difficulty in finding any jobs; many have difficulty finding good jobs. The U.S. economy is being restructured in ways that frequently eliminate the semiskilled manual jobs that would be most advantageous for a population with limited language skills. The option of setting up a business, even with the cost savings that result from the labor of family members, remains a risky proposition. The initial economic success of the Vietnamese refugees may thus have built-in limits. Upward mobility may be, as it has been for other immigrants at other times, effectively blocked (Gold and Kibria 1993; Haines 1987).

Even when economic progress is adequate, other problems endure. The situation of middle-aged and older refugees who were most active in the war and the government of the Republic of Vietnam deserves particular note. They do not appear to have fared as well in social and psychological adjustment as in economic terms. Most have not made a conscious effort to integrate themselves into American society, join professional organizations only when they have to, and infrequently interact socially with other Americans. Their social friends are predominantly Vietnamese. Even those with good jobs in mainstream American society lead a dual life—one in the office among their American coworkers and another at home and during off-hours among their Vietnamese compatriots. This phenomenon is prevalent especially among the educated and Westernized elements, for they have felt not only a loss of status but also a loss of motivation. Two early surveys of Vietnamese refugees provide useful information. One (Dunning and Greenbaum 1982) indicated that although 13 percent of Vietnamese refugees interviewed saw an improvement in their lives, about two thirds rated their lives as less satisfying than they had been in Vietnam. This discrepancy between economic success and psychological well-being is also supported by a survey of Vietnamese living in the southern Gulf Coast and in northern California (Starr et al. 1979; Roberts and Starr 1989). The findings show that economic success and psychological well-being are not consistently related among Vietnamese refugees and that the refugees who had greater educational attainment, higher social status, greater English proficiency, and a less traditional Vietnamese outlook—people generally thought of as better equipped for adjustment—tended to have higher incomes but also show greater strain from the process.

One important factor for these refugees is a "Vietnam syndrome" similar to the one experienced by American veterans of the Vietnam War. The syndrome causes withdrawal, a pessimistic outlook, and a negative attitude toward social participation. These refugees felt betrayed when South Vietnam was lost to the Communists and also believed that the U.S.-organized evacuation in 1975 was not actually meant to include them. They see the version of Vietnamese history prevalent in the American media and intellectual circles as distorted, unfair to them personally, and unfair to the cause in which they believed and for which they fought. They see themselves as losers and believe that there is no use in explaining the complexity of the Vietnam War to people who do not understand it or who refuse to accept their viewpoint.

This Vietnam syndrome is felt most acutely by former Vietnamese soldiers, especially by those who bore the brunt of the fighting and did not know why they had to withdraw during the last month of the war without having a chance to fight. It is also experienced by some generals who feel guilty about their performance during the last critical days of the war—and by Vietnamese who have arrived in the United States after having spent years in Communist reeducation camps. The Vietnam syndrome has often found a more active outlet among the former military than among the educated and the professionals who are doing better economically. Many of the former military, for example, have joined the various resistance movements, hoping one day to liberate Vietnam from the Communist regime. For these people, their presence in the United States is only temporary; their future is not in the United States but in a liberated Vietnam. Many of them also participate in activities against slanted histories of the Vietnam War, against human rights violations by the Hanoi government, and in commemoration of "National Shame Day" as the April 30 anniversary of the fall of Saigon is designated. Leaders of these movements know well the difficulty of their task but believe that the effort has an immediate beneficial effect in restoring a sense of self-confidence and self-respect to the refugees regarding their role in the war and their historical heritage.[9]

The situation of reeducation camp survivors is yet more difficult. Those who spent long years in the camps find it extremely difficult to adjust both to conditions in a new country and to the changing situation in Vietnam. Even reunion with relatives already resettled in the United States can be painful. Wives have become financially independent and have adopted different ways of thought and behavior. Some have even started new families after waiting for years with little hope of their husband's release. Their children were often too young when they left Vietnam to have any understanding of their father's trauma, may not have any appreciation for his political views, and often behave in ways that appear uncommunicative and disrespectful. Even with former colleagues, the experience of the camp survivors is difficult as they confront new gaps in status, financial situation, and political outlook. The trauma can be severe, leading even to suicide: Surviving the expected cruel treatment of enemies does not prepare them for the unexpected disappointment with their family and friends. For those who endure and attempt to create a new life in America—against such odds—a new kind of bravery is required.

Various other segments of the Vietnamese refugee population also face problems. The elderly, for example, often cannot compete effectively in the labor market; they usually cannot drive and thus have no independent means to get to a job, which is a particularly severe problem in southern California. Their traditional outlook and lack of English proficiency limit their ability to function effectively in the mainstream society. Although they may become more dependent on their children, their children are likely to have less and less time for them. There is little comfort in the company of their grandchildren, who tend to speak English more fluently than Vietnamese and to have a much more American outlook. For the older refugees who feel isolated in a changing family environment and in a strange world beyond the family, the need for peer support is obvious. Places of worship (such as Buddhist temples) and mutual assistance associations (such as Vietnamese senior citizens associations) can provide them with friendship and assistance. Participation in social and cultural activities of these organizations can be vital to a sense of self-worth and fortify them in their role as bearers of Vietnamese culture and tradition.

Vietnamese women have also had to adapt to changing circumstances. Many have to abandon a traditional role in the family and become wage earners—and often become the sole or primary wage earner. They may not be well prepared to cope with an unfamiliar Western world of work or with sullen husbands who find it hard to adjust simultaneously to their loss of status and to the changing role and behavior of their wives. This can cause serious tension in the family, can affect the welfare of the children, and sometimes leads to marital separation or divorce. On the whole, the Vietnamese family, which emphasizes the group over the individual, has weathered such storms of change. Vietnamese women, suggests Nazli Kibria (1990, 1993; cf. Tran and Nguyen 1994; Haines 1988), may believe that the "patriarchal" aspects of husband/wife roles need adjusting but seem to be committed to renegotiating roles without actually rupturing them. In addition, the more extended family, in which relatives live together and pool their resources, has helped many Vietnamese refugees to achieve economic self-sufficiency in a relatively short time.

If the adult refugees are faced with difficulties in their social and psychological adjustment, they can find much solace in their children. Despite the disruptions of resettlement, the temptations of a consumer society, and what many view as the poor influence of undisciplined American children, Vietnamese children are doing well in schools. Many Vietnamese have been valedictorians in their graduating classes. Others have graduated from colleges and universities and are pursuing careers in government and in the private sectors. A noticeable pattern among first-generation Vietnamese students has been their overwhelming concentration in science and engineering over the humanities. Kerry Penning (1992), for example, looked at courses of study pursued by Vietnamese in three Orange County community colleges and found Vietnamese about three times as likely to be in science, technology, and business areas as were other students. He, like others, stresses both the rationality of such an approach and the extent to which such a choice is an explicit family strategy toward enhancing the prospects of future generations. Again, it is the family that emerges as perhaps the key factor in identifying an improved future for Vietnamese in the United States and in mobilizing its members toward that goal.

BEYOND INITIAL RESETTLEMENT

The U.S. government and the voluntary agencies did a remarkable job in resettling a large influx of Vietnamese refugees into the United States in the aftermath of an unpopular war. This success was made possible by the traditional American compassion for refugees, by core features of Vietnamese society (a cohesive family structure, a capability to accommodate to change that is based on a turbulent history), and by important themes in Vietnamese culture (the need to live in harmony with nature, a high value placed on education).

Becoming economically self-sufficient has been, from the government's point of view, the immediate goal for newly arrived refugees. For most Vietnamese refugees, given some time for orientation to American society and some English-language and vocational training, this has been possible—despite a public welfare system that does not always provide an ideal combination of incentives and disincentives for beginning work at minimum-wage jobs. Many Vietnamese refugees have done much better than simple survival; others, through their children, will see a future move upward from what for now remains a bleak economic situation. As Vietnamese refugees have moved beyond the issues of minimal economic survival, they have become more active participants in a variety of American institutions, both "mainstream" and minority. Their future has become linked, sometimes in unpredictable ways, with that of other refugees, other immigrants, and other minorities. When Los Angeles exploded in race riots, for example, the Vietnamese were easily confused with other Asians, particularly the Koreans, who were the objects of much violence. Increased interaction inevitably leads to both cooperation and conflict, especially conflict between the refugees and people at the lower rungs of the social ladder who may feel their own position threatened by the newcomers. Government cannot legislate away such conflict, but civic leaders, both American and Vietnamese, and the opinion makers can at least minimize its impact by avoiding the temptation to exaggerate, distort, and stereotype.

Just as the Vietnamese became a more established part of the American scene, however, relations with the home country began changing. Increasing return visits to Vietnam by Vietnamese and by Americans, the loosening of economic restrictions within Vietnam, and the end in 1994 of the ban on economic relations between Vietnam and the United States began to make the divide between Vietnam and Vietnamese abroad less complete. One major refugee assistance organization, for example, turned its attention to economic assistance projects in Vietnam as one aspect of a broadened vision of Vietnam, and overseas Vietnamese linked together in at least some common causes. Vietnam became increasingly available to Vietnamese refugees in the United States, and the refugees became increasingly important to the Vietnamese government. An important political shift occurred. In the late 1970s and early 1980s, when the wounds of the war were still fresh and the Vietnamese occupation of Cambodia provided an opportunity for the resistance movement to develop international connections, anti-Communist activists among the refugees favored a military solution through the overthrow of the Communist regime in Vietnam. That position received considerable support from the Vietnamese refugees in the United States. However, the arrest and execution of resistance leaders who attempted to enter Vietnam from Laos, the withdrawal of Vietnamese troops from Cambodia, the reestablishment of relations between Vietnam and the Association of Southeast Asian Nations (ASEAN), and the collapse of Communist regimes in the Soviet Union and Eastern Europe all contributed to a shift away from military solutions toward political solutions. The resulting demands for human rights observation and democratization in Vietnam were effective enough that the Vietnamese government came to warn against the ''scheme of peaceful evolution.''

Nevertheless, there were significant changes in Vietnam. The government began economic renovation in 1986. It subsequently moved away from a centrally planned economy, made serious efforts to attract foreign investment, and attempted to involve overseas Vietnamese in the reconstruction of the country. By 1995 Vietnam was at peace with its neighbors, had established a liaison office in Washington, and had begun to shed much of its socialist dogma. Vietnamese refugees were divided in their response to that effort. Some advocated no cooperation with the regime until it became fully democratic and fully observant of essential human rights; others wished to cooperate in economic and technical areas to induce further change in government policy. Opponents of cooperation lost some ground as the overseas Vietnamese increased their visits to Vietnam and their financial support to relatives still in Vietnam. The visits and assistance to relatives, however, did not reflect direct support of the regime or a willingness to deal with it on a long-term basis. Although the support to relatives was about $750 million each year by middecade, the cumulative amount formally invested was less than $100 million—and even that money was devoted to trade and quick turn-around schemes rather than long-term investment. The overseas Vietnamese, more than other foreign investors, appeared to remain too skeptical about the sincerity of the regime to part with investment capital for more than a short period of time. At middecade the distance between the refugees and Vietnam had lessened, but the remaining gap was a formidable one.

NOTES

1. Published reports from the census provide two distinct ways to count Vietnamese. First is the count by country of birth (U.S. Bureau of the Census 1993b). Counts by country of birth only include those who are foreign born, thus missing: (a) children born in the United States (a considerable number); (b) children born in refugee camps (again, a considerable number); and (c) anybody else of Vietnamese extraction who might have been born outside Vietnam (presumably a very small number). The second is by self-reported ethnicity or race (U.S. Bureau of the Census 1993a). This number will include those missed by the foreign-born count and will also exclude those people from Vietnam who do not consider themselves ethnically Vietnamese (e.g., Chinese-Vietnamese who would classify themselves as "Chinese" rather than "Vietnamese"). In the text, this second, ethnic self-reporting figure is used.

2. The early French rule is portrayed vividly by Osborne (1969). Woodside's (1971) book on Vietnam and the Chinese model provides the classic introduction to the resurgent Vietnamese state during the early nineteenth century.

3. The photographs of the last helicopters leaving from the roof of the American embassy are well known. However, there were a variety of other escape routes, including earlier flights from Tan Son Nhat airport and various boats from Saigon and other harbors. Gail Kelly (1977) provides a particularly good description of the various escape routes in 1975 and the way in which this initial "wave" of Vietnamese refugees was resettled to the United States. Although many of those leaving were high-ranking military and government officials and their families, a very broad, if erratic, cross section of Vietnamese society also escaped at this time.

4. Interviews with recently arrived refugees who escaped from Vietnam after being released from "reeducation camps" about the reasons for their dangerous escape invariably provide an answer like: "We knew the chance of making it to safety was only ten percent, but we'd rather die than live with 'them.' "

5. Until spring 1978, the flow of refugees from Vietnam was about 2,000 to 5,000 per month. Mass exodus began in March 1978 (22,000), rose sharply in April (62,000), maintained that level through early 1979: May (60,000) and June (60,000) 1979. By August, however, the flow was down to 6,000. United Nations High Commissioner for

Refugees (UNHCR) data on refugee arrivals in Thailand indicate a total number of arrivals of 34,316 in 1977, doubling to 69,140 in 1978, peaking at 200,000 in 1979, and declining to 113,867 in 1980 and to 43,260 in 1981. (UNHCR figures for Thailand include both those fleeing by sea and the ''land'' people coming out from Cambodia and Laos during the same period.)

6. The term *dependents* was interpreted loosely to include not only spouse and children but also the spouse's parents, brothers, sisters, and sometimes other relatives. This made it possible for many Vietnamese who, through friendship or bribery, could pass themselves as spouses or dependents of U.S. citizens to get a place on the planes.

7. The Vietnamese government was willing to participate in the Orderly Departure Program for two main reasons: First, the plight of the boat people and international pressure during the 1978–1979 period forced Hanoi to put a tight control on clandestine escapes by boat and relax its control on legal exits. Second, Hanoi hoped a liberal emigration policy might help to improve its relations with Western nations, especially with the United States, at a time when Hanoi was diplomatically isolated because of its invasion of Cambodia.

8. See Kelly (1992) for comments on Amerasian children's lives in Vietnam; Ashabranner and Ashabranner (1987) for comments on unaccompanied refugee children, including Amerasians, in the United States; Mortland and England (1987) for a very good analysis of Vietnamese youth in foster care (with Caucasian families); and GAO (1994) for a more formal review of the Amerasian resettlement program.

9. A different type of active political participation can be found among younger Vietnamese and people who are concerned about their long-term role in the United States. Citizenship has been acquired by many. Especially in areas of dense concentrations, ad hoc and permanent groups have been formed to work in support of legislation or political candidates.

REFERENCES

Aames, Jacqueline, Ronald Aames, John Jung, and Edward Karabenick. 1977. *Indochinese Refugee Self-sufficiency in California: A Survey and Analysis of the Vietnamese, Cambodians, and Lao and the Agencies that Serve Them.* Report Submitted to the State Department of Health, State of California.

Ashabranner, Brent, and Melissa Ashabranner. 1987. *Into a Strange Land: Unaccompanied Refugee Youth in America.* New York: Dodd, Mead, and Company.

Caplan, Nathan, Marcella H. Choy, and John K. Whitmore. 1991. *Children of the Boat People: A Study of Educational Success.* Ann Arbor: University of Michigan Press.

Caplan, Nathan, John K. Whitmore, and Quang L. Bui. 1985. *Southeast Asian Refugee Self-Sufficiency Study: Final Report.* Ann Arbor, Michigan: Institute for Social Research.

Dunning, Bruce B. 1989. Vietnamese in America: The Adaptation of the 1975–79 Arrivals. In *Refugees as Immigrants.* Edited by David W. Haines. Totowa, New Jersey: Rowman and Littlefield. Pp. 55–85.

Dunning, Bruce, and Joshua Greenbaum. 1982. *A Systematic Survey of the Social, Psychological, and Economic Adaptation of Vietnamese Refugees Representing Five Entry Cohorts, 1975–1979.* Washington, D.C.: Bureau of Social Science Research, Inc.

Freeman, James A. 1989. *Hearts of Sorrow: Vietnamese-American Lives.* Stanford: Stanford University Press.

Gardner, Robert W., Bryant Robey, and Peter C. Smith. 1985. Asian Americans: Growth, Change, and Diversity. *Population Bulletin* 40(4).

Gold, Steve, and Nazli Kibria. 1993. Vietnamese Refugees and Blocked Mobility. *Asian and Pacific Migration Journal* 2(1):27–56.

Gordon, Linda W. 1987. Southeast Asian Refuge Migration to the United States. In *Pacific Bridges: The New Immigration from Asia and the Pacific Islands.* Edited by James T. Fawcett and Benjamin V. Cariño. Staten Island, New York: Center for Migration Studies. Pp. 153–173.

———. 1989a. The Missing Children: Mortality and Fertility in a Southeast Asian Refugee Population. *International Migration Review* 22(2):219–237.

———. 1989b. National Surveys of Southeast Asian Refugees: Methods, Findings, Issues. In *Refugees as Immigrants.* Edited by David W. Haines. Totowa, New Jersey: Rowman and Littlefield. Pp. 24–39.

Grant, Bruce, et al. 1979. *The Boat People: An "Age" Investigation.* New York: Penguin Books.

Haines, David W. 1987. Patterns in Southeast Asian Refugee Employment. *Ethnic Groups* 7:39–63.

———. 1988. Kinship in Vietnamese Refugee Resettlement: A Review of the U.S. Experience. *Journal of Comparative Family Studies* 19(1):1–16.

Kelly, Gail Paradise. 1977. *From Vietnam to America: A Chronicle of the Vietnamese Immigration to the United States.* Boulder, Colorado: Westview Press.

Kelly, Katie. 1992. *A Year in Saigon.* New York: Simon and Schuster.

Kibria, Nazli. 1990. Power, Patriarchy, and Gender Conflict in the Vietnamese Immigrant Community. *Gender and Society* 4(1):9–24.

———. 1993. *Family Tightrope.* Princeton, New Jersey: Princeton University Press.

Kim, Young Yun, and Perry M. Nicassio. 1980. *Research Project on Indochinese Refugees in the State of Illinois.* (5 vols.). Chicago: Travelers Aid Society of Metropolitan Chicago.

Le Ngoan. 1994. Profile of the Vietnamese American Community. National Congress of Vietnamese in America.

Mortland, Carol, and Maura G. England. 1987. Vietnamese Youth in American Foster Care. *Social Work* 32(3):240–245.

Nguyen Manh Hung. 1984a. Refugee Scholars and Vietnamese Studies in the United States: 1975–1982. *Amerasia Journal* 11(1):89–99.

———. 1984b. "Vietnam: A Television History": A Case Study in Perceptual Conflict between the American Media and the Vietnamese Expatriates. *World Affairs* 142(2):71–84.

Office of Refugee Resettlement (ORR). 1983. *Report to the Congress: Refugee Resettlement Program.* Washington, D.C.: U.S. Department of Health and Human Services.

———. 1995. *Report to the Congress: Refugee Resettlement Program.* Washington, D.C.: U.S. Department of Health and Human Services.

O'Hare, William P. 1992. America's Minorities–the Demographics of Diversity. *Population Bulletin* 47(4).

Osborne, Milton E. 1969. *The French Presence in Cochinchina and Cambodia.* Ithaca, New York: Cornell University Press.

Penning, Kerry. 1992. Tradition and Pragmatism: An Exploration into the Career Aspirations of Vietnamese Refugee College Students. In *Selected Papers on Refugee Issues*. Edited by Pamela A. DeVoe. Washington, D.C.: American Anthropological Association. Pp. 89–99.

Roberts, Alden E., and Paul D. Starr. 1989. Differential Reference Group Assimilation among Vietnamese Refugees. In *Refugees as Immigrants*. Edited by David W. Haines. Totowa, New Jersey: Rowman and Littlefield. Pp. 40–54.

Rumbaut, Rubén G. 1989. Portraits, Patterns, and Predictors of the Refugee Adaptation Process. In *Refugees as Immigrants*. Edited by David W. Haines. Totowa, New Jersey: Rowman and Littlefield. Pp. 138–182.

Starr, Paul D., Alden Roberts, Rebecca LeNoir, and Nguyen Ngoc Thai. 1979. Adaptation and Stress among Vietnamese Refugees: Preliminary Considerations. In *Proceedings of the First Annual Conference on Indochinese Refugees*. Fairfax, Virginia: George Mason University. Pp. 110–127.

Stull, Donald D., Michael J. Broadway, and Ken C. Erickson. 1992. The Price of a Good Steak: Beef Packing and Its Consequences for Garden City, Kansas. In *Structuring Diversity*. Edited by Louise Lamphere. Chicago: University of Chicago Press. Pp. 35–64.

Tran, Thanh V., and Thang D. Nguyen. 1994. Gender and Satisfaction with the Host Society among Indochinese Refugees. *International Migration Review* 28(2): 323–337.

U.S. Bureau of the Census. 1983. *Asian and Pacific Islander Population by State: 1980*. Washington, D.C.: Department of Commerce.

———. 1992. *1990 Census of Population. General Population Charactersitics—United States*. Washington, D.C.

———. 1993a. *Asians and Pacific Islanders in the United States*. (CP 3-5). Washington, D.C.

———. 1993b. *The Foreign Born Population of the United States*. (CP 3-1). Washington, D.C.

U.S. Committee for Refugees (USCR). 1984. *Vietnamese Boat People: Pirates' Vulnerable Prey*. New York: American Council for Nationalities Service.

U.S. General Accounting Office (GAO). 1994. *Vietnamese Amerasian Resettlement: Education, Employment, and Family Outcomes in the United States*. Washington, D.C.

Whitmore, John, Marcella Trautmann, and Nathan Caplan. 1989. The Socio-Cultural Basis for the Economic and Educational Success of Southeast Asian Refugees. In *Refugees as Immigrants*. Edited by David W. Haines. Totowa, New Jersey: Rowman and Littlefield. Pp. 121–137.

Woodside, Alexander B. 1971. *Vietnam and the Chinese Model*. Cambridge: Harvard University Press.

Part III

Comparative Material

Chapter 15

The Origins and Initial Resettlement Patterns of Refugees in the United States

LINDA W. GORDON

The material in this chapter is drawn primarily from official publications of the U.S. government, particularly the *Annual Reports* and *Statistical Yearbooks* of the Immigration and Naturalization Service and, later, the annual *Report to the Congress* of the Office of Refugee Resettlement (ORR).[1] Much of the statistical information is summarized in two tables. Table 15.1 lists the laws under which refugees have been admitted and shows the number entering under each law by decade. Table 15.2 displays the major countries of origin of the refugees, again by decade. All figures are complete through the end of federal fiscal year (FY) 1994.

In addition to basic data on refugee flows, the government sources provide a window into the prevailing thinking of their times with regard to the admission of refugees into the United States. Refugees—or displaced persons, as they were called in the 1940s—were initially seen as the unfinished business of World War II. They were thought to present a unique problem that called for a onetime solution.

THE AFTERMATH OF WORLD WAR II

When hostilities ceased in 1945, millions of people were outside their home countries without a reasonable prospect of being able to return. The Allies and many other countries responded by offering resettlement opportunities. In the United States, refugees were received under the immigration law of the time, whose organizing principle was the national origins quota system established in the early 1920s.

The quota system had been designed to give preference to persons wishing to immigrate from what were seen as the original (European) source countries

Table 15.1

Refugees and Asylees Granted Lawful Permanent Resident Status by Enactment, FY 1946–1994

	Total	1946-50	1951-60	1961-70	1971-80	1981-90	1991-94
Total	2,976,521	213,347	492,371	212,843	539,447	1,013,620	504,893
Presidential Directive of 12/22/45	40,324	40,324	-	-	-	-	-
Displaced Persons Act of 6/25/48	409,696	173,023	236,669	4	-	-	-
Orphan Act of 7/29/53	466	-	466	-	-	-	-
Refugee Relief Act of 8/7/53	189,025	-	188,993	28	2	2	-
Refugee-Escapee Act of 9/11/57	29,462	-	24,263	5,199	-	-	-
Hungarian Refugee Act of 7/25/58	30,752	-	30,491	258	2	1	-
Azores & Netherlands Refugee Act of 9/2/58	22,213	-	10,057	12,156	2	-	-
Refugee Relatives Act of 9/22/59	1,820	-	1,432	388	-	-	-
Fair Share Refugee Act of 7/14/60	19,800	-	-	19,714	82	3	1
Refugee Conditional Entrants Act of 10/3/65	142,103	-	-	39,149	102,625	329	-
Cuban Refugee Act of 11/2/66	520,107	-	-	135,947	252,119	105,898	26,143
Indochinese Refugee Act of 10/28/77	175,147	-	-	-	137,309	37,752	86
Refugee Parolee Act of 10/5/78	139,253	-	-	-	46,058	92,971	224
Refugee Act of 1980, 3/17/80	1,256,353	-	-	-	1,250	776,664	478,439
(a) Refugees	1,161,589	-	-	-	-	734,259	427,330
(b) Asylees	94,764	-	-	-	1,250	42,405	51,109

Note: "-" means not applicable.

Source: U.S. Immigration and Naturalization Service, 1995, *Statistical Yearbook of the Immigration and Naturalization Service, 1994.* Washington, D.C.: U.S. Government Printing Office.

Table 15.2
Refugees and Asylees by Region and Selected Country of Birth, FY 1946–1994

	Total	1946-50	1951-60	1961-70	1971-80	1981-90	1991-94
All countries	2,976,521	213,347	492,371	212,843	539,447	1,013,620	504,893
Europe	1,164,574	211,983	456,146	55,235	71,858	155,512	213,840
Albania	6,683	29	1,409	1,952	395	353	2,545
Austria	17,430	4,801	11,487	233	185	424	300
Bulgaria	6,825	139	1,138	1,799	1,238	1,197	1,314
Czechoslovakia	37,865	8,449	10,719	5,709	3,646	8,204	1,138
Estonia	11,754	7,143	4,103	16	2	25	465
Germany	101,626	36,633	62,860	665	143	851	474
Greece	31,423	124	28,568	586	478	1,408	259
Hungary	76,333	6,086	55,740	4,044	4,358	4,942	1,163
Italy	63,591	642	60,657	1,198	346	394	354
Latvia	39,728	21,422	16,783	49	16	48	1,410
Lithuania	28,069	18,694	8,569	72	23	37	674
Netherlands	17,638	129	14,336	3,134	8	14	17
Poland	209,602	78,529	81,323	3,197	5,882	33,889	6,782
Portugal	5,073	12	3,650	1,361	21	21	8
Romania	74,105	4,180	12,057	7,158	6,812	29,798	14,100
Soviet Union	330,328	14,072	30,059	871	31,309	72,306	181,711
Spain	10,652	1	246	4,114	5,317	736	238
Yugoslavia	85,198	9,816	44,755	18,299	11,297	324	707
Other Europe	10,651	1,082	7,687	778	382	541	181
North America	574,944	163	831	132,068	252,633	121,840	67,409
Cuba	537,920	3	6	131,557	251,514	113,367	41,473
El Salvador	4,507	-	-	-	45	1,383	3,078
Nicaragua	25,390	1	1	3	36	5,590	19,759
Other North America	7,127	159	824	507	1,038	1,500	3,099
South America	5,055	32	74	123	1,244	1,976	1,606
Chile	1,039	-	5	4	420	531	79
Other South America	4,016	32	69	119	824	1,445	1,527

Table 15.2 (Continued)

Asia	1,177,933	1,106	33,422	19,895	210,683	712,092	200,735
Afghanistan	31,569	-	1	-	542	22,946	8,080
Cambodia	127,413	-	-	-	7,739	114,064	5,610
China	42,770	319	12,008	5,308	13,760	7,928	3,447
Hong Kong	9,028	-	1,076	2,128	3,468	1,916	440
Indonesia	17,600	-	8,253	7,658	222	1,385	82
Iran	65,174	118	192	58	364	46,773	17,669
Iraq	21,454	-	130	119	6,851	7,540	6,814
Japan	4,542	3	3,803	554	56	110	16
Korea	4,622	-	3,116	1,316	65	120	5
Laos	192,836	-	-	-	21,690	142,964	28,182
Syria	4,484	4	119	383	1,336	2,145	497
Thailand	45,979	-	15	13	1,241	30,259	14,451
Turkey	6,968	603	1,427	1,489	1,193	1,896	360
Vietnam	585,993	-	2	7	150,266	324,453	111,265
Other Asia	17,501	59	3,280	862	1,890	7,593	3,817
Africa	53,647	20	1,768	5,486	2,991	22,149	21,233
Egypt	8,799	8	1,354	5,396	1,473	426	142
Ethiopia	33,174	-	61	2	1,307	18,542	13,305
Other Africa	11,674	12	353	88	211	3,181	7,786
Oceania	229	7	75	21	37	22	67
Not reported	139	36	55	15	1	29	3

Notes: Figures refer to those granted permanent resident status. "-" represents zero. China includes mainland China.

Source: U.S. Immigration and Naturalization Service, 1995, *Statistical Yearbook of the Immigration and Naturalization Service, 1994*. Washington, D.C.: U.S. Government Printing Office.

of the U.S. population and to restrict immigration from the nations of Southern and Central Europe, not to mention Asia.[2] Within that legal framework, few options existed to accommodate the large numbers of Poles, Germans, Latvians, Lithuanians, Russians, and many others in need of a place to live.

In this context, President Harry Truman issued a directive on December 22, 1945, providing that 90 percent of the immigration quotas for Central and Eastern Europe should be used for persons who could not or would not return to their prewar homes. The first ship bringing displaced persons arrived on May 20, 1946, and a total of 40,324 immigrants were admitted under the President's Directive from that day through June 30, 1948. Persons born in Germany or Poland made up more than two thirds of the total. Legislation was proposed to allow for displaced persons to be admitted in excess of quotas, but when it failed to be enacted, admissions continued under the President's Directive.

The Displaced Persons Act of 1948 finally became law on June 25, 1948. It initially allowed for 205,000 admissions over a period of two years, and it was later amended to permit up to 415,744 displaced persons to enter as immigrants over a longer period of time. This legislation provided for admissions to take place under the quota system by borrowing or ''mortgaging'' against a country's quota for future years. Over several years, the small quotas for many of the countries of Eastern Europe in combination with the large number of persons needing resettlement resulted in the mortgaging of those quotas for decades into the future. The law provided for persons of German ethnic origin who were born in other countries of Eastern Europe to be charged to the relatively large quotas of Germany and Austria, easing the pressure on the small-country quotas to some extent. The Displaced Persons Act also established the principle of adjustment to permanent resident alien (immigrant) status for qualifying persons who had entered the United States earlier on temporary visas and were unable to return home. Eventually, a total of 409,696 persons became immigrants under this legislation. Most of them had arrived by the end of FY 1952, and 80 percent of them were born in one of six countries: Poland, Germany, Latvia, the Soviet Union, Yugoslavia, or Lithuania.[3] All but 1 percent were Europeans.

THE 1950S: A DECADE OF AD HOC
REFUGEE LEGISLATION

The provisions of the Displaced Persons Act expired on different dates in the early 1950s, leaving some people in Europe and elsewhere still in need of resettlement. The ongoing problem of postwar refugees was one of the major issues addressed by the newly formed United Nations, and their work resulted in the 1951 Geneva Convention Relating to the Status of Refugees. The Geneva Convention established the definition of a *refugee* as a person having a ''well-founded fear of being persecuted for reasons of race, religion, nationality, membership of a particular social group or political opinion.'' It also tied this fear to events occurring before January 1, 1951. The United States did not, however, become a party to the Geneva Convention.

In the United States, the response to the continuing problem of refugees was to enact a series of laws in which immigrant visas were authorized outside the quota system for groups of special concern identified in the legislation. The first of these was the Orphan Act of July 29, 1953, which authorized the entry of up to 500 eligible orphans adopted by members of the U.S. Armed Forces or U.S. government employees serving abroad. A total of 466 orphans entered under this law in FY 1954 and 1955. Most were Japanese (287), with children born in Germany or Austria accounting for almost all of the rest. This was the first instance of U.S. refugee legislation being used to bring in a group that was primarily Asian.

The major U.S. response found expression in the Refugee Relief Act of 1953, which authorized 214,000 nonquota immigrant visas for a list of categories, each with a specific limit. The flavor of this legislation can be seen in the categories, which included 55,000 visas for "German expellees in Western Germany, Berlin, or Austria," 10,000 visas for "escapees in NATO countries or in Turkey, Sweden, Iran, or Trieste," 2,000 visas for "Polish veteran refugees in the British Isles," 45,000 visas for "Italian refugees in Italy or Trieste," 2,000 for "Far East refugees (non-Asian)," 3,000 for "Far East refugees (Asian)," 4,000 for "orphans," and many others. This legislation governed most of the refugee admissions during the 1950s after the expiration of the Displaced Persons Act. A total of 189,025 persons became immigrants under the Refugee Relief Act, of whom most arrived from FY 1954 through FY 1957. Europeans dominated this refugee flow. Italians were the largest group, with 30 percent; persons born in Germany, Yugoslavia, and Greece accounted for about 10 percent each. The largest non-European group was 6,906 Chinese. In the first response to the refugees created after the Hungarian uprising of October 1956 was crushed, 6,130 unused visas available under the Refugee Relief Act were allocated to Hungarians who had fled to Austria. The legislation expired on December 31, 1956, but adjustments of status under it continued in later years.

When the visas allocated under the Refugee Relief Act proved insufficient to respond to the Hungarian refugee crisis, the president announced that others would be admitted under the terms of the attorney general's parole authority, section 212(d)(5) of the Immigration and Nationality Act.[4] This was the first time the parole provision was applied to a relatively large number of people, and it set a precedent that continued for more than 20 years. By June 30, 1958, 31,915 Hungarians had been paroled into the United States, making a total of 38,045 Hungarian refugees. Existing legislation did not provide for the Hungarian parolees to become permanent resident aliens. Congress addressed the issue of their immigration status by passing the Hungarian Refugee Act of July 25, 1958, which allowed them to adjust status after 2 years' residence in the United States. Most of the Hungarians took this step soon after they became eligible in FY 1959 and FY 1960, and a total of 30,752 eventually did so.

The time lag between the arrival of these refugees in the United States and their adjustment to immigrant status, created by the use of the parole authority to admit large numbers of people in an emergency situation, gives rise to potential confusion for persons interested in the history of refugee admissions. The problem exists because the Immigration and Naturalization Service (INS) reports in greatest depth on persons at the time they receive immigrant (permanent resident alien) status. Refugees were admitted as parolees with the assumption that they would be residing indefinitely, but they did not appear in most of the official statistics until they became immigrants, so reference to the immigrant tabulations alone gives a false impression of the rise and fall in refugee admissions over time. In addition, refugees are not required to adjust their status, and some never do. Because the earlier postwar legislation provided immigrant visas for refugees, the discrepancy between initial admissions and admissions to immigrant status does not appear until the Hungarian refugee flow in FY 1957. Most of the subsequent refugee legislation has followed the model of parole or some other form of temporary admission with a waiting period before adjustment of status, so the distinction remains important for understanding later refugee movements. The time lag between arrival and adjustment of status is illustrated in Figure 15.1, which identifies the major refugee programs and highlights the larger refugee movements.

Gradually during the 1950s, the emphasis shifted from helping World War II refugees to resettling persons fleeing communism. The Refugee-Escapee Act of September 11, 1957, was passed in part to offset the expiration of the Refugee Relief Act by accommodating refugees other than the Hungarians. Part of the rationale for this legislation was the fact that nearly 20,000 visas allocated under the Refugee Relief Act had gone unused. Section 4 of the act provided for nonquota visas to be issued to refugee orphans arriving from abroad and for adjustment of status of orphans in the United States, while section 15 continued the practice of specifying particular groups to be admitted independent of the quotas: German expellees, Netherlands refugees and their relatives, and refugee-escapees. The law also restored the quotas that had been mortgaged under the Displaced Persons Act. Most of these refugees arrived in FY 1959 and FY 1960. They were a more diverse group than those admitted under the earlier laws. A total of 29,462 persons arrived under this law, of whom 57 percent were from Europe, primarily Hungary and Yugoslavia. An additional 37 percent were from Asia, with Korea and China being the leading countries; a substantial proportion of the Asians were orphans being adopted by Americans.

The next legislation was the Azores and Netherlands Refugee Act of September 2, 1958, which gave relief to Portuguese nationals displaced from their homes in the Azores by earthquake and flood and to nationals of the Netherlands who were refugees from Indonesia. This was the only instance of special refugee legislation in response to a natural disaster. A total of 22,213 persons entered as nonquota immigrants under this legislation, arriving mostly from FY 1960

Figure 15.1
Refugee Admissions

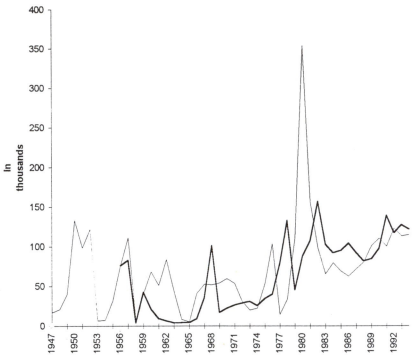

Notes: Light line represents initial admissions; *dark line* represents admissions to lawful permanent
    resident status. For the period 1946–1956, admissions to lawful permanent resident status and
    admissions were the same.
Source: U.S. Immigration and Naturalization Service, 1995, *Statistical Yearbook of the Immigration
    and Naturalization Service, 1994.* Washington, D.C.: U.S. Government Printing Office.

through FY 1962. Almost all of them were born in Indonesia, the Netherlands,
or Portugal.

The Refugee Relatives Act of September 22, 1959, among other provisions,
allowed relatives of persons who had been admitted under the Refugee Relief
Act to be admitted as nonquota immigrants. The number of persons admitted
under this legislation was only 1,820, most of them in FY 1960. The majority
were Italians, Hungarians, and Japanese.

THE 1960S: THE PAROLE AUTHORITY AND THE CUBANS

By 1960 the issue of refugees was a major international concern, as expressed
in the first World Refugee Year declared by the United Nations. The Fair Share
Refugee Act of July 14, 1960, was the U.S. response. It provided for the attorney

general to continue to use the parole authority to admit "refugee-escapees" and to adjust their status to that of permanent resident alien two years after their entry. The act placed a ceiling on these admissions tied to the resettlement activities of other nations; the number of such parolees was limited to 25 percent of the total number that had been resettled elsewhere. (The act also extended the provisions and raised the limits of several of the earlier refugee laws.) Arrivals began almost immediately, and these refugees appeared in the statistical record as immigrants beginning in FY 1963. A total of 19,800 persons eventually became immigrants under this provision, effectively all of those who entered under parole.[5] They arrived as parolees from FY 1961 through 1966, and most of them became immigrants from FY 1963 through 1968 at the rate of 2,000 to 4,000 yearly. A very wide variety of countries was represented, but nearly 80 percent were from four countries: Yugoslavia (33 percent), Romania (22 percent), Egypt (16 percent), and Hungary (8 percent).

The parole authority was also used outside the framework of the Fair Share Refugee Act for Chinese who had fled to Hong Kong from mainland China. This was done under a Presidential Directive of May 23, 1962, which specified that certain groups would be admitted: relatives of U.S. citizens and resident aliens, those with special skills needed in the United States, and those who had previously applied for entry as refugees but had been refused only because of numerical limitations. From the data of the directive through FY 1966, a total of 15,111 "Hong Kong Chinese" were approved under the program. Special legislation was not enacted for adjustment of status of this group. About 62 percent of them were able to become immigrants under the quota system based on their relationship to someone already living in the United States, and the rest adjusted status under other refugee legislation.

On October 3, 1965, a comprehensive new immigration act was signed, revamping the old quota system and adding, for the first time, a provision for the regular admission of refugees.[6] This law provided for the "conditional entry" of refugees under the seventh preference. It defined refugees as persons fleeing persecution on account of race, religion, or political opinion in a Communist country or the Middle East. Persons "uprooted by catastrophic natural calamity" were also defined as refugees. The yearly quota allocated to refugees was 10,200, 6 percent of the Eastern Hemisphere quota of 170,000. (A Western Hemisphere limit of 120,000 was imposed for the first time.) Not more than half of the refugee quota could be used for adjustment of status of persons meeting the definition of refugee who had been present in the United States for two years. Previous refugee laws were repealed. The first group to benefit from the adjustment-of-status provision in large numbers was the Hong Kong parolees, for whom no other laws were available.

Admission of refugees began immediately under the 1965 act, a mixture of new arrivals from abroad who entered with seventh preference immigrant visas and persons adjusting status. The new arrivals were counted as immigrants in their year of arrival, in spite of the fact that "conditional entry" meant that they did not gain *permanent* resident alien status until after two years' residence. During FY 1966 and 1967 about half of the admissions under this law were persons adjusting status (including the Hong Kong parolees), but thereafter the mix shifted so that in most years new arrivals were more than 90 percent of the total. Therefore, the yearly immigrant figures are a good reflection of the flow of people beginning in FY 1968. Admissions under this law ranged from 6,500 to nearly 10,000 yearly from FY 1966 through FY 1975. Amendments to the law on October 20, 1976, extended the preference system to the Western Hemisphere, which enlarged the seventh preference to 6 percent of 290,000, or 17,400. The number admitted grew accordingly, ranging between 10,000 and 14,000 yearly from FY 1976 through FY 1980.

Refugees from many countries were admitted under the seventh preference. Of the more than 39,000 who arrived during the late 1960s, 74 percent were from Eastern Europe, with 30 percent from Yugoslavia and 14 percent from Czechoslovakia. China accounted for 12 percent and Egypt for 6 percent. Europe continued to dominate among the sending countries during the 1970s, with 56 percent of the 102,000 arrivals. The Soviet Union was the largest sending country with 22 percent, and 11 percent were from Yugoslavia. Significant numbers also arrived under this law from China, Vietnam, Iraq, and Cuba in the 1970s.

The Cubans, of course, were the largest single refugee group to enter the United States during the 1960s. From the fall of the Batista government on January 1, 1959, large numbers of Cubans began arriving in the United States by any means available to them. Initially, most came on tourist visas and did not return. A sympathetic U.S. government allowed them to remain and, beginning in FY 1961, admitted large numbers of others as parolees. By FY 1962, the *Annual Report of the INS* described the Cubans as arriving "by common carrier, small boats, commandeered aircraft, and across the land boundary from Mexico." This was the first instance of a refugee flow from a Western Hemisphere country directly to the United States. On October 22, 1962, the Cuban "quarantine" was placed in effect, ending commercial flights between Cuba and the United States. Refugee arrivals slowed to a trickle but resumed again in large numbers in FY 1966 when an airlift was negotiated between the two countries. The 37-year history of refugee flows from Cuba to the United States consists of starts and stops of this nature characterized by varying degrees of cooperation between the governments; the details are beyond the scope of this chapter. A small number of clandestine arrivals by boat continued throughout.

For present purposes, the important point is the difficulty of saying with precision how many refugees have come to the United States from Cuba and when they arrived. This is because Cubans were admitted under many different laws over the years, and most people (including U.S. government officials) applied the term *refugee* generically to anyone from Cuba who arrived beginning in 1959, even those who were given immigrant status based on family relationships or other qualifications. The descriptions in successive *Annual Reports of the INS* do not paint a consistent picture of the Cuban flow. Beginning in FY

1962 the narratives refer to yearly arrivals from Cuba in temporary statuses and/ or as immigrants, cumulative arrivals since 1959, or both, but the categories vary, and the running totals are not always consistent with the reported yearly figures.

INS statisticians have attempted to reconstruct the Cuban flow from published and unpublished data. This effort indicates that from January 1959 through FY 1970, 446,000 Cubans arrived as parolees and visa overstayers. An additional 140,000 Cuban arrivals gained immigrant status, for a total of 586,000 Cubans admitted during that period. From FY 1971 through April 1, 1980 (the date the Refugee Act of 1980 took effect), an additional 105,000 Cubans were admitted via the parole authority, nearly 5,800 more were admitted under the seventh preference, and another 24,000 came as immigrants. In total, this means that nearly 557,000 Cubans arrived in what were generally considered refugee statuses, and 164,000 more were admitted as newly arriving immigrants, making 721,000 Cubans in all during the first 21 years and 3 months of this refugee flow.

The allocation of visas under the seventh preference of the 1965 act was clearly inadequate for a refugee movement of this magnitude. In addition, the direct arrival of many Cubans without the overseas selection and screening that had become the practice in the administration of other refugee programs posed a new situation. The response was the Cuban Refugee Act, enacted on November 2, 1966. This law authorized the adjustment of status of Cuban parolees, with the visas to be charged to the Western Hemisphere limit. It required a minimum of two years' residence before adjustment of status (later changed to one year), and it provided for the ''date of admission'' to immigrant status to be set as 30 months prior to the date of adjustment or the actual date of arrival, whichever was more recent.

Because nearly eight years had elapsed since the first Cubans began arriving, tens of thousands were eligible as soon as the law passed. In FY 1967 and 1968, 117,272 Cuban parolees were able to become permanent resident aliens, because the annual numerical limit of 120,000 Western Hemisphere immigrants established in the 1965 act did not take effect until FY 1969. From FY 1969 through FY 1975 the Cubans continued to adjust status at the rate of about 20,000 yearly, limited by the ceiling. Amendments to the Immigration Act of October 20, 1976, provided that the Cubans would not be charged to any numerical limits. This enabled 68,910 Cubans to adjust in FY 1977. By the end of the 1970s, 388,000 people had become immigrants under the Cuban Refugee Act. While this dwarfed all the earlier refugee programs except for the Displaced Persons Act, it represented only about 70 percent of those admitted in temporary statuses, a lower proportion than for other refugee groups that adjusted status after a waiting period. In summary, the figures on Cuban adjustments of status over time are a poor reflection of the number and timing of the actual Cuban arrivals, much more than is the case for any of the earlier refugee groups.

THE 1970S: THE PAROLE AUTHORITY AND
THE INDOCHINESE

During the entire decade of the 1970s, refugees continued to arrive under the seventh preference and the Cuban Refugee Act. In addition, the U.S. government responded to what were seen as refugee groups deserving of special consideration through the continued use of the parole authority. On October 1, 1971, the attorney general announced that he would use this authority to allow Soviet Jews who were able to leave the Soviet Union to enter the United States as refugees. At first, this movement was small, since few gained permission to leave. Then during 1972, the government of Uganda expelled thousands of its Asian nationals. On September 30, 1972, the attorney general announced that the parole authority would be used to admit a number of these Ugandan Asians, and by the end of FY 1973, almost 1,200 had been admitted. Other parole programs were used from 1977 through 1979 to admit Romanians, other Eastern Europeans, Lebanese, and political prisoners from South America.

The largest parole program of the 1970s was created for the Indochinese beginning in 1975. Early in April 1975, a group of 2,279 Vietnamese orphans were evacuated under a parole program authorized by Congress. On May 1 of that year, the parole of up to 130,000 Vietnamese and Cambodian refugees was authorized, and more than 100,000 of them had passed through Guam and arrived in the United States by June 30. An "Expanded Parole Program" in 1976 took primarily refugees from Laos. After a brief lull, refugees continued to escape from Indochina, and the first of a series of new parole programs was announced in August 1977. By FY 1979 the use of parole had grown to 61,875 places for Indochinese and 29,500 for others, far beyond the 17,400 who could be accommodated in the seventh preference.

As with the Cubans, the response again was to enact special legislation. The Indochinese Refugee Act of October 28, 1977, permitted Cambodian, Laotian, and Vietnamese parolees to adjust to permanent resident alien status after two years in the country. This made the approximately 130,000 refugees admitted in 1975 immediately eligible, and during FY 1978, 94,146 of them became immigrants. They continued to adjust their status in the next few years in high numbers, because the legislation remained in effect for those who arrived before January 1, 1979. More than 175,000 Indochinese have become permanent resident aliens under this law.

Other refugee groups were accommodated by the Refugee Parolee provision in legislation of October 5, 1978, which required only a one-year presence in the United States before adjustment of status. More than 18 percent of the refugees who became immigrants under this law were from the Soviet Union. This provision was used by Indochinese as well; nearly 72 percent of the beneficiaries were from Cambodia, Laos, or Vietnam. This law remains in effect for adjustment of status but has been little used since the mid-1980s. Still, more than 139,000 refugees have become immigrants under its provisions.

THE 1980S: THE REFUGEE ACT

The size of the refugee movements in the late 1970s and the discomfort of many officials about the use of the parole authority to handle them led directly to the Refugee Act of 1980. The act codified a revolution in thinking about the phenomenon of refugee movements and the desirable U.S. response to them. It adopted the UN definition of *refugee*. It acknowledged that the need to resettle refugees would be ongoing, requiring a permanent legal structure. It set up a yearly procedure in which the executive branch develops a proposal for the number of refugees to be admitted during the next year, based on an assessment of need worldwide and an appropriate U.S. response to that need. The proposal is presented to the Congress in formal hearings. Following the hearings, the president announces the final refugee ceiling figure for the year, including an allocation of the numbers among areas of the world. The Refugee Act provides for the ceiling to be adjusted upward during the year if needed to respond to a crisis, following consultation with Congress, and reallocation between areas of the world within a year's ceiling is also possible. This is the only area in U.S. immigration law that provides for annual assessment and adjustment of ceilings.

The Refugee Act repealed the seventh preference and all other preexisting refugee laws except the Cuban Refugee Act of 1966, an omission that was to have important consequences. (Refugees who had entered under the repealed laws were still able to adjust status under them.) This legislation also explicitly provided that the parole authority was not to be used to admit refugees except for "compelling reasons in the public interest." The Refugee Act established an orderly process in which potential refugee groups of "special humanitarian concern" to the United States are identified, and individual applicants from those groups are screened overseas to see if they meet the definition of refugee established in the act. While the usual picture of a refugee is one who has fled persecution and is in temporary refuge in a country of first asylum, the act also allows the president to designate people of special concern such as minority peoples or political prisoners who may be admitted as refugees directly from their home countries. The act also codified the idea of political asylum, applying the same definition as that of refugee. The only difference between the two is the location of application for the status: If people reach the United States and claim inability to return home because of persecution, they may apply for asylum.

The Refugee Act took effect on April 1, 1980, and it was tested almost immediately by a new outflow of Cubans. In late April, the Cuban port of Mariel was opened, and people were allowed to leave; many Florida-based Cubans used privately owned boats to bring their relatives out of Cuba. The Refugee Act did not provide for this kind of unmanaged flow, nor for large numbers of people to be accommodated in first asylum within the United States. After some discussion as to whether these Cubans could be considered refugees under the terms of the new act, it was decided that this mass outflow did not meet the requirements of the law. In June 1980, they were labeled *entrants,* a term with no existing basis in immigration law. Furthermore, a logical connection was drawn between the Cubans, who finally numbered 124,789 when the flow stopped in October, and approximately 40,000 Haitians who had been arriving in small boats in Florida during the late 1970s and in 1980. Although the flow of Haitians was smaller and took place over a longer time, in other ways it was judged comparable to the migration of the Cubans. A Presidential Declaration gave both the Cubans and the Haitians entrant status. A basis in law was established for entrant status in the Refugee Education Assistance Act of October 10, 1980. It defined entrants[7] and established a program for services to be provided to them in exact parallel to refugee program services. The Haitian flow into the United States continued in smaller numbers through 1980 and into 1981, finally ending in October 1981 when the Coast Guard was ordered to interdict small boats from Haiti and return suspected would-be migrants.

Because the status of entrant carried no provision for permanent residence in the United States, most Cuban entrants and some Haitians applied for political asylum. By the end of FY 1984 the number of claims pending by Cubans was nearly 122,000, and the number of Haitian claims was more than 7,000. Most of these asylum claims were held pending a decision on how to handle them. In FY 1985, the INS began disposing of the Cuban asylum claims by processing them for adjustment of status under the Cuban Refugee Act of 1966. From FY 1985 through FY 1990, 123,203 Cuban cases were closed without a decision; most of these people had arrived as entrants and were given immigrant status under the 1966 act. Because comparable legislation did not exist for the Haitians, no such remedy was available to them. However, one of the provisions of the Immigration Reform and Control Act (IRCA) of 1986 allowed Cuban and Haitian entrants to adjust status, giving them an artificial date of admission of January 1, 1982. Under this law, 31,595 Haitians and 4,579 Cubans became permanent resident aliens from FY 1987 through FY 1990.

Restrictions on all types of travel from Cuba after Mariel during most of the 1980s meant that relatively few Cubans migrated to the United States in that decade compared with the previous two. About 16,200 arrived under the Refugee Act, including 600 who received asylum. About 34,000 more Cubans arrived as immigrants during the decade, usually qualifying based on their relationship to someone already living in the United States. Beginning in 1989, exit permits for tourist travel became easier to obtain, and visits by Cubans to Florida increased severalfold. Some Cubans used the opportunity to stay for a year, until they could qualify to adjust status under the Cuban Refugee Act of 1966. INS research indicates that an average of 15 percent of the Cuban tourists did not depart during the period beginning in 1988, resulting in an estimate of 7,650 Cubans who might have chosen this method to immigrate from 1988 through 1990. This brought the cumulative total of Cuban refugees and persons treated like refugees (including the Mariel Cubans) to 706,000 and that of Cuban immigrants since 1959 to 198,000, a grand total of almost 904,000 by the end of the decade.

In the meantime, refugee admissions proceeded as envisioned in the Refugee Act. During the first decade (and six months) of its operation, 906,500 persons were approved for refugee status under its provisions. The countries of origin of the refugees continued to reflect the concerns of the earlier cold war decades and the history of U.S. involvement abroad. Thus, persons from Cambodia, Laos, and Vietnam made up 62 percent of those given refugee status during the 1980s, followed by Soviet[8] citizens (16 percent). A rather broad range of nationalities made up the remainder: Afghans, Ethiopians, Iranians, East Europeans, and Cubans being the most numerous. During the 1980s, 734,259 refugees adjusted to permanent resident alien status under the Refugee Act.

Applications for political asylum in the United States had been rare before the Refugee Act, on the order of 2,000 or 3,000 yearly during the 1970s when record keeping began. In 1980 the number of new asylum cases exceeded 26,000, and new filings continued at a high level for several years, due in part to cases filed by the Mariel Cubans. Asylum applications tapered off in the mid-1980s but then resumed their growth, reaching more than 101,000 in 1989. Most asylum applications are denied or closed; the number granted averaged about 4,800 yearly. The approximately 50,500 asylum *cases* granted during the 1980s contained about 66,000 *persons*. During the same decade, 43,655 persons adjusted to immigrant status after being granted asylum and observing the one-year waiting period.[9] The largest single nationality group was Iranians; many had been stranded in the United States after the 1979 revolution.

Much of the growth in claims for political asylum during the 1980s was fueled by recurring political upheaval in Central America. First from El Salvador and then from Nicaragua, thousands fled to the United States. Small refugee programs were created for both countries, but approximately 100,000 asylum cases were filed by nationals from each during the 1980s. More than 13,000 asylum claims by Nicaraguans were approved, but only about 1,400 Salvadoran claims were granted. Many more were able to gain legal status under the provisions of IRCA. Nearly 168,000 Salvadorans and 17,000 Nicaraguans applied for legalization, most of them based on having resided in the United States since before January 1, 1982, and the great majority of these applications were approved. During the late 1980s, the number of asylum claims from Guatemalans increased. At the end of 1990, 97,000 asylum claims were pending, including nearly 30,000 from Salvadorans, 25,000 from Nicaraguans, and 11,000 from Guatemalans.

Also during the late 1980s, the U.S. government was negotiating with Vietnam for the offspring of Americans born to Vietnamese mothers prior to 1976 to be allowed to leave Vietnam and enter the United States under the refugee program. The Vietnamese government objected to the use of the term *refugee* for these Amerasians, as they were called. The Amerasian Homecoming Act of December 22, 1987 (an amendment to an appropriations bill) provided a resolution in which these young people and their immediate relatives were given immigrant status but were resettled and provided assistance under the refugee program. A strong effort was then made to identify all eligible persons remaining in Vietnam, since the "children" were already teenagers or young adults. From 1988 through 1994, when the program was nearly complete, 19,333 Amerasians and 49,825 close relatives were admitted under this law.

Other legislation of the late 1980s modified the Refugee Act. An amendment to the Foreign Operations Act of November 21, 1989 (another appropriations bill) mandated relaxed standards to be applied to claims for refugee status filed by nationals of Cambodia, Laos, Vietnam, and the Soviet Union. It also provided for adjustment of status without regard to the quota system after a one-year waiting period to nationals of those countries who had been paroled into the United States after denial of refugee status. (Most of these persons were granted parole because they were related to persons already in the United States.) From 1991 through 1994, more than 27,000 Soviets and 15,000 Indochinese gained immigrant status under this law.

By the end of the decade, observers were remarking on the blurring of the distinction between *refugees* and *immigrants*,[10] as a result of the above legislation and the many other bills that were being proposed to provide immigration benefits to special groups. One prominent 1989 proposal would have created a category of up to 30,000 "special immigrants" to be admitted for foreign policy reasons; these were viewed as people whose situations fell short of the refugee definition but whose admission was deemed in the national interest. That proposal and most of the others failed to become law.

THE 1990S: THE END OF THE COLD WAR

The early 1990s brought the dissolution of the Soviet Union and the end of the cold war period. Despite these changes, refugee admissions under the Refugee Act during the 1991–1994 period continued to resemble those of the late 1980s. The number of persons approved remained steady at about 110,000 yearly, and the dominant countries continued to be the (former) Soviet Union, Vietnam, and Laos. However, fewer refugees were approved from Eastern Europe and Iran, while new areas of conflict were recognized by new programs for persons from Iraq, Haiti, Liberia, Somalia, and Bosnia-Herzegovina. From 1991 through 1994, 427,330 refugees were admitted to immigrant status.

In 1990, with immigration becoming increasingly an issue of public concern, Congress enacted major legislation revising the immigration visa preference system. The Immigration Act of 1990 also created Temporary Protected Status (TPS), designed to allow for the entry of groups of people in need of temporary refuge. It requires a finding that a country is the scene of ongoing armed conflict, environmental disaster, or other extraordinary but temporary conditions preventing its nationals from returning there safely. This was the first effort to create an explicit legal basis for allowing persons escaping danger to gain temporary refuge instead of permanent residence in the United States. In practice, this had been done for individuals and for some groups under the administrative discretion known as Extended Voluntary Departure (EVD). The law named nationals of El Salvador as the first group eligible for TPS, and it was clearly inspired by the experience of the 1980s with Central Americans. TPS is declared for periods of 6 to 18 months and may be renewed with a finding of continued danger in the country of nationality. Persons must apply for TPS and are required to renew their registration periodically. The law imposes a barrier to any future proposals for adjusting the status of groups in TPS by requiring a supermajority to enact such legislation.

A total of 187,128 Salvadorans registered for TPS during the initial registration period that ended December 31, 1991. Their TPS was not extended, but they were allowed to remain under a declaration of Deferred Enforced Departure (DED), which is now being used in place of EVD. The number of Salvadorans living in the United States in these temporary statuses is thought to be considerably larger than the number who registered, since in many cases it is likely that only the wage earners in a household registered. A number of other groups have been designated for TPS: nationals of Kuwait, Lebanon, Liberia, and Somalia in 1991, Bosnia-Herzegovina in 1992, and Rwanda in 1994. None of these groups proved to be as numerous as the Salvadorans. The largest was the Lebanese; more than 9,000 registered for TPS, and their protected status ended in 1993.

The use of legislation tailored for certain refugeelike groups also continued in the Immigration Act of 1990. A special provision allocated up to 1,000 immigrant visas for Tibetans who were living in exile, some of them for decades, in India and Nepal. In 1992 and 1993, 968 "Displaced Tibetans" were admitted to immigrant status. Most of these visas went to heads of households, who were expected to apply for the entry of their spouses and children later.

In another development, legislative relief was provided for persons from China, primarily students, who were present in the United States during the 1989 prodemocracy demonstration in Tienanmen Square. Some of them had spoken publicly against the crackdown by the government of China. They were initially given DED by an executive order. Their status was resolved by the Chinese Student Protection Act of October 9, 1992. It allowed Chinese who met certain requirements to adjust to immigrant status beginning on July 1, 1993, under the quota provided in the employment third preference category. Because that quota was not fully subscribed in FY 1993, the number of visas available was sufficient to meet the demand, and 48,212 persons became permanent resident aliens under the Chinese Student provision in FY 1993 and 1994.

Despite these developments on the legal front, events continued to unfold in ways that were difficult to accommodate under existing legal and administrative structures. The number of claims for political asylum grew in the early 1990s beyond anything that had been foreseen in the Refugee Act, reaching 104,000 in 1992 and about 145,000 annually in 1993 and 1994.[11] Guatemala and El

Salvador accounted for the most new claims filed from 1991 through 1994. Continuing unrest in Central America was not the only factor; the speed and affordability of air travel meant that people from all over the globe could reach the United States with relative ease and file a claim for asylum. Many claims were filed by persons from Asia and the former Soviet Union, and almost every country of the world was represented in the caseload. By the end of FY 1994 the pending caseload was nearly 425,000, including 127,000 claims from Guatemalans, 73,000 from Salvadorans, 27,000 from Chinese, 25,000 from Nicaraguans, and 21,000 from Haitians.

During 1991 the adjudication of claims filed with INS for asylum was assigned to a newly created Asylum Officer Corps, persons especially recruited and trained for this work. The number of claims granted from 1991 through 1994 remained at a yearly average of 4,800, despite the growth in claims filed. No single country dominated among the successful claims during this time. About 28,000 persons gained asylum during those four years, while more than 51,000 asylees were able to adjust to immigrant status during the same period.[12]

Cubans continued to arrive under the Refugee Act in the early 1990s at a rate of 3,000 or 4,000 yearly for a total of 13,400, and an additional 1,700 were granted asylum from 1991 through 1994. Tourist travel from the island also grew, as the Cuban government's age restrictions on travel were lowered in stages, beginning in 1991. The U.S. government suspended the issuance of tourist visas to Cubans several times, and strict standards were imposed to minimize the possibility of visa overstays. However, some Cubans did manage to arrive and remain; this number is estimated at 14,650 for FY 1991 to 1993. In the meantime, an average of 2,000 Cubans arrived yearly as immigrants, for a total of 8,000 from FY 1991 through FY 1994. These arrivals brought the cumulative totals since 1959 to more than 735,000 Cuban refugees (including those treated as refugees under the Cuban Refugee Act) and 206,000 admitted as new immigrants, for a total of 941,000 migrants since the Cuban revolution. At that level the Cuban refugees still slightly outnumber refugees from Vietnam (at 716,000) if Amerasians are not included. The two groups are nearly equal in total migration to the United States when the refugee and immigrant categories are combined.

Conditions in Cuba deteriorated when economic support from the Soviet Union was withdrawn, and increasing numbers of Cubans took to rafts and boats again, beginning in 1992. Several attempts to hijack ferries in Havana in the summer of 1994 touched off another migration crisis, as the Cuban government suspended its efforts to prevent departures. On August 19, the United States government announced a reversal in its long-standing policy of treating persons fleeing Cuba as refugees. The U.S. Coast Guard was instructed to intercept Cubans at sea and take them to the U.S. Naval Base at Guantánamo Bay in Cuba until the Cuban government could be persuaded to take them back. More than 30,000 Cubans were intercepted in this way before the outflow was restrained again in September.[13]

The Coast Guard embargo of Haiti had succeeded in stemming the flow of

Haitian "boat people" from its inception in October 1981 through the 1980s. However, many Haitians who did not qualify for entrant status were living illegally in the United States during the 1980s, and like the Central Americans, many of them were able to legalize their status under IRCA. Nearly 60,000 Haitians filed for legalization, 16,000 on the basis of having resided in the United States since before January 1, 1982, and 44,000 based on having performed seasonal agricultural labor under the terms specified in the act. Most of these applications were successful.

Haiti's first democratic presidential election was held in December 1990. However, after the president was ousted in a coup on September 30, 1991, increasing numbers of Haitians took to the sea despite the Coast Guard presence. Some were returned to Haiti, but many were held in a "processing center" set up at Guantánamo. Members of the new Asylum Officer Corps performed screening interviews to see if they had a "credible fear" of persecution, and those who did were brought to the United States to file formal applications for asylum.[14] Approximately 11,000 Haitians entered the United States in this way in the summer of 1992, and most filed claims for asylum in 1992 or 1993. In May 1992, because the increasing numbers of people fleeing could not be accommodated, the United States announced a program of in-country processing of Haitian refugee applications and resumed repatriating Haitians intercepted at sea.

The outflow of Haitians slowed thereafter but swelled again two years later. In May 1994, the United States announced a plan to resume screening for potential asylum claimants on ships or in processing centers. The number of fleeing Haitians grew rapidly to more than 21,000, and again they were housed at Guantánamo. After the deposed president of Haiti was restored in October 1994, most of the Haitians were repatriated, and the in-country refugee processing program ended.

To summarize the effect of the Refugee Act from its inception in 1980 to the end of FY 1994, 1.4 million persons have been approved under its provisions for refugee or asylum status, and more than 1.25 million of them have received permanent resident alien status in the United States. Data have not been compiled on the number who have gone on to become citizens, but preliminary analysis has established a higher propensity to naturalize among former refugees than among almost any other category of immigrant. Despite the successful operation of the act as shown in these numbers, mass migrations have continued that were not accommodated under the terms of the act, and policymakers have continued to seek alternative ways of dealing with them.

INITIAL SETTLEMENT PATTERNS
AND CHARACTERISTICS

In the years immediately following World War II, relatively little data were reported by the INS on the demographic and economic characteristics or the resettlement locations of the earliest refugee groups. However, from FY 1947 through FY 1952, INS tabulations of each year's immigrants by rural or urban area and major cities show displaced persons as a separate category.[15] This source shows that about half of the displaced persons admitted under the President's Directive of 1945 settled in New York City. Chicago was the second most common city of resettlement, with about 5 percent; 10 percent went to rural areas.

The Displaced Persons Act of 1948 gave preference to persons who would engage in selected occupations (agriculture, household work, and the construction, clothing, and garment trades) and persons with "special educational, scientific, technological or professional qualifications." In other ways as well, the concerns expressed in the language of this act sound familiar to anyone who follows the contemporary debate on immigration. It required assurances that persons admitted would "be suitably employed without displacing some other person from employment" and would not become public charges or displace others from housing. These preferences tilted the resettlement patterns toward a wider variety of places. In 1949 and 1950, nearly one fourth of the arriving displaced persons went to rural areas, and the proportion going to New York City fell to less than one fourth. In 1951 and 1952, the proportion going to rural areas fell back toward one eighth. New York City continued to be an attractive destination for displaced persons, but other cities in the East and Midwest (Chicago, Detroit, Philadelphia, and Cleveland) absorbed a significant share.

The Refugee Relief Act of 1953 continued to require "assurances" that refugees would not displace others from employment and housing and that they would not become public charges, but preferences were not based on occupational qualifications. A table in the FY 1957 *Annual Report of the INS* summarized the geographic distribution by state of nearly 188,000 of these refugees at their time of arrival. New York continued to be the major state of resettlement, with about one third. Illinois was second with 11 percent, and more than 10,000 each went to New Jersey, California, Ohio, Pennsylvania, and Michigan.

The FY 1958 *Annual Report of the INS* carried a table summarizing the demographic and occupational characteristics of the 38,045 Hungarians who had entered first under the Refugee Relief Act and later as parolees. About 62 percent were males, with a concentration of people in their twenties. They worked as skilled craftsmen, machine operators, or professional or technical employees. Their geographic distribution was not reported. Similarly, information on 13,619 Hong Kong parolees appeared in the FY 1965 *Annual Report.* They were divided evenly between males and females, with a median age of 20.7. Among the adults with reported occupations, most were professional, technical, or clerical workers.

The propensity of the Cuban refugees to settle in the Miami area is well known. During the 1960s a federal "resettlement" program was created to assist in relocating Cubans to other cities, to ease their perceived impact on south Florida. The INS annual reports did not treat this subject or publish tabulations of the places where Cuban refugees were settled. However, from 1961 through

1979, Cubans gaining immigrant status were tabulated by state and city of residence. The proportion of Cubans living in Florida ranged around 40 percent from 1961 through 1967 and rose to 59 percent in 1968, a year in which more than 90,000 Cuban refugees adjusted their status. From 1968 through 1972 it was about 37 percent, and through the 1970s, it rose gradually, reaching 60 percent in 1979. Initially, New York was the second most popular destination for Cubans, and New Jersey was third. New York's share of the Cubans fell from about 30 percent in the early 1960s to less than 10 percent by the late 1970s, while New Jersey's share rose from less than 10 percent to about 18 percent in the early 1970s before falling back to 11 percent in 1979.

The next large refugee group was the Indochinese, and the experience of the Cubans had an effect on their reception in the United States. During House debate on the Indochina Migration and Refugee Assistance Act of 1975, several speakers referred to the Cuban refugees as an asset to the country.[16] However, they went on to describe Dade County (Florida) as "inundated with Cuban refugees," and they referred repeatedly to the need to distribute refugees evenly about the country, to minimize impact upon specific labor markets and communities. This became the explicit policy of refugee resettlement for the Indochinese and under the 1980 Refugee Act, although its implementation has varied over time and with different groups.

At the end of December 1975, when the resettlement of the first Vietnamese and Cambodian refugees was complete, 21 percent had been placed in California, 7 percent in Texas, 5.5 percent in Pennsylvania, 4 percent in Florida, and the others were widely dispersed about the country. Data on the initial placement of refugees from Vietnam, Cambodia, and Laos after 1975 can be found in the subsequent publications of the refugee program (see "Further Sources"). Over time, the reunification of refugee families came to govern the resettlement patterns of newly arriving refugees. This meant that the internal or "secondary" migration of the early arrivals determined the geographic placement of latecomers. In the case of the Vietnamese, the proportion going to California increased from about one third in the early 1980s to more than 40 percent by 1987, where it stabilized.

After the first small group of Cambodians arrived in 1975, relatively few were resettled in the United States until 1981. The planning for their placement was done under an innovative program called the Cambodian Cluster Project or Khmer Guided Placement (KGP) Project. Federal officials working with voluntary agencies identified 12 favorable sites in nine states[17] around the country and prepared for them to receive Cambodian refugees by obtaining the cooperation of local officials and identifying housing and employment opportunities. These were generally medium-size cities without existing large refugee populations. About 8,000 Cambodian refugees were settled under this project, and most of the sites retained their Cambodian populations and continued to receive more in later years. This project is responsible for the Cambodian population being more widely dispersed than most other refugee groups. Still, by the late 1980s, about one third of the arriving Cambodians were going to California.

Like the Vietnamese, the Hmong from Laos have settled in a geographic pattern determined largely by the secondary migration of the earlier arrivals. During the early 1980s, many Hmong settled in places that were not historically centers of refugee settlement: the Central Valley of California, Minneapolis–St. Paul, and several small cities in Wisconsin. These communities have continued to receive the majority of the newer arrivals.

The Soviet Jews who arrived in large numbers beginning in the late 1970s, and the many smaller refugee groups who have arrived since 1980, all manifest distinctive patterns of geographic resettlement. These are usually governed first by the residence patterns of their compatriots who came earlier, even several generations earlier. Government policy promoting the dispersal of refugees has had a secondary effect, although a notable one for some groups. Beginning in FY 1983, the Office of Refugee Resettlement has published yearly data on the state of resettlement of all the major refugee groups who arrived during that year. This source shows that refugees are generally placed in the most populous states, with California and New York receiving the most overall. Since FY 1987, the *Statistical Yearbook* of the INS has carried a tabulation, by country of birth, of the metropolitan statistical area of residence of refugees and asylees at the time they adjust to permanent resident status. Examination of the variations in the geographic placement patterns of the different groups is beyond the scope of this chapter but may be carried out through these sources.

FURTHER SOURCES

The 9th Edition of the Immigration and Nationality Act, dated April 1992, includes appendixes of particular value for anyone interested in the legal framework of immigration. Appendix III, "Refugee-Related Provisions," reproduces the text of recent U.S. legislation on refugees, the 1951 Geneva Convention, and the 1968 Protocol Relating to the Status of Refugees. Appendix IV, "Current or Recent Alien Adjustment Provisions," reproduces the text of various laws providing for the adjustment to immigrant status of refugees or refugeelike groups in the United States. Appendix X, "Brief History of United States Immigration Policy," is an excellent summary of just what the title indicates, beginning in colonial times.

The annual publications of the federal agencies charged with administering the Immigration and Nationality Act contain detailed statistics on the refugees and quasi-refugee groups that fall within their areas of responsibility as well as narratives putting the numbers in context. Information on refugees who become permanent resident aliens has been published by the Immigration and Naturalization Service, in its *Annual Report* from 1945 through 1977 and in its *Statistical Yearbook* beginning in 1978. A series of reports to Congress on the Indochina Refugee Assistance Program was published beginning in 1975.[18] With the establishment in 1980 of the ORR, the series became the *Report to the Congress: Refugee Resettlement Program.* It continues to be published annually. This is the best source of data on the number and timing of actual arrivals of refugees and other persons eligible for programs administered by the ORR. It also provides detailed data on their age and sex composition and their places of initial resettlement.

NOTES

1. Data used in this chapter on the yearly arrivals of refugees refer to the federal fiscal years (FY) in effect at the time. From the 1940s through 1976, the fiscal year began on July 1 and ended on June 30; thus, FY 1976 ended on June 30, 1976. In that year the fiscal year was changed so that FY 1977 began October 1, 1976, and ended September 30, 1977. The calendar quarter of July, August, and September 1976 was designated the "transition quarter." In this chapter, data for the transition quarter are combined with FY 1976.

2. Numerical limits were not imposed on natives of the Western Hemisphere until 1965.

3. Because the United States never recognized the incorporation of Estonia, Latvia, and Lithuania by the Soviet Union, INS tabulations continued to display them as separate countries.

4. The parole authority was meant to allow for the temporary entry of individuals in situations where nonimmigrant visas are not appropriate, for example, when the individual is arriving to take part in legal proceedings or for specialized medical treatment. It is also used as a convenience for the INS and travelers whose travel documents are incomplete but who are thought to be admissible.

5. The 1966 *Annual Report* of INS states that 19,705 refugees entered under the parole authority of the Fair Share Refugee Act before it was repealed (p. 6).

6. Under this law, orphans adopted by U.S. citizens were defined as immediate relatives, admissible without regard to the preference system. This meant that special provisions were no longer needed to admit refugee orphans.

7. The law defines "Cuban and Haitian entrants" as persons granted parole with this designation, which had been given to most of those entering in 1980, and to any other national of Cuba or Haiti who enters under parole or who is an applicant for asylum or is the subject of deportation or exclusion proceedings but who has not received a final order of deportation. This wording meant that future as well as past arrivals from Cuba or Haiti were entitled to entrant status.

8. The number of refugees gaining permission to leave the Soviet Union declined after reaching a peak of 28,000 in 1980 to fewer than 1,000 yearly in 1984–1986. Emigration restrictions were gradually relaxed in the late 1980s, and refugee approvals for Soviets exceeded 50,000 in 1990.

9. The Refugee Act placed a limit of 5,000 yearly on adjustments of status by persons granted asylum; no limit exists on those adjusting from refugee status.

10. J. Biskupic, "Sweeping Changes Abroad Confound U.S. Policy," *Congressional Quarterly,* February 24, 1990, 592–596.

11. During 1995, new asylum regulations were put into place to discourage frivolous

claims, speed processing, and facilitate the deportation of persons whose claims were denied.

12. Another provision of the Immigration Act of 1990 increased the annual limit on asylees adjusting status to 10,000 and waived the limit entirely for persons who had already filed by a cutoff date. The main beneficiaries of this change were Nicaraguans. At the end of FY 1994, more asylees had adjusted status than had been counted as receiving asylum. This can happen for two reasons: Some persons are granted asylum in the immigration courts, and spouses and children who follow to join an asylee also receive asylum status.

13. In FY 1995, after the period covered by this chapter ended, more developments in U.S. immigration policy toward Cuba took place. The United States agreed to develop a special migration program in which at least 20,000 Cubans would be allowed to enter the United States directly from Cuba yearly in a combination of refugee, immigrant, and parole statuses. The United States also agreed to admit the 21,000 Cubans who remained in detention in Guantánamo in May 1995, counting them as part of the special migration program. However, future migrants who tried to enter without authorization would be intercepted and returned to Cuba.

14. The "credible fear" standard falls short of the standard of a "well founded fear" of persecution required under the Refugee Act for gaining asylum, but it establishes a reasonable basis for a formal claim. Most of the 11,000 claims filed by this group of Haitians had not been resolved by the end of FY 1994 and are included in the count of 21,000 active claims referenced above.

15. These tables are not cross-classified by country of birth. In most subsequent years from 1953 through 1979, the INS *Annual Report/Statistical Yearbook* contained tables cross-classifying that year's immigrants by country of birth for major countries and metropolitan area or state of residence. In years when refugees made up a substantial proportion of immigrants from a given country, these tabulations serve to indicate where the refugees settled.

16. *Congressional Record*—House, May 14, 1975, 14338–14377.

17. The nine states are Arizona, Florida, Georgia, Illinois, Massachusetts, New York, Ohio, Texas, and Virginia. In 1983, two new sites were developed in North Carolina.

18. The first three quarterly reports, in 1975, were prepared under the auspices of the Interagency Task Force for Indochina Refugees. From 1976 through 1977, the quarterly reports were authored by the Health, Education, and Welfare (HEW) Task Force for Indochina Refugees. In 1978 and 1979, the reports were produced annually by the newly created Indochinese Refugee Assistance Program.

Chapter 16

Public and Political Opinion on the Admission of Refugees

RITA J. SIMON

This chapter examines American attitudes toward refugees since the 1930s, looking, first, at political party platforms and, second, at public opinion surveys. Before considering these American attitudes about refugees, however, it is worth reiterating the slope of the refugee phenomenon itself.

Between 1933 and the outbreak of World War II, there were more than 1 million refugees on the European continent. Most of them were Jews who had left Nazi Germany, but some 700,000 remained in countries that were eventually occupied by Germany and Italy. As of 1938, there were between 65,000 and 70,000 refugees as a result of the Fascist dictatorship in Italy. Many of them migrated to North Africa. By May 1945, right after the end of the war in Europe, there were an estimated 40.5 million uprooted people in Europe; some 1.6 million had been displaced from Eastern Europe and refused repatriation to Soviet-controlled countries after the war.

In December 1946, the United Nations General Assembly approved the creation of the International Refugee Organization, which administered a network of camps and provided housing, food, medical care, rehabilitation, and retraining.

At the 1951 Geneva Convention on the Status of Refugees, a document was prepared that defined refugees as ''those persons who have a well founded fear of being persecuted for reasons of race, religion, nationality, membership of a particular social group or political opinion, are outside their country of nationality and cannot, or owing to such fear, are unwilling to avail themselves of the protection of that country.''[1] By December 1966, 50 governments had ratified that declaration, which went on to state: ''The refugee has a special status that sets him apart from the ordinary alien, because he is without any country's diplomatic protection.''[2]

Following the end of World War II and up through 1958, there were an estimated 1,335,000 French refugees from the former French colonies of Indochina, Tunisia, Morocco, and Algeria. Holland reported 300,000 Dutch refugees from Indonesia, and some 50,000 Tibetans fled Chinese occupation to India and Nepal. In other parts of Asia, with the independence of India and the establishment of the state of Pakistan, some 15 million people became refugees. In 1962, more than 1 million Chinese fled to Hong Kong, and in January 1966, there were an estimated 1 million refugees in Vietnam and Laos.

In Africa, between 1961 and 1967, an estimated 800,000 persons had fled into adjacent countries. Three hundred thousand refugees came to the Congo from Angola, Rwanda, and the Sudan. In the Middle East, as of June 1966, 1,317,000 refugees registered with the UN Relief and Works Agency: 707,000 in Jordan, 307,000 in Gaza, 164,000 in Lebanon, and 140,000 in Syria. Of the 1,210,000 immigrants to Israel between 1948 and 1964, the majority were refugees from Central and Eastern Europe, North Africa, and the Middle East.

In the Western Hemisphere, by October 1963, 350,000 Cubans had fled their island following the Cuban revolution and the establishment of the Castro regime.

By the mid-1990s, there were some 16 million refugees with an additional 25 million displaced persons seeking refuge within their home country. According to the International Refugee Committee, that number was "the highest total ever counted."[3]

MAJOR LEGISLATION AND PARTY PLATFORMS

In the years immediately following the end of World War II, no legislation was enacted that granted special immigration rights to refugees. But in December 1945, President Harry Truman directed U.S. consulate officers in Europe to give preference to displaced persons within the existing immigration quota stipulations. Following the Hungarian uprising in 1956, Congress enacted a law that allowed 21,000 Hungarian refugees to enter the United States without regard to the immigration quotas. In 1960, the Migration and Refugee Assistance Act facilitated the admission of more than 60,000 Cuban refugees to the United States.

The Indochinese Refugee Resettlement Program passed in 1975 allowed more than 200,000 Indochinese refugees to come to the United States. In 1980, the United States established an overall policy vis-à-vis the admission and resettlement of refugees to the United States. That policy is in effect as of the current time. Under the 1980 act, refugees were defined in accordance with the United Nations convention of 1951 as persons outside their homeland who were unable or unwilling to return because of persecution or fear of persecution. The 1980 act created the Office of the U.S. Coordinator for Refugee Affairs in the Department of State and the Office of Refugee Resettlement (ORR) in the Department of Health and Human Services.

Turning now to a review of the major political parties' positions on immigration, the presidential campaign of 1948 marked a switch in the Democratic Party's position on immigration from exclusionist vis-à-vis Orientals and restrictionist vis-à-vis everyone else to a moderately positive stance. For the first time in 20 years, the Democratic Party's platform contained a plank on immigration. In 1948, the party announced:

We pledge ourselves to legislation to admit a minimum of 400,000 displaced persons found eligible for United States citizenship without discrimination as to race or religion. We condemn the undemocratic action of the Republican 80th Congress in passing an inadequate and bigoted bill for this purpose, which law imposes un-American restrictions based on race and religion upon such admissions.[4]

In 1952, the Democratic Party's plank contained the following statement vis-à-vis refugees:

Solution of the problem of refugees from communism and overpopulation has become a permanent part of the foreign policy program of the Democratic Party. We pledge continued cooperation with other free nations to solve it. We pledge continued aid to refugees from communism and the enactment of President Truman's proposals for legislation in this field. In this way we can give hope and courage to the victims of Soviet brutality and can carry on the humanitarian tradition of the Displaced Persons Act.[5]

As the cold war intensified, President Dwight D. Eisenhower, in 1953, asked the Congress to pass a law that would admit 240,000 refugees over a two-year period from Soviet-controlled East European countries. This legislation was passed when the number of immigrants allowed to enter the United States was 150,000.

The Hungarian uprising in 1956 sparked the passage of the first of a series of acts passed by the Congress over the next 25 years. The 1958 Refugee Act allowed 21,000 Hungarian refugees to enter the United States without regard to immigration quotas. After a 16-year silence, the Republican Party platform included a plank on

immigration policy which is in keeping with the traditions of America in providing a haven for oppressed peoples, and which is based on equality of treatment, freedom from implications of discrimination between racial, nationality and religious groups, and flexible enough to conform to changing needs and conditions. We believe that such a policy serves our self-interest, reflects our responsibility for the world leadership and develops maximum cooperation with other nations in resolving problems in this area. . . . This Republican Administration sponsored the Refugee Relief Act to provide asylum for thousands of refugees, expellees and displaced persons. . . . We believe also that the Congress should consider the extension of the Refugee Relief Act of 1953 in resolving this difficult refugee problem which resulted from world conflict. To all this we give our wholehearted support.[6]

The Democrats in 1956 also included a rather long statement about immigration, which began: "America's long tradition of hospitality and asylum for those seeking freedom, opportunity, and escape from oppression, has been besmirched by the delays, failures and broken promises of the Republican Administration." It stated:

We favor eliminating the provisions of law which charge displaced persons admitted to our shores against quotas for future years. Through such "mortgages" of future quotas, thousands of qualified persons are being forced to wait long years before they can hope for admission.[7]

In 1960 the Migration and Refugee Assistance Act was passed, and it facilitated the admission and resettlement of more than 600,000 Cuban refugees. Immigration was a major issue in the 1960 presidential campaign. The Democratic platform supported adjusting immigration, nationality, and refugee policies to eliminate discrimination and to enable members of scattered families abroad to be united with relatives already in the United States.

The Republican Party platform held:

Immigration has historically been a great factor in the growth of the United States, not only in numbers but in the enrichment of ideas that immigrants have brought with them. This Republican Administration has given refuge to over 32,000 victims of Communist tyranny from Hungary, ended needless delay in processing applications for naturalization, and has urged other enlightened legislation to liberalize existing restrictions.[8]

In 1964, the Democratic platform reminded voters of its position on immigration in 1960:

We proposed to adjust our immigration, nationality and refugee policies to eliminate discrimination and enable members of scattered families abroad to be united with relatives already in our midst. The national-origins quota system of limiting immigration contradicts the founding principles of this nation. It is inconsistent with our belief in the rights of men. The immigration law amendments, proposed by the Administration, and now before Congress, by abolishing the national-origin quota system, will eliminate discrimination based upon race and place of birth and will facilitate the reunion of families. The Cuban Refugee Program begun in 1961 has resettled over 81,000 refugees, who are now self-supporting members of 1,800 American communities. The Chinese Refugee Program, begun in 1962, provides for the admission to the United States of 12,000 Hong Kong refugees from Red China.[9]

The Republican Party's plank was much briefer. It stated that "we pledge immigration legislation seeking to reunite families in continuation of the 'fair share' refugee program."[10]

Neither party had much to say about immigration or refugee policy again until 1984 when the Democratic Party included the following plank: "Our nation's outdated immigration laws require comprehensive reform that reflects our national interests and our immigrant heritage. Our first priority must be to protect the fundamental human rights of American citizens and aliens."[11] It stated opposition to "employer sanctions designed to penalize employers who hire undocumented workers . . . and identification procedures that threaten civil liberties as well as any changes that subvert the basic principle of family unification."[12] It also stated opposition to "bracero," a guest worker program, as a form of legalized exploitation.[13] Additionally, the platform promised that the Democratic Party would work to ensure that the Refugee Act of 1980 was complied with: "The party will provide the necessary oversight of the Department of State and the INS [Immigration and Naturalization Service] so as to ensure that the unjustifiable treatment visited upon the Haitian refugees will never again be repeated."[14]

The Republican Party's 1984 platform acknowledged the important and positive role that immigrants have played in U.S. history but then went on to state its central message:

We affirm our country's absolute right to control its borders. Those desiring to enter must comply with our immigration laws. Failure to do so not only is an offense to the American people but is fundamentally unjust to those in foreign lands patiently waiting for legal entry. We will preserve the principle of family reunification. With the estimate of the number of illegal aliens in the United States ranging as high as 12 million and better than one million more entering each year, we believe it is critical that responsible reforms of our immigration laws be made to enable us to regain control of our borders. The refugee problem is global and requires the cooperation of all democratic nations.[15]

Once again, in 1988, the Democratic Party platform did not contain a plank on immigration. The Republican platform included much the same message that appeared in its 1984 platform:

We welcome those from other lands who bring to America their ideals and industry. At the same time, we insist upon our country's absolute right to control its borders. We call upon our allies to join us in the responsibility shared by all democratic nations for resettlement of refugees, especially those fleeing communism in Southeast Asia.[16]

Neither party adopted an immigration plank in its 1992 platform.

PUBLIC OPINION TOWARD REFUGEES

National opinion poll data were first collected in the mid-1930s. By *public opinion* we mean the aggregate of views people hold regarding matters that affect or interest the community. Connecting that definition with the data referred to in this chapter, a more precise interpretation emerges: namely, the verbal responses that a representative sample of adults in the United States have made to questions about important issues affecting refugees and refugee policy.

In the 1930s, the United States was experiencing its worst economic depression, and the conflict that was to become World War II had already broken out in Asia and Europe. It was also a period of strong isolationist beliefs and policies. The United States did not join the League of Nations when it was organized following World War I, even though Woodrow Wilson, the wartime president, had been one of its major architects and proponents. A residue of bitterness remained as the result of the failure of almost all of the U.S. wartime Allies to pay back the loans extended to them during the war, a widely shared belief that the United States had been dragged into an essentially European conflict, and a feeling that Americans benefited not at all by the Allied victory.

As the prospects for war increased in the 1930s, warnings were heard from Congress, other public officials, and leading journalists that the United States should not be misled and allow itself to be involved in another European or Asian conflict. National polls conducted in 1937, 1939, and 1941 showed that not only did the public express dislike for the prospect of involvement in a future war, but also many respondents believed the United States' entry into the previous major conflict had been a mistake.

Predictably, the first items about immigration to appear on national polls in the 1930s asked about people who were forced to leave Nazi Germany and seek refugee. In May 1938 the public was asked:[17]

What's your attitude toward allowing German, Austrian, and other political refugees to come to the United States?

Response	*Percent*
Encourage, even if we have to raise immigration quotas	5
Allow them to come, but do not raise quotas	18
With conditions as they are, we should keep them out	68
Don't know	9

Although most respondents did not favor admitting refugees, there were some divisions on this issue. When responses were broken by the economic categories "rich-prosperous," "upper middle," "lower middle," and "poor," 30 and 29 percent of the rich and upper-middle respondents answered "encourage" or "allow them to come," compared with 15 percent and 22 percent of the lower-middle and poor respondents. Similarly, 43 percent of the respondents who were professionals encouraged or would have allowed them to come, compared with 15 percent of the factory workers. The respondents' sex and age made no difference on this item.

In January 1939, after Germany had annexed Austria and invaded Czechoslovakia, the following item appeared on a national poll:[18]

Should we allow a large number of Jewish exiles from Germany to come to the United States to live?

No—71 percent

If you were a member of the incoming Congress, would you vote yes or no on a bill to open the doors of the United States to a larger number of European refugees than are now admitted under our immigration quota?

No—83 percent

Following the end of the war, the public's opinion on U.S. responsibility to European refugees was polled:[19]

There are still a lot of refugees or displaced persons in European camps who cannot go back to the homes they had before the war. Which of these four statements comes closest to what you think this country should do about these refugees?

Response	Percent
1. We should admit all of these refugees who are well and strong to the United States, no matter what other countries do.	10
2. We should take only our share of these refugees and insist that other countries do the same.	43
3. There are still too many here now and we should not admit any more at all, but we should help to get them settled elsewhere.	23
4. They are a problem for the European countries to worry about, and we should let those countries handle the problem.	17
5. Don't know.	7

Once again, the more prosperous and more educated respondents were more likely to favor admitting at least "our share" of refugees. For example, 57 percent of the "rich" said they would be willing to take "our share," as opposed to 29 percent of the "poor"; 59 percent of the college-educated respondents, as opposed to 27 percent of the grade-school-educated, were willing to take at least "our share" of refugees.

In the June and August 1946 polls, the following question was asked:[20]

Would you approve or disapprove of a plan to require each nation
to take a given number of Jewish and other European refugees based
upon the size and population of each nation?

Response	June (percent)	August (percent)
Approve	37	40
Disapprove	48	49
No opinion	15	11

In November 1947, people were asked if they would vote yes or no on a bill
in Congress to let 100,000 selected European refugees come to this country in
each of the next four years in addition to the 150,000 immigrants now permitted
to enter each year under the present quota.[21] Seventy-two percent said they
would have voted no. Here again, the more educated and the richer respondents
were more likely to vote in favor of more immigration. Sex and age made no
difference.

Respondents' Economic Status	Yes (percent)	Respondents' Education	Yes (percent)
Rich	31	College	34
Upper middle	23	High school	16
Lower middle	17	Grade	10
Poor	12	None	14

Forty-seven percent of the American public approved of President Eisenhower's request to Congress that it pass a law that would admit 240,000 refugees
from Eastern European countries into the United States over a two-year period.
Forty-eight percent disapproved, and 5 percent had no opinion.[22] Predictably,
there was more support for the president's proposal from the more educated and
more prosperous respondents. The following figures describe the differences by
socioeconomic status.

Economic Level	Approve (percent)	Education	Approve (percent)
1 (highest)	67	College graduate	70
2	58	College (one-three years)	58
3	49	High school graduate	51
4 (lowest)	40	High school (ninth-eleventh grade)	40
		Grade school	44

In the midst of the Hungarian revolt in 1956, the U.S. public was asked:[23]

> Five thousand refugees from Hungary are being admitted to the
> United States. If you have room would you be willing to have one
> or more of the refugees from Hungary stay in your house for a few
> months or until such a time as this person could be on his or her
> own?

Fifty percent said they would be willing to have a refugee live with them, 35
percent said they would not be willing, and 15 percent did not know. Referring
to those 5,000 refugees, the public was asked a month later:[24]

> Do you feel that the United States is letting in too many refugees
> from Hungary, about the right number, or not enough?

Response	Percent
Not enough	11
About right	48
Too many	34
Don't know	7

Perhaps because only 5,000 people were involved and because those who
were admitted would not be eligible for citizenship, more people thought the
number was too small or about right than complained that it was too many.

A year after the 5,000 Hungarian refugees were admitted, the public was
asked how they felt about giving them permanent status:[25]

> Under the present immigration laws, the Hungarian refugees who
> came to this country after the revolt last year have no permanent
> residence and can be deported at any time. Do you think the law
> should or should not be changed so that these refugees can stay here
> permanently?

The responses were evenly divided: 42 percent favored changing the law, and
43 percent opposed a change. The other 15 percent had no opinion.

Between the time of the Hungarian refugee crisis and when the next groups
of refugees sought asylum, the U.S. public was asked whether they would be
willing to allow any refugees to enter and settle permanently in the United
States. The question posed was:[26]

> There are an estimated 15 million refugees in different parts of the
> world. These people have been forced to leave their home countries
> or have fled for various reasons. Are you in favor of or against

allowing any of those refugees to come to the United States to make
their homes?

Sixty percent said they would favor admitting some (the matter of how many
was not asked), 31 percent were opposed to admitting any, and 9 percent did
not know or did not answer.

Four years after the 5,000 Hungarian refugees were allowed to enter the
United States, the first wave of the anti-Castro, middle-class, professional Cubans sought asylum in the United States. From the time the first boatload landed
until the exodus was over, some 600,000 Cubans settled in the United States,
mostly in Miami.

In the decade of the 1970s, more than in any other period since the 1920s,
the United States was concerned with immigration policy. The issue was thrust
into the limelight as a result of four major factors: the defeat of South Vietnam
by North Vietnam; erratic changes in Soviet policy, whereby it opened and then
closed, or partially closed, its doors to Jews and other ethnic groups (Volga
Germans and Armenians) who wanted to emigrate; Fidel Castro's willingness
to allow Cubans to leave their island and make their way to the United States;
and the illegal movement across the border between Mexico and the United
States, with hundreds of thousands of Mexicans entering the United States. The
U.S. government responded more positively to the first three factors than it had
at any time since immigration restrictions were introduced in the 1920s.

Regarding the South Vietnamese who were evacuated to the United States at
the time the Communists were about to enter Saigon and the thousands who left
in small boats after the Communists gained control, the U.S. government passed
legislation that aided their evacuation and helped them resettle in the United
States. The first refugee act allowed for the entry of 7,000 Vietnamese per
month; in the summer of 1979, President Jimmy Carter doubled that number to
14,000. However, most Americans did not support their government's actions
on this issue. For example, in 1975, when the fall of Saigon was imminent, the
U.S. public was asked if these South Vietnamese were evacuated, should they
be permitted to live in the United States.[27] Fifty-two percent said they should
not be permitted to live in the United States, 36 percent said they should, and
12 percent had no opinion. For the first time, age was an important factor in
distinguishing responses. Fifty-six percent of the respondents under 30 years old
(between 18 and 29) favored allowing the South Vietnamese to live in the United
States, as opposed to 34 percent of the respondents who were between 30 and
49 years old and 25 percent of those who were older. Age was a significant
factor in many of the public controversies of the 1960s and 1970s. The slogan
"Don't trust anyone over 30" gained widespread support, and the anti–Vietnam
War and civil rights movements were led and supported by college-age youth
and other persons under 30.

Shortly thereafter, a Harris poll asked: "Do you favor or oppose 130,000
Vietnamese refugees coming to live in the United States?"[28] Forty-nine percent
opposed, 37 percent favored, and 14 percent were undecided. Forty-eight percent

of the college-educated public favored having the Vietnamese come to the United States, compared with 26 percent of those who had completed only grade school and 32 percent of those who had finished high school.

When the issue was posed .in personal terms, for example, "Would you, yourself like to see some of these people come to live in this community or not?"[29] Forty-eight percent said they would like to see some of these people come to live in their community, 40 percent said they would not, and the remainder had no opinion. Fifty-nine percent of the college-educated population and 58 percent of those with family incomes of $20,000 or more favored this point, as opposed to 37 percent of the high school–educated and 40 percent of those with family incomes of less than $5,000.

During the same period, the late 1970s, another group of people were leaving their homeland, getting into boats, and making their way to the United States. They had a much shorter distance to go before they landed on U.S. soil. The thousands of Cubans who arrived off the coast of Florida in 1978 were granted refugee status like the Cubans who had come almost two decades earlier, but unlike the Cuban refugees of the 1960s, many of the recent arrivals were not middle class and were not members of the professional and business community. Many came from rural areas, were poorly educated, and lacked urban occupational skills. When the American public was asked whether the U.S. government should permit these Cubans to come and live in the United States, the responses looked like this: should, 34 percent; should not, 57 percent; don't know, 9 percent.[30] More Americans opposed than supported their government's action. The division of opinion for and against admitting the Cubans matched that reported for the Vietnamese almost exactly.

A May 1980 Gallup poll asked the following general questions about refugees and the obligation of the United States to them:[31]

Some people say that the U.S. government should permit persons who leave other countries because of political oppression to come and live in the United States. Others say that the federal government should halt all immigration until the national employment rate falls below 5 percent. Which point of view comes closer to the way you feel—that political refugees should be permitted to immigrate to the United States, or that immigration should be halted until the unemployment rate in the United States drops?

Response	Percent
Allow immigration	26
Halt immigration	66
Not sure	8

In the 1950s and 1960s, the U.S. public responded more positively to the special circumstances of various ethnic communities who sought admission to the United States as a result of revolution in their homelands or other extraordinary chaotic or life-threatening events. However, in 1975, when the people seeking refugee status were Vietnamese rather than European, the direction shifted, and more opposed than favored their admittance. In 1979, when a new wave of Cubans sought refugee status, public opinion opposed their admission as well. A 1985 *Los Angeles Times* national poll about immigration and economic issues asked the American public:[32]

> Do refugee immigrants to the United States take more from the economy through social services and unemployment than they contribute to the U.S. economy?

Response	Percent
Take more	46
Contribute	19
Both	9
Not sure	10
Don't know	16

By more than two to one, respondents said refugees take more than they contribute to the American economy.

In 1992 the public was asked:[33]

> Do you agree or disagree with the recent U.S. decision *to refuse* to allow Haitian refugees to immigrate to the United States?

Response	Percent
Agree	67
Disagree	27
No opinion	6

Race was an important factor in the respondents' attitudes: 70 percent of white Americans agreed with U.S. policy, compared with 33 percent of black Americans' views and 42 percent of other nonwhite Americans' opinions.

How do public attitudes about the admission of refugees compare to public attitudes about admitting more or fewer immigrants into the country? Going back some 50 years, to 1946, the American public was asked what they thought the United States should do about "the refugees in European camps who cannot go back to the homes they had before the war" and "Should we permit more persons from Europe to come to this country each year than we did before the war, or should we keep the number about the same, or should we reduce the number?" The responses to these items are shown below.[34]

	Immigrants		*Refugees*
Reduce the number	37	We should not permit any more at all, but we should help them get settled elsewhere	23
Allow more to enter	14	They are a problem for the European countries to worry about and we should let those countries handle the problem	17

In 1953, the standard question about immigrants appeared on a national poll: "Should immigration be kept at its present level, increased, or decreased?" About refugees, the public was asked about whether they supported the law that President Eisenhower was asking the Congress to pass that would admit 240,000 refugees to enter the United States over a two-year period. The responses looked like this:[35]

	Immigrants		*Refugees*
Decrease the number	39	Do not admit	48

In 1965, the standard immigration question was asked, along with, "Do you think the United States' immigration policy should or should not have provisions for admitting people who escape from communism?"[36]

	Immigrants		*Refugees*
Decrease the number	33	Should not have provisions	23

After the 1960s, the refugees items that appeared on national pools focused on non-European refugees. The 1978 and 1979 items asked about Indochinese and Cuban refugees; and in 1980, a general question was asked about whether the U.S. government should permit persons who leave other countries because of political oppression to come and live in the United States. In 1977 and 1981 the standard immigration questions were included on national polls:[37]

	Immigrants			*Refugees*		
	1977	**1981**		**1978**	**1979**	**1980**
				(Indo-Chinese)	**(Cuban)**	
			Do not			
Decrease			allow			
the number	42	65	to enter	57	57	66

In 1986, a national poll asked the same question about refugees that it has asked about immigrants since the late 1940s. The results were as follows:[38]

Recommend	*Immigrants*	*Refugees*
Same number	35	43
Increase	7	7
Decrease	49	39
Don't know	9	11

On the whole, the public support for refugees was slightly higher than it was for immigrants, but most of the time, especially when the refugees were non-Europeans, support for their admission dropped.

Further evidence for the public's antipathy toward non-Europeans coming to this country may be seen in responses to the following items asked on a national poll in 1982:[39]

Since the beginning of our country, people of many different religions, races, and nationalities have come here and settled. Here is a list of some different groups. Would you read down that list and, thinking both of what they have contributed to this country and have gotten from this country, for each one tell me whether you think, on balance, they have been a good thing or a bad thing for this country?

Nationality	*Good*	*Bad* (in percent)	*Difference*
English	66	6	60
Irish	62	7	55
Jews	59	9	50
Germans	57	11	46
Italians	56	10	46
Poles	53	12	41
Japanese	47	18	29
Chinese	44	19	25
Mexicans	25	34	−9

Koreans	24	30	−6
Vietnamese	20	38	−18
Haitians	10	39	−29
Cubans	9	59	−50

There are two things that should be especially noted about these responses. Immigrants who arrived earlier, no matter from where (e.g., the Chinese and Japanese) are viewed more positively than immigrants who are arriving in large numbers at about the time the question is being asked. And the most recent arrivals, the Haitians and the Cubans, receive much more negative responses than the Koreans and the Vietnamese.

How does American public opinion vis-à-vis refugees compare to other countries in the world? In 1975, in response to a question about whether they favored or opposed 130,000 Vietnamese refugees coming to live in the United States, 37 percent said they favored such a move; 49 percent wanted to keep them out. In 1979 when asked about Cuban refugees, the responses were roughly the same: 34 percent would allow them to enter, and 57 percent would keep them out. In 1979, when the Australian public was asked, "Should Australia take in more or less, or about the planned number of Vietnamese refugees?" 11 percent favored allowing "more to enter," 54 percent wanted to allow fewer to enter, and 30 percent supported having the planned number enter.[40] A few months later, the same question was asked, and 5 percent more of the public favored allowing more Vietnamese refugees into the country.

In 1986, 7 percent of Americans polled favored increasing the number of refugees permitted to enter the country, 39 percent favored decreasing the number, and 43 percent wanted to keep the number allowed to enter what it currently was.[41] In Great Britain in 1989, 11 percent of the public favored increasing the number of refugees permitted to enter, 52 percent wanted to decrease the number, and 26 percent thought about the right number were being allowed to come in.[42] When the same question was asked in 1992, 14 percent thought "too few" refugees were permitted to enter, 42 percent thought "too many," and 35 percent thought the number was about right.[43]

In 1990 when the German public was asked, "Are you for a change of laws regarding political asylum so as to prevent so many asylum seekers from coming into the country?" 60 percent favored a change, 24 percent opposed a change, and 16 percent were undecided.[44]

CONCLUDING REMARKS

Public responses to national poll data suggest that refugees do not enjoy a special status in the hearts and minds of the American public. Much of the antiimmigrant sentiment that has been pervasive in American society over the past 50-plus years extends to refugees as well. But it is important to differentiate attitudes and feelings about refugees in general with the responses Americans make when they hear about the troubles or obstacles that a particular refugee family has to overcome. For a specific family, or an individual, there is usually sympathy and a willingness to help. But refugees or immigrants "in general" are viewed with indifference, fear (they will compete for my job or my child's place in school), and hostility. "There are already too many of them in this country" and "Many are living off the public trough" are common expressions. In comparing American attitudes against those in other countries, especially those countries that have also had a traditional immigrant receiving policy, American responses are not atypical. The countries of the West—be it Canada or the United States, Australia, or those in Western Europe—all are anxious to close and, at times, lock their doors to most immigrants or refugees seeking admission or asylum.

NOTES

1. Suny Kim, "Gender-Related Persecution: A Legal Analysis of Gender Bias in Asylum Law," *Journal of Gender and the Law* (spring 1994):114.
2. Ibid., 115.
3. *International Rescue Committee,* Annual Report (New York: IRC 1993), 1.
4. Rita J. Simon and Susan A. Alexander, *The Ambivalent Welcome: Print Media, Public Opinion and Immigration* (Westport, Connecticut: Praeger, 1993), 23.
5. Ibid.
6. Ibid., 24.
7. Ibid.
8. Ibid., 25.
9. Ibid., 26.
10. Ibid.
11. Ibid.
12. Ibid., 27.
13. Ibid.
14. Ibid.
15. Ibid.
16. Ibid.
17. Ibid., 31.
18. Ibid.
19. Ibid., 33.
20. Ibid.
21. Ibid., 34.
22. Ibid.
23. Ibid., 35.
24. Ibid.
25. Ibid., 36.
26. Ibid.
27. Ibid., 37.
28. Ibid., 38.

29. Ibid., 39.
30. Ibid.
31. Ibid.
32. *Los Angeles Times* poll, April 1985.
33. Gallup poll, 1992.
34. Simon and Alexander, 41–43.
35. Ibid.
36. Ibid.
37. Ibid.
38. Ibid.
39. Ibid., 45.
40. Gallup International Organization, 1979.
41. *New York Times*/CBS News poll, July 1986.
42. Gallup International, 1989.
43. Gallup International, 1992.
44. Gallup International, 1990.

Chapter 17

Hardening the Heart: The Global Refugee Problem in the 1990s

BILL FRELICK

The lack of protection from one's own government is a key element in the concept of refugee. A refugee has been denied the rights associated with citizenship—the social contract between a government and its citizens has been shattered. Rather than protect them, the government either comes to represent a direct threat or is unable to protect its citizens against threats from other quarters. Denied rights due them as citizens, refugees become a unique human rights concern, as they are forced to seek protection from outside their homeland.

Although the logic of refugee status dictates some form of asylum, a place where the refugee can stay safely outside the dangerous home country, in fact, international law is decidedly weak on the right to asylum. Although the non-binding Universal Declaration of Human Rights states, "Everyone has the right to seek and to enjoy in other countries asylum from persecution," the meaning of "to enjoy" is rather vague. Governments grant asylum; individuals "enjoy" it. The refugee's right to enjoy asylum is therefore limited by the willingness of other governments to proffer it.

International refugee law defines refugees as persons outside their home countries who fear return because of persecution due to their race, religion, nationality, membership in a particular social group, or political opinion; and the United Nations machinery for refugee protection and assistance has, for the most part, traditionally not started up until displaced persons cross the line separating them from their home country, thus putting themselves into exile and becoming "refugees." The countries—usually contiguous—to which refugees initially flee have become known as countries of "first asylum" and have traditionally borne the greatest burden in caring for refugee populations. Since World War II, the goal of the international community has been to develop a system of "burden sharing" to relieve the Thailands, Pakistans, and Malawis of the cost and threat to stability presented by offering asylum to hundreds of thousands of refugees, often for many years. The development of programs to resettle refugees in the United States and other industrialized nations far removed from the scenes of the original refugee flows was intended in large measure to preserve first asylum, to keep the doors open to allow refugees to escape to the neighboring country.

For nearly 50 years, any discussion of "refugees" presupposed "exile" as a tautological given, the starting point either for providing temporary asylum or for solving the refugee problem. During this time, the United Nations High Commissioner for Refugees (UNHCR) promoted three durable solutions for refugees—voluntary repatriation, local settlement, or third-country resettlement—each of which took exile as its starting point and two of which accepted exile as a permanent fact. Although voluntary repatriation was designated the preferred solution, in most cases during the cold war, the prospects for voluntary return seemed remote, even illusory. A few lucky refugees made the best of exile, resettling in Canada, the United States, or some other far-off country; but the overwhelming majority remained in a holding pattern, languishing for years in grim, Third World refugee camps.

These millions of refugees, many of whom were exiled directly or indirectly due to the cold war, often spent a decade or more in what seemed to be a hopeless wait. During that time, however, refugees were often tolerated, even encouraged to flee their countries of origin, because they had a supporting role to play in the cold war. Refugees from Communist-dominated countries, at the least, could win propaganda points by having "voted with their feet." Often, they served foreign policy goals of host countries more directly, for example, by continuing actively to destabilize their home countries, seen as enemies by the host governments and their patrons. Afghan, Cuban, Cambodian, and Nicaraguan refugee camps, among others, were used by resistance groups to draw support, new recruits, and sympathy for their causes.

THE SEARCH FOR ROOT CAUSES

The need to address "root causes" of refugee flows has been discussed—without practical effect—for years. It has been an idea that seems obviously right, a truism: Prevent the cause of a person becoming a refugee, and avoid forcing other countries to bear the burden of caring for the refugee in exile. Identifying root causes became a cottage industry of sorts among refugee policy analysts during the 1980s. Given the preponderance of refugee movement from the Southern Hemisphere, much of the debate about root causes took on a North-South flavor, reflecting, as well, the cold war ideological biases of the time. Analysts identifying themselves with the liberal democracies of the North tended to identify root causes in terms strictly internal to the refugee-producing states, emphasizing repression and human rights abuses—persecution—associated with the violation of civil and political rights. Analysts on the other side of the ideological and hemispheric divide tended to emphasize economic imbalances and poverty, arms proliferation, and other structural forms of oppression not strictly indigenous to the refugee-producing country. This latter root cause theory, by placing much of the blame for the existence of refugee populations outside the country of origin, laid the groundwork for moral and political claims upon host countries to be responsive to refugees due to their shared responsibility for their creation. Regardless of where the blame was placed, however, everyone could talk about the need to reduce political violence and injustice and to prevent people from becoming refugees. But no one really had much of a clue how to do it.

When the international community has actually tried to address root causes of refugee flows, the response has more often than not been a case of too little, too late. By the time help arrives, great human suffering has usually already occurred, and tens or hundreds of thousands have been displaced from their homes. For example, by the time help arrived in Somalia, in November 1992, up to a half million Somalis already had died from war, famine, and disease. UN peacekeepers remained holed up in the Mogadishu airport, and critically needed humanitarian assistance remained warehoused. In Haiti, before the U.S. intervention, perhaps irreparable damage was done not only to institutions of civil society but to the very ecology of the country, as military and paramilitary forces spent three years stripping the country bare.

In general, the mechanisms of international response are cumbersome and slow moving. Just as often, however, as in the case of Bosnia, governments find it difficult to reach agreement on concerted action to avert or redress man-made disasters. Finally, the costs—political as well as financial—are often deemed too great to justify a meaningful expenditure of international resources and commitment. As a consequence, governments may find it easier, cheaper, and more in their immediate interest not to address the root *causes* of refugee flows but to deal rather with the *effect*—the refugees themselves—and treat them as the problem, rather than the massive human rights violations that caused them to flee.

PREVENTING REFUGEE FLOWS: KURDS AND HAITIANS

Post–cold war experience suggests a growing preference among governments to prevent the flow of refugees rather than to prevent the abuses, violence, and social inequities that cause them to flee. Croatia pushing back Muslims attempting to flee Bosnia, Pakistan denying entry to new flows of Afghans fleeing ethnic violence, Italy summarily returning Albanian boat arrivals, Kenya trying to close its borders to Somalis—these are but some of the early post–cold war examples of would-be refugees being forced to remain in their home countries, despite their fears of remaining and their desire to leave. These examples illustrate a new paradigm for the international community's response to refugees that has emerged in the post–cold war world: Would-be refugees are prevented from becoming refugees at all; asylum outside their country is denied, as the world community pledges to protect them inside the country where they fear persecution or violence.

This paradigm shift started with the first post–cold war refugee crisis. As Iraqi President Saddam Hussein turned the guns of his defeated army on his own troublesome Kurdish and Shi'a minorities, more than a million refugees fled toward the Iranian and Turkish borders. Turkey, engaged in civil war with its own Kurdish minority, was unwilling to allow a massive flow of Kurdish refugees across its borders. The international community came to Turkey's aid with UN Security Council Resolution 688, which was framed not as a condemnation of Saddam Hussein's repression of the Kurds but rather as a response to the "massive flow of refugees towards and across international frontiers." Its focus was on the instability created by the Kurds themselves—that their flight across borders would "threaten international peace and security in the region." In short, the refugees were defined as the problem.

Resolution 688 was used to authorize "Operation Provide Comfort," the creation of a "safe zone" in northern Iraq. While the rhetoric of Operation Provide Comfort was humanitarian, and the military was, in fact, mobilized for purposes that were, in part, humanitarian, something else was going on: the prevention of a refugee flow. This was not an effort to address the root causes of the refugee flow so that potential refugees would feel secure enough to choose not to leave. In fact, they had no choice; asylum in neighboring Turkey was denied, and the assistance that did arrive came as much to shore up political alliances with friendly governments and to challenge the enemy regime as it did to assist the refugees. In short, the Kurdish refugees were prevented from seeking asylum in Turkey, and despite the carving out of a safe zone, Saddam Hussein continued to cast a shadow over the area.

The U.S. response to Haitian refugees following the September 1991 overthrow of democratically elected President Jean-Bertrand Aristide followed a similar pattern. At first, continuing a long-standing U.S. policy, Haitian boat people were interdicted by the U.S. Coast Guard and screened for potential refugee claims aboard the cutters. As the numbers swelled, however, the Haitians were off-loaded at the U.S. naval base at Guantánamo, Cuba. As the numbers of Haitians at Guantánamo grew, the United States took the extraordinary step between May 1992 and July 1994 of automatically returning every Haitian interdicted on the high seas without even a cursory interview to determine whether the person might be in danger of persecution if returned.

Rather than create a "safe haven zone," as in northern Iraq (a similar effort would come later, with the use of the Guantánamo naval base in Cuba), the initial justification for returning Haitian asylum seekers to Haiti was that they would be able to apply for refugee status through the U.S. embassy in Port-au-Prince.

IN-COUNTRY REFUGEE PROCESSING

As long as the United States maintained the policy of automatic return, and the refugee problem was "solved" by sending them back, the U.S. government had little incentive to push hard to bring about the changes that would convince Haitians to stay home. As Haiti kept plummeting into a deepening hole of repression and misery, the much-vaunted U.S. refugee processing procedure directly out of Haiti, inherently flawed from the start, failed to protect the most vulnerable. Applicants were forced to wait, unprotected, often for months while their cases were pending, and, amazingly, were required to produce a passport— for which they needed to be fingerprinted by the Haitian authorities—before being admitted to the United States. State Department statistics show that the approval rate for applicants for refugee status in Port-au-Prince stood at 7.7 percent from the beginning of refugee processing from Haiti, February 1992, through January 1994 (in contrast to 84 percent approval for all nationalities applying for refugee status through U.S. diplomatic posts abroad in Fiscal Year [FY] 1993). But that only told part of the story; out of 49,928 preliminary applications received by the U.S. embassy in Port-au-Prince during that time, only 817 cases had been approved. Most applicants had no hope of ever having an interview.

The in-country refugee processing procedure was not unique to Haiti. In fact, it had become the cornerstone of U.S. refugee resettlement policy in the early 1990s, demonstrating, at times, more of a convenience for government bureaucrats than an attempt to save the most vulnerable refugees. What protection was really being offered for people claiming to fear for their lives? They were basically told to "take a number and wait your turn." And, they were left to their own devices to figure out how to avoid arrest during the wait.

In-country processing sends the implicit message: You can only be protected if you are willing to wait in line. In-country refugee processing may do some good for some people under certain circumstances, but it cannot substitute for the right to seek asylum outside the country of persecution for those for whom the danger is too great to wait. Since overseas refugee admissions procedures are completely discretionary, the U.S. government could designate as a refugee for U.S. admission almost anyone it chose; it was compelled to take none. Because the number of applicants was so high, and the number of refugees to be admitted to the United States was determined by budgetary and political requirements, there were far more applicants than could ever be admitted, even if high numbers had bona fide claims. Therefore, for a time, the U.S. refugee adjudicators in Haiti created a screening standard requiring applicants to show a higher level of threat than what is required under international law to establish refugee status.

A similar in-country procedure for processing refugees was created at the height of the Vietnamese boat exodus. However, those who decided to flee by boat were never turned back because such a program existed. In the 1980s, it would have been unthinkable for the United States to have said that the existence of an Orderly Departure Program from Vietnam would mean that Vietnamese boat people could be summarily returned without a hearing.

In-country processing has also been used for resettling Soviet Jews and Evangelical Christians out of Moscow. In fact, due to the direct admissions from Haiti, Cuba, Vietnam, and the former Soviet Union, roughly three quarters of "refugee" admissions to the United States in 1994 were not even refugees by international definition, because they were not outside their home countries when they were so designated. Long before in-country refugee processing had started for Haitians, Ricardo Inzunza, the deputy commissioner of the Immigration and Naturalization Service (INS) in the Bush administration, identified the problems associated with in-country processing:

Unfortunately, in most cases, those most in need of this legal remedy [i.e., in-country processing]—those most vulnerable to abuses and with least access to any viable alternative—are least likely to be able to take advantage of it. Those in active flight are unlikely to get into the U.S. embassy, or even to it, without being noticed and/or arrested. . . . It is slow and many persons with a "well-founded fear of persecution" simply cannot wait for such processing to be completed.[1]

Inzunza's critique was downright prophetic. In June 1992, then-Representative Stephen Solarz testified before the House Western Hemisphere Subcommittee that the use of in-country processing to justify the summary return of boat people was "a ludicrous argument."[2] He said, "In the Soviet Union, Cuba, Vietnam, and Romania, in-country processing has been an alternative option for those with the inclination, courage, and gumption to use it. But it has never been the exclusive option, and it is clear that making it the exclusive option does not conform to international law."

Solarz, then-chairman of the Subcommittee on Asian and Pacific Affairs, and a prime mover within Congress in defense of Vietnamese refugees, commented on the damage the Haitian policy would do for refugee protection in Asia:

I pity the poor American diplomat who in the future is asked to go to the British or the Bangladeshis or the Malaysians or the Thais and say, "Respect the principle of first asylum." There will be peals of laughter in the room. They will say, "Who are you kidding? You guys don't respect the principle yourself. Why should we?" We are forfeiting our moral authority here. And we are compromising our capacity to come to the defense of refugees all over the world.

Solarz need not have limited his comments to East Asia. In October 1992, Spain reached an agreement with Morocco, by which Morocco agreed to step up its patrols in the Strait of Gibraltar to prevent Moroccans from leaving for Spain; Yemen and Kenya both briefly refused to allow boats carrying Somali refugees from landing in 1992. In mid-1991, Italy began patrolling the Adriatic, interdicting Albanian boats and, in August of that year, summarily returned

19,000 Albanians who arrived by boat, including about 2,000 who refused to leave a stadium where they were being held until they were promised that their asylum claims would be considered. However, they, too, were rounded up and summarily deported with nary a murmur of international protest.

REPATRIATION: VOLUNTARY OR FORCED?

These developments on the international front may have occurred with or without the U.S. precedent. At the least, however, Solarz's point about the "poor American diplomat" is well taken. The United States lost its moral authority to protest, even when it thought the treatment of refugees and asylum seekers by other governments was wrong. On December 10, 1991, after Hong Kong forcibly repatriated 28 Vietnamese, the U.S. State Department expressed "regret" that the returnees had not been allowed to apply for a voluntary return program run by the United Nations.[3] No sooner had he spoken than the State Department spokesman was confronted with the question why the United States opposes forced returns to Vietnam but not to Haiti. He awkwardly responded that "the United States believes that country conditions in Haiti are such that the persons who are returned will not face persecution" but that in Vietnam "the United States opposes forcible repatriation under present conditions in that country." The State Department spokesman's answer held Haitians to a standard of facing actual "persecution" but seemed not to require a persecution standard for Vietnamese, talking rather only of "present conditions" there. His formulation did not actually say that human rights conditions were any worse in Vietnam than in Haiti, and, indeed, a comparison of the State Department's own human rights reporting on the two countries at that time would indicate just the opposite.[4] By August 1992, at which point the U.S. policy of summarily returning all Haitians was in full swing, the U.S. government remained silent when Hong Kong deported 200 Vietnamese from its camps for boat people. "In the space of four years, the U.S. State Department completely reversed its position on the forced repatriation of Hong Kong refugees, even going so far as to effect a policy in the fall of 1993 that permitted the Hong Kong government to attempt to send all Vietnamese asylum seekers home and force them to apply for immigration to the U.S. from Vietnam."[5]

As human rights conditions in Haiti deteriorated beyond the point at which the U.S. government could continue to maintain with any semblance of credibility that in-country refugee processing represented a sufficient and adequate protection mechanism, and under increased political pressure from the congressional Black Caucus and civil rights activist Randall Robinson, who waged a hunger strike to protest the policy, President Bill Clinton relented in July 1994 and resumed screening interdicted Haitians to determine if they were refugees. Soon overwhelmed by the number who took that opportunity to flee the country, Clinton reestablished a detention center for interdicted Haitians at the Guantánamo naval base in Cuba.

With a renewed refugee "problem" at hand, Clinton finally did take positive and firm actions to restore democracy to Haiti. U.S. soldiers occupied Haiti, and the military junta was forced out. Within six months of reestablishing the Guantánamo safe haven camp, sufficient political change had occurred in Haiti to convince at least three quarters of the Haitians at Guantánamo to repatriate voluntarily. By early 1995, the U.S. government unilaterally decided that it was safe to repatriate the remaining Haitians forcibly after brief and cursory refugee screenings.

But country conditions do not change overnight. In its rush to repatriate the Haitians, the U.S. government failed to take seriously the needs of persons who had suffered past persecution, who had a right to be assured that the changes that had occurred in Haiti since the return of Aristide would be permanent. Instead, they were told to go back before their own government had gotten on its feet and while it was still under the protective umbrella of U.S. troops. UNHCR told the State Department that it would not participate in "cursory screening" of the Haitians at Guantánamo, saying that the screening procedures "deviate significantly from international and U.S. law."

Pushing refugees home too soon has been a too-common phenomenon in recent years. By focusing on the cost of hosting refugees, and seeing them as a burden to be avoided, host countries have been pushing more and more for premature or involuntary repatriation. In various places in the early to mid-1990s, refugees have been pressured to "choose" repatriation: Bangladesh pushed hard for the repatriation of Rohingya refugees from Burma; Thailand cajoled Laotians on its soil to go home; Iran pressured Afghan refugees to leave; India strongly coaxed Tamils to go back to Sri Lanka; Mexico strongly encouraged Guatemalans to repatriate. In such cases, UNHCR, whose mandate includes the promotion of voluntary repatriation when it determines that conditions have changed sufficiently to allow their safe return, is put in an uncomfortable position. It cannot *promote* voluntary repatriation when conditions have not improved sufficiently. On the other hand, UNHCR is authorized to *facilitate* repatriation of any refugees whenever they choose, as long as the refugees are fully aware of the dangers upon return. UNHCR has walked a thin line between not promoting repatriation into unsafe conditions, yet facilitating such repatriations.

Donors have failed to meet UNHCR appeals for programs that could maintain refugees outside their home countries (and for reintegration programs for returnees, as well). At the same time, the countries of first asylum are pushing hard to close the camps that UNHCR is no longer able to fund. In such cases, the drive for repatriation appears to come less from the refugees themselves than from the host countries, who call upon UNHCR, which is no longer able to support their stay, to facilitate the repatriation.

The distinction between *facilitating* versus *promoting* return is most likely lost on the refugees. In any case, Tamils have returned to a highly volatile situation in Sri Lanka, and Rohingyas have returned to Burma with few assurances that the Burmese authorities will desist from the abuses that led the Rohingyas to flee. In many cases, it appears that refugees are repatriating from situations where the original reasons for their flight still exist, yet the international community has not shown itself to be particularly concerned with carefully determining risks and fully informing refugees about their options, including that of remaining in asylum outside their home countries.

Even in the best-run and best-financed repatriation program of recent years, in which all Cambodians repatriated from Thailand, there was still a high degree of uncertainty on the part of the returnees and a tendency to slip from encouraging repatriation to coercing, then to pushing and shoving the last refugees out. Many of the 360,000 who returned voluntarily quickly became dislocated, if not actually displaced, in Cambodia. Many who could not return to their original villages accepted cash incentives. Soon the money ran out, and they had not become reestablished. A relative handful of "refuseniks"—573—refused to go home, saying that they still feared persecution. On May 7, 1993, Thai soldiers forced them onto buses and took them across the border into Cambodia.

How is the success of repatriation measured? For Thailand, it was a great success—they closed the Cambodian refugee camps so they could then turn their attention to ridding themselves of the remaining Vietnamese, Laotian, and Burmese refugees in the country. The international community also saw it as a success: one less refugee population in need of international assistance. But for the Cambodian repatriates themselves, it was more of a mixed bag.

Hong Kong, Malaysia, the Philippines, and Indonesia joined with Thailand in saying it was time for the remaining Vietnamese refugees and asylum seekers to go home and set the end of 1995 as the deadline for doing so, leaving few options for the refuseniks among them. The United States, wanting to "solve" the Southeast Asian refugee problem, has gone along.

The Vietnamese refugee problem represented one of the long-term caseloads of a country that still fit the cold war profile. The solution, while still worrisome to many, did evolve over a number of years. In most new refugee situations, however, in the post–cold war era, there has been a rush to keep potential refugees in their home countries or to get them back as soon as possible.

CONCLUSION: THE WANING OF ASYLUM?

The post–cold war refugee system has become so intensely solution oriented that when confronted with impending refugee crises the international community is jumping ahead to solutions—either preventing the refugee flow or repatriating those who manage to escape—before paying adequate attention to the interim need to provide protection while the situation that caused the displacement is still unresolved or uncertain. The trend in U.S., Canadian, and European refugee policy suggests that "managing" or preventing refugee flows has surpassed both the goal of stopping the violence that forces people to flee and of assisting and protecting those who have managed to escape. Canada and the United States have passed laws or regulations that will allow them to enter into an agreement to permit either country to block access to asylum seekers who travel through the other's country. The European Community has signed a similar multilateral agreement, the Dublin Convention, which will allow European states also to turn away asylum seekers at the border. There is a great danger in pushing asylum seekers back to countries through which they transit without looking at the merits of their claims to refugee status. They might eventually wind up in countries to which they first fled that have less regard for due process and are already overburdened with refugees and their own human rights problems. The United States, Canada, and other liberal democracies will be able to point to their asylum procedures as being fair and lawful, but they will be on paper only. Access to these systems will be blocked to all but a select few. Iranians and Iraqis will be sent back to Turkey; Central Americans to Mexico; and Bosnians to Croatia. What happens to them at that point is anyone's guess.

By closing their own doors to asylum seekers and condoning push-backs by countries bordering refugee-producing states, the U.S. government and its closest allies have acquiesced in—if not actively promoted—the most serious compromise of the most fundamental principle of refugee protection: the right of refugees to flee their own countries and seek asylum from persecution in other countries and not to be returned into the hands of their persecutors. Until these countries are willing to act in a way that allows them to reassert moral authority to speak on behalf of refugees, the worldwide system of refugee protection is bound to founder. And those countries seem unlikely to change the way they act so long as they don't change the way they think—to see refugees not as a threat but, once again, as victims who have a right to our concern and our protection.

NOTES

1. Ricardo Inzunza, "The Refugee Act of 1980: Ten Years After—Still the Way to Go," *International Journal of Refugee Law* 2, no. 3 (1990):421–422.

2. *Refugee Reports* 13, no. 6 (June 19, 1992):14.

3. "Hong Kong Ousts More Boat People, U.S. Expresses Regret," *New York Times,* December 11, 1991 (quoting State Department spokesman Daniel Rochman).

4. U.S. Department of State, *Country Reports on Human Rights Practices* (Washington, D.C.: Government Printing Office, February 1992). The report on Vietnam, 1026–1036, cites no known executions of political prisoners or politically motivated extrajudicial killings in 1991, no documented cases of disappearances, and says that "recently released reeducation camp detainees report that camp conditions have been relaxed since 1989" (1027) and that "it remains easier to travel abroad and inside the country than was the case a few years ago. People talk much more freely with foreigners, and there is an increasing separation between the party and the State" (1026). The 1992 State Department Country Report on Haiti (633–642) says, "Haitians suffered frequent human rights abuses throughout 1991, including extrajudicial killings by security forces and partisan mobs, disappearances, torture and other mistreatment of detainees and prisoners,

arbitrary arrest and detention. . . . Following the coup, . . . the army resorted to brutality and massacre to control the population; credible estimates placed the dead nationwide at between 300 and 500'' (683).

5. Brian McCalmon, ''Winding It Up in Hong Kong: The Increasing Impatience with Vietnamese Asylum Seekers,'' *Georgetown Immigration Law Journal* 8 (1994):340.

Chapter 18

Documentary Films about Refugees

BEATRICE NIED HACKETT

Suddenly, in the 1980s, there was a burst of documentary films about refugees in the United States. That burst was the result of a combination of elements that have, in turn, changed so that documentaries about refugees today are different from those earlier ones. Of the three basic kinds of documentaries made in that decade—films about global refugee situations, instructional or training films, and documentaries about adaptation—the last marks the decade most clearly. Films like *Moving Mountains* (1989), about the Yiu Mien from the mountains of Laos, resettled in the Pacific Northwest and "catapulted from one century to another," showed how difficult it was for resettled refugees to put down new roots.[1] Today, documentaries about refugees are more likely to be about broader issues like the political, military, economic, and social reasons forcing a group of people to flee than about resettlement.

In the first section of this chapter, I survey some documentary films and videos about refugees, their purposes, range of concerns, and how they differ from each other and over time. In the second section, I discuss the elements that came together in the 1980s to encourage documentary films about refugee adaptation and how these have changed. In the third section, without becoming overly technical, I discuss some of the skills, resources, and problems involved in making documentaries about refugees and the implications of these dynamics for viewers. Finally, after some concluding remarks, I suggest how to find these films.[2]

Before the 1980s, there certainly were journalists' filmed accounts of resettled refugees[3] and newsreels about people having been driven from their homes by war or persecution: Chinese from Manchuria in 1938 or Hungarians in 1956, for example. There were videotaped oral histories and Hollywood films about other refugee populations including the Jews of the Holocaust. Here, however,

I am not concerned with journalistic accounts, newsreels, or Hollywood films but with contemporary broadcast-quality documentaries produced in the United States about refugees. By *broadcast-quality documentaries* I mean video and film presentations of factual political, social, or historical events or circumstances produced with sufficient professionalism and interest that they are suitable for (at least) public television or cable television broadcasting and commercial distribution. These are films dealing with real people and real events, as opposed to staged scenes of imaginary characters and fictional stories made in studios (Jacobs 1971:2). Nor do I discuss training films here, those short films never intended for broadcast but instead for specific audiences of health workers, police, teachers, refugee workers, and so on.[4] Many were made with Southeast Asians in mind and are now less relevant than they were as that refugee flow diminishes, programs change, and other procedures are established to bring in newcomers and help them adjust.

There are differences between working in film and working in video—video is much less costly and the production process faster, among other things—but for the purposes of this chapter, I refer to those who shoot either or both and those who often combine roles as camerapersons, directors, and/or producers as "filmmakers" and the products generally as "films."

SURVEYING DOCUMENTARIES ABOUT REFUGEES

Most of the documentary films about refugees produced in the 1980s in the United States were about Southeast Asians and their new lives.[5] They focus on those aspects of the resettlement experience that intrigued, puzzled, or delighted the filmmaker and others. Their general purpose was to educate and inform an adult audience. Any categorization of the films is arbitrary, but I think there are discernible themes, and grouping the films as I have at least gives an idea of the range of these documentaries.

By far the largest number of documentary films about the resettlement experience are those that concentrate on the themes of being caught between two worlds, of the trade-offs made in struggles to adapt, of trying the new and maintaining the old.[6] For example, there are *Survival of Sonthery Sou* (1984), about one Cambodian refugee's experience after the fall of Phnom Penh and her struggles to fit into a new culture in America; *Best Place to Live: A Personal Story of the Hmong Refugees from Laos* (1982), about Hmong families in Rhode Island still experiencing the stressful process of cultural and economic adjustment five years after their arrival; *Letter Back Home,* about Lao and Cambodian young people now in San Francisco's Tenderloin District; *Safe Haven* (1987), about 982 European Jews who found refuge in Oswego, New York, during World War II; and a film about Polish refugees, *After Solidarity: Three Polish Families in America* (1987).[7]

Some films about the resettlement experience are concerned with identity. The struggle to understand and reconcile old and new selves acquires immediacy and drama when the filmmaker concentrates on the story of an individual refugee. For example, *Thanh's War* (1990) is the story of a Vietnamese-American who, as a boy, was wounded severely in the throat during a firefight in his Vietnamese village that killed his widowed mother.[8] Loaded onto a helicopter by GIs and airlifted to the United States, he undergoes surgery, is taken in by an American family, and grows up American. As an adult, he reflects in his still-scratchy voice that he didn't flee his home, didn't choose to come to the United States, is grateful for the chances given him, yet has a sense of incompleteness. He acknowledges and celebrates his Americanness but mourns that missing part of himself. He resolves the lack by going back to Vietnam, seeking out surviving relatives, and finally, by marrying a Vietnamese woman.

Other films that explore the theme of incompleteness that is at least partly resolved by going back to the homeland are *From Hollywood to Hanoi* (1993), by Tiana, a Vietnamese-American film actress and filmmaker who returns to Vietnam partly for herself and partly to please her grandfather; and *Back to Kampuchea,* which focuses on the protagonist's return to Cambodia and his impressions of the country after Pol Pot.[9]

A different kind of adaptation film, *Blue Collar and Buddha* (1988), focuses on conflict between resettled refugees and their hosts. The film tells the story of Lao Buddhist refugees struggling in their new home in Rockford, Illinois. The historical background of Rockford is established with old still photographs and music. The situation of the unemployed "blue-collar" workers is juxtaposed to the Lao, who are finding jobs, although menial ones, and appear to be moving upward. The scenes in a dark bar with its half-drunken customers, their faces contorted as they insult Lao they confuse with Vietnamese, contrasts greatly with the daylight-lit temple ceremonies and the serene and prayerful faces of the Lao. The differences and moods produced are intentional and provocative.[10]

Other films that focus on adaptation through conflicts between the newcomers and the host communities include *Ben Da, USA* (1981) and *Fire on the Water* (1982), which both explore the conflict between Vietnamese refugees and native Texas shrimp fishermen along the Gulf coast, and *Monterey Boat People,* which does the same among fishermen in California.[11]

Still another view of adaptation is represented in *Dance of Tears,* made by the National Council for the Traditional Arts in 1986.[12] This film depicts the new lives of members of a Khmer classical dance troupe. The story of their dogged attempts to stay together, to build their art and their repertoire, and to practice and give performances in the face of the demands of complicated work schedules is a general view of problems resettled refugees face, enriched by scenes of traditional and spectacular dances. There are other short documentaries about resettled refugees' traditional arts and cultural heritage, some shot in performance locations: *The Common Thread* (1981); *Cambodian Dance Troupe: Los Angeles Festival* (1990); *Khmer Historical Mural of Khao-I-Dang* (1986); and *Lao Natasin Dance Troupe.*[13]

The Story of Vinh[14] stands out as a film about the darker side of adaptation.

The cassette description claims the film is the "story of Vinh Dinh, son of a U.S. serviceman and a Vietnamese mother, who makes the journey from Vietnamese culture, from youth to manhood, and from false dream to harsh reality." The description gives no hint that Vinh does this by getting into trouble first with two sets of American foster parents and then with the law, until, finally, he winds up in prison. He says that being in prison is not so bad; it is like the reeducation camps in Vietnam.

There are documentary films that include the experiences of refugees from several regions of the world and, sometimes, of immigrants who may not technically be called refugees. For example, *Stories of Survival: Refugees in Atlanta* (1988) is a four-part series in which a Cambodian woman and men from Vietnam, Afghanistan, and Cuba relate their experiences to an interviewer. A 25-minute video for high school and college students, *The New Pilgrims* (1984) examines the adjustment of both refugees and immigrants from Central America, Mexico, Vietnam, Korea, and the Philippines and their effect on the labor force. *Between Two Cultures* (1990) has intergenerational conflict as its theme. The film follows Vietnamese and Salvadoran young people trying to fit in their new society yet still attempting to fulfill the expectations of their parents.[15]

Generally, however, documentaries focused on Central American refugees are less about adaptation than about flight. *Camino Triste: The Hard Journey of the Guatemalan Refugees* (1983) is the story of some 125,000 Guatemalan, mainly Maya Quiche, Indians who fled a brutal counterinsurgency program and live a precarious existence in southern Mexico. Another film, *Todos Santos: The Survivors* (1989), is about the flight to Guatemala City and Mexico of villagers who survived the terror of a night in 1982 when they were herded and sealed into their church for destruction by the Guatemalan army.[16]

While the films about Southeast Asians going home have identity and the incomplete person as their themes, films about Central Americans going home are concerned with repatriation from refugee camps and the problems of starting anew in their old homes. For example, *Refugees Do Return Home* (1990) is about Salvadorans returning to their homes in 1989; *Peace Peeping Up* (1988) is concerned with Mayan refugees from Nicaragua who are being repatriated from camps in Honduras to their traditional homelands; and *Return of the Maya* (1992) describes the plight of Mayan refugees from Guatemala living in refugee camps in Mexico and working with Mexican archeologists at excavation and restoration of ancient Mayan ruins.[17]

Films about contemporary refugee-producing situations and their political, social, and economic backgrounds can be quickly outdated as circumstances change; as emphasis shifts from the refugees themselves to the situation that produced flight, the point of view of the film often changes as well to one of open advocacy. The film *Haiti Dreams of Democracy* (1987) is about Haiti's social and economic crisis at the time and only incidentally about refugees. It focuses on music and song and the importance of radio in a country with an 85 percent illiteracy rate; so it is useful in a limited way. *Cuba: The Shadow of*

Doubt (1986) examines the origins of Castro's revolution, U.S.-Cuban relations, and everyday Cuban life as background for refugee flight; much has changed since the film was made. *Against the Wind and Tide* (1982), however, is about the Mariel boat lift and the experiences of Cubans seeking asylum in the United States.[18]

Documentaries about refugee adaptation in the United States may have slowed, but they have not ceased. *Cambodian Doughnut Dreams* (1990) is about Cambodians who own and operate doughnut shops in Los Angeles, trying to build new lives and dreams in America. Refugees themselves have begun to make films about their experiences, and fresh products have been the result. For example, the Refugee Youth Video Project in Oregon has produced *What Is My Homeland Now? The Refugee Experience* (1994) and *So They Will Know Who I Am: Traditional Artists in Refugee Communities* (1994). Another film shot by a young Cambodian with a camcorder, *a.k.a. Don Bonus* (1995), chronicles his own senior year of high school, struggling to graduate in spite of family crises and peer pressures. But films like *Who Are Refugees?* (1993), *Central Americans* (1993), and *Rwandan Nightmare* (1994) signal an increasing interest in broader concerns in the 1990s.[19]

BEHIND THE SCENES: 1980 AND BEYOND

The large numbers of Vietnamese, Laotians, and Cambodians resettled in the United States in the aftermath of involvement in the "Indochina" wars were the first refugees many Americans knew; the refugees impressed them greatly. As refugees settled into cities and communities all over the United States, their hosts wondered about and wrestled with the newcomers' different appearances, languages, religions, and traditions; the sense of responsibility and sympathy for these newcomers was not always, but mostly, real and generous. The refugees, for their part, found the reality of their new lives brought economic, mental, and physical problems. As Southeast Asians were trying to adapt, the decade's turmoil in Central America drove Salvadorans, Guatemalans, and others to the United States, and Americans' attention was drawn to their different situations.

This influx of large numbers of resettled refugees, then, became the catalyst in a mix that included newsreel and journalistic experience, a well-developed technology, and numbers of trained filmmakers, enabling more specific elements to interact. First, there was the interest of documentary filmmakers in the resettled refugees; the filmmakers were practitioners and boosters of a medium they felt ideal for exploring and telling refugees' stories with the excitement they themselves felt.

Second, federal, state, and local governments were interested in how the newcomers were adapting and what could be done to accelerate the process with compassion and efficiency. Grants were made to research these questions, and scholars and refugees began talking to each other about problems and adaptation.

Third, there were mutual assistance associations (MAAs) and other groups of refugees who themselves wanted the larger community to understand them and their stories. From the refugees' point of view, the "progress" they were making in their new lives coexisted with their need to maintain and record what was good and useful from their old lives.

Fourth, there were audiences in the host communities who wanted to learn more about these newcomers.

Fifth, there was the ready agency of public television and cable stations across the country to show the films to large audiences and the likelihood of ongoing commercial distribution.

Sixth and finally, in those early days, there was funding from several sources for those willing to go through the process of proposal writing and competitive appeals. Nonprofit and church groups, state arts and humanities agencies, and private foundations made grants for research, story development, production, and postproduction phases of films about the newcomers. Each funding source had its own guidelines and requirements, which, in turn, affected the final products.

While these elements still exist, they have changed. Funding for documentary films has become much harder to secure as funders redefine their own goals and images and shift their dollars accordingly. Funding films is an expensive risk many foundations and arts and humanities councils are no longer willing to take. At the same time, the flood of refugees has slowed, and interest in newcomers' problems, from wherever they come, has diminished. News accounts draw our attention to faraway places as refugee environments. Filmmakers, too, are finding other locations to document refugee experiences. For example, *Tibet in Exile* (1991) tells the story of Tibetan refugees living in India. [20]

MAKING DOCUMENTARY FILMS ABOUT REFUGEES

Documentary filmmakers have points of view when they make films or videos. A point of view is not the same thing as the story, nor is it an ulterior motive or a devious manipulation. A viewpoint means merely that filmmakers, the persons who ultimately organize, form, and present the material of the story (Foss 1992:5), have not only the story in mind but the manner in which it is to be told. They look at the story from a particular vantage point (Foss 1992:5), just as the author of a book does. They are not ethnographic filmmakers, nor are these films ethnographic films. [21]

Certainly filmmakers strive for some objectivity when they point the camera here or there, but why here and not there? The camera may record an event, but the viewer does not see everything that was shot nor, especially, what was *not* shot. Close-ups may grab our attention, but they are designed to do so, and we accept the filmmaker's decision to emphasize one thing or other; we might have chosen something or someone different.

Editing, the process of choosing, arranging, and linking (cutting) suitable and visually satisfying film footage into logical sequence with appropriate narrative or internal dialogue and other background sound and titles, likewise reflects the filmmaker's point of view. Editing is the expensive postproduction process that gives the film the smooth finish we've come to expect.

Just as filmmakers have points of view, so, too, does the folk ensemble or temple or MAA or individual refugee who wants or consents to have a film made. The process starts with an idea for a film about something or someone. If the idea originates with the filmmakers, they must build rapport and trust with the person or group to be filmed. If the idea originates with a group, they must find a congenial, sympathetic, and skilled filmmaker they can trust. Together the filmmaker and the protagonist or representatives of the group, sometimes with an outside expert, work out a general storyline or treatment in plain language (Baddeley 1973:12) and a tentative plan to film the visuals that will carry the story forward, give it dramatic interest, evoke the feeling or mood intended, and fit the point of view. (Usually by this point, serious efforts are made to find funding.)

Much serendipity is involved in documentary filmmaking. For example, a demonstration by neighbors against parking cars along their properties during a celebration at a Buddhist temple erupts, and the county sheriff appears. The filmmaker had set out to record the ceremony itself but winds up filming the unpredicted and visually exciting confrontation. Should it be used? Would its use change the original intent of the film? What is the filmmaker's proper role (Barnouw 1993:272)? Whose concerns are paramount; whose ethics prevail?

Even the manner in which an event or person is filmed is important to skilled filmmakers, who can lovingly light and display a sympathetic subject as easily as they can harshly hold an unsympathetic one in the unrelenting lens. The point of view of some filmmakers is more openly political than others, but generally, documentary filmmakers do not set out crassly to manipulate viewers' feelings and emotions, though they may wind up doing so. Manipulating audiences by arranging moving images is nothing new for filmmakers; think of the propaganda films on all sides in World War II or even Vietnam (Barnouw 1993:272).

Beyond the point of view, there are other levels at which filmmakers' skill and the time, money, and other resources available to them influence the final product. There is, first of all, the conception, the idea of what the film is to be about, its purpose and decisions about how best the story can be expressed on film. There are the visuals to be considered. A dramatic story or event usually makes a good film, but without good visuals to show action and to translate the story, the job is more difficult. There are also limits of scope, depth, and intended audience as well as limits of time, money, and resources. The story must be one that can be sufficiently explored and contained within designated time limits. Documentary filmmakers usually work to an approximate 27-minute or 58-minute format to fit public television programming requirements. The film about the Khmer classical dance troupe, *Dance of Tears,* had seed money from a Swiss television network through the Swiss cameraman working on the film, and they wanted two 45-minute segments to fit their programming requirements.

This was done and then redone for American television requirements—an expensive and time-consuming editing process.

There is the actual shooting of the film, the production. Depending on funding, the filmmaker may shoot film at a ratio of 7:1, that is, seven feet of film shot for every one used. With less expensive video, a 10:1 or 11:1 ratio is not unusual. Documentary filmmakers do not always have the luxury of planning shots far in advance, nor can they ask for a special event to be repeated. Some filmmakers shoot everything in sight and worry about putting it together later. Some, necessarily more frugal of time, money, or story, shoot only carefully planned events, hoping to bridge them with narrative. Generous money and time budgets can allow for shooting reenactments or travel. Many documentaries make use of voice-over narrators or include "talking heads" to explain, interpret, or bridge action and further the theme.

There is, most importantly, the postproduction editing already discussed, which melds the elements together into a whole. And there is the distribution, which guarantees that a large viewing audience will enjoy the film for as long as possible. For example, the rights to one of the films mentioned here was sold to the Discovery Channel on cable for three years. The filmmakers were able to pay off some debts and were assured of more viewers than through other kinds of distribution. Rarely does anyone involved in the kinds of documentaries described here receive a salary. Most filmmakers who make documentaries about refugees hope to produce a worthwhile film and to break even doing it.

Making documentaries is much like creating an exhibit (without the funding anxiety); curators and their teams designate a story—what is to be explained and understood about some phenomenon—and the theme that will best support that message or explanation. The curators do their research, choose and arrange artifacts, and prepare captions to support the theme in a logical way and lead the viewer to the desired conclusion.

Like exhibits, films run into problems in planning and execution. Funds run out, new material or ideas must be taken into account, committees disagree, subjects of the film demand a voice in production, an expert is unavailable at crucial times, or the protagonist becomes ill or moves. I know of a film seven years in progress that illustrates some of the problems that occur in making films about refugees. Let me give the example.

Some members of a Lao community wanted to commission a film about the Lao temple and its important role in the lives of their refugee community, both for themselves and to educate their neighbors about Lao Buddhism. In this community was a skilled professional cameraman who had already been videotaping temple activities without any thematic organization. The cameraman was joined by an American who would act as producer, and together they agreed to undertake to find funding for the project. A principal source of funds at the time required the applicants to assemble an advisory committee including community representatives and scholars familiar with the community through their research.

This suited everyone involved; the proposal was successful, funds were granted, and work started.

Tensions developed, however, when some footage, exciting to the filmmakers, alarmed the monks because it showed an aspect of adaptation they thought unflattering and unfair to the Lao community and unsuitable for the film. The original concept was rethought, and agreement (or compromise) was reached. But this took time and money as the film was reedited and more film was shot. Money ran out and other funds were sought as the months passed. Unexpectedly, the filmmakers, because they were considered "experts" by the Lao, encountered increased difficulty getting the community advice and discussion they wanted.

A rough cut (a tentative and roughly edited version of part or all of a film in approximate sequence) that took into account the monks' concerns was put together for the full committee. Committee members had varying experiences and knowledge of filmmaking and of the Lao refugee community. All agreed on the film's artistic merits but found the theme unclear. The filmmakers concurred but, having run out of funds, had to put the project on hold while they sought funds for the final postproduction phase. The film was only completed after seven years and the support of many individuals and institutions.[22]

The dynamics of filmmaking have implications for viewers. Just as an aware reader approaches a book, a viewer who approaches a film, understanding not only the story but the filmmaker's point of view, purposes, and devices, derives more satisfaction from the film. The levels at which the filmmaker's skills and resources make a difference have corresponding levels in an audience's own skills and experience as viewers.

At the level of film as medium, striking and sharp images, changing camera angles, smooth transitions, color and lighting awareness, appropriate and judicious use of "talking heads" or reenactments—all contribute to a visually satisfying film. Audiences know that badly held cameras distort and disturb, just as badly conceived themes confuse. Heavy-handedness is boring, and clunky transitions (usually the result of insufficient funding for postproduction) give a home-video feeling.

At another level, the level of story, the same skills used to examine a book or article apply. What do the filmmakers (authors) intend, and do they succeed? The description on the videocassette or in the catalog tells something about the story. Does the filmmaker tell that story clearly and fairly? (A documentary is an account of reality, after all, not a work of imagination.) Are the characters presented with dimension? Do we care about them? Is the use of narration appropriate? Is information unnecessarily duplicated (Foss 1992:36)? Is the point of view of the filmmaker intrusive? Does it matter? Does the filmmaker achieve dramatic interest and/or excitement?

Another level at which we view films is to look at the issue examined. Most documentary filmmakers look at issues differently from social scientists. Filmmakers look for the tension, the drama, the excitement in the story, not for the elements social scientists hope to isolate and analyze. Yet for many who see the film on their television sets, the emotions, decisions, and actions of people made real on screen may impress more deeply and their problems make more sense than any case study in a journal.

Do the documentaries discussed here examine issues of interest to social scientists? The broadcast-quality films about refugees made in the 1980s and early 1990s are generally concerned with violence, human rights, or some facet of the experience of resettlement and the complex realities of identity, ethnicity, survival strategies, culture maintenance and the traditional arts, and even intergenerational conflict, but not gender roles. I know of only one Canadian-made film concerned exclusively with women refugees: *Women at Risk.* The film presents portraits of three women refugees living in camps in Malaysia, Zambia, and Costa Rica.[23] Films that explore class, caste, or power among refugees are more likely to have been made in the homeland before flight or after repatriation and are referred to as films about social change in film catalogs.

Issues examined in films about Central Americans differ from those about Southeast Asians. Aside from training films meant to instruct, most concentrate on such issues as the situations that caused flight, the dangers of flight, the legalities of the newcomers' status, obstacles to the asylum procedure, or the sanctuary movement itself. It may be there are fewer documentary films about Central American resettled refugees and their adaptation in the United States than there are about Southeast Asians because their status and reception are ambiguous. There is little doubt Central Americans fled their homes under many of the same conditions as other refugees. But as long as their legal status (as refugees, asylees, asylum seekers, or undocumented persons) is uncertain and public and governmental reaction to them is ambivalent—and they consequently try not to call attention to themselves—films about their adaptation seem unlikely. Another reason for the lack of films about Central Americans' adaptation may be that they have only recently begun to think of themselves as making permanent communities in the United States.[24]

CONCLUSION

There are documentary films about global refugee situations, training films, and films about specific refugee experiences. In the 1980s, when attention to refugees was focused on Southeast Asians newly resettled in the United States, most documentary films, encouraged by a full complement of factors unique at the time, explored issues and problems of the resettlement experience. As American attention came to include Central Americans, documentary films about Salvadoran and Guatemalan refugees reflected what was different about their situations. In the 1990s, some documentary films continue to be made or completed about adaptation. But there is an increasing trend perceptible in documentaries about refugees, perhaps fueled by on-the-scene accounts of refugee situations in Europe, Africa, and Asia, to reflect growing concern and interest in refugees in general and in the worldwide and particular political situations that force increasing numbers of people to flee.

The several films shot by refugees themselves and mentioned earlier, however, may signal a new genre of documentary about refugee adaptation in the United States; we may see more of them.

Documentary films about refugees put faces on the impersonal numbers we read about. They make people, situations, and problems we have not personally experienced real for us. They can explore universal themes or immediate political issues; they can be the total of what we think we know about refugees or be tools to help us learn more.

HOW TO FIND DOCUMENTARY FILMS ABOUT REFUGEES

There are many, many more films about refugees than those mentioned in this chapter; they vary in quality, length, and point of view. University and public libraries often have segments of news accounts about refugees and refugee situations for loan. They also have films and videos like those discussed in this chapter, especially in states where there are large resettled refugee populations. State arts and humanities councils, which have funded films on refugees and newcomers, often have resource centers with copies of the films they funded for loan. State refugee programs or their equivalent agencies for newcomers can also provide information about films.

The Office of Refugee Resettlement (ORR) in Washington, D.C., updated its 1991 directory of films about refugees in 1995. University Film and Video of the University of Minnesota (UFV-UM) in Minneapolis has a large selection of films about refugees listed in its 1995–1997 catalog. The Educational Film and Video Locator in audiovisual sections of libraries has an index entry for refugees and provides descriptions and distribution information.

I have found the large standard video directories and locators (e.g., *Bowker's, Variety's,* the *Video Source Book*) not very useful for finding documentaries of the kind described here because many are never copyrighted. The catalogs of smaller distributors who specialize in political or social issues, such as *First Run/Icarus Films* and the *Human Rights Film Guide,* are more likely to handle films about refugees and refugee situations. Others are named in the notes at the end of this chapter.

Other resources to check for films about specific refugee situations include organizations interested in human rights and political and social issues and change, such as Amnesty International, the Institute for Policy Studies, and the U.S. Committee for Refugees, all in Washington, D.C., and the American Friends' Service Committee. Some of these videos are unedited but can be useful. Newer films about refugee situations are often categorized and listed not under *refugee* but under the name of the particular country or group involved.

The notes that follow act as a kind of catalog for the films discussed here and suggest distribution outlets to continue your search. I have listed films with their dates and distributors wherever possible. I've failed in some cases. Occasionally, production companies were put together to make a single film and are hard to trace. Another caution: phone numbers do change. Finally, a reminder that reference librarians in the audiovisual sections of libraries are always helpful people.

NOTES

1. *Moving Mountains,* 1989, by Elaine Velazquez, distributed through Filmmakers Library (212-808-4980), belongs to the "early period," although it was released in 1989.

2. I am grateful to Cliff Hackett, Ruth Landman, and Priscilla Coudoux, husband, anthropologist, and filmmaker, respectively, for their comments and advice on early versions of this manuscript.

3. For example, the old *Omnibus* television show, a sort of cultural magazine, first on CBS and then on ABC, showed segments about Russian refugee dancers in the United States in 1954 and on Hungarian refugees in Austrian refugee camps in 1957 (Library of Congress Motion Picture, Broadcasting & Recorded Sound Division, VBD 9570–9571 and VBE 2407–2408).

4. These include films as different as *Refugee Mental Health; Psychiatric Interviewing of Refugee Patients,* 1988, available from the Refugee Assistance Program of the Mental Health, Technical Assistance Center of the University of Minnesota Hospital, 612-627-4325; and *Gift of Rice: Police and the Refugee Affairs Center,* 1988, available on loan from Chief of Police, Dallas Police Department, 214-670-3692.

5. Of the films listed in the 1991 ORR *Directory of Films and Videotapes on Refugees,* excluding instructional films, 34 are about Southeast Asians, 1 about Central Americans, 1 about Poles, 3 about Haitians, and 1 about Cubans. Five other films include segments about refugees from more than one place.

6. Of the 32 films and videos about refugees listed in the 1995–1997 *University Film and Video Catalog of the University of Minnesota,* 30 were produced in the 1980s, 2 in 1991. Twenty-five of the 1980s films are about resettlement experiences, adjustment, and adaptation. The remaining 5 are training films, films about refugee camps, and films about the refugee selection and admission process in Canada. Both of the films produced in 1991 could be roughly categorized as forms of adaptation films, although 1 includes immigrant and refugee experiences.

7. *Survival of Sonthery Sou,* 1984, is available from University Film and Video, University of Minnesota (UFV-UM), 1-800-847-8251; *Best Place to Live: A Personal Story of the Hmong Refugees from Laos,* 1982, is distributed by UFV-UM, 1-800-847-8251; *Letter Back Home,* by Nith Lacroix, is available through Independent Producers; *Safe Haven,* 1987, is available from UFV-UM, 1-800-847-8251; *After Solidarity: Three Polish Families in America,* 1987, through UFV-UM, 1-800-847-8251.

8. *Thanh's War,* 1990, by Elizabeth Farnsworth, was produced by KQED in San Francisco and is available through that station, 415-553-2892.

9. *From Hollywood to Hanoi,* 1993, by Tiana, is available from Friendship Bridge Productions in New York, 212-735-3970; *Back to Kampuchea,* by Martin Duckworth, is distributed by First Run/Icarus Films, 1-800-876-1710, and Cornell University Media Center.

10. *Blue Collar and Buddha,* 1988, by Taggart Siegel, is available from Filmmakers Library in New York, 212-808-4980.

11. *Ben Da, USA,* 1981, by David Hogoboom, is available from Cinemantics in Norwalk, Connecticut, and the University of Texas at Dallas Media Center; *Fire on the Water,* 1982, by Robert Hillman Associates, is available from Cinergy Films in Emeryville, California; *Monterey Boat People,* by Vincent Digirolano in Berkeley, California, is available from him, 415-845-2733.

12. *Dance of Tears,* 1986, is available from the producer, National Council for the Traditional Arts in Washington, D.C., 202-639-8370.

13. *The Common Thread,* 1981, is available from UFV-UM, 1-800-847-8251; *Cambodian Dance Troupe: Los Angeles Festival,* 1990, is available on loan at no cost through the Bureau of Refugee Services, Des Moines, Iowa, 515-283-7999; *Khmer Historical Mural of Khao-I-Dang,* 1986, is available through Insight MCC, Inc., Santa Cruz, California, 408-458-1628; *Lao Natasin Dance Troupe,* through the Coordinator of Information Services and Special Projects, Bureau of Refugee Services, Des Moines, Iowa, 515-283-7903.

14. *The Story of Vinh,* by Crosscurrent Media, is available through the National Asian American Telecommunications Association, San Francisco, California, 415-552-9550 or 415-863-0814.

15. *Stories of Survival: Refugees in Atlanta,* 1988, by Debbie Bowling, is available through Georgia Mutual Assistance Consortium, Hapeville, Georgia, 404-763-4240; *The New Pilgrims,* 1984, is available through UFV-UM, 1-800-847-8251; *Between Two Cultures,* 1990, through the International Counseling Center, Washington, D.C., 202-483-0700.

16. *Camino Triste: The Hard Journey of the Guatemalan Refugees,* 1983, through UFV-UM, 1-800-847-8251; *Todos Santos: The Survivors,* 1989, by Olivia Carrescia, available from First Run/Icarus Films, New York, 1-800-876-1710.

17. *Refugees Do Return Home,* 1990, from Refugee Voices, Washington, D.C., 202-832-0020; *Peace Peeping Up,* 1988, by Ana Carrigan, is available from First Run/Icarus Films, New York, 1-800-876-1710; *Return of the Maya,* 1992, by Judith Mann and John DeGraf, is available from the Video Project, 1-800-4-PLANET.

18. *Haiti Dreams of Democracy,* 1987, through UFV-UM, 1-800-847-8251; *Cuba: The Shadow of Doubt,* 1986, through UFV-UM, 1-800-847-8251; *Against the Wind and Tide,* 1982, by S. Bauman, J. Burroughs, and P. Neshamkin, through Filmmakers Library in New York, 212-808-4980.

19. *Cambodian Doughnut Dreams,* 1990, by Charles Davis, is distributed by First Run/Icarus Films in New York, 1-800-876-1710; *What Is My Homeland Now? The Refugee Experience,* 1994, and *So They Will Know Who I Am: Traditional Artists in Refugee Communities,* 1994, are available on a single videocassete from IRCO in Portland Oregon, 503-234-1541; *a.k.a. Don Bonus,* 1995, is a coproduction of the National Asian American Telecommunications Association (NAATA) and Wayne Wang and is available from them, 415-863-0814; *Who Are Refugees?* 1993, is available from Refugee Voices, Washington, D.C., 202-832-0020; *Central Americans,* 1993, by Rhonda Fabian and Jerry Baber, is distributed by Library Video Company; *Rwandan Nightmare,* 1994, is distributed by First Run/Icarus Films in New York, 1-800-876-1710.

20. *Tibet in Exile,* 1991, by Barbara Banks and Meg McLagan. Contact UFV-UM at 1-800-847-8251.

21. Heider (1976:6) states that the goal of ethnographic filmmakers is ethnography,

that is, a detailed description and analysis of human behavior based on long-term ob-
servational study on the spot. For a successful ethnographic film, he continues, filmmakers must think ethnographically, or scientifically, and ethnographers must think
cinematographically, or visually (ix). For more on ethnographic films, see *Films as Ethnography* (Crawford and Turton 1992) and *Films for Anthropologial Teaching* (Heider
1977).

   22. *Too Much Air to Breathe,* 1995, by Priscilla Coudoux and Sylvain Coudoux, is
available from Samsara Communications, 202-543-1672.

   23. *Women at Risk,* by the Société de radio-télévision du Québec, is available from
Filmmakers Lab in Quebec, Canada.

   24. I am indebted to Lori Kaplan of the Latin American Youth Center in Washington,
D.C., for this insight.

REFERENCES

Baddeley, W. Hugh. 1973. *Documentary Film Production.* London & New York: Focal
      Press.
Barnouw, Erik. 1993. *Documentary: A History of the Non-Fiction Film.* New York and
      Oxford: Oxford University Press.
Crawford, Peter Ian, and David Turton, Editors. 1992. *Films as Ethnography.* Manchester
      and New York: Manchester University Press.
Foss, Bob. 1992. *Filmmaking: Narrative & Structural Techniques.* Los Angeles: Silman-
      James Press.
Heider, Karl G. 1976. *Ethnographic Film.* Austin & London: Voltex Press.
————, Editor. 1977. *Films for Anthropologial Teaching.* Washington, D.C.: American
      Anthropological Association.
Jacobs, Lewis. 1971. *The Documentary Tradition.* New York: Hopkinson & Blake.

Chapter 19

An Annotated Introduction to the Literature

DAVID W. HAINES

The following citations provide an introduction to the vast and scattered literature on refugees in the United States. Because the literature is so extensive, considerable selectivity has been necessary. I have been guided by three principles: The first principle is relevance. I have tried not to stray from the specifics of refugees in the United States into the situation of refugees in other countries, other immigrants to the United States, or the situation of refugees in their countries of origin. Nevertheless, a few references appear for general immigration and refugee items that may serve as a starting point for a more general search. As well, some references to Central Americans are included, even though the legal changes of the 1986 Immigration Reform and Control Act have tended to mute their claims to refugee status.

The second principle is availability. Items that are not readily available (such as out-of-print reports, articles in defunct or rare journals, papers presented at meetings) are not included. Most of the items included here should be available in a reasonable university library or through on-line bibliographic services. NTIS (National Technical Information Service) will be useful for government-sponsored research reports.

The third principle is parsimony. I have refrained from multiple references to a single source. There are thus no separate references to items found in a single listed book or journal volume. Multiple citations of individuals are also generally avoided; no one, however voluminously published, has more than two direct citations to his or her individual credit here. Also excluded for reasons of parsimony are popularized accounts, journalistic reports, and personal narratives—useful as these may be for understanding the difficulties that refugees face and overcome.

The result is an introduction to the academic literature that excludes many good items. I bear the responsibility for these trade-offs in selection and for the content of the annotations. Both reflect an involvement with this kind of bibliographic effort that began 15 years ago when I went to work for the federal government's refugee resettlement program to conduct a review on the then fairly limited research on refugee adjustment in the United States.

Adelman, Howard, Editor. 1991. *Refugee Policy: Canada and the United States.* Staten Island, New York: Center for Migration Studies. 455 pages. Series of 20 papers from a 1990 conference. The volume covers both overseas and domestic resettlement and asylum issues for both countries. For resettlement, the more germane papers are on the 1980 Refugee Act (Zucker and Zucker), the economic progress of Southeast Asian refugees (Bach and Argiros), and the mental health of Southeast Asian refugees (Rumbaut). However, the other papers on asylum and on comparisons with Canadian resettlement are also of interest.

Aguirre, Benigno E. 1974. Differential Migration of Cuban Social Races: A Review and Interpretation of the Problem. *Latin American Research Review* 11(1):103–124. Analysis of the factors leading to the predominantly white racial composition of early Cubans coming to the United States. The author reviews the existing data on the various waves of Cuban refugees and notes that although occupational levels have gradually fallen, racial homogeneity has increased. The explanation offered is that Afro-Americans are seen as "both a major bulwark of the revolution and one of its main beneficiaries." The tendency for black Cubans in the United States to have a distinctive geographical distribution is also mentioned.

Airriess, Christopher A., and David L. Clawson. 1991. Versailles: A Vietnamese Enclave in New Orleans, Louisiana. *Journal of Cultural Geography* 12(1):1–13. Readable introduction to the unique Vietnamese enclave in New Orleans. As the authors note, New Orleans Vietnamese are Catholic, rural, and North Vietnamese in origin. The active efforts of the Catholic Church, the availability of large blocks of apartments, and the relatively familiar climate have combined to create a setting somewhat similar to Vietnam itself. The authors highlight religion, extensive vegetable gardens, and the ethnic commercial strip, producing an unusually clear portrait of an active refugee community.

Airriess, Christopher A., and David L. Clawson. 1994. Vietnamese Market Gardens in New Orleans. *Geographical Review* 84(1):16–31. Intriguing review of gardens maintained by elderly Vietnamese in New Orleans. The authors note the emotional and economic value of the gardens and then provide a review of three distinct gardening environments: backyard gardens, densely grown levee gardens, and somewhat more extensive and market-oriented supplemental levee gardens. Description of the specific plants grown, the yearly planting cycle, and the use of fertilizers, pesticides, and equipment is also included. "In sum," the authors note, "gardening gives the elderly population of Versailles emotional well-being and economic empowerment."

Amerasia Journal. Annual. Selected Bibliography. Los Angeles: UCLA Asian American Studies Center. Annual bibliography on all aspects of Asian-American life. *Amerasia Journal,* always a valuable resource, produces this annual bibliography as part of one (sometimes two) of its regular issues. The journal is attentive to

Southeast Asian refugees, and its bibliography is probably the single best source for recent citations on a wide range of topics and ethnic groups. Very short annotations are included if for some reason the cited title does not provide adequate information.

Amerasia Journal. 1993. Special Issue: The Asian American Subject. *Amerasia Journal* 19(3). Special issue addressing neglected areas of Asian-American literature and text. Relevant pieces include an analysis of how Southeast Asian refugees have been portrayed in the media (Thomas DuBois), a review of some Vietnamese-American texts that have been incorporated and distorted in essentially non-Vietnamese-American work (Monique Thuy-Dung Truong), general themes in Hmong students' essays on Hmong history (Franklin Ng), themes of exile and home in the writing of overseas Vietnamese women writers (Qui-Phiet Tran), and a short reflection by a Vietnamese on his youth in America (Khanh Ho). The two Vietnamese-related pieces are particularly direct and valuable in presenting internal views of the refugee experience.

Ashabranner, Brent, and Melissa Ashabranner. 1987. *Into a Strange Land: Unaccompanied Refugee Youth in America.* New York: Dodd, Mead, and Company. 120 pages. Very readable introduction to refugee minors and the programs designed for them. The book is aimed at young readers but is also a useful starting point for others. The particular problems of unaccompanied minors are well described, particularly the double loss of culture and family and the unpredictability of the new country. The major portion of the book concerns Southeast Asian refugees, including a chapter on Amerasians, and provides roughly equal attention to exodus, the minors' experience in America, and the programs supporting them—especially placement in foster families.

Ashmun, Lawrence F. 1983. *Resettlement of Indochinese Refugees in the United States: A Selective and Annotated Bibliography.* DeKalb: Northern Illinois University, Center for Southeast Asian Studies. 207 pages; 1,037 entries. Bibliography through 1981 on Southeast Asian refugees, including books, dissertations, articles (journals, magazines), program documents, and miscellaneous papers. Ashmun incorporates and adds to a variety of existing bibliographies to produce a useful compendium. This is a very comprehensive and useful source for the early years of the Southeast Asian refugee resettlement effort.

Bach, Robert L., and Jennifer B. Bach. 1980. Employment Patterns of Southeast Asian Refugees. *Monthly Labor Review* 103(10):31–38. Early analysis of Southeast Asian refugee employment in the United States based on the Immigration and Naturalization Service Alien Address Report and Opportunity Systems Incorporated surveys. Bach and Bach note that refugee labor force participation rates are lower than those for the U.S. population as a whole but rise consistently with length of residence in the United States. Data also indicate that refugees consistently work more hours per week than the general U.S. population but still, in many cases, have marginal earnings.

Baker, Reginald P., and David S. North. 1984. *The 1975 Refugees: Their First Five Years in America.* Washington, D.C.: New TransCentury Foundation. 165 pages. Analysis—largely statistical—of the adjustment of the initial wave of Southeast Asian refugees. After a review of the refugees, their exodus, and the policy context in the United States, the authors focus on three major issues: settlement patterns, labor force participation, and earnings. The general conclusions suggest the relative success of 1975 arrivals and the particular success of those with better education and occupational skills (including military service for men). The possible movement of refugees into the cash, "underground" economy is noted. The analysis is based on a painstaking recreation and linking of the "Indochinese Evacuee Master File" from 1975 with Immigration and Naturalization Service and Social Security Administration data files. The authors' comments on the difficulty of that process are of additional interest.

Bankston III, Carl L. 1995. Vietnamese Ethnicity and Adolescent Substance Abuse. *Deviant Behavior* 16(1):59–80. Analysis of the correlates of self-reported substance abuse based on a 1994 survey of high school students. The general argument is that community interaction in itself has strong negative effects on drug and alcohol use—and thus should be analyzed in addition to issues of family environment and peer groups. The author considers Vietnamese language use to be particularly important. (The Vietnamese community in New Orleans is unique; see separate citations to Airriess and Clawson.)

Barger, W. K., and Tham V. Truong. 1978. Community Action Work among the Vietnamese. *Human Organization* 37(1):95–100. Overview of the constraints and options of community action work based on experience with a Vietnamese association in Lexington, Kentucky. The authors were involved in facilitating the incorporation of the association and the establishment of a small model business. They recommend the following as basic elements in such work: (1) establishing communication and mutual respect, (2) identifying areas of mutual involvement, (3) negotiating roles, (4) identifying goals with emphasis on the community's explicit interests, and (5) assessing the nature of the community.

Baron, Roy C., Stephen B. Thacker, Leo Gorelkin, Andrew A. Vernon, William R. Taylor, and Keewhan Choi. 1983. Sudden Death among Southeast Asian Refugees: An Unexplained Nocturnal Phenomenon. *Journal of the American Medical Association* 250(21):2947–2951. Review of the sudden unexplained deaths of 51 Southeast Asian refugees from 1977 to 1982. A variety of case study material, results from questionnaires, and autopsy findings are adduced to determine the causes of these sudden nocturnal deaths, almost universally of males and disproportionately common among Laotians. No clear explanation emerges, although stress is suggested as a significant factor.

Bender, Lynn Darrell. 1973. The Cuban Exiles: An Analytical Sketch. *Journal of Latin American Studies* 5:271–278. Brief analysis of the early Cuban refugee flow largely in terms of the factors affecting the departure decision. "Without question, Cuba's most successful 'export' from the very beginning of the Castro period has not been revolution, but the physical removal of its domestic enemies." Bender notes the generally upper-class origins of most refugees and their decreasing involvement in formal political opposition to Castro. A brief description of the different periods of Cuban emigration is also presented.

Benson, Janet E. 1990. Households, Migration, and Community Context. *Urban Anthropology* 19(1–2):9–29. Review of Vietnamese and Laotian households in Garden City, Kansas. As part of a broader study of immigrants involved in the meat-packing industry, the author examines the structure of refugee households and the forces that affect that structure, concluding that the "mobility and flexibility of households . . . can be explained . . . not only by cultural values but by the insecure nature of refugee employment." The discussion benefits from some clear examples of particular households and from a well-honed sense of the cultural basis of household economic strategies.

Boone, Margaret S. 1980. The Uses of Traditional Concepts in the Development of New Urban Roles: Cuban Women in the United States. In *A World of Women: Anthropological Studies of Women in the Societies of the World*. Edited by Erika Bourguignon. New York: Praeger. Pages 235–269. Analysis of the changing roles of Cuban immigrant women in the United States, based largely on the author's fieldwork in the Washington, D.C., area. The author notes the traditional schism between male and female roles in Cuba but also the significant equality and importance of women in some public domains. In the United States, Cuban women have maintained a semblance of ideal traditional roles. They have also participated actively and effectively in the world of work. The major portion of the article involves a description of various women's roles, both formal and informal.

Boone, Margaret S., Editor. 1981. Metropolitan Ethnography in the Nation's Capital. Special issue of *Anthropological Quarterly* 54(2). 55 pages. Set of seven articles (plus editor's introduction) on different ethnic groups in the Washington, D.C., area. Separate articles deal with Vietnamese (Haines, Rutherford, and Thomas), Cubans (Boone), and Hungarians (Schuchat), as well as Sephardic Jews, Palestinians, Armenians, and Serbs. Together, the articles are particularly useful in dealing with the maintenance of dispersed ethnic communities and with the unique effects of the nation's capital on immigrant and refugee adjustment.

Boswell, Thomas D., and James R. Curtis. 1984. *The Cuban-American Experience: Culture, Images, and Perspectives*. Totowa, New Jersey: Rowman and Allenheld. 200 pages. Comprehensive review of the Cuban experience in America. The authors provide initial overviews of Cuban history, the various waves of Cuban exodus to America, and the demographic and geographical profile of the resulting Cuban-American population. They also address an unusually broad range of subjects: development of Miami as the "Cuban Capital of America"; language; religion (both the dominant Catholicism and also Protestantism, Judaism, and Santéria); the arts (particularly music and painting); cuisine; and politics. The book closes with a discussion of the family, generational changes, and the likely course of Cuban assimilation.

Breyer, Chloe Anne. 1993. Religious Liberty in Law and Practice: Vietnamese Home Temples and the First Amendment. *Journal of Church and State* 35(2):367–401. Review of the legal implications about disputes on home temples in Orange County, California. The author uses a 1991 zoning case to examine competing legal approaches to the First Amendment's guarantee of the free exercise of religion (i.e., traditional "balancing" versus more recent "strict neutrality" approaches). In the process, the competing concerns of the refugees (temples as residences for monks, lack of resources to build large temples) are presented. The case finally resulted in an imposed compromise: reduction in noise and number of people in the temple in return for continued operation for a limited period of time.

Buchanan, Susan Huelsebusch. 1983. The Cultural Meaning of Social Class for Haitians in New York City. *Ethnic Groups* 5(1/2):7–30. Review of the persistence of social class among New York City's 300,000 Haitians. Haitian views of social class rest on a mix of fact and perceptions about wealth, ancestry, birthplace, residence, education, and comportment. Although economic opportunities in the United States have caused some shifts and narrowing in class differences, the structure of social class in Haiti continues to pervade social relations among Haitians in New York. In fact, that structure expands to "create mental maps of social space and to structure interpersonal interaction." The author is particularly attentive to the specific Creole words used to convey class distinctions.

Burns, Allan F. 1993. *Maya in Exile: Guatemalans in Florida.* Philadelphia: Temple University Press. 208 pages. Accessible review of Mayan refugees, focusing on Indiantown, the major end point of exodus to Florida. The author has extensive research and advocacy experience with the Maya and presents a mix of qualitative and quantitative data. The chapter on work provides a lucid review of the problems in assessing the refugees' status as asylum applicants, illegal immigrants, and applicants for legal status under the 1986 Immigration Reform and Control Act. A highly evocative, personal introduction is provided by Jeronimo Campo- seco.

Camino, Linda A., and Ruth M. Krulfeld, Editors. 1994. *Reconstructing Lives, Recap- turing Meaning: Refugee Identity, Gender, and Culture Change.* Amsterdam: Gor- don and Breach. 253 pages. Anthropological perspectives on refugees. The papers focus on identity and gender, with representation of Cubans (Boone), Cambodians (Mortland, Kulig), Lao (Krulfeld), Soviet Jews (Markowitz), Afghans (Omidian), Southeast Asians in general (Benson), and refugee students in general (DeVoe). The papers provide a variety of useful insights based on first-person research but are probably most notable for very extensive attention to women and the structure of family and community relations. Useful and readable.

Canda, Edward R., and Thitiya Phaobtong. 1992. Buddhism as a Support System for Southeast Asian Refugees. *Social Work* 37(1):61–67. Review of the services pro- vided to refugees by three midwestern Buddhist temples—two Lao and one Khmer. The discussion of the 1987–1989 research is very general but does pro- vide a useful overview of temple services and how they compare with secular American services. The integration of social services with the temples' normal religious activities is perhaps most striking. Given the nature of Buddhist doctrine, the authors point out that "all Buddhist services are fundamentally spiritual in intent."

Caplan, Nathan, Marcella H. Choy, and John K. Whitmore. 1991. *Children of the Boat People: A Study of Educational Success.* Ann Arbor: University of Michigan Press. 197 pages. Survey-based analysis of the educational progress of Vietnam- ese, Chinese-Vietnamese, and Lao. The book is the result of extensive survey work in Seattle, Orange County (California), Chicago, Houston, and Boston, sup- plemented by school transcripts. Although the authors provide a general review of these refugees' resettlement, their main emphasis is on the cultural values and family structures that they argue have led to impressive educational achievement. This is one of the most important quantitative research projects on Southeast Asian refugees and one of the most direct in its conclusions: Culture and family are central to educational success.

Capps, Lisa L. 1994. Change and Continuity in the Medical Culture of the Hmong in Kansas City. *Medical Anthropology Quarterly* 8(2):161–177. Review of the medical beliefs and practices of Christian Hmong. The Hmong community in question is firmly Protestant and has forsaken much of its prior animist beliefs and practices. The author provides a succinct analysis of the implications of Protestantism for beliefs in spirits and ancestors and discusses the areas in which continuity with prior beliefs exists. The article's main subject is the mix of Christianity, Chinese medicine, and modern Western medicine that constitutes the "medical culture" of these Hmong.

Card, David. 1990. The Impact of the Mariel Boatlift on the Miami Labor Market. *Industrial and Labor Relations Review* 43(2):245–257. Statistical analysis based on census and Current Population Survey data from 1979 to 1985. The 1980 Mariel influx of about 125,000 Cubans led to a 7 percent increase in Miami's labor force and a 20 percent increase in the Cuban labor force. The author provides a description of the influx and then an interesting—if technical—analysis that indicates the influx had little effect on either Cubans or other workers in low-skilled jobs. Three factors are noted that help explain the lack of effect: (1) existing industries that could easily absorb more workers; (2) the viability of Spanish as a de facto second language; and (3) a drop in migration to Miami from other areas in the United States.

Casal, Lourdes, and Andres R. Hernandez. 1975. Cubans in the U.S.: A Survey of the Literature. *Cuban Studies* 5:25–51. Review of the literature on Cubans in the United States through 1974. The discussion is organized in terms of the following 12 topics: (1) causes of the migration, (2) demographic composition, (3) exiles as sources of information about Cuban society, (4) assimilation and acculturation, (5) political behavior and attitudes, (6) family and sex roles, (7) mental health, (8) occupational adjustment, (9) youth problems, (10) special "at risk" groups (such as blacks and the elderly), (11) relationships with other ethnic groups, and (12) impact of the Cubans on U.S. society. A short annotated bibliography is included.

Catanzaro, Antonino, and Robert John Moser. 1982. Health Status of Refugees from Vietnam, Laos, and Cambodia. *Journal of the American Medical Association* 247(9):1303–1308. Report of results from early medical evaluations of 709 Southeast Asian refugees in San Diego. Screenings, all conducted within two months of arrival, indicated a variety of medical problems, including anemia, hepatitis, and intestinal parasites. The authors present findings separately for Vietnamese, Cambodians, Hmong, and Laotians and stress the considerable variation in the health problems faced by all of these groups.

Celano, Marianne P., and Forrest B. Tyler. 1991. Behavioral Acculturation among Vietnamese Refugees in the United States. *Journal of Social Psychology* 131(3): 373–385. Research with 60 Vietnamese using an acculturation scale developed and used earlier with Cuban refugees. The results are unusual in suggesting a movement *away* from acculturation with increased time in the United States. However, those from higher socioeconomic backgrounds, and those currently employed, had higher acculturation scores. The authors note that the data—which involve relatively recent arrivals—are insufficient to determine whether this pattern of rejection is a continuing or temporary one.

Chan, Sucheng, Editor. 1994. *Hmong Means Free: Life in Laos and America*. Philadelphia: Temple University Press. 267 pages. Set of Hmong narratives, prefaced by the editor's 60-page overview of the Hmong in Laos and in the United States. The narratives are particularly valuable in providing related views from within four distinct families. Stories from each family were taped and transcribed by a student son or daughter of the family, who also wrote his or her own narrative. Two other free-standing narratives are also included: one by a major community leader. The multiple perspectives from within families make this a unique resource.

Cichon, Donald J., Elzbieta M. Gozdziak, and Jane G. Grover. 1986. *The Economic and Social Adjustment of Non–Southeast Asian Refugees*. 2 vols. Dover, New Hampshire: Research Management Corporation. Two-volume, federally funded study of Afghans, Ethiopians, Poles, and Romanians. The study aimed to assess the adjustment of these groups, the nature of their interaction with the refugee resettlement system, and the ways in which their resettlement could be improved. Volume 1 provides the general findings, and Volume 2 provides reports from the study's five sites (Dallas, Chicago, Washington, D.C., Los Angeles, and New York City). The research included discussions with service providers at each site, reviews of agency records, and native-language interviews with some 200 refugees. The study is an important counterbalance to the voluminous federally funded research on Southeast Asian refugees.

Clarke, Greg, William H. Sack, and Brian Goff. 1993. Three Forms of Stress in Cambodian Adolescent Refugees. *Journal of Abnormal Child Psychology* 21(1):65–77. Results of psychological testing and interviewing of 69 Cambodian refugee youth in Oregon who had lived through the Pol Pot years. The authors look separately at war-related trauma, the strains of resettlement, and recent stressful events common to the general population. The results indicate the continuing effects of war-related events. In addition, the results indicate a clear division between PTSD (posttraumatic stress disorder) and depression, with depression linked to more recent events. The general suggestion is that while depression may wane over time, PTSD is likely to continue.

Cole, Ellen, Oliva M. Espin, and Esther D. Rothblum, Editors. 1991. *Refugee Women and Their Mental Health: Shattered Societies, Shattered Lives*. New York: Haworth Press. 308 pages. Collection of papers on the psychological impact of refugee status on women. The papers range widely in topic and approach but do a good job of conveying both the disorientation of exile and the sharply brutal treatment that refugee women receive throughout the stages of exodus, transit, and resettlement. Of most relevance to the United States are articles on Afghan, Cambodian, Salvadoran, Soviet Jewish, and Vietnamese refugees.

Cooney, Rosemary Santana, and Maria Alina Contreras. 1978. Residence Patterns of Social Register Cubans: A Study of Miami, San Juan, and New York SMSAs.

Cuban Studies 8(2):33–49. Examination of the residential patterns of middle- and upper-middle-class Cubans in three urban areas, based on data from the Cuban Social Register (1974) and the U.S. census. Cubans, the authors found, were most segregated by class in San Juan and least segregated in New York, with Miami falling in between. In all three cities, social register Cubans "live in high quality neighborhoods differing from other upper-middle-class areas only in terms of ethnic exclusivity." The high degree of residential clustering of upper-class Cubans in San Juan is attributed by the authors to the homogeneity of the original migrant stream to Puerto Rico.

Davis, Donna G., and Janet C. McDaid. 1991. Identifying Second-Language Students' Needs: A Survey of Vietnamese High School Students. *Urban Education* 27(1): 32–40. Brief results of a survey of Vietnamese students in San Diego. The survey included 311 grade 10 and 11 Vietnamese students (of whom 75 were Chinese-Vietnamese). The results show the generally positive experience of the students and the increase in their English-language competence with increased length of U.S. residency. The authors, however, also note problems: great concern about finances, considerable concern about safety in their neighborhoods, and some experience of discrimination—particularly by other students but also occasionally by teachers.

Delgado-Gaitan, Concha. 1994. Russian Refugee Families: Accommodating Aspirations through Education. *Anthropology and Education Quarterly* 25(2):137–155. Broad review of Russian immigrants and their use of education in a California city. The discussion includes, but is not limited to, recent non-Jewish refugees. Church support (Orthodox, Pentecostal, and Baptist) of the immigrants and refugees is of particular interest, as is the discussion of the benefits and difficulties of interaction within a Russian community that has a broad range of cultural backgrounds and emigration experiences.

DeVoe, Pamela A., Editor. 1992. *Selected Papers on Refugee Issues.* Washington, D.C.: American Anthropological Association. 145 pages. First in a series of selected anthropological papers on refugee-related issues. Selections relating to refugees in the United States include concepts of community and nation among the Lao (Krulfeld); elderly Afghan refugees (Omidian and Lipson); second-generation Latvians (Carpenter); biculturalism (Hopkins) and women's roles in acculturation among Cambodian refugees (Rasbridge and Marcucci); aspirations of Vietnamese refugee college students (Penning); general problems in refugee health (DeVoe); and Vietnamese refugees in Hong Kong camps (separate papers by Donnelly and Knudsen). This is an accessible set of insights into a wide range of groups and resettlement settings.

Donnelly, Nancy D. 1994. *Changing Lives of Refugee Hmong Women.* Seattle: University of Washington Press. 224 pages. Anthropological study of the Hmong in Seattle based on extensive personal involvement and interviewing. The author focuses on gender roles, providing invaluable insight on Hmong women's views but also a balanced view of age and gender in general and the competing forces of change and adherence to tradition. The book is especially attentive to the way in which the research developed from personal involvement with the Hmong and provides useful information on Seattle itself, Hmong textiles, development projects, and courtship and marriage. The extended life history material is helpful.

Downing, Bruce T., and Douglas P. Olney, Editors. 1982. *The Hmong in the West: Observations and Reports.* Minneapolis: University of Minnesota, Southeast Asian Refugee Studies Project. 401 pages. Collection of 20 papers originally presented at a research conference on the Hmong held in 1981. The conference was the first of its kind in the United States, and the papers, although varying in topic and method, represent an important advance in research on this refugee population. A keynote historical review by Yang Dao is followed by separate sections on cultural continuities and changes, Hmong language and communication, issues in Hmong learning of Western languages, and resettlement problems and prospects in the United States.

Duany, Jorge. 1993. Neither Golden Exile nor Dirty Worm: Ethnic Identity in Recent Cuban-American Novels. *Cuban Studies* 23:167–183. Review of three Cuban writers who bridge the Cuban and American experiences. The author notes that first-generation Cuban-American writers have tended to be concerned with issues of exile, whereas future Cuban-American writers will likely emphasize more general ethnic themes. In the middle are the three writers he discusses, for whom the "literature of exile gradually becomes a literature of resettlement." The author's analysis is anthropological—and clearly written.

Dunning, Bruce B., and Joshua Greenbaum. 1982. *Survey of the Social, Psychological, and Economic Adaptation of Vietnamese Refugees in the U.S., 1975–79.* Washington, D.C.: U.S. Department of Health and Human Services. (SSA Publication No. 13-1 1755, December 1982.) 43 pages. Executive summary of a far longer report on a survey of 555 Vietnamese refugees living in the Los Angeles, Houston, and New Orleans areas. An overview of the study itself is followed by summaries of the refugees' backgrounds, their economic adjustment to the United States, their sociocultural adjustment, and their perception and use of services. This is an important data set, particularly strong in its inclusion of attitudinal and social information and in its representation of refugees arriving in each of the five years from 1975 to 1979.

Eaton, William W., and Roberta Garrison. 1992. Mental Health in Mariel Cubans and Haitian Boat People. *International Migration Review* 26(4):1395–1415. Survey-based comparison of 1980 Cuban and Haitian arrivals in the Miami area. The authors provide a cautionary analysis that shows very different patterns for psychosis, depression, anxiety, and alcohol problems as measured by standardized interview protocols. Cubans generally show a worse situation in all four areas. Those with lower economic status also tend to show more problems. However, the relationships are neither consistent nor linear. The authors conclude that such mental health patterns are "likely to be unique to each distinct immigrant group."

Ebihara, May, Carol A. Mortland, and Judy Ledgerwood, Editors. 1994. *Cambodian Culture since 1975: Homeland and Exile.* Ithaca, New York: Cornell University Press. 194 pages. Set of anthropologically oriented papers on the survival and recreation of Khmer culture. This is an important collection of papers that address Khmer culture both in the homeland and abroad. Although only a minority of papers are focused entirely on refugees in the United States, many others have at least some comment on the situation of those settled in the United States who face the difficulties of resettlement in addition to the need to confront a holocaust

that they somehow survived. Articles by Carol Mortland (religion), Judy Ledgerwood (gender), John Marcucci (pain and its treatment), and Frank Smith (refugee viewing of television) are relevant and important.

Eckels, Timothy J., Lawrence S. Lewin, David S. North, and Danguole J. Spakevicius.
1982. *A Portrait in Diversity: Voluntary Agencies and the Office of Refugee Resettlement Matching Grant Program.* Washington, D.C.: Lewin and Associates.
125 pages. Final report of an early study of the Matching Grant Program conducted under contract to the federal government. The program involved a match
of up to $1,000 for each refugee served by participating voluntary agencies. The
report describes the operation of the program and the variations in the way different agencies use the program. Those served through the program include Soviet
Jews, Armenians, Poles, Romanians, Afghans, and Ethiopians.

Edelman, Joseph. 1977. Soviet Jews in the United States: A Profile. In *American Jewish
Yearbook, 1977.* Edited by Morris Fine and Milton Himmelfarb. New York: The
American Jewish Committee. 24 pages. Useful early overview of the Soviet refugees who had come to the United States through the end of 1975. The author
covers the following areas: general migration patterns; the problem of dropouts
(*noshrim*); places of origin in the Soviet Union; age and sex distribution; geographical distribution in the United States; problems in adjustment and
integration; job placement (with emphasis on the problems of professionals); and
the current stress on the issue of Jewish identification.

Erickson, Roy V., and Giao Hoang. 1980. Health Problems among Indochinese Refugees.
American Journal of Public Health 70(9):1003–1006. Report on the findings from
194 medical evaluations of Indochinese refugees seen at the University of Connecticut between June 1979 and January 1980. The prevalence of intestinal parasites, tuberculosis, tuberculin skin test positivity, hepatitis B, and other infectious
diseases was similar to that noted in a variety of previous studies. However,
significant levels of hematologic, dermatologic, psychiatric, and endocrine ab-
normalities were also detected.

Espiritu, Yen Le. 1989. Beyond the "Boat People": Ethnicization of American Life.
Amerasia Journal 15(2):49–67. Broad discussion of ethnicization in America. The
author's central distinction is between groups that go through a process of ethnicization after arrival and those "twice-minorities" who have already constructed an ethnic identity and community in their home country. The discussion
eventually includes a short but well-drawn distinction between ethnic Vietnamese
and Chinese-Vietnamese refugees in the United States. The economic advantages
of the Chinese-Vietnamese as a "twice-minority" with solid ethnic ties are
stressed.

Evans, Jeffrey, and Wendy Baldwin, Editors. 1987. Migration and Health: Special issue
of *International Migration Review* 21(3):491–865. Wide-ranging set of articles,
including several on refugee groups. Four deal with Southeast Asian refugees:
Kwok B. Chan and David Loveridge on Hong Kong camps for refugees; Thanh
van Tran on ethnic community supports for Vietnamese; David Peters, Earl
Hershfield, David Fish, and June Manfreda on tuberculosis; and Amos Deinard
and Timothy Dunnigan on Hmong health care. In addition, Lynn August and
Barbara Gianola provide a comparison of psychiatric disorders of Southeast Asian

refugees and Vietnam veterans; Lucia McSpadden discusses Ethiopian refugees; and Rosalie Young, Allen Bukoff, John Waller, and Stephen Blount discuss a set of Asian, European, and Middle Eastern refugees.

Fagen, Richard R., Richard A. Brody, and Thomas J. O'Leary. 1968. *Cubans in Exile: Disaffection and the Revolution.* Stanford, California: Stanford University Press. 120 pages of text plus appendixes. Analysis of the factors leading to the early exodus from Cuba, with emphasis on the period from 1959 to 1962. The findings are based on 209 self-administered questionnaires and some cross-correlations with the files of the Cuban Refugee Center in Florida. Chapters deal with the following areas: (1) demographic characteristics, including comparison with the general Cuban population; (2) attitudes toward the revolution; (3) levels of political participation before, during, and after the revolution; and (4) analysis of the individual reasons for exile. The book emphasizes the exodus for what it implies about the Cuban revolution.

Fahti, Asghar, Editor. 1991. *Iranian Refugees and Exiles since Khomeini.* Costa Mesa, California: Mazda Publishers. 296 pages. Collection of papers on the origins, results, and meaning of exile. The editor provides introductory comments on the 1979 revolution and the nature of the Iranian exodus. Separate sections then address some historical concerns (the Baha'i community, overseas students), Iranians in Europe, Iranians in the United States, the exile media, and literature in exile. Of particular relevance to the United States are papers on exiles in Los Angeles (Mehdi Bozorgmehr and Georges Sabagh), name changes (Betty Blair), political demonstrations (Ron Kelly), and Iranian television (Hamid Naficy).

Fein, Helen. 1987. *Congregational Sponsors of Indochinese Refugees in the United States, 1979–1981.* Rutherford, New Jersey: Fairleigh Dickinson University Press. 165 pages. Valuable review based on personal involvement and more formal interviewing. The author focuses on the nature of altruism and draws a direct parallel between the Holocaust and the plight of Indochinese refugees. The descriptive material covers the general dynamics of how group sponsorships develop: first, with a view of refugees as victims, next, with a strong initiating person in a congregation, and finally, with the snowballing of support. The widely varying courses of actual sponsorships are also discussed. The book provides important insights on a neglected aspect of U.S. resettlement efforts.

Feingold, Henry. 1978. Soviet Jewish Survival, American Jewish Power. *Midstream* 24(2):11–22. Analysis of the historical similarities and connections between Soviet and American Jewry. Feingold notes that both American and Soviet Jews have been caught up in a process of secularization and assimilation into a wider society, although in the Soviet Union, these processes have had a more forced nature. In regard to Soviet Jewish emigration at that time, the major conclusion is that the prime reason for emigration was the perceived decline in future upward mobility, rather than any actual restriction of current activities.

Feldman, William. 1977. Social Absorption of Soviet Immigrants: Integration or Isolation. *Journal of Jewish Communal Service* 54(1):62–68. Review of the social integration of early Soviet Jewish arrivals in Cleveland, Ohio, based on a survey of 148 families drawn from the caseload of the Jewish Family Service Association. In general, the émigrés had adjusted well, with rapid rises in English-language competence and income levels. A continuing residential concentration in the heavily Jewish neighborhood of Cleveland Heights is notable, as is the general increase in Jewish religious activities. Feldman concludes that the Soviet Jews were relatively satisfied with their new life and actively desired to be part of the American Jewish community.

Fernandez, Damian J., Editor. 1992. *Cuban Studies since the Revolution.* Gainesville: University of Florida Press. Set of papers and comments from a 1990 Florida "dialogue among Cubanists." Several of the papers directly address Cubans in the United States, but even those directed at Cuba reflect the highly political concerns of U.S. Cubans. Topics covered include the overall status and bibliographic basis of Cuban studies, historiography, political science and international relations, economics, and the humanities. Of particular relevance are comments by Gerald Poyo, Silvia Pedraza, and Lisandro Perez.

Ferreé, Myra Marx. 1979. Employment without Liberation: Cuban Women in the United States. *Social Science Quarterly* 60:35–50. Analysis of labor force participation and domestic roles of Cuban women in the Miami area. The research included interviews with 122 Cuban-born women selected through random sampling of telephone listings of Spanish surnames. The importance of female labor participation for the level of household income is noted, but the major conclusion is that this extensive participation by Cuban women in the labor force is not in conflict with the maintenance of their traditional domestic roles in the home.

Ferris, Elizabeth. 1987. *The Central American Refugees.* New York: Praeger. 159 pages. General overview of the patterns in Central American refugee origins and movements. The author introduces the policy context and the situations in El Salvador, Guatemala, and Nicaragua that generated the refugees. She then addresses in separate chapters the Mexican, Costa Rican, Honduran, and U.S. responses to the refugees. The section on the United States is brief but helpful.

Finnan, Christine R., and Rhonda Ann Cooperstein. 1983. *Southeast Asian Refugee Resettlement at the Local Level: The Role of the Ethnic Community and the Nature of Refugee Impact.* Menlo Park, California: SRI International. 259 pages. Final report of a two-part study conducted under contract to the federal government. Part I examines the structure and function of refugee communities, including the importance of kinship groups, informal social networks, and formal organizations—and the variety of tangible and intangible supports provided through such social relations. Part II examines the effects that refugees have on the localities in which they settle, including such topics as housing, employment, public assistance, and education. The report is based both on secondary analysis and on field research in five counties across the United States.

Freeman, James A. 1989. *Hearts of Sorrow: Vietnamese-American Lives.* Stanford: Stanford University Press. 446 pages. Series of carefully edited refugee narratives covering all aspects of the Vietnamese refugee experience. The major parts of the book cover the narrators' experiences growing up in Vietnam, the experience of war itself, the situation following reunification in 1975, the exodus from Vietnam, and the process of adjusting to life in the United States. The book is well balanced and well crafted. There is variety in the experiences presented, much narrative that rings true, and good attention to the cultural, familial, and religious underpinnings of the Vietnamese experience.

Gallagher, Dennis, Editor. 1986. Refugees: Issues and Directions. Special issue of *International Migration Review* 20(2). 360 pages. Special issue covering international and domestic refugee issues. In addition to general articles on causes of, and solutions to, refugee flows, six articles cover U.S. resettlement, most with a survey research orientation: Haitian refugees (Stepick and Portes); Southeast Asian refugees in general (separate articles by Bach and Caroll-Seguin, Rumbaut and Weeks, and Yu and Lin); Sino-Vietnamese (Desbarats); and Hmong (Fass). The volume is valuable for its insights into the concern (and frustration) with the global refugee situation in the mid-1980s as well as for its reflection of the increasing quantitative sophistication of research on refugees in the United States.

Gardner, Robert W., Bryant Robey, and Peter C. Smith. 1985. Asian Americans: Growth, Change, and Diversity. *Population Bulletin* 40(4). 44 pages. Overview of Asian-Americans based largely on special data runs from the 1980 census. The authors present a balanced and accessible review of Asian immigration and then discuss such specific issues as geographic location, age and sex distribution, fertility, mortality, health, families/households, education, work, youth, poverty, use of public programs, and future prospects. Perhaps of most value are the graphs and charts that provide a comparison among Asian-Americans and between Asian-Americans and other segments of the U.S. population. The Vietnamese, in particular, emerge as a rapidly growing segment of the population and an unusual one in terms of fertility, household size and structure, education, occupation, and income. Vietnamese generally appear as less advantaged than other Asian-American groups. (Some limited information on other Southeast Asian refugees is also included.)

Gerber, Lane. 1994. Psychotherapy with Southeast Asian Refugees: Implications for Treatment of Western Patients. *American Journal of Psychotherapy* 48(2):280–293. Reflective consideration based on the author's clinical experience. The two main stimuli for the reflection are a Cambodian and a Laotian patient. The accounts are vivid ones on their own terms, but the author uses them primarily to look at what they imply for more effective therapy with Westerners. Her central argument is that some of the Asian concerns with family and spiritual embeddedness might be usefully applied to Western patients.

Gitelman, Zvi. 1978. Soviet Immigrants and American Absorption Efforts: A Case Study in Detroit. *Journal of Jewish Communal Service* 55(1):72–82. Review of the adjustment of Soviet Jews, based in part on interviews with a random sample of 132 refugees in Detroit. Gitelman stresses the need to understand the differing backgrounds of Soviet Jews, particularly the distinction between "Westerners" and "heartlanders." Major findings from the survey are (1) high levels of general satisfaction with life in the United States, (2) positive economic expectations for the future, (3) disappointment with the isolation and lack of sociability among Americans, (4) concern about crime, and (5) ambivalence about the level of social freedom in the United States.

Gold, Steven J. 1992. *Refugee Communities: A Comparative Field Study*. Newbury Park, California: Sage Publications. 257 pages. Comparative analysis of the adaptation of Vietnamese and Soviet Jewish refugees. The book is unusual and valuable for its detailed concurrent treatment of two very different refugee groups, based on extensive field research supplemented by interviewing. The dual approach easily explodes stereotypes of refugee adaptation and thus helps bring these two groups into the broader framework of newcomer adaptation to an increasingly multicultural United States. The book provides a theoretical overview, summarizes the Vietnamese and Soviet Jewish exoduses, and then turns to the details of community life. Resettlement agencies, self-employment, and forms of ethnic organization each receive a full chapter's attention.

Gold, Steven J. 1994. Chinese-Vietnamese Entrepreneurs in California. In *The New Asian Immigration in Los Angeles and Global Restructuring*. Edited by Paul Ong, Edna Bonacich, and Lucie Cheng. Philadelphia: Temple University Press. Pages 196–226. Intriguing review of Chinese-Vietnamese and their role in a complex southern California "ethnic enclave." The author reviews the size and growth of Chinese-Vietnamese entrepreneurship, and the complex economic and ethnic dynamics by which Chinese-Vietnamese "re-establish a middleman economic role similar to the one that they occupied in Southeast Asia." The Chinese-Vietnamese, for example, not only rely on each other but also use ethnic Vietnamese as a clientele, Latinos as inexpensive labor, and other Chinese as sources of capital. This complex enclave is presented as a counterpoint to the more ethnically homogenous Cuban enclave in Miami. Both positive and negative aspects of the enclave are discussed.

Goldstein, Edgar. 1979. Psychological Adaptation of Soviet Immigrants. *American Journal of Psychoanalysis* 39(3):257–263. Informal overview of psychological problems faced by Soviet refugees, written by a former Soviet psychiatrist. Particular problems noted are (1) the "totalitarian state" that the refugee carries within himself; (2) an unclear sense of ethnic and religious identity; (3) the great loss of status as an immigrant in the United States; (4) a letdown as refugees realize that they are less important to the United States than they had expected; and (5) a strong tendency to deny psychological problems.

Gordon, Linda W. 1989. The Missing Children: Mortality and Fertility in a Southeast Asian Refugee Population. *International Migration Review* 22(2):219–237. Demographic analysis of the Southeast Asian refugee population. The author develops overviews of the age structure and fertility of the separate national groups (Vietnamese, Laotian, Cambodian) based on federal government statistics. She compares the results to other available data, particularly from California, and then provides estimates of the total Southeast Asian refugee population. Vietnamese are estimated to be the fourth largest Asian-American group. The article is valuable not only for its conclusions but as an example of the painstaking demographic analysis necessary to estimate population size for particular refugee groups.

Grant, Bruce, Michael Richardson, et al. 1979. *The Boat People: An "Age" Investigation*. New York: Penguin Books. 225 pages. Review of the dramatic exodus by sea of refugees from Vietnam in the late 1970s. The book is a well-written, compelling narrative based on the reports of correspondents for the Australian newspaper *The Age*. It is particularly useful in sorting out the different flows by time (1976–1979), by cause (e.g., the increasingly anti-Chinese stance of the Vietnamese government), and by route (e.g., the flows east and north from northern Vietnam versus those south and west from southern Vietnam).

Granville Corporation. 1982. *A Preliminary Assessment of the Khmer Cluster Resettle-ment Project.* Washington, D.C. 180 pages. Review of the implementation of a special resettlement project for Cambodian refugees. The purpose of the project was to encourage the clustering of Cambodian refugees in numbers sufficiently large for effective community support but away from areas of dense, "impacted" resettlement. The hope was that resources could be more efficiently utilized, "secondary" migration (especially to California) would be reduced, and employment opportunities would be enhanced. The report does not include any definitive evidence of project success but does include detail on the development and implementation of the project on the national level and at 4 of the 12 resettlement sites (Boston, Jacksonville, Columbus, and Houston). The central involvement of Cambodian mutual assistance associations is of particular interest.

Hagan, Jacqueline Maria. 1994. *Deciding to Be Legal: A Maya Community in Houston.* Philadelphia: Temple University Press. 200 pages. Anthropological case study of Maya from San Pedro (Totonicapan). The author reviews their emigration and the course of settlement in Houston. The focus of the book, however, is the social process of deciding to become legal (under the provisions of the 1986 Immigration Reform and Control Act) and the effects of that legalization on their lives. These particular Maya are less "refugees" than many other Maya and thus provide a useful counterpoint to the experience of the Quiché and Kanjobal Maya.

Haines, David W., Editor. 1989. *Refugees as Immigrants: Cambodians, Laotians, and Vietnamese in America.* Totowa, New Jersey: Rowman and Littlefield. 198 pages. Collection of articles reviewing the major survey research efforts during the first decade of Southeast Asian refugee resettlement. Projects covered include the federal government's annual survey of refugees (Gordon); two early surveys of Vietnamese (Dunning; Roberts and Starr); an early, multigroup survey in Illinois (Kim); two broad, multigroup surveys in San Diego (Strand; Rumbaut); and a multisite survey of Vietnamese, Lao, and ethnic Chinese (Whitmore, Trautmann, and Caplan). The editor provides an introduction to the nature and historical context of this body of research, and the chapters follow a common format to facilitate comparison. Methodological issues receive considerable attention.

Hamilton, Nora, and Norma Stoltz Chinchilla. 1991. Central American Migration: A Framework for Analysis. *Latin American Research Review* 26(1):75–110. Review of internal and international migration in Central America from a historical, theoretical perspective. The authors begin with a standard sociological emphasis on capitalism and its effects on core and peripheral areas and then trace migration from the nineteenth century, with emphasis on the postwar period and particularly detailed information on El Salvador. They note that the political violence and repression of the 1970s and 1980s created a change in the magnitude of migration, although that migration often flowed through traditional channels. The article provides a balanced, coherent framework for understanding the overall nature of Central American migration.

Harding, Richard K., and John G. Looney. 1977. Problems of Southeast Asian Children in a Refugee Camp. *American Journal of Psychiatry* 134(4):407–411. Description of the efforts made to meet the mental health needs of Vietnamese children at Camp Pendleton in 1975. The authors found that children generally received strong emotional support from their multigenerational Vietnamese families and adapted well to their new surroundings. However, children separated from their families demonstrated emotional vulnerability, and their foster placement as unaccompanied minors led to serious problems. Some of these problems stemmed from the sponsoring process that removed the children from families to which they had become attached in an informal way.

Hein, Jeremy. 1993. Refugees, Immigrants, and the State. *Annual Review of Sociology* 19:43–59. Overview of the last several years of sociologically oriented research on refugees. The author raises the basic question of whether refugees are fully different from immigrants or simply a set of immigrants with a special political designation. Both world system issues and the histories of specific refugee groups receive attention—including issues of adaptation to the new host societies. This article is a good place to begin a broad, theoretical examination of refugee and immigrant issues from an academic perspective.

Hein, Jeremy. 1994. From Migrant to Minority: Hmong Refugees and the Social Construction of Identity in the United States. *Sociological Inquiry* 64(3):281–306. Analysis based on structured interviews with 40 Hmong leaders in Wisconsin. The author distinguishes a migrant versus a minority orientation on the basis of whether interviewees see their problems as reflecting their newness to America or as due to the essential inequality of American society. The Hmong lean sharply toward a migrant orientation. The police killing of two Hmong youths provides a particularly telling test case for the two orientations.

Hendricks, Glenn L., Bruce T. Downing, and Amos S. Deinard. 1986. *The Hmong in Transition*. University of Minnesota, Southeast Asian Refugee Studies Project. Published jointly with the Center for Migration Studies, Staten Island, New York. 464 pages. Proceedings of a University of Minnesota conference on the Hmong. The conference brought together a very wide range of researchers and practitioners. Separate sections address culture and change, adaptation, language and literacy, and health care issues—each with a brief introduction. The 20 papers in the volume are essential reading for anyone with a particular interest in the Hmong or for anyone who wishes to understand the unique situation and background of highland minority groups who are often ignored in the larger migration of lowland, agriculturally based groups.

Hopkins, MaryCarol, and Nancy D. Donnelly. 1993. *Selected Papers on Refugee Issues— II*. Arlington, Virginia: American Anthropological Association. 196 pages. Second in a series of selected anthropological papers on refugees. Papers relating to refugees in the United States include a reconsideration of U.S. resettlement policy (Haines), reflections on conducting life histories with Cambodian refugees in Dallas (Rasbridge), how Vietnamese and Cambodian refugees construct predictable environments out of camp life (Geiger), Vietnamese refugee interpretations of Western and traditional medicine (Stephenson), the role of mutual assistance associations (Van Arsdale), and factors influencing fertility changes among Lao refugees (Zaharlick, Tobrack, and Calip-Dubois).

Howell, David R., Editor. 1982. Southeast Asian Refugees in the U.S.A.: Case Studies of Adjustment and Policy Implications. Special issue of *Anthropological Quarterly* 55(3). 62 pages. Set of five articles by anthropologists, with an introduction

by the editor about the role of anthropology in refugee resettlement and public
policy. Articles deal with segmental kinship among the Hmong in Minnesota
(Dunnigan), refugees in the fishing industry in California (Orbach and Beckwith),
ethnic solidarity among the Hmong in California (Scott), community influences
on the occupational adaptation of Vietnamese refugees (Finnan), and the overall
interactions of refugee kinship and American public policy (Haines).

Jacobson, Gaynor, Nina Dorf, Nancy Jacobs, Morton Schrag, Marvin Bienstock, Irwin
Gold, and Marina Cunningham. 1979. A Symposium on the Soviet Immigrant.
Journal of Jewish Communal Service 56(1):50–76. Set of papers on early Soviet
refugees delivered at the annual meeting of the Conference of Jewish Communal
Services in Toronto, 1979. The following papers are included: "Today's Jewish
Immigrant" (Jacobson), "Impact of Soviet-Jewish Culture on the Problem-
Solving Process" (Dorf), "New Culture Learning in the Day-Care Center" (Ja-
cobs), "How the Center Helps Russian Jews" (Schrag), "Soviet Jewish
Resettlement in the Small Community: Working with Volunteers" (Bienstock),
"Resettlement of Soviet Jews in Toronto" (Gold), and "Prenatal Group for So-
viet Immigrants" (Cunningham and Dorf).

Jenkins, Shirley, and Mignon Sauber. 1988. Ethnic Associations in New York and Services to Immigrants. In *Ethnic Associations and the Welfare State*. Edited by Shirley Jenkins. New York: Columbia University Press. Pages 21–105. Overview of
ethnic associations in New York based on survey and interview data from a 1985
study for the Community Council of Greater New York. New York remains a
major and diverse immigrant mecca, and the range of associations covered is
unusually broad, including many refugee groups (Ethiopians, Poles, Soviet Jews,
Cambodians, Vietnamese, Sino-Vietnamese, Cubans, and Haitians). The study
aimed at determining general types of associational structure and purpose but
provides some interesting asides about particular refugee groups.

Jesilow, P., G. Geis, H. Pontell, and J.H.L. Song. 1992. Culture Conflict Revisited: Fraud
by Vietnamese Physicians in the United States. *International Migration* 30(2):
201–222. Analysis of the 1984 arrest of 34 Vietnamese doctors and medical
personnel for Medicaid fraud in the Los Angeles area. The analysis is based on
the events themselves and 60 subsequent interviews of Vietnamese to determine
their reactions to those events. The arrests were conducted in a highly publicized
sweep with initial (later retracted) statements about very sizable amounts of
money. The authors consider the police action to have been discriminatory in its
excessiveness. They also describe the shame the episode evoked in the Vietnamese community and the way it changed doctor-patient relations.

Jones, Allen K. 1984. Iranian Refugees: The Many Faces of Persecution. Washington,
D.C.: U.S. Committee for Refugees. 20 pages. Review of the situation of Iranian
refugees, with special attention to the religious and ethnic groups most at risk
after the overthrow of the shah in 1979. Baha'is have borne the worst of it, but
Jews, Christians, and Zoroastrians have also fared poorly. Ethnic groups (Kurds,
Baluchs, Arabs) have also suffered, as have the middle classes. The article was
written at the time when significant numbers of Iranians were beginning to be
accepted as refugees in the United States, largely through applications for asylum
of those already in the United States. The presence of some 50,000 Iranian students at the time of the shah's overthrow is noted.

Jones, Allen K. 1985. *Afghan Refugees: Five Years Later.* Washington, D.C.: U.S. Com-
    mittee for Refugees. 24 pages. Review and recommendations regarding the Af-
    ghan refugee situation. The major portion of this issue paper details the generally
    successful effort to maintain a workable asylum situation for Afghan refugees in
    Pakistan. The relative porousness of the Afghanistan/Pakistan border in cultural
    terms is noted. Although third-country resettlement is limited, the author does
    provide a cogent summary of the problems Afghans face in resettlement, partic-
    ularly a deep malaise about leaving Afghanistan, a very high level of social
    isolation (that is most severe for women), and an Islamic religious tradition that
    sometimes hinders cultural accommodation to life in a new country.

Justus, Joyce Bennett. 1976. Processing Indochinese Refugees. In *Exploratory Fieldwork
    on Latino Migrants and Indochinese Refugees.* Edited by Roy S. Bryce-Laporte
    and Stephen R. Couch. Washington, D.C.: Smithsonian. Pages 76–100. Report
    on exploratory fieldwork carried out at Camp Pendleton (California) in 1975. The
    research included both interviews and participant observation. Specific findings
    about the refugees include overreporting of previous occupation (particularly un-
    nerving, considering the importance placed on occupational background in much
    research on refugees); misunderstanding of the resettlement process; and strong
    desires for secrecy. This article is invaluable in delineating the divergence be-
    tween the perceptions of refugees and those of camp managers.

Kelley, Ron, Jonathan Friedlander, and Anita Colby, Editors. 1993. *Irangeles: Iranians
    in Los Angeles.* Los Angeles: University of California Press. 396 pages. Impres-
    sive collection of photographs, articles, and interviews involving Iranians in Los
    Angeles. Separate sections provide reviews of Iranian history, ethnic and religious
    diversity, family and gender issues, wealth and economics, political life, and pop-
    ular culture. The articles themselves are well written. In addition to various con-
    tributions by Ron Kelley, there are very good discussions of ethnic and religious
    diversity (Bozorgmehr, Sabagh, and Der-Martirosian), gender issues (separate ar-
    ticles by Nayareh Tohida and Shideh Hanassah), and popular culture (Hamid
    Naficy). Coverage includes Muslims, Jews, Baha'is, Armenians, Assyrians, Zo-
    roastrians, and Kurds.

Kelly, Gail P. 1986. Coping with America: Refugees from Vietnam, Cambodia, and Laos
    in the 1970s and 1980s. *Annals of the American Academy of Political and Social
    Science* 487:138–149. Review of the early stages of Southeast Asian refugee
    resettlement in the United States. The author notes the distinctive waves of ref-
    ugees and the basic problems in resettlement. The discussion is general and rel-
    atively positive—although the precarious economic situation of refugees in the
    early 1980s recession is noted. The author argues that the government consistently
    attempted to make refugees a nonissue, thus undermining efforts to understand
    the progress (or lack thereof) of refugees in adjusting to American society.

Kelly, Gail Paradise. 1977. *From Vietnam to America: A Chronicle of the Vietnamese
    Immigration to the United States.* Boulder, Colorado: Westview Press. 254 pages.
    Review of the initial Vietnamese refugee exodus of 1975. The book is based on
    written documents and on the author's interviews conducted at Fort Indiantown
    Gap (Pennsylvania). The first part of the book is a compelling account of the
    exodus, including a description of the types of people who were able to escape.

The second part concerns the camp experiences of the refugees, with emphasis on the areas of education and cultural orientation. The third section describes the initial adjustment of the refugees after being sponsored out of the camps. Kelly stresses the way in which the United States tried to force the refugees into being ordinary immigrants.

Kibria, Nazli. 1990. Power, Patriarchy, and Gender Conflict in the Vietnamese Immigrant Community. *Gender and Society* 4(1):9–24. Balanced analysis of Vietnamese refugee women's options and constraints within the "patriarchal bargain." The article begins by noting the way Vietnamese women traditionally maximized their flexibility—especially in economic exchanges and informal neighborhood social groups. In the United States, these same factors are strengthened by the increasing importance of women's economic contributions to the family. Nevertheless, several fieldwork observations suggest that women continue to support an unequal balance of power with men because of the perceived benefits to them, especially in terms of family solidarity. The author concludes that "the effects of migration on gender relations must be understood as highly uneven and shifting in quality, often resulting in gains for women in certain spheres and losses in others."

Kinzie, J. David, Kiet Anh Tran, Agatha Breckenridge, and Joseph Bloom. 1980. An Indochinese Refugee Psychiatric Clinic: Culturally Accepted Treatment Approaches. *American Journal of Psychiatry* 137(11):1429–1432. Report on the evaluation and treatment of 50 Indochinese patients at a clinic established by the authors in 1978 in Portland, Oregon. Most of the patients seen at the beginning of the program were psychotic and severely impaired. However, later patients suffered from a wider variety of problems. A flexible approach to treatment was adopted that would be compatible with the cultural expectations of the refugees. One of the results was an emphasis on the medical approach of the physician. The process by which the clinic gained acceptance in the community is also discussed.

Koehn, Peter H. 1991. *Refugees from Revolution: U.S. Policy and Third-World Migration.* Boulder, Colorado: Westview Press. 463 pages. Broad analysis of both the global dynamics and U.S. resettlement experience of key refugee groups. The author argues that "[r]efugee issues provide a particularly revealing illustration of the interconnected nature of foreign and domestic policy and the growing power of the Third World to direct attention to previously neglected concerns." The book focuses on five groups: Cubans, Vietnamese, Iranians, Ethiopians, and Eritreans. There is considerable original research, particularly on Iranians, Ethiopians, and Eritreans (specifically Los Angeles and Washington, D.C.).

Kogan, Deborah, Patricia Jenny, Mary Vencill, and Lois Greenwood. 1982. *Study of the State Administration of the Refugee Resettlement Program (Final Report).* Berkeley, California: Berkeley Planning Associates. 166 pages. Final report of a study conducted under contract to the federal government. Based on field visits to nine selected states, the authors describe and analyze the influence of the general state context on the refugee program, the structure of the program within the overall state government, the design of the program, issues of coordination at the state and local levels, and the ways in which accountability is maintained within the program. A concluding chapter presents suggested standards for examining the

management of the program and a set of key program issues. The resulting portrayal of the refugee program is balanced, thoughtful, and sometimes provocative.
The states included were California, Iowa, Massachusetts, Minnesota, Ohio, Pennsylvania, Texas, Utah, and Washington.

Kogan, Deborah, and Mary Vencill. 1984. *An Evaluation of the Favorable Alternate
Sites Project.* Berkeley, California: Berkeley Planning Associates. Federally
funded evaluation of a special resettlement project. The project arose from the
federal government's desire to encourage geographic dispersal in resettlement
through formal "placement policy." The project included two sites for Vietnamese refugees in Arizona (Phoenix and Tucson) and two sites for Cambodian refugees in North Carolina (Charlotte and Greensboro). The project was generally
successful in its goals, with positive employment outcomes. The authors provide
a thoughtful review of key program components such as the clustering approach,
careful site selection, provision of adequate resources, strong coordination, and
extensive flexibility at the site level. The main report is approximately 300 pages
and includes profiles of refugees at the sites. A 21-page executive summary was
produced separately.

Kritz, Mary M., Editor. 1983. *U.S. Immigration and Refugee Policy: Global and Domestic Issues.* Lexington, Massachusetts: Lexington Books (D.C. Heath and Company). 415 pages. Series of papers originally presented at two conferences in
1981. Separate parts deal with the international context, global refugee problems,
domestic impacts in the United States, Caribbean migration, pluralism in the
United States, and general conceptual and policy issues. There is an introduction
by the editor and a foreword by Victor Palmieri, the former U.S. coordinator for
refugee affairs. This is a useful policy review reflecting the situation immediately
after the passage of the Refugee Act of 1980.

Kunz, E. F. 1973. The Refugee in Flight: Kinetic Models and Forms of Displacement.
International Migration Review 7(2):125–146. Uniquely influential article on refugee fight and transit. Kunz's basic contention is that the kinds of dynamics
("kinetics") through which the refugee moves from country of origin to eventual
resettlement condition ultimate resettlement outcomes. His distinction between
anticipatory and acute refugee movements, his analysis of "vintages" and forms
of displacement, and his general emphasis on the need for comparative work on
different refugee flows are all widely echoed in the literature on refugees.

Laguerre, Michel S. 1984. *American Odyssey: Haitians in New York City.* Ithaca: Cornell
University Press. 198 pages. Important study of Haitians in Brooklyn, Manhattan,
and Queens. After an initial overview, the author's major chapters cover the
ideology and pragmatics of emigration from Haiti; the neighborhoods and their
social, religious, educational, and ethnic structure; the organization of the family
(including continuing relations with kin in Haiti); economic adaptation; health
beliefs and practices; and political life. The presentation is balanced and accessible.

Lamphere, Louise, Editor. 1992. *Structuring Diversity: Ethnographic Perspectives on the
New Immigration.* Chicago: University of Chicago Press. 257 pages. Set of six
articles covering multidisciplinary team research on interethnic relations. The editor provides an introduction to the book's focus on the institutions that mediate

ethnic relations. The article most completely directed at refugees is on textile and construction work of Cuban and Haitians in Miami (Grenier, Stepick, Draznin, LaBorwitt, and Morris); however, most of the papers deal at least partially with such refugee groups as Guatemalans, Hmong, Poles, and Vietnamese. The research for each of the papers was conducted with funding from a special Ford Foundation project ("Changing Relations: Newcomers and Established Residents in U.S. Communities").

Lamphere, Louise, Alex Stepick, and Guillermo Grenier, Editors. 1994. *Newcomers in the Workplace: Immigrants and the Restructuring of the U.S. Economy*. Philadelphia: Temple University Press. 309 pages. More detailed analysis of three cities studied as part of the Ford Foundation's "Changing Relations" project (see immediately preceding citation). The volume provides four chapters each on Miami, Philadelphia, and Garden City (Kansas). The discussions of Cubans and Haitians in Miami are particularly valuable, as is an analysis of work and family linkages among Lao and Vietnamese in the Kansas meat-packing industry—in which Janet Benson provides a particularly incisive analysis of the multiple-wage-earning strategies used by refugee families and the enormous toll such strategies can take on individuals and on family life. Refugees also appear intermittently in the discussions of jobs in Philadelphia.

Lese, Karen P., and Steven B. Robbins. 1994. Relationship between Goal Attributes and the Academic Achievement of Southeast Asian Adolescent Refugees. *Journal of Counseling Psychology* 41(1):45–52. Quantitative analysis of the goals of 39 Cambodian and Vietnamese students in a bilingual vocational education program in 1990. Overall, the authors find that goal stability and commitment were significantly related to grade-point average and goal attainment. General acculturation was not significantly related. As expected, the range of goals given by the students emphasized family, academic achievement, and career plans. The authors describe the specific scales used and provide extensive warnings about the methodological difficulties in conducting this kind of research on a cross-cultural, multilingual basis.

Light, Ivan, Georges Sabagh, Mehdi Bozorgmehr, and Claudia Der-Martirosian. 1993. Internal Ethnicity in the Ethnic Economy. *Ethnic and Racial Studies* 16(4):581–597. Survey-based analysis of the structure of the Los Angeles Iranian ethnic economy. The authors argue very clearly that there is no single homogeneous Iranian ethnic economy. Instead, there are four distinct economies (Armenian, Baha'i, Jewish, and Muslim) that have distinct occupational and structural characteristics and that are only "weakly tied to an encompassing Iranian ethnic economy." In support of this argument, the authors present data regarding high levels of self-employment and ethnic segregation. The paper also provides a very useful introduction to sociologists' fascination with ethnic economic activity, including distinctions between ethnicity and internal ethnicity, and between non-localized ethnic economies and the more famous, highly localized ethnic enclave economies such as Miami.

Lin, Keh-Ming, Laurie Tazuma, and Minoru Masuda. 1979. Adaptational Problems of Vietnamese Refugees: Health and Mental Health Status. *Archives of General Psychiatry* 36:955–961. Report on approximately 300 interviews conducted with Vietnamese refugees in Seattle, Washington. Based on separate administrations of the Cornell Medical Index in 1975 and 1976, the authors note high and continuing levels of physical and mental dysfunction. There were also shifts between 1975 and 1976, including an increase in anger and hostility and a decrease in feelings of inadequacy. The article provides valuable baseline data on the initial Vietnamese refugee arrivals.

Liu, William T., Maryanne Lamanna, and Alice Murata. 1979. *Transition to Nowhere: Vietnamese Refugees in America.* Nashville, Tennessee: Charter House. 214 pages. General description of the 1975 Vietnamese refugees from the time of departure to initial sponsorship and resettlement in the United States. The research was conducted at Camp Pendleton (California), with an emphasis on mental health problems, and included the use of various standardized protocols, such as the Cornell Medical Index. The authors also cover the general demographics of the refugee population, American public reactions, and the special problems of unaccompanied children.

Loescher, Gil, and John A. Scanlan. 1986. *Calculated Kindness: Refugees and America's Half-Open Door, 1945 to the Present.* New York: The Free Press. 346 pages (219 pages text). Solid review of U.S. refugee policy since World War II. The authors stress the tension in refugee admissions between humanitarian and foreign policy considerations—especially the overwhelming importance of anti-Communist ideology. They are very attentive to the roles of the executive and legislative branches (e.g., the importance of President Eisenhower's creation of presidential parole authority) and to the policy influence of the media and concerned citizens both within and outside government. The concluding discussion of increasing restrictionism remains current. Displaced persons, Hungarians, Cubans, Haitians, Southeast Asians, and Central American refugees are all covered.

Loescher, Gilburt D., and John A. Scanlan, Editors. 1983. The Global Refugee Problem. *Annals of the American Academy of Political and Social Science* 467. 253 pages. Set of 13 articles on refugees. Five deal directly with refugees in the United States: Loescher and Scanlan on the effects of U.S. foreign policy on Cuban refugee flows; Ronald Copeland on the Cuban boat lift of 1980; Naomi Zucker on the legal contest over Haitian refugees; Arnold Leibowitz on the Refugee Act of 1980; and Norman Zucker on U.S. resettlement policy. The other articles provide an overview of the global refugee problem in the early 1980s.

Long, Lynellen D. 1993. *Ban Vinai: The Refugee Camp.* New York: Columbia University Press. 242 pages. Thoughtful, engaging analysis of what was one of the major Thai refugee camps on the Lao border, based on extensive work in refugee camps overseas and with refugees in the United States. The author examines the structure of the camp, camp life, and "refugee consciousness," focusing on five families (three Hmong, one ethnic Lao, and one Lao-Khmu). Three introductory chapters provide an overview of the camp and the way it reflected the international relief system. The remaining chapters are generally narrative and take the reader through the days and seasons of a setting that is both local and transnational. The book is a valuable—and personal—guide to the complex social and organizational dynamics of refugee camps.

Lorentzin, Robin. 1991. *Women in the Sanctuary Movement.* Philadelphia: Temple University Press. 229 pages. Review of the sanctuary movement of the 1980s. The author provides a general overview of the movement and its internal tensions—particularly between humanitarian and political goals—and then discusses in detail women's roles in, and influence on, the movement. Chicago receives the most attention, but the 29 interviews that provide the substance of the book include eight local sanctuary sites.

MacDonald, Jeffrey L., and Amy Zaharlick, Editors. 1994. *Selected Papers on Refugee Issues: III.* Arlington, Virginia: American Anthropological Association. 188 pages. Third in a series of anthropologically oriented papers on refugees. Of most direct relevance to refugee resettlement in the United States are papers on Guatemalan refugee women in Los Angeles (Gabriele Kohpahl), Mayan refugees—mostly in Florida (Nancy Wellmeier), the inconsistency between American policies and the family life of Cambodian refugees (MaryCarol Hopkins), and the difficulties in conducting fieldwork "at home" among Laotian refugees (Ruth Krulfeld). The volume also includes interesting papers on refugees in Europe and an intriguing comparison of Salvadorans and Nicaraguans in asylum in Honduras.

Majka, Lorraine, and Brendan Mullan. 1992. Employment Retention, Area of Origin, and Type of Social Support among Refugees in the Chicago Area. *International Migration Review* 26(3):899–926. Analysis of some 3,300 refugee statistical profiles for the Chicago area in 1988. The authors focus on job retention and define that by two measures of employment (same job, any job) after 90 days. They provide a valuable review of research on refugee employment and then present findings that are useful for two main reasons. First, Chicago has an unusually broad range of Southeast Asian, Eastern European, and Soviet refugees, all of whom are included in the analysis. Second, the findings are an important addition to the existing research as they document the importance of age, gender, education, and household structure to employment retention. Of particular interest is the extent to which access to mainstream support sources (as opposed to ethnic self-help efforts) is correlated with higher job retention.

Markowitz, Fran. 1993. *A Community in Spite of Itself: Soviet Jewish Émigrés in New York.* Washington, D.C.: Smithsonian Institution Press. 317 pages. Ethnographic study of Soviet Jewish refugees in the Brighton Beach area of Brooklyn. The author, an anthropologist, lived in the area in 1984–1985 and focused on the formation of a "community" among 1978–1980 arrivals. She notes that the resulting community does not match stereotypes of ethnic immigrant communities and has certain "post-modern" qualities. The book provides a solid review of the reasons for emigration from the Soviet Union, social relations among the émigrés, the life cycle, and the way in which the moral community is developed and defined. There are some interesting comments at the end about the way these refugees view more recent arrivals.

Marsh, Robert E. 1980. Socioeconomic Status of Indochinese Refugees in the United States: Progress and Problems. *Social Security Bulletin* 43(10):11–20. Review of existing data on employment, income, and receipt of public assistance among early Indochinese refugees in the United States. The article is based largely on the first six surveys conducted by Opportunity Systems Incorporated but also includes a section on refugee earnings written by Harold Grossman. In general, the early refugees showed significant improvement in employment and earnings levels by the end of 1978. Marsh suggests that later-arriving refugees are likely to face more difficulties because of their lower educational and occupational backgrounds.

Martin, Philip, and Elizabeth Midgley. 1994. Immigration to the United States: Journey to an Uncertain Destination. *Population Bulletin* 49(2). 47 pages. Overview of U.S. immigration for a general audience. Issues covered include the history of U.S. immigration and immigration policy, the demographic and economic effects of immigration, and the perceptions of and by immigrants. Issues are illustrated with reference to some of the major studies and selective compilation of census data. A short but valuable list of ''suggested readings'' is included. This is a solid, balanced, and accessible primer on U.S. immigration that helps place the situation of refugees in perspective.

Masuda, Minoru, Keh-Ming Lin, and Laurie Tazuma. 1980. Adaptation Problems of Vietnamese Refugees: Life Changes and Perceptions of Life Events. *Archives of General Psychiatry* 37:447–450. Analysis of the coping and adaptation problems of early Vietnamese refugee arrivals in Seattle, Washington. Data derived from about 300 interviews conducted during 1975 and 1976, with an emphasis on the Social Readjustment Rating Questionnaire (SRRQ). Results indicate a high level of life changes during the evacuation year of 1975 but also indicate continuing high levels of change during 1976. In particular, problems associated with work, finances, lifestyle, marriage, and school continued to adversely affect the refugees and, in fact, increased during 1976.

Masud-Piloto, Félix Roberto. 1988. *With Open Arms: Cuban Migration to the United States.* Totowa, New Jersey: Rowman and Littlefield. 148 pages. Review of Cuban emigration to America. The author covers basic background issues and early Cuban emigration, then chapter by chapter describes Eisenhower's initiation of the program, Kennedy's involvement with Cuba and its refugees, the boat and air migration from 1965 to 1973, the 1980 Mariel exodus, and the aftermath of Mariel. A final chapter raises comparative considerations regarding Haitian and Central American refugees. The book is based largely on historical documents, supplemented by some informal interviewing.

Matsuoka, Jon K. 1993. Demographic Characteristics as Determinants in Qualitative Differences in the Adjustment of Vietnamese Refugees. *Journal of Social Science Research* 17(3):1–21. Report on a questionnaire-based study of 112 Vietnamese and Chinese-Vietnamese in San Diego. The multivariate statistical approach yielded relatively independent measures of acculturation and mental health. Men were higher on acculturation measures, but women were higher on mental health measures. There was a general increase in problems with age and with religiosity, married people were generally more positive, and Chinese-Vietnamese fared better than ethnic Vietnamese. Also noted are the effects of loss of status for some refugees versus the increased opportunities for those with lower status in country of origin.

Mattson, Roger A., and Dang Dinh Ky. 1978. Vietnamese Refugee Care: Psychiatric Observations. *Minnesota Medicine* 61(1):33–36. General observations on the situation of Vietnamese refugees during their brief stay on Wake Island in 1975.

Authors note the age distribution, class structure, large family groups, and general good health of the refugees. Relatively few adjustment problems appeared. Of those that did occur, the following were the major ones: (1) problems with the high protein and fat in the American diet; (2) frequent psychosomatic complaints, such as headaches, stomach pain, and insomnia; and (3) some anxiety during the ultimate move away from Wake.

McInnis, Kathleen. 1991. Ethnic Sensitive Work with Hmong Children. *Child Welfare* 70(5):571–580. Brief review of critical problems in service provision to Hmong children. The author stresses the way in which Hmong children are torn between a traditional group-oriented culture and an American individualistic culture. She then discusses three areas of Hmong culture: the importance of the clan; the centrality of the family (including the importance of children and the need for discipline of them); and Hmong views of physical and mental illness. Also noted are the special problems of Hmong children and the comparatively constructive way Hmong have faced serious poverty in the United States.

McNall, Miles, Timothy Dunnigan, and Jeylan T. Mortimer. 1994. The Educational Achievement of the St. Paul Hmong. *Anthropology and Education Quarterly* 25(1):44–65. Results of a longitudinal survey of high school students that began in 1988. The authors found relatively high social adjustment and academic achievement among the Hmong students. They also found impressive support for education by the students' parents, despite the parents own lack of extensive schooling. The obstacles to academic achievement (e.g., very early marriage for women) are also noted.

Meinhardt, Kenneth, Solen Tom, Philip Tse, and Connie Young Yu. 1986. Southeast Asian Refugees in the "Silicon Valley": The Asian Health Assessment Project. *Amerasia Journal* 12(2):43–65. Review of a 1981 survey of 1,684 Cambodians, Chinese (both immigrant and refugee), and Vietnamese. The survey provided extensive demographic and mental health–related information in a format permitting direct comparisons with the general population. Not surprisingly, refugees were in much worse economic situations and had much higher levels of psychological strains, with Cambodians by far facing the most serious problems. The article provides a considerable amount of descriptive information and is particularly valuable in sorting out refugees versus nonrefugees and Cambodians versus Vietnamese versus Chinese.

Menjivar, Cecilia. 1994. Salvadoran Migration to the United States in the 1980s. *International Migration* 32(3):371–401. Review of migration from El Salvador to the San Francisco area, based on a survey of 150 people and follow-up, in-depth interviews with 40 of them. The author provides an accessible, reasoned analysis leading to three main points. First, the reasons for migration were both political and economic. Second, the existence of kin links in America was essential in the complicated exodus from El Salvador through Honduras and Mexico to the United States. Third, those same kin links were strained and sometimes ruptured once the newcomers reached the United States—largely because of extremely limited employment opportunities.

Mesa-Lago, Carmelo, and June S. Belkin. 1982. The Cuban Exodus: A Symposium. Special combined issue of *Cuban Studies* 11(2) and 12(1). 103 pages. Series of four articles, with separate comment sections, on the Cuban exodus to the United States. The articles address (1) the incorporation into the United States of 1970s arrivals (Portes, Clark, and Lopez); (2) the Cuban entrants of 1980 (Bach, Bach, and Triplett); (3) the political structure of the Cuban community in the United States (Azicri); and (4) a comparison of Cubans and Mexicans in the United States (Bailey). Comments on the articles are provided by Rogg, Fernandez, Baloyra, and Perez.

Migration World. Bimonthly. Staten Island, New York: Center for Migration Studies. *Migration World* (formerly *Migration Today*) provides general information on migration-related topics, a guide to sources, and relatively informal articles. Refugees receive considerable attention. Libraries may not keep back issues, but if they do, this is a valuable resource. *Migration World* articles are not included in this bibliography. (The Center for Migration Studies also publishes the academic journal *International Migration Review.*)

Mindel, Charles H., Robert W. Habenstein, and Roosevelt Wright, Jr., Editors. 1988. *Ethnic Families in America: Patterns and Variations.* (3rd Edition). Englewood Cliffs, New Jersey: Prentice-Hall. 505 pages. Series of chapters on different ethnic family structures, including Cuban and Vietnamese. Jose Szapocznik and Roberto Hernandez review the multiracial origins and central importance of the Cuban family, how its rigid patriarchal form has moved toward greater egalitarianism in the United States, and the challenges posed to it by intense intergenerational conflict. Thanh Van Tran reviews Vietnamese history and the post-1975 diaspora, then focuses on the traditional, multigenerational, hierarchical family and the problems it has faced under the stresses of life in the United States—particularly economic demands and different rates of acculturation of the different generations.

Miralles, Maria Andrea. 1989. *A Matter of Life and Death: Health-Seeking Behavior of Guatemalan Refugees in South Florida.* New York: AMS Press. 172 pages. Study of Mayan refugees in a small Florida town. The book is a revised version of a master's thesis that has anthropological origins and a strong applied orientation. The author's emphasis is on Mayan medical beliefs and the refugees' use of health services, but she also provides background on the origins of this refugee group, the stresses of migrant work, and the way this particular group fits into an unusually complex local community.

Mitchell, Christopher. 1994. U.S. Policy toward Haitian Boat People, 1972–93. *Annals of the American Academy of Political and Social Sciences* 534:69–80. Coherent review of U.S. policy on Haitian refugees. The author briefly sketches the origins of legal, then nonlegal immigration to the United States. The article then focuses on the legal and political aspects of interception of boat refugees with particularly useful analysis of the Bush and early Clinton administrations. He finds U.S. policy ''on balance a discreditable affair'' but also notes how policy on Haitians is becoming less an anomaly than an emerging general policy for all refugee groups.

Model, Suzanne. 1992. The Ethnic Economy: Cubans and Chinese Reconsidered. *Sociological Quarterly* 33(1):63–82. Intriguing review of competing ''ethnic economy'' theories based on 1980 census data. The author outlines three approaches: first, the classic middleman minority hypothesis; second, the ethnic enclave perspective; and third, an ethnic hegemony perspective. These are all well-

established streams in sociological thought on immigration, and the author provides a succinct overview. The actual statistical examination is technical, but—
to generalize—the results suggest that the advantages of enclave economies for
immigrant workers are quite limited.

Montero, Darrel. 1979. *Vietnamese Americans: Patterns of Resettlement and Socioeconomic Adaptation in the United States.* Boulder, Colorado: Westview Press. 72
pages of text, plus front matter and appendixes. General description of the demographic characteristics of the early Vietnamese refugees and their adjustment to
the United States through 1977, based largely on the first five surveys conducted
by Opportunity Systems Incorporated under contract to the federal government
and provided to interested researchers. A general model of what the author terms
"spontaneous international migration" is also presented.

Morgan, Scott, and Elizabeth Colson, Editors. 1987. *People in Upheaval.* New York:
Center for Migration Studies. 241 pages. Series of anthropological essays from a
1983–1984 seminar at the University of California (Berkeley). The papers range
greatly in topic and character, but several deal with refugees in the United States:
Marilyn Lacy and Gisele Bousquet in separate articles address the situation of
the Lao and Vietnamese in asylum camps; Jonathan Habarad and Louisa Schein
in separate articles analyze the resettlement of two Laotian minorities (Hmong
and Iu Mien); and Steven Gold assesses the interaction of refugees and service
providers.

Mortland, Carol, and Maura G. England. 1987. Vietnamese Youth in American Foster
Care. *Social Work* 32(3):240–245. Solid review of unaccompanied minors placed
with Caucasian foster families, based on a combination of interviewing and direct
program experience. The authors provide a succinct review of the literature on
unaccompanied Vietnamese minors and then discuss five key strategies used by
the minors in adjusting to American life: (1) adherence to the goals for which
they came to America; (2) basing conclusions on previous information; (3) acquiring the culturally proper material possessions; (4) seeking information from
all possible sources; and (5) maintaining their previous, extensive independence.
Conflicts with the foster families are inevitable as the minors embark on "an
erratic search for a continuity of purpose . . . and a resolution to the conflict en-
gendered by their loss."

Mortland, Carol, and Judy Ledgerwood. 1988. Refugee Resource Acquisition, the Invisible Communication System. In *Cross-Cultural Adaptation: Current Approaches.*
Edited by Young Yun Kim and William B. Gudykunst. Newbury Park, California:
Sage Publications. Pages 286–306. Analysis of the patronage system in refugee
resettlement. The authors review the sharply divergent Southeast Asian and American views of public assistance and how they coexist by being largely invisible
to each other. On the refugee side, a system of patronage makes sense as a
mechanism for navigating an unknown system to gain desired benefits. What is
unusual in resettlement is that young refugees are able to develop roles as patrons
because of their literacy in English. Much of the invisibility of this patronage
system to American service providers results from the fact that gifts and labor
are provided by the client in small increments spread over time. The article is a
very balanced introduction to the structural miscommunication that occurs in resettlement programs.

Muecke, Marjorie A. 1983. Caring for Southeast Asian Refugees in the USA. *American Journal of Public Health* 73(4):431–438. Overview of key problems medical practitioners are likely to face when treating refugees from Cambodia, Laos, and Vietnam. After providing brief cultural backgrounds, Muecke lucidly explains and "demystifies" typical practitioner problems, including (1) essentials of etiquette in initial patient contacts, (2) use of interpreters, (3) gaining patient consent, (4) reasons for client unresponsiveness, (5) cultural restraints, (6) social supports, and (7) traditional attitudes toward healing.

Muir, Karen L. S. 1988. *The Strongest Part of the Family: A Study of Lao Refugee Women in Columbus, Ohio.* New York: AMS Press. 191 pages. Field research-based dissertation on the Lao in Columbus. The book includes general information on Lao resettlement and refugee programs, but the heart of the discussion involves the shifting roles of women as Lao and as refugees in the United States. The author provides some intriguing comparisons with Lao refugees in other locations and some sensible analysis of male and female role tendencies—particularly male competition and factionalism versus female cooperation and cohesion.

Muzny, Charles C. 1989. *The Vietnamese in Oklahoma City: A Study in Ethnic Change.* New York: AMS Press. 200 pages. Review of refugees in Oklahoma, based on a variety of survey and interview information from the late 1970s and early 1980s. Major chapters cover cultural background, exodus, initial resettlement experiences, public sector activities (employment, education), private sector activities (language use, family, kinship, ceremony), and group organization (the Vietnamese American Association specifically). The book benefits from frequent use of extended interviewee comments.

Naficy, Hamid. 1993. *The Making of Exile Cultures: Iranian Television in Los Angeles.* Minneapolis: University of Minnesota Press. 283 pages. Interesting analysis of Iranian exile television covering the 1980s. Iranian TV is the largest non-Spanish ethnic television in the Los Angeles area and, to the author, a window on how exiles process their "experiences of separation, liminality, and incorporation, as well as their resistance to incorporation and their efforts at differentiation and dissimilation" (xvi). The book includes both objective detail on the media and also more interpretive material (e.g., on textual politics, fetishization, and hybridity).

Nguyen-Hong-Nhiem, Lucy, and Joel Martin Halpern, Editors. 1989. *The Far East Comes Near: Autobiographical Accounts of Southeast Asian Students in America.* Amherst: University of Massachusetts Press. 213 pages. Set of essays written by refugee students in the United States. The essays cover home country memories, exodus, and adaptation to life in the United States. They reflect all three countries (Vietnam, Cambodia, and Laos—although with less representation of the Laotian experience). Together the essays provide a very effective introduction to the refugee experience, partially because the student views are fresh and removed from the rhetoric that affects other adult-centered refugee accounts. Two introductory pieces by the editors are balanced and useful in their own right. This is an excellent place to begin to understand the Southeast Asian refugee experience.

Nguyen Manh Hung. 1984. Refugee Scholars and Vietnamese Studies in the United States, 1975–1982. *Amerasia Journal* 11(1):89–99. Review of the problems and potential of refugee scholars. The author notes the various barriers to refugee scholars, particularly lack of facility in English, complete unfamiliarity with grantsmanship, lack of time, lack of knowledge of the specific scholarly standards that permit publication, and a highly politicized environment in which refugees tend to the Right and established American scholars tend to the Left. Concluding comments note the unique advantages of experience and perspective that refugees have and why their contributions are so important to the "search for the evasive truth about Vietnam."

Nicassio, Perry M. 1983. Psychosocial Correlates of Alienation: Study of a Sample of Indochinese Refugees. *Journal of Cross-Cultural Psychology* 14:337–351. Assessment of Southeast Asian refugee alienation based on interviews with 460 heads of household in Illinois in 1979. The sample included, and separate analyses were conducted for, Vietnamese, Cambodians, Hmong, and Lao. Overall, Lao and Vietnamese tended to be less alienated than Hmong and Cambodians. However, the key correlates of alienation appeared to be lack of economic progress, low English proficiency, and a great self-perceived difference from nonrefugee Americans.

North, David S., Lawrence S. Lewin, and Jennifer R. Wagner. 1982. *Kaleidoscope: The Resettlement of Refugees in the U.S. by the Voluntary Agencies.* Washington, D.C.: New TransCentury Foundation. 139 pages. Final report of a study conducted under contract to the federal government. An overview of the 15 voluntary agencies involved in the resettlement of refugees is followed by separate chapters on the allocation process, structural and organizational issues, services provided to refugees, and refugee use of public assistance programs. Although sympathetic to the great variability among the voluntary agencies and their historical seniority in resettlement, the report generally favors the more uniform and rationalized program operations and stronger government oversight that, in fact, emerged in the 1980s.

Office of Refugee Resettlement (ORR). Annual. *Report to the Congress: Refugee Resettlement Program.* Washington, D.C.: U.S. Department of Health and Human Services. Annual report to the Congress on the operations, accomplishments, and goals of the refugee program during the preceding fiscal year. The reports typically include reviews of the overall program, with emphasis on domestic assistance. Particularly useful are sections on refugee population characteristics and economic adjustment. Extensive appendixes include tables on arrival rates, nationality, state of destination, et cetera; reports from other public and private agencies; and a list of state refugee coordinators.

Orleck, Annelise. 1987. The Soviet Jews: Life in Brighton Beach, Brooklyn. In *New Immigrants in New York.* Edited by Nancy Foner. New York: Columbia University Press. Pages 273–304. Engaging essay on Soviet Jews in New York, their adaptation, and their effects on a well-established Jewish community. The author provides a succinct history of Brighton Beach and how Soviet Jewish resettlement was crucial in avoiding the community's decline. Separate discussions of the elderly, working-age adults, and children show their varied adjustment, with especially intriguing insights about the very successful adjustment of the elderly— who found a congenial existing community of other elderly Jews. The article concludes with a description of the unique restaurants whose activities transform Brighton Beach into "Little Odessa" after dark.

Owan, Tom Choken, Editor. 1985. *Southeast Asian Mental Health: Treatment, Prevention, Services, Training, and Research.* Washington, D.C.: U.S. Department of Health and Human Services. 559 pages. Collection of 19 practitioner-oriented papers on refugee mental health. The volume is the result of a multiagency federal government effort to bring together insights about, and treatment approaches for, Southeast Asian refugees. The papers are generally accessible, relatively terse, and written by well-credentialed authors. The result is a good sampler of the mental health issue as it appeared in the mid-1980s. Its sections mirror the book's title (treatment, prevention, services, training, and research).

Pedraza, Silvia, Editor. 1994. Immigration, Race, and Ethnicity in America. Special issue of *Social Problems* 41(1):1–176. Series of papers mostly on recent immigrants and refugees. Of particular interest on the refugee side are an intriguing comparison of African-American and Cambodian day-haul farmworkers in Philadelphia (Pfeffer); a comparison of Cuban and Iranian ethnic enclaves (Light, Sabagh, Bozorgmehr, and Der-Martirosian); household structure and ideology among Vietnamese (Kibria); and labor market incorporation of Central Americans in Washington, D.C.—where there was no major existing Latino population (Repak).

Pedraza-Baily, Silvia. 1985. Cuba's Exiles: Portrait of a Refugee Migration. *International Migration Review* 19(1):4–34. Review of the progressive stages of the Cuban exodus. The author focuses on the changes in those fleeing Cuba, the implications of those changes for the exiles, the exile community, and the way in which the United States and Cuba constructed a system of political international migration that met both countries' immediate goals. This is a relatively accessible introduction to the over 20 years and nearly a million people that constituted the Cuban exodus at the time the paper was written.

Perez, Lisandro. 1986. Immigrant Economic Adjustment and Family Organization: The Cuban Success Story Reexamined. *International Migration Review* 20(1):4–20. Succinct analysis of the Cuban immigrant "success story" in terms of the family household. The author provides a brief, clear review of competing individual-oriented (e.g., human capital) and structural (e.g., dual labor market) frameworks for explaining immigrant adjustment and then examines the role of the household. Three factors help explain Cuban success: high rates of female labor force participation, low fertility, and the contributions of the coresident elderly. Although based on 1980 census data, this remains a very good general introduction to household-based perspectives on immigrant achievement.

Perez, Lisandro, Editor. 1990. Cuban-Americans in Miami. Special section of *Cuban Studies* 20:3–63. Set of four useful articles on the Miami experience. Lisandro Perez provides an overview of "Cuban Miami at the Crossroads"; John Stack and Christopher Warren discuss "Ethnicity and the Politics of Symbolism"; Guillermo Grenier looks at "Ethnic Solidarity and the Cuban-American Labor Movement"; and Isabel Castellanos writes on "The Use of English and Spanish among Cubans." The papers share a general focus on the tension between Cubans as exiles and Cubans as part of U.S.-based ethnic divisions.

Phillips, Bruce A., and Mitra Kahrize Khalili. 1995. The Iranian Jewish Family in Transition. *Journal of Jewish Communal Service* 71(2/3):192–199. Brief review of
Iranian Jews in Los Angeles, based on the authors' general knowledge and a set
of 20 in-depth interviews. The authors stress the importance of the family to the
Iranian Jews, and the strain that develops between individuals' desire for some
increased autonomy and their concurrent desire to maintain a close, traditional,
extended family. The tendency for Iranian Jews to be involved in religious activities is noted, as is their potential as a bridge to the wider Iranian, Middle Eastern,
and Muslim communities.

Portes, Alejandro. 1969. Dilemmas of a Golden Exile: Integration of Cuban Refugee
Families in Milwaukee. *American Sociological Review* 34:505–518. Classic article about the integration of Cuban families in Milwaukee, based on 48 in-depth
interviews conducted jointly with husbands and wives. Portes's general hypothesis
is that the level of integration is a function of the rewards available from current
socioeconomic status. The correlation between economic rewards and level of
integration is described as a result of the rational-individualistic ethic of those
Cubans who came to the United States.

Portes, Alejandro, and Robert L. Bach. 1985. *Latin Journey: Cuban and Mexican Immigrants in the United States*. Berkeley: University of California Press. 387 pages.
Analysis of Cuban and Mexican immigration during the 1970s, based on a sequence of three surveys for each of the populations. The authors provide a theoretical overview, reviews of post-1890 immigration in general and Cuban and
Mexican immigrant flows in particular and then present considerations of basic
adjustment patterns, the Cuban enclave in Miami, the nature of secondary labor
markets, immigrant perceptions of America, and the development of immigrant
social relationships. The book is rich in quantitative data and particularly influential in its analysis of the economic development and implications of ethnic
enclaves.

Prieto, Yolanda. 1986. Cuban Women and Work in the United States: A New Jersey
Case Study. In *International Migration: The Female Experience*. Edited by Rita
James Simon and Caroline B. Bretell. Totowa, New Jersey: Rowman and Allenheld. Pages 95–112. Analysis of the widely noted high labor force participation
of Cuban refugee women, based on a 107-person survey in an area of dense Cuban
settlement near New York. The author's basic argument is that an increasing
involvement of women in paid production is justified by the desire for a better
life. However, the author also notes a surprisingly high level of paid employment
of these women when they were still in Cuba, the intrinsic value of work to many
of them, and the extent to which work outside the home and women's responsibilities within the home are not in conflict. Most of the women surveyed worked
in the apparel and textiles industries.

Rahe, Richard H., John G. Looney, Harold W. Ward, Tran Minh Tung, and William T.
Liu. 1978. Psychiatric Consultation in a Vietnamese Refugee Camp. *American
Journal of Psychiatry* 135(2):185–190. Review of the author's experience providing psychiatric consultation at Camp Pendleton during 1975. Their major recommendations as a consulting team were related to the stage of camp
development: Early recommendations concerned easing adaptation to the camp
setting; later efforts included creating a psychiatric crisis clinic and carrying out

a mental health survey with a random sample of refugees. Many of their recommendations were successfully implemented, but the authors do note problems in adequately identifying the camp's structure and particularly in resolving the problems facing unaccompanied minors.

Reder, Stephen, Mary Cohn, Judith Arter, and Steven Nelson. 1984. *A Study of English Language Training for Refugees: Public Report.* Portland, Oregon: Northwest Regional Educational Laboratory. 66 pages. Summary of an important federally funded study conducted from 1981 to 1983. The study had three phases: (1) a mail survey of service providers; (2) a series of site visits with emphasis on classroom observation—but also including surveys with 400 households; and (3) pretest/posttest analysis of actual English-language acquisition. The study is a very important one, combining interesting statistical material with a qualitative appreciation of the classroom and the varying needs of students (e.g., students not literate in their own native language).

Reder, Stephen, et al. 1985. *The Hmong Resettlement Study.* Portland, Oregon: Northwest Regional Educational Laboratory. Major federally funded study of the Hmong conducted in association with the University of Minnesota's Southeast Asian Refugee Studies Project and Lao Family Community, Inc. The 262-page final report (Volume I of the study) includes background on the Hmong, general patterns of Hmong resettlement in the United States, and Hmong progress in employment, English-language acquisition, and children's education. Separate volumes published at various times in 1984 and 1985 cover economic development and employment projects (Volume II by Simon Fass and Diana Bui), exemplary projects (Volume III), and site-specific material (separate 50-plus page reports) on Orange County (California), Fresno (California), Portland (Oregon), Minneapolis–St. Paul, Dallas–Ft. Worth, Fort Smith (Arkansas), and Providence (Rhode Island).

Rodriguez, Nestor P. 1987. Undocumented Central Americans in Houston: Diverse Populations. *International Migration Review* 21(1):4–26. Review of the estimated 100,000 undocumented Central American migrants in Houston. The author discusses the origins, settlement patterns, employment, and reasons for emigration, based largely on a series of interviews by a mixed team of Mexican and Central Americans. Particularly emphasized are the recentness of this immigration, its cultural and racial diversity, and the dynamics of household formation. The largest segment of the population (Salvadorans) were the most clearly politically driven refugees, although such reasons appeared sporadically for Guatemalans, Hondurans, and the few identified Nicaraguans.

Rogg, Eleanor Meyer. 1974. *The Assimilation of Cuban Exiles: The Role of Community and Class.* New York: Aberdeen Press. 241 pages. Influential description and analysis of research conducted on Cuban refugees during 1967–1968 in the New York City area. The research was conducted under funding from the Department of Labor and included interviews with 250 randomly selected Cubans in the high-density Cuban area of West New York, New Jersey. Rogg focuses on the relationships between adjustment and the presence of a strong ethnic community and between adjustment and occupational and class backgrounds in Cuba. Other areas covered include the restructuring of family relations, ethnic relations, and intergenerational conflicts.

Rollwagen, Jack R., Editor. 1990. Southeast Asian Refugees in the United States. Special issue of *Urban Anthropology* 16(3–4):273–304. Set of four useful papers. Marjorie Muecke looks at Lao reconstructions of identity in Seattle through the incident of a Lao ghost who haunts the refugees. Carol Mortland and Judy Ledgerwood look at both government and refugee perceptions of so-called secondary migration. Amy Zaharlick and Jean Brainard look at the effects of ethnicity and demographics on resettlement, both nationally and locally (Franklin County, Ohio). Finally, Carol Mortland looks at the ways in which overseas processing centers (specifically the one in the Philippines) transform refugees but often do so in ways that increase their dependence both in the camps and subsequently in the United States.

Rubin, Burton S. 1975. The Soviet Refugee: Challenge to the American Jewish Community Resettlement System. *Journal of Jewish Communal Service* 52(2):195–201. Reflective article on Jewish communal services and their appropriateness to Soviet refugees. Rubin reviews the mismatch between the values and behavior of the service agencies and the attitudes and experiences of Soviet Jews. He concludes that it "seems abundantly clear that our ability to adapt and redefine our social services, as well as our attitudes, are as vital and important for the successful immigration of the Soviet Jew as is his own ability to adapt and modify his value system to our own cultural milieu."

Ruefle, William, William H. Ross, and Diane Mandell. 1992. Attitudes toward Southeast Asian Immigrants in a Wisconsin Community. *International Migration Review* 26(3):877–898. Intriguing analysis of 458 telephone survey responses on public attitudes toward Hmong refugees in La Cross, Wisconsin. The respondents were about evenly split in being positive or negative toward the sizable Hmong population (4 percent of La Cross's 50,000 people). Statistical analysis showed predictable correlation between positiveness toward the Hmong and the respondents' income, education, and optimism about economic conditions. However, the most important predictor was a separate "ethnocentrism" factor. The analysis suggests that attitudes toward immigrants reflect people's basic attitudes toward in-groups and out-groups more than they reflect economic or demographic characteristics. The authors warn that neither the Hmong as a people nor La Cross as a site is typical.

Rumbaut, Rubén D., and Rubén G. Rumbaut. 1976. The Family in Exile: Cuban Expatriates in the United States. *American Journal of Psychiatry* 133(4):395–399. Frequently cited overview of the adjustment of Cubans in the United States, with emphasis on the interplay between uprootedness and the opportunity for new accomplishments. The authors note the following factors in explaining the relative success of Cuban adjustment: (1) high occupational and educational levels, (2) formation of vigorous ethnic communities and the support they furnish in maintaining a positive ethnic identification, and (3) an effectively organized reception by the United States.

Rutledge, Paul James. 1992. *The Vietnamese Experience in America*. Bloomington: Indiana University Press. 173 pages. Overview of the Vietnamese refugee experience. The author provides a sound, though abbreviated, review of exodus and asylum, the different refugee waves, initial resettlement, community development, societal integration, and personal adjustment. The author's research in Oklahoma City provides the best material in the book, particularly regarding religion. Some of that material is presented in more detail in his prior monograph *The Role of Religion in Ethnic Self-Identity* (Lanham, Maryland: University Press of America, 1985).

Rynearson, Ann Manry, and Pamela A. DeVoe. 1984. Refugee Women in a Vertical Village: Lowland Laotians in St. Louis. *Social Thought* 10(3):33–48. Overview of the Laotian community in St. Louis, with a major focus on a single apartment building with 122 refugees. The authors convey very clearly how the public spaces of the apartment were transformed into shared social space. Gender roles receive particular attention. The analysis suggests that relations between men and women have many egalitarian aspects, and the sharing of work, home, and child care duties is an important asset in resettlement. Differences in roles—particularly on formal occasions—are also noted.

Sabagh, Georges, and Mehdi Bozorgmehr. 1987. Are the Characteristics of Exiles Different from Immigrants? *Sociology and Social Research* 71(2):77–84. Attempt to test for refugee/immigrant differences based on the 1980 census. The analysis concerns Iranians in Los Angeles and notes in passing the sharp concentration of students in the populations, the widely varying estimates of Iranians in the area, and the known preeminent status of Los Angeles as a home for Iranian immigrants and exiles. The statistical analysis suggests that the exiles are more frequently from minority groups and represent a broader demographic slice of society. Information on economic differences is less clear. The very high levels of English-language competence and self-employment are also noted.

Salter, Paul S., and Robert C. Mings. 1972. The Projected Impact of Cuban Settlement on Voting Patterns in Metropolitan Miami, Florida. *Professional Geographer* 24(2):123–131. Early analysis of the impact of Cubans on the political system in Miami. The article is based on voting patterns, estimated ethnic concentrations, and a street corner survey of 502 Cubans. The results indicate that Cubans ''will have a strong tendency to support candidates who take a strong anti-communist position, particularly in international affairs, and who in general express conservative ideals.'' Salter and Mings's contention that Cuban voters would turn Miami from a traditional Democratic stronghold to a source of conservative strength has been at least partially borne out by subsequent events.

Schulz, Nancy, and Ann Sontz. 1983. *Voyagers in the Land: A Report on Unaccompanied Southeast Asian Refugee Children.* Washington, D.C.: United States Catholic Conference. 86 pages. Report on 420 minors resettled by one of the two agencies involved with such refugee minors. Although limited to mail surveys, the report provides an interesting snapshot of the minors and their adjustment to the United States. Considerable progress is seen in educational, occupational, and social areas (including relations with relatives—especially siblings—and American friends). The study pays particular attention to changes in placement, the effects of different kinds of placement (e.g., ethnic foster parents), and the correlates of frequent depression.

Scott, George M., Jr. 1988. To Catch or Not to Catch a Thief: A Case of Bride Theft among the Lao Hmong Refugees in Southern California. *Ethnic Groups* 7(2):

137–151. Absorbing account of the abduction of a woman to become a bride. The author discusses the case and the cultural background for the practice and notes that this is simply the best documented of several reported cases. Roughly following traditional practice, the man abducted a 16-year-old girl and hid her at a clansman's apartment. Normally, the abduction would have been followed by marriage arrangements. However, in this case an appeal to American agency staff interrupted the normal sequence of events and resulted in a serious rift in the Hmong community.

Shaw, Robert, Jr. 1977. Preventive Medicine in the Vietnamese Refugee Camps on Guam. *Military Medicine* 142(1):19–28. Review of the health situation in, and general management of, the refugee camps on Guam in 1975. Major medical-related problems included water supply, food, waste disposal, insect and rodent control, and disease surveillance and control; major refugee complaints were conjunctivitis, upper respiratory tract infections, diarrhea, skin problems, gastroenteritis, and other relatively mild problems. Shaw also reviews camp management and suggests areas in which improvements could be made, such as communication, understanding of cultural differences, and recreation.

Simon, Rita J. 1983. Refugee Families' Adjustment and Aspirations: A Comparison of Soviet Jewish and Vietnamese Immigrants. *Ethnic and Racial Studies* 6(4):492–504. Comparison of Soviet and Vietnamese refugees, based on interviews of parent/adolescent-child pairs in Chicago. Because Southeast Asian and Soviet refugees are rarely the subjects of a single research effort, Simon's findings of differences (particularly in economic adjustment) and similarities (e.g., parental expectations for the children) are particularly intriguing.

Simon, Rita J., Editor. 1985. *New Lives: The Adjustment of Soviet Jewish Immigrants in the United States and Israel.* Lexington, Massachusetts: Lexington Books. 190 pages. Set of quantitative and qualitative papers reflecting the situation of Soviet émigrés around 1980. Some papers include both Israel and U.S. data; others focus on only one country. Of relevance to the United States are general survey data on social and economic adjustment (Rita Simon and Julian Simon); attitudinal data on quality of life (Zvi Gitelman); an interesting narrative account of two families (Lenora Greenbaum); and separate analyses of émigré small-business owners (Nancy Lubin) and artists (Marilyn Rueschemeyer).

Skinner, Kenneth A., and Glenn L. Hendricks. 1979. The Shaping of Ethnic Self-identity among Indochinese Refugees. *Journal of Ethnic Studies* 7(3):25–41. Analysis of the development of ethnic identity among Indochinese refugees, with emphasis on college students at the University of Minnesota. The refugee's major options for self-identification are as a refugee, as a member of a particular group (such as Vietnamese or Lao), or as an Asian-American. The authors note the different rewards for self-placement in each of these categories. Minnesota college students, for example, have access to considerable financial support as members of the Asian-American minority. Potential problems with other minorities are also discussed.

Smith-Hefner, Nancy J. 1994. Ethnicity and the Force of Faith: Christian Conversion among Khmer Refugees. *Anthropological Quarterly* 67(1):24–37. Analysis of the causes and consequences of conversion among Khmer in Boston. The article is based on extensive fieldwork and interviewing in the 1989–1991 period and includes useful, competent general comments on Khmer culture, exodus, and resettlement in Boston. The heart of the article is the review of the very small proportion of the Khmer who have converted and the generally favorable social and economic results of that conversion. The counterpoint between a traditional Buddhism (that is interwoven with the very essence of Khmer ethnicity) and an often evangelical reborn Christianity is very well drawn.

Southeast Asian Refugee Studies (SARS) Project. n.d. Assorted Bibliographies. Minneapolis: University of Minnesota, Institute of International Studies and Programs. Series of specialized, annotated bibliographies. SARS has long been a force in the study of the Hmong but also maintains a broader collection of materials on Southeast Asian refugees. It has published bibliographies on elderly refugees (Laura Boyer, 1991), nursing research and practice with refugees (Marjorie Muecke, 1990), the Hmong (Douglas Olney, 1983; J. Christina Smith, 1987), refugee youth (Ruth Hammond and Glenn Hendricks, 1988), and Cambodia and Cambodian refugees (John Marston, 1987).

Stanley, William Deane. 1987. Economic Migrants or Refugees from Violence? A Time-Series Analysis of Salvadoran Migration to the United States. *Latin American Research Review* 22(1):132–154. Attempt to test statistically the political versus economic motivations of Salvadorans coming to the United States. The author provides a succinct review of the question and then describes several statistical analyses based on economic and political factors (e.g., level of political assassinations) as they related to the monthly number of Salvadorans apprehended as illegal immigrants. The results strongly support the importance of political motivation for exodus to the United States.

Starr, Paul D., and Alden E. Roberts. 1982. Community Structure and Vietnamese Refugee Adaptation: The Significance of Context. *International Migration Review* 16(3):595–615. Examination of the significance of the social context of the receiving community on the adjustment of Vietnamese refugees in the United States. The analysis is based on interviews with 350 refugees in 1978 in northern California and along the central Gulf Coast. Starr and Roberts argue, on the basis of statistical analysis, that although refugee background characteristics have important effects on adjustment, such features of the local community as employment opportunities, ethnic heterogeneity, and general educational level also have demonstrable effects.

Stein, Barry N. 1979. Occupational Adjustment of Refugees: The Vietnamese in the United States. *International Migration Review* 13(1):25–45. Influential article on the occupational adjustment of Vietnamese refugees to the United States. Data on the refugees come largely from the first five Opportunity Systems Incorporated surveys funded by the federal government and cover the period from 1975 to mid-1977. Stein's emphasis is on downward occupational mobility, and he suggests that after four years in the United States refugees are likely to be close to their permanent economic status. The article benefits greatly from its attention to comparative information on other recent refugee groups.

Stein, Barry N., and Sylvano M. Tomasi. 1981. Refugees Today. Special issue of *International Migration Review* 15(1–2). 398 pages. Collection of 30 articles and documentary notes on various aspects of refugee exodus and resettlement, of which about a fourth bear on the recent resettlement of Southeast Asian refugees in the United States. The volume, the first effort of its kind in the United States, brought together the disparate perspectives of research, policy, and program operation, as well as a good range of comparative material from different countries. The contributions are organized into separate sections on policy, resettlement, and adjustment, with initial sections on more theoretical issues and a concluding and useful article by Stein on some likely parameters of the refugee experience as a field of study.

Stowers, Genie N. L. 1990. Political Participation, Ethnicity, and Class Status: The Case of Cubans in Miami. *Ethnic Groups* 8(2):73–90. Review of patterns in Miami voting from 1955 to 1985. An analysis of voting in local elections shows a very high voting turnout of Cubans throughout the period and a turnout that is sharply higher than for Anglo and black groups. Statistical analysis confirms the importance of ethnicity and, for Cubans, indicates some interesting, if not always consistent, effects of class status.

Strand, Paul J., and Woodrow Jones, Jr. 1985. *Indochinese Refugees in America: Problems of Adaptation and Assimilation.* Durham, North Carolina: Duke University Press. 182 pages. Overview of Indochinese refugee adjustment in San Diego. The book is divided approximately in half, dealing first with general background considerations (history, resettlement policy) and then with the results of a survey conducted in 1981. Particular attention is paid to health, educational, and employment issues. This was one of the first survey efforts to aim at multivariate statistical analysis of multiple Southeast Asian refugee groups.

Stull, Donald D., Editor. 1990. When the Packers Came to Town: Changing Ethnic Relations in Garden City, Kansas. Special issue of *Urban Anthropology* 19(4): 303–427. Set of six articles on Southeast Asians, Hispanics, and Anglos in Garden City, relating to the meat-packing industry. The editor provides an overview, then Michael Broadway discusses the meat-packing industry itself, Arthur Campa describes immigrant and resident Hispanics, Janet Benson describes "good neighbors" in the trailer courts, Ken Erickson looks at social service agency involvement, and Mark Grey discusses immigrant students at the local high school. (See also the two citations for Lamphere provided above.)

Sue, Stanley, Charles Y. Nakamura, Rita Chi-Ying Chung, and Cindy Yee-Bradbury, Editors. 1994. Asian American Mental Health. Special issue of *Journal of Community Psychology* 22(2). Set of quantitatively oriented papers. Two of the papers, based on data from the same very large California needs assessment survey in 1986, address Southeast Asian refugees. In the first, Rita Chi-Ying Chung and Keh-Ming Lin address changes, continuities, and intergroup variation in the ways medical help is sought. The size of the survey is important here since it permits adequate statistical analysis of Cambodian, Chinese-Vietnamese, Hmong, Lao, and Vietnamese refugees. In the second paper, Jennifer Abe, Nolan Zane, and Kevin Chun look at refugees suffering from posttraumatic stress disorder. They stress the significance of anger and the independent effects of culture.

Sullivan, Teresa A. 1984. The Occupational Prestige of Women Immigrants: A Comparison of Cubans and Mexicans. *International Migration Review* 18(4):1045–

1062. Analysis of nationality and gender differences, based on data from the 1970 census. The author notes the limited attention paid to women immigrants and then provides an illustrative analysis of how different factors affect immigrants' occupational prestige. Significant differences appear between men and women, although those gender differences are slighter than the nationality differences between Cubans and Mexicans.

Szapocznik, José, Mercedes Arca Scopetta, Maria de los Angeles Aranalde, and William Kurtines. 1978. Cuban Value Structure: Treatment Implications. *Journal of Consulting and Clinical Psychology* 46(5):961–970. Examination of the relationship between cultural variables and psychological treatment models for Cubans in the Miami area. The article is based on clinical experience and on research with more than 500 Cuban and native-born American adolescents. By developing four factorially derived subscales, the authors demonstrate that Cuban immigrant adolescents tend to prefer hierarchical social relations, subjugation to nature, and actions phrased in the present tense. Anglo-Americans, on the other hand, prefer individuality, mastery over nature, and a future orientation. In discussing treatment models, the authors stress that the therapist must accept the importance of his or her authority and emphasize concrete objectives.

Taft, Ethel. 1977. The Absorption of Soviet Jewish Immigrants—Their Impact on Jewish Communal Institutions. *Journal of Jewish Communal Service* 54(2):166–171. General assessment of the effects of early Soviet émigrés on the Jewish community and on Jewish social services in particular. Taft suggests that long-range effects will be limited because of the current institutional rigidity of American society and the lack among the émigrés of any strong Jewish involvement. However, there have been some discernible effects including increased cooperation between family and vocational services, expansion in the range of activities provided by Jewish centers, and redefinition of the role of clients in the formulation of social service policy.

Teitelbaum, Michael S. 1980. Right versus Right: Immigration and Refugee Policy in the United States. *Foreign Affairs* 59:21–59. Review of the policy implications and alternatives regarding immigration to the United States. Teitelbaum notes the rising level of immigration, the predominance of Spanish speakers, and the laxness of Immigration and Naturalization Service enforcement practices. He emphasizes the need for the development of a coherent policy that fulfills three conditions: (1) adequate expression of traditional American humanitarian values; (2) protection of the civil liberties and human rights of U.S. citizens and legal immigrants; and (3) actual enforceability. The effects of immigration on labor markets, fertility, and political consensus are stressed. The article provides useful insight into views on refugee policy at the end of the Carter administration.

Tenhula, John. 1991. *Voices from Southeast Asia: The Refugee Experience in the United States.* New York: Holmes and Meier. 247 pages. Solid introduction to the Southeast Asian refugee experience in America. The interview segments with refugees cover traditional values, the American involvement in Southeast Asia, exodus, initial adjustment to the United States, and longer-term adaptation. The book very much reflects the author's long experience in resettlement work and his consequent concern for the practical (and spiritual) dilemmas of adaptation. The interview segments are quite abbreviated at times, but the inclusion of translated poems provides a counterbalance. The book is bracketed by short—but strong—essays by two noted refugee advocates: Le Xuan Khoa and Liv Ullman.

Tillema, Richard G. 1981. Starting Over in a New Land: Resettling a Refugee Family. *Public Welfare* 39(1):34–41. Informal review of one congregation's experience in sponsoring a five-member Hmong family who had already spent five years in a refugee camp in Southeast Asia. Tillema describes initial health problems, cultural conflicts over medical practices, problems in dealing with social service agencies, congregational resources, and educational issues. Major recommendations involve the utility of explicit service plans and the need to coordinate a wide variety of public and private resources.

Tollefson, James W. 1989. *Alien Winds: The Reeducation of America's Indochinese Refugees.* New York: Praeger. 205 pages. Critique of U.S. resettlement programs, largely because they force onto refugees American values and behavior that are not necessarily in their best interest. Based on 16 months in Southeast Asian refugee camps in the mid-1980s, the book reviews some general issues of refugees and refugee policy but focuses on the specific content and process of refugee education in the camps, the complex bureaucracy running the camps, and the way that bureaucracy intruded on refugees' liberty and even their health. The critique is an important one, but it is very sharp and should be balanced with some recognition of the inherent difficulties in educational efforts.

Tran, Thanh V., and Thang D. Nguyen. 1994. Gender and Satisfaction with the Host Society among Indochinese Refugees. *International Migration Review* 28(2):323–337. Statistical analysis of gender as it relates to refugees' satisfaction with life in America. The analysis is based on prior survey work in 1982 and in many ways raises as many questions as it resolves. What does emerge is a clearer appreciation of the related effects of gender, age, and education on the specific issue of satisfaction with life—as opposed to the more typical quantitative emphasis on employment and income. The authors speculate that the results indicate that men focus on socioeconomic issues, while women focus more on social relations.

Uba, Laura, and Rita C. Chung. 1991. The Relationship between Trauma and Financial and Physical Well-being among Cambodians in the United States. *Journal of General Psychology* 118(3):215–225. Statistical test of the effects of trauma based on a sample of 590 Cambodians in California. The authors hypothesize that previous traumas will negatively affect refugees' current employment and physical health. The data support those hypotheses even though separate measures for age, gender, general psychopathology, psychosocial dysfunction, anxiety, and depression were also included in the analysis. Interestingly, the number of years in refugees camps did not show significant effects; the authors suggest that may indicate that the traumas of camp life do indeed dissipate over time.

U.S. Commission on Immigration Reform. 1994. *U.S. Immigration Policy: Restoring Credibility. A Report to Congress: Executive Summary.* Washington, D.C.: U.S. Government Printing Office. 250 pages. Interim report of the commission established by the Immigration Act of 1990 to assess existing policy and to submit a final report in 1997. The interim report makes a variety of recommendations—

the most widely publicized at the time being the use of the Social Security number as the core identification for ensuring that illegal aliens do not obtain work in the United States. In addition to the broad recommendations on immigration policy and a valuable synopsis of the 1990 act is a short section ("Immigration Emergencies") that addresses refugee and refugeelike situations.

U.S. Committee for Refugees. Annual. *World Refugee Survey* (1717 Massachusetts Avenue NW, Suite 701, Washington, D.C. 20036). Annual publication on refugees throughout the world. Although the content varies from year to year, the general format entails a review of the year followed by articles on different issues, ranging from general policy and program concerns to the specific situations of particular refugee groups in countries of temporary and permanent asylum. Also included are summaries of refugee statistics, quite-detailed reports on individual countries (both as sources and destinations for refugees), and a useful directory of refugee-related organizations.

U.S. Committee for Refugees. Monthly. *Refugee Reports* (1717 Massachusetts Avenue NW, Suite 701, Washington, D.C. 20036). Monthly newsletter on current developments regarding refugees and the refugee program. The newsletter focuses on the U.S. refugee program and is probably the best single source for an updated knowledge of legislation, policy, and program directions. Lead articles are typically followed by program updates, resources, and statistics sections.

U.S. General Accounting Office (GAO). 1979. *The Indochinese Exodus: A Humanitarian Dilemma*. Washington, D.C. 106 pages. Particularly useful review of the Southeast Asian refugee situation, published during the height of the boat exodus from Vietnam. Separate chapters discuss the growth of the refugee problem in Southeast Asia, the role of the international agencies, camp conditions in Southeast Asia, U.S. selection and processing of refugees, and the resettlement program in the United States.

U.S. General Accounting Office (GAO). 1982. *Improved Overseas Medical Examinations and Treatment Can Reduce Serious Diseases in Indochinese Refugees Entering the United States*. Washington, D.C. 66 pages. Report on the incidence of serious diseases among Indochinese refugees and the existing or necessary procedures to identify and treat such diseases. The report suggests that serious diseases too frequently go undetected and untreated. GAO recommended the improvement of treatment overseas as the safest and most cost-effective solution to the problem. Most recommendations were subsequently implemented.

U.S. General Accounting Office (GAO). 1983. *Greater Emphasis on Early Employment and Better Monitoring Needed in Indochinese Refugee Resettlement Program*. Washington, D.C. 122 pages. Review of the refugee resettlement program conducted at the request of the House Committee on the Judiciary. The report focuses on four major problem areas: (1) a family reunification policy that caused significant concentrations in few localities; (2) the great extent to which refugees were receiving public cash assistance; (3) an insufficient emphasis on rapid employment for refugees; and (4) the fragmented management of the program.

U.S. General Accounting Office (GAO). 1994. *Vietnamese Amerasian Resettlement: Education, Employment, and Family Outcomes in the United States*. Washington, D.C. 81 pages. Review of the experiences of the 75,000 Amerasians and family members resettled under the Amerasian Homecoming Act of 1987. The report provides a solid review of the special circumstances of the Amerasians, based on existing demographic and program data, supplemented by interviews in two localities, a survey of resettlement agencies, and discussions with program personnel at the national level. The results portray a population that faces difficult educational and employment problems but also one that is generally pleased with a U.S. environment more tolerant than the one they left in Vietnam. The importance of family connections is stressed.

U.S. Immigration and Naturalization Service. Annual. *Statistical Yearbook of the Immigration and Naturalization Service.* Washington, D.C.: Government Printing Office. Key source on immigration and naturalization. The annual report provides an overview of program operations and extensive supporting tables and appendixes (e.g., listing of all U.S. immigration laws). Areas of most relevance are general immigration (which includes refugee adjustment of status), refugee applications and arrivals, and asylum applications and determinations. Nonimmigrants (e.g., students, tourists), naturalization, and enforcement are also covered.

Van Arsdale, Peter W., Editor. 1993. *Refugee Empowerment and Organizational Change: A System Perspective.* Arlington, Virginia: American Anthropological Association. 189 pages. Collection of papers on refugees. The editor provides introductory comments on the need for a system perspective and a typology of models of empowerment. Papers on refugees in the United States include Carol Mortland on patron-client relations and mutual assistance associations, Vang Pobzeb on Hmong advocacy, Pamela DeVoe on employer-employee relations and perceptions for Southeast Asian refugees, and Myrna Adkins and Barbara Sample on Colorado's Spring Institute and its training programs.

Vigil, James Diego, and Steve Chong Yun. 1990. Vietnamese Youth Gangs in Southern California. In *Gangs in America.* Edited by R. Huff. Newbury Park, California: Sage. Pages 146–162. Important introduction to Vietnamese youth gangs. The authors note the external (racism, school problems) and internal (war trauma, family stress) factors that make some youth susceptible to gang activity. One important factor is their inability to succeed in educational terms, thus failing at both their parents' and American society's expectations for them. Vietnamese youth gangs differ in important ways from other gangs. They are strongly focused on making money (rather than claiming territory), are highly pragmatic (as they usually only rob other Vietnamese), and are extremely fluid in membership.

Vignes, A. Joe, and Richard C. W. Hall. 1979. Adjustment of a Group of Vietnamese People to the United States. *American Journal of Psychiatry* 136(4):442–444. Brief review of early research conducted mainly with 50 newly resettled Vietnamese families in Baton Rouge, Louisiana. The major focus of the research was the construction of a social adjustment index, which was then tested for statistically significant correlations with age, religion, income, education, and marital status. The only significant relationship was with income. More generally, Vignes and Hall suggest that the Vietnamese are adjusting well, although they do echo other research that has found that previously high-status individuals face particular problems because of the extent of their downward mobility in the United States.

Wain, Barry. 1979. The Indochina Refugee Crisis. *Foreign Affairs* 58(fall):160–180. Review of the Southeast Asian refugee exodus from 1975 to 1979. Wain discusses the different waves of refugees (ethnic Vietnamese, ethnic Chinese, Highland Lao minorities) and analyzes them in terms of Hanoi's foreign policy vis-à-vis the Soviet Union, China, and Southeast Asia. The major recommendation is for direct U.S. negotiations with the Vietnamese government, since it remained the most important instigator of the refugee flows. (Wain's 1981 book *The Refused* [New York: Simon and Schuster] deals with the same period in greater detail.)

Wallace, Steven P. 1986. Central American and Mexican Immigrant Characteristics and Economic Incorporation in California. *International Migration Review* 20(9):657–671. Overview of Central American and Mexican immigrant differences based on the 1980 census. Central American immigrants were better educated, more urban, and more frequently women. Earnings for men were similar; Central American women earned more than Mexican women but less than men. The author notes the recentness of Central American immigration, its more political origins, its distinctive settlement patterns, and the mixed support this information provides for structural versus assimilationist perspectives on immigration.

Waters, Tony. 1990. Adaptation and Migration among the Iu Mien People of Southeast Asia. *Ethnic Groups* 8(2):127–141. Exploratory consideration of the estimated 10,000 Mien who have settled in the United States. The Iu Mien (or Yao) appear as an unusually adaptable minority population originating in China and moving later into Laos. They were the most adept of the highland peoples at Chinese culture and relatively unstructured in political and linguistic terms. Nevertheless, their identity endured, largely through a central cultural emphasis on ancestor worship. The paper concludes with a broad consideration of how the Mien can endure as a distinct people in the United States—particularly given the inability to maintain or re-create traditional agricultural practices.

Welaratna, Usha. 1993. *Beyond the Killing Fields: Voices of Nine Cambodian Survivors in America.* Stanford: Stanford University Press. 285 pages. Set of narratives that bridge life in Cambodia, the Khmer Rouge period, and exodus and resettlement in the United States. An introduction and two concluding interpretive chapters bracket the narratives themselves. The narratives and interpretation benefit from the author's own experience as an immigrant Asian woman with particular sympathy for the Buddhist tradition, the attacks upon it by the Khmer Rouge, and its continuing centrality to Cambodians in America. Many of the narrators were quite young when they left Cambodia, which makes their description very direct.

Westermeyer, Joseph, Tou-Fu Vang, and John Neider. 1984. Acculturation and Mental Health: A Study of Hmong Refugees at 1.5 and 3.5 Years Postmigration. *Social Science and Medicine* 18(1):87–93. Early assessment of changes in Hmong refugee self-ratings, based on 89 respondents interviewed initially in 1977 and reinterviewed in 1979. Although there were few social changes in their lives, there were distinct changes (improvements) in self-rating. There was a particularly significant reduction in depression (SLC-90 and Zung scales). Nevertheless, distress remained higher than that reported for other populations.

Williams, Carolyn L., and J. W. Berry. 1991. Primary Prevention of Acculturative Stress among Refugees. *American Psychologist* 45(6):632–641. Overview of local, national, and international approaches to alleviating the stress of refugees as they move to a new society. The authors focus on "acculturative stress" and the way it is affected by the experiences of refugees. They then provide examples of programs to help refugees cope with that stress. At the local level, they note efforts in Washington state to use native rituals to ease the trauma of Khmer children; at the national level, they note both U.S. and Canadian program initiatives; and at the international level, they describe efforts in Khmer refugee camps in Thailand. The need for cross-cultural training, understanding, and cooperation is stressed. (The same issue also includes an article by Elizabeth Gong-Guy, Richard Cravens, and Terence Patterson on delivery of mental health services to refugees.)

Winsberg, Morton D. 1979. Housing Segregation of a Predominantly Middle Class Population: Residential Patterns Developed by the Cuban Immigration into Miami, 1950–74. *American Journal of Economics and Sociology* 38(4):403–418. Statistical analysis of shifts in ethnic residential concentration in Miami from 1950 to 1974. Winsberg notes that although Cubans have assimilated economically, they have not assimilated residentially. Initial analysis of the data indicated the rapid expansion of Cubans throughout the city. The net effect, however, was a significant rise in residential segregation involving not only Latins but also blacks, Jews, and the elderly.

Woldemikael, Tekle Mariam. 1989. *Becoming Black American: Haitians and American Institutions in Evanston, Illinois.* New York: AMS Press. 191 pages. Important study of the approximately 2,000 Haitians in Evanston (on the outskirts of Chicago) in 1978–1980. Chapters address the structure of Evanston; the distinct periods of Haitian migration to Evanston; Haitian community life; Haitians and religious institutions; Haitians and educational institutions; second-generation Haitians; and community advocacy. The author's two major points are, first, that Haitians are caught between their own cultural identity and a receiving society that sees them in racial rather than cultural terms; and second, that second-generation Haitians tend to lose that cultural identity as they become absorbed into a black American identity. The study is based on fieldwork and some life histories, both of which yield compelling descriptive material.

Wong, Cindy. 1989. Doing Fieldwork on Chinese Vietnamese in America. *Amerasia Journal* 15(2):179–185. Engaging reflection on fieldwork in the Los Angeles area. The author, a middle-class immigrant from Hong Kong, describes her field entry into a Chiuchow Buddhist temple. Over time, she became increasingly involved with temple-related activities and even began receiving cash gifts (in traditional red envelopes) for her errands and services. Her parents subsequently worked for the temple as well. The comments on trying to de-exoticize films of temple activities and trying to sort through self/other distinctions in fieldwork are thoughtful.

Yang, Teng, Shoua Vang, Paoze Thao, David North, John Finck, and Bruce Downing. 1985. *An Evaluation of the Highland Lao Initiative.* Washington, D.C.: Coffey, Zimmerman, and Associates. 133 pages. Federally funded review of a special resettlement initiative. The project arose from a concern about increasing concentration of Highland Lao (mostly Hmong but also Iu Mien, Lao Lue, and Lao Theung) in central California—and with high rates of welfare utilization. Special funds were provided for non-California localities, with an attempt to involve ethnic mutual assistance associations. The evaluation staff contacted 32 of the 47 funded organizations. The report provides a review of services provided and some of the outcomes, which were generally positive although limited.

Zhou, Min, and Carl L. Bankston III. 1994. Social Capital and the Adaptation of the Second Generation: The Case of Vietnamese Youth in New Orleans. *International Migration Review* 28(4):821–845. Case study of Vietnamese in New Orleans. The authors review the unique Vietnamese settlement in the Versailles area (largely Catholics who were previously refugees from North to South Vietnam) and the way in which the Vietnamese family and community foster a strong emphasis on education—even though the adults themselves do not have any extensive educational background. Specific data from a survey of 198 students are included. At the most general level, the authors suggest the need to examine what they call "social capital" in addition to the more conventional sociological emphasis on "human capital."

Zucker, Norman L., and Naomi Flink Zucker. 1987. *The Guarded Gate: The Reality of American Refugee Policy.* New York: Harcourt Brace Jovanovich. 342 pages. Broad, relatively informal review of American refugee policy. The authors begin with a review of American immigration, then turn to a discussion of refugee law, the specific resettlement programs in place in the 1980s, and the dilemmas faced in asylum determinations. The authors are advocates for a more activist and equitable refugee policy and see the Refugee Act of 1980 as an adequate legal basis for such a policy. The book is at its best in sketching three critical asylum issues of the 1980s: the special burdens placed on Haitians (chapter 5), the legislative dispute over Central Americans (chapter 6), and the development of the sanctuary movement (chapter 7).

Index

About the Contributors

MEHDI BOZORGMEHR is an assistant professor of sociology at the City College, City University of New York. He was project director of a survey of Iranians in Los Angeles (funded by the National Science Foundation) and has published extensively on Iranians in the United States—including entries in *Encyclopedia Iranica* and *Encyclopedia of American Immigrant Cultures*. He received his Ph.D. from the University of California at Los Angeles.

JOSEPH COLEMAN first participated in the Cuban refugee program when he worked in human services at the state and federal levels. Later, in 1975 he coordinated the Department of Health, Education, and Welfare's processing of Southeast Asian refugees arriving at Fort Indiantown Gap in Pennsylvania, and then spent the next 20 years with the federal refugee program, mostly at the U.S. Department of State. His major focus was on involving and informing refugee groups in both the domestic and overseas aspects of the program. From 1988 to 1993 he coordinated the roles of the federal agencies that were part of the private resettlement program of the Cuban American National Foundation— a program that he and the foundation developed. He is a graduate of Vanderbilt University.

FREDERICK J. CONWAY has conducted both academic and applied research on agriculture, health practices, and religion in Haiti, as well as comparative applied research in Francophone Africa. In 1980, he served as an adviser to the Cuban-Haitian Task Force in Miami and as acting director of the Krome South camp for unaccompanied Haitian minors. More recently, he has conducted research on immigration policy in California and currently teaches at San Diego

State University. He is a graduate of Yale University and subsequently received his Ph.D. in anthropology from American University in 1978.

PAMELA A. DEVOE has carried out research on culture change and cross-cultural interaction, including work with American Indians in the United States, American expatriates in Central America, and Taiwanese Chinese in Taiwan. In 1980 she began her involvement in refugee issues, conducting research in St. Louis, examining issues of refugee policy and program development, and contributing to the American Anthropological Association's Committee on Refugee Issues—of which she is currently the chair and formerly editor of its 1992 *Selected Papers on Refugee Issues.* Her Ph.D. is in anthropology.

TIMOTHY DUNNIGAN is an associate professor of anthropology at the University of Minnesota. His primary research interests are linguistic acculturation, cultural semantics, written translation, and oral interpretation—as well as language-based problems of ethnographic description. His published work focuses on both Native American and Southeast Asian cultures: specifically, the Pima, Ojibwa, Dakota Sioux, and Hmong. He received his Ph.D. from the University of Arizona.

BILL FRELICK is a senior policy analyst with the U.S. Committee for Refugees, a nonprofit organization dedicated to defending the rights of refugees and asylum seekers in the United States and throughout the world. He is coeditor of the monthly *Refugee Reports,* associate editor of the annual *World Refugee Survey,* and widely published in his own right—both in technical policy publications and the popular press. His major geographic areas of interest are North America and the Caribbean, Europe, and the Middle East. He is a Phi Beta Kappa graduate of Oberlin College and subsequently received his M.A. from Columbia University.

STEVEN J. GOLD is an associate professor of sociology at Michigan State University and a senior fellow at the Wilstein Institute. He is the author of *Refugee Communities: A Comparative Field Study* (1992); has published numerous articles on immigrant adaptation, ethnic self-employment, and community development in both academic journals and edited volumes; and is the former president of the International Visual Sociology Association. Most recently, he has been involved in studies of Israeli immigrants in Los Angeles and Jewish philanthropy. He received his Ph.D. in sociology from the University of California at Berkeley in 1985.

LINDA W. GORDON is a demographer who has worked for extensive periods at both the federal Office of Refugee Resettlement and the Immigration and Naturalization Service—where she is currently the acting director of statistics. Her publications focus on the demographic characteristics of refugees, their geographic distribution, and their adjustment in the United States; immigration from Asia; and women in migration. She is a graduate of the University of Michigan and received her Ph.D. in sociology from Ohio State University.

ELZBIETA M. GOZDZIAK, a native of Poland, is an assistant professor at the Howard University School of Social Work and a lecturer at the Johns Hopkins School for Advanced International Studies. Her academic work covers displaced populations, research methods, and various aspects of Eastern European society and politics. She has also worked in policy analysis and project development, both on refugees in the United States and on development projects in Poland and Slovakia. Dr. Gozdziak is a cultural anthropologist by training.

BEATRICE NIED HACKETT is an anthropologist-in-residence at American University and the former executive director of the D.C. Community Humanities Council. She has conducted field research on Chinese-Cambodian refugees in the Washington, D.C. area, and has also conducted historical research on refugees in Europe, particularly Germans from Pomerania and East Prussia who fled the Soviet advance in 1945. Her collection of refugee narratives, *Pray God and Keep Walking: Stories of Women Refugees* was published in 1995. She received her Ph.D. in anthropology from American University.

DAVID W. HAINES is a social anthropologist whose involvement with refugee issues began in 1979 and has included policy-related work for the federal government and both small- and large-scale research projects on the adaptation of refugees. He is the editor of *Refugees in the United States* (1985) and *Refugees as Immigrants: Cambodians, Laotians, and Vietnamese in America* (1989). His academic writing includes Vietnamese social history, refugee adaptation, and American culture and society. He received his M.A. in Southeast Asian Studies and his Ph.D. in anthropology from American University.

PHILIP A. HOLMAN spent most of his government career working directly or indirectly with the refugee program. He worked for the Cuban Refugee Program from 1962 to 1964 and returned to that program for the period from 1969 to 1975. He then worked with the Indochinese Refugee Assistance Program from 1975 to 1980 and finally with the newly formed Office of Refugee Resettlement (ORR) from 1980 to 1995. He was ORR's Director of Policy and Analysis for 14 years until his retirement in 1995. He is a graduate of Princeton University.

JULIENE G. LIPSON is professor of nursing and medical anthropology at the University of California at San Francisco (UCSF) where she teaches international/cross-cultural and community health nursing. Since 1982, she has conducted research on the health and adjustment of immigrants and refugees to California from the Middle East and, since 1986, from Afghanistan. She is co-director of the UCSF-based health resource center for Middle Eastern immigrants and health and service providers. She also directs the Afghan Health Education Project, a community health assessment among the San Francisco area's Afghan community. She is an R.N. and received her Ph.D. in anthropology.

MILES A. MCNALL is a doctoral candidate in sociology at the University of Minnesota. His dissertation research concerns the adaptation of Eastern Europeans to emerging post-Communist social structures. In addition, he has published a number of articles pertaining to the adjustment of Southeast Asian refugees to life in the United States.

CAROL A. MORTLAND has been involved with research and programs with Southeast Asian refugees since 1981. She is the coeditor of *Cambodian Culture since 1975: Homeland and Exile;* her own published work deals with refugee patronage, refugee camp life, resettlement, and belief systems. She has also worked both as a director of local resettlement programs and as director of refugee programs for a national volunteer agency. Most recently, she has become involved in archaeological excavation in Cambodia. She received her Ph.D. in anthropology from the University of Oregon.

NGUYEN MANH HUNG is currently an associate professor of government at George Mason University and director of its Indochina Institute. Prior to leaving Vietnam in 1975, he was a professor at the National School of Administration and subsequently Deputy Minister of National Planning and Development for the government of the Republic of Vietnam. He has written extensively in both English and Vietnamese on issues relating to Vietnam and its foreign policy. He received his Ph.D. in international relations from the University of Virginia in 1975.

DOUGLAS P. OLNEY has conducted a variety of research on ethnicity, kinship, and refugee adaptation and currently works as a research consultant focusing on refugee issues. His major academic work relates to the development of Hmong self-help organizations in the United States. He received his Ph.D. in anthropology from the University of Minnesota in 1993.

PATRICIA A. OMIDIAN is a lecturer in the Department of Anthropology at California State University at Hayward. Her major research focused on family conflict and life-course issues in an Afghan refugee community in northern California and reflected her more general concern with the formulation, production, and reproduction of identity among Middle Eastern and Central Asian immigrants and refugees. She has also worked directly as coordinator for both a community health resource center and an Afghan health education project. She received her Ph.D. in medical anthropology.

RITA J. SIMON is currently a university professor at American University—having formerly taught at the University of Chicago, the University of Illinois, and the Hebrew University in Jerusalem. She has authored or edited some 30 books of which 3 are particularly relevant to this volume: *The Ambivalent Welcome* on media coverage of immigration, *International Migration: The Female Experience* (coedited by Caroline Brettell), and *New Lives: The Adjustment of Soviet Immigrants in the United States and Israel.* Dr. Simon received her Ph.D. in sociology from the University of Chicago in 1957.

MARLINE A. SPRING is currently a research associate at the University of Minnesota's Community-University Health Care Center and a doctoral candidate in anthropology, also at the University of Minnesota. As an applied anthropologist, she has produced health education materials for Southeast Asian refugees and published articles on such health issues as the adequacy of reproductive services provided to Hmong patients.

SUSAN BUCHANAN STAFFORD is currently the director of Corporate and Foundation Relations for Queens College, City University of New York. Her major academic research focused on Haitian immigrants and refugees in the United States. She has worked for various branches of the federal government on Cuban and Haitian resettlement programs, for a refugee resettlement agency, and for a national advocacy organization on Haitian causes. More recently, she has been involved in grants and development in the area of higher education. She received her Ph.D. in anthropology from New York University.

JOHN K. WHITMORE, an historian of Vietnam, is currently a research associate of the Center for South and Southeast Asian Studies and an adjunct associate professor of the Department of History, both at the University of Michigan. He has published extensively on Vietnamese history—particularly the Lê dynasty—and was involved in a set of major surveys of Vietnamese, Chinese-Vietnamese, and Lao refugees in the United States, including coauthorship of *The Boat People* (1989) and *Children of the Boat People* (1991). He received both his M.A. in cultural anthropology and his Ph.D. in Southeast Asian history from Cornell University.

TEKLE M. WOLDEMIKAEL is currently an associate professor of sociology and anthropology at the University of the Redlands and also taught at the University of Gezira in the Sudan in the early 1980s. He has published articles on Haitian immigrants, ethnicity and nationalist movements in Eritrea, and ethnic relations in the Sudan and is the author of the 1989 volume *Becoming Black Americans: Haitians and American Institutions in Evanston, Illinois.* He received his B.A. in economics from Addis Ababa University and his Ph.D. in sociology from Northwestern University.

ISBN 0-313-29344-9

90000>

EAN

9 780313 293443

HARDCOVER BAR CODE